World Christianity and Indigenous Experience

In this book, David Lindenfeld proposes a new dimension to the study of world history. Here, he explores the global expansion of Christianity since 1500 from the perspectives of the indigenous people who were affected by it and helped change it, giving them active agency. Integrating the study of religion into world history, his volume surveys indigenous experience in colonial Latin America, Native North America, Africa and the African diaspora, the Middle East, India, East Asia, and the Pacific. Lindenfeld demonstrates how religion is closely interwoven with political, economic, and social history. Wide-ranging in scope, and offering a synoptic perspective of our interconnected world, Lindenfeld combines in-depth analysis of individual regions with comprehensive global coverage. He also provides a new vocabulary, with a spectrum ranging from resistance to acceptance and commitment to Christianity, that articulates the range and complexity of the indigenous conversion experience. Lindenfeld's cross-cultural reflections provide a compelling alternative to the Western narrative of progressive development.

David Lindenfeld is Professor Emeritus in the Department of History at Louisiana State University. He has been researching cross-cultural religious interactions worldwide for nearly two decades and is coeditor, with Miles Richardson, of *Beyond Conversion and Syncretism: Indigenous Encounters with Missionary Christianity, 1800-2000* (2011). Lindenfeld is an active member of the World History Association and the Yale-Edinburgh Group on Missionary Christianity.

World Christianity and Indigenous Experience

A Global History, 1500–2000

DAVID LINDENFELD
Louisiana State University

CAMBRIDGE
UNIVERSITY PRESS

CAMBRIDGE
UNIVERSITY PRESS

University Printing House, Cambridge CB2 8BS, United Kingdom

One Liberty Plaza, 20th Floor, New York, NY 10006, USA

477 Williamstown Road, Port Melbourne, VIC 3207, Australia

314–321, 3rd Floor, Plot 3, Splendor Forum, Jasola District Centre,
New Delhi – 110025, India

79 Anson Road, #06–04/06, Singapore 079906

Cambridge University Press is part of the University of Cambridge.

It furthers the University's mission by disseminating knowledge in the pursuit of
education, learning, and research at the highest international levels of excellence.

www.cambridge.org
Information on this title: www.cambridge.org/9781108831567
DOI: 10.1017/9781108917643

© Cambridge University Press 2021

First published 2021

A catalogue record for this publication is available from the British Library.

Library of Congress Cataloging-in-Publication Data
NAMES: Lindenfeld, David, author.
TITLE: World Christianity and indigenous experience : a global history, 1500–2000 /
David Lindenfeld, author.
DESCRIPTION: Cambridge, United Kingdom ; New York, NY, USA : Cambridge University
Press, 2021. | Includes bibliographical references and index.
IDENTIFIERS: LCCN 2020042270 (print) | LCCN 2020042271 (ebook) |
ISBN 9781108831567 (hardback) | ISBN 9781108926874 (paperback) |
ISBN 9781108917643 (epub)
SUBJECTS: LCSH: Christianity and culture–History. | Conversion–Christianity–History. |
Indigenous peoples–Religion. | Agent (Philosophy)
CLASSIFICATION: LCC BR115.C8 L555 2021 (print) | LCC BR115.C8 (ebook) |
DDC 270.089–dc23
LC record available at https://lccn.loc.gov/2020042270
LC ebook record available at https://lccn.loc.gov/2020042271

ISBN 978-1-108-83156-7 Hardback
ISBN 978-1-108-92687-4 Paperback

Contents

Maps and Illustrations

Tables

vii

Acknowledgments

This book was roughly sixteen years in the making, as it involved my shifting of research fields from European to world history. A sabbatical in 2003 enabled me to accept a visiting fellowship at the Center for History, Society, and Culture at the University of California, Davis. Among those at Davis who provided helpful advice and encouragement in getting me started were John R. Hall and Jacob Olupona. In 2008, the Georgetown University Department of Theology provided me the opportunity for organizing a workshop on indigenous encounters with missionary Christianity, together with my Louisiana State University colleague in anthropology, the late Miles Richardson. Georgetown faculty members Peter C. Phan and Joseph Murphy were instrumental in providing this venue, with the help of Anh Q. Tran, SJ. The other participants contributed greatly to my understanding of the field: Saurabh Dube, C. Mathews Samson, Elizabeth Elbourne, Richard Fox Young, Sylvia Frey, and Anne Keary. This workshop led to the publication of a collection of essays, *Beyond Conversion and Syncretism* (New York: Berghahn Books, 2011).

A number of specialists in different cultural regions generously reviewed individual chapters and the articles that fed into them, providing invaluable criticism and advice along the way. Foremost was my longtime colleague and friend, the late John Henderson, an East Asian scholar with a broad comparative perspective, who reviewed most of the manuscript. Others included Katherine Benton-Cohen, Gibril Cole, Philip J. Deloria, Carter Findley, Susan Schroeder, Peter Sutherland, Joel Tishken, Catherine Wessinger, Deanna Ferree Womack, William Worger, and Richard Fox Young. The manuscript reviewers for

Cambridge University Press provided many valuable suggestions as well. Cartographer Mary Lee Eggart provided invaluable assistance with maps.

For a book that deals centrally with religion, readers are entitled to know an author's upbringing, affiliation, and biases. Raised in the religions of my parents, namely Judaism and Quakerism, I found my way to Unitarian Universalism in the 1970s and have remained there ever since thanks to a vibrant church community in Baton Rouge, Louisiana. The theme and approach of this book have been inspired by that faith, which finds human wisdom to be distributed among all cultures, with no one tradition having a monopoly.

Finally, I dedicate this book to my wife, Jerri Becnel, who has lovingly shared me with this project for most of our marriage.

Introduction

RELIGIOUS INTERACTION AND THE STUDY OF
GLOBAL HISTORY

What can the study of cross-cultural interactions tell us about religions and how they operate in world history? The purpose of this book is to address that question. It does so by investigating a particular arena of such interaction, namely the strategies which a variety of peoples worldwide have employed in dealing with the presence of imported Christianity, often as conveyed by missionaries, in their midst. The terms "World Christianity" and "global history" have become widespread in recent decades, in part reflecting the state of the highly interconnected world we live in and in part attempting to move away from an exclusively Western interpretation of how that world works. For example, the study of World Christianity is in large part a response to the dramatic growth of Christianity in the Southern Hemisphere, particularly in sub-Saharan Africa, so that there are now more Christians south of the equator than north of it.[1] And global history generally subscribes no longer to a single master narrative of "development" that applies to all regions (a notion that betrays a Western bias) but instead to a variety of interactions and "connections" that cross national, regional, and cultural divides.

Nevertheless, these ideas have genealogies that are important to understand. Global history as a field of study, for example, is practically synonymous with world history, a term that is also currently in use, and has roots that go back far in time.[2] The desire to understand the world as a whole, as was known at the time, can be traced to the ancient cultures of Greece and China. In the early modern West it took the form of philosophy of history, as practiced by such thinkers as Vico, Voltaire, Herder, and Hegel, and in the twentieth century by such figures as Spengler and Toynbee.

A closely associated term was "universal history," which usually had strong Christian connotations, as found in the chronicles of the Middle Ages, which began with the creation story from Genesis. And World Christianity may be viewed as but the latest expression of the aspiration of universal Christian outreach that goes back to Jesus' injunction to "go therefore and make disciples of all nations" in Matthew 28:19 – an aspiration that would become associated with the word "mission." It is important to note that "mission" did not always have this association, but began to be used in this way only in the sixteenth century with Ignatius of Loyola and the Jesuits.[3] This, of course, coincided with that great eruption of European power that led to the exploration and conquest of much of the globe. Missionaries were frequently, though not invariably, a part of such expansion, as in the Portuguese and Spanish empires. But the Jesuits also regarded as their "mission" winning back the Protestants in Europe, and ventured to places like Japan and China, where no Western conqueror had yet appeared. In other cases they acted independently of the colonizing power, as in French Canada. Still, missionaries became active agents of globalization and were generally seen as sharing a common purpose with colonizers even when they did not directly collaborate, namely to bring a "superior" way of life to those not yet exposed to it. Thus, however benevolent the intentions of individual missionaries were, they tended to view indigenous peoples as static, unchanging, "traditional" – in contrast to the dynamism of the Europeans.[4]

It is this conception that this book seeks to correct. Its aim is to investigate the strategies that a variety of indigenous peoples worldwide employed in dealing with the presence of imported Christianity in their midst during the colonial era. Thus, rather than view the global spread of Christianity through the eyes of missionaries, it seeks to reverse the telescope, so to speak. It takes as a given that, even in conditions of extreme subjugation, people have some degree of agency to control their own circumstances, creating a situation of interaction with agents from outside. Missionaries could not possibly have succeeded in converting numbers of people to Christianity without the help of such indigenous agents. And in many cases – often underestimated in the literature – the latter proved to be quite capable of spreading Christianity on their own (e.g., the "south-south" movement between Africa and South America).[5]

The focus of this study, however, is not so much the spread of Christianity per se but rather as an illustration of how people interact with novel stimuli from outside (including their rejection). Moreover, it should be remembered that such new connections across geographical or cultural divides, however exploitive or destructive they may have been (as in the cases of slavery or the spreading of diseases), could also offer opportunities. As the great world historian William H. MacNeill once put it, "It seemed obvious to me ... that historical change was largely provoked by encounters with strangers, followed by efforts to borrow (or sometimes to reject or hold at bay) especially attractive novelties ... encounters with strangers ... [are] the main drive wheel of social change."[6]

World Christianity, then, is obviously part of global history. Yet it is noteworthy that, along with religion in general, it has been relatively neglected by world historians of the modern era, at least when compared to other types of interactions. For example, in his 2003 survey of the field of world history, Patrick Manning writes, "It is remarkable, in contrast [to earlier periods], how little discussion of religion appears in the world history literature for recent centuries."[7] Manning attributes this to two causes: (1) the tendency to interpret modern religious phenomena in secular terms, and (2) the prevalence of local studies, which historians have been reluctant to place in the context of larger patterns.

The first point is perhaps less surprising if one looks at the genealogy of the field of world history itself as it has emerged as a recognized subdiscipline within the Western historical profession since the 1960s. The pioneers of the field tended to focus on the material sorts of cross-cultural interactions such as trade and commerce, technological transfer, and the spread of diseases. Cultural issues, perhaps by virtue of their relative intangibility, tended to lag behind. To argue for their inclusion is obviously not to deny the reality or importance of factors such as economic or political motives in determining the dynamics of religious interchange, but only to move the discussion toward a more complete picture.[8]

There is a more subtle factor at work as well, which applies more broadly to historical scholarship as a whole. However willing we Western historians may be to acknowledge the role of religion in principle, it can be difficult to translate this into practice because of biases that derive from a "disenchanted" worldview, which may persist at an unconscious level.[9] Insofar as religion is concerned with the supernatural, there is an impulse not to deal with the latter directly, but to explain it away as attributable to other more "rational" factors (such as the function it serves in holding a society together), rather than accept at face value the explanations given by the peoples under study. How many of us feel uncomfortable in taking animistic explanations – the active agency of spirits – at face value in accounting for historical change?[10] What are we to make of the traders on the Mumbai stock exchange who chant the 108 names of the Hindu god Ganesha daily before the opening?[11]

Ironically, similar biases can be found not only among secular scholars, but also among religious scholars as well. Here too, one finds traces of a bias in favor of disenchantment, operating indirectly. I am thinking of the distinction between "world" and "traditional" religions which still pervade textbooks in comparative religions as taught in American colleges and universities—however respectful their authors in fact are of religious diversity and cognizant of cross-cultural inter-actions.[12] The canon of "world" religions has in fact changed little since the 1893 Parliament of the World's Religions.[13] The criterion of mem-bership in this canon is, for the most part, a set of written scriptures, as in Judaism, Christianity, Islam, Hinduism, Buddhism, Confucianism, Taoism, Janism, Zoroastrianism, Sikhism (Shinto is an exception). Religions that lack a clear written scriptural tradition are still character-ized as "traditional," "primal," "basic," "tribal," or "indigenous," no matter how elaborate their cosmologies or how widespread their adher-ents may be (a case is currently being made that the *orisha* devotions stemming from the West African Yoruba deserve such a designation, as they are to be found among former slaves in Brazil, the Caribbean, and North America).[14]

Regarding Manning's second point, one can attribute the preference for local studies – conducted in this case by anthropologists as well as historians and religious scholars – to the pressures of academic specializa-tion. Add to this the influence of postmodernism and its distrust of grand narratives since the 1970s, which makes many historians leery of the whole notion of world history – however committed they may be to exploring "transnational" connections and influences that cross cultural or political borders.[15] A parallel reaction has developed within mission-ary studies against the master narratives of the past, the very impetus that gave rise to World Christianity, which has been characterized as "partly the product of missionaries' and missiologists' postcolonial guilt."[16] In its place has emerged a plethora of local studies, frequently positioned to take advantage of the close contacts between missionaries and native peoples that missionary records reveal.[17] Such local studies, combined with the work of anthropologists and secular historians, make a compara-tive study such as this one possible.

Yet the question remains: why have we found the transition from the local study to a broader framework – however defined – more difficult in the area of religion than in other topics that comprise world history? Certainly religion is no less "global" than commerce or disease – one could point to the outreach of missionaries in the nineteenth and twentieth centuries to places as remote from the West as Melanesia, or the widespread acceptance of Buddhist practices in the West today.

To answer this question, I believe we must add a third factor to the two which Manning adduces: a relative paucity of vocabulary and hence of theoretical frameworks in order to make sense of a wide variety of these data. It is this deficit that this book seeks to remedy, at least in part, by presenting and testing a more variegated vocabulary of indigenous encounters with missionary Christianity, drawn from extended comparative research.[18] Note that a vocabulary is not a typology. It does not automatically imply a scheme for classifying and pigeonholing such encounters. We will find many instances of multiple types of interactions operating concurrently. Still less does this framework imply a single master narrative. Rather it provides a matrix from which multiple narratives can be constructed. Whether any broader theoretical generalizations do in fact emerge from this comparative study is a question to be considered in the conclusion.

Before proceeding, however, it should be pointed out that there already is, ready-at-hand, a broad interpretive framework – which could be characterized as a grand narrative – to account for missionary encounters with non-Western peoples. This is the view that missionaries have been agents of Western cultural imperialism, imposing their values and practices on others in all corners of the globe. This view is mirrored in a certain popular image of missionaries as rigid and disrespectful of the people they seek to convert, which has found its way into novels such as James Michener's *Hawaii* (1959) and Barbara Kingsolver's *The Poisonwood Bible* (1998).[19] Although this narrative contains some truth, it has increasingly come to be an overly simplistic take.[20] One can point to at least as many counterexamples of missionaries' extraordinary self-sacrifice, heroism, and kindness, which surely made a positive impression on indigenes.[21] To be sure, one finds many such stories in the hagiographical literature generated by the missionary movement itself, which was often written for the purpose of fundraising. In fact, the historical sources provide abundant evidence for both stereotypes. Missionaries spent much time issuing prohibitions, telling people what they could not do or what they must give up, while at the same time providing services and assistance that were greatly beneficial, such as healing, tools, literacy, and love.

This is just one instance of the complexity and many-sidedness of the missionary-imperialism issue. In an obvious way, as already noted, the global outreach of missionaries in the modern era *coincided* with the expansion of European powers beyond the continent. It is also obviously true that missionaries often consciously and arrogantly carried Western mores and cultural values to other places on their own, independently of any colonial military or political backing. The connection between the three C's – "Christianity, commerce, and civilization" – was widely upheld in missionary circles in the nineteenth century, though rarely without debate.[22] Yet during that same period, missionaries frequently worked at cross-purposes with colonial authorities. In parts of French West Africa, the colonial authorities preferred Muslim local rulers to Christian ones as better keepers of order. In the companion volume on missions to the *Oxford History of the British Empire*, Norman Etherington concludes, "All things considered, the trajectories of missions and empire hardly bear comparison."[23] This, however, may be more evident to those who have studied missionary sources and actions than to indigenous peoples, who were likely to view missionaries and colonial officials as part of the same wave.[24] Nevertheless, as Etherington stresses, the "cultural imperialism" argument ignores the fact that many of the most active proselytizers of Christianity outside of Europe were natives themselves. This points to a major weakness of the more simplistic versions of the "cultural imperialism" thesis: its tendency to deny agency to non-Western peoples. Critics have discerned in this argument a polarizing mindset that, by reifying the categories of "Western" and "non-Western," replicates the master narrative it seeks to overturn.

There is, however, a more sophisticated version of the "cultural imperialism" interpretation – found in the work of anthropologists Jean and John Comaroff – which seeks to complicate the picture. The Comaroffs' purpose is to show

"how modernity, rooted in the development of capitalism in Europe, took on its particular forms in Africa and elsewhere; how these forms emerged out of the interplay of religion and political economy, meaning and power, both 'back home' and abroad; how the metropole was itself affected in the process of its confrontation with 'others'; how this process gave rise to cultural struggles, accommodations, hybridities, and new hegemonies."[25]

Their method is a massive study of a single case: the Anglican and Methodist missions to the southern Tswana in South Africa in the nineteenth century. They emphasize that colonialism can take many forms, that political, economic, and cultural processes of domination are different, and that the indigenous peoples are active agents in the process, accepting at times, subverting at others. Thus, rather than "conversion," they posit a "conversation," albeit between unequal parties of colonizer and colonized, which they characterize as "that curious mix of consent and contestation, desire and disgust, appropriation and accommodation, refusal and refiguration, ethnicization and hybridization – subsumed in the term 'the colonial encounter.'"[26] They call this process a "dialectic of domination and resistance" while rejecting the implication that dialectics involves some kind of linear formula or teleological assumption.[27] They devote separate chapters to the missionaries' introduction of – and the Tswanas' differentiated response to – agricultural techniques, money, Western-style clothing, architecture, and medicine. The richness of detail of the Comaroffs' study has been acknowledged and praised even by those who are skeptical of its overall gist. Such skepticism takes several forms: (1) whether the authors actually succeed in freeing themselves from the teleological assumptions they so strenuously strain against (e.g., whether they impute to the missionaries a degree of power and control greater than they actually possessed), and (2) whether their general formulations, such as "cultural imperialism" or "colonization of consciousness," are in the end accurate characterizations of the religious and cultural changes that the southern Tswana experienced.[28]

Nevertheless, the more nuanced treatment of colonialism by the Comaroffs points in the direction of post-colonialism, as exemplified in the subaltern studies movement that originated in India, which likewise seeks to give voice and agency to non-Western peoples. The term "post-colonialism" itself is ambiguous: for some it expresses the antagonistic stance to Western hegemony and self-proclaimed cultural superiority noted in the previous section. But one can distinguish this "oppositional" version from "complicit" postcolonialism, as Vijay Mishra and Bob Hodge have defined it.[29] The latter direction points to a variety of native responses, ranging from subversion to accommodation and imitation. By seeking to get to the native voices and outlooks, it offers a certain corrective to the cultural imperialist approach.[30] These postcolonialists tend to stress the various mixtures and combinations of native and foreign elements as the norm, encapsulated in such terms as "syncretism" and "hybridity."[31]

The present study takes off from this point by adopting the postcolonial perspective of viewing missionary encounters from indigenous points of view. Yet it also finds that terms such as "syncretism" and "hybridity" are still too general to provide the enrichment of theoretical insight that is needed to do justice to this perspective. It proposes a more variegated vocabulary of cultural encounter.

An ambitious work such as this one necessitates some self-imposed limitations. First, it makes no claim to completeness: the attempt to study all countries or all cases would have exhausted the reader's patience. Second, I have avoided the temptation to delve deeply into primary sources, thus going against the grain of my training as an historian. To do so with any assurance would have required language skills that far exceed my capacity. It seemed more prudent to rely on the work of other scholars who have mastered the languages and sources and write from long familiarity with the cultures they study. The availability of such scholarships makes this work feasible. Third, and perhaps more damagingly, a study of cultural *inter*actions implies that influence is a two-way street, in this case that missionaries and the societies that sent them were affected by the encounter as well as the people they sought to convert. The Comaroffs' work, for example, underlines this. However, an attempt to do justice to the influences on both sides of the encounter would have stretched the project beyond the bounds of manageability. Fourth, and most damagingly – and least subject to the author's control – this study is hampered by the asymmetrical distribution of resources among academic institutions in different continents, reflecting the current inequalities of wealth in the world at large. Ironically, some of the most creative centers of Christianity today are in places where those resources are the thinnest, such as Africa. Thus, a Sierra Leonean mission historian noted in 2006 that none of the five histories of African Christianity in the previous decade had been written by an African.[32] The vast bulk of world history that is written today comes from the West, a fact ameliorated in part by the increasing presence of non-Western scholars in Western colleges and universities. Nevertheless, this is bound to produce limitations on insights that a greater number and prominence of native scholarly voices would provide. In that sense, this study is a product of the limitations of its time.

A further premise of the study is that no society is monolithic; thus any foreign religious encounter will generate a variety of native strategies to deal with it. In this connection, it is also my belief that colonialism is not monolithic either. Philip Curtin has provided a helpful typology to begin sorting out the differences. He distinguishes between three general types of foreign domination: (1) settler colonialism, in the sense of migrants establishing a colony in a new place, numerically overwhelming the indigenous inhabitants, as in the United States and Canada, Australia and New Zealand; (2) territorial empire, in which a minority of foreigners dominates a large indigenous population, as in British India or Nigeria; and (3) plural societies in which foreign settlers live alongside native peoples, as in South Africa, Israel, parts of the former Soviet Union, and some Latin American countries.[33] Each of these types of situations presents indigenous peoples with a different range of choices and limitations.

The premise of complexity obviously also applies to Judeo-Christianity itself. The different approaches of Catholicism, Protestantism, and Eastern Orthodox come immediately to mind, and within each of these, there had developed a great variety of components – mythical narratives, ethical precepts, rules for living, ceremonies, artistic expressions, and self-conducted rituals (such as prayer). The effect of this complexity has been to provide any number of *cultural hooks* that could serve as points of compatibility with an indigenous culture, no matter how alien their values and practices may at first appear. Thus missionary Christianity was rarely, if ever, met with total incomprehension, and native peoples were able to find something with which they could identify.

The premise of complexity also applies to two commonly used notions as applied to cross-cultural religious interactions, namely conversion and syncretism. A major reason for introducing a more elaborate set of terms is to move away from the imprecision that each of these terms carry with them.

The term "conversion" derives from Judeo-Christianity, where it is defined as "turning," indicating a radical transformation of one's beliefs or identity (there is no terminological equivalent to it in Islamic discourse).[34] But how this transformation occurs is subject to a great variety of conditions. Conversion is sometimes individual, sometimes collective, usually voluntary, but sometimes coerced. It can occur for a great variety of reasons, whether strictly religious, or social, economic, or political. For our purposes, it is worth noting that "conversion" may mean quite different things to the missionary and the indigene in any given cultural encounter.

Fortunately, several studies of conversion as a general phenomenon appeared in the 1990s which took account of these multiple dimensions.[35] This literature draws attention both to the fact that conversions are often not total, that is, they incorporate significant elements of the culture and religion that existed beforehand and also to the converse, namely that despite such continuities, people who see themselves as converts often – though not invariably – express a sense of rupture with their past. Thus the "turning" expressed in the original definition is not just a fiction or a construct in many cases. This is true at an individual level, in that converts often find themselves breaking ties with their families or peers, and also at a social level, where, as this study will reveal, there are innumerable cases of collective idol-smashing and other forms of destruction of the artifacts of one's past affiliation.[36]

A valuable contribution of this literature is its drawing our attention to macrohistorical processes affecting religious change–even though such broad views are rarely without controversy. Thus Robert B. Hefner, in his introduction to *Conversion to Christianity*, points to the long-term success of some of the world religions. He writes, "they are the longest lasting of civilization's primary institutions," outliving empires and world economic systems.[37] Building on the theories of Max Weber, Hefner claims, "the doctrines of the world religions ... *do* seem to be organized around a unified view of the world derived from a consciously systematized attitude toward life. ... These religions regularize clerical roles, standardize ritual, formalize doctrine, and otherwise work to create an authoritative culture and cohesive religious structure."[38] He further claims that the development of world religions tends to highlight "transcendence," by which he means a shift in concern toward other-worldliness and salvation. Unity in this world seems to be achieved, in other words, by setting one's sights on another world above and beyond it. [39] In so emphasizing uniformity, Hefner anticipated J. R. and William H. McNeill's macrohistorical interpretation of world history in their work *The Human Web*, wherein interconnectedness over long stretches of time results in a disappearance of diversity – a trend empirically demonstrated in such phenomena as the disappearances of human languages and in animal and plant species.[40]

The latter emphasis finds reinforcement in what is doubtlessly the most discussed theory of conversion in recent times, that of Robin Horton, whose ideas likewise continue to provoke discussion by virtue of their overarching generality. If Hefner, following Weber, invokes universality of religious change by a positing a "vertical" image of a transcendent otherworldly God, Horton achieves the same result with a "horizontal" image of a supreme being whose powers extend geographically, taking precedence over local gods as societies become more cosmopolitan. An African specialist, Horton noted that many African religions operated on a "two-tiered" system: a multitude of "lesser spirits," which were concerned with more or less local affairs, and a "supreme being" or creator-god whose sphere was the world as a whole. The creator god was often not the object of direct worship, because it had little relevance to the day-to-day affairs of the community. But with trade and improvements in communications, the local community came increasingly to confront forces outside it, which increased the relevance of spirits whose powers have a broader geographical range, hence the tendency to embrace the universal gods of Islam and Christianity. Horton emphasized that these world religions acted as mere catalysts for reconfigurations within the existing beliefs and practices of the African religions. He based this contention on his belief that African religions were every bit as "rational" in their own terms as modern secular thought, in that they represented a consistent system of "explanation, prediction, and control" of the world, including the ability to adapt to change. Horton did not restrict this story to modernization per se; he also traced the African receptiveness to Islam in earlier centuries to the presence of mobile groups such as traders and pastoralists.[41]

Such theories inevitably give rise to the question of how different cultural aspects of local and world religions are combined – the question of syncretism. The dictionary definition – "the combination of different forms of belief or practice" – indicates both the term's relevance and its uninformativeness, or, as one ambivalent commentator puts it, "the term has precipitated frustration and confusion over the centuries since Plutarch first foisted it upon us—and ... despite all, it remains ever stimulating, ever useful."[42] Although still widely used by scholars, the term has aroused a great amount of debate and even heated opposition from a variety of circles, suggesting that some deeply emotional issues are at stake. Within Christianity, the term often connotes an undermining or adulteration of the core tenets of its distinctive message. For some indigenous peoples, it connotes colonialist oppression. Among anthropologists, its changing use reflects the impact of the culture wars of the late twentieth century.[43]

My criticism of syncretism as a theoretical concept is threefold:

1) As already stated, the term covers a great variety of operations and combinations. It can mean, for example, the synthesis or fusion of deities from different traditions, as between Shinto gods and Buddhist Bodhisattvas in Japan, or the juxtaposition of different religious practices, as in an Afro-Brazilian religion where Catholic rituals take place in the front part of the house, African ones in the back. Its uses overlap with terms such as "bricolage," "hybridity," "creolization."

2) Like the term "conversion," syncretism may thus mean different things to any two or more parties in a given cross-cultural encounter. A good example is the so-called Aladura (praying) churches that arose among the

Yoruba in southwestern Nigeria in the 1920s and 1930s, breaking away
from the denominations that had previously been established by missionaries. The emphasis on faith healing in these churches might well appear to a
westerner to be a syncretic incorporation of African elements. But the
Aladuras themselves vigorously rejected this characterization, claiming it
was a new form of Christianity which rejected traditional African
medicine.[44]

3) It tends to focus on the content of cross-religious combination, and by doing
   so fosters a certain one-dimensionality in the analysis of cross-cultural interaction. Thus there is a temptation to treat syncretism in a somewhat mech-
   anical fashion, a blending or compounding of elements which can be traced
   back to divergent cultural roots (e.g., practice x and practice y come from
   Africa in the case of African-American slaves, while z comes from Western
   missionaries). Cross-cultural interaction is in fact more complex than this,
   taking place at a variety of levels and in a number of different ways simultaneously. What needs to be classified, in other words, is not merely contents but
   also the processes which produced them, i.e., the *strategies* of how societies
   deal with new religious forces to which they are exposed.

All this is not to deny that blending or juxtaposition of deities or rites
occurs. As Mircea Eliade points out in his *History of Religious Ideas*,
"syncretism has played an important part in the formation of Hittite,
Greek, and Roman religions, in the religion of Israel, in Mahayana
Buddhism and in Taoism."[45] But the question of determining what quali-
fies as syncretism at any given time depends on who controls the discourse. What counts as false syncretism vs. true religion was undoubtedly
different for the Council of Trent than for Vatican II. Some scholars
distinguish between "syncretism from above" and "syncretism from
below," depending on whether the combinations are formulated by elites
or by the common people.[46] While tracing the different meanings of
syncretism may be an effective way of uncovering these power relations,
the process can be rendered more complete and more precise by consider-
ing syncretism together with its obverse, namely *selection*. To put it
differently, any analysis of cross-cultural mixing or blending should take
account not only of what is included, but also what is left out. This is
simply a restatement of the fact that indigenes and missionaries are both
active agents in the interactive process. The following vocabulary seeks to
take account of this complexity.

A VOCABULARY OF STRATEGIES

For convenience of exposition, the following types are ordered on analogy
to a spectrum, ranging from rejection at one end to acceptance on the

other. It cannot be overstated that this is an analogy, nothing more. It should not be taken to mean that different cases can be neatly lined up on a linear continuum; as previously stated, religious interactions are typically multileveled, so that any one case will exemplify several types simultaneously or at different times. Still less does this ordering imply a chronological sequence. Indeed, as many mission scholars will attest and as subsequent chapters will demonstrate, rejection is frequently *not* the first response of a native group to foreign missionaries. Rather, it often stems from subsequent disillusionment when Christianity is perceived to fail in delivering its initial promise.

1. **Resistance and Rejection.** The term "resistance" is often used in postcolonial discourse very broadly, as practically synonymous with "resilience," to refer to the ability of indigenous cultures to survive in the face of oppression.[47] In fact, indigenes have resorted to a wide variety of strategies to achieve this end. I use the term here in a fourfold, more delimited sense: first, to point to cases of violent collective action against missionaries or Christians; second, to refer to cases of noncompliance or noncooperation, but without widespread violence; third to refer to simple nonacceptance or indifference to Christianity; and fourth to point to theological movements that highlight struggle against poverty and injustice.

Some well-known examples of violent resistance would include the Boxer Uprising in northern China at the turn of the last century and the Pueblo Revolt against the Spanish in 1680 in what is today New Mexico. In both cases, missionaries and churches were singled out as targets of attack – in north China spontaneously, especially in the initial stages, in New Mexico as the result of a planned coordinated attack by a native leader.[48] Both were products of simmering resentment against foreign intrusion, exacerbated by missionary contempt for native practices, combined with droughts which served as a short-term "trigger effect."

Such cases of violent resistance are easy to locate and describe, while nonviolent (sometimes called *passive*) resistance may be more elusive. It is easier to spot in places where missionaries functioned as landowners and were in charge of native labor. Susan M. Deeds enumerates the behaviors of the Indians in northwest Mexico on Jesuit estates in the seventeenth and eighteenth centuries. Not surprisingly, these came about in the wake of unsuccessful revolts. They included "foot dragging, evasion of or minimal compliance with communal labor obligations, and dissimulation," reinforcing missionary stereotypes of the Indians as lazy. Other actions included pilfering of agricultural surpluses or cattle, casting spells on priests (who in some cases nearly died from strange illnesses), and, more mildly "expressions of disrespect, mimicry, grumbling, and gossip."[49] One means available to the natives here as in many other situations was simply flight – although this depended considerably on geographical conditions.

Such expressions of non-compliance often shade into a more general refusal to accept Christianity, sometimes in spite of prodigious missionary efforts to the contrary. This response is in fact quite widespread. According to Lewis Rambo, "from a careful reading of the literature it is clear that in fact most people say no to conversion."[50] In most societies, far more people choose not to convert than do. An interesting case is that of Brazilian and Peruvian Amazonia, where there was no massive conquest, and where missionaries actually sought to protect natives from enslavement. The missionaries' attempts to convert these groups met with short-term success and long-term failure. One reason is not far to seek: the Jesuits' method of bringing Indians together into villages in the sixteenth century increased their vulnerability to disease and led to massive population loss. This seems to have immunized the Amazonians against later Catholic missionary attempts, which were uniformly unsuccessful.[51] In the mid-twentieth century, Protestant groups such as the Summer Institute of Linguistics had a burst of success and left behind some important educational reforms, but even their conversions were temporary, and over time people simply forgot about the religious message. Anthropologist Peter Gow concludes, "indigenous Amazonian people respond ... to missionaries with the same bizarre mix of fervent enthusiasm and total indifference. It is not that indigenous Amazonian peoples cannot understand Christianity, for they clearly can and do. What they do not seem to be willing to accept is why that understanding is supposed to matter so much."[52]

At the same time, there have been movements *within* Christianity that have put issues of poverty and injustice front and center, leading to resistance to the groups in power. While these have often originated with theologians and other intellectuals, it is fair to say that they have had an impact on actual social, economic, and political struggles. The best-known example is probably Liberation Theology, which started in Latin America in the 1960s and 1970s and soon influenced similar movements in places like South Africa and Korea. This was clearly one manifestation of the broader trends of those decades with their emphasis on democratization, anti-colonialism, and Marxist theory. While Liberation Theology has often been criticized for remaining a "top-down" phenomenon, claiming to speak for the voiceless without letting them speak for themselves, there is no denying that many priests and laity paid witness to it with their lives, as in places like El Salvador, where Archbishop Oscar Romero was murdered while preaching a funeral mass.[53]

2. Selective Incorporation. In this type, a society responds to missionaries by incorporating a relatively small number of foreign features into their cultural pattern, which nevertheless remains clearly dominant. A more precise term for this process would be "inculturation," but this might lead to confusion, given the Roman Catholic use of this term since the Second Vatican Council.[54] In the latter use, there is a strong emphasis on missionary agency, spreading the gospel through the symbols and customs of a native culture. It also stresses that this is a two-way process, i.e., the meanings and interpretations of Christian symbols and customs may be enriched and modified. The focus, however, remains the gospel and the Christian message. In viewing such transactions from a native perspective, however, it is clear that the principles of selection may be different, and that the gospel may not be at the center of what is "inculturated." In any event, the main purpose of this type is to highlight how native cultures can retain their identity and characteristics while allowing inputs from outside.

A vivid example of selective incorporation comes from Homi K. Bhabha's book *The Location of Culture*.[55] The scene is a grove of trees just outside Delhi, India, in 1817. About five hundred men, women, and children are gathered there, reading and discussing the Bible. An Indian catechist comes upon them and asks them about the book. They claim it was sent from God (whose name was Jesus) to them via an angel who appeared at Hurdwar fair (the angel was probably a missionary). The catechist objects that this was the Europeans' book, translated for the natives' use: "'Ah! No,' replied the stranger, 'that cannot be, for they eat flesh.'" The Indians are also selective about what they incorporate: when the catechist explains to them the communion sacrament, they reply, "To all the other customs of Christians we are willing to conform, but not to the Sacrament, because the Europeans eat cow's flesh, and this will never do for us."

One pattern of incorporation that is found in a great variety of cases is to conceive of the Christian God and His earthly messengers primarily in terms of a power or force capable of controlling physical events and of entering into daily life, thereby doing great good or harm. The Westerners' technologies were clear manifestations of the greater power or force of their God. The first impression made by the large seagoing ships – the Algonquians of Canada described them as moving islands – not to mention the gunfire and metal tools could not but reinforce this view.[56] In the twentieth century, the mystery of flight had the same effect, leading to the famous cargo cults in the South Pacific. Much of the initial enthusiastic reception to Western missionaries can be attributed to this belief. At the same time, it was also a source of later disillusionment, when the new religion did not lead to an amelioration of daily life. This led to another widespread pattern: the suspicion that the Westerners were withholding secret knowledge not contained in the Bible.[57] At the same time, Jesus' and the missionaries' ability to heal the sick served as a *cultural hook*, fitting in well with the interpretation of spirituality as power to alter one's day-to-day existence.[58]

3. **Concentration of Spirituality.** In these cases, indigenes use foreign incorporations to sweep away large portions of their native religion, thus narrowing the focus to one or few features and thereby ridding the previous religion of its distorting or "superstitious" practices. Anti-idolatry campaigns furnish the most readily visible examples, as we will find when discussing the Aladura revival in Nigeria and the Taiping Rebellion in China. Clearly the injunctions of the First Commandment and the Second Commandment against multiple gods and graven images constituted a powerful *cultural hook* in these two movements.

I believe that, as a strategy, concentration of spirituality lies at the heart of a number of well-known religious phenomena in a wide variety of societies. For one thing, it probably helps to account for the increasing popularity of Islam and Christianity, with their monotheistic and monolatric doctrines and their commitment to a single prophet as divinely inspired or incarnated above all others. Together these two religions account for over half of the world's population today. One can also find plenty of examples of the same strategy in indigenous religions prior to the arrival of Islam or Christianity. In fact, concentration of spirituality may often work as a radicalized version of selective incorporation, reinforcing patterns that existed previously. This is the case in central Africa, where the spread of new religious movements periodically brought with them the destruction of charms and fetishes, again well before the arrival of Christianity. On the island of Biak in the former Dutch East Indies, idols were simply smashed, sold to traders, or thrown into the sea when they no longer proved effective.[59] In Chinese folk religion, one finds the same phenomenon. As is well known, such spiritual housecleanings have periodically occurred within Christianity and Islam as well in the form of various religious reform movements.

The desire to cleanse religion of its superfluous, distracting, or corrupting elements has rightly been characterized as a "quest for purity." A 1988 collection of essays under that title stressed the cross-cultural nature of this quest, with case studies of Calvin's Geneva, Puritan New England, Dutch Evangelicalism, the Wahhabi movement in Arabia, the Fulani jihad in West Africa, the Iranian Revolution, the Taipings, and communism, among others. The editors of the collection stressed the inexhaustible struggle against evil as common to all of these movements.[60] Certainly the preoccupation with sin, including the desire to restrict or repress much of human sexuality, would come under this heading. Yet, upon closer inspection, one finds that the struggle against evil is too restrictive a formulation. The asceticism associated with sexual restriction or abstinence, for example, is not necessarily a condemnation of evil, but can also be a means of concentrating one's energies for other, more urgent tasks at hand, contributing to an *intensification* of spirituality, not to mention a more disciplined and focused lifestyle. Gandhi's renunciation of sexual activity also comes to mind as a means of focusing his energies. The link between concentration of one's spiritual resources and asceticism will also be familiar to students of Max Weber, who characterized asceticism itself as "a methodical procedure for achieving religious salvation."[61]

Thinking of concentration of spirituality as a means of energizing and intensifying one's religion sheds light on another widely noted pattern: cultural revitalization. Coined by anthropologist Anthony Wallace and initially derived from his study of the Seneca prophet Handsome Lake at the turn of the nineteenth century, it was intended to cover a great variety of revival and reform movements. Wallace's main focus is the internal means which a culture has to heal itself when in crisis or in need of renewal – an emphasis that will be fleshed out in subsequent chapters.

Wallace observes, "With a few exceptions, every religious revitalization movement with which I am acquainted has been originally conceived in one or several hallucinatory visions by a single individual."[62] This suggests yet another form of concentrated spirituality that is related to revitalization movements but extends far beyond them: those abnormal, exceptionally intense experiences that go under the name of "altered states of consciousness." Such states, C. J. Jung suggests, are close to the core of what it means to be religious: the numinous experience of being seized by a higher power independent of one's will. Creeds and rituals, according to Jung, are only congealings and codifications of such original religious experience.[63] Hallucinations, trances, and dreams on the part of individuals obviously play a major role in their establishing charismatic authority as prophets or shamans, as Wallace pointed out. But it is also clear that other such states may be induced collectively (e.g., the "speaking in tongues" of the Pentecostals). A study conducted by anthropologist Erika Bourguignon of 488 societies worldwide found that altered states of consciousness were institutionalized parts of their culture in 90 percent of the cases.[64]

Concentration of spirituality can be manifested in different ways in space and in time. Certainly one way to concentrate one's spiritual energies – and to attain a pure life – is to segregate oneself spatially from the rest of society by creating an isolated community. This is the impulse behind the Puritan settlements in the New World, not to mention the later socialist utopias. It was also an impulse that shows up in many missionary efforts: to insure that natives were genuinely and not superficially converted, they needed to be physically separated from their pagan contemporaries and concentrated in "Christian villages" – an experiment that was repeated time and time again. A Spanish name for such settlements – *reducciónes* – expressed the mentality of concentration. One finds the same language in English proclamations in the seventeenth and eighteenth centuries: the purpose of colonization in the New World with respect to the Indians, as found in statements from King James I to George Washington, was to "reduce" them from a state of savagery to one of civility. This frequently meant changing their habits from moving their villages about to staying in one place.[65] At the same time, such spatial concentration could also be desired by indigenous peoples themselves as a haven or refuge from the turbulence going on around them – most famously, perhaps, by the Guaraní people of the Rio de la Plata region of South America, who flocked to the Jesuit mission settlements by the thousands in order to escape forced labor by the Spanish settlers and slave-raids by the Portuguese.[66]

With respect to time, concentration of spirituality finds expression in millennialism: the conviction that many of the most important events in all of world history are concentrated in the age in which one happens to live. The notion of the "end time" serves as an energizing factor, an approaching deadline, as it were, for salvation.[67] The Chinese historian Lian Xi has traced how this fervor has been responsible for the phenomenal growth of Christianity in China since the mid-twentieth century, despite – or perhaps because of – its being persecuted under the communists. He also shows how this represents a continuity with previous Buddhist and Taoist beliefs in a similar vein.[68] In the Christian tradition, millennialism finds its scriptural justification in the Books of Daniel and Revelations, the study of which in itself can become the basis of a Christian community's identity, as in the case of the Seventh-Day Adventists.[69]

One should add that concentration of spirituality is sometimes achieved not by reduction of superfluous elements but by subsumption, the bringing together of multiple beliefs and practices under a single powerful symbol. A clear example is the idea of the Devil as the embodiment of evil, a belief that grew in Europe in the late Middle Ages and reached a climax in the early modern period. As multitudes of evil spirits and demons came to be viewed as agents of a single Satan, that spirit became greatly more powerful and dangerous – as, so it was believed, were the human beings, mostly women, who secretly trafficked with him. As is well known, the result was an increase in torture, persecutions, and killings of women who confessed to be witches. The same logic could later be found in many missionaries' reactions to the beliefs of many Native American, African, and Asian societies that embraced multiple spirits, both good and evil. They were seen as incompatible with Christian doctrine and hence the work of the Devil.[70]

This example leads me to make one final observation on this subject. If concentration of spirituality is a widespread and many-faceted process to be found in the dynamics of religious change at all levels, then the same may be said of its conceptual opposite, namely the beliefs in and interaction with multiple spirits, as found in many societies throughout the world. Thus it will be convenient to refer throughout this book to the notion of *diffuse spirituality* as representing one aspect of religion with which missionaries have often had to deal. One can think of multiple spirits as typically crossing boundaries, operating throughout nature, negating such distinctions as between the natural and supernatural, the material and immaterial, the living and the dead, the sacred and the secular. One obvious consequence of this belief is that it is easier to incorporate new deities from outside, making the adoption of Christianity in some form or other as less problematical than it might otherwise seem. In the history of religion, such beliefs are often associated with the term "animism," which continues to have connotations of an evolutionary view from "primitive" or "primal" to "advanced." Alan Strathern has chosen the name "immanentism" to refer to these phenomena in a way that closely maps my notion of diffuse spirituality.[71] I would further claim that examples of diffuse spirituality can also be found in so-called advanced societies (as does Strathern), just as concentrated spirituality can be found in "primal" ones. The bases for this contention will hopefully become clear in the individual chapters and the conclusion.

4. Conservation of Form. In this type, a society will identify itself as Christian, appropriating much from missionaries by way of content, while at the same time preserving the deeper structures of its own group, which may be quite different culturally from that of the missionary. Such deeper structures include forms of social organization, such as clans, families, or ethnicities, as well as intellectual structures and behavioral patterns.

An illustrative example comes from the highlands of central Suwalesi, an island in the Indonesian archipelago. The Tobaku people in the region are 99 percent Protestant and think of themselves as devout, even fanatic, having received Salvation Army missionaries since the early twentieth century. Moreover, they associate their devotion with Western modernity. According to Lorraine Aragon's study published in 2000, most families "attend church regularly, sponsor church-supervised rites, wear Western-style clothes, send their children to government-approved schools, pay taxes, and purchase clinic medicines."[72] Their hymns are European words and tunes in Indonesian translation. Nevertheless, at a broader and deeper level, the Tobaku highlanders retain a strong belief in the efficacy of propitiating the deities in order to ensure such things as good harvests and good health – but the deities are now Christian ones. One thing this has meant is the continuation of sacrifice of plants and animals; they interpret Protestant blessings of these as promises to God, while retaining the practice of slaying chickens and pigs on important ritual occasions. If Western Christians interpret sacrifice symbolically, as in communion, the Tobaku people continue to interpret it literally.[73]

A more familiar, if inverted, example of conservation of form may be found in the modern Western notion of the secular.[74] The term derives from the Latin *saeculum*, which meant an era or age (the French *siècle* derives from the same root). Among the early Christians, it came to refer to the era between the first and second comings of Christ, which believers were expectantly awaiting. As this "age" became indefinitely extended, the term came to serve as an expression of the duality between Christianity's otherworldly orientation, which posited salvation in the next life, and its need to address the concerns of people in this world. The duality between the "spiritual" and "temporal" realms thus became an enduring feature of medieval Christianity. This can be viewed as a version of the contrast between concentrated and diffuse spirituality, as became evident when, over time, the otherworldly orientation was channeled into monasticism, and those who chose the monastic life became known as "religious," in contrast to the clergy who did not take such vows, known as the "secular." With the Reformation, monasteries in Protestant lands were disbanded, hence "secularized." It seems that this breakup of Western Christianity opened up the possibility to think of "religion" and "the secular" as more general terms, applicable beyond a specifically Christian context. Thus, the *Oxford English Dictionary* lists the first generalized use of "religion" (outside of poetry) to mean a belief in a higher power in 1535, and the first use of "secular" to refer to the present or visible world in 1597. Of course, the meanings of these terms would change drastically as the Enlightenment thinkers such as Voltaire, Diderot, and later Feuerbach and Marx attacked the notion of religion itself. A central concept in that attack was the notion of superstition, a notion by which Christians, both Catholics and Protestants, had previously attacked what they considered to be irrational aspects of pagan religion in Europe, in other words the remnants of diffuse spirituality. The enlightenment thinkers then turned this notion against Christianity itself.[75] Thus, however much the *contents* of these terms were inverted, the binary *form* of the contrast has largely persisted as a habit of thought.[76] By this I mean the tendency to associate the secular with such things as rational thought and scientific approach to nature and society, as arrayed against the irrational and supernatural, which was the realm of religion.

5. **Vernacular Translation.** My use of this term is derived from and builds on the work of Indian historian Saurabh Dube, who in turn builds on that of Vicente Rafael on the Tagalog peoples in the Philippines under the Spanish.[77] I find the term apposite to describe a particular type of interaction, namely when a group arrives at their own understanding of the meaning of Christianity (or Judeo-Christianity) as a whole, rather than piecing together individual aspects. This admittedly presupposes a rather distinct appropriation of the term "translation" – not in the sense of a glossary or a line-by-line operation, but in the sense that one needs to understand how a language works as a total system before one can arrive at an authentic translation of any of its parts. This obviously also presupposes a degree of familiarity and exposure on the part of the indigenous group to missionary Christianity over a period of time. Thus initial attempts at vernacular translation may indeed be fragmentary. Dube and Rafael both draw from a postcolonial perspective, where translation, like hybridity, is a key term. It seeks to establish a relationship between languages – and hence the worldviews – of two cultures of unequal power

that results neither in total domination by one side nor in total rejection
by the other. In other words, one would not expect the colonizer's world
to be completely or transparently assimilated by the colonized; nor one
would expect the colonized to be totally mute or uncomprehending, as
implied in Gayatri Chakravorty Spivak's negative answer to her question,
"Can the Subaltern Speak?"[78] In Dube's formulation, to vernacularize is
not merely to find linguistic equivalents to the foreign terms, nor even to
arrive at a "faithful" rendering of them, but to reinterpret them in a way
that meets the needs of the colonized people, a "transmutation of distinct
categories and discrete concepts."[79] Obviously selectivity plays a central
role here.

Now this use of the term "translation" is remarkably congruent with
its use among Christian scholars in describing the missionary impulse.
Andrew Walls puts translation at the heart of the Christian message when
he writes, "Incarnation is translation. When God in Christ became man,
Divinity was translated into humanity as though humanity were a recep-
tor language."[80] Moreover, *vernacular* translation is seen as basic to
Christian missionary work ever since Paul began spreading the word to
the Gentiles. In his influential book *Translating the Message*, the African
theologian Lamin Sanneh asserts that "the recipient culture is the authentic destination of God's salvific promise and, as a consequence, has an
honored place under 'the kindness of God,' with the attendant safeguards
against cultural absolutism."[81] Sanneh provides an appendix which lists
the entire or partial Bible translations into no less than 1,808 different
languages.[82]

Thus translation in a missionary encounter, at least in its initial stages,
is always a double process. Both missionary and indigene are translating,
interpreting what they perceive to be the other's worldview in terms of
their own. Both of these processes are interdependent, in that missionaries
have to rely on native speakers to begin their work, and indigenes have to
deal with unfamiliar new stories and concepts that refer to unheard-of
times and places. With greater familiarity, however, native translations
tend to assume a life of their own, which may distance them from the
missionaries rather than drawing them closer together. Translation does
not necessarily mean harmonization.[83]

Like concentration of spirituality, the strategy of vernacular translation can assume different forms in time and in space. In the former case,
it means finding an appropriate place for indigene peoples in the Judeo-
Christian narrative. Here, it made a considerable difference whether the
missionaries were Protestant or Catholic, since the Protestant emphasis

on the vernacular Bible provided the tools for natives to arrive at their interpretation of the narrative presented therein. The timing of the translations of the Old and New testaments was a key feature in determining the shape of indigenous Christianity. This also explains why Judaism could sometimes assume great importance, sometimes eclipsing the importance of Christ himself. The appeal of Old Testament Judaism was threefold: (1) the customs of the nomadic Hebrews were points of identification with pastoralists in various parts of the world, such as Africa; (2) the central themes of enslavement, liberation, exile, and return to the promised land constituted a narrative which many colonized or oppressed groups could easily relate to; the very term "diaspora," so central in the history of African Christianity, derives from its application to the Jews;[84] (3) the story of the Ten Lost Tribes of Israel in effect provided a point of entry into the narrative for peoples who had no prior contact with Western culture and thus had no obvious place to fit in. Missionaries and natives often agreed on tracing the origins of peoples such as the Native North Americans or the New Zealand Maori to the Lost Tribes. The Native American Pequot missionary William Apess came to the same conclusion in the early nineteenth century.[85]

Indigenous Catholics could and did draw on other types of narrative, such as the life of Christ. This came to play a central role in Filipino Christianity, where a rendition of the passion story, extended to include Creation and the Last Judgment, was chanted and dramatized every year during Lent. Again, there was emphasis on the downtrodden: Christ's humble origins were emphasized.[86] Certainly in many parts of the world today, Christ's identification with the poor informs the way natives translate the Christian message as a whole, as in Liberation Theology.

By spatial forms of vernacular translation, I mean systems of correspondence between elements of different religious worldviews. The Catholic company of saints, for example, afforded ready opportunity for establishing a comprehensive system of equivalences between native spirits and saints via juxtaposition. The Afro-Caribbean and Afro-Brazilian religions such as Santería and Candomblé form clear examples of this type, as a later chapter will demonstrate. Andrew Walls points out that these equivalences can actually give rise to new religions that are no longer identifiable as a form of Christianity.[87]

Correspondences can occur in widely differing ways, depending on how language functions in a culture. David K. Jordan provides a numerological illustration from Taiwan in recounting a conversation with a college-educated Methodist on the parable of the loaves and fishes in 1985:

"Jesus' miracle of the five cakes and two fish," Mr. Wáng explained, "was something often done by ancient miracle workers in China, which is how we know that it really happened. It shows the connection between the Bible and Chinese tradition, for the two fish, pressed into a circle, are none other than the *Yīn-Yáng* symbol, and the five cakes are five because that corresponds with the five elements."

"In the West," I objected, "it is the small number of loaves and fishes rather than the numerology that impresses people."

"If you told Chinese that Jesus had performed the miracle with six or four cakes, they would never believe it," he answered, "for everyone knows that is impossible. Because he used five, people believe in his miracles, for everyone knows that great Taoists could multiply fives. They did it all the time."[88]

Jordan also presents another illustration of material correspondence in China, based on the complexity of individual Chinese characters. These can be broken down into their constituent strokes, each of which has a meaning of its own. Finding hidden correspondences at this level, known as "glyphomancy," was a technique that Chinese Christians sometimes used to convert their countrymen, i.e., pointing to specifically Christian symbols or ideas embedded in Chinese characters, which they claimed were intentionally planted by ancient sages.[89]

Finally, one might consider *dialogue* to be an end-product of vernacular translation, the exploration of commonalities and differences between different religious points of view. One can view interreligious dialogue as incorporating vernacular translation but necessarily going beyond it. Each side must make the effort of interpreting another's faith in terms that one finds comprehensible. But this cannot be the final step; rather the goal is to understand the other in the other's terms – to devernacularize, in a sense. By the same token, dialogue does not necessarily imply transformation of one's own religious point of view, or the expectation that one will transform the other.[90]

6. Dual Religious Participation. This type may be thought of as the inverse of the previous one, referring to the simultaneous practice of two distinct traditions, without any attempt to translate one into the other. The term was coined by anthropologist William K. Powers, based on his work with the Oglala Lakota Sioux on the Pine Ridge Reservation in South Dakota. He views it as an understudied type, often confused with syncretism, when in fact no blending or combination is envisaged. For the Sioux, the pattern developed as a direct result of white interdiction:

during the years when most traditional rituals such as the sun dance were prohibited, from 1883 to 1934, the only way of preserving them was to carry them out in secret. Meanwhile, many Sioux accepted the Christianity of the missionaries. This perhaps could be seen as an example of passive resistance, but Powers suggests a more positive interpretation: "It is much more reasonable to assume," he writes, "that the Oglala became at least nominal members of Christian churches because the latter provided a kind of sanctuary from that part of the white world that regarded them as savage and hostile."[91] Significantly, when the prohibitions were lifted, the dual pattern held as well. Thus, according to Marla Powers (William's wife and fellow anthropologist), writing in 1986, the Oglala Sioux observe christenings, marriages, and the Christian religious holidays, but may also visit a medicine man for help in curing an affliction.[92] Such a pattern is probably quite widespread in many cultures, perhaps a witness to the human capacity to compartmentalize. But it can also be seen as an expression of societies that feature diffuse spirituality and the ability to accommodate diverse spirits within their pantheon.

7. **Selective Acculturation.** The term "acculturation" suggests the opposite of inculturation or incorporation, namely change to or toward a foreign model. Yet its usage is also problematical, as it was the preferred term of American anthropologists in the early twentieth century to refer to cultural mixing in general. Melville Herskovits used it along with syncretism. Yet despite the subtlety of his analyses, the term came to be seen as having an implicit subtext, namely that of long-term assimilation to a predominately European cultural model.[93] Thus it has become dated, as demonstrated by the fact that it merited an article in the 1968 *International Encyclopedia of the Social Sciences* , but not in the 2001 *International Encyclopedia of the Social and Behavioral Sciences.*

Still, a term is needed to denote those cases where groups are drawn to and identify with a culture that is not their own. This type, then, seeks to do justice to the kind of attraction which drew many non-Western individuals, particularly those living in colonial enclaves such as trading posts or port cities, to Western culture, as embodied in such terms as "modernity" and "civilization." Needless to say, missionaries and their institutions played a key role as attractors in these situations. Many of them had conceived their mission as a culturally "civilizing" one from the outset, inseparable from their spreading the Christian message of salvation. Frequently it was that cultural mission – as distinct from the latter message – that was most readily accepted, most overtly through the vehicles of Western medicine and education.

For purposes of analysis, I use the term "selective" here to mean one of two things, depending on who is doing the selecting: the foreigner or the indigene. In practice, the two are extremely difficult to disentangle. Much of the literature on colonialism emphasizes the former by claiming that, while originally based on coercion, colonialism continues to operate at a subconscious level, foreclosing alternative worldviews by setting the very terms of discourse. To quote the Indian psychologist Ashis Nandy, "the ultimate violence which colonialism does to its victims ... [is] that it creates a culture in which the ruled are constantly tempted to fight their rulers within the psychological limits set by the latter."[94] This aspect emerges clearly in the Comaroffs' study of the Tswanas in southern Africa. By showing how the introduction of such things as agricultural tools and techniques, money, Western dress and architecture, and legal and political concepts all gradually changed the Tswanas' day-to-day existence, they make a persuasive case for what they call the "colonization of consciousness," even allowing, as they do, for native choice within these frameworks.[95] They stress that much of this occurs at the level of form as well as content, by creating the categories within which negotiation takes place – the *assimilation* rather than conservation of form. Thus, for example, African indigenes have adopted for themselves the national identities as created by the colonial maps, even as they struggled for independence; both the "ethnic subject" and the "modernist citizen" can be seen as examples of such assimilative categories.[96]

I would argue, however, that the framing of acculturative interactions exclusively in terms of colonial domination tends to minimize the extent of genuine attraction exerted by Western civilization for non-Westerners (not that the West had a monopoly on this – Islamic civilization exerted a similar pull for many in sub-Saharan Africa, for example), and the role of indigenous selection in the process. Indeed, a common thread in accounts of missionary education in many places is the indigenes' demand for instruction in a European language. The ability to read and understand colonial directives was obviously an urgent need on the part of indigenous leaders. This often worked at cross-purposes to the missionaries' project of spreading the message in the vernacular, especially among the Protestants. Thus, we find the Sioux chiefs Red Cloud and Spotted Tail petitioning President Hayes in 1877 for Catholic missionaries rather than Protestants because they provided instruction in English. In West Africa as well, Anglicans introduced English instruction in the early 1900s for fear of losing students to the Catholics.[97] A similar story can be told for Beirut, Lebanon in the nineteenth century, which became known as the "city of schools," but where the dominant language was French.[98]

If this demand for language instruction and Western knowledge may still be seen as enabling indigenes to operate within the parameters set by the Western colonizer, the attraction could also operate at a deeper level, namely the empowerment that comes with a feeling of belonging to a wider world. For example, the anthropologist Joel Robbins, in his work with the small Urapmin language group in remote Papua New Guinea writes of their conversion to Christianity: "When Urapmin pray with everyone else in the world on Sunday, they see themselves ... as linking up with the 'white' Christian world as opposed to what they take to be the disappointing 'black' nation of Papua New Guinea, a nation that is full of chaos and danger and that has marginalized the Urapmin and rendered them peripheral."[99]

Perhaps the most dramatic demonstration of the power of this long-term acculturation came with the African-American colonization of Liberia. Despite the idealistic hopes of its founders of returning American slaves and free blacks to their ancestral roots, the colony faced a continual struggle against tremendous odds: an appalling death rate of 50 percent for the first two decades due principally to malaria, attacks from hostile natives, poverty, and uprootedness. One thing became instantly clear to the settlers, however: they were not like the Africans. The identity they forged in this desperate situation was the one they had willy-nilly acquired in the New World: that of civilized Westerners, which they opposed to the native "savages." And the Judeo-Christian narrative provided the vessel that carried this identity to their new home. In the words of the first inaugural address of the new republic in 1848 by Joseph Roberts, the settlers were "[a] mere handful of isolated Christian pilgrims ... surrounded by savage and warlike tribes bent upon their ruin and total annihilation ... determined in the name of the 'Lord of Hosts' to stand their ground." Their purpose was "the redemption of Africa from the deep degradation, superstition and idolatry in which she has so long been involved."[100] Citizenship could be granted to natives provided they "abandoned all the forms, customs and superstitions of heathenism." There were some native parents who voluntarily placed their children in settler homes so that they could learn the ways of civilization.[101]

8. Acceptance and Commitment. The vocabulary would be incomplete without an attempt at grasping what it means for different non-Westerners to accept Christianity wholeheartedly. Yet this is far easier said than done. Certainly there are abundant biographies of converted

and committed individual native Christians that dot the missionary literature. But how is one to evaluate these? The question of bias plays a big
role here, as it was in the interest of missionaries to parade as many
converts as they could for the benefit of readers back home. Yet the
scholar who approaches this material from a purely secular starting point
is equally prone to bias, namely to minimize or explain away the evidence
in the sources for a genuinely spiritual encounter. In his study of
conversion, Rambo lists five major themes that recur in his conversations
with about two hundred converts of different orientations: (1) an intimate
relationship with God; (2) a sense of relief from guilt; (3) a sense of
purpose for living, including social commitment; (4) a sense of belonging
to a community; (5) an enlarged view of reality and the cosmos.[102] One
might ask whether these themes hold up under widely differing cultural
conditions. As far as I know, there are no good answers to this question,
because the study of comparative confession or autobiography is in its
infancy.[103]

Public and collective expressions of Christian commitment are obviously easier to categorize and discuss. One can always look at statistics of
how many Christians there are in a given place, their percentage of the
population as a whole, and how these change over time. Certainly these
numbers indicate an impressive growth of Christianity worldwide in the
twentieth century. But, aside from questions of reliability, the numbers
beg the question of the meanings that people attach to being a
Christian.[104] As with the cases of resistance and rejection, there are
obviously many gradations of acceptance from passivity to activity.
Furthermore, trying to dissect these expressions makes it very difficult
to disentangle the "how" of acceptance from the "why," – that is, the
varied motivations and reasons people have for accepting Christianity in
the first place. One way of keeping such a discussion within bounds is to
focus on the ways in which Christians demonstrate their commitment
over an extended period of time. There are several ways one can do this:

(1) One is to look at what indigenous Christians have done, in areas
    such as public service, charitable work, education and compare
    these to the records of other religious or secular groups.
(2) A number of commentators have noted that the appeal of
    Christianity in many parts of the world today is its ability to foster
    a sense of community, particularly in those countries where urban-
    ization is a powerful trend. Andrew Walls notes, "African peoples
    who have long resisted Islam and shown little interest in Christian

missions in their homelands have divided between church and mosque when migration has got underway to the cities."[105] The *cultural hook* of Jesus's outreach to the poor and the sick is a prominent theme in this appeal.

(3) One can look at the ability of a Christian community to survive in the face of adversity. In a number of East Asian countries, for example, Christians have been objects of persecution. Yet their numbers remained steady or even increased. In Japan, when Christianity was reintroduced in the 1860s after having been banned by the Tokugawa shogunate for over two hundred years, it was discovered that there were some 20,000 "Hidden Christians" that had remained true to their faith.[106] Vietnamese Christians suffered intermittent but bloody persecutions at the hands of the Nguyen dynasty in the nineteenth century, yet their numbers continued to grow.[107] Korean Christianity has sustained three waves of persecution: that of the Confucian Choson Dynasty, the Japanese occupation, and communist North Korea. Yet today it is stronger in South Korea than anywhere else in Asia. Christianity has thus been associated with Korean patriotism by virtue of its history.

(4) Another way is to look at indigenes as taking an active role in the spread of Christianity themselves, either as missionaries or as aides to them. It is recognized that they did so in practically every case, but also that they rarely left written records. Nevertheless, there are group patterns that emerge, apart from the narratives of individuals. Certain countries have strong missionary movements – Korea being one of them, second only to the United States in the 1990s in numbers of missionaries sent abroad.[108] Another remarkable case is the Polynesian Pacific Islands, where natives have embraced Christianity with a breadth and depth rarely equaled elsewhere. Once the European missionaries had succeeded in converting the chiefs in Tahiti and nearby islands in the early nineteenth century, natives began to form auxiliary societies that spread the religion to other islands. Most remarkably, the tiny atoll-nation of Tuvalu, the fourth-smallest country in the world in area and the second smallest in population (as of 2018), has sent at least seventy-nine missionaries to eight different parts of the Pacific.[109] One can speculate that the desire to leave the confines of home which spurred the Polynesians to row across vast distances also spurred them to actively embrace an expansive and proselytizing religion.

Clearly, the desire to expand and proselytize can also involve violence, as does the willingness to fight to defend one's faith. Jenkins devotes a chapter in his book *The Next Christendom* to "the next crusade," in which the confrontation between Christianity and Islam most immediately comes to mind. Yet perhaps an equally intriguing challenge to world Christianity in the future is how it will deal with the phenomenon of indigenous cultural revival among peoples (e.g., Native Americans, Australian Aborigines, and Maori) who had been exposed to prolonged missionary activity. To what extent do such movements entail a rejection of Christianity? How adaptable is Christianity to such revivals of indigenous cultural expression? These are questions which the subsequent chapters will seek to address.

2

Colonial Latin America

The Nahuas (Aztecs) and Their Neighbors

PRECONDITIONS

The Spanish conquest of central Mexico offers an exceptionally favorable set of circumstances for posing many of the issues surrounding indigenous/missionary encounters with relative sharpness and clarity. The compactness of the core of the Aztec Empire, the Basin of Mexico, with its dense concentration of peoples who mostly shared the same language – Nahuatl – offers a good basis for comparison with the more rugged and remote areas of the Spanish colonies, which often contained a diversity of language groups. The decisiveness of the 1521 Spanish military victory over this core and the resolve and brutality with which Cortés and his followers destroyed the Aztec temples and removed their priests in the years immediately following left no doubt as to their intentions to impose a new religion. The smallpox epidemic's role in contributing to the Spanish victory is universally acknowledged; it turned out to be merely the first in a wave of epidemics that seemingly decimated the society, reducing the population of southern Mexico to as little as 10 percent of the estimated preconquest numbers by the early seventeenth century. If nothing else, these scourges taxed the indigenes' powers of explanation, because the cyclical theories of fortune of their previous belief systems could not account for them.[1] It is hardly surprising, then, that they tended to attribute superior power to the new religion.

Another set of favorable preconditions for the spread of Christianity was the relative sophistication of the members of the Mendicant orders who did the work of missionization. The first to arrive were, symbolically, twelve Franciscans in 1524, followed by Dominicans in 1526,

Augustinians in 1533, and Jesuits in 1572. The Franciscans dominated the early phase; their idealistic desire to create a Christian paradise in the New World and their asceticism remind one of the New England Puritans.[2] Yet, like the other orders, they were also schooled in Erasmian Renaissance humanism and, consequently, were determined to understand as much as they could about the peoples they sought to convert. This meant learning their languages, which, in turn, meant collaborating with native speakers. The early friars became conversant in a total of ten Mexican languages and published books in at least six of them.[3] The creation of written vernaculars in Latin alphabets constituted one of the missionaries' greatest gifts to their target peoples – a theme we will see repeated in culture after culture worldwide. In the words of one scholar of Nahua literacy, "[a]lthough its place in Christian iconography is relatively minor, the book should be nearly as central a symbol of the church as the cross."[4] The friars also created schools, again with the help of native collaborators, for instruction in the catechism, plus technical and moral education, the latter for girls as well, although this was abandoned in ten years. The Franciscans separated the sons of the nobles from those of the commoners and trained the former in a European curriculum at a special college, the Colegio de Santa Cruz at Tlatelolco, thereby fostering a literate Nahua elite whose members were soon writing their own works in their own language.[5] Most of the information we have on preconquest Mexico was compiled by this generation of postconquest writers. Although the friars' commitment to such schools declined by the end of the sixteenth century, most villages in the Basin had their own Nahuatl scribe by then.

These linguistic achievements should not lead one to underestimate the significance of the arts as means of communication. Christian imagery in churches was especially important, and Indians had assimilated Western-style painting and sculpting by the 1580s.[6] The friars also had the good sense to incorporate music and dance into worship, thereby drawing on native enthusiasms and traditions. Elaborate processions and dances became the rule on feast days, including theatrical performances by the Nahua. One type of performance was the staging of mock battles between Christians and Moors, which could be found both in Spanish tradition and – with different players – in the Aztec tradition as well. Such scenes probably served as masks for anti-Spanish sentiments. Beginning in 1539, however, a council of bishops found it necessary to draw boundaries between these spectacles and Christian worship by a series of restrictions and prohibitions. But controlling their exuberance remained a chronic problem.[7]

Friars did what they could to relieve the suffering caused by disease. Although they founded few hospitals, they were at least as able to care for the sick as the native shamans who, they noted, perished while the friars did not. They organized public scourges to express penance for sins and provided spiritual support in the form of administering the sacraments, particularly baptism.[8]

It is clear that the natives often demanded, and the missionaries acceded to, mass baptism, even though this went against the requirement that converts be given a minimum of instruction beforehand.[9] Once baptized, attendance at mass, including sermons, was required, as was catechism class and yearly confession. One was expected to know the basic doctrines and prayers by heart.[10]

There were occasions when the friars imposed their religion by force, punishing those who disobeyed by whipping – in violation of Spanish law – but it is easy to exaggerate the extent of this practice. According to Louise Burkhart, "[O]n the whole friars were, for their time, a peaceable lot who preferred to do their persuading with words, with pictures explained in words, and with the example set by their own lifestyle."[11]

A third set of favorable preconditions consisted in the Nahuas' predisposition to acquiesce in many of the measures that the conquerors imposed. True, the idea that the Nahuas had been expecting Cortés's arrival in the form of the return of their god Quetzalcoatl has been effectively put to rest by recent scholarship – although it did become widely accepted in the mid-sixteenth century, since it was both flattering to the Spanish and mollifying to the Nahuas in the light of their defeat.[12] But the state that the Spanish had vanquished in 1521 was itself an empire, which had treated its conquered subjects in much the same way that the Spanish did – with the notable exception of regular human sacrifice. The Nahuas were thus used to paying tribute in terms of labor; moreover, the sons of their nobility had been required to go to school in the capital. The Aztecs had also burned the temples of the peoples they conquered, and the latter incorporated the gods of the victors into their pantheon. As James Lockhart and Stuart B. Schwartz put it, "Given the fact of conquest, the sedentary peoples by and large took conversion for granted. The question was one of learning just what a converted person should do and how much of the old could be retained. Thus the emphasis was on instruction rather than conversion, on teaching Christian duties, beliefs, and sacraments."[13]

This is not to deny the overall oppressiveness and exploitiveness of Spanish rule, particularly when it came to extracting labor and mineral wealth. Indeed, Charles Gibson, one of the foremost scholars of colonial Mexico, concurs with the basic truth of this so-called Black Legend. Yet Gibson's evidence also points to certain mitigating factors that deserve mention. For one, the drastic loss of native population resulted in a much more favorable ratio of people to land in the crowded Basin than before the conquest. For another, the Spanish control of the economy was not matched by its domination of native political structures. There were simply too few settlers or officials to do so, with the result that the local nobility remained in power, even as new municipal institutions were established. True, the Spanish had plans for resettlement of the Indians into more compact villages, as they did throughout their empire, but in the Basin, these were limited in extent.[14] Thus native peoples were able to exercise a degree of control over their local circumstances that the Black Legend – an eighteenth-century European term in any case – would not lead one to expect.[15]

PRISM OF SOURCES

Given this scenario, what can we tell about indigenous attitudes and behaviors toward Christianity? The answers vary widely depending on the type of source one reads. On the one hand, there is good evidence for Nahua *resistance*, not necessarily in the form of violent uprisings, but by secretly carrying on their traditional practices – often in caves – while outwardly acquiescing to Christianity (*dual participation*). This might have been expected during the twenty-odd years immediately following the taking of the capital city, as the Spanish were still consolidating their control. Some calendars and religious art survive from this period, and there are accounts of nobles pretending to send their sons to the mission-ary schools but sending their slaves instead, bedecked in noble finery, while girls were locked up to prevent them from going.[16] At the same time, there is some evidence of genuine native affection for the friars, particularly the Franciscans, who were at least kinder than the Spanish landowners. The evidence of secret "idolatry" continues, however, during the latter half of the sixteenth century and into the seventeenth century, as that initial affection appears to have evaporated. Spanish authorities noted a decline in church attendance in the 1550s.[17] A memorial by the bishops of New Spain in 1565 states, "The great readiness with which these newly converted Indians revert to their idolatries, rites, sacrifices, and superstitions is notorious."[18] Statues of gods were sometimes con-cealed behind altars in churches, so that Christian prayers could apparently be directed to the Nahua deity.[19] Perhaps the most damning indictment of the seeming failure of the missionaries to win over their charges comes from two of the friars, Diego Durán and Bernardino de Sahagún, who devoted their lives to understanding and recording the customs of the Nahuas. The more familiar they became with those customs, the more they realized the extent of the cultural and religious divide. Durán's account reveals the troubled anomie, the feeling of being at home in neither religion that many of his subjects experienced.[20] Nor, as he admits, were these practices limited to outlying regions of New Spain; they could be found in Mexico City itself.[21]

The Spanish search for "idolatry" in the New World intensified in the seventeenth century, as the Catholic Reformation in Europe brought with it a renewed commitment to orthodoxy and vigilance against its violators, resulting in multiple inquisitions on both sides of the Atlantic. Indeed, some of the most detailed descriptions of native non-Christian practices come from clergy who were part of these campaigns – although they were infrequent and mild in Mexico in comparison to Peru. References to the Devil as the unifying cause of these violations become more frequent. Nevertheless, by the end of the century this zeal was diminishing, and similar reports of pagan practices were received with greater equanimity.[22] Still, as late as 1803, a town in the Central Basin of Mexico was found to be worshipping "idols" in caves.[23]

These accounts might invite a certain amount of skepticism, because their sources are almost entirely Spanish and perhaps tell us as much about the mentality of the missionaries as about the Nahuas themselves.[24] They bespeak disappointment, an inverted reflection of the inflated expectations with which the friars came, including expectations of what it meant to be converted.[25] Still, missionaries like Sahagún and Durán knew their subjects well, and their conclusions have been confirmed by many subsequent local studies.[26] But while such "idolatrous" practices undoubtedly existed, the natives' interpretation of their meanings were not necessarily those of the friars. In any case, missionary complaints about the lack of sincerity of their converts will echo throughout the following chapters as a kind of refrain.

A very different picture emerges when one turns to the vernacular documents written by the local scribes as they became literate in the new alphabetic written language. These are mostly legal documents – the Nahuas were enthusiastic litigants – and undoubtedly better reflect the views of the Nahua elite than of the lower classes. Nevertheless, they do show how religion was intertwined with society and politics at the local

level. They certainly do not convey the impression of insincerity in the
practice of Christianity; on the contrary, they reveal a proliferation of
churches built by local residents with their own labor, in addition to the
monastery churches in the larger towns that enlisted tribute labor. The
church was located either on or near the site of the former temple, which
had served as the focal point of municipal religious life. This proliferation
may explain the decline in church attendance noted by the Spanish, since
most of these village churches operated independently of a priest, except
for an itinerant visit (hence their label *iglesias de visita*).[27] The chief officer
of the church, the *fiscal*, was a prestigious figure drawn from the noble
families that constituted the ruling elite of the municipality. He not only
kept financial records but also performed many of a priest's functions in his
absence. Other staff members had various titles, often in connection with
music and singing.[28]

The extant wills and testaments shine a most revealing spotlight on the
assimilation of at least one Christian concept. This was the practice of an
individual's willing that his or her property be sold to pay for masses to be
said after death. A few documents make explicit reference to the soul's time
in purgatory, which might thereby be reduced. In some cases, the subject
stipulated that the land was to be rented to pay for an ongoing endowment
for such masses. These arrangements obviously affected how much wealth
would be passed on to one's family and were not infrequently a cause of
dispute. The church obviously benefited from such bequests, but the fact
that the proceeds were not always donated to the church as a whole, but
instead to a mass for one's soul, suggests that individualistic as opposed to
communal notions of religiosity were taking hold. Women were more
likely to write such provisions into their wills than men.[29]

Another institution that served to support the church, including payment for masses, was the *cofradía* (brotherhood). Borrowed from the
Spanish, these institutions multiplied greatly among the Nahuas in the
seventeenth century. They functioned in part as burial societies, since the
expense of a proper funeral was considerable. They also became a mark of
local identity. Despite the name, the membership, in one case, was over half
female.[30] Later, in the nineteenth century, when church practices were
under attack from the secular government, the local *cofradía*s tended to
merge with the municipal offices, creating a so-called civil-religious hierarchy as the native village was thrown back on its own resources.[31]

A still different picture emerges from a third type of source: Christian
writings in Nahuatl (sermons, catechisms, psalms, religious plays, etc.)
done under the auspices of the friars, but probably often formulated by

their native students and assistants, on whom the missionaries depended for translations of the message they sought to convey. Here, one can see a distinctive set of meanings that the Nahuas brought to the new religion (*vernacular translation*). Experts in the language have analyzed these texts, looking closely at the religious terms and their meanings in order to determine just how that intended message was transformed in the process. For example, the word chosen for "sin," *tlatlacolli*, was derived from the verb "to damage, spoil, or harm," conveying something of the this-worldliness of the Nahua interpretation – one answered for one's sins through one's misfortunes in this life rather than in the next. Also, there was no generic term for "evil" in Nahuatl.[32] To be sure, the vocabulary contained contrasts that could help convey in a metaphorical sense the dichotomy between good and evil, such as light and dark, cleanliness and filth, health and disease. But the underlying Nahua belief system did not dichotomize them in the same way. According to Burkhart, "[F]or Nahuas the basic cosmic conflict was between order and chaos, for Christians between good and evil." Maintaining order meant that the equilibrium between light and dark forces had to be maintained, giving each its proper place. "The Nahuas and their gods coexisted in a relation of reciprocity, a contract: if humans behaved in socially and ritually prescribed fashion [including offerings], the gods were expected to grant them the things that they thereby merited."[33] The notion of divine grace or forgiveness was absent. Correcting for chaos meant that there was room for repentance and confession, another point of overlap between the two religions that served as a *cultural hook*, but, again, with different meanings attached. The Nahuas eagerly lined up for confession, sometimes traveling great distances to do so. Yet confession did not necessarily involve a feeling of contrition; it was rather an act of setting things right. Confession had a legal meaning as well in preconquest times; one could be absolved from punishment if one obtained a letter certifying confession.[34] These are just some examples that bespeak a fundamental difference of outlook: Nahua religion was animistic, drawing no sharp distinction between the material and spiritual worlds, thus rendering somewhat irrelevant the missionaries' distinction between the "sincere" and the "idolatrous."

PATTERNS: CONSERVATION OF FORM, SELECTIVE ACCULTURATION, AND SELECTIVE INCORPORATION

How then best to characterize the Nahuas' interactions with Christianity? Among Mesoamerican specialists, the term "syncretism" has often been

used to express the fusion of old and new elements that presumably
occurred. Those who do so not only recognize its past imprecision but
also believe it can be refined.[35] A majority of scholars nevertheless have
weighed in against it, finding it too pat and static, failing to capture the
dynamics of a complex process.[36] Certainly, we are dealing here with a
multiplicity of adaptations, sometimes sequential, sometimes occurring at
several levels simultaneously, and invariably reflecting local customs
and conditions.

In my view, a term that better describes this multilevel quality is
conservation of form, by which I mean that the Nahuas absorbed much
of the content of Catholic imagery and ritual imported from Europe while
adapting it to the formal structure of their previous beliefs about the
world and the supernatural – more often than not, however, as expressed
in their practices rather than in words. This pattern persisted alongside
the *dual participation* mentioned earlier; the relative distribution of these
depended largely on geographical conditions, with *conservation of form*
predominating in the central Basin.

This is evident in what is undoubtedly the predominant expression of
Nahua Christianity, which took shape in the late sixteenth century, the
veneration of saints. Lockhart puts it well:

Saints leap out of wills, municipal decrees, sales, leases, annals, primordial titles,
indeed almost everything the Nahuas wrote down without supervision and primarily for their own eyes. No other aspect of Christian religious belief and ritual
had a remotely comparable impact on the broad range of their activity (especially
if we consider that Jesus Christ and often the cross were in effect treated as so
many more saints), with the possible exception of the rites associated with
death.[37]

Each municipality had its patron saint, which was a focus of communal
identity much as local deities had been in preconquest times. The distinctive open-church architecture of early colonial Mexico reflects this, providing an example of preconquest forms preserved. Unlike European
churches, those in Mexico included an enclosed open space, just as
Aztec temples had been, a patio where the priest could conduct mass
outdoors (Fig. 2.1).[38]

The arched structure on the right housed an altar plus room for
musicians for the outdoor masses. In addition, each household had its
saint or saints, with a special structure set aside for their images. These
were neither limited to one particular patron nor at the household or
communal level; there was a plethora of images in homes and churches,
the latter creating a crowded exuberance of color that has come to be

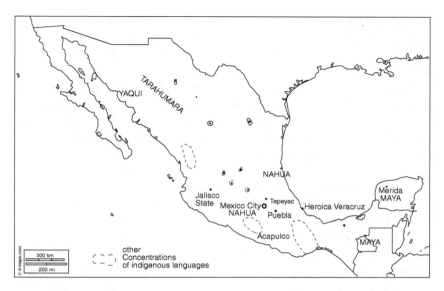

Figure 2.1 Mexican indigenous languages
Source: Modified from Tony Burton, *Major Indigenous Groups*, in "The Geography of Languages in Mexico: Spanish and 62 Indigenous Languages," *Geo-Mexico*, April 23, 2010

known as "indigenous baroque."[39] Multiple images of Christ were incorporated into this pantheon. These images were viewed as animated. According to Serge Gruzinski, "Saints were persons. Images moved, walked, sweated, bled, cried like people as only people can."[40] They were recognized as landowners in whose name individuals and churches acted as custodians. In the twentieth century, one finds cases of images being assigned godparents to care for them.[41] One sees in this the fusion of materiality and spirituality that characterized the preconquest religion, not to mention the conservation of belief in multiple spirits.

Local studies have uncovered a good deal of continuity between the veneration of saints and the pre-Hispanic gods, particularly as regards their functions (e.g., bringing rain, where St. John the Baptist became identified with the Aztec god Tlaloc). Saints' feast days were often adjusted to meet the local agricultural calendar.[42] On the other hand, there was a certain randomness to this process; one looks in vain for the elaborate tables correlating saints and spirits that one finds, for example, in Afro-Caribbean or Afro-Brazilian religions. According to J. Jorge Klor de Alva, the grandchildren of the preconquest generation had already forgotten the names of the gods.[43] Moreover, the preconquest Aztec practice of blood offerings through ritual killing and dismemberment as a means of insuring rebirth and fertility had been erased.[44] But the form of ritual, that of making an offering to the saints so that they will favor the living, was conserved.[45]

These practices have also survived in the well-known Day of the Dead (November 2), now a prominent tourist attraction notable for portraying death in a carnivalesque, lighthearted way. Observed throughout the Catholic world as All Souls Day, it is the occasion of a special mass for the departed souls in purgatory to aid in their purification. Thus, like the endowment of special masses, it derives from a concern with one's fate in the afterlife. Offerings to the dead, including food, are common in Spain and Latin America. In Mexico, however, it has achieved a prominence and intensity unparalleled elsewhere. It is widely regarded as a syncretic fusion par excellence, in which the dead are said to return for a visit to partake of the offerings and in which figurines representing the dead are consumed. In fact, however, we have little information about preconquest funereal practices, except for kings, so it is entirely possible that, like the veneration of saints, it is a variation on a Catholic custom that took shape during the colonial period. If nothing else, it illustrates the creative and inventive possibilities of such popular religious practices, as is the case in most religious festivals throughout the world.[46]

The veneration of Mary, which eventually culminated in the shrine of the Virgin of Guadalupe at Tepeyac – just outside Mexico City – becoming the Western Hemisphere's greatest pilgrimage site, suggests yet another pattern, namely *selective acculturation*. To be sure, Mary was introduced to Mexico by Cortés, who presented her as a victorious conqueror, which the Nahuas might have identified with the fearsome war goddess Coatlicue. But under the friars, the Marian image evolved into something quite different, that of a tender and merciful intercessor, no longer resembling the Aztec goddesses temperamentally. The virgin came to fill a need that other available divine figures could not provide. Told that their own gods and spirits were demons and manifestations of the Devil, Mary represented a figure of positive emotional attachment.[47]

The site at Tepeyac was just one of many where the Nahua had come to venerate the Virgin in their local areas. The notion that the site had previously been a temple of an Aztec goddess has been shown to be implausible, since her name, Tonantzin ("our revered mother"), is a form of address rather than a specific goddess.[48] The earliest references to it go back to 1556, not to an apparition but to an image of a dark-faced madonna painted by an Indian; it is unclear whether it is the same as the present one, but stylistically the latter is consistent with Nahua painting of the time.[49] Its location close to the capital made it a favorite site for Spaniards as well, as other witnesses of the sixteenth and early seventeenth centuries attest. Its gradual rise to prominence beginning in the mid-seventeenth century can be seen as a manifestation of growing *acculturation* of at least some Nahuas to Spanish society at that time.[50] More Indians were becoming bilingual and able to serve as intermediaries between the Spanish and native populations.[51] What emerged as central in both Spanish- and Nahuatl-written versions of 1648 is the story that the Virgin had appeared to an Indian peasant, Juan Diego, in 1531, just as Christianity was becoming established. This was an imported Spanish theme: the notion that the Virgin miraculously appeared to someone of humble origin was a standard feature in the Old World. Thus, we might see this as *assimilation* of a foreign form rather than conservation. But making that person an Indian became crucial in eventually making Guadalupe a symbol for all Mexicans, notably in the War of Independence from Spain. The canonization of Juan Diego by Pope John Paul II in 2002 as the first indigenous saint from the Americas marked the ultimate validation of the Indian component.[52]

Various local studies of Nahua villages might lead one to question the degree of acculturation that occurred in relation to the Guadalupe devotion. An ethnographic study conducted in the 1970s by James A. Taggart provides a nice illustration of the differences between *selective acculturation* and *selective incorporation*. Taggart recorded and analyzed stories from fifteen renowned storytellers in two villages in the Sierra Puebla, a rugged mountain range located between central Mexico and the Atlantic coast. One of these villages was purely Nahua; the other had a mixed Nahua-Hispanic population. The Spanish minority had settled there during the nineteenth century and developed coffee plantations. They remained the dominant class, both economically and politically, at the time of the study. Although bilingual, they lived apart from the Nahuas, who were dependent on them for employment and patronage. Taggart compared a number of stories from the two villages, as well as the Aztec versions found in Sahagún. The differences in the stories reflect the degree of Spanish influence. In the first village, one story of the origin of the sun and moon once again identifies the sun with Jesus and the moon with Mary. In the latter, Jesus's birth is still identified with the dawn, but follows roughly the Biblical Christmas account, no doubt due to the fact that the Christmas pageant was celebrated there regularly. Other stories illustrate different views on women, with the Spanish-influenced one being more patriarchal.[53]

THE SPANISH FRONTIER

The picture changes as one looks beyond the Basin of Mexico, the core area of Spanish control. Several factors combined to delay and attenuate the Christian impact in other parts of the colony – among them ethnic and linguistic diversity, sparse population, and geographical obstacles – not only the rugged mountains, but also the coastal areas, whose inhospitable climate made them "the least Catholic states of Mexico," according to Robert Ricard.[54] As the Spanish control weakened, the spectrum of indigenous responses broadened. As one might expect, they included numerous examples of violent *resistance*, and not just in the early years. Sometimes these rebels deliberately attacked the missions and enacted bloody parodies of their rituals, as in the case in 1541, when Caxcan warriors in Jalisco killed and mauled the speech organs of a preaching Franciscan lay brother in return for his preaching. They then made his habit into an object of worship with a special feast day to celebrate the triumph of idolatry.[55] The famous Pueblo Revolt of 1680 was equally specific; not only were clergy targeted and churches demolished, but the Indians bathed to undo the effects of baptism.[56]

Given such conditions, the dynamics of native-missionary encounters were likely to be considerably different from those of the core region. In the absence of heavy Spanish settlement, missionaries tended to take over the role of colonizer, controlling as much as possible all aspects of native life. They were more likely to undertake resettlement, use physical punishment, and were less likely to have mastered the local languages.[57] In northwestern Mexico, Susan M. Deeds discerns a common rhythm to the indigenous response: (1) initial acceptance and even invitation of missionaries; (2) disillusionment and rebellion after about a generation, often with a millenarian motive; (3) passive and sullen *resistance* following defeat. In some cases, this led to the disappearance of a tribe, as its members assimilated into the mixed labor force.[58] In others, such as the Yaqui and Tarahumara peoples, it led to survival, as the natives managed to incorporate certain aspects of the new culture, including its religion, but maintaining enough of the old ways to sustain a sense of identity. The reasons for the initial acceptance would include physical desperation, as the waves of disease frequently preceded the missionaries, seeking shelter from Spanish slaving, or recognition of the material advantages of their agricultural techniques. Disillusion could result from the realization that the missionaries could not prevent disease or that the concentration of peoples even furthered it; also, the natives increasingly viewed the missionaries as part of the exploitive labor system. Passive resistance included refusal to resettle in the mission communities, pilfering, and showing disrespect (e.g., during sermons). In general, the *selective incorporation* that took place among the Yaqui and Tarahumara peoples meant that their acceptance of Catholic rituals and festivals while consciously rejecting its doctrine.[59]

YUCATAN AND THE ANDES

In some ways the model of the frontier applies to the missionary impact on the Mayans in the Yucatán Peninsula, at least at the beginning. It took the Spanish several tries to conquer the peninsula between 1526 and 1546, due in part to the climate and the population's dispersal, which was conducive to guerilla warfare. Even afterward, it remained an economic backwater. Spanish penetration was on the whole more gradual and shallow, unable to prevent a revolt from breaking out as late as 1847.

If the contours of Spanish colonialism in the Yucatán were milder than in central Mexico, those of religious interaction were more jagged, at least in the early years. The Franciscans, who arrived in 1544, never learned the native language to the same extent as in central Mexico. As in other frontier areas, they often took the lead in subjugating the natives, for example in resettling them into compact towns. They were nevertheless able to marshall into school in Mérida some two thousand sons of the nobility, who obediently learned the Christian religion and acquired literacy in a new Mayan alphabet. In 1562, however, the missionaries discovered that the Mayans, including those closest to them, were worshipping idols in caves, sacrificing children on crosses, and performing their own version of the mass. This was probably less parody than imitation, as the nobles sought to incorporate the key elements of the new faith into their own. We know this from an indigenous written source: the books of *Chilam Balam*, secretly recorded by the educated Mayans in the new alphabet, in order to preserve their old wisdom. One of these reduces Christianity to an epoch in cyclical Mayan history, one that will eventually come to an end.[60]

In any case, the immediate reaction of the friars to the discovery was a feeling of intense betrayal, which resulted in a massive inquisition, with over 4,500 Indians being tortured and 158 deaths, some by public execution at a huge idol-burning ceremony.[61]

These measures, harsh as they were, did have the effect of subduing Mayan religious resistance, and the Indians gradually settled into the pattern of venerating the saints, much as in central Mexico.[62] Noble families who had preserved Mayan rituals in secret ceremonies now served the church as fiscal officers and cantors. If there were any differences from the Nahuas' case, they lay in: (1) the relatively greater role of the cross, which was associated with a powerful Mayan symbol, the Tree of Life; (2) the communal public aspects of veneration of the saints continued to outweigh the private individual ones; (3) pre-Christian deities and spirits play a greater role in rituals, meshing with prayers to the Father, Son, and Holy Spirit.[63] Over the long run, the Mayans retained more of their indigenous culture than was the case with the Nahuas.[64] According to Nancy Farriss, the revolt of 1847, almost 301 years to the day after the one that sealed the Spanish conquest, signaled that "the time had come to fulfill the prophecies foretelling that the Spanish, like the Itza and other foreign oppressors before them, would be driven out."[65]

The case of Andean religion in South America represents yet another variation of the frontier scenario. There was a contrast between the cities of Cuzco, Quito, and Lima (the latter founded by the Spanish in 1535), which served as centers of *selective acculturation* (e.g., of European techniques of painting and sculpture), and the countryside, where the rugged terrain combined with the shortage of priests worked against any quick and easy conversion. Thus, when the Spanish attacked the Incan temples and priesthood in Cuzco in 1532, it had little initial effect on the mountain peoples. Over time, however, they proved responsive to miracles and visitations of the Virgin, as they had previously absorbed the Incan worship of the sun.[66] Nonetheless, Andean spirituality proved exceedingly difficult to root out, because its embodiments, known as *huacas*, could be found almost anywhere. The Spanish tended to think of these *huaca* spirits as idols, typically inhabiting mountains and caves, but they could also be places, and the term could also be applied to anything extraordinary, whether good or bad.[67] Otherwise, the frontier pattern is clearly evident: a slow conquest beginning in 1532, a major rebellion in 1564, in which the *huacas* were predicted to rise up and overthrow the Lord God. This was followed by a long period of partial assimilation and *resistance* – so timed, in this case, to catch the full wind of the Counterreformation and the Catholic determination to extirpate false idols. This *Extirpation*, as it was called, lasted throughout much of seventeenth century, albeit sporadically. It was distinct from the Inquisition, on the grounds that the Indians were too new to the faith to commit heresy. There were public trials and burnings, but no one was put to death (the Inquisition in Peru was reserved for persons of Spanish descent). Extirpations were also accompanied by intensive instruction on Christian doctrine. The trials ironically provided the perfect arena for the practice of passive *resistance*, as local specialists soon learned to manipulate the points of law in their favor (e.g., by claiming to be imposters rather than actual sorcerers and witches, a lesser offense).[68] There were certainly some signs of a nascent fusion between Andean religion and Christianity, just as Christian scholars sought to find Andean and Inca counterparts and translations of basic theological concepts. But the extirpations contravened these impulses, reinforcing the deep divide, in the minds of the missionaries, between the work of the Lord and that of the Devil. The result was a form of *dual participation* – of Catholic ritual observance on the one hand and the preservation of the *huacas* on the other. Neither of these observances was completely airtight – for example, one had to get permission from a *huaca* to attend a Christian festival – but the twin systems persisted.[69] As Nicholas Griffiths formulates it, "In this way, neither religion absorbed the other; but then, nor were they simply juxtaposed; they were articulated into a symbiotic relationship, whereby one system was subordinated to the other ... yet both functioned as alternative sources of supernatural support."[70]

CONCLUSION: CONCENTRATED VS. DIFFUSE SPIRITUALITY

Let us step back from the canvas we have sketched out and try to draw some observations about the larger patterns of native-missionary interaction. We may characterize these in terms of differences and similarities between the two sides.

On the side of differences, as we have seen, the Spanish tended to recognize the tension between good and evil as primary, the Nahua between order and chaos. They did not divide the world between the spiritual and material to the same extent, but instead sought equilibrium among opposing forces. Most obviously, the Christian creed was monotheistic, the Nahua polytheistic.[71]

On the side of similarities, there were a good many *cultural hooks* between the Nahuas' religion and Christianity that helped facilitate the *conservation of form*. The Nahuas acknowledged the immortality of souls and had rituals that resembled baptism and confession. They both recognized the importance of supernatural intercessors between themselves and the more remote deities or deity. Also, as we have seen, the church had

learned the value of spectacle and ceremony, which constituted an important attraction to the Indians.

Students of medieval Europe will recognize here a common repertoire
of beliefs and practices to fulfill these purposes: the veneration of saints,
the adoration of the Virgin Mary, the sacred shrines, the votive offerings,
even as the specific expressions of these beliefs and practices varied from
one region to another.[72] Historians such as William Christian emphasize
the adaptability of Catholicism and its ability to incorporate local
customs rather than dwelling exclusively on its dogmatic proclamations,
as scholars have often done.[73] This can be related to a tendency to locate
faith more in a set of common observances and rituals rather than in a
creed, something that could be found in both medieval Europe and
colonial Mexico. One might indeed view sincere belief as the product of
habituation that comes from repeated performance of ritual over time,
rather than as necessarily existing prior to such actions. Moreover, the
collective performance of rituals was a powerful bonding mechanism in
creating a feeling of common identity.[74]

Clearly the success of Christianity in reaching the peoples of northern
Europe had been based in large part on its ability to accommodate these
local pagan practices.

And it should come as no surprise that scholars of these accommodations should reach for the label of syncretism to describe them.[75] Yet it
should be clear, both from the history of medieval Europe and of Spanish
America, that such accommodation was only half the story. For the gap
between Christian monotheism and Nahuan polytheism could only
incompletely be bridged. Accommodation alternated with the Christian
impulse to condemn multiple spirits and their human agents as extensions
the Devil and to destroy the idols that embodied them.

The changes that were brewing within Christianity around
1500 involved the reassertion of its claims as an exclusive religion,
emphasizing the divergences between itself and paganism, whether in
the guise of superstition or devil worship. This is most evident in the
Protestant Reformation, with its widespread condemnation of ritual itself,
but also in the Catholic Reformation, which also reemphasized the
importance of doctrine.[76] One can already see this in the sixteenth-
century Mexican friars' doubts about the sincerity of their converts, a
concern based on the proposition that the genuineness of one's
Christianity lay ultimately in one's inner state of mind and the beliefs
that one held, rather than the correctness of their practices. The latter was
often difficult for missionaries to accept, as shown by the controversies

over how much instruction in doctrine should precede baptism. It also is an indication of how Christian attitudes were changing when compared to the Middle Ages.

In colonial Mexico, these changes worked to the disadvantage of the Indians over time, undoing the initial favorable conditions that obtained immediately following the conquest. Thus the missionaries' success in educating a literate Nahuan elite raised the question of whether they should be given access to the Bible in translation. In the early 1500s, there was no prohibition against this. But by the end of the century, the prohibition had been put in place, on the grounds that the Indians were incapable of grasping the true meaning of the sacred writings. Similarly, there were Spanish advocates of allowing Nahuas to be ordained as priests, but they were also overruled. Most tellingly, the ethnographic work of Sahagún and his native collaborators, which preserved in writing the recollection of Aztec civilization, was banned by King Philip II for fear that such memories might spark renewed idolatry.[77] All of this contributed to the growing belief that Indians were permanent children incapable of achieving the spiritual heights attained by the Europeans.

Thus, to generalize, Christianity in the modern era has been marked just as much by conflict between opposing tendencies across religious and cultural divides as by compromise and accommodation between them. This brings us to the question of how best to characterize these differences in a way that does justice to both the conflictual and accommodative dimensions. I would formulate this as follows: both traditions have tendencies both toward *concentration* of whatever constitutes spirituality on the one hand, and toward the complementary *diffusion* of that spirituality on the other. It is argued throughout this book that both tendencies are present in all religions and periods – thus contravening an evolutionary perspective – provided one pays attention to the full range of behaviors and pronouncements that go under the name of religion, not just its belief systems. In Catholicism, for example, the veneration of saints represented the diffuse aspect, offsetting the doctrine of the Trinity and the notion of an only begotten Son of God. On the other side, the Aztec religion, while encompassing many gods, also had its temples which constituted a center where religious ritual was concentrated. One can also view a highly trained priesthood, entrusted to interpret and preserve sacred writings, whether the Holy Bible of the Christians or the calendrical cycle of the Aztecs, as an expression of concentrated spirituality, as opposed to a clergy where anyone who feels "called" can assume leadership of a congregation (as in the American Baptist tradition, for example), thus diffusing spiritual authority by drawing from a wider sector of the population – a tendency to be found in Protestantism, offsetting the concentration of its creed on justification by faith alone.

These two basic tendencies can combine in various ways, depending on the crosscurrents of economic, political, social, technological, and intellectual history that exist in any given time. In the case of Mexico and Peru, the anti-idolatry campaigns tended to run out of steam over time in the face of native resistance. But if local adaptability of Catholicism was the outcome, it was often the result of a struggle – a struggle that never seemed to be put to rest for very long, but recurred in the long run with different terminologies and parties as people sought to purify the religion that in their minds had become superstitious and corrupt.[78] In the nineteenth and early twentieth centuries, the parties in the conflict became the secular state versus the Catholic church as a whole, with the state assuming the role of the anti-idolater in anti-clerical campaigns promoting separation of church and state. These were promulgated by liberals over the course of the nineteenth century and supported by the small groups of Protestants that appeared in Mexico at the time. These strictures were written into state law beginning in the 1850s but not always enforced. A decisive confrontation came in the 1920s, when President Plutarco Calles decided to enforce these provisions, leading to a three-year guerilla war known as the Cristero revolt.

The second half of the twentieth century witnessed another shift in alignment, this time more between factions within the church than between church and state. Although battle lines soon reemerged, one can detect an overall shift toward accommodation to popular needs and to diffusion of religious authority. This fermentation began in the 1950s as the Vatican, increasingly aware of the threat of communism, sought to bolster the Latin American church via missionaries and teachers, and supporting a regional bishops' conference (CELAM) that turned to social and economic issues. Some 600 Latin American bishops attended Vatican II, and many soon applied its mandates in the Medellín Conference of 1968, heavily influenced by Liberation Theology's "preference for the poor." Despite heavy criticism from the conservative members of the hierarchy (including the future Pope Benedict XVI), the number of priests in Mexico more than doubled between 1960 and 2000, from 5,834 to 13,173.[79] Catechists and women religious increased as well. Part of this effort was directed to indigenous peoples, and many of their languages received Bible translations for the first time.[80]

In any event, these initiatives were in the process of being outflanked by another from the Protestant side, namely Pentecostalism. To quote an

Figure 2.2 Facade and open chapel of the Parish of the Purisima Concepcion in Otumba, Mexico State. The arched structure on the right housed an altar plus room for musicians for the outdoor masses.
Source: Photo by Leigh Thelmadatter, March 2,, 2010. Used by permission

anonymous but oft-cited phrase, "liberation theology opted for the poor, and the poor opted for Pentecostalism."[81] Over time, its appeal spread to the middle classes as well and clearly benefited from the changes in media, from radio to the internet, that facilitated mass communication. What Pentecostalism had to offer was, among other things: (1) experiential and participatory communication with the Holy Spirit through movement, music, and speaking in tongues – examples of concentrated spirituality; (2) physical and psychological healing; (3) an appeal to women, who were empowered by these techniques to confront the *machismo* atmosphere in the home; (4) diffusion of spiritual authority, guaranteed by the sheer proliferation of small churches, so that, according to David Martin, "anyone could rise to the top if equipped with spiritual gifts, and if those gifts did not find room in one Pentecostal church another church rapidly appeared where room could be found."[82]

Catholics soon learned to imitate some of the Pentecostals' techniques, forming charismatic groups of their own. In order to differentiate themselves from the Protestants, they continued to highlight the Virgin Mary as the medium for the gifts of the Spirit. And perhaps it is not surprising that Mexico, despite registering some seven million Protestants in 2000, had proportionately fewer than in most other Latin American countries. This suggests that the Virgin of Guadalupe continues to exert her magnetic attraction.[83]

3

Native North America

The Colonial Northeast, the Cherokees, and the Sioux

INTRODUCTION

The picture of North American societies at the time of European conquest is, in many ways, the inverse of the Mesoamerican one. Although both contained considerable cultural diversity – there were an estimated 350 mutually unintelligible languages in Mesoamerica and at least 200 in North America – one does not find the few well-defined centers of power such as the Basin of Mexico or the Yucatán Peninsula.[1] Native North American nations were dispersed, making it impossible to combine their stories into a single narrative or even a few intelligible patterns, and treatments of them are invariably broken down by region. Moreover, unlike Mesoamerica, there was no single European conqueror, but rather a multiplicity of rivals, thereby compounding the complexity. In addition, neither the English nor the French combined colonizing and missionary activities under a single agency, as did the Franciscans and Jesuits in northern Mexico. Add to this the plurality of English colonies, each with their own governors and councils, creating further opportunities for confusion and conflict.

If there is nevertheless one generalization that holds across a wide variety of North American peoples in different regions, it is that they made no sharp separation between religion and the rest of their culture. Many Europeans at first thought they had no religion at all, given the absence of such markers as temples and/or specialists visibly marked off from the rest of the population; many Native languages have no word for "religion" itself. In this sense, Native American societies generally exemplify what we have called "diffuse spirituality." Spirits could be found in a wide variety of forms throughout nature, such as animals, plants, and minerals, in addition to deities. A review of the diverse cultural traditions reveals that some posited a supreme spirit over all the others (such as *Gitche Manitou* among the Algonquins), while other traditions did not, and some acquired this idea only after contact with the Europeans.[2] Spirits were often likely to be characterized in terms of their *power* to affect good or ill fortune, which helps explain the centrality of ritual, by which power can be invoked and channeled. Relative concentrations of spirituality occurred through individuals – shamans – who were particularly gifted accessing this power, but by no means held a monopoly. All in all, Michel Foucault's idea of power and knowledge as twin aspects of a single phenomenon is an apposite formulation for this type of spirituality in its relation to human beings, although Foucault had a very different context in mind when he conceived the idea.[3]

Some Native American societies were settled, based on agriculture, while others were hunter-gatherers, and many practiced a combination of both. One finds many cases of movement and migration, either to follow the movements of animals or to cultivate new grounds when soil or forests were depleted. This meant interaction with neighboring groups, resulting in the high cultivation of the arts of war and diplomacy. One indication of the cultural and ethnic fluidity that often ensued was the widespread practice of adopting war captives into one's tribe, a process that was extended to whites as well. Its purpose, according to Thomas Ingersoll, was "to replace lost family members, recruit dynamic tribal members who would raise children, and maintain ancestral lineages and clans that structured the social calendar."[4] A related practice was the so-called mourning war to be found in the northeast, in which women who were grieving the loss of a household member could demand that the men conduct a raid to replace the loss – although the "adopted" captives were often tortured and executed if the grief was not yet assuaged.[5] This is an example of the authority and power that women could attain in some Native North American societies, particularly in the east.

Complicating the picture even further was the fact that the *type* of colonial relationship between Europeans and Native Americans changed drastically over a short span of time, from what Curtin calls territorial empires to settler colonies, thus radically reducing the range of options that the Indians had open to them.[6] In many cases, their first exposure to European influences had come in the form of deadly diseases which sometimes arrived even before the colonists themselves appeared in any numbers. This was the case in southern New England, for example, where an epidemic that killed between 70 and 90 percent of the population – the exact disease is still unknown – swept through in 1616–17, in advance of the Plymouth colony of 1620. Nevertheless, the Europeans did not always have the upper hand during the early years of colonization; rather a certain balance of power obtained. This was due to a number of factors: (1) the relatively small number of European colonists in the seventeenth and eighteenth centuries; (2) the predominance of trade as a major source of interaction; and (3) the scarcity of women among the colonists and the liaisons with native women that followed. All of these resulted in situations that called for much mutual accommodation and understanding. Richard White has ably conceptualized this situation in the Northeast as a "middle ground," a set of meanings that emerged from the attempts of two very different cultures to arrive at an agreement. The processes he describes to achieve this end resemble the initial stages of *vernacular translation*, albeit with unexpected results. White writes:

On the middle ground diverse peoples adjust their differences through what amounts to a process of creative, and often expedient, misunderstandings. People try to persuade others who are different from themselves by appealing to what they perceive to be the values and practices of those others. They often misinterpret and distort both the values and the practices of those they deal with, but from these misunderstandings arise new meanings and through them new practices—the shared meanings and practices of the middle ground.[7]

Some of the most conspicuous fruits of this process were the ceremonial practices surrounding diplomacy between Europeans and natives that flourished as the Anglo-French rivalry escalated in the eighteenth century, such as the exchange of wampum belts and other gifts and the use of kinship terms to address one another (such as "father" to refer to the English king).[8]

White's book also chronicles the decline of this middle ground in the early nineteenth century as European settlers poured into North America in unprecedented numbers, threatening and eventually driving the Indians from their lands. The New Zealand historian James Belich has recently elaborated this latter phenomenon for the English-speaking world, noting its explosive quality not only in North America, but also in places like Australia and New Zealand. In the Old Northwest of the United States, that increase was twenty-eight-fold between 1810 and 1860, from 250,000 to 7 million.[9] Significantly, Belich dates the onset of this explosion in North America from 1815, precisely the year that White chose for his obituary of the middle ground. The explosion came in the form of fits and starts of cyclical booms and busts, and Belich points to an increase in the number of Indian wars during the boom phases and a decrease during the busts.[10] As part of this overall shift, the "Indian" became less a party in negotiation and more of a stereotype, often the object of racial denigration and hatred. Another effect of the shift, albeit with a certain time lag, was an increasing if often unacknowledged sense of guilt among part of the white population, a mentality that found expression in the sharply contradictory images of the Indian that coexisted within white culture. As Robert Berkhofer and others have pointed out, Indians were simultaneously denigrated as lazy, dirty, violent, and crude but idealized as courteous, brave, simple, modest, and in touch with nature.[11] The use of stereotyped images of "the American Indian" continues to this day. All this has not been lost on the Indians themselves, as the case studies that follow will illuminate.

The tortured history of US–American Indian relations, with all its injustices, broken treaties, removals, and cultural crusades, further complicates the writing of that history today. For Native writers, dealing with missionary Christianity has been a difficult topic, since missionaries were long associated with some of the most oppressive practices, such as sending Indian children to distant boarding schools. The Cherokee scholar Jace Weaver noted that Native academic treatments of missionary encounters were lacking prior to the 1990s.[12] One of the first works to remedy this gap, *Missionary Conquest* by George Tinker, put forth an interpretation of missionaries as agents of cultural genocide.[13] As regards the Indian perspective, Tinker speculated that:

The process of Christianization has involved some internalization of the larger illusion of Indian inferiority and the idealization of white culture and religion...[which] surely results in a praxis of self-hatred...Just as an abused child slowly but inevitably internalizes a parent's abuse as a consistent demonstration of the child's own shortcomings and may even regard the life of the abusive parent as exemplary, so communities of oppressed peoples internalize their own oppression and come to believe too many of the stereotypes, explicit and implicit, spoken by the oppressor.[14]

Since then, there has been a reaction to this view, with several works highlighting Indian agency and the ways in which Natives adapted Christianity to their own cultural ways and needs. These scholars make the claim that the choice between being genuinely native and genuinely Christian was, and is, a false one.[15] Yet this emphasis raises some important questions about the degree of continuity between missionary Christianity and native traditions. Older scholars such as Robert Berkhofer have pointed out that, for many Native Americans,

Christianity presented a stark choice, not merely between competing religious beliefs and practices, but between accepting or rejecting Western culture as a whole.[16] This approach calls into question the long-term viability of a middle ground. But these are questions that can only be answered on a case-by-case basis.

COLONIAL NORTHEAST

A brief overview of the colonial Northeast, the subject of a voluminous literature, introduces these complexities while providing a basis for comparison of various native strategies in dealing with missionaries. Not only was there a three-way contest between French, Dutch, and English colonists, but also a heterogeneous variety of Native groupings. There were two different language groups, Algonkian and Iroquoian, and a multiplicity of "tribes" or nations within each one (including the "Algonquians" and the "Iroquois" – i.e., those whose labels resembled those of the larger language groups, but were in fact only one of many within the latter). The Algonquins tended to be hunters and fishermen, living in scattered and mobile communities in the coastal areas of what is now Canada and northern New England, the lower St. Lawrence Valley, and extending to the upper Midwest. Their food sources were abundant for the most part, providing a level of health comparable to the Europeans of the time.[17] In between these groups were the Iroquoians such as the Wendats (or Hurons, as the French called them), who practiced sedentary agriculture and lived in much larger concentrations. In this they resembled their longtime enemies to the south, the Haudenosaunees (or "Iroquois"), a federation of five nations (the Mohawks, Oneidas, Onandagas, Cayugas, and Senecas) in what is now New York State.

The juxtaposition of Catholic missions in French Canada and Protestant ones in New England also affords a basis for comparison of these from indigenous perspectives and for testing the assertion, frequently made, that "sacramentalism gave Catholic missions an entrance into the Indian mental world and a functional purpose in the Indian daily world denied to Protestants."[18] In support of this view, one can point to the effectiveness of an emphasis on ceremony and ritual; the use of objects such as vestments, chalices, pictures and statues; not to mention the practical fact that the Catholic missionary orders could devote their full efforts to converting the natives, whereas Protestant clergy had to take on this task in addition to ministering to their settler congregations. Certainly the numbers were impressive: the Jesuits claimed to have baptized over 16,000 natives between 1632 and 1672 and maintained with pride that these were not mass baptisms as in Spanish America, but based on the ascertainment of genuine understanding and conviction. About one-third of these, however, were performed close to death, certainly an act of compassion for those who believed that the alternative was eternal damnation, but leading one to question the extent of prior instruction in Catholic doctrine.[19] Nevertheless the ritual emphasis does help to explain the relative success of Catholicism in French Canada in the long run – i.e., by the mid-eighteenth century. A closer look from an indigenous perspective, however, reveals a more complicated and uneven picture.

The notion of the middle ground is plausible if one gives due weight to the misunderstandings and divergent interpretations that went into the shaping of it and persisted, to a great degree, thereafter. A good example is the matter of trade. Clearly this, rather than religion, was at the forefront of the French colonists' minds when Jacques Cartier first sailed up the St. Lawrence in 1534: no priests or missionaries were aboard.[20] Likewise the desire for European goods such as metal tools, wool blankets, and glass beads constituted the earliest attraction of natives, having been exposed to these by European fishermen possibly as early as the 1480s – leading to a tumultuous reception of Cartier's ships by the Mi'kmaqs at Chaleur Bay, New Brunswick.[21] Meanwhile, the Indian behavior indicated that they, on the contrary, regarded the strangers as healers as well as traders; they brought their invalids to them to be cured and demanded immediate baptism–evidence of their regard for the foreigners as possessing spiritual power (*Manitou*). The initial attraction bespoke *selective incorporation* rather than *acculturation*, a fact that the French refused to recognize for many years.[22]

Cartier promised to bring priests on his next voyage, a promise that was not kept; he did, however, erect a large cross and unceremoniously captured several natives to bring them to France in order to immerse them in European culture, which they would then carry back to their "savage" brethren. Like most other Indians subjected to such experiments, they did not survive the transplant, but were baptized before they died prematurely.[23] Such actions soon provoked disillusionment and hostility on the part of the Indians, combined with their observations of the colonists' lack of survival skills in the New World. The Indians succeeded in driving away the French in 1541; they were not to return until 1608. The result of the initial encounter, then, was to convince both sides of how divergent their religious views actually were.

The French continued the acculturative strategy with the help of the Recollects, an order of Franciscans, again with no success. This led to their replacement by the Jesuits in 1625, who had by then developed, based on their work in India and China, a certain appreciation of native culture and the need to work with the leaders of the existing power structure. Their annual reports on the Canadian mission, the *Jesuit Relations*, continue to serve as an invaluable ethnographic source. For their part, the Indians would only host the missionaries if trade channels with the French would be kept open. This put the missionaries in a delicate position, since the French fur traders were not exactly embodiments of Christian virtue. The Jesuits sought to keep the Indians away from French settlements, in part to protect them from the destructive effects of alcohol, although they never completely solved this problem. They did, however, achieve a healthy balance between cooperating with the French merchants and keeping their distance from them. This led to their focusing on the Wendats, who were both eager fur traders and practiced sedentary agriculture, enabling the missionaries to concentrate their efforts.

Unfortunately, the arrival of the Jesuits coincided with a massive smallpox epidemic, and the Wendats not unreasonably attributed this to the new black-robed shamans. According to one source, "people literally plugged their ears, jeered, and shouted at the unwelcome visitors; sometimes they brandished hatchets and chased them away."[24] A faction emerged urging that the missionaries be put to death as sorcerers; they were saved partly by their connection with the French merchants and by a small group who had already accepted baptism as a healing power.[25]

Nevertheless, the Jesuits approached their task with patience and persistence, which extended to learning the native languages and mastering them to the point of being able to debate their shamanic counterparts, which led them to an appreciation of the Wendats' sharpness of mind.[26] Finding ways to translate concepts such as sin proved to be as daunting here as with the Nahuas. However much they denigrated the authority and practices of the shamans as superstitious, their technique was basically to adopt shamanic logic, namely that their ability to predict and alter the course of nature was superior, albeit in the name of the Christian God. Praying for rain or for better crops or success in war, if done often enough, was bound to be effective some of the time. More impressive was their ability to predict eclipses of the sun and the moon, if prepared with proper ceremony. To the Natives, their books and writings seemed were similarly endowed with invisible power, even witchcraft.[27]

Moreover, their belief that shamanic power could be used both for evil and good enabled more and more Wendats to gradually overcome their suspicions of the Jesuits as the cause of the epidemic.

This view of native Christianity as enhanced shamanism should not, however, lead us to ignore the fact that the missionaries' willingness to accommodate to native customs was highly selective, to put it mildly. James Axtell itemizes the practices that converts were required to give up:

The Jesuit list of cultural proscriptions...included not only narrowly "religious practices, such as sorcery, dreaming, and sacrifices, but also customs from nearly every aspect of Indian life: health care (curing dances, games, feasts, and sweats), warfare (revenge, killing of children, cannibalism , and torture, though not war itself), domestic relations (slander, nudity, polygamy, adultery, divorce, and premarital sex), and death (suicide, excessive mourning, fancy dress of the corpse, and the indiscriminate mixing of Christian and pagan remains)."[28]

If Christians were understandably outraged at the Wendats' practice of torturing captured enemies to death, the natives were similarly shocked at the Christians' notions of discipline and punishment of their own people, which included the beating of women and children.[29] This was especially true at the first Jesuit settlement of Sillery near Quebec, founded in 1637, where residents felt the full force of Christian asceticism and monastic zeal, featuring as it did both daily prayers and public floggings. At the same time, Sillery was also the site of Christian compassion, as Ursuline nuns ran a hospital on the premises which ministered to hundreds of sick natives.[30]

The effect of these mixed messages was not so much to bring about a blending with native religion, but rather a bifurcation of response. On the one hand, there emerged a small but dedicated cadre of native Christians for whom its *concentration of spirituality* and asceticism constituted a welcome alternative to the breakdown of their own society, whether from disease, war, or cosmological confrontation. Sillery, for example, not only produced 167 zealous converts, but also brought requests from neighboring tribes for missionary instruction.[31] These conversions came not only from individuals, but also from families, who tended to convert together. On the other hand, many if not most natives came to perceive the extent of the threat that the missionaries posed to their society and values. Particularly disturbing was the missionaries' *style* of proselytizing, which involved verbal confrontation and attack on the shamans, something quite alien to the manners of the natives and the high value they placed on consensus. A particularly jarring moment was the occasion of a traditional Wendat ceremony of reburial of their dead, which occurred when a village moved, and involved the mixing of the bones of different individuals to symbolize unity – a practice that the newly converted Native Christians refused to participate in.[32] This was symptomatic of a developing crisis of cohesion within Wendat society.

The Wendats were thus already weakened internally when disaster struck in 1648: a massive attack by the Haudenosaunees from the south, designed not merely to capture prisoners but to also wipe out as many Wendat villages as possible. The Haudenosaunees had also suffered unprecedented losses in the 1640s from smallpox and other epidemics; they now resorted to mourning wars on an unprecedented scale, using firearms for the first time, to replenish their numbers and to capture the Wendats' fur trade.[33] The attacks went on for two years with forces of as many as a thousand warriors. The Wendats were driven from their lands; many took refuge on an island in Georgian Bay, where they faced mass starvation in the winter of 1650. The remnants scattered throughout the Great Lakes region, where they became known as the Wyandots; some of them joined the Haudenosaunees as adoptees. During these years, baptisms increased dramatically, suggesting that the crisis itself was conducive to accepting the new faith. One of the Wendat Christian communities founded in the aftermath survives to this day.[34]

In the midst of these horrific wars, there occurred an event that again illustrates the convergence of European and native views, albeit from diametrically opposed assumptions. This was the torture unto death of two missionaries to the Wendats on March 16, 1649. We know that one of them, Jean de Brébeuf, had come to anticipate a martyr's death by this time, given the increasing obstacles he faced as Wendat resistance grew. Indeed, one his former charges, who had gone over to the other side, dramatized his apostasy by pouring boiling water over the priest's head in a parody of baptism. Brébeuf withstood his torture, mocking his captors and proclaiming his faith to the very end. The Haudenosaunees, for their part, acknowledged his courage with the supreme compliment of ritual cannibalism, incorporating his strength by eating his body and drinking his blood.[35]

The missionaries' narrative of martyrdom was of course thoroughly grounded in Christian tradition and had become a way of rationalizing the unsuccessful mission in French Canada.[36] Evidence that the Haudenosaunees did not share this narrative and bore no particular animus against their victims as Christians is provided by the fact that, three years later, they invited missionaries themselves, partly to minister to the adopted ex-Wendats among them. Furthermore, as many now saw the advantage of a French alliance, a further invitation brought some 50 priests, laymen, and soldiers to settle among the Onondagas, one of the five nations, in 1656. Over the next few decades, the pattern of bifurcation repeated itself, with a considerable number of baptisms (an estimated 20 percent of all Haudenosaunees), confrontations with native practices and traditions, and, by the 1670s, separation of traditionalists and Christians, as the latter migrated of to newly established communities in French Canada.[37] Former Wendats were numerically prominent among the migrants, as were women. Once again, these communities were the centers of Christian piety and asceticism, leading one Jesuit to comment that "our Iroquois are much better Christians than the French."[38] Again, the spatial *concentration of spirituality* served to preserve native identity in the midst of upheaval. The communities were free of the factionalism that had come to divide the nations outside. In the case of the Mohawks, these communities became the basis for reservations that exist today.

The most famous of the Mohawk migrants to the Canadian settlements was Kateri Tekakwitha, a young woman whose life exemplified the multiple victimizations that natives suffered at this time. The daughter of an Algonquin mother and a Haudenosaunee father, she lost both to smallpox at age four, which also scarred and blinded her. Living with her relatives, she became a Christian at age nineteen, over the opposition of her family. She came to the Canadian settlement at Kahnawake two years later, but the intensity of her devotion outstripped even the routine that the Jesuits offered there. Her self-mortifications soon weakened her to the point of death at age twenty-four. Two Jesuit missionaries who knew her wrote down her life story soon after, again assimilating her into the narrative of martyrdom.

Kateri's story may well illustrate George Tinker's version of missionaries as reinforcing low Indian self-esteem. In any case, what is most significant about her is her posthumous fame, particularly in the twentieth century. Veneration of her increased at first among non-native Catholics, leading not only to the growth of her shrine in New York state, but also to the establishment of annual Tekakwitha Conferences beginning in 1939. Since the 1970s, the participation of Native Catholics in these conferences has increased, and Kateri has drawn increasing attention from Catholics across the nation. Aside from Juan Diego of Mexico, she is the sole Native American to be canonized as a saint. She seems to symbolize and express the wounds that Native Americans have suffered over the years, as well as the pride that Native America could produce a saint, not to mention the guilt and contrition that their colonizers have come to feel. At the same time, she also serves to divide Native Christians from those groups who seek to revive traditional religion.[39]

Over time, then, the settlement strategy came to predominate in French Canada and provided a basis for the middle ground.[40] By the end of the seventeenth century, the French had largely given up their goals of acculturation to French ways; and for their part, many Natives were willing to accept living in settlements for at least part of the year. The missionaries were now more willing to incorporate Native festivals into their liturgical calendar than had been the case at Sillery; Natives were better able to integrate Christian rituals and beliefs into their way of life and even their mythology. The result was that Catholicism became firmly rooted in many Algonquin tribes, enabling them to resist British incursions in the eighteenth century. Only belatedly did the British realize that they too needed missionaries as tools of diplomacy to stem the flow of Haudenosaunees to New France.[41] Still, the main appeal of Christianity appeared to be its rituals rather than its beliefs.[42] Thus the pattern of *selective incorporation* still held.

Turning to the Algonkian-speaking areas to the south in New England, the well-known theological differences between Catholics and Protestants played a role in the missionary-Native encounter there. Protestants regarded Catholicism as "baptized heathenism," and the animosity was reciprocated.[43] Protestants tended to eschew visual spectacle, dances, and chants (but not hymn singing). They concentrated on instruction – translating the Bible, teaching it, and training Natives to carry on this work. Their results were not unimpressive: before the American Revolution, southern New England could claim 133 Native preachers and teachers, and 91 Christian villages (or praying towns, as they were called) – in contrast to New France, which could not boast a single indigenous priest before the nineteenth century.[44]

The nations of southern New England relied on both farming and hunting. Their political arrangements were decentralized, with chiefs (known as *sachems*) relying heavily on popular consent. Their numbers were of course severely depleted by the epidemic of 1616–17, and they were about to face a wave of settler colonialism in the form of Puritanism, in which families from England were arriving in ever increasing numbers in the 1630s and 1640s, hoping to establish the kingdom of God on Earth. Approximately three thousand settlers arrived by 1633; a decade later there were some thirteen thousand.[45] The Puritans regarded the Indian loss of life in the epidemics as a sign of God's plan for clearing the land to make way for His true followers (ironically, the Indians even welcomed the settlers initially to replenish their depleted lands). The settlers had no qualms about using brutal violence to defeat any resistance, as they did with the Pequots in Connecticut in 1637, casting themselves as the Old Testament Israelites making war on the Canaanites.[46] There was little room here for a middle ground: interaction with missionaries began only after the English had firmly established political control of eastern Massachusetts.[47]

It is clear that the Puritans believed that Christianization of the Indians must begin by "reducing them to civility," i.e., acculturating them to English customs, and that spatial concentration into segregated settlements was the prime means of doing so. This pattern was the main point of resemblance to the French efforts as they eventually developed. Also, the list of Puritan taboos that were to be enforced in these settlements – against polygamy, fornication outside of marriage, blasphemy, immodesty, indolence, and idolatry – were not very different from those of the Jesuits.[48] For their part, the Indians who moved to the settlements found in them a means to carve out a space for themselves within the engulfing English colony: concentration was first and foremost a means to survival. In the words of one Indian who accepted the mission, "I saw the English took much ground, and I thought if I prayed, the English would not take away my ground." Or another, "[I] loved to dwell at that place...and therefore I thought I will pray to God...not for the love of God but for the love of the place I lived in."[49] The theme of community also comes through: "When I first prayed to God, I did not pray for my soul, but only I did as my friends did, because I loved them."[50] Ironically, all of these statements were made as confessions of sins along the path to experiencing grace and true conversion. Evidently these "praying Indians," as they were called – approximately 1,100 by one estimate – had internalized the Puritan *concentration of spirituality*.[51] At the same time, native religious practices persisted in areas where English control was weaker.

Massachusett and Wampanoag Indians were initially drawn to the mission towns by their desire for literacy and access to English goods. Whatever these initial reasons, the Indians soon found that a demanding form of Christian spirituality was part and parcel of the spatial arrangement. Already in 1646, the colonial legislature had levied a £5 fine for worshipping false gods. The most vivid illustration was to be found in the first praying town of Natick, founded in 1650 by the most visible and energetic missionary, John Eliot, who had learned the Massachusett language and would soon translate the Bible into it, along with fourteen other works – the first such translation in the New World.[52] As Axtell put it, "if true theocracy was ever practiced in Anglo-America, Natick was the place."[53] More importantly, Natick was the hub of a network of praying towns, each with its own native ministers, church officials, and teachers.[54]

Although Eliot certainly believed in salvation by grace rather than works, he conceded that human actions such as prayer were essential to establish a relationship with God and were particularly important for bringing non-Christians into the fold. Thus, he encouraged prayer not only in formal services, but at mealtime, in the fields, and even prescribed the proper posture for praying. In this respect, ritual remained central to the communities, at once maintaining a link to Algonquin spirituality while disrupting its traditional rhythms and ritual cycles, replacing them with Christian ones.[55] In this way also, the Natives' New England Protestant experience was not as far removed from the French Catholic one as might first appear.

Prayer, however, was but the first stage in the process of conversion to become a member of the elect, a process for which few were chosen (baptism was an intermediate stage). In order to establish a church at Natick, Eliot had to produce confessions of eight such chosen Indians for examination by English Puritan elders to demonstrate the thoroughness of their religious education and the sincerity of their convictions. At the heart of these confessions, just as for the much larger number of praying Indians, was the experience of sinfulness, central to the Puritan theology and all the more important to instill in those whose previous culture had deprived them of a sense of their own unworthiness. In this sense, the centrality of sin lends support to Tinker's interpretation of missionary work as an act of cultural denigration at the psychological level. Observers of the Natick confessions and prayers noted how emotional they often were, with tears flowing in a manner quite uncharacteristic of the Indians' previous stoicism. At the same time, a scholar of Algonkian spirituality, Kenneth Morrison, points to the personal and intersubjective relationship of people with spirits ("other-than-human persons"), which existed long before the settlers arrived and which the confessional would certainly reinforce.[56] Morrison views the adoption of Christianity less as a rejection of previous traditions and more as a pragmatic readjustment of these.

If Puritan worship could be an exercise in psychological humiliation, it did not thereby simply reduce the Indians to passivity. Question-and-answer periods were part of the standard service and included a time for Natives to ask questions. As they became more familiar with Christian stories and beliefs, the more challenging their questions became, probing inconsistencies in the Bible as well as the problem of evil.[57] Catechism, of course, enabled the English to pose questions to the Indians as well, and it became the core of religious instruction in the towns. Eliot again expressed satisfaction at the degree to which his parishioners mastered the catechism.[58] The praying towns were also sites of schools, with instruction at first in Massachusett, later in English. These appeared to be more successful than the boarding schools, which generally ended in failure. In 1675, Natick could boast a 30 percent literacy rate; each praying town had a native teacher, either full- or part-time.[59]

While the establishment of the praying towns clearly preserved a sense of community and thereby contributed to the Indians' survival, the extent to which their customs were also preserved has been debated.[60] However one interprets the data, the degree of *selective acculturation* was significant. Inhabitants of some praying towns were taking up sedentary agriculture, learning English crafts, wearing English clothes, partitioning their wigwams to enforce Puritan standards of modesty, and obtaining guns to fend off their neighbors. Perhaps most symbolic yet profound was the requirement that Indian men cut their long hair. To quote Axtell, "a willingness [of an Indian man] to cut his long hair signaled his desire to kill the Indian in himself and to assume a new persona modeled upon the meek, submissive Christ of the white man's Black Book."[61]

Because these changes had a disruptive effect on native family and kinship structures, sometimes dividing family members from one another, it is not surprising that they should lead to resentments and *resistance*, thus replicating the pattern of bifurcation we saw among the Wendats. The result was King Philip's War of 1675–76, under the leadership of Metacom (his Indian name), the son of Massassoit, the sachem who had initially supported the Pilgrims.[62] This was an exceedingly bloody conflict on both sides: the casualty rate among the Indians was 40 percent, and one in sixteen Englishmen of fighting age was killed.[63] After the bloodshed had lifted, the number of praying towns were drastically reduced from fourteen to four.

The decades that followed witnessed alternating patterns of acculturation and resistance, leading eventually to the expropriation of Indian lands and the migration of many New England Indians westward. Prior to the American Revolution, Indians in Massachusetts lived interspersed, albeit as an underclass, with European settlers. Although prone to indebtedness, poverty, and alcoholism, Native churches still provided a focus and sense of community for many, and the network of itinerant preachers and teachers reconstituted itself. One can speak of a brief period of middle ground, a genuine combination of economies and cultures in which Indians worked as farmers, day-laborers, and whalers.[64] Pre-contact religion persisted, but interacted with popular magical practices among the settlers, and also of the increasing number of African Americans in New England.[65] Massachusetts Indians remained largely immune to the revival known as the Great Awakening, which swept through colonial New England in the 1740s, though this was not true for their neighbors in Connecticut and Rhode Island.[66] Unfortunately, renewal of warfare between England and France in 1744 and again in 1756, put an end to this era of relative stability. The pressure of white settlement resumed, especially after the end of the French and Indian War in 1763, and most of the Indian communities disintegrated. By 1778, only twenty-one Indians remained in Natick. Nevertheless, Indians were as a result developing a broader consciousness of pan-Indianness, even as racism directed against Indians was spreading among the white population. This attitude helped fuel the violence of the Revolutionary War on the frontier, which led to scorched earth campaigns and massive destruction of Indian farms and villages.[67] The victory of the colonists meant no reprieve for the Indians: even those who had fought on the American side found their lands taken away.[68] The Revolution clearly represented a tipping point in the transition from territorial empire to settler colonialism.

As might be expected, the late eighteenth and early nineteenth centuries witnessed an increasing *resistance* to settler colonialism. This took the form of resurgent nativism, transmitted by a number of visionary prophets, of whom Neolin (the Delaware Prophet), Tenskwatawa (the Shawnee Prophet), and Handsome Lake (Seneca), are the best known. The first two inspired warriors such as Pontiac and Tecumseh (Tenskwatawa's brother) to engage in warfare against the whites, while Handsome Lake's movement was an internal reform. Although all three resisted missionary Christianity, one is still struck by the convergence of these nativist movements with the Christian ones at the level of basic strategy, namely *concentration of spirituality*, as a means to revitalize their peoples and cultures.[69]

Nativism was, however, still a part of a bifurcated pattern in which Native Christianity continued to play an important if smaller role. This involved the resettlement westward of Native Christian communities from New England who maintained the strategy of *selective acculturation*. An individual who became a leader in this trend was Samson Occom

(1723–92), a Connecticut Mohegan. Occom came to Christianity through the fire-and-brimstone sermons of the Great Awakening but also exemplified a desire for empowerment through English education and literacy.[70] He became an ordained Presbyterian minister, although his pay was less than a quarter of that of white clergymen.[71]

Perhaps Occom's most significant achievement was to conceive and help lead an exodus of members of seven tribes from the increasingly hopeless conditions in southern New England to form an intertribal Christian community, called Brotherton, in Oneida country in New York. Occom conceived of this a few years before the Revolution, and the actual move was not completed until the 1780s, after its conclusion; the intensity of the hopes attached to this utopian experiment must be seen in the light of the bloodshed and destruction of villages that the Revolution had wrought on the Indians. The Oneidas, members of the Six Nations, welcomed the newcomers as a way of strengthening their numbers against future white incursions; they also embraced *selective acculturation* as a means to this end.[72] They were soon joined by a group of Mahicans from Stockbridge in western Massachusetts[73] who had fought on the American side but had subsequently been displaced by white settlers. As David J. Silverman puts it, "their task...was not to impress colonial society—they had already experienced the futility of that exercise over the years—but to attract God's smile."[74] In other words, they remained true to the Calvinist theology of the Puritans: only by acknowledging their past sins and by accepting God's word could the Indians survive the crisis. Occom saw the Brotherton community as setting an example for surrounding tribes; he and the other leaders were quick to grasp the parallels with the Jews of the Old Testament and the promised land, as well as the imminence of God's final judgment. They roundly rejected the racial theories of other Indians and of the whites and sought peaceful relations with the settlers in the name of Christianity and civility, often mediating between them and other tribes. They clung to these beliefs in the face of mounting evidence to the contrary, as they were driven further westward in the subsequent decades, first to Indiana and then to Wisconsin, where a community of Stockbridge Indians still survives, falsifying the myth of the "Last of the Mohicans."[75]

CHEROKEES

The Cherokees were and remain one of the largest Indian nations in North America. In 1700, their population was estimated at 22,000, and their hunting range encompassed 40,000 square miles. Speakers of an Iroquoian language with three distinct dialects, they inhabited the mountainous region of the South Appalachians, but extending to the fertile lands on either side. Their location gave them a strategic importance in the conflicts between the British, Spanish, and French and enabled them to maintain autonomy from colonial powers for well over two centuries (they had encountered the Spanish during DeSoto's expedition in 1540; the first contacts with English settlers took place in 1673). At the same time, the terrain favored decentralized authority, with some 40 towns that were largely self-governing. By 1730, there were three recognized groupings of these towns, on the eastern, center, and western sides of the Appalachians respectively. A clan social structure spanned these units, with each of seven clans represented in each town.

The history of their interactions with Christians is one of sharp contrasts, perhaps reflecting what one anthropologist has called the Cherokees' concern with "categorical tidiness." According to this interpretation of their worldview, the order of the cosmos is threatened when elements which do not belong together are allowed to mix, and the primary purpose of ritual was to remove such pollution when it occurred.[76] A prime example would be the separation of peace and war. Each town had a separate chief for each, marked by the colors white and red, respectively. The decision for war was a matter of town deliberation; if the decision was in favor, the war chief, generally younger than the peace chief, would assume authority. Each condition was associated with different behaviors: in peacetime, one was to avoid giving offence or showing strong emotion; in wartime, the passions of the young were deliberately stoked.[77] Women played an active role in both groups, often mediating in case of disagreements. Warfare was seasonal, and warriors underwent ritual purification both before departing and upon return. During the summer, young men found an outlet in a ball game that frequently turned violent. The Cherokees had a well-deserved reputation for ferocity in war, perpetuated by their belief in clan retribution, which was based on the notion that natural balance required the taking of a life for a life. At the same time, their diplomatic skills were equally well-developed, as witnessed by the 22 separate treaties they signed with the Anglo-Americans between 1721 and 1835.[78]

The most conspicuous feature of Cherokee-Christian interactions during the colonial period is their almost total absence, a state of affairs for which both Natives and colonists were responsible.[79] Cherokee spirituality was characterized by a certain conservative pragmatism, focused on maintaining harmony and order through a cycle of six annual rituals and being markedly averse to individual expressions of religious fervor. The Cherokee of course had their religious specialists, known as *adonisgi* (conjurers), who presided over knowledge of cures and cast spells to help or harm individuals as the need arose. But generally, wise elders were favored over charismatic prophets.[80] The dignified bearing and rhetoric of the leading chiefs seemed to satisfy the white stereotype of the noble savage, and the 19-year-old Thomas Jefferson was highly impressed by one such speech that he heard, even though he could not understand a word of it.[81] Reinforcing this image was the popular European notion that the Indians were descendents of the Lost Tribes of Israel. One visitor to the Cherokees, James Adair, devoted a 230-page book in 1775 to arguing for this proposition.[82]

More surprising is the lack of initiative from the British side, especially in the light of the founding of the Anglican Society for the Promotion of the Gospel in Foreign Parts (SPG) by royal charter in 1701, an organization specifically aimed at the American colonies. It was not for want of trying: the SPG sent a number of missionaries to South Carolina. The reason may be gleaned from a statement from its disillusioned commissary, who judged the white colonists there to be "the Vilest race of Men upon the Earth ... being a perfect Medley of Bankrupts, pirates, decayed Libertines, sectaries, and Enthusiasts of all sorts."[83] These colonists had minimal interest in attending church, and making money seemed to be their primary focus. Traders were uncooperative when it came to helping the missionaries, and the king's emissary turned rather to Native *adonisgi* to win the support of the Cherokees.[84] Trade, then, was the first channel of interaction between Cherokees and colonists beginning in the 1700s, in which huge numbers of deerskins were exchanged for firearms, metal tools, beads, and rum. As was the case elsewhere, trade was accompanied by intermarriage, a means by which Native women contributed to diplomacy by furthering and cementing commercial ties. By tapping into the wealth of the traders in this way, the Cherokees created over time a wealthy class of mixed bloods. For the Carolinians, a prominent commodity in trade was slaves, which led them to foment wars among the Indians in order to provide them with captives who were then sold as slaves. The Cherokees were at first victims of this practice, then participants, which led the wealthier among them to incorporate slavery into their own society.[85] The Cherokees were also quite willing to exchange land for commodities, and the early treaties provided for numerous land cessions. It was only during the 1770s that the Indians realized the full threat of white encroachment on the land. All in all, the colonial period can be characterized as one of *selective incorporation*, in which the Indians largely preserved their political, economic, and cultural autonomy, despite certain borrowings from the English.

For all their independence and sense of self-worth, the Cherokees were not immune to the depredations that accompanied European colonialism. An epidemic of smallpox in 1738–39 destroyed about half the nation; hundreds of warriors committed suicide rather than live disfigured by the disease, and conjurers discarded their sacred paraphernalia as useless.[86] Firearms greatly increased the scale and human cost of wars, which spiraled out of control in the 1750s and again in the 1770s and 1780s, due in large part to the inability of either Natives or colonists to coordinate their internal efforts in order to maintain peace.[87] Carolinians could no more control the actions of neighboring Virginians than peace chiefs could assuage the mounting demands of aggrieved clansmen and women for retribution. The same situation applied during and after the American Revolution, when a faction of young Native warriors split off and founded their own towns to mount a sustained resistance to settlers, and militant American frontiersmen formed the independent state of Franklin in defiance of the federal government's treaties. Atrocities such as the burning of entire villages and the destruction of crops became routine. As a result, the Cherokee population had declined to about 12,000 in 1775 and to around 10,000 in the 1780s, with half of their towns destroyed and three-quarters of their lands taken away.[88] The six annual ceremonies had been telescoped into one, the Green Corn Festival. The belief in an orderly and harmonious universe had been severely disrupted.

The Cherokees had already responded to these challenges in the mid-eighteenth century by introducing more tribal-level government, although it was unable to prevent the factional split of the 1770s. But in 1794, the war faction had admitted defeat, ending organized military resistance to the United States.

In the following years, the Cherokees underwent a dramatic, even revolutionary, shift in strategy from *selective incorporation* of Anglo-American ways to *selective acculturation* to these. This was spearheaded by the mixed-blood minority, which had already gone much further in this direction than the full-bloods. Against a background of worsening white-Indian relations, *acculturation* was designed to refute the charge of "savagery" and demonstrate that Indians could be as "civilized" as their white neighbors, thus reinforcing their claims for sovereignty. It involved such practices as sedentary agriculture, the dissolution of clan loyalties in favor of nuclear families (including the formal ending of clan retribution in 1810), a written language devised by a Cherokee, and a series of laws culminating in a constitution modeled on that of the United States in 1827. At the beginning, the Cherokees received encouragement and aid from the federal government, which embraced such a civilizing policy for Indians in general during Washington's presidency. But the Cherokee surpassed all others in the alacrity with which it was embraced and implemented. By 1825, the nation could boast 31 gristmills, 14 sawmills, 62 blacksmith shops, and 19 schools. The population had increased by 30 percent over 1809.[89] At the same time, of course, the pressure of white settlement continued and with it the increase in racist attitudes on the part of the frontier settlers.

As part of this new strategy, the council began inviting missionaries to come to Cherokee territory for the purpose of providing education. This set up a conflict of priorities between Natives and the missionaries, the former wanting education, the latter wanting conversion. The first to arrive, the Moravians in 1799, did not want to establish a school until they had made a minimum number of converts; they believed in the segregated settlement as the proper way to imbue the true religion. When, after three years, neither the converts nor the school materialized, the council asked them to leave. Not ones to give up, however, the Moravians reluctantly set up a boarding school with seven students.[90] Much more ambitious and successful were the New England Congregationalists, whose American Board of Commissioners for Foreign Missions – the Natives were considered foreign – arrived in 1817. It established eight schools, including a model farm. Its attitudes reflected Calvinist Puritanism, with strict standards for conversion, rigorous discipline, and high academic standards. Nevertheless, these schools conveyed the practical skills that the Indians were demanding. They appealed especially to the mixed bloods, who bought into the Congregationalists' identification of their religion with progress and civilization in general, thus enhancing their own sense of empowerment. The ABCFM also served as a lobbying group for the Cherokee cause in Congress, and sponsored a highly effective speaking tour of 15 eastern cities by one of its converts, who confounded his audiences' expectations by dressing in a suit and tie rather than in traditional costume.[91] The Congregationalists were, however, by no means free of racial prejudice, and closed a school in Connecticut to train native missionaries when two of them became engaged to white women there.[92]

The full bloods often found themselves excluded from these enterprises, but soon two other denominations arrived that catered more
directly to their needs: Baptists (1819) and Methodists (1823–24). These
missionaries had less formal education themselves and were more egalitarian in their approach. In contrast to the other denominations, the
Methodists welcomed people who were initially hesitant about
Christianity and included them as converts.[93] They also abjured concentrated settlements in favor of itinerant preaching and schooling – a
practice that the Baptists then adopted as well. The most effective missionary to the Cherokee of all was the head of the Baptist mission, the
Reverend Evan Jones, the only one who took the trouble to learn
Cherokee. This enabled him to train a cohort of Native exhorters and
preachers, through whom a number of full blood Cherokees could eventually embrace Christianity as their own. The council eventually made
Jones a Cherokee citizen.[94]

These processes of *acculturation* and Christianization did not always
go smoothly, and, as in the colonial Northeast, were part of a bifurcated
pattern. Part of this was due to the attitudes of many mixed bloods
themselves, who, under the influence of their missionary teachers, went
from selective acculturation to complete identification, i.e., "to become as
much like whites as possible," in the words of William G. McLoughlin.
This led them to look down on the traditions of their own people as
superstitious and savage.[95] For example, the most prominent Cherokee
intellectual, Elias Boudinot, called the Plains Indians "American
Arabs."[96] Such condescension inevitably brought a backlash in the form
of several nativist revivals during the period and an upsurge in traditional
practices.[97] This was greatly aided by the invention of the written language, Sequoyan, named for the Cherokee who invented it. Sequoyah's
syllabary enabled the *adonisgi* to write down and spread their formulas
and spells, largely unnoticed by the missionaries and mixed bloods.

These tendencies nevertheless failed to cripple the *acculturation* movement in the 1820s and 1830s, thanks to several factors. First, for those
who disagreed, the option of voluntary emigration to lands west of the
Mississippi was open, and some 5,000 Cherokees had done so by 1828.
Second, the Sequoyan syllabary worked to the advantage of integration in
the long run. The council published laws both in English and Cherokee,
where they could be read and discussed by all, and published the bilingual
newspaper, the *Cherokee Phoenix* under Boudinot's editorship. The missionaries soon came to use Sequoyan for Christian pamphlets and Bible
translations. Third, the mixed blood chief, John Ross, made it his business

to be in contact with the full bloods as well – he took the unusual step of converting to Methodism – and gained their support in the struggle for survival that was about to occur. In a memorandum to Congress in 1835, Ross used the idea that the Indians were descended from the Israelites to argue that they deserved to stay in the homeland that God had given them.[98] The theory of Israelite descent reinforced the acculturationist position that the Indians were the equals of whites and could be educated to their level. Still, the aristocratic lifestyle of Ross and the men around him – women were no longer in the circles of power – continued to provoke resentment among less well-off mixed-bloods as well, fueling factionalism which persisted throughout the nineteenth century. The days of government by consensus were over.

The central event in Cherokee history was undoubtedly the forced removal from Appalachia to eastern Oklahoma in 1838 – the infamous Trail of Tears. Sadly, the removal crisis, ushered in by the federal Removal Act of 1830, undid many of the bonds within the Cherokee nation that had gradually built up in the previous decade. At first, most missionaries to the Cherokees supported the Nation in opposing removal, and 12 of them signed a manifesto to this effect. Two ABCFM missionaries, Samuel Worcester and Elizur Butler, went to jail in Georgia for defying a law designed to remove them from Cherokee territory – a law that was declared invalid by the Supreme Court in the spring of 1832. But Andrew Jackson's decision not to enforce the court's decision, plus his reelection in the fall of that year, demoralized much of the opposition. The missionaries on the ground gradually lost the support of their national organizations, and Worcester and Butler concluded in December that the struggle was futile. The same issue was to split the Cherokee themselves. Although a majority clearly favored resisting, a group opposed to the Ross faction took shape in 1932, headed by Boudinot. It was this group that signed the Treaty of New Echota in 1835, which acquiesced in the removal to Oklahoma and, although declared illegitimate by the majority, gave the US government its excuse to do so forcibly.

All of this served to undermine the missionaries' credibility and enhanced the prestige of traditional religion. Yet Ross relied heavily on Biblical imagery in these years to buoy the spirits of his people – imagery drawn mainly from the Old Testament such as the Book of Job and and the Book of Exodus. In the end, Ross was allowed to organize the removal and lead his own people in the Trail of Tears. Evans was one of three missionaries who went with them, recording the suffering in his diary. Yet he also recorded that "the gospel is making advances altogether unprecedented in the Christian history of the Cherokees," even as the traditional ceremonies also increased in popularity. In the traumatic situation, each allowed the other to offer its own brand of consolation.[99]

The years immediately following the removal, by contrast, were ones of disorientation, anomie, and factionalism in which interest in both traditional and Christian religion declined and the rule of vengeance again prevailed (targeting, among others, Boudinot and the other signers of the Treaty of New Echota). Thanks in large part to Ross's efforts, however, stability returned by the mid-1840s, ushering in a "golden age" that lasted until the Civil War, which was to divide the Cherokee nation yet again over the issue of slavery and bring even greater loss of life and property than had the removal itself.

Contributing to the era of stability were the missionaries, whom the Council had invited to return in the 1840s (and again in the 1860s following the Civil War). The various denominations cooperated in a vigorous temperance movement; the Reverend Worcester took up residence in Indian territory, translating and printing portions of the Bible, hymnals, primers, and tracts.[100] In one area, missionary influence declined: education, as the council instituted an ambitious public school system, surpassing those of whites in neighboring states. Instruction was in English, which again benefited the mixed-bloods more than the full-bloods, categories which themselves became increasingly defined by one's language rather than ancestry, and kept the tension between these two groups alive. Nevertheless, even though poor in comparison to the mixed-bloods, the full-bloods also improved their material position between the removal and the Civil War.

During the years before and after the removal, there gradually took shape a remarkable accommodation between traditional Cherokee religion and Baptist/Methodist form of Christianity – often to the chagrin of the Congregationalists, Presbyterians, and Moravians. McLoughlin, the leading authority on Cherokee Christianity, maintains that it spread beyond actual church membership (12–15 percent of the nation as a whole in 1860), and evidence for it persists into the mid-twentieth century.[101] McLoughlin calls it a syncretic movement, a label that fits the case provided we understand it as encompassing a number of different types of interaction which deserve to be distinguished.

The first and the earliest to take shape, roughly between 1800 and 1830, was the *vernacular translation* of the Biblical story, or at least parts thereof, and its incorporation into the body of Cherokee mythology.[102]

One finds a great variety of creation stories loosely based on the model of Genesis during these years, probably devised by different *adonisgi* to explain things that their earlier creation stories could not account for. Cherokee stories of the earth's origins did not contain a reference to a single Great Spirit or creator; the earth was a single island suspended from the heaven by four cords, and the ruling spirits were animals acting in council. This picture had to be modified to explain the arrival of people from other shores, as well as the existence of different races. The grafting of a creator God to explain these phenomena was probably the most powerful move of *vernacular translation* on the part of the southeastern Indians, enabling them to talk of God as interchangeable with the Great Spirit. In this way, the evolution of Cherokee beliefs paralleled the nativist revitalization movements of the Northeast, even though the Cherokees themselves remained relatively impervious to these. Beyond this, the question of how the Great Spirit fashioned the races was a matter of great divergence of opinion. We have seen the Israelite connection which appealed to the mixed-bloods. But the full-bloods leaned toward more ethnocentric explanations, claiming that God created the races separately (polygenesis), each on their own continents – a balance that was disfigured by the arrival of the whites and the African slaves they brought with them. Some versions found the red men to be the original race, to whom God had given the "Great Book," which the whites stole from them. In any case, the Indians emerged as a chosen people, clearly a translation of the Old Testament idea of a covenant between God and a nation, markedly different from the notion of individual salvation which appealed to the white Protestants. Over time, this *vernacular translation* of Biblical passages came to include the belief in the coming millennium as well, which enhanced the Mormons' popularity when they arrived in 1847.

A further example of *vernacular translation* at work would be a convergence at the level of ritual. There are fewer instances of this, but one seems very important: the Baptist rite of total immersion, which took place in a river or stream, corresponded to a traditional Native purification ritual.[103] Evans was willing to perform this repeatedly, which contravened Baptist theology of immersion as the one-time sign of being accepted into the church. One might also point to the three-day Methodist camp meetings, drawing people in from 40 to 50 miles away, which the Baptists soon adopted as well, as replicating the intensity of traditional festivals and dancing. One can also view such meetings as an instance *of conservation of form*, affording opportunities for maintaining sociability, cooperation, and the sharing of food that traditional festivals had also provided.[104]

Finally, one can point to *dual participation*, a willingness to accept or tolerate practices of another religion even if not compatible with one's own. This did not happen overnight, as one sees in Jones's record of his itinerant preaching in the early years and his confrontations with the *adonisgi* he inevitably encountered. Jones shared the Christian view of Native dances and medical incantations as idolatry and sought to persuade the *adonisgi* of this. He was able to pose questions to them to which they had no answer, but he was unable to extirpate the practices themselves, and most Cherokees retained what they found useful from the old religion, even as they found hope and consolation in Christian prayer and song.[105] In the years following the removal, however, the mutual understanding and tolerance seems to have increased. Christians were now willing to interpret some of the Native practices as more secular than religious, and hence acceptable, such as the medicine of the *adonisgi* and the ball plays; some *adonisgi* even became church members.[106] Unlike the other denominations, Methodists and Baptists tolerated attendance at the Green Corn Ceremony, even though they did not much like it.

In the 1850s and 1860s, this tolerance moved toward more active cooperation under the pressure of the slavery controversy. This came with the formalization of a secret society in favor of abolition known as the Keetoowah in the 1850s. This society, which still exists today, was restricted to full-bloods only. It had roots among the Indians going back before the removal, but now became a rallying point where Christians and traditional leaders came together. As the slavery controversy drove a further wedge between the wealthier, slave-owning mixed-bloods and the poorer, non-slave-owning fulls, it also brought many missionaries under suspicion of spreading abolitionism, including, of course, Jones. Evidence points to him as the instigator of the new initiative to counter the pro-slavery faction, and its early leaders were his Native protégés. The society was non-sectarian, however, and its purpose was to promote full-blood political power. But both types of rituals were incorporated: according to McLoughlin, "meetings took place around a council fire; tribal dances were encouraged; sacred myths were recited (along with Christian hymns and prayers), and meetings were conducted by ancient procedures rather than those copied from the whiteman's political system."[107] A measure of the society's success lies in the fact that two elected chiefs after the Civil War were Native Baptist preachers who spoke only Cherokee.[108]

Neither the acculturative strategy of the mixed-bloods nor the revitalization of the Keetowahs were strong enough to withstand the next great wave of settler colonialism, beginning with the intrusion of thousands of white squatters in Indian territory in the 1870s and culminating in Oklahoma statehood in 1907 – and with it the end of Cherokee self-government. Some of the mixed-bloods profited by the allotment of Indian lands to individuals that was part of the process, and some became part of the Oklahoma political elite, while the full-bloods sank back into greater poverty and isolation – some of the worst of any tribal group. The imperialism was cultural as well as political and economic, as the Federal Bureau of Indian Affairs took over the Cherokee schools and established boarding schools where the Cherokee language was forbidden. As is well known, this "fifty-year period of dormancy" was followed by a reversal of these policies and trends, as the Indian renaissance across the country gathered momentum in the 1970s. The Cherokee were able to draw on the strength of their combination of Native and Christian worship to further these aims.[109]

The leadership of the Cherokee nation following World War II reflects the divergent constituents of the nation itself. From 1949 to 1975 the chief was W. W. Keeler, a mixed-blood who rose to prominence as head of Philips Petroleum Corporation. He used his influence and expertise to gain advantages for the Nation from the federal government. He was succeeded by Ross Swimmer, a Republican banker who went on to become head of the Bureau of Indian Affairs in Washington. Swimmer was replaced in 1985 by Wilma Mankiller, the first elected female chief, who grew up in the impoverished rural area in eastern Oklahoma in the 1940s and 1950s. Her family celebrated Christmas, went to Baptist church occasionally, but learned little about Christianity; at the same time, she also secretively attended traditional ceremonies. She participated in the occupation of Alcatraz Island as part of the Indian movement of the 1970s. As an adult, she became a more regular churchgoer, but describes her cultural situation as follows:

The Cherokee Nation and our people have a well-known reputation for being able to adapt to the non-Indian world and of running a well-organized tribal government. But what people do not realize is that we live within two realities, and the two are very different. One reality is the acceptance of and ability to deal with the non-Indian world around us, and the other reality is our being able to hold onto and retain our ancient Cherokee belief systems, values, customs and rituals.[110]

At the same time, one can point to the statement of a practicing *adonigsi* in North Carolina to an ethnologist in 1961, claiming that today's conjurers all consider themselves to be good Christians: "If it wasn't [for] the power of the Creator, you couldn't make anything move."[111] Perhaps the invocation of a single creator God is the lynchpin that continues to hold the divergent strands of Cherokee spirituality together.

THE OCETI SAKOWIN (SIOUX)

The term "Sioux" is not a Native label, but a foreign one, a French corruption of an Ojibwa word meaning "enemy" or "little snake." The Indians themselves referred to a group of seven tribes (*Oceti Sakowin*, the "Seven Fireplaces"), grouped into three divisions which are known either by generic name (Santee, Yankton, Teton) by their dialect (Dakota, Nakota, Lakota, all of which meant "friends" or "allies"). The Lakota or Tetons, the largest group, came to be further subdivided into seven tribes, the best known being the Oglala, the Brulé, and the Hunkpapa (Sitting Bull's tribe).[112] The three major divisions were spread geographically roughly from east to west, from Minnesota and Nebraska to the Dakotas. The three dialects were, however, sufficiently similar to be mutually intelligible – a fact of obvious advantage for the missionaries, who could rely on translations in one area to be understood in another. Thus the existence of these differences did not seriously impede the spread of Christianity.

The Lakota Sioux in particular have formed the basis for the stereotypes that most Euro-Americans and Europeans have of Indians in general – whether as the warriors who defeated Custer at Little Big Horn, or as the spiritual peoples who cherish the earth, as popularized in the film *Dances with Wolves*. Neither of these stereotypes takes into account, or seems at first glance compatible with, the fact that most Sioux accepted Christianity, as conveyed to them by missionaries, at some time between 1860 and 1930. Statistical documentation for this process is as always questionable, but points to a general trend that was well under way by the First World War. An article in *Harper's New Monthly Magazine* in 1893 fondly estimated the number of Protestants to be between 10,500 and 11,000 (out of some 26,000 total population), and the number of Catholics at 4,740.[113] A study conducted on the Pine Ridge Reservation in the 1940s claimed that "all the Pine Ridge Indians profess belief in Christianity and nominal membership in some church."[114] As recently as 1987, a study claimed that "most Sioux people maintain membership in, and belief in the efficacy of, some Christian denomination."[115] These observations stand in marked contrast to those of Native Americans as a whole. An interdenominational survey conducted in 1921 revealed that slightly less than half of the 400,000 Native people were nominal Christians.[116] A 1998 article states that "today, only between 10 and 25 percent (depending on what set of statistics one chooses to believe) of Natives consider themselves Christians."[117] Such numbers, of course, beg the question of what it means to be a Native or Sioux Christian, and how one combines it with one's previous religious practices and beliefs.

Certainly no small part of the explanation for the growth of Christianity among the Sioux lies in the preparedness, persistence, timing, and clout of the missionaries themselves. With every major defeat of the Sioux, missionaries were present, equipped with ritualistic and linguistic tools, and working largely hand in hand with the US government. The rhythm of this process varied with the three regional divisions. Not surprisingly, the eastern Dakota were the first to be subjected to the shift from flourishing trade with Euro-Americans to settler colonialism, a transition that caught them largely unawares as they ceded more and more of their territory in Minnesota to the whites beginning in 1837.[118] Protestant missionaries from the ABCFM played a leading role in the process, having arrived in the early 1830s. After some small initial successes, mostly with women and mixed-bloods, they faced increasing *resistance* in the 1840s. In the words of one of them, Stephen R. Riggs, "From the time that the chief men came to understand that the religion of Christ was an exclusive religion, ...they set themselves in opposition to it," sometimes persecuting the converts, preventing their children from going to the mission school, and killing the cattle of the missionaries.[119] This led Riggs and his fellow missionary, Thomas Williamson, to advocate a far-reaching program of total cultural assimilation. According to a statement from the American Board:

[T]here are still influential advocates, in government circles, of the theory that you can only treat the Indian as a member of a clan. It is the belief and experience of your missionaries that this is a profound error, and that it lies at the bottom of the government's acknowledged ill success in many cases...You must disintegrate the clan if you would elevate the man. And then nothing should bar them from all the rights and responsibilities of American manhood, as fast as they are able to assume them.[120]

This vision included transforming the Sioux from hunters into farmers, setting up boarding schools, and eventually disintegrating tribal lands into individual holdings – the program that became government policy for much of the following century. It must be emphasized that this was the program of many well-meaning white humanitarian circles (e.g., the so-called Indian Rights Association, founded in the 1880s) who saw such assimilation as the only alternative to physical extermination that other settlers were advocating. Thus paradoxically, white guilt over treatment of the Indians fed and intensified the assimilation effort rather than dampening it. The most visible examples were the boarding schools, such as the one founded by Richard H. Pratt at Carlisle, Pennsylvania, where children were sometimes separated from their families for years and subjected to barracks-like regimentation. To quote Robert Warrior, "a simple look at the graveyards at off-reservation boarding schools attests to the killing power of homesickness set against an ideology of eradicating all traces of Indianness from a young person's life."[121] By 1902, there were 154 such government-run boarding schools, in addition to the mission schools.[122]

Meanwhile, the Dakotas themselves were experiencing the same kind of bifurcation that had occurred earlier east of the Mississippi, with tragic results. In 1862, a minority of Dakotas made war on white settlements, killing some 500, thereby unleashing among whites a groundswell of calls for vengeance. The attackers fled westward or into Canada, as did many who had opposed the war but feared persecution. Most of those who remained, whether friendly or hostile, were interned while preparations were made for their removal from the state. Thirty-eight were executed. As with the Cherokee removal, these traumatic conditions provided an opportunity for the missionaries: Riggs and Williamson, who intensified their efforts with the internees, affecting several hundred "prison conversions." Many of those who were executed went to their deaths singing a Christian hymn.[123] In the years immediately thereafter, the Dakotas were forced to move several times before finding permanent settlements. Under conditions of overcrowding, extreme deprivation, and death that accompanied these removals, not to mention the Indians' uncertainty about their fate, the wave of conversions continued. At the time the missionaries were the only group of whites who showed them any compassion. As they settled into the reservations on the eastern plains, their life became marked by "the singing of hymns, the daily routine of the classrooms, and the seasonal round of planting and harvest."[124]

The middle, or Yankton, Sioux had moved into the eastern plains in the late eighteenth century. Unlike their neighbors, they preferred to live in sedentary villages for much of the year. Their relations with the US government remained peaceful. According to one of their members, Vine Deloria Jr., this was a point of honor, because Lewis and Clark had ceremoniously wrapped the chief's son in an American flag at birth.[125]

An 1858 treaty established the reservations and gave the Yankton unrestricted use of a quarry in Minnesota that provided clay for the sacred pipes (this lasted until 1893). They were largely receptive to missionary Christianity while continuing their previous religion in secret.[126]

The western Lakotas, by contrast, underwent a dramatic transition from conquering to conquered nation. Since the late eighteenth century, they had migrated westward into the Great Plains, turning to hunting the buffalo, which was their main source of subsistence and profit in trade. This proved to be highly successful, partly because their mobility enabled them to escape the epidemics which undermined other nations. Their population increased from 5,000 in 1804 to 25,000 in 1850, outnumbering the other two Sioux divisions combined.[127] The further they ranged, the more horses they required, which led to more and more raids on their neighbors whom they came to dominate, causing them to be widely feared. Both hunting and war valorized individual acts of male bravery, and the women likewise encouraged the men to avenge their lost relatives. The Lakotas' clearing the plains of their enemies helped ease the way for white settlers, and the two expansionist powers began to clash in the 1850s, leading to the well-known wars of the 1860s and 1870s.

In the words of James O. Gump, "United States Indian policy was driven by the contradictory impulses of greed, compassion, guilt, and self-righteousness."[128] Thus, even as General William T. Sherman was fighting the Lakota war bands to extinction, President Ulysses S. Grant was pursuing his "Peace Policy" on the newly formed but ever-shrinking reservations. This was in response to the increasing protests of religious and civic leaders in the late 1860s against the corrupt administration of Indian lands, and it gave missionary societies a prominent role to play in Indian education. For convenience, individual denominations were assigned to different reservations, and five Sioux reservations were given to the Episcopal Church. This policy was designed to eliminate sectarian rivalry among Protestants, but it had the opposite effect where Catholics were concerned. Catholics were given only 8 out of some 130 agencies, including two Sioux, and understandably felt slighted; after a decade the plan was disbanded because of disputes over religious liberty.[129] The Catholics had been evangelizing in breadth, so to speak, in the middle decades of the century, with Jesuit missionary Pierre Jean de Smet traveling throughout the region, performing baptisms, distributing crosses and generally trading on the image of the Black Robe as a "big medicine man."[130] By the 1880s, both the Episcopal and Catholic churches were served by energetic bishops, namely William Hobart Hare and Martin

Marty, who, for all their rivalry, promoted similar programs of Indian evangelization and education (both boarding and day schools).[131] The churches also supported the prohibition of most Lakota religious rituals; the principal one, the Sun Dance, was banned in 1883.

These efforts coincided with the increasing material deprivation of the Lakotas following the military defeats of the 1870s. Part of Sherman's war policy had been to undermine the basis of the Indians' livelihood, which meant the mass killing of the buffalo. By the 1880s, only a few hundred survived. As attempts at raising cattle and growing crops failed, the Lakotas became increasingly dependent on government rations. To add further injury, the Dawes Act of 1887 instituted the allotment policy which opened the reservations to individual white settlers, involving the further partitioning and reduction of Indian territory. In addition, the Sioux were faced with a reduction of rations, bringing many to the edge of starvation by the end of the decade.

In these desperate circumstances, it is not surprising that the Lakotas should have grasped at a message of hope emanating from Wovoka, a Native prophet in Nevada, whose ghost dance was spreading to some thirty nations in the West. This was but one of a number of prophetic dances in the middle and late nineteenth century coming from the Pacific Northwest.[132] Wovoka promised a day, soon to come, when Indians could return to their abundant lives before the whites arrived, complete with the return of the buffalo and the reuniting with their departed loved ones. This would not involve war – God would see to it on his own that whites were removed – but did require a circular dance that Wovoka claimed to have learned in heaven and that would hasten the coming. Nor is it surprising that Christian elements should be interwoven in this message. Wovoka had worked for a devoutly Christian white family, and while witnesses differed on whether Wovoka claimed himself to be Christ returned, the Lakota visitors certainly believed it, claiming they could see the wounds from the cross on his back. It made sense that the savior whom the whites had killed should now return to rescue the Indians from them. At the same time, the dance was predominantly made up of elements that stemmed from Indian traditions, and many interpreted it in that way.[133]

It should be noted, however, that a majority of Lakotas probably did not participate in the Ghost Dance. In a recent study, Jeffrey Ostler estimates the number to be between one-fourth and one-third; James Mooney, in his classic work, gives the figure of one-half.[134] Many remained skeptical; there is evidence that some Christians crossed over and became followers of Wovoka, but others remained loyal. At the height of the dance in October 1890, one Jesuit missionary complained that no one attended mass; yet in the same month Elaine Goodale, the government supervisor of education, witnessed an Episcopal convocation with 1,700 communicants.[135] Certainly the churches opposed the Ghost Dance, as did the government, which saw it as a threat, with the tragic consequence of the massacre at Wounded Knee, with 270–300 casualties, mostly women and children.[136] It marked a further and decisive stage in Lakota demoralization.

In this context, what meanings did the countless baptisms, catechisms, and sermons of Christianity have for the Sioux? Certainly, as in the colonial northeast, the churches helped to preserve community at a time when most other institutions that served that purpose were falling down around them. Beyond this, one can begin to answer the question by looking briefly at Sioux conceptions of spirituality. These have been characterized as being very flexible in beliefs and rather more conservative in rituals, though never static.[137] A key belief was that the cosmos itself was fundamentally incomprehensible. On the question of whether the Sioux ever postulated a supreme being before the missionaries came on the scene, the term *Wakan Tanka*, which the missionaries used to translate as God, referred not to a single being but a mysterious power or force of holiness (*wakan*) that was diffused throughout all things. Certain manifestations of *wakan* were particularly great, however (*tanka* = great); sometimes one sees these grouped symmetrically. Thus, one finds references to sixteen aspects of *Wakan Tanka* in groups of four; but this was by no means a universally held classification, and different holy men had different conceptions of *Wakan Tanka* without finding a particular need for agreement.[138] Indeed, a hallmark of Sioux spirituality is the latitude it gave to individual interpretation; religion was primarily a matter of one's experience rather than of formal doctrine.

The very diffuseness of the manifestations of *Wakan Tanka* meant that incorporating an outsider's God into Sioux cosmology posed no great problems of conscience or belief. As one convert, George Sword, explained:

When I believed the. . . *Wakan Tanka* (Great Spirit) was right I served him with all my Powers. . .In war with the white people I found their *Wakan Tanka* the Superior. I then took the name of Sword and have served *Wakan Tanka* according to the white people's manner with all my power. . .I joined the church and am a deacon in it and shall be until I die. I have done all I was able to do to persuade my people to live according to the teachings of the Christian ministers.[139]

Admittedly, Sword was an extreme case in that he advocated *acculturation* and the suppression of Lakota religious practice.[140] But others used similar pragmatic arguments to opt for a more selective acceptance of Christianity that did not necessarily exclude traditional forms.[141] As we have seen, this flexibility could also work the other way: at the time of the Ghost Dance, many new Christians suddenly forsook their new faith and briefly found a greater power in the millennial movement.

Another point of convergence between the two religions was a central myth of the Sioux that posited a single intercessor figure: White Buffalo Calf Woman, who appeared to the Sioux and gave them the sacred pipe that was to be the direct link between them and *Wakan Tanka*. Upon leaving, she turned into a white buffalo calf, showing that the *wakan* buffalo would provide for the tribe.[142] The pipe was to be used for peacemaking and obviously represents a feminine principle to offset the warrior ethos. The analogies to Jesus were noted by Sioux leaders such as Red Cloud, who stated in 1876 that "when God sent His Son, Jesus, to the Whites, He had sent his daughter, Buffalo Calf Woman, to the Lakotas."[143] According to Red Cloud, she had prophesied that Indians would merge with whites within the next ten generations.

Sioux rituals were less open to adaptation, although there was no rigid protocol or central authority to regulate them. For all the flexibility of beliefs, the rituals reveal a deep commitment to ascetic, *concentrated spirituality* in practice, as seen in a number of examples such as the vision quest, the sweat lodge, and the Sun Dance. As part of their initiation into adulthood, young males were expected to conduct a spiritual retreat in isolation, usually on a hilltop, going without food or water for several days, until they received a vision from the spirits. An exceptionally intense vision marked one as a shaman and imposed an obligation to live out the direction of the spirits for the rest of one's life.[144] During the rituals, the shamans spoke a special language to communicate with their spirit helpers. The sweat lodge was a purification ceremony and was held (among other times) prior to a great ritual such as the Sun Dance (and later the Ghost Dance). The Sun Dance was intended to bring the various roving bands together; a witness to an 1881 dance estimated that 3,500 people attended.[145] A four-day ritual, its climax featured men demonstrating their courage by inserting skewers in their flesh while dancing around a sacred pole until they collapsed. The symbolism of the rite pointed to the hunt and to war.[146]

Given the ban on the Sun Dance and most other traditional rituals, which lasted from 1883 to 1934, the only way of preserving them was to carry them on in secret, as indeed was done. Thus the predominant strategy for dealing with the missionaries, at least among the Lakota, was *dual participation*.[147] According to the anthropologist William K. Powers, most Natives continued to believe the traditional religion while they acquiesced in Christian ceremonies in order to preserve their social customs and language or even to obtain food.[148]

In Powers's version of *dual participation*, the Sioux participated in the rituals of Christianity while holding steadfast to their traditional beliefs. But given the flexibility of those beliefs, this interpretation is at least open to question. Certainly for some Sioux, one can point to the active and enthusiastic role which they played in the churches – not only as worshippers and hymn-singers, but also as catechists and priests, as missionaries to other tribes to the west, both Sioux and non-Sioux, and sometimes as communicators to the surrounding white population. The Episcopalians, under Hare's leadership, vigorously promoted a native clergy. Vine Deloria Jr. writes of the "Big Four" Native priests who "were regarded by the Sioux Episcopalians as their most important spiritual leaders."[149] Catholics admittedly present a different story, in that no Sioux became a priest until 1985.[150] Nevertheless, Native catechists came to perform many of the duties of priests, including giving sermons, visiting the sick, and administering funeral rites; perhaps a dozen Native women became nuns.[151]

An important part of Christianity's appeal lay in the practice of annual convocations within each denomination, which proved to be extremely popular, with people traveling several hundred miles to attend. These provided opportunities for the dispersed members to congregate, as the Sun Dance had done, thus showing *conservation of form*. Estimates of attendance at the Episcopal Niobrara convocations, held annually since the 1870s, varied between 3,000 and 10,000.[152] The Catholic congresses began in 1891, perhaps in response to their poor showing during the Ghost Dance.[153] They consciously borrowed some of the elements of the Sun Dance which they found unobjectionable, namely a tall pole at the center which now served as an altar for mass and was topped with an American flag. Marty delivered a sermon to show Jesus's sacrifice on the cross was a higher form than the self-torture of the Sun Dance.[154]

Another important way in which the missionaries conserved Native culture, despite all their pronouncements about quashing it, was by creating a written vernacular language. By the time of the Dakota uprising of 1862, the early Protestant missionaries had already accomplished this. Teaching literacy played a key role in the prison conversions of 1862–63, and the few Indians who had learned it taught it to the other male prisoners, who eagerly wrote letters to their families.[155] The commitment to preserving the vernacular extended to the early missionary schools among the Presbyterians, Congregationalists, and Episcopalians, until the federal government banned the practice in 1889, requiring English instead.[156] The Dakota language persisted, however, in hymnals and prayer books, and not least the Bible itself, which was translated in full by 1879, and extended as well to several bilingual newspapers published by the denominations. The Presbyterian/Congregationalist journal, *Iapi Oaye/The Word Carrier*, began in 1871 and continued to 1939. In 1878 it had achieved a circulation of nearly 1,600.[157] The Episcopalian paper *Anpao Kin/Daybreak* began publication in 1876. The Catholics were slower to embrace the vernacular, but eventually came to recognize its usefulness. The Lakota *Sinasapa Wocekiye Taeyanpaha* (*Catholic Herald*) was published from 1890 to 1936.[158] Several German Jesuit missionaries took an interest in Native culture in the '90s, and one of them, Eugen Buechel, published several books in Lakota, including a grammar.[159] The Catholic catechism, which built on the work of the earlier linguists, utilized different combinations of the word *wakan* to present the seven sacraments, conveying them as sacred power.[160]

The significance of a new written vernacular as a means of empowering an ethnic minority in the face of colonialism is well documented. One needs to be careful, however, about identifying it exclusively with the preservation of native culture. For example, the masthead of the *Iapi Oaye/Word Carrier* (published by the missionaries) read as follows: "OUR PLATFORM For Indians we want American Education! We want American Homes! We want American Rights! The result of which is American citizenship! And the Gospel is the power of God for their Salvation!"[161] In 1890, the paper strongly condemned the Ghost Dance.[162] Conversely, one cannot conclude that because the vernacular in the schools was the choice of the missionaries it was also necessarily the choice of the Indians. In 1877, the Lakota chiefs Red Cloud, Little Wound, and Spotted Tail specifically requested Catholic missions rather than Protestant because the Catholics used English in the schools, thereby granting easier access to the white man's ways.[163] One should recall that even the distant boarding schools, oppressive as they were, could serve as sites of native empowerment, for example in fostering athletic talent.[164] Nevertheless, in the view of Lakota anthropologist Beatrice Medicine, the use of the vernacular in church did help to preserve the language, in both spoken and written forms, into the period of revival in the late twentieth century.[165]

Over time, however, the efficacy of these measures tended to diminish; by the 1940s, the long-term effects of being in a position of dependency, coupled with harsher economic times, were making themselves felt, and the signs of self-abnegation that Tinker alluded to were beginning to multiply.[166] As Indian children learned English, the enthusiasm of their parents to use Dakota as a written language began to wear thin.[167] Missionary sources from this period likewise reveal a sense of failure.[168] Moreover, the Indian Reorganization Act of 1934, by creating new organs of political expression for Native Americans, led to the diminution of the church's role in providing indigenous leadership. Both the Episcopal and Catholic churches became less interested in promoting Native clergy.

In the face of these obstacles, however, one can point to the creativity and activism with which a number of Sioux intellectuals and spiritual leaders responded to this situation, drawing on Christianity as a means of engaging the conscience of the surrounding white population. The most famous of these was undoubtedly Black Elk (1863–1950). The life and work of this Lakota holy man illustrate both the intricacies that *dual participation* could assume and also the ambiguities and unresolved difficulties of communication between Natives and whites. The twists and turns of his spiritual biography have generated a voluminous literature, much of it focused on who was the "authentic" Black Elk.[169] Moreover, as someone who was literate in Lakota but spoke little English, his own pronouncements were mediated by white interlocutors to such a degree that it is difficult to distinguish the man from the myth.[170] His views first became known outside the Lakota because of his meeting with John G. Neihardt in 1930. Neihardt, the poet laureate of Nebraska, was working on an epic poem about the American west, and sought out Black Elk for material on the Ghost Dance and the massacre at Wounded Knee. Black Elk felt a strong affinity for the visitor and, in a series of interviews, poured out his early life story and knowledge of the Lakota religion he had once practiced. The interviews became the raw material for Neihardt's *Black Elk Speaks*, which was eventually translated into eight languages. The book was not a literal rendering of the transcripts, but a poet's attempt to capture their spirit. It became a key text in the revival of Native traditions in the 1960s and 1970s and in the appreciation of these by whites.[171]

As a boy of nine, Black Elk had experienced an extended vision that marked him as someone destined to be a spiritual leader and healer. As Black Elk told it: "In my vision they had predicted that I was chosen to be intercessor for my people so it was up to me to do my utmost for my people and everything that I did not do for my people, it would be my fault."[172]

Part of the fascination of *Black Elk Speaks* was undoubtedly that it bore witness to the major events of Sioux history during his lifetime: Black Elk observed the Battle of Little Big Horn as a teenager; in the 1880s he traveled with Buffalo Bill's Wild West Show to Europe, as did seventy-five to one hundred Indians each year, reflecting a desire to learn more about the white man's ways.[173] As a condition, he was required to accept Christianity and briefly become an Episcopalian. Upon his return, he participated in the Ghost Dance and fought the US troops in the aftermath of the Wounded Knee massacre. Neihardt's version ended at this point, presenting Black Elk as a "pitiful old man" whose vision had failed him. In other words, Neihardt's version represented the romanticization of the vanishing Indian, an image that could soothe the conscience of a white readership while retaining the Social Darwinist vision of white superiority. In fact, as the full transcripts reveal, Black Elk's intent was just the opposite: by telling these things to Neihardt, he had hoped to revive and strengthen Lakota culture by communicating it to whites. This is just one of many significant omissions in Neihardt's version.

Another is that, thirteen years after the Wounded Knee massacre, Black Elk converted to Catholicism. The reasons for the conversion have never been fully elucidated. There is evidence for personal, pragmatic, and ethical motives. We do know that, two years after Wounded Knee, Black Elk married, and it is likely that his wife was a Catholic, for their sons were baptized in the 1890s. When asked later by Neihardt about his Catholicism, Black Elk simply replied, "My children had to live in this world." Also, Black Elk had continued to practice traditional healing into the early 1900s. He had been performing these rites in 1904 on a boy who had been baptized when a Jesuit entered, grasped Black Elk by the neck, and said, "Satan, get out!" The Jesuit also invited the holy man to accept instruction in Christianity, and after two weeks of instruction, Black Elk was baptized and given the name Nicholas (for the saint on whose feast day the baptism occurred).[174] In addition, there were ethical considerations. According to his vision, Black Elk was to make war using a lethal herb; he now shrank from the possibility of using it to kill innocent women and children.[175]

Whatever his motives, after his conversion Black Elk quickly assumed a leadership role within the Catholic mission. He became one of the first Native catechists, filling in for priests as they traveled from church to church. Soon he was going on missionary expeditions to other Indian nations such as the Arapahoes and the Winnebagos. One Jesuit missionary praised his zeal in doing so, comparing him to St. Paul. He was said to have effected 400 conversions.[176]

Black Elk's decision to talk to Neihardt in 1930 and the publication of *Black Elk Speaks* constituted another turning point in his development, one which ushered in a period of simultaneous practice of Lakota and Catholic religion. Once again, his motives are obscure, but it is quite possible that he perceived the same deterioration of life on the reservation that had struck other observers, and concluded that Christianity alone was failing to provide sufficient spiritual meaning to his people.[177] In any event, the publication of *Black Elk Speaks* scandalized the missionary community and proved to be an embarrassment to Black Elk and his younger children. He was persuaded to issue a statement repudiating the ending and to proclaim the superiority of Catholicism[178] Nonetheless, this did not prevent him from resuming some sacred dances and from continuing to educate the white public about Lakota religion. This took the form of his participation, for most of the rest of his life, in an Indian pageant for tourists each summer on a site on the way to Mount Rushmore. According to Raymond DeMallie, he was the main attraction, reenacting the healing cures, a burial, and the sun dance.[179] As in all previous phases of his religious life, Black Elk thought it important to make religion manifest through public performative utterances.

Black Elk's thinking did not remain static during the last years of his life, but evolved in the direction of underscoring the parallelisms between Lakota religion and Christianity. The product of this was a final book, *The Sacred Pipe*, again told to a white writer, Joseph Epes Brown (who had been inspired by *Black Elk Speaks*), published posthumously in 1953. In this case, it is impossible to sift out the role of Brown's editing, since there is no alternative version of the conversations. The book presents seven sacred rituals as central to the Lakota, intended to parallel the seven sacraments. There is no attempt to interpret one in terms of the other, rather to inform white readers about Lakota rituals themselves. In the preface, however, the Christian belief in Jesus as the Son of God is presented as similar to the Lakota belief in *Wakan Tanka* sending the White Buffalo Calf Woman – and the belief on both sides that the end of the world is not far off. Black Elk/Brown also emphasized that the book had a universal message beyond that of helping the Lakota people: "to help in bringing peace upon the earth, not only among men, but within men and between the whole of creation."[180] Thus the message pointed in the direction of convergence, namely that Lakota religion and Christianity ultimately worship the same God in different ways.

It should be noted, however, that this notion of convergence was highly selective, in that Christianity served as a filter through which certain Lakota elements were retained and others left out from what otherwise appeared to be an "authentic" Native discourse. For example, the limitation of the basic rituals to seven ignored some major ones, not least the healing ceremony that Black Elk had been practicing on the eve of his conversion.[181] Also, the impact of Christianity as an agent of pacification is evident: the function of the Sun Dance as a preparation for war is passed over. Perhaps most profoundly, Black Elk/Brown's reference to *Wakan Tanka* in the singular reinforced its function as a translation for "God," which followed missionary practice but not necessarily past Lakota usage.[182] One might see this as resembling what the Comaroffs called "colonization of consciousness" or what we have labeled *assimilation of form*, in that the colonizers shaped the form of the presentation even while indigenous content was preserved. It is also clear, however, that this meaning has caught on with many Sioux. Even those who have embraced the revival of traditional religion tend to claim that they and Christians worship the same God.[183]

Not all Indian leaders, however, acquiesced in this interpretation of Native American Christianity. A distinguished representative of a different, *resistant* view was the Yankton intellectual Vine Deloria Jr. (1933–2005). Deloria's Christian pedigree was impeccable: he came from a family of distinguished Episcopalian leaders, his great-grandfather having converted in 1871. His grandfather Philip was revered as an orator – there is a statue to him in Washington National Cathedral – and his father, Vine Sr. followed in his footsteps. In addition, his aunt, Ella Deloria, trained as an anthropologist and transcribed and translated Lakota and Dakota materials. Although Vine Jr. earned a Bachelor of Divinity degree from Augustana Lutheran Seminary in 1963, he soon became convinced that legal rather than religious expertise was the more valuable tool to revitalize the Indian nations, and went on to law school. His main reputation, however, was as a broad-ranging intellectual, addressing issues in natural science, anthropology, history, and religion, provocatively questioning the basic assumptions of Western thought in each case. As a spokesman for the American Indian movement of the

1960s and 1970s, he authored such books as *Custer Died for Your Sins* (1969), *We Talk, You Listen* (1970), *God Is Red* (1973), *Behind the Trail of Broken Treaties* (1974), and *Red Earth, White Lies* (1995). With his polemical and easily readable style, he was able to simultaneously inspire and lead Native Americans to greater autonomy and to successfully appeal to the consciences of the surrounding white majority.

Vine Jr. tackled the differences between Christianity and Native American religion in *God Is Red*. "Both religions," he stated, "can be said to agree on the role and activity of a creator. Outside of that specific thing, there would appear to be little that the two views share."[184] Christianity is based on a revelation that occurs at a specific point in time, which generates a linear view of history with a definite beginning and end. Native religions are based on revelations that occur at specific points in space – holy sites and lands that generate a view of the sacred that is tied to land and its stewardship. A fundamental difference is that, in the Judeo-Christian story, man receives domination over creation, opposite the veneration of nature that is at the heart of Indian religions. Deloria also insisted on the tribal specificity of religions; the rites and obligations that are established between god(s) and peoples cannot be simply transferred from one group to another under the guise of a vague universalism. In this way, he gave voice to the view of many Native Americans that white interest in their religion – as in the New Age movement, for example – amounted to a kind of cultural poaching. Deloria went on to mount a critique of the notion of cultural hybridity itself:

I suggest...that we have on this planet two kinds of people—natural peoples and the hybrid peoples. The natural peoples represent an ancient tradition that has always sought harmony with the environment. Hybrid peoples are the product of...an ancient genetic engineering that irrevocably changed the way these people view our planet. I can think of no other good reason why the peoples from the Near East—peoples from the Hebrew, Islamic, and Christian religious traditions —first adopted the trappings of civilization and then forced a peculiar view of the natural world on succeeding generations. The planet, in their view is not our natural home and is, in fact, ours for total exploitation. We are today reaching the "nth" term in this sequence of exploitation and face ecological disasters of such complete planetary scope as to surpass our wildest imagination.[185]

Nevertheless, Deloria held that Indian spirituality contains wisdom which modern-day Christians desperately need to hear and learn from, since in his view Christianity lacks the tools to cope with the ecological crisis of the present. One might view the preservation of an earth-centered spirituality as a gift that Native Americans have made to the white world.

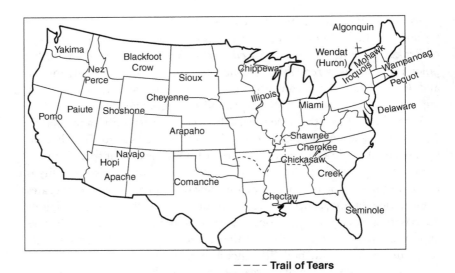

Figure 3.1 Native North America
Source: Modified from Instructional Resources Corporation map, 2005

4

Sub-Saharan Africa and the Diaspora

INTRODUCTION: AFRICAN CHRISTIANITY AND ISLAM

In sub-Saharan Africa, Christianity has grown faster than in any other part of the world in the twentieth century except the Pacific islands – from 9 percent of the population in 1910 to between 48 and 57 percent a hundred years later. Islam, by comparison, grew from 14 percent to between 29 and 41 percent in the same time span, while so-called African Traditional Religion declined from 76 percent to between 8.7 and 13 percent.[1] This is all the more remarkable in view of the inevitable and understandable association many Africans made between Christian missionaries and European colonialism in the first half of the twentieth century.

Yet these numbers are misleading, because they imply that Christianity (or Islam) and African religions are mutually exclusive categories. In fact, by common consensus, indigenous pre-Islamic and pre-Christian practices continue to live on in the midst of the two monotheistic faiths. The term "syncretism" still finds widespread use to describe this situation, though not without criticism as being too general.[2] Quite often, this relationship appears to take the form of *dual religious participation*, i.e., simply compartmentalizing one's religious behavior. The Nigerian historian E. A. Ayandele put the matter crisply in an address at the University of Ibadan in 1975:

Scratch the African pastor and you would discover that he has greater faith in the charms and amulets he wears surreptitiously and in the 'witch-doctor' to whom he pays nocturnal visits than in the Holy Bible and Jesus Christ; scratch the Christian medical doctor and you would discover that he pays greater attention to the diviner and the psychical fears instilled by his village *milieu* than his scalpel and the white man's tablets; scratch the prominent layman politician and you discover that his public bold face and animal courage are against the background of his secret endless groveling before masters of supernatural forces in traditional society.[3]

Yet such mixing may be an expression of a genuinely felt pluralism, a belief in the reconcilability of different religious expressions, each appropriate to different situations. Thus, according to Stephen Ellis and Gerrie ter Haar:

Religious belief operates at every level of society in Africa...so that an individual may be a member of several religious congregations simultaneously, and in many parts of the continent may even practice religious rituals regarded in the West as belonging to different systems of belief, such as Christianity and Islam, or Christianity and 'traditional' religion, or Sufism and reformed Islam, as in Sudan.[4]

A Catholic man from Mozambique puts it more precisely: "It's not that we have one foot in the church and one foot in tradition, . . . but both feet in the church *when we're there*, and both feed on the ancestral grounds *when we're there*."[5]

This pluralism is grounded in two fundamental assumptions which, despite the diversity of African societies, are commonly agreed to apply across many of them:

1) a profound belief in *diffuse spirituality*, an expandable multiplicity of invisible spirits and their ubiquity in everyday life, capable of absorbing such Christian deities as God, Jesus, the Holy Spirit, and Satan, but without necessarily extinguishing what had gone before.[6] This would suggest a strategy of *selective incorporation* – selective in that, over time, many aspects of Christianity as imported by Western missionaries have been shed in favor of practices that are more recognizably African. At the same time, Christianity has had to come to terms with the preexisting parts of the spirit world. A good example is the pervasiveness of witchcraft as a social fact, grounded in the belief that evil spirits operate through possession of individual bodies and souls, so that any misfortune or evil that a person experiences is traceable to the malevolent thoughts and actions of others. In times of economic or political instability, such as Africa has recently experienced, these beliefs have flourished. Thus, the accusation, exile, torture and killing of presumed witches has continued and even increased in some areas, such as in parts of South Africa after the end of

Apartheid.[7] To meet the challenges posed by such beliefs in their quest for deliverance from evil, African Christians have necessarily drawn on aspects of their faith that would seem to be distinctly "unmodern" in the West (although by no means entirely absent from it), such as demonology and spirit possession.[8]

2) The pervasiveness of spirits also entails rejection of a sharp dividing line between spiritual and material worlds. As Adrian Hastings put it:

> African tradition was inherently holistic. Here less than anywhere could you mark off the secular from the sacred. The religious permeated pretty well everything or—one might well say—the secular permeated everything. Thus you can analyse ancestor veneration in almost entirely secular terms, and many good social scientists have done so, or you can analyse it in entirely religious terms. But you certainly cannot separate the two.[9]

This means, for one thing, that contemporary politicians have not infrequently turned to invisible spirits for power and advantage, employing divination and sacrifice.[10] For another, there is little or no problem with religious practice in pursuit of such this-worldly goals as health, wealth, security, or getting ahead.[11] This, in turn, promotes a certain pragmatism with respect to innovations from outside. For example, the sociologist Ann Swidler finds that, for all their "traditional" practices, sub-Saharan Africans are also open to Western science, medicine, and education.[12]

This openness can be found in the past history of the importation of foreign religions. Thus, it would surely be too simplistic to portray African Christianity (or Islam) as mere overlays riding above a relatively unchanging indigenous substrate. The interaction was much more complex and profound. Over time, Africans have reached out to Islam and Christianity because they wanted to broaden their horizons and benefit from contacts with the wider world, both material and spiritual, that these religious messengers brought with them. Taken as a whole, African religion was probably never static for very long.[13] As historian David Maxwell and others have pointed out, people in central and southern Africa moved about for religious reasons, going on pilgrimages extending hundreds of miles, long before Christianity appeared.[14] The same could be said of the trans-Saharan caravans, or the Pentecostals of today with their international outreach. Such cosmopolitanism fits in well with the aforementioned assumptions of spiritual multiplicity and integration of religion with the other spheres of life, and indeed suggests that the label "African traditional religion," insofar as it suggests stasis, is quite inappropriate to begin with. If "traditional" implies a reluctance to change, then "world" religions, with their orthodoxies based on written texts, may often be more "traditional" than those based on more fluid oral transmission.

It further follows, or so I will argue in this chapter, that if one compares sub-Saharan Africans' encounters with Islam and Christianity in terms of basic strategies, then one finds that they share many more similarities than differences.[15] This is so despite the fact that the chronologies of the two processes are quite different, with Islamic contacts across the Sahara dating back to the eleventh century (not to mention the Indian Ocean cultural basin), while Christianity had to await the Portuguese voyages of the fifteenth century, with its cultural impact generally coming much later.[16] But in general, given their integration of spiritual and material interests, Africans associated both new religions with new opportunities for trade, as well as with "civilization" – in the sense of providing new and more effective means of attaining a well-ordered society, e.g., through literacy, law, education, and moral codes. Thus, the familiar triad of "Christianity, commerce, and civilization," so often discussed in connection with nineteenth-century European colonialism, can be seen as a variant of this broader pattern, one that was fueled as much by African demand as by foreign imposition. These factors probably outweighed the significance of specific beliefs about God, although the fact that many African religions acknowledged a high creator god in some fashion doubtless served as a *cultural hook*.[17] Missionaries and Christian scholars have eagerly fastened on these connections, often while ignoring the indigenous contexts in which they occurred.[18]

A comparison of African Christianity and African Islam has the further advantage of highlighting the dynamism of African religions themselves, for in the extended processes of encounter, these exhibited some dramatic alterations and swerves. One can discern, moreover, a broad, rough pattern in these changes. The British historian Islam Humphrey Fisher identified such a pattern in a seminal article in 1973 and urged its use for comparative purposes.[19] He posited three stages of interaction between Islam and sub-Saharan Africa: (1) quarantine, (2) mixing, and (3) reform. In the first stage, Muslim traders and clerics dealt with kings and princes but largely kept to themselves and made few converts. In the mixing stage – Fisher also consciously avoided the term "syncretism" – Islam attracted many new followers, and institutions such as Quranic schools spread literacy. Islam proved to be quite accommodating to local customs and religious practices, moreso than Christianity was later to do, most notably regarding polygamy. The third stage, reform, represents a revulsion against such mixing and a movement toward *concentration of spirituality* in the desire to attain a pure form of Islam – ironically, Fisher maintains, fueled by the very literacy acquired in the second stage. The best-known historical example is the Fulani jihad of the early nineteenth century under Uthman dan Fodio. But there were others, such as the works of fifteenth-century scholar Al-Maghili. The example shows that Fisher allows for considerable flexibility in his stage-theory, not insisting on a strict linear progression. The parallels with African Christianity are not exact, but I think still applicable – though my interpretation will differ in some important respects from Fisher's on the details.[20] I also find evidence for a cyclical view, consisting of an oscillation between mixing and reform, similar to the one developed by Willy de Craemer, Jan Vansina, and Renee C. Fox in a widely cited study of religion in central Africa.[21] They suggest that new movements occur every twenty to thirty years, which appear better able to meet the villages' practical needs and alleviate their misfortunes; in the process old charms and symbols are discarded. One finds similar stories in the adoption of Christianity elsewhere.[22] One can see this as illustrating a dialectical relationship between diffuse and concentrated spirituality, considerably complicating the pattern of selective incorporation.

Initial acceptance of Islam and Christianity by sub-Saharan Africans often hinged on one or both of two conditions: (1) the work of native missionaries and teachers, or at least peoples of African descent, working with foreigners but often doing the bulk of the work; (2) the existence of a powerful centralized monarchy that was willing to promote the new religion.

The first was a similar feature of African Islam and Christianity, although the mode of transmission varied greatly depending on the nature of barrier that happened to separate sub-Saharan Africa from its foreign shores – in one case the desert, in the other the oceans. The first case has been described as a relay, with Berbers bringing Islam by caravan to the southern shore, from whence it spread to the edges of the tropical forest. Throughout, peripatetic clerics were accompanied by their students, as well as those who established themselves in Muslim quarters.[23] People from the south could accompany the caravans to the Islamic centers in Egypt and Arabia. When the barrier was the ocean, relations tended take place on either shore. East Africa had long since become part of a homogenous Indian Ocean culture in which Arabic influences were paramount; here the most likely form of transmission was intermarriage. Later, however, in the nineteenth century, Islam would penetrate inland, largely peacefully.[24]

For Christianity, native transmitters were essential to the process of creating written languages and for translating the Bible into them. The credit for these multiple translation efforts usually goes to the European missionary linguists, but their accomplishments were unthinkable without active native participation. The Anglican bishop John Colenso wrote of his efforts in the nineteenth century:

I have no special gift for languages, but what is shared by most educated men of fair ability. What I have done, I have done by hard work—by sitting with my natives day after day, from early morn to sunset, till they, as well as myself, were fairly exhausted—conversing with them as well as I could and then listening to them conversing—writing down what I could of their talk from their own lips, and, when they were gone, still turning round again to my desk to copy out the results of the day.[25]

To be sure, these linguists constituted a tiny percentage of the European missionary cohort, but their influence far outweighed their numbers. The fact that the Bible and other religious tracts were the first available reading matter in print had much to do with shaping people's religious imagination.

As for the second condition, Muslim and Portuguese clerics alike believed that the surest way to spread their religion was to target the rulers. Moving from North Africa across the Sahara, Muslims were fortunate to encounter a number of powerful empires in the Sudanic belt on the southern side of the desert and were able to secure their cooperation and in many cases their conversion. They ingratiated themselves by claiming Allah's superior power at bringing practical results, such as by praying for rain. Their European Christian counterparts were neither as fortunate nor adept. Most of the coastal areas they reached were not controlled by large states, and their penetration was shallow and ephemeral. The reasons are not far to seek: the shortage of clergy, given the vastness of the Portuguese Empire and its proselytizing ambitions; the vitality of Islam in much of the continent; the hostility of the interior disease environment. In his treatment of West African Christianity, Lamin Sanneh characterizes the period from 1450 to 1750 in terms of "a sterilized European institution, safely quarantined in hygienic enclaves along the coast whence it occasionally timidly emerged to make local contact. Often it returned from such wavy ventures still effectively insulated against cross-cultural influences..."[26] Such quarantines were not about to lead to mixing.[27]

There were, however, exceptions, and these demonstrate that strong monarchs were indeed important to the spread of Christianity. But they were by no means a sure guarantee of acceptance; too many other variables needed to be in place. The Kingdom of Benin, the wealthiest and most renowned kingdom in West Africa at the time the Portuguese arrived, is a case in point. The oba, or ruler, did indeed express an interest in Christianity in 1514, and coupled it with a request for guns. The Portuguese, however, insisted on his conversion prior to such a trade, and despite the arrival of a few missionaries, nothing lasting was achieved.[28] Attempts to reach the kingdom in subsequent years were hampered by factional rivalries, both within the court and on the European side as well, as British and Dutch traders eventually made their appearance. The smaller and poorer neighboring kingdom of Warri illustrates the point even more graphically, for here the ruler was interested enough to travel to Portugal for priestly training but never succeeded in conveying his enthusiasm to the people. Part of the problem was again European rivalries: Portugal obstructed any attempts to send more missionaries from the Roman office of propaganda, suspecting this to be an attempt at Spanish infiltration.[29]

THE KINGDOM OF KONGO

The one place where the Portuguese succeeded in reaching the mixing stage, instigating a form of Christianity that struck deeper roots on the African continent was central Africa, particularly the Kingdom of the Kongo. Some scholars point to the fact that, according to Kongolese belief, that the color of the inhabitants of the land of the dead, who possessed superior knowledge, was white, and that the Portuguese, who first appeared in 1483, must have been from this spirit world. When the Portuguese took hostages and returned two years later with them alive and well (unlike the Algonquians in Quebec), this convinced the Kongolese of their superior power.[30] The distinctiveness of the Kongo Kingdom was the product of a number of factors: First, it was at the time relatively centralized and stable, which enabled successive kings to establish a continuity of political-religious practice that lasted, despite later upheavals, for some three hundred years.[31] Second, natives and missionaries were fortunately able to establish quite quickly some common interpretations of their religious experiences which, although neither side meant the same thing by them, worked to the satisfaction of both, thus creating a middle ground. The Iberians, like the Kongolese, both had a strong sense of the miraculous and of the tutelary function of local spirits. John Thornton has called these "co-revelations" and gives the following example:

Shortly after the first official Catholic priests arrived in Kongo, two Kongo nobles dreamed simultaneously of a beautiful woman who beseeched the Kongo to follow Christianity. Moreover, one of them also found a stone, which was "black and unlike any others in the country" near his house, which was shaped like a cross. When King Nzinga a Nkuwu heard these tales, he asked the Christian clergy present for an explanation. They unhesitatingly explained that the woman in the dream was the Virgin Mary and that she and the stone were "signs of grace and salvation" and that the events were "miracles and revelations."[32]

An even more compelling case occurred a few years later, when King Nzinga's son was battling rivals for the throne and an apparition of a white cross and of St. James appeared over the battlefield, scattering his enemies. St. James' Day, July 25, became a national holiday.

This second king, baptized Afonso in 1491, ruled from 1506 to 1543 and was responsible more than anyone else for the spread of Christianity in the Kongo. He was open to Portuguese influence, read deeply in Christianity, established a school system for the nobility, and sent some of its members to study in Portugal. Portuguese influence, however, did not mean control; under Afonso, Christianity was chosen rather than imposed from without and provided a means to reinforce royal authority over rivals. Rather than relying exclusively on foreign missionaries, the nobility took an active part in teaching Christianity, and foreign observers in the capital city were impressed with the widespread knowledge of basic teachings and prayers; over time this was extended to the countryside.[33] Belief was secondary to ritual, however; Catholicism provided an ensemble of practices and symbols which allowed it to be incorporated into existing Kongolese religion. According to Thornton, "conversion did not involve a fundamental change in religious outlook by anyone in the country, but was largely a product of renaming existing institutions and concepts."[34] Thus the term for "holy" was *ukisi*, derived from *nkisi*, the Kikongo term for physical receptacles for spirits, or "idols" in Christian terms. The Holy Spirit was *Moyo Ukisi*, the Holy Bible *nkanda a ukisi*, and the translation of "priest" was the Kongolese term for "shaman," which was *nganga*. Similarly, the missionaries accommodated the native practice of polygamy by labeling one spouse a wife, the rest as concubines.[35] This did not mean that all aspects of Kongolese religion were equally acceptable, and missionaries engaged as elsewhere in periodic campaigns to quash native cults. But this was not as alien to African practice as one might think, as African rulers themselves, including Afonso, also indulged in destroying fetishes and images as a way of enhancing their own spiritual power vis-à-vis their rivals. Afonso tore down the "house of idols" in the capital and erected a church on the site – a ritual that was replicated throughout the region.[36] On the whole, it appears that the Kongolese had become thoroughly comfortable with their Christianity, while at the same time retaining many if not most of their previous practices – an example of mixing, or in our terminology, *selective incorporation*.[37]

By the mid-seventeenth century, the political stability of the Kongo had disintegrated, and the country was plagued by civil warfare, exacerbated by the spread of the slave trade. Christianity nevertheless withstood the test and produced a prophetess – one of several prominent women in Kongolese religion and politics at this time.[38] This was Dona Beatriz de Kimpa Vita, who had been a *nganga* but became possessed by St. Anthony, a popular saint in the Kongo. She claimed that the end of the world was imminent, a sign of divine punishment for the degenerate political situation, and also that both Jesus and St. Francis had been born in the Kongo (contrary to the claims of the foreign missionaries). Her movement can be seen as an instance of reform or *concentration of spirituality*, discarding the superficialities and getting to the core religious experience, though still within the framework of Kongolese practice. A prayer that has come down to us reads in part, "*Salve* you say and you do not know why. *Salve* you recite and you do not know why. *Salve* you beat and you do not know why. God wants the intention, it is the intention that God takes."[39] It was also a protest against the use of Christianity by the nobility exclusively, and not surprisingly she was regarded as a heretic by the authorities. She was burned at the stake, but her movement survived her, although many of her followers were sold into slavery. The high volume of slaves from the Kongo in these years meant that, in all probability, many had learned their Christianity in Africa. The Stono Rebellion in South Carolina was conducted by Kongolese slaves trying to break out of the Protestant colony to Catholic Florida.[40] Grassroots Christianity continued in the Kongo as well, although many outside observers in the nineteenth century preferred to view it as syncretic and therefore not genuine. Nevertheless, when American Baptist missionaries arrived in the Kongo in the 1880s, they found an enthusiastic reception.[41]

THE AFRICAN DIASPORA AND CATHOLICISM

The contrast between journeys of Muslim converts across the Sahara and the horrors of the Atlantic middle passage for enslaved West Africans could hardly be more striking. It might seem self-evident that the association of European Christians with the burgeoning slave trade would present a formidable obstacle to the conversion of Africans. Yet paradoxically, it was precisely through enslavement that masses of them were baptized and thus "became" Christians in a minimal sense. True, as Linda Heywood and John Thornton have demonstrated, many of the Kongolese and Angolan slaves in the seventeenth century had become Christians prior to the journey, and that the bulk of slaves in the early and middle decades of the seventeenth century came from these regions.[42] Yet for millions of others who came later, this "becoming Christian" must have been most superficial, consisting of sprinkling holy water over masses of captives prior to embarkation.[43] For the Catholic Church, slavery meant primarily a harvest of souls to be saved, and baptism remained compulsory in the Portuguese, Spanish, and French colonies. Article 2 of the French *Code Noir* of 1685 mandated that slaves were to be both baptized and instructed in the Catholic religion, although the latter was largely honored in the breach. Christianity thus served to support the slave system, as witnessed by the fact the clergy themselves owned 21 percent of the slaves on the Canary Islands in the sixteenth century, and the Jesuits were probably the largest group of slaveholders in Portuguese Angola in the mid-seventeenth.[44] True, beginning in the 1680s a few voices were raised within the Church against the abuses of the slave trade, but these failed to stop its ever-expanding scope; a greater concern was that slaves might eventually be sold to Protestants.[45]

Although such "converts" were generally acknowledged to be Christians in name only, it marked the beginning of a series of encounters and negotiations between Africans and Christianity that eventually spread back to Africa. Aside from the Kongo and Angola, the story of these encounters begins in the diaspora.

The most common interpretation of this process is that it led to a family of syncretic religions, which combined elements of both indigenous religion and Catholicism in varying degrees and forms, the best known being Vodun in St. Domingue/Haiti, Santería in Cuba, and Candomblé in Brazil.[46] Because the church prohibited African "superstitious" practices, they were first carried on in secret, under the guise of worshipping the Catholic saints. This was abetted by a structural homology between the beliefs of Catholicism and many African religions, namely the acknowledgment of a supreme god (*Bondye* in Vodun, *Olodumare* or *Olofi* in Santería, *Olorun* in Candombé), although this figure was distant and unapproachable in the African cases, together with a panoply of more accessible mediator or intercessor spirits (*Lwas* in Vodun, *Orishas* in Santería, *Orixas* in Candomblé).

Naturally the term "syncretism" has been no less problematic here than in other parts of the world, not only for scholars but also for practitioners of these religions, for whom it became a loaded term. In the twentieth century, after slavery was abolished and religious restrictions lifted, there arose, beginning in the 1930s, an effort to preserve the native religions in "pure" form, which meant stressing their African-ness as the seat of their fundamental values and shedding any Catholic accretions. In this context, "syncretism" became a pejorative term, indicative of colonial religious oppression which had now outlived its usefulness. The most famous spokesperson for this view in the later twentieth century was the Candomblé priestess Mae Stella, but examples can be found in Santería as well.[47]

Neither the view of Afro-Catholic syncretism nor the search for pure African-ness can, however, do justice to the complexity of this cross-cultural interaction. The phenomenon of religious combination must rather be viewed as part of the larger process of African adaptation to the New World, in which Catholicism was only one element among many, and one that has probably received undue attention.[48] James H. Sweet's extensive study based on Brazilian and Portuguese archives (including its Inquisition) reveals the persistence of such African practices as divination, healing, and cursing ("witchcraft") into the eighteenth century.[49] The process might fruitfully be compared to Darwinian natural selection: faced with the traumas and brutalities of slavery, Africans sought and found niches in which their societies could survive and eventually flourish by shedding those behaviors that no longer served the purpose and retaining those that did. The specific traits that survived in this process were determined by the vicissitudes of the environments in which the slaves found themselves. As the environments themselves changed, so did the selection, creating a process of evolution which continues to this day. Spiritual factors had a privileged role to play in the process because of their transportability. As Roger Bastide eloquently put it:

As his lineages, clans, village communities, or kingdoms were destroyed, the African clung more and more tenaciously to what remained to him of his native country, to the one treasure he had been able to bring with him—his myths and his gods. They lived on in his mind as mnemonic images subject to the vagaries of memory, but they were also inscribed in his body in the form of motor responses, dance steps or ritual movements, instantly aroused by the dull throbbing of drums.[50]

Among the many factors that shaped the development of the new religions, one might mention the work environment. Many if not most slaves in Brazil and the Caribbean worked on large plantations in which the black slaves far outnumbered the white masters; these were relatively conducive to the formation of slave societies, especially when compared to work in the mines. Slaves after all arrived in America equipped with organizational and adaptational skills: Africa had states, armies, and slavery, so the experience of being uprooted was not entirely novel. Slavery was also found in the cities, where Africans had greater freedom of movement which enabled them to form associations, including religious ones, which also had not been lacking in Africa. Cities also contained free people of color: in mid-nineteenth-century Cuba, they comprised one-third of the black population.[51]

In these work environments, a goodly amount of spiritual selection occurred in the New World among the different African religions, quite independently of Christianity. Certain spirits disappeared from the pantheons, while others were redefined. For example, slaves on the Brazilian plantations felt no obligation to feed the spirits of agricultural fertility, since this would only benefit the masters. Probably the most sweeping change was the reduction in the number of spirits, from as many as 601 *Orishas* in Africa to a few dozen in Cuba and Brazil.[52] Whereas each spirit would have its own priest and temple in Africa, in the New World they were combined into single dwellings under one priest.

This said, the role of the Catholic Church in furthering the religious combination was far from negligible, even though its obligation to instruct the slaves via catechism was, as we have said, rarely carried through. Certainly the clergy were at one with the slaveholders in reinforcing the social order and discouraging rebellion. This involved not only preaching acceptance of the slaves' station in life, but also in providing them with some organizational outlets for sociability. These were the religious brotherhoods and sisterhoods, which the church viewed as organs for the propagation of Christianity among the Africans. Thus the Portuguese organized the Brotherhood or Our Lady of the Rosary of the Blacks, with branches on both sides of the Atlantic, in Brazil, the Kongo, and Angola. They were organized by "nation," even allowing one of them to elect a king and a queen, including a coronation festival. All of this meant that the church acted as an agent of selection, deciding which native practices could be interpreted as compatible with Christianity and which were to be condemned as inspired by the Devil.[53] In this way the brotherhoods became, willy-nilly, incubators of the Afro-Latin religions: the first Candomblé houses in the early nineteenth century were formed by members of these Catholic brotherhoods and sisterhoods.[54] A parallel development took place in Cuba, where the church sponsored clubs called *cabildos*, which served the functions of sociability, mutual aid, and burial society. The *cabildos* marched, drummed, and danced in the Catholic festivals of Epiphany, Carnival, Holy Week, and Corpus Christi.[55] Again, Santería grew directly out of these organizations.

In St. Domingue/Haiti, the situation was somewhat different. Here, the church took a more uncompromisingly hostile attitude toward African practices, which evolved into Vodun largely outside of church-sponsored institutions (though not to the exclusion of Catholic imagery and ritual). The slaveowners feared – rightly, it turned out – that these practices would encourage rebellion, as happened in 1791. During the Haitian Revolution, the church was almost entirely absent, and the new government did not succeed in reestablishing relations with Rome until 1860, by which time Vodun had become more firmly established. Institutional relations continued to be tense into the twentieth century, with the church conducting anti-superstition campaigns resulting in persecutions and massacres. The fact that Afro-Catholic religion has survived this relationship at all is remarkable.[56]

We may now ask: How did this relationship with Catholicism look from the Africans' point of view? What strategies did they employ in interacting with it? At first glance it might seem that, like the Lakota Sioux, the slaves practiced dual participation, going to mass, taking the sacrament, while continuing their dances and sacrifices in secret. Yet several examples strongly suggest that something quite different was taking place. One is the runaway slave kingdom of Palmares, in the interior of northern Brazil and consisting of some eleven thousand escaped slaves at its height. The kingdom's longevity, its successful defenses, sophisticated economy, and effective government and police system all attest to the slaves' organizational talents brought from Africa. The kingdom also contained churches, statues of Jesus, the Virgin and the saints, and people praying. If Christianity were a mere pretext, there was no evidence of it there.[57] A second comes from colonial St. Domingue, where, despite the hostility of the church, Vodun ceremonies incorporated Catholic rituals such as taking the communion wafer or sprinkling holy water. According to a scandalized Catholic witness: "In regard to...the little bit of water that is consecrated during the Sunday Mass, it is rare that one finds one drop of it when the ceremony has ended; they carry it in little calabashes and drink some drops when they rise . .and pretend that it will guarantee their welfare against all the witchcraft that might befall them."[58]

Clearly in these cases, Catholicism was seen as efficacious in providing access to a reservoir of spiritual power.

Pressed to explain the relationship more precisely, scholars have turned to linguistic analogies, seeing a form of *vernacular translation* as the fundamental strategy. Thus Roger Bastide, in conducting his fieldwork in Brazil, determined that his native subjects believe that "the saint is the *orixa* under a Portuguese name."[59] Following this suggestion, Joseph Murphy in his study of Santería, proposes that "the way of the *orishas* and the way of Catholicism are two different languages and that the *santero* is competent in both."[60] Paul Christopher Johnson takes the idea further: "The *orixas*...are also a grammar, a cognitive program, and a map of relations by which practitioners are both embedded in an ordered world and enabled and emboldened to change that order for their and their community's benefit."[61] The saints become part of that program; translation is possible because they shared in a system of correspondences in which individual saints are matched with individual *orishas* by virtue of their specific powers.

This system is best understood not as a comprehensive cosmology or theology, but as a language, developed through practice rather than mere belief. Thus the pairings could vary widely from Cuba to Brazil, or within different regions of Brazil. For example, one of the best-known *Orishas*, both in Africa and the New World, is Shango, who once lived as a powerful king in the Yoruba city of Oyo, and became the *Orisha* of fire and lightning. Like other *Orishas*, Shango appears dressed in specific colors (red and white), is fed with specific foods, and invoked with specific drum patterns and dance steps. In Cuba, his Catholic counterpart is the martyr Santa Barbara, so chosen because her pagan father was miraculously struck dead by lightning after having tried to behead her for remaining a Christian. Shango is celebrated on Santa Barbara's feast day of December 4 (as with most *orishas*, the Catholic calendar determined the schedule).[62] Yet in Brazil, Santa Barbara is identified with Shango's wife Yansan, who was able to acquire his magic of spitting lightning. Shango is paired with different saints depending on the region, among them St. Jerome, St. Peter, and St. Michael the Archangel.[63] In Vodun, St. Peter is identified with Legba, the gatekeeper, while in Santería, he is paired with Ogun, the *Orisha* of iron.

While the contents thus vary, there appears to be a common underlying principle, that of comprehensive connectedness, a form of African cosmopolitanism: the more spirits that can be brought into the system, the more efficacious it will be. In Trinidad, *Orisha* devotion encompasses Hindu and Jewish traditions, reflecting the island's ethnic composition; in Brazil, there are variants of Candomblé that incorporate Amerindian traditions; and throughout region there has been a growing appeal of non-Christian spirit mediums, some claiming to be "scientific." The most influential figure in this "spiritism" was the Frenchman Allan Kardec, who quite self-consciously sought to include multiple ethnic traditions in his pantheon, which the Brazilians keyed into *Orixa* spirits.[64]

While the language of correspondence might suggest that saints and *Orishas* are identical, practices clearly indicate that they are thought of as juxtaposed rather than fused. Symbiosis rather than synthesis is the preferred way of characterizing the relationship. In both Santería and Candomblé, the altars to the two are kept separate, and the integrity of Catholic worship services is observed. Part of the initiation process for a Candomblé priestess is attending mass and taking the sacrament. In Vodun, perhaps to compensate for the rocky relations with Catholicism in the past, there is a figure known as *prêt savann* (bush priest) present at important rituals to recite Catholic prayers and chant hymns (and sprinkle holy water), though his role is more symbolic than efficacious.[65]

Overall, however, it appears that African traditions predominated, indicating a pattern of *selective incorporation* of Catholic features into indigenous religion.[66] This can be seen in several features that are acknowledged as common to African religions which are found in the New World but not to the same degree in European Catholicism. Perhaps the most conspicuous is possession and trance, which initiates regularly aspire to and achieve. This is not, as sometimes conceived, a hysterical or uncontrolled state, but one that is carefully regulated as part of a larger ritual in which dance plays a central role. One talks of the *Orisha* "mounting" the initiates, and this can involve a great deal of switching and variation of gender roles.[67] A second difference is the centrality of offerings and sacrifices that sustain the *Orishas*, going well beyond the Catholic notion of praying to the saints. Finally, African religions have a variety of techniques for dealing with everyday life and problems that are not found in nearly the same degree in Catholicism. These include divination, of which the Yoruba *Ifa* technique is the best known but by no means the only one; the casting of spells, often in conjunction with herbal medicine; and the use of charms and amulets.[68] Perhaps underlying all these is the notion that even the highest god, Olodumare, is subordinate to a fundamental force or energy (*Axe*) which permeates the universe – a sign of diffuse spirituality.

THE AFRICAN DIASPORA AND PROTESTANTISM

In contrast to Native Americans, Protestantism affected the African slaves in the United States in a profoundly different manner than did Catholicism. The main reason is that Protestantism, unlike Catholicism, did not provide a system of intermediary spirits between human beings and the high God which could be brought into alignment with the Africans' own. Instead there developed a personal relationship between the slave and the high God and the intermediary of his only son (or the Holy Spirit). In her study of the evolution of an Afro-Baptist faith, Mechal Sobel states that, "in the new view, Jesus becomes *the* intermediary, *the* messenger, *the* doctor, and *the* spirit with whom blacks had contact."[69] In his broader study of slave religion in the antebellum South, Albert J. Raboteau formulates it as follows, "The African gods with their myriad characteristics, personalities, and myths do not 'mount' their enthusiasts amid the dances, songs, and drum rhythms of worship in the United States. Instead it is the Holy Spirit who fills the converted sinner with a happiness and power that drives him to shout, sing, and sometimes dance."[70] In other words, diffuse spirituality gave way to concentrated spirituality, and in turn the authority of the diviner and conjurer made room for that of the preacher.

This is not to deny that important elements of African spirituality and memory survived, such as dance rhythms, song styles, and the congregational response known as "shouting," all of which persist to this day. A powerful strand of continuity with several African regional rituals, serving to bring them together, was the circular dance known as the ring shout, which was incorporated into Christian services, and hence could be seen as evidence of Africanization of Christianity itself.[71] In addition, many of the practical aspects, such as casting of spells, herbal medicine, and divination, continued to be practiced at least through the antebellum period.[72] These drew from Native American herbal knowledge as well (one particular herb, the source of good luck, was known as "Cherokee").[73] Nevertheless, while the degree of African cultural continuity in North America has been the subject of much discussion and research, it seems clear that accommodation to the Protestant version of Christianity involved greater change on the Africans' part than what took place in the Caribbean or Latin America. Clearly, also, this change did not occur overnight. It is the merit of Sobel's study to have delineated the stages by which it occurred, from the predominance of an "African sacred cosmos" in the early years to a transitional period of confusion and contradiction, eventually regaining coherence in the form of Baptist Christianity.[74] The latter generally occurred in the first quarter of the nineteenth century. Still, the proportion of genuine converts on the eve of the Civil War, although difficult to determine, probably constituted less than half the black population; an estimate for Virginia puts it at 22 percent.[75]

In North America, this change was facilitated by the fact that the black population was much less heavily concentrated in large plantations. Although this varied by region, in 1860, 47 percent of bondsmen lived on holdings with fewer than twenty slaves, and the white slave owners of these holdings represented 88 percent of slave owners overall. Another contrast between the Protestant and Catholic colonies was the lack of an official requirement for conversion and instruction in the former. Although many slave owners were indifferent or even hostile to providing this in both cases, the lack of a requirement gave greater scope and incentive for missionaries to enter the scene voluntarily, so that missionaries in fact played a greater role in the Protestant regions. This is not to say that all missionaries who desired to convert the Africans were equally well suited to the task. The disconnect between the formality of Anglicanism and African spirituality was especially pronounced – not to mention the fact that blacks were expected to sit in the back of the church, in deference to English ideas of social hierarchy.[76]

It was quite otherwise with the Great Awakenings, those periods of intense revival that preceded and followed the American Revolution. The emotionalism of the preaching and of the congregations' involvement obviously resonated with African experience, and some have suggested that whites actually welcomed blacks to the meetings as more adept at emotional expression than they.[77] To quote Raboteau, "The Anglican usually taught the slaves the Ten Commandments, the Apostles' Creed and the Lord's Prayer; the revivalist preacher helped them feel the weight of sin, to imagine the threats of Hell, and to accept Christ as their only savior."[78] Moreover, the Methodists' practice of circuit riding, visiting countless small rural communities, pioneered by John Wesley himself, made the revivals a shared biracial experience, in which women were also included as equals.[79]

Not only the tone, but also the content of the Methodist message appealed to Africans: the equality of souls in God's eyes and their equal capacity to be saved. This was epitomized in one of Wesley's first conversations with a slave woman in South Carolina as he was working out his version of Protestantism. He promised her that in the Christian heaven she would "want nothing, and have whatever you can desire. No one will beat or hurt you there. You will never be sick. You will never be sorry anymore, nor afraid of anything."[80] The ability of the Christian story to address the fact of suffering as a central theme formed a powerful bond of identification with the slave experience. The belief in God's justice both eliminated the need for intermediaries and enhanced one's sense of worth as an individual. This translated, among other things, into blacks assuming a leadership role in their congregations and becoming eloquent preachers themselves, sometimes ministering to whites.[81] Such examples of interracial harmony were found in the early revivals, but generally did not last, and most churches built after 1800 had separate galleries and entrances for blacks.[82]

It was not long before Baptists began vying with Methodists for the allegiance of African-Americans and soon overtook them. Both stressed the centrality of the conversion experience and the passage from the dark feelings of sinfulness to the joy of being saved, but the Baptists combined this with a ritual, that of immersion. The passage from a state of near-death to rebirth would have been familiar to many Africans through initiation rituals. Also, baptism itself may have been known to some slaves from their Congolese background, as the Capuchins had been baptizing thousands in Africa. But there was much that was new – in the Congo, baptism was by salt rather than water and it signified protection against harm. But immersion in water signified a more profound experience of rebirth, and also something that Africans from different regions could share together.[83] Another advantage the Baptists had over the Methodists was autonomy of individual churches, which often arose spontaneously. Black Baptists were able to successfully maintain their independence from white control in a number of cases; it is clear that slaves devoted a major portion of their meager resources to building and maintaining their churches.[84]

Over time, African-American Protestants fashioned their own *vernacular translation* of the meaning of Christianity. If the Catholic version had been based on notions of spatial correspondence, the Protestant version was based on a narrative extending over time, drawing on Biblical stories from the Old Testament and the New Testament passed along orally and in song. Needless to say, the travails of the Israelites and their Exodus from slavery in Egypt to the promised land of Canaan played a central role, as did the Second Coming. Several commentators stress the importance of the image of a journey as part of this understanding.[85] The promised land, the fabled Canaan, came to mean freedom, manifest in a variety of hopes at different times – whether in the bliss of heaven, or escape to the free states of the North, or an end to slavery, or later to racial discrimination, or for some, when these promises failed, in a return to Africa, a gleaming symbol of hope.

It should not be surprising that the enhanced self-worth among African-Americans should eventually find expression in slave revolts. Denmark Vesey's 1822 revolt was inspired by the Bible, and Nat Turner, leader of the bloodiest US uprising in 1831, was a lay Baptist preacher. Turner's rebellion in particular marked a turning point in black-white relations: slave owners now turned to an aggressive program to instruct the slaves in a Christianity that stressed order and obedience. As this took hold in the following decades, the black churches stiffened their *resistance* by going underground with secret prayer meetings. Their belief in the millennial ending of the Christian narrative convinced them that slaveowners were destined for hell. They derided the hypocrisy of such injunctions as "Thou shalt not steal" when, as they said, their ancestors themselves were stolen from Africa.[86]

At the same time, the Biblical narrative, together with the ideas of God's justice and love, equally bestowed, could form a powerful engine of *selective acculturation* to white society. After all, the Exodus story is what the Puritans told themselves when they settled in New England, and their high expectations eventually broadened into the notion of American exceptionalism. Moreover, these ideas formed a confluence with those of the Enlightenment, particularly the belief in natural equality, all strong enough to launch antislavery movements in England and the United States by the end of the eighteenth century. Free blacks in New England were able to avail themselves of these currents, and they actively fought in the American Revolution. By the turn of the century, slavery had ended in half of the country.[87] This acculturative trend continued to take hold in urban areas where strong black churches existed. At the same time, this also meant distancing oneself from the African dances and rituals which persisted in rural areas.[88]

This confluence of African-American Christianity and Enlightenment ideas was especially effective in toppling the slave-owning class in

Jamaica, where the emancipation of slaves in 1833 was preceded by the so-called Baptist War in 1831. As in St. Domingue, the huge numbers of slaves meant that the rule of the planters was exceptionally oppressive, and also that African religions continued to thrive. The countervailing antislavery movement was fueled by the combined efforts of blacks and whites from both England and the United States. Wesley's encounters with slaves in South Carolina provided the foundation for his principled support of abolition on return to England. Among the black Baptist preachers who went to Jamaica, the most prominent was George Liele, an ex-slave who had already founded a church in Savannah and moved to Jamaica in 1784, where he established a congregation in Kingston that grew to eight hundred members. Liele was also instrumental in enlisting the active involvement of British Baptists.[89]

Liele was careful to admit to his congregation only slaves who had permission of their masters, thus illustrating the dilemma of the early missionaries, who tended to focus more on personal conversion than on institutional change. For their part, the slave owners thought that a tightly regulated missionary movement could be a stabilizing force, discouraging rebellion, the possibility of which was always present. What eventually undermined this equilibrium in the 1820s was the pressure from the Baptist and Methodist churches in England, who had embraced the abolitionist cause. They proved very effective at pointing to physical abuses on the part of slaveowners such as flogging, thereby rendering the missionaries' support of the owners increasingly untenable. The decisive moves came from the slaves themselves, the Christian converts who planned and instigated the 1831 revolt. The quashing of the revolt only led to greater brutality and thus indignation in British public opinion. In the end, the moderates and slave owners were caught in a pincer movement between black insurgency on one hand and pro-abolitionist forces in England on the other. Missionaries themselves came to see the incompatibility of their message with the slave system in practice. When emancipation arrived in 1834, thousands flocked to the churches and a British Baptist received a hero's welcome.[90]

This euphoria was soon to prove ephemeral. The cultural differences between British and African Christians soon came to the fore as economic problems plagued the island. Yet the autonomous black Baptist churches continued to thrive, incorporating African beliefs and practices and differentiating themselves from the European missions.[91] Their ongoing vitality meant that Jamaica would serve as a prominent source of Christian renewal efforts in the twentieth century, most notably Marcus

Garvey's Universal Negro Improvement Association with its aim of uniting Africans throughout the diaspora.

IN SLAVERY'S WAKE: SIERRA LEONE AND LIBERIA

The twin movements of abolition and back-to-Africa were joint products of the Christian-Enlightenment synthesis. A growing number of literate, acculturated ex-slaves on both sides of the Atlantic imbibed these ideals in the late eighteenth century and, working with white businessmen, philanthropists, and humanitarians, gave birth to them. Olaudah Equiano's autobiography (1789) is probably the best-known product of this process; William Wilberforce, the great advocate of abolishing the slave trade and then slavery itself, was likewise associated with the back-to-Africa scheme. During the American Revolution, thousands of African Americans faced the prospect of freedom; some fought with the colonists, believing in the promises of the Declaration of Independence, while others, faced with the British promise of emancipation if they joined the loyalists, did so. Following their defeat at Yorktown, the British decided to resettle many of these loyalists in Nova Scotia, while others wound up on the streets of London. Conditions in both places were adverse: aside from the unfriendly climate, the new arrivals in Nova Scotia were not given the plots of land they had been promised. At the same time, the Great Awakening was sweeping through Nova Scotia, and the new settlers were highly receptive to proselytization. So it was that one of them, Thomas Peters, traveled to London to present their grievances in 1791, where he became an instant celebrity. A Yoruba by birth, Peters had been sold to a French slave ship in 1760, sold twice more in America, fled his third master in 1776, fought with the British, and resettled in Nova Scotia. Meanwhile, a group of London businessmen and philanthropists had founded the Sierra Leone Company to settle the London poor in West Africa, but the initial scheme had failed. Peters eagerly agreed to send the Nova Scotians there, and some 1,200 arrived in 1792, battered from the voyage, but still hopeful. The parallel with the Hebrews did not escape them.[92]

In the course of their struggles, these ex-slaves had developed a truly free society which made them no less feisty and rebellious than the American colonists they had fought against. It was they, not the British, who planned and founded the settlement of Freetown. They demanded the Company establish a rule of law, including trial by jury, and took up arms against it for failure to live up to its promises and for unfair taxation.[93] Women played a prominent role, both as preachers and church leaders and as property owners and entrepreneurs.[94] Devoutness and a strong work ethic were widespread: one English observer claimed she heard someone preaching somewhere whenever she awoke at night.[95] Their industry is shown by the fact that when their agricultural schemes failed, they turned to trade, making Freetown a major port on the West African coast.

The circumstances surrounding the founding of the American Colonization Society in 1816 and subsequently the Republic of Liberia were rather different. By then the immediate hopes for the abolition of slavery from the Revolutionary era had faded, and the sectional tensions arising from slavery were increasingly difficult to ignore. In these circumstances, the idea of back-to-Africa could serve as a safety valve, even a panacea, attracting a strange collection of bedfellows. For some it seemed to be a more hopeful alternative to abolition; for others, it expressed a disbelief that the two races could ever live in harmony; for still others, it served as a means to propagate the Gospel. The initial impetus came in part from the efforts of Paul Cuffe, a free mixed African-American and Native American New England entrepreneur, and in part from a group of whites who viewed free blacks with suspicion, potential instigators of insurrection, but who, it was thought, could exercise unfettered liberty in the lands of their ancestors. This understandably aroused the suspicion of many free blacks themselves. Nonetheless, given the traumas that African-Americans endured in the course of the nineteenth century, some sixteen thousand eventually migrated there.[96] Once again, Biblical analogies dominated the rhetoric of both whites and blacks in the back-to-Africa movement, and were taken a step further – slavery itself was now seen as part of God's providential design, to bring the slaves into contact with the greatness of Western civilization, which they could now pass on to their benighted African cousins. The African American Episcopalian missionary Alexander Crummell, a freeman born in New York City, who studied in Cambridge, served in Monrovia from 1853 to 1873, expressed this view with eloquence:

Among other providential events the fact, that the exile of our fathers from their African homes to America, had given us, their children, at least this one item of compensation, namely, the possession of the Anglo-Saxon tongue... the Almighty has bestowed upon us, in having as our own, the speech of Chaucer and Shakespeare, of Milton and Wordsworth, of Bacon and Burke, of Franklin and Webster.....[By contrast], within this wide extent of territory are grouped a multitude of tribes and natives with various tongues and dialects...[and] there are . .definite marks of inferiority connected with them all, which place them at the widest distance from civilized languages.[97]

In reality, such sentiments were undercut by two major adversaries: the malaria-bearing mosquito, which inflicted a mortality rate of 15–25 percent in the major towns, and the opposition of the indigenous leaders, who rightly viewed the settlers as colonialists.[98] Crummell was no more successful than others in persuading the indigenous inhabitants of Liberia of the superiority of Christianity – according to an 1843 census, only 353 had converted – and the antipathy between the Americo-Liberians and indigenes only increased over time.[99] When the Grebo, a nation that has been receptive to Episcopal missionaries, revolted in 1876, the missionaries sided with them against the government, and henceforth the Americo-Liberians actually prohibited further missionary work in the interior, although citizenship was open to those who were willing to renounce native culture.[100] Meanwhile, mainline Christianity became more and more closely identified with the ruling elite, culminating in an informal interlocking directorate of political leaders and church officials – to the exclusion of independent or "syncretistic" Christian movements – which lasted until a coup in 1980.[101]

The development of Sierra Leone took a very different turn, despite the fact that the attitudes of the settler elite toward the indigenous peoples were scarcely more generous than those of the Americo-Liberians (the stories of both groups slavishly imitating European dress are legion). The difference is marked by two factors. First, the location of Freetown gave it a peculiar advantage of being both a port and an entrepot, accessible both by sea and by inland trade routes which extended northeast to the Niger River; it thus stood at an intersection, as it were, of two great trading basins, the Atlantic and the Trans-Saharan. Before long, it was receiving merchants and migrants from the interior as well as by sea, making it a melting pot – a German linguist found over a hundred different languages spoken there in 1851.[102] This meant, among other things, a steady increase in Muslims in the town. At first, relations between the Christian and Muslim communities were tense, and the British actually destroyed a mosque in 1840. But the folly of alienating these valuable contributors to the economy became evident soon thereafter, and relations became quite friendly in subsequent decades, with Christians and Muslims attending each other's weddings and funerals; missionaries sometimes employed Muslim translators in their proselytizing efforts.[103] These were symptoms of the fact that a new and distinctive society, known as *Krio*, defined neither by ethnicity nor by religion, had emerged in Freetown in the course of the nineteenth century.[104] Often caricatured as "black Englishmen," they were capable of displaying the same cultural arrogance vis-à-vis the peoples of the interior as we observed in Liberia. But on close inspection they represented a genuine fusion of multiple traditions, not least African ones.[105]

The second distinguishing factor was the steady influx of liberated Africans, or recaptured ex-slaves following the British government's decision to outlaw the slave trade in 1807 and its making Sierra Leone a crown colony the following year. British vessels now patrolled the coast of West Africa, intercepting slave ships and transporting their cargo to Freetown, thus continuing to fulfill the aspirations of the original anti-slavery organizers. Because the Yoruba were the major victims of the slave trade in these years, they came to constitute the largest group of liberated Africans as well. All in all, some 60,000 slaves were so resettled by 1864 (compared to 5,700 in Liberia).[106] From the outset, the British were faced with the formidable responsibility of caring for these people, and a policy evolved after several years of trial and error. In 1816, a new governor, Charles MacCarthy, worked out an arrangement whereby missionaries from the Anglican Church Missionary Society (CMS) would serve both as religious and administrative leaders in an expanded network of Christian villages in the vicinity of Freetown. Each village would have a church, a school, and enough land to make it self-supporting. MacCarthy's vision was not only to instill Christianity, but also the virtues of "order, neatness, and tidiness," the hallmarks, in his view, of civilization.[107]

How well did this scheme work? The results were mixed. Where the missionaries had the right combination of personality traits, it was quite successful, winning the loyalty and appreciation of the ex-slaves. In other cases, they suffered from heavyhanded, harsh discipline.[108] More often than not, missionaries felt unsuited to take up both religious and political burdens, and the numbers soon proved overwhelming, so that many of the villagers were left to fend for themselves. In any case, the liberated Africans soon developed the same habits of resourcefulness and independence as the Nova Scotians had done. Religiously, their main strategy appears to have been *dual participation*, attending church as required but continuing the practice their ancestral rituals, with drumming and dancing lasting far into the night. The Muslims among them responded to attempts to snuff out their religion by taking up arms in 1826, eventually leading to the government's establishing a separate village for them.

Others were able to profit from the new educational opportunities, moving to Freetown and entering into *Krio* society.

Still others eventually returned to their homelands, carrying Christianity with them, the first generation of African missionaries. It should be noted, however, that the preponderance of native missionaries in West Africa during the early nineteenth century was due just as much to the high mortality rate of Europeans in the tropical disease environment before the widespread use of quinine in the 1850s. The CMS sent seventy-nine missionaries and their families to Sierra Leone between 1804 and 1826, of whom only fourteen remained in service. Most of the others had died.[109] The CMS realized it had no alternative but to train Africans to be missionaries, and accordingly established a seminary in Freetown, Fourah Bay College, in 1827. At least one hundred Anglican Africans, most from Sierra Leone, were ordained by 1899, many of whom had been trained at Fourah Bay.[110]

The man who exemplified and came to symbolize the extraordinary achievements – and vicissitudes – of these liberated, acculturated Africans was Samuel Ajayi Crowther. Ajayi was born in Yorubaland, probably in 1806. At the age of fifteen, his town was burned to the ground by Moslems invading from the north, a part of the Fulani jihad. He was captured and sold into slavery, undergoing four different masters in a year and in 1822 was put on board a Portuguese slave ship that was intercepted by the British just after it left port. He was taken to Sierra Leone, learned to read and write, and was baptized as an Anglican, with an English name, in 1825. He once wrote, "I have considered the Church my mother, which has taught me to pray, as it were upon the Prayer-Book, when I knew not how to utter a word."[111] Two years later, he became the first student enrolled at Fourah Bay College. He became a teacher, studied both Greek and local languages, and later published *A Vocabulary of the Yoruba Language* in 1843, the same year he became ordained. He went on to translate the New Testament into Yoruba. Crowther had learned to thrive in the pluralistic environment of Freetown, not shying away from trying to convert Muslims and *Orisha* worshippers (who likewise had found a place in *Krio* society), but avoiding confrontational techniques in doing so and thereby winning the admiration of his fellow Yoruba, regardless of their religious affiliation.[112] He had meanwhile also become a missionary, participating in an unsuccessful expedition up the Niger River in 1841. In 1845, he returned to Yorubaland, where he was reunited with his mother, whom he baptized three years later. His combination of scholarly, missionary, and diplomatic talents won him the ultimate recognition: he was given a Doctor of Divinity by Oxford and consecrated Bishop in Canterbury Cathedral in 1864. At the same time, he represented the trend of acculturation to the British Empire; an interview with Queen Victoria and Prince Albert in 1851 was decisive in persuading the British to intervene in the Yoruba civil wars.[113]

QUARANTINE, MIXING, AND REFORM IN WEST AFRICA

In 1839, a group of Yoruba Freetown merchants petitioned the governor of Sierra Leone to establish a colony at Badagri in Yoruba territory in what is today Nigeria. The expedition included missionaries, "so that the Gospel of Christ can be preached throughout our land."[114] The missionaries consisted of an Englishman, a German, and Crowther. The people of Badagri accepted, seeing it as an opportunity to open trade with the British, a motive that was replicated in several other coastal towns. Some of the rulers were willing to make substantial concessions to the missionaries, such as the ending of human sacrifice; but at least as many rejected the newcomers. In the western areas, the Sierra Leonians (or Saros, as they were called) were essentially returning home; but as they moved eastward they became foreigners, speaking a different language – a problem that only increased over time after Crowther's bishopric extended to the Niger River. And even at home, they often remained a distinct group and were often perceived as no different from whites.[115]

At the time, the Yoruba were experiencing a series of civil wars that were themselves conducive to enslavement, creating obstacles to the Saros' attempts at proselytization in some areas and opportunities in others. The result was a broad spectrum of responses, ranging from a massive expulsion of missionaries in 1867 in the town of Abeokuta to a thriving minority of acculturated neo-Englishmen in Lagos (a community that included Muslims), to a massive conversion of a proud group, the Ijebu, who had resisted the British until being thoroughly defeated by them in 1892.[116] Lagos also received a number of ex-slaves from Brazil, creating the first Catholic population in Yorubaland. They remained under lay leadership until the 1860s, when French missionaries arrived, shocked at the retention of "pagan" customs among them.[117] Lagos also served as an entry point for liberated Muslim ex-slaves, both from Sierra Leone and Brazil, introducing a more Western-oriented group into the Muslim communities. Islam in Africa was in a "mixing" stage, growing much faster than Christianity (even the mass conversion of the

Ijebu in 1892 netted more new Muslims than Christians).[118] By the end of the century, only about 1 percent of the Yoruba had become Christian.[119]

It would appear then that for most of the nineteenth century, Christianity in Yorubaland remained in a "quarantine" stage – despite the fact that the CMS missionaries, both African and European, were not shy about preaching in the streets or in engaging *Orisha* devotees or Muslim Imams. That they were able to do so in an atmosphere of relative cordiality was a tribute to Yoruba pluralism and tolerance.[120] Crowther's gifted translations were able to draw on the Muslim presence in his choice of terms (e.g., *Alufa*, the Muslim term for "cleric," used for Christian pastor or priest).[121] If Christianity remained nevertheless isolated, particularly in the early nineteenth century, it can be traced to the attitudes of the missionaries – their reluctance to baptize people without proper instruction and their tendency to condemn broad swaths of African religion as sinful. This bespoke a deep divide between the religious views of the Europeans from those of the Yoruba, views which the Muslims did not share and which the Saros were unable completely to bridge. The Europeans located true conversion and redemption from sin in an inward state of mind as distinct from a set of rituals and practices. This was particularly characteristic of German Pietism, which was strongly represented among the European missionaries, both in Yorubaland and elsewhere, and was quite alien to the Yoruba point of view. Missionaries looked in vain for the "change of heart" that went beyond the mere following of rules, and frequently expressed dissatisfaction and distrust of their new converts (as in colonial Mexico).[122]

The issue that, more than any other, brought this opposition to a head was polygamy, clearly marked as a sin by European Christians, and no less essential to family structure in much of Africa, including living arrangements in family compounds. Thus acceptance of Christianity often meant breaking relations with one's own family, and this, in turn, drove the missionaries to provide a space for them. In Yorubaland, this took the form of mission houses, which were designed to serve as havens for the souls who had been won over against overwhelming odds. They often included schools on the premises. These stopped short of being boarding arrangements, unlike the Catholic Christian villages, which were introduced as well. But they were part of a pattern that could be found in many parts of Africa – the villages surrounding Freetown were another example. For the Africans, they served as places of refuge in a chaotic world, much as in North America.[123]

In these circumstances, it is not surprising that the initial converts to Christianity were people on the margins of society, either of low status or displaced, such as ex-slaves or refugees, of which there were many in war-torn Yorubaland. The attraction of Christianity to outsiders is poignantly portrayed in Chinua Achebe's novel *Things Fall Apart*, set among the Igbo of southeastern Nigeria. Here the tender-minded boy Nwoye rebels against his harsh warrior father Okonknowo by joining the Christians; the missionary greets him with the words "Blessed is he who forsakes his father and his mother for my sake."[124]

Under these conditions it might be difficult to imagine a transition to a "mixing" stage, and Fisher maintains that none really took place. As evidence, one can point to a pattern that occurred among the second generation of converts, namely a reversion to previous ancestral practices (the missionaries' name for it was "backsliding.") The disruption of social life that the Christians demanded was often too much to bear, and *dual participation* was frequently the result, particularly where polygamy was concerned.[125]

If one takes a longer view, however, one can see several types of mixing taking place. Even by the middle of the century, missionaries were discovering that they could no longer afford the luxury of such an introverted view of conversion. They learned to adjust their message by shifting emphasis away from sin and salvation in favor of making claims that God had the power of affect practical changes, such as making rain and curing disease. They drew on the effects of industrial technology to demonstrate Christian civilization's superior power. The magic lantern, an early version of a slide projector, was a favorite missionary device, and one mission house had a generator to demonstrate that electricity was not caused by Shango, the *Orisha* of lightning.[126] Writing was construed as a manifestation of a greater power because it enabled people to transmit content across space and time without having to remember it. A common Yoruba name for Christians was *Onibuku*, the book-people.[127]

For many Africans, however, the decisive impetus to pursue "mixing" was the upheaval to their societies caused by European colonialism following the Great Scramble of the 1880s. Africans found themselves subject to new borders, administrative units, taxes, and employment opportunities. To quote Hastings, "If Nigerians, Ugandans, Zaireans, and Zambians exist[ed] as such at the end of the twentieth century, so that Yoruba and Igbo are united in being Nigerians while Fon or Akan never can be...it is due to the arbitrary decisions of colonialists at the end of the nineteenth century."[128] At the same time, there was an influx of missionaries, many of them women, numbering some ten thousand by 1910, backed, so it seemed, by the new imperialists. Africans sought to partake of the new power by adopting the religion of the powerful, regardless of whether missionaries were present or not. The Church Missionary Society, for example, counted 51,750 baptized in Nigeria in 1914.[129] The number of native Catholic catechists among the Igbo jumped from 33 in 1906 to 552 in 1918, while the number of non-native clergy stayed almost the same. The number of Catholics went from 1,488 to 13,042 in the same period.[130]

Within this framework, one can distinguish two types of mixing that were taking place. The first was *selective acculturation*: to survive in this new world, or at least to take advantage of the new jobs in the cities, required literacy and some Western education, and missionaries who provided it were suddenly indispensable. "Teachers, teachers, teachers, are what the natives are demanding," wrote a bishop in Rhodesia. In parts of Africa, the word for "reading" was the same as the word for "Christian."[131] There was a "race for schools" as various missionary groups competed with each other in a given district, heightening denominational rivalries, especially between Protestants and Catholics.[132] Catholics were less attached to vernacularization and more willing to teach in English, which significantly heightened their appeal. The mission schools in fact served as generators of *acculturation*, preaching the superiority of Western civilization, though the selective character of that acculturation is attested by the persistence of customs such as polygamy. The schools also served as generators of a new political elite; most of the leaders of the independence movement were products of them.

The second type was in many ways the inverse of the first: a movement toward African cultural nationalism and *resistance* to the intrusions of the foreigners, especially as the latter became more overtly racist. The movement had a significant cultural impact, yielding a new interest in ancestral religion, mythology, and history.

"Why should there not be an African Christianity as there has been a European and an Asiatic Christianity?" asked James Johnson, a fiercely independent Anglican Saro clergyman serving in Lagos, in 1905.[133] This movement occurred within the previously acculturated elite and was certainly brewing prior to the Great Scramble. Indeed, it is hard to imagine that at least some members of a group with a history of anti-slavery and equal justice would have reacted otherwise to the increasing high-handedness of European missionaries and officials.

Much, though not all of this movement came to be subsumed under the label of "Ethiopianism." Here was ready-at-hand a symbol, at once religious, cultural, and political, that linked the earlier back-to-Africa movement with this later *resistance*. It was rooted in a passage from the Old Testament (Psalm 68:31) that prophesied a role for Africa in the Judeo-Christian narrative, "Princes shall come out of Egypt; Ethiopia shall soon stretch her hands unto God." This was interpreted as reinforcing the slavery-as-redemption story that had fueled the hopes of the returnees. Moreover, the fact that Ethiopia had survived as an independent Christian kingdom, strong enough to defeat the Italian invaders in 1896, added strength to the symbol. "Ethiopianism" came to mean a variety of things in West, East, and South Africa during this time, not to mention identification with the work of Marcus Garvey and the Rastafarians.[134]

The growing racist stereotypes that accompanied European colonialism in the 1880s and '90s only heightened this resistance, as acculturated Africans found themselves no longer taken seriously. Once again, Bishop Crowther, now advanced in years, served as both exemplar and symbol of this shift in attitudes. Given the growing administrative problems in his diocese, an investigation was launched by the CMS in London, conducted by young missionaries who had no appreciation of the achievements of the Saros. As one of them put it, "the pastors. . .must be changed, the message preached must be changed, the time, mode, and place of worship must be changed, the school children must be changed and the course in the school must be changed."[135] Crowther, humiliated, resigned his office in 1890.

The affair triggered a wave of anger throughout the acculturated community and led to the formation of a series of independent churches free from missionary control – no less than fourteen in Nigeria by 1917. This was a dynamic situation, with multiple schisms and reunifications over time.[136] One has the impression that each was groping, rather self-consciously, to find a proper degree and kind of mixing – e.g., whether and how far to incorporate African music, whether polygamy should be permitted for clergy or only for members, and so on. A number of leaders shed their European names and adopted African ones – or hybrids. There was much ambivalence – Johnson refused to baptize children with English names but also refused to change his own. Many congregations wanted to be free of foreign leadership but did not want to give up their Anglican or Methodist liturgy. One might summarize this as a strategy of *assimilation of form* – the form being European.[137]

This kind of mixing, with all its ambiguities and contradictions, had as its representative figure Edward Wilmot Blyden (1832–1912), a great writer and teacher who gained wide recognition for his book *Christianity, Islam and the Negro Race*, which appeared in 1887. Blyden, although an ordained Presbyterian minister, provocatively maintained that the cultural influence of Islam in Africa was beneficial when compared to that of Christianity. Born in the Virgin Islands in 1832, educated in the United States during slavery and denied admission to seminary because of his race, he became an advocate of the back-to-Africa movement and dedicated much of his life to the Liberian cause. He became no less disillusioned, however, by the abuses of the Americo-Liberian government, which he attributed primarily to the sense of superiority of the mixed-blood emigrants vis-à-vis the native population. He came to believe that the best solution to Liberia's political problems was for it to become part of the British Empire and was celebrated in London high society for his views.[138] Yet this existed in his mind alongside a vigorous cultural nationalism, promoting African pride and unity. His seemingly contradictory views exemplify the assimilation of European form in two respects: his beliefs in the historical law of progress and in the immutability of races (he vehemently opposed race mixing). Thus, he subscribed to the "civilizing mission," whether at the hands of African-Americans or colonialists, which would lead to the flowering of a pan-African nationalism based on the unity of the black race.[139]

If the African nationalism of the elite may be seen as an assimilation of European form, just the opposite was taking place among peoples all across Africa around the same time in a movement that fits the category of "reform" in Fisher's sense, namely not merely converting to Christianity but experiencing an intensified commitment to it. This also fits the notion of "revival," a common phenomenon throughout Christianity, but exceptional in its extent in Africa from about 1910 to 1940. It deviates from Fisher's model in not being a consecutive "stage" but rather a distinct *aspect* of African Christian development. It manifested itself in a bewildering variety of new churches and splinter groups – a 1968 study tagged no less than 5,000 – under various labels, some depending on the region (e.g., African Independent Churches, African Initiated Churches, Aladura, Zionist, Pentecostal, prophetic healing churches). There have been notable attempts to categorize these, but Allan Anderson is probably right in emphasizing their futility, given the fluidity of the situation and the ease with which people could pass from one group to another.[140] More helpful is an approach via common strategies which underlie a great many of these movements. Two in particular stand out: (1) *concentration of spirituality*, in combination with (2) *conservation of African form*. Thus on the one hand the elements of religious practice were reduced, simplified and thereby energized, leading to a shedding of many aspects of ancestral religion, while on the other the basic outlook and purpose of the latter were preserved and strengthened. While these movements can be seen as a response to the upheavals brought about by colonialism, they may be also and no less validly seen as a product of a maturing of African Christianity, reflected in people's ability to read and understand the Bible – in their own terms, rather than those presented by the missionaries.

In West Africa, one can discern two phases of this reform: (1) the appearance of individual prophets who attracted huge followings beginning in the 1910s, and (2) the growth of the Aladura (from the Arabic word for "prayer") churches in the 1920s and '30s. The prophets, William Wade Harris of Liberia, who wandered the Ivory Coast and into the Gold Coast, and Garrick Patrick Braide of the Niger Delta, both came from Christian backgrounds and were well versed in the Bible, had visions that confirmed their divine callings. Both were known for their healing powers and miracles, staying well within the African tradition of invoking God's greater power. Harris performed mass baptisms, contrary to the missionary practice of requiring instruction in Christian doctrine before being baptized. Neither Harris nor Braide were opposed to missionary work, however; indeed, Harris told his followers to "wait for the men with the Bibles" who would give them further guidance on how to live a Christian life. The result of both movements was that conventional churches were swamped with thousands literally seeking entry into church buildings. As the movements spread, both Harris and Braide delegated their charismatic powers to assistants; at the same time, the movements became less orderly and controllable. This disturbed the authorities, who were jittery in any case because World War I was in progress. As a result, both prophets were arrested, in 1914 and 1916 respectively. Harris was sent back to Liberia, while Braide spent two years in prison. Both spawned independent churches which survived them, as well as drawing new converts to established ones.[141] A further parallel can be drawn to the case of Simon Kimbangu in the Belgian Congo, whose career followed a similar trajectory to Braide's, but with his prison sentence lasting thirty years, from 1921 to 1951. In 1996, the Kimbanguist Church was the largest independent church in Africa, with an estimated seven million members.[142]

The various churches that come under the label "Aladura" likewise originated in the visionary experiences of their founders.[143] Many of them started out as movements within the Anglican church in Yorubaland, but their participants soon became aware of the incompatability of their worship styles. Worship in the missionary-run churches seemed heartless and insincere, especially in the light of widespread dual participation. An early convert described his experience as follows:

Odubanjo [an Aladura] preached on God's power to heal, protect, and bless. All this was new to me—that God was still doing this today. I'd never heard this in the Methodist church, nor that God meets our financial needs also, and protects us from all dangers and perils. As Methodists we had relied on juju as our parents had done; we had gone to native doctors, and that meant bowing to idols.[144]

We might itemize the components of this strategic combination as follows:

1. **Visions, trances, and dreams** were not merely the property of founding prophets, but a part of shared congregational life (in one case, members actually slept in the church and were awakened to share their dreams and visions in the middle of the night).[145] The Aladuras found ample precedent for such altered states in the Bible, particularly the Old Testament. The 1938 constitution of the Church of the Lord Aladura states as follows: "We believe in dreams and visions because those of ancient days used to speak to God through visions and dreams. People like Abraham, Isaac, Moses, Jacob, Joseph, Solomon, etc . . . And we are directed by the Holy Spirit."[146] The Old Testament contained plenty of examples of polygamy as well, and many (though not all) of the prophetic movements allowed it.

One result of the reliance on visions as a mark of charismatic leadership was the tendency toward factionalism and fragmentation within each of the Aladura churches. Visions could be multiplied indefinitely, with no decisive means of testing their validity. Thus the Church of the Lord Aladura experienced no less than twenty-one secessions as of 1961, while another prominent church, the Cherubim and Seraphim, experienced fifty-one as of 2006, although many of these were temporary.[147]

2. **The destruction of "fetishes."** The landscape of these prophetic and praying movements was dotted with bonfires, with people throwing their old sacred objects and charms into the flames. Braide, Harris, and Kimbangu urged this sort of cleansing, as did the Aladuras. Hastings describes one such preacher, Joseph Babalola, in 1930, "Several times a day, armed with Bible and handbell, he called on the people to bring out all their idols and juju to be burnt. God alone was sufficient. Never in

Yorubaland was there such a mass movement and never such bonfires of the implements of traditional religion."[148] The effect was doubtless a liberating one, as the old system of propitiating multiple spirits as a way of warding off harm and evil was not proving to be effective in the transition to colonial rule.

3. Asceticism. Another expression of spiritual concentration, familiar to readers of Max Weber's *Protestant Ethic,* is asceticism, the distrust or deliberate denial of the sensual or the impure – as a means to channeling one's energy and focusing one's attention on spiritual matters. In several Aladura churches, this took the form of fasting, which is closely associated with effective prayer. The cofounder of one Aladura church, the Cherubim & Seraphim, Moses Orimolade, claimed that "prayer and fasting are the only ways through which man can reach God."[149] Members were expected to fast during the day on Wednesdays and Fridays plus the forty days of Lent.[150] In the Celestial Church of Christ, the prohibition of alcohol, tobacco, and pork is written into the constitution; some commentators suggest a Muslim influence here.[151] The Kimbanguist church added prohibitions against dancing and bathing and sleeping naked.[152]

Students of Weber might also expect to find a correlation between such attitudes and a strong work ethic and sense of social advancement, and in some cases this would be correct. J. D. Y. Peel's study of the Aladura in the '20s and '30s found that it attracted young men who had moved from the countryside into the city, often employed as clerks and hence well educated.[153] In some ways, however, this sense of discipline reinforced traditional ideas and roles, notably in the case of women. Menstruating women were thought to be unclean and were – and still are – excluded from worship, even though women were disproportionately attracted to Aladura churches. The role of women in leadership positions today varies from one church to another, but in most cases they are excluded from top positions. David Laitin's claim that "Christianity appears to be a woman's religion run by men" is apposite.[154]

4. Prayer as a means to healing. The centrality of prayer, indicated by the name "Aladura," nicely illustrates the synthesis of concentration and conservation that comprised the reformist strategy. According to Akinyele Omoyajowo, prayer is "the pivot on which hangs the entire faith of the Cherubim & Seraphim," with members expected to pray at least five times daily (the resemblance to Islam is more than coincidental).[155] For the Church of the Lord Aladura, the ideal regimen was every three hours, including 3 AM.[156] Prayer was a substitute for consulting diviners and making sacrifices to lesser gods; the belief was that "God answers all prayers."[157] Reliance on the efficacy of prayer as a way of curing illness goes back to the origins of the first Aladura churches, which occurred at the time of the terrible influenza pandemic of 1918. Neither the native techniques of ancestral religion nor those of Western medicine were of any use to stop it; faith healing thus offered a new strategy.

The use of prayer to combat illness may serve as an illustration of a broader struggle, namely against suffering and evil in general, sometimes known as *deliverance*. Here the belief in a multiplicity of spirits was not so easily eradicated. The early years of the Cherubim & Seraphim were marked by active witch hunts on the part of its members, to the alarm of the colonial authorities but with the approval of local chiefs.[158] A Celestial Church of Christ hymn goes, "Angels of the lord descend in all perfect holiness. All the wizards and the witches, all herbalists and all heathens, they surround us. Angels of the Lord descend in all our tribulations."[159] Yet the strategy of simplification and concentration was evident here as well: the figure of Satan came to serve as a collecting point for the replacing the varieties of malevolent forces – though not always with success.[160]

The prophetic and Aladura churches experienced a remarkable longevity, thriving in the postindependence period, despite the aforementioned tendencies of splintering and schism. They retained their dynamism, striking roots in Sierra Leone, Liberia, and Ghana in the 1940s and '50s, and since the 1960s establishing branches in Europe and North America, where they provide a "home away from home" to West Africans abroad.[161]

Nevertheless, we can observe a pattern with the Aladuras that we have seen earlier in the nineteenth century, namely an oscillation between concentration of spirituality and its hefty demands on the one hand, and a reversion to ancestral practices on the other. There were signs that the Aladuras were following this pattern in the second half of the twentieth century. An example would be a certain prophet Wobo, duly baptized in the Church of the Lord Aladura, who in 1960 established his own church. Wobo's ministry consisted largely of individual consultations in the form of predictions about their life events, much in the manner of *Ifa* divination. Wobo's clientele came not only from his church, but from the mission churches, who visited him in secret.[162]

EAST AFRICA: THE PERFECT STORM OF BUGANDA

East and Central Africa are today strongholds of Christianity. East Africa has gone from 49.4 percent Christian in 1970 to 65.9 percent in 2010.[163]

This increase has occurred largely in the second half of the twentieth century: in 1938, only 8 percent of Kenyans and 25 percent of Ugandans were Christian.[164] The contrast is even stronger in central Africa, where in 1910 only 1.1 percent of the population was Christian, compared to 73.9 percent in 1970.[165]

These were regions where Catholicism experienced much growth and vitality, relatively more than in West Africa. The initiative came from Rome in the years between the two world wars, as the popes concentrated on sending more missionaries beyond Europe. This was a theologically conservative movement that made no concessions to African culture, although the emphasis on sacraments and ritual undoubtedly served as *cultural hooks*. In a few cases, such as the Belgian Congo, conversion was accomplished by force. More often, however, the missionaries themselves were often sensitive to cultural and linguistic differences, thanks to the order of the White Fathers, founded in 1868, whose founder, Charles Lavigerie, emphasized accommodation to indigenous dress, language, and food. And more missionaries meant the training of more native catechists, who actually did most of the work. They were frequently teachers as well as religionists, and one spoke of the three Rs: Reading, Writing, and Religion. In the words of Adrian Hastings, "to their people, and even to themselves, they [the catechists] stood for and were linked with a world of religious and secular power, the world of the bishop, of a cathedral, even of the Pope."[166]

Space does not permit the exploration of the multiple cases of religious change in East and Central Africa, much less sample the rich scholarly literature that portrays it.[167] We will instead have to limit discussion to a single case, that of Uganda. Today there are more practicing Anglicans in Uganda than in England, though they are outnumbered by Ugandan Catholics.[168] This state of affairs owes its origin to a history in which most of the factors affecting cross-cultural religious interaction were at play in a span of two decades, and in a sequence optimally suited to lead to this result.

The Kingdom of Buganda, the nucleus of present-day Uganda, occupied a fertile and densely populated area on the north shore of Lake Victoria in East Africa. It was a highly centralized state, and it had developed a political system that made it exceptional: the king (*kabaka*) had developed over the years a network of chiefs appointed by him, independent of the hereditary clan structure that had originally structured Gandan society. At the same time, his new layer of leaders and the *kabaka* himself appeared to have loosened their ties to ancestral religion which

was associated with the clans. These appointed chiefdoms offered opportunity for men from any social level to come to the royal court and to
prove their worth, though tenure in these positions was extremely
unstable and subject to much maneuvering. Questions of succession to
the kingship were frequently resolved by force of arms. None of this,
however, completely dissolved the clans, which remained intact and could
exert a moderating influence on the extremes to which this system might
otherwise have led.[169]

Buganda had remained isolated until the mid-nineteenth century, but
Christianity was able to make an impression in the early stages of foreign
contact. True, Islam had been first to arrive, via Swahili traders who
exchanged Gandan slaves and ivory for guns; the *kabaka*, Mutesa I,
had shown a strong interest in Islam. But when faced with the threat of
an Egyptian invasion, his enthusiasm cooled. At this point (1875), he
received a visit from the famous (or infamous) journalist-explorer-pro-
moter Henry Morton Stanley, who persuaded him to accept Christian
missionaries in the kingdom. This appealed to Mutesa probably as a
check to Muslim influence, and two years later, the first CMS missionaries
arrived. They were followed in 1879 by Catholic White Fathers, their first
major thrust into sub-Saharan Africa. Mutesa insisted that these missionaries remain at court, a form of quarantine. But this had the opposite
impact from quarantine in West Africa, in that it reached the young,
ambitious opportunity seekers – the most rather than the least influential
people in society.[170] It seems that, at first, the presence of both Anglicans
and Catholics at court created an atmosphere of intellectual excitement
and debate that increased Christianity's appeal among these young men
(they apparently also had an aversion to circumcision, which markedly
decreased the appeal of Islam). Already by 1882 a collective conversion
movement was underway.[171]

The "mixing" stage of the Bugandan story, largely independent of
missionaries, began with the death of Mutesa in 1884, followed by a
decade of political instability which quickly degenerated into civil war.
Much of this was due to the weakness, paranoia and occasional tyranny
of the next *kabaka*, Mutesa's son Mwanga, who reigned for most of this
period. When the Christian pages at court resisted his homosexual over-
tures, he had thirty-one of them burned alive. This only created a sense of
persecution and martyrdom among the rest, many of whom found refuge
in their clans. Mwanga himself was deposed temporarily in 1888, and
there followed a four-way struggle between Muslims, Protestants,
Catholics, and followers of ancestral religion, including several

intermittent combinations of these forces. Thus the "mixing" took the form of these religions being absorbed into the Bugandan political culture of power struggles – though the combatants were no less sincere and fanatical in their convictions for all that. In this way the Buganda of the 1890s resembled the wars of religion sixteenth-century Europe. The Protestants soon gained the decisive political advantage thanks to the arrival of the British in the person of Captain Frederick Lugard, representing the British East African Company. Lugard had no scruples about training his machine gun on the Catholics and allowing them to be sold into slavery, but he eventually presided over the pacification of the kingdom, again with minority Protestants being awarded the most offices but with Catholics and Muslims given assured representation.[172] Lugard's pacification resembled the French Edict of Nantes (1598) by segregating the warring faiths territorially. Catholics were given the province of Buddu, and a population transfer of some 15,000 people followed. Muslims were deliberately scattered across the whole territory, further weakening them politically.

The wars and subsequent pacification set the stage for mass conversions to Christianity, much as was happening elsewhere in Africa. In this case, the appointee-chiefs played a leading role, their faith having been steeled in war. Many who served under them simply followed their lead. Protestants and Catholics pursued parallel paths in their respective regions, and European missionaries reentered the picture as translators and teachers. Once again, the scale of conversion was astounding. Reading houses were set up to teach literacy, increasing from twenty to two hundred in the course of a single year; Catholic open-air catechisms were reported to draw as many as three thousand. The Bible translation by Anglican missionary George Pilkington, completed in 1895, sold 1,100 copies, plus 4,000 New Testaments, 13,500 single gospels, and 40,000 collections of Bible stories.[173] According to Roland Oliver:

The missionaries were constantly being stopped as they walked about the streets with people racing out of their houses with books in their hands to ask the meaning of obscure passages. What was a winepress? How far was it from Jerusalem to Jericho? In what died the wealth of Capernaum consist? The embarrassed clergymen had to write home to headquarters for reference books and commentaries.[174]

Meanwhile, Catholic Buddu became the site of the one and only diocese in Africa controlled by native priests during the interwar period. The clergy at its headquarters, Masaka, were more comfortable in Latin than in English.[175]

This zeal quickly translated into an evangelistic impulse to spread Christianity into neighboring territories, an impulse which was part of Bugandan imperialism and nicely fit British aims as well, somewhat to the latter's surprise.[176] Gandan missionaries did not stop there, however, but extended to eastern Congo, Rwanda, western Kenya, and northern Tanzania.

Of course, such intensity could not be sustained indefinitely, and by the 1920s there was a general feeling that the level of commitment in the Anglican church was slackening. Chiefs were returning to ancestral religion and to polygamy. This was the background to the Ugandan wave of reform, known as *Balakole* (the saved ones) which took place in the 1930s. The initiative came from an English missionary in Rwanda, Dr. Joe Church, who worked with Gandan missionaries there. They brought it into the Anglican church in Uganda as a way of purifying it, and it spread through East Central Africa, reaching its peak in the 1950s. One finds here the familiar narrowing of religious concerns to a few elements – in this case focusing on the blood of Christ – to the exclusion of indigenous tradition. Asceticism figured prominently as well. Hastings writes: "Young revivalists ... threw away their bracelets and necklaces, they denounced the spirit cults practiced in their homes, they ate taboo foods, red ants and grasshoppers. They refused to go to dances. They cut down their beer banana plants and even their coffee trees, claiming that they sought no riches on earth."[177]

Inspired by John Bunyan's *The Pilgrim's Progress*, which had been translated into several local languages, the *Balakole* cut themselves off from family and kin to become pilgrims. Many became millennialists, convinced that the end of the world was at hand.[178] Thus here, too, *concentration of spirituality* triumphed.

Yet when the kingdom of Buganda was absorbed into the independent nation-state of Uganda in 1962, the role of Christianity was altered. Resentments against the domination of the kingdom led to the rise of new authoritarian leaders Milton Obote, who abolished the office of *kabaka*, and his rival Idi Amin. When the Anglican archbishop Janani Luwum criticized Amin's dictatorship, he was brutally murdered in 1977. He was one of several high-ranking Christian clergy in Africa who took a stand against authoritarian rulers in the postindependence period.[179]

That the churches were, however, not necessarily immune to political involvement that resulted in morally compromising actions was demonstrated in neighboring Rwanda, where churches actually served as killing sites in the genocide that occurred there in 1994, and where majority

Hutus routinely portrayed minority Tutsis as "cockroaches." In his book
Christianity in the Twentieth Century, Brian Stanley provides a detailed
account of the macabre twists and turns that led to this result. His sober
conclusion is that "wherever churches have become large and influential
human institutions, they tend to prioritize the maintenance of political
access over the safeguarding of moral independence."[180] The sheer variety of scenarios in African church-state relationships, however, shows
that this is not always the case, as the example of South Africa will show.

AFRICAN CHRISTIANITY IN THE SETTLER COLONIES: SOUTHERN AFRICA

In those areas of sub-Saharan Africa that saw large numbers of European
settlers, one understandably finds *resistance* playing a greater role on the
African side, especially in the latter part of the twentieth century. The
rhythm of oppression and resistance in settler Africa was, however, quite
irregular, interspersed with periods of economic opportunity and educational advancement for Africans. There were several reasons for this.
First, settlers came in unpredictable waves, triggered by chance occurrences or local circumstances, such as the discovery of diamonds in
Kimberley in 1867 or the influx of settlers to Kenya and Rhodesia
following the Second World War. While each wave inevitably brought
with it some form of exploitation, the character of that exploitation could
change from one wave to another. Thus the initial Dutch settlers
(Afrikaners) on the southern Cape enslaved the native Khoi people beginning in the seventeenth century but frequently intermarried with them, in
contrast to the racial taboos that characterized twentieth-century apartheid; this did not, however, eliminate frontier violence or alleviate mutual
distrust and fear, with the result that the early settlers tended to oppose
Khoi baptism, since that would signify acceptance into the community of
whites.[181] Second, South African peoples were buffeted about not only by
advancing white settlers but also by the native expansion emanating from
the Zulus known as *mfecane* ("grinding," "crushing") in the 1810s and
'20s, creating further waves of refugees and resettlement among peoples
who did not necessarily share the same language or ethnicity.

   Third and not least, the same geographical and climatic conditions that
made southern Africa (and Kenya) attractive to white settlers also enabled
white missionaries to survive and flourish, in sharp contrast to West
Africa. Thus South Africa became, in Noel King's words, "a kind of

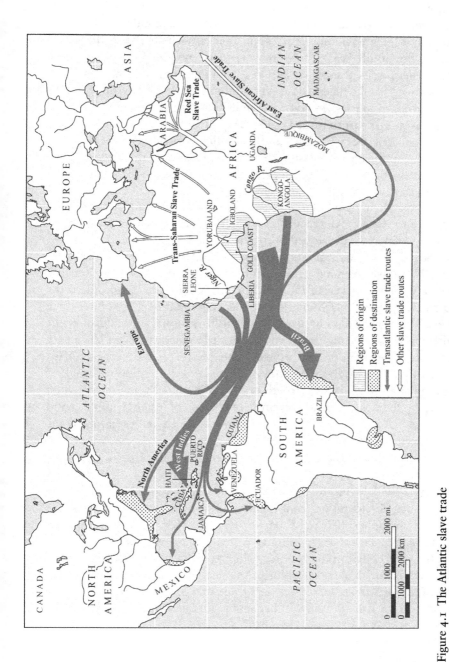

Figure 4.1 The Atlantic slave trade

Source: Modified from Strayer, Robert W. *Ways of the World: a Brief Global History with Sources.* 2nd ed. Boston: Bedford/St. Martins, 2013. P. 689

Drawn by Mary Lee Eggart

happy hunting ground for every denomination under the sun." By 1911, there were over 30 missionary organizations and 1,650 individuals there – probably a greater number per capita than anywhere else in the world (except the South Seas).[182] Moreover, these missionary societies were often beneficiaries of large land grants from the colonial powers; a "mission station" could encompass several thousand acres.[183] While it might seem that missionaries would thus be indistinguishable from other settlers in native eyes, the truth turned out to be quite different. Many missionaries, particularly from England and the United States, held liberal views which sympathized more with the Africans than with the settlers. They were products of the same reform movements which had led to the abolition of the slave trade and slavery itself, and held to the belief that God loved all humans equally – the same strand of Christianity that appealed to African-American slaves.[184] This was quite at odds with the view the Afrikaners developed over time, namely that God had developed specific covenants with specific nations, each according to their status and rank. These two seemingly incompatible interpretations of what it meant to be a Christian nevertheless did not entirely preclude compromise: the Dutch Reformed Church interpreted their covenant as a missionary one to evangelize the Africans, and the English missionaries could often be quite comfortable with a gradual approach to equality which left plenty of room for segregation. Nonetheless, the differences were crucial. Thus in the case of the Khoi, for example, missionary intervention on behalf of their rights in the early nineteenth century eliminated some of the worst abuses by the Afrikaners and eventually caused the latter to move inland from the Cape Colony – the "Great Trek," which only reinforced the Afrikaners' sense of special mission.

At first, the foreigners were no more successful in gaining converts than in other parts of Africa. The best-known missionary of the nineteenth century, David Livingstone, turned to the explorations that made him famous out of frustration from failure to win over his initial targets, the Tswana of southern Africa.[185] More often than not, Africans responded to messages of everlasting life and a loving God with incredulity and skepticism. The Christian notion of sin proved just as difficult to export here as in colonial Mexico or North America.[186] Gradually, however, the appeal of Christianity increased, partly due to missionary initiative, partly by several revival movements beginning in the 1860s, and partly by Africans forming their own churches.[187]

The pattern of indigenous encounters with Christianity in South Africa is thus that of a complicated mosaic: a variety of strategies pursued by different groups simultaneously. To begin with the Khoi, the willingness of missionaries to stand by them in their violent struggles with the Afrikaners in the early 1800s drew several hundred converts who followed them to a mission station at Bethelsdorp; from here Christianity spread rapidly over the next decades, leading to some Khoi even serving as missionaries themselves to people in the interior. Beginning in the 1840s, however, they became increasingly disillusioned with the British, who supported the landed interest of white settlers – resulting in a rebellion in 1850.[188]

In contrast, their immediate neighbors to the east, the Xhosa, had produced two rival visionary prophets in response to the settlers by the 1810s, after a particularly brutal onslaught by the British. One, Nxele, preached an ongoing war between the God of the whites, as taught by the missionaries, and the God of the blacks; the other, Ntsikana, converted to Christianity. He composed a hymn, which is still sung today, in praise of "the one who brings together herds which oppose each other."[189] Ntiskana inspired a number of leaders in subsequent generations to develop a distinctive Xhosa Christian tradition largely independent of missionary influence. The Xhosa were particularly receptive to the Christian millennialist ideas of the resurrection of the dead, as their previous beliefs had regarded death as the supreme impurity which had to be cleansed. The indigenous and Christian strands came together – tragically – in another prophetic vision of a young girl, Nongqawuse, in 1856, which directed the Xhosa to slaughter all their cattle, who had recently been stricken with lung disease, and whose sacrifice would enable her people to rise again. It is estimated that 40,000 people died of starvation as a result.[190]

Contrasts also abounded in the political realm. Warrior peoples like the Zulu found missionaries useful as go-betweens with their European adversaries, but drew the line at their religious ideas. The Zulu king Dingane, after a long and exasperating dialogue with a missionary in 1837, ended the conversation by telling him, "I and my people believe that there is only one God—I am that God...I do not want you to trouble me again with the fiction of you English people."[191] On the other hand, certain kings adopted Christianity as their state religion, particularly among the Tswana. One of them, Khama III of the northern Tswana, who was always pictured in European dress, traveled to London in 1895 to secure the protection of his kingdom from Cecil Rhodes's territorial ambitions, giving eventual rise to the modern state of Botswana.[192] Not all of the king's subjects followed suit, however: a 1946 census put the number of Christians at less than 20 percent.[193] In fact, by this time, many Tswana and other South Africans had developed a strong sense of cultural relativism, insisting that missionary Christianity was inappropriate for them.[194]

What generalizations, if any, can be drawn from this mosaic? One can say that the scope of missionary activity promoted a degree of cultural mixing that served to counter the segregationist impulses of the Afrikaners. Paradoxically, the very size of missionary land holdings meant that these could serve as incubators for native empowerment. The fact that the stations served as places of refuge for the homeless and outcast, as well as residences for migrant laborers, protected the members of these Christian villages from many of the settlers' harsh laws that bore on natives outside.[195] Norman Etherington's study of Natal shows that these residents were recognized as a separate class, the *kholwa* (believers). With missionary encouragement, they quickly built on the security provided by the mission stations to acquire more livestock, wagons, and ploughs, and to sell agricultural goods to a wider market. The missionaries' introduction of the plough radically changed gender relations, as agricultural planting now became men's rather than women's work. African entrepreneurs also established ox-drawn transport businesses which did much of the hauling of the newly discovered diamonds.[196] Stories of native agricultural prosperity could be replicated throughout settler Africa in the nineteenth and early twentieth centuries, though it is not clear how much of it stemmed from missionary estates. In any case, native economic advancement gradually presented a threat to white settlers, and the government soon began to place legal restrictions on native rights to buy and sell property. Nonetheless, missionary efforts continued as Africans moved from the rural areas to the cities, and a strong urban "social gospel" movement persisted into the twentieth century.

Meanwhile, these trends had created a great indigenous demand for education, which the missions provided, including a number of racially integrated, high-quality secondary schools in the Cape Colony. The largest of these was Lovedale, founded in 1841 by the Glasgow Missionary Society. By 1887, it had taught over 2,000 students, including 538 women. White and black students ate and slept separately, but attended classes together. As elsewhere in Africa, the most prominent nationalist leaders were products of the mission schools, including Nelson Mandela. The unwillingness of Afrikaners to finance black education led to a de facto monopoly of mission schools into the 1920s and '30s. As elsewhere, Africans demanded instruction in English and Afrikaans as keys to advancement.[197] It could be argued that such advancement became decisive in triggering the institutionalization of apartheid itself – or so one if its architects, D. F. Malan, implied in 1938, ten years before apartheid was enacted: "[F]or a white minority to stand against the overwhelmingly superior power of civilized and educated non-whites who wish to share our way of life and to strive in every respect for equality with us ... makes our generation's struggle for a white South Africa infinitely more difficult."[198]

The eventual result was the notorious Bantu Education Act of 1953, which removed the missions from control of the schools.[199]

The success of the missionary movement in appealing to Africans in the first part of the twentieth century may be gauged by the numbers of African members of the white-controlled missionary churches: in 1938, out of 792,872 African Christians, 463,349 belonged to one of the mainline denominations, leaving 329,473 as probably belonging to one of the independent African churches.[200] This despite the undeniably paternalistic attitudes of the missionaries themselves: however sincere was their desire to "uplift" the African, their cultural bias shone through in their unwillingness to delegate authority and ordain African clergy.

In these circumstances, it is not surprising that Ethiopianism should also have taken root among urban and educated Africans as a form of religious *resistance* to the missionary churches. As in West Africa, the form of worship remained European, but there seems to have been less flirtation with indigenous culture. Continuing the strategy of mixing, these churches quickly sought affiliation with denominations abroad. In order that Ethiopia might stretch out its hands to God, Ethiopian churches stretched out their hands to America. The reasons were in large part practical. These African churches desperately needed financial support, and organizations like the African Methodist Episcopal Church in the United States with some 800,000 members, were potential sources. The AME bishop, H. M. Turner, made a sensational visit to South Africa in 1898, and African membership ballooned to some 10,000.[201] The desire for an institute of higher education was high on the Africans' list of priorities, and it eventually came to pass in 1916, based on Booker T. Washington's Tuskegee Institute. This was acceptable to whites as well, who preferred it to African students going to America to study and picking up revolutionary ideas.[202] One man who did study in the United States, the Reverend John Dube, also a Methodist clergyman, became the first president of the African National Congress, the group that would eventually lead the struggle against apartheid. According to

Steve De Gruchy, Christians who followed constituted "a who's who of ANC leadership down the years."[203] Thus the links between Christianity, education, and black independence were forged in the early twentieth century, albeit in a moderate, gradualist form.

As white restrictions on blacks' freedom of movement increased, many turned to *concentration of spirituality* as a way of gathering strength by turning inward and looking to a utopian future. Many of these African churches adopted the label "Zionist," inspired partly by Alexander Dowie's apocalyptic Christian community in Zion City, Illinois. One is struck by the relatively greater emphasis on spatial imagery in these groups, in comparison with the Aladuras, for example. There were several attempts to establish holy cities, modeled on the New Jerusalem, which served as places of pilgrimage, refuge and hope, perpetuating in a way the missionaries' notion of a Christian village.[204] One of the first acts by Isaiah Shembe, South Africa's most famous prophet, was to purchase land in 1914 to create such a refuge, a representation of heaven on Earth. Shembe conceived this sacred space as a spiritual alternative to political space, which had just been restricted the previous year by the Native Lands Act, preventing from blacks from purchasing property outside their reserves. Shembe himself had a view similar to that of the African-American emigrationists on slavery: settler colonialism was part of God's plan for Africans, teaching them suffering as atonement for previous sins and as a preparation for their eventual redemption.[205]

Apart from Shembe's movement, Zionist churches were characterized by much schism and fusion, offering Africans, including women, opportunities for organization and leadership that were denied them in the larger society. In this way, as with the imagery of spatial separation, these churches found a way of living with apartheid.[206]

As white intransigence in the face of black demands increased, however, and struggle between the two groups became more violent beginning in the 1960s, and with the general failure of both the mission and prophetic churches to confront apartheid, it appeared that Christianity was losing its relevance compared to secular movements such as communism. This, however, proved to be just an interlude: inspired and energized by liberalizing and ecumenical movements such the World Council of Churches and drawing on their own preexisting networks, African Christian clergy, both black and white, gradually found the strength to mount an opposition to apartheid based on theology and moral principle, a case of *acceptance and commitment*. African students took the initiative in formulating a Black theology in the 1970s, based on the notions of liberation and struggle, similar to what was happening in the United States and Latin America.[207] In the mid-1980s the churches moved from issuing pronouncements to joining with other organizations with demonstrations and boycotts in the face of increasingly violent repression. The churches thus played a key role in the collapse of the regime in 1990 and the efforts to dampen the violence in the years immediately following.[208] By this time, the number of adherents to the independent churches had increased from 21 percent in 1960 to 47 percent of the African Christian population in 1991, while the mission churches had declined from 70 percent to 33 percent in the same period.[209]

NEW PENTECOSTALS

The decades following independence were ones of economic hardship and political instability across sub-Saharan Africa, due in part to the fluctuations in the world economy (such as the oil crisis of 1973) and in no small part to the behaviors of the political leaders themselves, which lent themselves to massive corruption. This has been described as "clientelism" or "patrimonialism," in which authoritarian leaders built up large numbers of followers who are indebted to them. The public display of wealth and status was part of their exercise of power (the "big man" syndrome).[210]

The same decades also witnessed the dramatic upsurge of Christianity, from c. 75 million to c. 351 million between 1965 and 2000.[211] Catholics played a significant role in this story, thanks to the reforms of Vatican II, which led to the growth of African clergy and religious orders, with women outnumbering men in the latter by about five to one.[212]

The most striking development, however, was the growth of Pentecostal churches of all sizes. Difficult to quantify, their most obvious manifestations are the megachurches in the cities, the appeal to youthful members, the use of electronic media, as inspired and spurred on by American tele-evangelists. The new flavor of this Christianity is vividly conveyed by Birgit Meyer:

Nothing can better evoke what is at stake than the salience of the contrast between the familiar image of African prophets from Zionist, Nazarite, or Aladura churches, dressed in white gowns, carrying crosses, and going to pray in the bush, and the flamboyant leaders of the new mega-churches, who dress in the latest (African) fashion, drive nothing less than a Mercedes Benz, participate in the global Pentecostal jetset, broadcast the message through flashy TV and radio programs, and preach the Prosperity Gospel to their deprived and hitherto-hopeless born-again followers at home and in the diaspora.[213]

Nonetheless, this is a misleading picture of the movement as a whole, for alongside these glamorous cases were innumerable small local African-initiated charismatic ministries, numbering some ten thousand by one estimate, many of them doubtless ephemeral.[214] Women not infrequently played a leadership role in these, since the charismatic gifts of preaching and healing are distributed across gender lines. In the case of a rural region in Malawi, for example, women members are believed to be responsible for the churches' rejecting polygamy in favor of monogamy.[215] One result of the massive drift to these new churches has been to force some of the older ones to incorporate charismatic elements into their services, however awkward this was at first.[216] Indeed, the "Pentecostalization" of the older churches is one of the most notable features of this period.

The question arises whether this surge should be seen as something radically new in African Christianity or as a continuation of already-existing trends. There is evidence for both views, but I believe the formula of *concentration of spirituality* combined with *conservation of form* begins to describe it. In this respect, the cyclical pattern as presented by De Craemer, Vansina, and Fox retains its suggestibility.[217] To support this, let us look at Nigeria, whose leaders have exerted an influence on religious formation throughout sub-Saharan Africa. While older Pentecostal denominations had been in Nigeria in small numbers since the 1920s, the movement took off in the 1970s with the Deeper Life Bible Church founded by William Kumuyi, which began as a fifteen-member Bible study group in 1973 and grew to a membership of over 200,000 by 1988.[218] This should be viewed against the background of American evangelists who preached in Nigeria at the time, but also the political instability of those years and the wild fluctuations in the economy that accompanied it. As the above quote by Meyer suggests, the Deeper Life church rejected the Aladuras, who had allowed traditional ritualistic practices to creep in to their churches, diluting the concentration of spirituality that had originally characterized it.[219] Nevertheless, we can observe many similarities between the two movements.

For the concentration, there is the emotional intensity and fervor that characterize Pentecostal meetings worldwide, expressed in such altered states of consciousness as speaking in tongues. But there is also the rejection of "traditional" ceremonies and specialists, and of multiple spirits in favor of communing with a single Holy Spirit, which becomes the focus of the practices previously directed toward the many.[220] Particularly important is the belief that each individual can experience the Spirit directly, rather than through the medium of a clergy member – a priesthood of believers, in other words.[221] The Deeper Life church was also characterized by asceticism and anti-materialism, in sharp contrast to the conspicuous displays of wealth by the political leaders of the time.[222]

Beginning in the 1980s, however, a new wave of Pentecostal churches took shape that emphasized material prosperity in this world as God's gift to the faithful. Examples of this trend would include the Winners' Chapel, founded in 1983 by David Oyedepo and active in thirty-eight African countries by 2000, and the Church of God Mission, founded by Benson Idahosa. His Christ for All Nations Bible School trained charismatic pastors across West Africa. By the '90s these churches had developed sophisticated media technologies to record and broadcast their services, which took on the shape of theatrical performances. As Nigeria's economy spiraled downward, these preachers increasingly emphasized the miraculous; Jesus the miracle worker overshadowed Jesus the teacher or the Sermon on the Mount. All of this required money, and congregants were expected to give if they were to receive the material blessings. There was likewise a concentration of authority in the hands of the clergy, as they gave themselves titles of bishop and archbishop, or acquired honorary degrees from Bible colleges. In their flaunting of wealth and status they mirrored the "big men" of the political elite.

All of this naturally created a certain tension with the more humble and egalitarian values of the earlier phase, and it seems that the majority of Pentecostals fell between these two extremes.[223] For many, the motivation provided by the energy of the Pentecostal church served not to bring great material success, but rather simply to get by and survive in uncertain and precarious times (in 1980, half the population of Nigeria lived on less than thirty cents a day).[224]

In all this, we can see several instances of *conservation of form*. First, the gospel of prosperity itself, which, for all its modern capitalistic accoutrements, expresses a fundamental African belief that religion is directed to material well-being no less than spiritual – in fact, they are one and the same. No less important, however, is the way in which Pentecostals grapple with the tensions and contradictions within their faith, such as the discrepancy between the promise of prosperity and its actual absence. There is no escaping the reality of evil, and it is approached via notions of diffuse spirituality. To be sure, evil is embodied in the single figure of Satan. But Satan turns out to preside over a multitude of demons which are everywhere and which seemed to multiply in times of crisis such as the 1990s. In Ruth Marshall's words, "powders, charms, wizards, witches, ancestor spirits, *orisa, obanje,* juju, Ifa, voodoo, Mami Wata, other water or marine spirits, snakes, owls, vultures crocodiles, cats, and other animals, but also a whole pantheon of Biblical demons...apparently, there is no end to evil."[225] Witches, as human agents who enlist such evil spirits, proliferated as well. Such a web of evil was useful in accounting for abuse of power in high places and occasionally rebounded on pastors themselves. This applies also to medicine: there is the emphasis on healing through the laying of hands, embodying the assumption that illness is spiritual as well as physical, and that evil spirits can be driven out by means of exorcism. Jesus's own practice, as recorded in the New Testament (Mark, 9), is cited as evidence. To quote David Martin, "African Christianity...proclaims a Jesus who is victor over evil and death rather than a lamb brought to the slaughter."[226] In sum, the strategy of deliverance, articulated during the Aladura period, remained prominent among the Pentecostals.

Here, we find again a pattern of oscillation between concentration and so-called backsliding, moving back and forth between Christian and indigenous observance as circumstances require.[227] Meyer interprets the Pentecostal sequence of possession by evil spirits, exorcism, and possession by the Holy Spirit as a reenactment of this oscillation, capable of multiple repetition.[228] Thus the form of oscillation is conserved within the concentrated setting of Pentecostal worship.

If there is anything new in this, it is perhaps the content rather than the form: the way that indigenous and Biblical imagery is interwoven with that of modern capitalism – not only the brand names of cars and watches, but the metaphors of business and investment. Kwabena Asamoah-Gyadu points to four basic symbols which he believes characterize contemporary Pentecostalism: the dove, the eagle, the globe – and the microphone.[229] The reach of electronic media to remote areas of the world provides a common, blanketing set of cultural references. This gives new meaning to the notion of *acculturation*: there is no need to "reach out" to modern culture: it is already there, reaching out to one. In this regard, African Pentecostalism is part of an international phenomenon, and this in itself is a status symbol for its leaders: many churches include "international" in their names. Asamoah-Gyadu's image of the

South Africa language groups

Figure 4.2 South African language groups
Source: Drawn by the author

soaring eagle indicates that Pentecostals are no less eager to spread their enchanted version of Christianity to neighboring countries and beyond. African Pentecostal churches are among the largest of African churches in Europe, and leading evangelists regularly make tours to the United States. There is a reversal of roles here in that Africans can rightly regard secular "Dark Europe" as a heathen region.[230] This sort of outreach, however modern it appears to be, preserves the form of cosmopolitan activity that has characterized Africa for many centuries.

Given the demographic shift of World Christianity to the southern hemisphere, these developments are likely to have an impact on the West as well. One can see this in the tendency of African Christians to align with Western conservatives rather than liberals on questions of gender and sexuality. At the same time, one may question whether the interplay of concentrated and diffuse spirituality represented by the deliverance strategy is something that is readily transferable from the relatively impoverished African continent to the affluent West. One can see the influence of Christianity in localizing and channeling the belief in multiple spirits, both by subsuming them under a single Satan and by treating them more in the context of personal and interpersonal situations rather than in the political realm. Yet the language and imagery of spiritual warfare remains prominent, which could easily fuel the fire of conflict, especially with equally concentrated and militant Islamic groups. The belief in God's love remains strong, but faces some stiff competition.

5

The Middle East

As the birthplace of the three major monotheistic faiths, the Middle East has been the focus of Christian missionary activity throughout much of its history. Although the region's population today is overwhelmingly Muslim – estimated 93 percent in 2010, including North Africa – it also contains the world's largest concentration of Jews; Christians continue to comprise a significant minority (6.1% in 2010) – although that percentage has been declining (from 7.3% in 1970) and is expected to decline further.[1]

As is all too familiar, the Middle East has been the scene of recurring war, persecution, and political instability for at least the last hundred years. It is tempting to attribute this in part to a rhythm of jihad and crusade that seems for some to have characterized the overall history of Christian-Islamic relations since the time of Muhammad, often portrayed as a "clash of civilizations." Such formulas have elicited no less impassioned rebuttals, insisting on the wide-ranging similarities and shared values of these two monotheistic traditions.[2] Quite aside from the fact that Muslim "Civilization" extends far beyond the Middle East, the long-term history of Arab society is replete with examples of Muslims, Christians and Jews coexisting peacefully on a day-to-day basis for long periods of time, living near each other, doing business with each other, sharing each other's rituals and saintly figures to the point of syncretism, and even occasionally collaborating with each other militarily.[3]

A more accurate portrayal of the conflictual aspect might be termed a clash of *concentrated spiritualities* rather than civilizations: the belief that the Supreme Being finds its quintessential manifestation at a particular point in historical space and time; in a single individual in the case of Christianity and a single book in the case of Islam; or, in the case of Judaism, in a series of covenants with a single group at specific points on a historical timeline. This concentration promotes a tendency to exclusivity, which, in the case of Christianity and Islam, is paradoxically reinforced by their claims to be also universally true, for all people at all times and places subsequent to the defining event. This poses problems of how to treat people of different faiths – particularly within a polity where one of these is the state religion, a problem that previous polytheistic empires in Europe and Asia did not have to face.[4] It also sparked a rivalry among the three religions over their supremely Holy Places, with Jerusalem serving to incite the Christian imagination as a pilgrimage site, while the Dome of the Rock contains the inscription, "O People of the Scripture! ... say not 'Three' ... Allah is only One God. Far is it removed from His Transcendent Majesty that He should have a son."[5]

It might be further argued that these claims created a predisposition for groups *within* both Christianity and Islam to claim infallibility, that one's particular interpretation of the quintessential event or scripture is the only true one. How else can one explain that, at certain times and places, both monotheisms have devoted as much energy to combatting "heretical" or "schismatic" versions of their own faiths and within their own cultures as to vanquishing the "other"(e.g., Catholic vs. Protestant vs. Orthodox, or Sunni vs. Shia) – clashes that surely cut across the "clash of civilizations"?

None of this is to assert that religion was or is the sole cause of conflict and instability in the Middle East, although the reality of the holy wars can hardly be denied. At other times, as we will see, religion could act as kind of flammable fuel to intensify existing economic or political differences, thereby rendering these conflicts more violent than they might have been otherwise, and seemingly overnight (as in the case of former Yugoslavia in the 1990s, an example from a neighboring region).

One obvious consequence of this attitude is that Christian missionaries over the centuries have been almost uniformly unsuccessful in winning Jews and Muslims over to their faith – an obstacle reinforced by a strong Islamic prohibition on apostasy, punishable by death according to shari'a law. In other words, the predominant indigenous strategy in dealing with Christian missionaries has been *resistance*. Consequently, we will be dealing more often with Christian-Christian missionary encounters than with Christian-Muslim ones. Given the seemingly insurmountable barriers to proselytization which Islam presented, Western missionaries turned their attention to their supposedly less advanced Eastern brethren, in the hope that the latter's "improvement" as Christians would eventually set a shining example for the Muslims in their midst.

At the same time, insistence on these doctrinal cores should not lead us to fall into the opposite trap of reductionism. It should be obvious that, as both Christianity and Islam spread and evolved, they adapted to changing circumstances and developed new varieties. This occurred at times by combining with surrounding religions through processes such as *incorporation* and *acculturation*, at other times by splitting from previously existing versions of one's own faith. Nowhere, in fact, was this latter process more fully developed than in Middle Eastern Christianity in the centuries prior to the coming of Muhammad and extending into the early Islamic period. The highly variegated strands of Christian doctrine, many of which persist to the present day, were traceable partly to multiple powerful bishoprics in the Middle East that traced their origins to the Apostles (Antioch in Syria, Alexandria in Egypt, Caesarea in Palestine) and which could pose threats to Rome and later to Constantinople. These power plays found expression in doctrinal disputes, largely over the question of how to interpret the incarnation: whether the human and divine aspects of Jesus were separate, fused, or somehow otherwise combined. These disputes reflected Christianity's increasing exposure to Greek philosophy and its emphasis on abstract concepts rather than concrete events. Despite the efforts of several church councils to resolve them, these disputes left a legacy of schism and factionalism, giving rise to a bewildering variety of positions.[6] Several of the churches which emerged from this churning play an important role in our story and deserve introduction here:

1. *Nestorians* trace their origins to the bishop of Constantinople, who emphasized the "two-ness" of Jesus' nature. This proved unacceptable to the Council of Ephesus (431) and Nestorius's followers eventually migrated to Persia. Known as the Church of the East, their own missionary work stretched as far east as India, the Mongol Empire, and China. They suffered a drastic decline in the fourteenth century but survived in northern Mesopotamia into modern times.

2. *Coptics (Egypt) and Armenians* both embraced the "fusion" position ("Monophysite," or more properly "miaphysite"), contrary to the Council of Chalcedon (451), which opted for combination, reinforcing the doctrine of the Trinity. The Armenian king

Tiridates had been the first ruler to embrace Christianity as a state religion in the early fourth century.

3. *Syrian vs. Greek Orthodox.* The Syrian Christians were also divided over the decision of the Council of Chalcedon. Those who opposed it called themselves "Syrian Orthodox" as distinct from pro-Greek Orthodox who supported it. Another splinter group which also accepted Chalcedon was

4. *Maronite,* presumably named for a third-century Syriac saint. They eventually settled in Mount Lebanon, established an autonomous community there, and eventually declared their loyalty to Roman Catholicism in 1182.

The geographical proximity of Europe and the Middle East that created favorable conditions for war also fostered interaction in terms of commerce and exchange of ideas. The European medieval synthesis of Christian theology and Greco-Arab philosophy is well known, and the eastern Mediterranean has been characterized as a "cultural melting pot."[7] Perhaps less well known is the fact that the Middle East itself remained a shared space and zone of interaction between Islam and Christianity for several centuries after the Muslim conquest. The speed and breadth of that conquest did not lead to instant or forced conversion – far from it. The conquerors regarded Islam at first as an exclusively Arab religion; the idea of a universalistic faith began to take hold only in the 700s.[8] This meant that Christianity remained a majority religion in the region for several centuries, encompassing roughly 50 percent of the world's Christian population.[9] The shift from majority to minority occurred only gradually, with the Crusades serving as the approximate tipping point. Meanwhile, Christians served as translators and interpreters of Greek philosophy in the early Abbasid Caliphate (late eighth century), contributing to the flourishing of Islamic culture in Baghdad. They also produced works of Christian theology and apology in Arabic, including epistolary exchanges with Muslim scholars.[10] Christian mystics also probably played a role in stimulating Sufism.

One factor that doubtless eased the eventual process of conversion to Islam for Christians was the fact that Jesus had already been *incorporated* into Muslim theology, beginning with Muhammad himself. The Qu'ran portrays Jesus as a divinely inspired prophet, one who stands out from the line of earlier Hebrew prophets. Jesus is a model of piety and devotion, a healer, and a performer of miracles. Absent of course are the incarnation and the crucifixion. In subsequent Islamic writings, Jesus was also given a role in Islamic eschatology, to reappear at the end of the world.[11] Over time, however, this picture of Jesus was brought into line with the belief in Islamic exclusivity. The true revelation of God to Jesus, it was said, had pointed to the coming of Muhammad, but this had been suppressed in the corrupt texts of the various Christian gospels. Thus the New Testament gave a distorted picture of Jesus and as a result was harmful to the faith of true Muslims. Over time, then, the "melting pot" aspect receded in favor of Christians and Muslims reading their own scriptures but not that of the other – despite the absence of any such prohibition in the Qu'ran itself.[12] This, however, did not prevent Muslims from adoring the Virgin Mary, who is also celebrated in the Qu'ran, or from sharing the Feast of the Annunciation with their Christian neighbors.[13]

If Christians – in their fragmented churches – and Jews nevertheless managed to survive intact over centuries of Islamic imperial rule, this was due mainly to the protected status (*dhimmi*) extended to them by Islamic law itself.[14] Although they were accorded special status as "Peoples of the Book" in the Qu'ran, the same arrangements were extended to other communities such as the Zoroastrians and later Hindus when the Muslims reached India. *Dhimmi* status was more a product of pragmatic necessity of maintaining peace and order in ruling a heterogeneous empire than of any theological – much less liberal – set of principles. It drew on precedents already established in the Roman and Persian empires. It was eventually codified in the so-called Pact of Umar, which became part of Islamic law in the ninth century.[15] The central provision was that non-Muslims would be allowed to practice their religions, according to their own laws, in return for a special tax (*jizya*). To be sure, protection did not mean equality: other provisions were gradually added to ensure that everyone realized the subordinate status of non-Muslims. These included such measures as: not to build any new churches or repair old ones, not to ring bells to summon to worship, or hold public processions, not to ride horses or camels but only donkeys or mules, not to teach the Qu'ran to their children, not to wear certain colors reserved for Muslims and to wear distinctive clothing. Non-Muslim men were forbidden to marry Muslim women, but a Muslim man could take a non-Muslim woman for a wife, provided the children were raised Muslim. Except for the *jizya*, most of these were not consistently enforced. There are accounts of Christian festivals where Muslims looked on or took part.[16]

While certainly humiliating, the *dhimmi* laws generally afforded religious minorities a degree of peace and security unmatched by their counterparts in Europe. To be sure, laxity of enforcement could work the other way, in failing to stem popular anger in times of interreligious hostility. The Crusades were an obvious case in point: Arab Christians had to pay a double price, both in terms of European military occupation and Muslim retribution, particularly under the Mamluk sultans in Egypt and Syria in the thirteenth century, when popular attacks on Christians increased.[17] In addition, *dhimmi* regulations tended to be more rigorously enforced at these times, bringing increased hardship on the Christians. In the long run, in any event, the predominance of Islam served as a magnet for *acculturation* on the part of the other religions – for example, in the use of Arabic as opposed to the Syriac language. The end result of this process was frequently conversion. To quote Robert Haddad, "At few times in the course of the Muslim centuries was it other than perfectly clear to the non-Muslim that most mundane interests would be served by conversion to the faith of the prophet."[18] For those who were not so inclined, however, there was the option of seeking outside help, and one place to look was Rome.

It is safe to say that the Western missionary impulse toward the Muslim world originated with the Crusades, epitomized by St. Francis of Assisi's visit to the sultan of Egypt in 1219 in the midst of the Fifth Crusade. Contemporary accounts indicate that Francis was willing to accept death should his preaching fail. The sultan, however, who had just offered a negotiated peace to the crusaders, sent him back to his camp in one piece. But a number of other missionaries – Franciscans and Dominicans – followed and succeeded in meeting their deaths; subsequent Franciscan accounts of the 1219 meeting portrayed the saint as actively seeking martyrdom.[19] Later, after the Franciscans were granted a presence in Jerusalem as protectors of the Holy Places by the Mamluk sultan, martyrdom remained a part of their mind-set vis-à-vis their religious adversaries into the nineteenth century.[20]

In the wake of the Crusades, missionaries helped spread the message of Roman Catholicism, specifically recognizing the supremacy of papal authority, vis-à-vis the Orthodox churches, giving rise to the so-called Uniate movement. Given the varieties of Eastern Christian churches, they were only partly successful but won support among the Maronites and to a lesser extent the Armenians.[21] Negotiations between the Byzantine and Roman churches on the question of union did take place, however, climaxing in a fragile agreement in 1439 in Florence that nevertheless failed to hold. Fourteen years later, the Ottomans conquered Constantinople.

OTTOMAN RULE, SIXTEENTH TO EIGHTEENTH CENTURIES

In many ways, the early centuries of Ottoman rule represented a recapitulation of the early Islamic expansion: the conquest of the largely Orthodox Christian Balkan Peninsula meant that Muslims were once again in the minority, pointing to a continuation of *dhimmi* status for Christians and Jews, generally following the provisions of the Pact of Umar. The empire thus famously served as a haven for many Sephardic Jews at the time of their expulsion from Spain in 1492. The major exception to this (though not the only one) was the practice of *devshirme*, the drafting and converting of boys from the Christian territories to serve in the army, an Ottoman innovation that was contrary to existing Islamic law but was implemented for reasons of state. *Devshirme* both provided these boys with opportunities for upward mobility within the government but brought hardship and loss to families whose sons were taken away.[22]

Over time, the Ottomans applied the *dhimmi* principles to more and more specific groups, as new leaders and communal structures sought official recognition. These groups became known as *millets*, based on a real or imagined bestowing of communal rights in the past and organized by confession.[23] Some trace this system back to the conquest of Constantinople itself in 1453, for even as the conqueror, Sultan Mehmet II, was converting churches into mosques, he continued the office of Christian patriarch of Constantinople and appointed a Greek Orthodox monk to fill the position. Although the exact circumstances surrounding the appointment are unclear, it made a statement that the new sultan saw himself not merely as an Islamic ruler, but also as the successor to the emperors of Rome and Byzantium. It had the further virtue, from Mehmet's perspective, of driving a further wedge between the Orthodox and Roman churches, effectively burying the union of 1439. It also helped to solidify the predominant position of the Greek Orthodox Church among the several Orthodox churches in the Balkans: the patriarchate of Constantinople was to remain in Greek hands. This did little to resolve tensions between the different churches; in fact, the more groups that emerged, the more contentious did this process become. Later, in the nineteenth century, the *millets* were to serve as the cradles of ethnic as well as religious particularism.[24]

All of this was to have consequences for the Arab peoples after the Ottomans added them to their empire in 1517. For Muslims, this initially meant little more than a change of ruler at the top; Christians found their *dhimmi* status more secure than under the Mamluks. In practice, the rule from above was light, and local religious communities had control over their own affairs.[25] This was to change, however, as new dynamic forces emerged in the sixteenth and seventeenth centuries.

The sixteenth century has aptly been called the "age of confessionalization," pointing to intensifications of religious commitment and *concentration of spirituality* in both Christianity and Islam that were at once parallel and interdependent.[26] The Protestant and Catholic reformations in the West were matched by a sharpened antagonism between Sunnis and Shia in the East, represented by the Ottoman and Persian Safavid empires, respectively. These dividing lines encouraged an increased insistence on doctrinal purity and suspicion of heterodoxy and heresy, as witnessed by the Catholic Inquisition on the one side and the "Sunnitization" of Ottoman rule under Süleiman the Magnificent (1520–66) on the other.[27] Such internal conflicts in no way diminished Christian-Muslim antagonism, at least at the level of rhetoric. In the West, the call for a crusade against the "terrible Turk" spanned the entire period, going back to before the fall of Constantinople itself and lingering on until the reign of Louis XIV in the seventeenth century – although the internal divisions within Europe, political, as well as religious, prevented such a call from coming to fruition.[28] On the Muslim side, Ottoman conquests were accompanied by a steady rhetoric of *jihad*.[29] Martyrology was also rife, with the Greek monks at Mount Athos providing counseling in preparing men who had converted to Christianity from Islam – thereby committing apostasy – to face their deaths.[30] Religious militancy was laced with apocalyptic expectations, whether of the coming of Christ or the Shia redeemer (*mahdi*). These hopes reached a peak in the early sixteenth century, fueled by the claims to universal monarchy by both Charles V, the Holy Roman Emperor, and Süleiman.[31] In addition to all this, the hostility between the Roman Catholic and Greek Orthodox churches retained its intensity, leading some Orthodox clergy to flirt briefly, if unsuccessfully, with Protestantism.[32]

Needless to say, this atmosphere fostered a tremendous impetus to missionary activity, preeminently among Roman Catholics. The founding of the Jesuit order dates from this period (1534); its founder, Ignatius of Loyola, initially wanted it to serve in the Holy Land. Missionaries served the project of the Uniate movement, i.e., winning over Eastern Christians to what they viewed as the only true church, namely the Roman Church. To this end, the popes established a Greek college in Rome in 1576 and another for Maronites in 1584, to train natives in the process of converting their own people. The Maronite college established a printing press, publishing the Gospels and other prayer books in Arabic.[33] The Office of the Propagation of the Faith (Propaganda) came in 1622 and devoted much of its attention to the Ottoman Empire.

The relative success of missionaries' physically penetrating the realm of Islam over the next century stems from the intertwining of religious and secular motives, both on the part of Europeans and Ottoman rulers, as well as Arab Christians themselves. There was a desire for commerce on all sides, and diplomatic activity was rife, well in advance of establishment of formal embassies. Such activity, including treaties, was admissible under Islamic law, which interpreted them as truces in the holy war against the infidels.[34] Foreigners who engaged in these activities were granted protection and special legal status, *ahdname* in Turkish, meaning roughly safe-conduct, and "capitulations" (from Latin *capitularium*) in Western languages. In order to facilitate these contacts, foreigners were allowed to hire native intermediaries to serve as translators and other functions (*dragomans*). The Ottomans were willing to let native Christians serve in this capacity. Moreover, they were willing to extend this protection to foreign missionaries – partly on the grounds that as Muslims they themselves were immune to such proselytization, which only concerned intra-Christian relations.[35] If this seems naïve in retrospect, it probably did not seem greatly important at the time: Western trade comprised only 5–10 percent of Ottoman commerce as a whole.[36]

In all such business, the French were destined to play a preeminent role. This is traceable to the fact that they shared a common adversary with the Ottomans, namely the Habsburgs. The first, highly secret agreement between the French and the Ottomans occurred when the French king, Francis I, had been taken prisoner by Charles V in 1525. It was followed by further agreements in 1534, 1569, 1604, 1690, and 1740.[37] Through these agreements, the French formally assumed the role of protectors of missionaries in the Ottoman Empire. Of course, by the eighteenth century, the role of commerce had grown immeasurably as the Europeans gained economic and military strength, and the number of Christians who applied for *dragoman* status grew out of control.

The exceedingly complex religious geography of Arab Christianity requires us to differentiate by region in determining how locals negotiated these changes. Much of the Christian population was located in Syria, particularly in urban areas. The city of Aleppo stood out as a commercial center; its Christian population, largely Greek Orthodox, welcomed both the French and the missionaries. One reason was that the French could offer protection from raids on Ottoman ships by pirates, and it was understood that the price of such protection was submission to Rome. But Roman Catholicism had its own attractions. Missionaries were valued for their medical knowledge, by Muslims as well as Christians, during an outbreak of plague. Their schools provided instruction in valuable foreign languages and bookkeeping, in addition to religious instruction in Arabic. They opened schools for women as well, and women were encouraged to participate in worship.[38] In 1680, there were 24 Latin priests and 14 French merchants in Aleppo.[39] The movement spread to Damascus as well, where missionaries taught approximately 400 students in 1760.[40] Missionaries initially took a non-combative approach, avoiding theological debates, and working within the home. Gradually they succeeded in instilling a more Western sense of religiosity, focusing on examination of one's inner states through the vehicle of confession.[41] Soon, Aleppans were forming their own religious orders and creating monastaries.[42] The first Arabic printing press in the Ottoman Empire was introduced there in 1706, and Catholics were able to participate in the mass in their own tongue – centuries in advance of the Latin mass being abandoned by the Vatican. Bruce Masters concludes that Roman Catholicism gave Aleppans a rare opportunity for control over their own affairs.[43]

The Maronite church, with a long history of good relations with Rome, was especially responsive to the new missionary wave. The Maronites were concentrated in the rugged mountains of southern Syria known as Mount Lebanon, where they were relatively free from Ottoman interference. There they practiced what they considered to be a relatively pure form of Christianity. They shared the region with an independent Muslim sect, the Druzes. Relations between the two religious groups were nevertheless relatively peaceful and tolerant, illustrating the larger pattern within the empire. Maronites and Druzes shared power, sometimes within a single village, because both sides recognized a supposedly immutable social hierarchy of ruling families.[44] Symptomatic of their willingness to cooperate was their willingness to respond to a call to crusade: beginning in 1603 a Druze emir, Fakhr ad-Din II, staged an abortive uprising against the Ottomans and invited the Maronites to join his army. He made his way to Europe and had an audience with the pope, promising 20,000 Máronite soldiers. Fakhr-ad-Din eventually converted, and wore a crucifix when he was beheaded by the Ottomans in 1635.[45]

The Maronite College in Rome counted 280 pupils between 1580 and 1788 (though not all returned home).[46] Its daily routine followed that of the Jesuits, "meditation, examination of conscience, rosary, spiritual readings, catechism, confraternities, daily assistance at mass, more than monthly frequency of confession and communion."[47] The curriculum was that of the Roman seminary, with no concessions to oriental sensibilities, except for instruction in Arabic. There is evidence that the Maronite clergy actively sought instruction in literacy that the missionaries provided.[48] One of the graduates, Istifan Duwayhi, became a most energetic patriarch who brought Maronite ritual into line with that of Rome. Under his tenure (1670–1701) the Maronites expanded in number, with new monastaries and churches (in contravention, incidentally, to the Pact of Umar).

The Holy Land itself did not have a large Christian population–that of Jerusalem hovered around 10 percent in the sixteenth century – but was obviously of great symbolic importance and as a place of pilgrimage. European pilgrims dwindled in the seventeenth century, thanks to the danger posed by pirates, while those from the Ottoman Empire soared. One French observer counted only 80 Western pilgrims compared to the 6,000 from the East.[49] Relations with Muslims at these times were not always peaceful; a Good Friday procession was likely to be greeted by Muslim hecklers. But the main source of conflict was the rivalry between the Catholic, the Greek Orthodox, and the Armenian guardians of the Holy Places. The question of which party should conduct mass could lead to fistfights and even death.[50] Under Süleiman, the Greeks were favored and the Franciscans were excluded, but the French later made sure they were brought back. Europeans spent vast sums in order to maintain the Western presence there.[51] Perhaps the most striking feature, however, was the varying interpretations that the different Christian churches gave to the events of Holy Week. Western pilgrims focused on the suffering of Christ on Good Friday, retracing the stations of the cross. For the Greek and Armenian churches, the highlight was Saturday evening and the celebration of the "holy fire," stemming from a passage in the Old Testament (I Kings 18) when a fire was said to come from heaven to the prophet Elijah. Worshippers sought to receive the fire with candles and touch it with their garments or directly on the body in the belief that this contact would preserve them from the fires of hell. Needless to say, Western observers viewed this as the height of superstition.[52]

A third group of Arab Christians, the Egyptian Copts, remained largely impervious to missionary activity. The Copts had undergone drastic diminutions of numbers prior to the Ottoman conquest. They were mostly peasants, indistinguishable from their Muslim neighbors except in religion. Those in the cities were artisans or civil servants. They remained true to their miaphysite traditions and resisted attempts of Jesuits and others to convert them to Roman Catholicism. Only in the eighteenth century did migrations of Syrian merchants to Cairo give Catholicism much of a foothold.[53]

With the eighteenth century, the conflictual aspects of the Christians' attraction to Rome and the West began to emerge. In Egypt, tensions rose between Catholics and Copts, causing the latter to be more self-conscious about their traditions and to increase their sense of discipline.[54] In Aleppo, the drift of some Greek Orthodox bishops to Roman Catholicism now triggered a sharp reaction. This led to a series of conflicts over control of the church in Aleppo and Damascus, which became violent on occasion.[55] The Catholics survived through a combination of their own determination (sometimes holding services in private homes), French consular protection, and payoffs to local officials as the occasion demanded. Thus the attempt of Rome to unite the Arab Christians under its wing had just the opposite effect. To quote Haddad, "Where two Churches, the Maronite and [Greek] Orthodox ... had claimed the loyalty of upward of 90 percent of Syrian Christendom, there now stood three. And although the Orthodox maintained a numerical superiority over their Uniate kinsmen they lost to them some of their most elite elements."[56]

Such conflicts generated a certain amount of uncertainty over how far one should imitate the intensely pious ideals of the Jesuits. One can see this in a controversy within the Maronite community surrounding a female mystic, Hindiyya al-Ujaymi, the daughter of a prosperous Aleppo family and educated by the Jesuits. She engaged in bouts of frequent confession and extreme asceticism in a manner reminiscent of the Mohawk woman Kateri Tekakwitha; later she claimed that Jesus was speaking directly through her body. She founded an order of nuns in 1750 and moved to Mount Lebanon. All of this provoked suspicion from the Jesuits themselves and from Rome, while some Maronites came to her defense. Her order was suppressed, but she was eventually allowed to live in seclusion. She proved to be an embarrassment, however, to the Maronite community, poised as it was between its traditionalist Muslim and Orthodox neighbors.[57]

All in all, it is safe to say that the impact of these Western practices on Arab Christianity, while profound, were not so extensive as to overturn indigenous religion or society for the majority.[58] The process was more one of *incorporation* than of acculturation. To be sure, the emphasis on an individual's religious state, the spread of literacy, and the opening of opportunities to women within the church were significant changes. But the basics of Eastern ritual – the liturgy, calendar, icons, and so on – remained. Unlike the Western church, clergy retained the ability to marry. But the stage was set for further upheavals in the nineteenth century.

NINETEENTH CENTURY

For many Ottoman subjects, the nineteenth century, particularly the second half, might well be called the age of *unrequited acculturation.* On the one hand, European military, technological, economic, and cultural trends penetrated more deeply than ever before. Aside from steamship, telegraph, and railroad communication, more people were drawn into the market economy – both from the growing urban middle class and the farmers. The number and types of schools proliferated, creating a reading public with the development of newspapers, magazines, and novels. Western-style dresses and furnishings were evident in the cities. On the other hand, the indigenes' embrace of these trends collided with that bundle of negative stereotypes on the European side that Edward Said analyzed as Orientalism – "the self-containing, self-reinforcing character of a closed system," in his words.[59] Said showed how these stereotypes were increasingly based on secular categories such as race, character, temperament, and culture during the nineteenth century, in addition to generalized notions of progress that relegated Orientals to a backward status. Their characterization of the Ottoman Empire as the "sick man of Europe" was part of this, and the European powers did not hesitate to intervene in Ottoman affairs whenever it suited their imperialistic purposes – often under the pretext of protecting Christians, as in the Balkans.

Missionaries were of course active participants in this process, often penetrating into remote areas ahead of merchants and diplomats. They did not always subscribe to the secular narrative at first, having their own Biblical one, or see their role as necessarily dispensing secular knowledge. But over time the demands of their prospective converts, combined with the disruptions created by European penetration themselves, tended to bring missionaries over to the secular goals in the course of the century.[60] Of necessity, missionaries shifted their goals from outright evangelization to good works and living by example. They nevertheless doubtless contributed to the rigidification of boundaries between Christians and Muslim communities.[61]

The common political currency that emerged, so to speak, of both the imperialist incursions and the indigenous response to them proved to be nationalism: the Europeans supported the Christian groups in the Balkans against the Ottoman Empire to form their own nation states, and the Ottomans and their Middle Eastern subjects eventually adopted this European form of political expression in response – regardless of whether or not their ethnic, linguistic, or religious composition was well suited to the homogeneity and territorial integrity that nationalism presumed.

Let us trace these developments in several select instances in which negotiations with missionaries were involved.[62]

Syria and Lebanon

In the middle decades of the nineteenth century, Muslim-Christian relations, which had remained largely peaceful for centuries, underwent a change in parts of Syria that can only be described as a meltdown. In Mount Lebanon, within the space of four weeks in 1860, an estimated 12,000 Christians were killed and 100,000 were left homeless, creating a refugee problem for cities such as Beirut. Further incidents of mass violence occurred in Aleppo, Nablus, Mosul, Jeddah, and Damascus between 1850 and 1860.[63] Far from being an expression of primordial antagonisms, however, the causes of this deterioration were complex and time-specific. They might best be viewed as the end result of a chain reaction that began with the shock of Napoleon's invasion of Egypt in 1798. A common Muslim response to this was to suspect Arab Christians, regardless of sect, as being in collusion with the enemy (some were), a feeling that was reinforced by the next major blow, the Greek War of Independence in the 1820s.[64] Meanwhile, an Albanian soldier, Muhammad Ali, had taken power in Egypt, consciously integrating its economy with that of Europe and introducing Western learning – processes that favored Christians who were equipped to serve as mediators. Muhammad Ali's ambitions led him to invade and occupy Syria in the 1830s at the expense of the Ottomans, where he enacted similar policies. In order to win European favor, Christians were granted tax exemptions and accorded privileges normally accorded to Muslims.[65] Under Egyptian occupation, Beirut grew in importance as a port city, its population growing from 10,000 to 15,000, and Christian merchants were able to afford luxurious houses in Damascus as well. But cheap European imports undercut local artisans and traders, and many in the countryside chafed at the increased taxes and military conscription which the Egyptians had introduced, so that disenchantment was widespread by the end of the decade. The Druzes were the first to revolt, and the Egyptians responded by arming the Maronites. Eventually the European powers intervened, forcing the Egyptians to withdraw and restoring the Ottoman government.

The Ottoman response to these and other challenges was the series of decrees known as *Tanzimat*, or reorganization, over the next two decades. They were designed partly to assure the dynasty's survival by creating an army that could stand up to the Europeans; this would involve a more thorough system of taxation as well as conscription. But they were also intended to counteract the European stereotype of the Turks as backward and despotic, and also to bolster the loyalty of subjects to the Ottoman state itself. The initial rescript of 1839 combined conformity with shari'a law and European-style rights, but was widely misunderstood in the West; the subsequent declaration of 1856 was more emphatically European, stating that "every distinction or designation pending to make any class whatever of the subjects in my empire inferior to another class, on account of their religion, language, or race, shall be forever effaced from administrative protocol."[66] These represented an historic break with the *dhimmi* status that had governed the "peoples of the book" since the earliest days of Islam. It meant, among other things, that Christians felt they could publicly display crosses, conduct religious processions, and build new churches and cathedrals. It seems that this public display was the most galling of all to Muslims in cities like Aleppo, where such a procession touched off a riot in 1850. The protesters mentioned the ringing of church bells along with taxation and conscription in their list of grievances.[67]

The mere existence of the *Tanzimat* decrees on paper was a far cry from their being actualized on the ground. At first Ottoman authorities were at a loss to interpret them, much less enforce them.[68] The result was a vacuum of authority in which the simmering Druze-Maronite hostility in Mount Lebanon, stemming from the Egyptian occupation, would gradually intensify. Both factions appealed to European powers to bolster their case. The Maronites looked to the French, as they had done in the past; the Druzes, in response, looked to the British. As long as these disputes, over land and local control, were primarily among the ruling elites, they could be contained. But popular discontent welled up, motivated in large part by resentment against the new rich. In 1858, a charismatic muleteer named Tanyus Shahin led a revolt of villagers against the notables, driving them out. He appealed to the equality of all based on *Tanzimat*. Shahin was a Christian and soon began advocating the rights of all Christians, even in areas controlled by Druzes. By 1860, his followers were marching into Druze villages. The resultant highly charged atmosphere throughout the region was such that any individual act of violence – and there were many – could and did trigger mass slaughter. As word spread to Damascus, the massacres spread there as well.[69] This time the Ottoman army intervened with mass executions. The French intervened as well, arranging a settlement with the Ottomans whereby Mount Lebanon would become a semiautonomous region ruled by a non-Lebanese Christian governor – setting a precedent for the French mandate after World War I and the eventual establishment of Lebanon as an independent state in 1943.

With regard to the missionaries, the period was marked by a momentous change: the entry of British and American Protestants on the scene, a consequence of the second Great Awakening at home. Like the Catholics earlier, the Middle East, in particular the Holy Land, captured their imagination: the American Board of Commissioners for Foreign Missions (ABCFM) spent at least 45 percent of its entire budget on the region in 1860.[70] Protestant activity spurred competition from the Catholics, who returned in the 1830s after a hiatus and attracted many indigenous entrants into the religious orders by the end of the century. The Russians got into the act in the 1840s, supporting the Orthodox churches. The missionaries were protected by the foreign consulates, with the British covering for the Americans at first. Under pressure from the French, the Ottomans recognized the Syrian Catholics as a *millet* in 1830; British pressure brought similar recognition to the Protestants in 1847. The Protestant-Catholic rivalry became aligned with the Druze-Maronite conflict in Mount Lebanon.[71] Missionaries thus contributed to the sectarian tensions, although they too were shocked by the horrors of the 1860 massacres. That upheaval led them to turn away from purely evangelical activities toward secular ones.[72]

In general, one is struck by the huge discrepancy between the ambitious aims of these missionaries, particularly the Protestants, and their results. This discrepancy may serve as a gauge of indigenous attitudes and responses, for which we have very little independent evidence.[73] These aims may be summarized under three headings: (1) conversion of the Jews, stemming from the millenarian beliefs in the imminent second coming and the prophecy in the Book of Revelation that its first stage would be the conversion of Jews and their return to the Holy Land; (2)

reform of the Orthodox churches, which both Catholics and Protestants considered to be Christian in name only; their conversion to Western Christianity was still seen as setting an example that would result in the eventual conversion of the Muslims; (3) providing access to the Bible and to Christian practices and morals through translation and education, as well as medical assistance. These were not seen not as ends in themselves, but as a means for producing a new generation of Christians. Women's education was stressed, since women were crucial in conveying habits and values from one generation to another.

The first two of these aims failed spectacularly, while the third aim achieved considerable success, if not always in ways the missionaries had imagined.

The London Society for Promoting Christianity among the Jews, founded in 1809, was the most prominent of several such organizations.[74] Its influence in English ruling circles, together with similar sentiments in Germany, led to the founding of an Anglo-Prussian bishopric in Jerusalem in 1841. The response of the local rabbinate was decisive: to destroy the mission's literature and to forbid Jews any contact with it, including its medical service, on pain of total ostracism and denial of any legal protection under *dhimmi* status.[75] This did not entirely deter subsequent initiatives, but the goal of converting the Jews certainly receded by the second half of the century.[76] Jerusalem remained, however, the center of missionary interest, and became the site of multiple schools, orphanages, churches, and hospitals, constructed in Western architectural styles. Another missionary center was Nazareth, where, according to contemporary reports, Christians and Muslims lived in harmony.[77]

As for the Eastern Christian churches, the Protestants approached them with a full array of Orientalist stereotypes, which merged seamlessly with their anti-Catholic views. The missionaries' initial approach was confrontational; one depicted the pope as a mere "bit of clay."[78] As with the rabbinate, the response of the Maronite clergy to such insults was uncompromising: the patriarch's condemnation of 1823 portrayed the Protestants as agents of Satan; among their sins were the use of Arabic, preaching, journeying among the poor (the missionaries met regularly with beggars), and distributing unauthorized Bibles (the Protestant version, unlike the Catholic, omitted the Apocrypha). Maronites were forbidden to have any contact with them, on pain of excommunication. The patriarch was as good as his word; when the young As'ad Shidyaq, a highly educated member of a prominent Maronite family, went over to the Protestants, he was imprisoned, tortured, and died in solitude in 1830. The missionaries had their first martyr.[79]

By contrast, the missionaries' early success in education exceeded their fondest hopes. This began in Beirut, where the Americans had established a base in 1823. Because the first missionaries did not know the Arabic language, which limited their ability to preach, they decided to emphasize the distribution of printed literature to transmit the word of God, to be accompanied by schools with instruction in Arabic. This of course involved the hiring of native teachers. The first such "schools," begun in 1824, were highly informal, located in the missionaries' homes, which involved their wives as well. Within the first few months, the number of students rose from seven to almost 50, in the next year to 80 or 90, and by 1827 to about 600. Most of the students were from Greek Orthodox homes, which continued into the 1830s in spite of a ban from the patriarch.[80] When the missionaries had to leave temporarily in 1828 due to the Greek-Turkish War, they received a fond farewell from "droves of natives."[81] Although the numbers fluctuated in the subsequent turbulent years, by 1858 the missionaries could boast 30 primary schools with 1,020 pupils, all taught by native teachers.[82]

Of these pupils, 277 were girls. Female education began as early as 1824 in homes, with a separate school established in 1834 and a boarding school in 1847.[83] As a precursor of these, the missionaries instituted a system of "adopting" girls into their homes, helping with chores while receiving instruction. They were allowed one overnight visit at home per year. While Puritan virtues such as industry, punctuality, and cleanliness were emphasized, care was taken not to overly "Europeanize" them in terms of dress, for example. While this may sound like a harsh regime, genuine ties of affection could develop between the missionaries and their "adoptees," some of whom then formed the nucleus of a native Protestant church. One girl, Rahil Atta, married a Maronite named Butrus al-Bustani, who became an "adopted" son-in-law, worked and taught for the mission, converted to Protestantism, and went on to become one of Syria's foremost intellectuals.[84]

Despite these advances, the number of initial converts was small: only 75 in 1858. The numbers compared unfavorably with the ABCFM's successes in other parts of the world, such as Hawaii. Part of the problem was the missionaries' own high bar for admission, insisting on an interior conversion experience on the part of the individual, and their concomitant distrust of the sincerity of those who otherwise expressed interest. Matters came to a head in 1847, when a group of converts under

Al-Bustani's leadership petitioned the Americans for the formation of a church, saying, "We have forsaken our churches, prepared to undergo disgrace and persecution and loss . . . If we remain in our present unorganized state, we shall be weak in ourselves and appear so to those around us." Under pressure from Boston, the missionaries acceded in the following year.[85]

The sharp contrast between the numbers of students and converts is a telling indicator of indigenous interests and demands; they saw in mission schools a means of access to Western secular knowledge rather than purely religious inspiration. The history of the Protestant printing press in Beirut tells the same story: while it produced religious works and eventually a new translation of the Bible, it also printed school books in a variety of subjects, including geography, arithmetic, and algebra.[86] The Jesuits were especially adept at cultivating these demands, combining Christian education with Francophile cultural allegiance.[87]

The inclusion of secular education proved controversial for the Protestants: the head of the ABCFM at mid-century, Rufus Anderson, decidedly disagreed with any such pedagogy. "Civilization is not conversion," announced an ABCFM circular in 1856.[88] Anderson objected to the teaching of English in missionary schools rather than Arabic, on the grounds that pupils thus acculturated to Western ways "will be rendered unfit by their expensive tastes and habits to become the wives of the native preachers and pastors living on small salaries . . ."[89] The greater the trend toward secular education, the more Anderson dug in his heels. But, thanks largely to competition from Catholic schools, he eventually lost the battle to the missionaries in the field – and to the Syrian Protestants themselves.[90]

The massacres of 1860 constituted a low point from which Syrian society was able to recover. Christian and Muslim elites alike realized they had to actively keep the peace and search for commonalities to overcome sectarianism. Al-Bustani reflected this trend: having left the ABCFM mission in 1851 (where he had earned a mere $300 a year), he established in 1863 a "national" boarding school, with students deliberately recruited from a variety of sects – over the objections of both the Maronite and Protestant clergies. He had already begun to advocate an Arab cultural awakening and a Syrian patriotism in print.[91]

The peacemakers of the 1860s and '70s were aided by several factors. First, the centralizing measures and promotion of Ottoman loyalty by Sultan Abdulhamid (r. 1876–1909), while regarded as cruel and repressive in much of the empire and in the English-speaking world, was actually welcomed by his Arab subjects for including local notables in his bureaucracy. Second, the region was benefitting from the fruits of the industrial revolution in terms of improved communications (telegraph, railroads, steamship travel). Not the least of these fruits was a burgeoning press, so that missionary publications became part of a larger stream of literature. There were 16 printing presses in Syria in 1868.[92]

All this provided a setting for an Arab modernist literary renaissance. The role missionaries played in starting it has been the subject of controversy.[93] They certainly deserve credit for developing a standard Arabic font for use in print, and Christian intellectuals played a prominent role in the early stages. But this argument minimizes the fact that Islamic cultural tradition, with its embrace of reason and science, provided a sufficient basis for such modernism, and Muslim schools and institutions were able to respond to the stimulus from the West on their own accord. Muslim and Christian reformers held oddly parallel views; each identified their religion with its civilizational accomplishments rather than with any particular belief or ritual.[94]

At the same time, this situation provided a classic case of genuine if *selective acculturation* to Western ways on the part of Syrian Christians. This was evident not only in the reception of European fiction in the Beirut literary periodicals, but even more strikingly in the countryside of Mount Lebanon, where it triggered a huge wave of emigration to the Americas - over one-third of the population – between 1890 and 1915.[95] This was due partly to a population explosion, partly to the loss of income from the silk export industry on which many peasants had depended. In any case, a significant portion of these emigrants returned home, bringing Western dress, marriage and childrearing customs, and educational ideals back with them. This by no means amounted to a complete rejection of Eastern ways, but it did dramatically increase the demand for missionary education, both for boys and girls. It was estimated that by the turn of the century, there were some 10,000 girls and 60,000 boys attending school, numbers far greater than in other parts of the Ottoman Empire.[96] An annual report from the American School for Girls in Beirut cites a number of parents as saying, "Yes; we want English, but we want more than the language, we want American manners and spirit instilled into our daughters."[97]

The behavior of the missionaries themselves in this situation seemed curiously contradictory. On the one hand, they embraced more than ever the Arab demand for nonreligious instruction and Western knowledge. The founding of Syria Protestant College in 1866 was the most notable example, ostensibly to "open the door for giving the Arab race the treasures of literature, science, art and religion, which are stored in the European languages, and help repay the East for its contribution to the revival of letters in Europe in centuries past," though an internal memo stated another reason, namely to prevent Protestant youth "from being drawn into papal institutions."[98] (The Jesuits responded with St. Joseph's University in 1875). In addition, the mission press published a number of periodicals designed to acquaint Arab readers with Western science and culture. The monthly *al Muqtataf* (The Digest) had a circulation of some 3,000 in the 1880s and became the preeminent journal for transmitting Western science in the Arab lands; the weekly *al-Nashra al-Usubu'iya*, on a variety of subjects with a circulation of 1,100, contained many articles written by Syrian Protestants themselves, including women.[99] An analysis of these writings reveals a striking difference of tone when compared to the missionaries' writings themselves: the Syrians showed a greater degree of civility and respect for Catholics, Orthodox, and Muslims.[100]

On the other hand, as part of a wave of heightened evangelistic activity and self-confidence worldwide, and encouraged by the official proclamations of religious equality of the *Tanzimat* era, Christian missionaries now started turning their attention to converting Muslims, a goal that proved to be scarcely less delusional at the end of the nineteenth century than the conversion of Jews had been at the beginning.[101] But it produced a good bit of defamatory rhetoric along the way, particularly against the Ottoman Empire, whose days they regarded as numbered and whose understandable attempts to regulate schools within its borders were portrayed as religious intolerance. Most vitriolic of all was William Ewart Gladstone, British prime minister intermittently between 1868 and 1894, who referred to the Turks as "the one great anti-human specimen of humanity." A *Punch* cartoon from 1895 depicts him in a crusader's armor.[102] Missionaries rejoiced at the British occupation of Egypt in 1882, which they hoped would be a prelude to her control of the entire region.[103] All this was to do irreparable harm to their cause and foment long-term *resistance*.[104]

One way in which missionaries sought to reconcile these opposing tendencies was to adopt a bastion mentality with regard to the institutions they had established. Thus, for example, the Syrian Protestant College was open to students of all faiths, but once admitted, all were required to attend prayers twice a day plus two services on Sunday and Bible study every Wednesday. A similar strategy obtained for a proposed CMS hospital in Nablus, Palestine: within its four walls, missionaries would be free to proselytize Muslims, e.g., by reading the Bible to patients in waiting rooms. Such strategies only invited hostility and conflict: residents of Nablus sought to obstruct the project, while Muslim and Jewish students at Syrian Protestant College struck against compulsory church attendance.[105] Moreover, the limits of Protestant openness to science were shown in the College's censure of a faculty member who lectured on Darwin's theory of evolution, an incident which divided the faculty and the student body. Islamic modernists responded by claiming there was no conflict between Darwin and Islam.[106]

Arab modernists, like their contemporaries in West Africa and many other parts of the world, faced a corresponding dilemma: they were attracted to Western technology, culture, and values on the one hand, but were rejected by Westerners themselves as inferior on the other hand. It was becoming clear that the Westernizing reforms such as the *Tanzimat* measures did not bring the Ottomans acceptance into the European club.

Muslim modernist intellectuals were increasingly and painfully aware of this contradiction in the 1870s and '80s. One result was a turn toward *resistance* in the form of pan-Islamism, which sought to unite Muslims from across the Asian continent.[107] For these intellectuals, this turn by no means entailed a rejection of Western humanistic values or rationalism, but only of the West's own double standard in living up to them. A good example is the Turkish thinker Halil Halid, whose book *The Crescent Versus the Cross* (1907) criticized the West's civilizing impulse and its Christian bias.[108] Thus, the Western powers were willing to promote independence for such Christian minorities as Bulgarians and Armenians, while simultaneously conquering and occupying Muslim areas like Egypt, Tunisia, and later Libya in violation of international law. At the same time, there was a revival of interest in the Ottoman sultan in his capacity as caliph, i.e., protector of Muslims throughout the world – a position which had been explicitly mentioned in the constitution of 1876. This prospect stirred considerable debate both in the empire and abroad. Abdulhamid did not actively promote the idea in the hopes of sustaining friendly relations with Britain and France as in the past. But he did unofficially promote Pan-Islamic ideas and connections to the extent that he could.[109] He also showed increasing *resistance* to missionary penetration by building government schools to compete with the Christian ones, by monitoring the latter, and even sending Sunni missionaries to groups which showed signs of deviating from Islam.[110]

The appeal of Pan-Islamism would eventually be outstripped by that of nationalism itself, as was already demonstrated in the Balkan Peninsula and later adopted by the Turks themselves. But nationalism was especially problematic in the Middle East – moreso than in other parts of the Ottoman Empire. Was the nation to be Ottoman? Muslim? Syrian? Lebanese? Arabic? No clear answer had emerged by the time of the First World War.

Egypt

This dilemma is well illustrated by the Egyptian Copts. In contrast to previous centuries, the Copts experienced a remarkable growth in numbers, wealth, and confidence in the course of the nineteenth century. Missionaries played no small role in this, though not an exclusive one. Copts were able to advance in government positions that the Ottomans had vacated during the Napoleonic invasion and made further gains under Muhammad Ali. The latter's modernization policies also invited an influx of Europeans to Egypt, especially from Latin countries, doubling the size of the Catholic population. Protestant missionaries came in two waves, the first from England, the second from the United States, focusing on the urban and rural populations, respectively. The American Presbyterians outfitted a riverboat and sailed up and down the Nile selling Arabic Bibles. The response was positive, since Coptic, the language of the church, was little used beyond it, while Arabic was the true vernacular. Soon Egyptians themselves were doing the selling. Moreover, the Coptic clergy did not object to Bible distribution at first, though their resistance mounted sharply as the missionaries gained steam and were winning converts themselves, leading to small but resilient Catholic and Protestant churches.[111] Nevertheless, according to Heather J. Sharkey, "by the early twentieth century, the Coptic Orthodox Church had fully embraced the Arabic Bible and the culture of Bible-reading, and was arguably developing evangelical strains of its own."[112] The American and British Bible societies sold a total of 7,622 volumes of scripture in a single year.[113] Moreover, the influence of missionary education could be seen in the curriculum of the school that the Copts themselves established under Patriarch Cyril IV in 1855, which attracted the sons of the elite, furthering their position in Egyptian society. By 1891, the landholdings of the wealthiest Copts ranked just behind the descendants of Muhammad Ali and other high officials.[114] For good reason, the late nineteenth century has been called the golden age of Coptic history.

Such prominence was bound to provoke resentment, which became acute under the British occupation. As had occurred many times in the past, Christians were tarred by association with a foreign power, whether justifiably or not, and this applied to both missionaries and the Copts themselves. The growing pan-Islamic movement played on such sentiments. But the Copts could – and did – claim that *they* were the original true Egyptians, and that subsequent groups, including Arab Muslims, were the foreign invaders. These competing nationalisms were played out in the press, and in 1910 a Copt minister was assassinated. The outcome of these tensions was to increase pressure for a purely secular Egyptian nationalism, which the First World War only intensified, and which would lead to increasing waves of anti-missionary activity in the 1920s and 1930s.[115]

Nestorians ("Assyrians") and Armenians

Mention should be made of these two non-Arab peoples, who were most receptive to Western missionaries in the nineteenth century – with huge unintended consequences both for the missionaries and themselves.

Members of the now shrunken Church of the East, known variously as Nestorians, Chaldeans, Syrians, and later Assyrians, were dispersed across the regions that spanned the Ottoman, Persian, and Russian empires.[116] Many of them lived in feudal subordination to the Kurds, who were accustomed to tolerate the great variety of religious allegiances that existed in the region. In the nineteenth century, these Christians became increasingly caught in the crossfire of great power rivalries, including the British, who were seeking a land route to India. Competing groups of missionaries – Catholics, Anglicans, and American Presbyterians – were frequently aligned with these interests, creating situations not unlike the crisis of 1860 in Lebanon, as when the Kurds, reacting to perceived threats, massacred some 7,000 Christians in 1843.[117] At the same time, it is clear that the Nestorian leaders themselves sometimes welcomed missionary aid precisely because they were seeking foreign political and military protection. Toward the end of the century, some 10,000 Nestorians in Persia signed a petition to unite with the Russian Orthodox Church.[118] This did not prevent the growth of a flourishing American-run Protestant church, with an impressive network of schools and publications, in northwestern Persia, particularly in the city of Urmiah, with about 3,000 members on the eve of the First World War.[119]

It is through these publications that Nestorians learned of the archaeological discovery of the ancient Assyrian palace at Nineveh in 1843 along with some 22,000 clay tablets reinforcing much of the Old Testament story, and by the end of the century, they had come to think of themselves as descendants of the Assyrians.[120] This "invented tradition" was part of their growing sense of nationhood, marked also by the appearance of a nationalist biweekly newspaper, *The Star*, in 1906 and a National Assembly in 1907.[121]

The tragedy of the Armenian genocide in the Ottoman Empire is well known, and even commentators sympathetic to the missionary enterprise attribute to it a certain role in contributing to that tragedy, if only by fostering a heightened national consciousness through a written vernacular and by creating unrealistic expectations as to what the Armenians could achieve on their own.[122] But the missionary component was only a part in a much more complex story.

The Armenians' past had been exceptionally fragmented. Not only were they dispersed across the three empires, speaking multiple dialects, but there was a sharp division between rural and urban populations. The latter formed the basis of the Armenian merchant and banking community in places like Istanbul and Smyrna (though there were also significant class differences within these communities). In 1700, there were about 60,000 Armenians in Istanbul, including 8000 Catholics. By 1808, the latter number had increased to 30,000.[123] The Armenian elite was active in establishing schools before the missionaries arrived in Istanbul, but once they did, Armenians made up a large part of the student body in the missionary schools and colleges.[124] The attraction of Bible study in the growth of an Armenian Protestant church has been well documented.[125] During the *Tanzimat* era, the Ottomans recognized separate *millets* for both Catholic (1834) and Protestant (1850) Armenians, though not without outside pressure from the French and the British, respectively. By the end of the century, Armenians, mostly from the Istanbul elite, were able to enter the civil service; a study of 366 files of bureaucrats between 1850 and 1908 revealed 52 Armenians.[126] By this time, the community had already fashioned a national constitution with representative bodies with the aim of providing self-government for the *millet*.[127]

All this bespeaks a significant degree of *acculturation*, both toward Western culture and ideas and to Ottoman society as it moved in the same direction. Admittedly, this process was not entirely smooth: there was resistance from the patriarch of the Armenian church and reprisals from the Ottoman government on occasions when its Western "friends" turned hostile (as when the French destroyed the Turkish fleet at Navarino Bay in 1827, leading to the temporary expulsion of the

Catholic missionaries). But the overall process was clear and gave no indication of what was later to come.

Even more remarkable was a similar process occurring in the rural areas of eastern Anatolia. In 1855 an American Protestant missionary arrived in the remote province of Kharpert, the site, as legend had it, of the Garden of Eden. By 1890 the mission consisted of 25 churches and almost 2,000 members. It boasted a complete educational system, from primary school through college, including schools for women. Literacy was the main hook; the Bible as the principal text.[128]

The force that reversed this tide was clearly nationalism, which in the Armenian case was inspired more by secular than by religious ideas. A group of Armenian intellectuals living in western Europe brought with them the idea of national independence, which had an anti-clerical twist; the Western missionaries opposed it as well.[129] The main inspiration came from the Balkans, where nationalities such as the Bulgarians were liberating themselves from the Ottoman Empire with Western and Russian assistance. The Armenians hoped to get similar guarantees from the Western powers at the Congress of Berlin in 1878, but had the misfortune of coming to these ideas later than the others, when Ottoman resistance had already stiffened. The Western powers had used the excuse of protection of Christian minorities for interference one time too many. In these circumstances, the requests of the Armenian assembly for autonomy proved futile, and by the 1880s more young people were embracing revolutionary methods and parties, leading to a cycle of violence and counterviolence. The revolutionaries held out the hope of triggering British assistance, as the Bulgarians had done. But despite Gladstone's urgings, the British declined to respond.

The Ottomans' response to these challenges, as it developed in the wake of the loss of their Christian territories in the Balkans, was one of "exemplary repression," to quote Ronald Grigor Suny.[130] In 1890, Abdulhamid established extra regiments of Kurds to deal with any local disturbances in eastern Anatolia. These regiments were exempt from regular military discipline and would play a key role in the atrocities that were to come.[131] Although the radical revolutionary movement was hardly representative of the entire Armenian population, the authorities came to believe that it did so, and this belief was widely shared by the neighboring Muslim population. Economic resentment toward the more prosperous and educated Armenians played a powerful role as well. The result was a series of massacres resulting in the deaths of an estimated 100,000–300,000 Armenians in 1895–96, with massive flights of refugees to neighboring countries – foreshadowing the even larger killings that took place during the First World War. Missionaries witnessed these massacres firsthand. Although none lost their lives and no schools were closed, thanks to government protection, the Ottomans became convinced that the missionaries had played an active role in fomenting the insurgency.[132] Missionary involvement in the Middle East had increased sevenfold in the previous decade, and much of the ABCFM's work was with the Armenians.[133] As also might be expected, tensions between the Armenians and the surrounding Muslim population also increased. Another massacre in 1909 at Adana, the ancient Armenian capital, half of which was burned to the ground, appeared to be more a product of this local hostility than of state-sponsored terrorism.[134]

The underlying cause of the Armenian and Assyrian tragedies was the incompatibility of the national principle, based as it was on ethnic or linguistic or religious homogeneity, with the actual existence of multiple interspersed nationalities that characterized the region. Sadly, this was to become the main narrative of the Middle East in the twentieth century – and into the twenty-first century.

TWENTIETH CENTURY

In contrast to much of the world, World War I in the Middle East may be viewed less as a turning point in itself than as the middle phase of a revolution that began with the Young Turk revolt in 1908 and ended with the proclamation of the Turkish Republic in 1923. As the missionary historian Kenneth Latourette noted in 1945, the upheavals resulting from this revolution meant that there were fewer Christians in proportion to the total population of the region than any time since the second or third century.[135] Events since 1945 have depleted that proportion much further.

The Young Turks consisted of several factions, one of which espoused European values such as constitutionalism and representative government, while another leaned toward authoritarian nationalism. Unfortunately, the next few years witnessed the the Ottoman Empire's further dismemberment in Europe, leading to the dominance of the authoritarian wing. Once again, Britain and France showed no interest in helping the Ottomans, acceding to the Italian annexation of Libya in 1911 and the conquests of the Balkan League in 1912, which virtually drove the Ottomans off the European continent – a loss of almost four million inhabitants.[136] The Balkan Wars also witnessed instances of "ethnic cleansing" on all sides, as each nation-state sought to make its territory ethnically homogenous. This meant the killing and expulsion of Balkan Muslims, largely at the hands of Christians; these refugees fled to Anatolia. Thus the effect of the Balkan Wars was to turn the Empire into much more of a Muslim region than it had been previously. Small wonder, then, that the Ottomans turned away from Britain and France and toward Germany as an ally and toward Pan-Islamism and Turkish nationalism as ideologies.[137] It was small wonder also that their desire for retribution would be visited on the Christians who remained – primarily the Greeks and Armenians.

Once war broke out, the government wasted no time in abrogating the centuries-long capitulations for the British and French; in November 1914, it formally declared jihad against the Triple Entente. While the declaration did not mention Christianity, in deference to their German and Austrian allies, the propaganda appeals to Muslim solidarity probably had the effect of unleashing further hatred of Christians by local populations. At a more mundane level, these proclamations ruptured the financial links between missionaries and their western European benefactors, leading to a drastic reduction of Christian orphanages, schools, and hospitals and an exodus of Catholics. The United States, however, remained neutral, in order to protect its trade and its missionaries, and the Ottomans allowed them to remain.[138] They were, of course, exposed to the dangers of being in a war zone, which engulfed much of the Middle East, as the Turks fought the Russians on one side and the British and French on the other. The Armenians lived on both sides of the Turco-Russian border and thus were caught in the war zone; this fed the Ottomans' suspicion that they were collaborating with the enemy, especially after a major defeat in the winter of 1914–15. Persia was also drawn in to this war zone, and it is estimated that as much as one-quarter of its population died, mostly from famine and disease.[139]

The Great War in the Middle East brought with it the massive slaughter of Christians – not only the Armenians, but Syrian Orthodox, Assyrians, and Maronites as well.[140] On the eve of the genocide, the Interior Minister Talaat Pasha informed the Armenian patriarch that "there was no room for Christians in Turkey," and advised him to leave the country.[141] Soon the government, in full control of the Ottoman bureaucracy, was methodically rounding up Armenian men throughout Anatolia and killing them, torturing and deporting the women and children to Syria and Lebanon under inhuman conditions. Churches were also deliberately destroyed – although American missions and schools were allowed to remain, in Beirut as in Istanbul. By the end of the revolutionary period in 1923, an estimated 1.5 million Armenians had perished, while the Syrian Orthodox lost over 90,000, more than one-third of its population in the Middle East.[142] Further to the east, the Assyrian Christians fled the avenging Turks to join the Russians, while others found refuge in Persian Urmiah. This was the scene of an act of great missionary heroism in 1915, as the American and French Catholic missions organized a safe area for some 20,000 Assyrians. Urmiah changed hands several times, however, and at the end of the war, the Christians, no longer safe, fled en masse, becoming another group of homeless, stateless refugees.[143] The end result of all these dislocations and massacres was an estimated loss of some 250,000 Christians other than Armenians – collectively remembered as the *sayfo* (the sword) and now seen as the result of deliberate Ottoman policy.[144]

The great suffering brought on by these ruptures – not to mention the famine in Beirut stemming from the disruption of Anglo-French trade – led to an impressive American relief effort in 1915 that, though spurred and financed in large part by missionaries, channeled these charitable impulses toward a nonsectarian humanitarian organization, in effect secularizing the missionary project. The American Committee for Armenian and Syrian Relief, chaired by the foreign secretary of the ABCFM, was made up of clergy (including a rabbi), college presidents, and businessmen. Within two years it raised over four million dollars.[145] It later became known as Near East Relief.

The appeal to Muslim solidarity led to the diminution of Christian influence in yet another respect. Responding to the propaganda of an Islam based on Turkish nationalism, the British and French now saw fit to present themselves not so much as protectors of Christianity but as advocates of a freshly minted Arab nationalism, and found ready support among Egyptian spokesmen. Here is part of a proclamation from Muslim scholars at Al-Azhar University in Cairo in 1916:

The Turks have a grudge against the Arabic language, the language of the Prophet and the Qur'an, the language of prayer, and seek to destroy it and substitute their own. Therefore our language, hunted down everywhere in Turkey, was able to find asylum only in two regions that have escaped the hold of the Turks, thanks to France and England: Syria and Egypt.[146]

The allies succeeded in engineering an Arab revolt against the Turks and raised hopes for independence at the conclusion of the war. These were reinforced by Wilson's Fourteen Points, which specifically mentioned the nationalities under Turkish rule. But the British and French had other plans, which called for dividing the region into spheres of influence and acceding to Jewish Zionists' request for a homeland, formalized respectively in the secret Sykes–Picot Agreement of 1916 and the public Balfour Declaration the following year. Faced with the contradiction between these aspirations, the victors at the Paris Peace Conference arrived at the compromise formula of "mandates" under the League of Nations, which would preserve colonial rule until the Arabs became sufficiently "developed" to govern themselves – a formula that Wilson found acceptable but most Arab leaders did not. The arbitrariness of the Sykes–Picot borders created a formula for disaffection and instability that has plagued the region ever since.

The wartime plans of the allies also called for the partition of Anatolia, written into the Treaty of Sèvres in 1919, which provided for an Armenian and a Kurdish state. But this time the Turks had other plans, as Mustafa Kemal ejected the occupying powers from the region and created the Turkish Republic, which was recognized by the powers at the Lausanne Conference in 1923.[147] The principle of ethnic and religious homogeneity was reinforced as Turks in Greece moved east to Anatolia, while Greek inhabitants of Anatolia were moved westward – about 1.4 million – removing the last remaining sizable Christian minority from Turkey. The bulk of the Armenian survivors of the genocide, many of them orphans, were concentrated in the cities of Syria and Lebanon. The Near East Relief was able to care for about 132,000 of them.[148]

Another example of the lingering instability was the fate of the Assyrian Christian refugees. Fleeing from Persia at the end of the war, they turned to the British for protection, who resettled them in the area north of Mosul in what became Iraq; the British also armed them in order to defend themselves – and British interests as well. At Lausanne, the Turks made it clear that they had no interest in repatriating them, so they remained an armed minority in Iraq – until that country gained nominal independence from the British mandate in 1930. Soon clashes between the Assyrian and Iraqi armed forces developed, leading to more massacres and burning of villages. Many Assyrians then fled to northeastern Syria, where they settled in a fertile region and were granted Syrian citizenship in 1941. Many had emigrated, and the patriarch of the Assyrian church resided in the United States from 1940 until 2015.[149]

As peacetime conditions returned, so did the missionaries, who more often than not faced an increasingly hostile reception, although this varied from country to country. The Turkish Republic was avowedly secular, having broken its ties with Islam by renouncing the caliphate; but it was no more open to Christian conversion and outlawed the teaching of Christianity in schools and hospitals to non-Christians. The schools themselves were still welcome, however, as desirable centers of Western learning.[150] In Persia, now Iran, the government also embraced Westernization, but likewise restricted Christian instruction and in 1934 expelled all foreigners, including missionaries, from the Urmiah region, fearing more unrest.[151]

The situation was quite different in the areas under the French and British mandates. The French had justified their claim to Syria and Lebanon partly on their long-standing and extensive missionary institutions, and now asserted that they taught over half the schoolchildren in Syria, Lebanon, and Palestine. The Jesuits alone had 150 schools, not to mention the St. Joseph University in Beirut.[152] They still maintained an air of Western, especially French, superiority. Along with other missionary schools, they were responsible for the high level of literacy in Lebanon—the highest in the Arab world—but also to its cultural fragmentation. According to Elizabeth Thompson, "Most [students] went to a myriad of private and foreign schools, each with its own curriculum, its own literature, its own history books. Maronites learned that Lebanon's origins were in ancient Phoenicia. Arabist schools taught their Greek Orthodox and Muslim students that Lebanon was part of the great Arab civilization that bloomed in the Middle Ages."[153]

On the Protestant side, the Syrian Protestant College underwent a development parallel to that of the Near East Relief in philanthropy: its board of trustees dropped the religious affiliation, renaming it the American University of Beirut in 1920, partly in response to its prior difficulties in appealing to Muslim, Jewish, and Eastern Christian students. Its academic reputation as a liberal arts college drew students from all over the Arab world, but Its identity as an American-run institution made it the focal point of violent protest over US pro-Israel policies in the 1960s and '70s.

The British mandate in Palestine had the effect of opening the floodgates to Protestant missionaries, especially from the United States. There were over thirty such societies operating there in the 1920s, in addition to Catholic and Orthodox organizations.[154] Such efforts largely ran aground, however, in the face of British support of Zionism, which Arabs – Muslim and Christian alike – generally opposed. Palestinian Christians played an especially active role as spokesmen for this opposition early on, as they had benefited from missionary education and were highly acculturated to Western ways (one of them, Edward Said, was named after the Prince of Wales).[155] Two Arab newspapers that took the lead in opposing Zionism were owned by Christians; following the Balfour Declaration, a number of joint Muslim-Christian associations were formed.[156] In short, the growth of Zionism leading to the state of Israel created the conditions for a dominant strategy of *resistance* to missionaries among Christians themselves.

Following the creation of Israel in 1948, the new government banned missionary activity but was anxious to maintain good relations with the West and to promote religious tourism. Once they gained control of the Holy Places in Jerusalem following the 1967 war, the Israelis faced the same dilemma of placating the different Christian groups that had existed since medieval times. The Vatican had long called for the internationalization of the city and did not recognize the state of Israel until 1994. The churches also had the dilemma of working with the state while ministering to their Palestinian congregants, many of whom had been expelled along with Muslims when Israel was create – some 50,000 Christians out of 700,00–800,000 Arabs. Given their educational advantages, many Palestinian Christians chose to emigrate: in the occupied territories they constituted about 3 percent of the Arab population, compared to 10 percent during the mandate period, while in Israel itself the decline was from 21% in 1950 to 9% in 2003.[157] At the same time, the state of Israel was attractive to a growing generation of Evangelicals, who saw it as a step toward the fulfilment of the millennial prophecy. They tended to support Jewish settlers on Palestinian territory, bringing them into conflict with the older churches.[158]

The case of Egypt offers an exceptionally clear outline of the trajectory followed by most Arab states as they extricated themselves from colonial ties. At the end of World War I, Egypt was still under British control, but the movement for independence had grown quite strong, leading to the first steps in that direction in 1922. Still, there were about 450 missionaries in Egypt in 1930, with a native staff of about 1,400.[159] Moreover, Britain had allowed missionaries to try and convert Muslims. A highly vocal proponent of this, the American Samuel Zwemer, took to distributing missionary tracts in the courtyard of Al-Azhar, the venerable center of Islamic learning in Cairo. In the 1920s, the consequences of such tactics came home to roost, and Zwemer's actions prompted a strike of some 3,000 students in 1928 and later a strong anti-missionary manifesto from Al-Azhar clergy.[160] At the same time, a number of Muslim associations were formed to actively promote Muslim culture, some of them

borrowing missionary tactics such as the distribution of tracts. One of
them, the Muslim Brotherhood, eventually became the most famous. Like
the others, it publicly opposed missionary activity. Then, in 1933, an
incident in a Christian orphanage inflamed public opinion across Egypt:
a Muslim orphan girl, Turkiyya Hasan, was caned for refusing to stand
for Christian prayer; in the same year, the Muslim Brotherhood doubled
its branches throughout Egypt.[161] In 1934, the government enacted the
first of a series of laws restricting missionary education, culminating in a
1958 measure requiring that school directors be Egyptian. This meant
that foreign missions had to transfer their school properties to the native
Coptic Protestant church. By this time, missionaries had long since given
up their conversion efforts, focusing instead on service projects.[162]

As elsewhere in the Middle East, American and British recognition of
Israel only enflamed Egyptian public opinion further, for which missionaries paid a price, regardless of their own attitudes toward the Jewish
state. In 1953 a book appeared by two Lebanese Muslims, Mustafa
Khalidi and'Umar Farrukh, entitled *Evangelism and Imperialism in the
Arab World*, which went through six Arabic editions in the next thirty
years. The authors argued that missions represented the most dangerous
aspect of Western imperialism and revived the rhetoric of the crusade to
characterize them.[163] Even the missionaries' translations of the Bible into
vernacular dialects came under suspicion as a strategy of divide-and-
conquer. Only classical Arabic, the language of past cultural glory, was
fitting.[164] The ignominy of Egypt's defeat in the 1967 war with Israel
marked the crowning blow, and the last American missionaries were
forced to leave Cairo under the cover of darkness.[165] Some returned,
but only as guests of the Coptic Evangelical Church. This pattern of
collaborating with local churches has become typical in subsequent years.

Meanwhile, the Copts themselves developed a missionary movement
directed to sub-Saharan Africa. They could claim to be historically the
original Christian church of Africa and also free from the taint of Western
imperialism. In 2014, they could claim approximately 400,000 members
south of the Sahara.[166]

The 1967 war and its aftermath proved to be a marker in a number of
respects – not a turning point, in that it merely perpetuated the cycle of
artificial borders, disaffected peoples, armed militias, civil warfare, and
refugees that had plagued the region since World War I. In this instance
the victim was Lebanon, which had achieved some measure of stability
from the 1940s to the early 1970s. But the Israeli-Palestinian conflict
spilled into Lebanon thereafter, hollowing out the society and creating

a conglomeration of militia-run ghettoes in Beirut. In another way, Israel's occupation of the Holy Places has had an unexpected effect: a rare missionary success story that brought genuine conversions from Jews. The missionaries here were Evangelicals, who saw in the retaking of the temple a fulfilment of their prophecy. This prompted a change in attitude toward Jews, embracing them as the chosen people, pointing toward the second coming of Christ. For some Israelis disillusioned with Zionism and the warfare it has brought, this was an attractive alternative. The resultant "messianic Judaism" is a genuine syncretism of the two religions, combining Jewish and Christian holidays and prayer books. The estimated number of Messianic Jews in Israel in 2012 was between 10 and 20,000.[167]

Messianic Judaism has little to say about Arabs and Islam; but here too one can point to a genuine change of attitude on the part of many Christians, especially their higher institutions. Thus the Second Vatican Council issued a proclamation in 1965 calling for mutual understanding with Muslims; the Protestant World Council of Churches issued a set of guidelines for interfaith dialogue in 1979. In his 2006 contribution to the *Cambridge History of Christianity* on Christian-Muslim relations, David Thomas asserts that "the changes in these attitudes have been more fundamental than in any other period in the fourteen hundred years of shared Christian and Muslim history."[168] At the same time, he finds that neither Catholics nor Protestants have entirely succeeded in overcoming the tension between the need for dialogue and the pull of mission.[169] The Lebanese-American Muslim scholar Mahmoud Mustafa Ayoub, who has devoted much of his professional career to promoting Muslim-Christian dialogue, also concludes that thus far neither side is willing to accept the other's faith in their own terms – the age-old problem of exclusivism.[170]

The upheavals of the second decade of the present century – the civil wars resulting from the Arab Spring and the growth of radical Islamist movements such as ISIS – have only increased the persecution and displacement of Arab Christians. As Eleanor Tejirian and Reeva Specter Simon conclude in their study of Christian missions in the region, "The Middle East has become more than ever the Muslim world."[171] Muslim *resistance* to Western secularism is strong, and Arab resistance to missionary Christianity as an extension of Western imperialism is bound up with it, reinforced by American Christians' widespread support of Israel.

Given these undeniable trends, it may be tempting to accept the picture of a "Clash of Civilizations" as becoming more and more true in the Middle East. Yet this ignores a powerful alternative narrative that applies

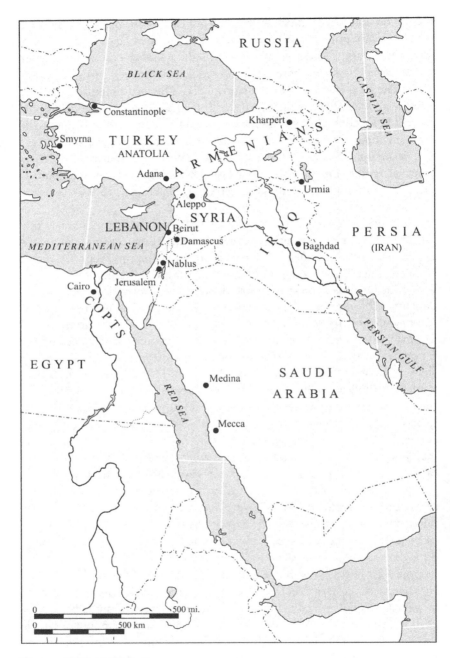

Figure 5.1 The Middle East
Source: Drawn by Mary Lee Eggart

both to the past and the present, namely one of interconnectedness via migration. The very persecutions of Arab Christians in recent times has led to waves of emigration, with strong diasporas among Maronites, Assyrian Christians, and Syrian Orthodox. The need for guest workers in Europe, primarily in Sweden and Germany, contributed to this trend in the late twentieth century. At the same time, the demand for immigrant labor in the Arab Gulf states has brought a significant increase of Christians to the Middle East. Naturally these situations pose challenges of balancing acculturation with preserving one's cultural and religious identity.[172] Yet the strong pull of the latter impulse can create temptations of its own toward simplification and reification of the past. As the historian Bernard Heyberger eloquently writes:

The massacres of 1860, of 1915, and of the Lebanese civil war, in addition to recent attacks against Christians in Egypt and Iraq, are always remembered and often recalled. In these ways, the narratives of Eastern Christians produced from within the community remain, for the most part, mired in polemics. The production of a discourse based on the methods and ethics of the humanities could help people to move beyond these traumas, to calm the suffering of the memory, and to begin to discover new facets of the history of Eastern Christians .... . As Paul Ricoeur eloquently puts it, the historian helps the society to treat the pain of remembrance and contributes in this way to leaving the dead to rest in peace.[173]

6

India

INTRODUCTION

It is generally acknowledged that Hinduism, as the name of a distinct religion, did not exist before the nineteenth century. Before that, the term "Hindu" had simply meant "Indian" and was derived from the Persian name for the Indus River, referring also to the people who lived in the region. With the expansion of Islam into India beginning in the eighth century CE, the meaning changed to cover all those Indians who were not Muslims.[1] But this did not mean that these shared a common religion, either in their own eyes or necessarily in those of foreigners. Westerners, however, tended to lump them together as heathens or gentiles – hence the name "Gentoo." In the eighteenth century, the term "Hindu" gradually replaced "Gentoo," retaining the implication that they were more or less alike.[2] Western missionaries, writing around the turn of the nineteenth century, appear to have been the first to append the suffix "-ism" to the word "Hindu."[3] Moreover, it is widely agreed that Indians' own appropriation of the term developed in no small part out of interaction and confrontation with the missionaries, just as "Hindu" had earlier evolved out of interaction with Muslims.

In fact, Hindus held (and continue to hold) a great variety of religious beliefs and practices that were not always compatible. Some looked to the polytheism of the *Rig Veda*, the oldest portion of scriptures known as the Vedas; others postulated a monistic impersonal ultimate reality (Brahman), found in the Vedas and elaborated in the philosophical texts known as the *Upanishads*. In later centuries some focused on Vishnu as the supreme god (Vaishnavism), others on Shiva (Shaivism), and still others on Mahadevi, the great Goddess, also called Shakti. The familiar notions of karma, yoga, and reincarnation entered the history in the *Upanishads* and thereafter remained more or less constant in the diverse religious orientations in the subcontinent. Nevertheless, the idea of bringing all of these beliefs together under a single concept would be roughly analogous to lumping Judaism, Christianity, and Islam together under the label of, say, "Abrahamism."[4]

Not surprisingly then, Hinduism was and remains a container of contradictions – even more so than the other great religious traditions, of which the same can be said. It seems that, for every one of its religious actions that one can think of, there is an opposite and almost equal reaction. Hinduism encompasses polytheism, philosophical monism and monotheism, eroticism and asceticism, tolerance and intolerance, priestly elitism (the Brahmins) and popular devotion, drawing in part on the multiple ethnicities (so-called tribal religions) that survived the Aryan conquest (1500–1000 BCE). While this pluralism has been the hallmark of Hindu religious life, the coexistence of these multiple forms in close geographical proximity has nevertheless led to a certain fluidity of boundaries between them. One expression of this, which has gained in prominence since about the sixth century CE, is the emphasis on personal devotion (*bhakti*) in which the individual establishes a bond with a chosen deity.[5] These attachments were furthered through the two epics, the *Mahabharata* and *Ramayana*, through collections of myths known as the *Puranas*, and through music, dance, and ritual. This coincided with the proliferation of temples to these deities throughout India. All of this afforded a great scope for imaginative interplay between the various components, encompassing both the natural and the supernatural worlds, and extending to freely incorporating figures from foreign religious traditions. This *diffuse spirituality*, the dynamic ability to combine and incorporate, some scholars maintain, lends an inclusivity to Hinduism that underlies the pluralism.[6]

Thus if, prior to the nineteenth century, the word "Hindu" referred to non-Muslim Indians, it follows that there were Hindu Christians. Indeed, the term was not unheard of even in the 1800s.[7] In fact there were Christians in India long before the arrival of modern missionaries, quite possibly dating back to within a century of Jesus's death. These were the so-called Thomas Christians, followers of the Apostle Thomas, who is said to have traveled to India and met his martyrdom on the southeast coast near the present city of Chennai (formerly Madras). Whether this actually happened, or whether Thomas Christians actually go back that far, no one is sure. But the story remains a vibrant and living part of their oral tradition (more definite evidence dates back to 345 CE). They were also known as the Syrian Christians, because they followed the rites and language of the Syrian Orthodox church.

The Thomas Christians became thoroughly assimilated into Indian society, illustrating the aptness of the designation "Hindu Christian" and the strategy of *selective incorporation* that underlay it. Robert Eric Frykenberg describes them as "Hindu in culture, Christian in faith, and Persian or Syrian (Orthodox) in doctrine, ecclesiology, and ritual."[8] The Thomas Christians settled and expanded on the Malabar coast in the present state of Kerala, an area both prosperous and warlike, that was divided into some 20–30 competing kingdoms. Martial virtues were magnified via the figures of warrior gods and goddesses. The Syrians made themselves welcome by proving their fighting prowess, and their churches and rites became accepted parts of the religious landscape. The Christians often built their churches in the vicinity of Shaivite temples, and the two groups participated in each other's rituals, including animal sacrifices. In some places, St. Thomas himself became a part of the Hindu pantheon; in others, worship of him merged with a Hindu warrior god – and also with a local Muslim warrior.[9] A further illustration of this flexibility of incorporation is the presence of a Jewish menorah in one church in Kerala, a shrine to saint Marttasuni, who lived 137 years *before* Christ and met her martyrdom by defying the orders of King Antiochus (known through the story of Hannukah) to worship idols and eat pork – a sign of an ancient Jewish presence in the region.[10]

EARLY MODERN PERIOD

The Portuguese of course had little or no foreknowledge of these relation-ships and little appreciation of them after they arrived, beginning in 1498. The most notable exception, the Jesuit Roberto de·Nobili, who resolved to convert the Brahmins by completely adopting their lifestyle, was Italian. While the Syrians initially looked to the Portuguese as potential allies in their ongoing local political struggles, these Hindu Christians were soon offended by the Europeans' habits such as slaughtering cattle and eating beef. Moreover, as we have seen in colonial Mexico, Roman Catholicism became less tolerant as the sixteenth century wore on. Thus began a series of confrontations and struggles for control of the Thomas Christians between the Latin and Eastern churches which lasted until the twentieth century (the Anglicans were no more tolerant when they arrived in the 1800s). In the Portuguese colony of Goa, regulations of non-Christian worship became increasingly repressive. In 1559, all images were to be destroyed and feasts banned, and Hindu orphans were ordered to be handed over to Christians for instruction and baptism; the Inquisition was formally established in 1560.[11] As may be imagined, such measures were met with subversion and occasional violence.[12]

This is the appropriate place to introduce the fact of caste, because it pervades the entire history of Hindu-Christian relations.[13] Here is another apparent contradiction: between the fluidity of spiritual boundaries and the rigidity of social ones. The terminology of caste can be confusing. On one hand, there is the familiar Brahminic written classification, going back to the Vedas, of broad class distinctions: the four *varnas* (colors) of Brahmins (priests, white), Kshatriyas (kings and warriors, red), Vaishyas (merchants, yellow), and Shudras (laborers, black). These are actually umbrella-like terms, for within each *varna*, there are innumerable groups of *jatis* (birth) defined by hereditary occupation, marriageability, and other marks of exclusivity such as food taboos. The *jatis* constitute what are properly known as "castes." Outcastes, or untouchables (*avarna*, colorless), were those considered to be engaging in unclean occupations and therefore polluting by definition. A great variety of occupational identities exist under the name of "caste" – some 2,000–3,000 over all of India – varying considerably from one region to another. Moreover – and contrary to the stereotype of India as a static society – caste was often a dynamic arena of struggles for social mobility – not with the view of abrogating caste distinctions, but of elevating a group's rank within the hierarchy, e.g., from untouchable to Shudra or from Shudra to Vaishya. Religious conversion was one way of doing so. The Syrian Christians, encompassing multiple occupational *jatis*, seem to have been considered either Kshatriya or Vaishya.[14] Paradoxically, the very rigidity of caste boundaries helped preserve the integrity of Christianity as a badge of identity. There was no blending of Christ and Shiva; still, the spatial proximity of these plural religious traditions allowed for a variety of combinations and borrowings on a smaller scale.[15] At the same time, the need to maintain one's distance from the lower or impure groups meant that these struggles could continue within Christianity, as with other Hindu religions.

A good example of a cohesive and enduring caste group is the Paravars, the communities of Tamil fishermen along the southeast Indian coast, and the first group to convert en masse to Catholicism after 1500. The Paravars became specialists at diving for pearls in the oyster

beds that lay off the coast. Though profitable, this was strenuous and
dangerous work and was considered relatively unclean by the surrounding society; hence they were classified as untouchables. In the early 1500s
the Paravars were engaged in conflict with Muslim fishermen and merchants in the area who sought to impinge on the trade. Hearing about the
Portuguese, they sent a delegation to appeal for help in 1532, and over
20,000 had been baptized within months. Realizing that this act was little
more than the sealing of an alliance, the Jesuits sent a charismatic personality, Francis Xavier, to bring about a more thorough conversion. Robert
Eric Frykenberg describes his methods as follows:

> With no knowledge of Tamil, he and three Tamil-speaking assistants spent many
> months walking from village to village, building prayer houses, baptizing children,
> and drilling children in rote recitations of the Lord's Prayer, *Ave*, Creed, and
> Commandments. These doctrines were to be recited aloud every morning and
> evening at the sound of a bell. Attempts were made to install a *kanakkapillai*
> (catechist/accountant) for each village, to keep track of births, deaths and mar-
> riages for each lineage (*vamsha*). When families from other communities ... asked
> for baptism, they too were drawn into the fold.[16]

In 1555, the Jesuits further reinforced the Paravars' religious loyalty by
bringing a statue of the Virgin from Manila and placing it in a local
chapel. She was known as Our Lady of Snows, and gradually became the
focus of a 10-day festival in which the statue was paraded through the
streets in a grand car, pulled by the members of the community, much as
Vaishnavite, Shaivite, and goddess images were feted. The festival drew
worshippers from other Hindu regions and became one of several
Christian processions that were thus incorporated into Indian religious
life. They are still thriving today, with one of them, Our Lady of Health at
Velankanni, drawing as many as a million participants from as far away
as Mumbai (Bombay).[17]

   Several commentators have noted that the religious orientation of these
festivals is little different than what one finds in early modern Spain, or
many other parts of the Catholic world. Nevertheless, the fact of caste
was and is often a distinguishing feature.[18] The Paravars, for example,
were able to maintain most of the markers of their caste identity, including decisions about whom to marry, which were left to the caste headmen.
They did not remain static in their occupations, however; when the Dutch
arrived in south India, the Paravars met an increasing demand for other
maritime occupations such as navigation. But over time, their rising
wealth, status, and ostentation put them at increasing odds with other
castes and also with the Jesuits who had originally sponsored them. This

became an issue in the nineteenth century, when the Jesuits returned to India after having been banished in 1773. They now found that the caste headmen had assumed authority that belonged to a priest, such as who may take communion. In addition, their own attitudes toward caste were no longer as accommodating as in the sixteenth century. In one case, after unsuccessfully trying to remove the authority of the headmen, the Jesuits tried erecting a rival shrine. But this led to conflicts over who should have the right to process on what streets, a conflict typical of caste rivalries. Such a situation was likely to lead to riots, and did so in 1877.[19] Further examples of such disputes could be multiplied in southern India, where they frequently became linked to Catholic-Protestant competition. One solution to such caste rivalries was to segregate worship spaces by building a wall around a church, or even partitioning the interior – in one case, a wall 20 feet high down the center of the nave.[20]

It might seem that the proclivity to express one's religion through images, processions, and the like would predispose Hindu Christianity to favor Catholicism over Protestantism. This, however, would not be completely correct, even though Catholics continued to outnumber Protestants in Tamil-speaking areas. Admittedly, the German Pietist missionaries who began arriving in the Danish colony of Tranquebar in Tamil country in 1706 doubtless abhorred such "idolatries" as much as they despised Catholicism itself. But they brought with them a distinctive set of tools, which proved to be likewise effective in creating communities of devout Hindu Christians – provided one allows for an incubation period of 30–50 years.[21] These tools were: (1) education and (2) translation, combined with a remarkable organizational effectiveness in mobilizing indigenous participants. Following the example of their home base in Halle, they began establishing schools for the poor and orphans within a year of their arrival. Also within that year, the prodigious Bartholomaus Ziegenbalg, one of the first two missionaries, had mastered the Tamil language to be able to give a sermon in it, and went on to compile two dictionaries, a grammar, and a translation of the New Testament by 1714. Ziegenbalg quickly developed an appreciation for Tamil culture and literature; in this he resembled the Catholic Nobili, but with an important difference: Nobili's primary identification was with the Brahmin elite, while Ziegenbalg, again following the Pietist example, sought to make literacy available for the lower castes as well. That appreciation was manifest in his creation of Tamil hymns set to Indian melodies (as well as to German chorales), in his extensive collection of indigenous literature which he sent back to Halle – and likewise in importing European science and literature to India – and perhaps above all, in his ability to recruit and enlist the cooperation of native teachers and catechists. All of these strengths were passed on to the missionaries who followed – 56 in the course of the eighteenth century. During that time the mission employed about 500 Indians, including more than 200 catechists, teachers, and assistants, as well as 9 ordained clergy. By 1798, this network was estimated to have 6,000 converts (including a caste of ex-thieves and robbers).[22] The momentum of translation and education was transferred to other Protestant missionary organizations. By 1858 the Bible was available in ten languages spoken in India, and the New Testament in four more.[23] And in the Tamil region, according to the 1901 census, about 14 percent of the Christian population was literate as compared to 6 percent of the Hindus and 7 percent of the Muslims. As many of these were lower caste, the Protestant effort did have real effects in improving the status and opportunities of these people.[24] It seems clear that the appeal of Christianity, like that of Islam, lay in its offering of salvation to all people regardless of status.

Although the eighteenth-century German missionaries like Ziegenbalg disapproved of caste, they were forced to accommodate to it if they were to have any success at all. For most Indians, to renounce caste, even the lowliest, was to cut oneself off from one's family and community, a price they were not willing to pay. The accommodation was made again in terms of establishing spatial divisions within Christian worship – but by segregated seating rather than by walls and structures. Thus when the New Jerusalem Church in Tranquebar was constructed in 1718 in the form of a crucifix, the north and south arms were reserved for upper caste (Vellalar) men and women, respectively, while the east and west wings were for untouchable (Paraiyar) men and women. Europeans sat on benches, Vellalars on mats, while Paraiyars sat on the floor. The two caste groups drank from separate communion cups; one extremely talented Paraiyar-born catechist was passed over for ordination because it was said that no Vellalar would take communion from him.[25] Yet this arrangement constituted a middle ground, a shared belief or ritual with two divergent interpretations. For the Tamils, it meant that Christians acknowledged the existence of separate communities as part of the God-given order of things, which was quite compatible with the availability of salvation to all. The missionaries, on the other hand, tended to rationalize their position by claiming that caste was part of the social and cultural order of things rather than the Godly one (much as they also did with Cherokee healing practices or Chinese ancestor veneration).[26]

The Brahmins were generally the caste most concerned with preserving their purity and therefore least likely to be among the Christian converts. Still considered upper-caste were the Vellalars, a group that included large landowners who controlled large numbers of untouchable agricultural laborers. Some of them were more receptive to Christianity and were often given leadership positions.[27] Thus, ironically, despite the opening to the untouchables, the hierarchical relationship between landowner and worker was preserved within the church.[28]

We know something of the initial Tamil upper-caste attitudes toward Christianity from their exchanges with the German missionaries that are preserved in the latter's records. These included objections to the foreigners' uncleanliness (including not only the eating of beef, but also ingesting the body and blood of Christ); their drinking and gluttony (probably referring to the colonists rather than the missionaries themselves); and their perfunctory burial and marriage rites. Some sought to explain to the missionaries that the worship of lesser divinities did not preclude the belief in a Supreme Being, and others maintained that temple rites are after all not as important as personal devotion – the notion of *bhakti*, which actually resembled the Pietists' practice of faith.[29]

For the Paraiyars (origin of the English term "pariah") we have no such voices, but their story can be told through numbers. Thanks to the proselytizing efforts of largely indigenous catechists, mass conversions in Tirunelveli near the southern tip of India began to explode in 1797 and continued in successive waves throughout the nineteenth century. It began among a group known as the Shanars (a name associated with excrement) who, like the Paravars, had developed an occupation that others regarded as dirty, namely climbing palm trees and tapping the sap from them. They eagerly turned to Christianity as a way of escaping this stigma and eventually rechristened themselves as Nadars (lords). Entire villages became Christian, and temples were turned into schools. This triggered a furious backlash from the landlords who feared the loss of their labor and sent in gangs to smash their houses and prayer centers. This, in turn, led to the formation of Christian villages of refuge, where in some cases the Halle model of voluntary welfare organizations and schools was replicated. This drew in more converts, so that the number of evangelical Christians in Tirunelveli rose from 11,186 in 1836 to 46,047 two decades later.[30] Similar movements sprouted in other parts of India as well. Clearly the Paraiyars looked to Protestant Christianity as a source of stability and material support. This often troubled the missionaries as being less than pure, but one should beware of imposing a dualism of material and spiritual motives on a society which did not make such a distinction.[31]

Vernacular translation occurred through literary activity. The Tamil language is, next to Sanskrit, the oldest written language in India and one of the oldest in the world. It had long since developed a rich tradition of religious literature, dating back to the first century CE, including *bhakti* devotional poetry going back to the sixth century.[32] Thus literature provided an arena of expression for interaction, on the part of poets and scholars, between Christians and other Hindus. A Tamil poet, H. A. Krishna Pillai, would compose a version of Bunyan's *Pilgrim's Progress* in 1894. The best-known exponent, however, was the remarkable Tamil Protestant poet Vedanayaka Sastri (1774–1864). His creation of a body of Christian literature epitomizes the strategy of vernacular translation. At the same time, his later life serves as an illustration of the disruptive transformations that Hindu Christians were to experience in the early nineteenth century.

Born the son of a Vellalar convert, Sastri was sent to missionary schools run by the Halle Pietists, where he was exposed to Western science. While there he also developed a lifelong friendship with Serfoji, the future ruler of the kingdom of Tanjore, a center of literary and artistic activity, and who shared Sastri's admiration for Western knowledge. Sastri himself became headmaster of a school for catechists at age 19 and taught mathematics and astronomy, where he remained for 35 years. At the same time he was writing Tamil Christian hymns and poetry, some of which was meant to be performed in song and dance. He performed these throughout the region and was duly honored as "the Evangelical Poet." His masterpiece was probably *Bethlehem Kuravanci* (The fortune teller of Bethlehem), in an indigenous genre of "fortune teller" poems that was already well established. These poems contained a love story, which Sastri made into an allegory of the daughter of Zion in love with Jesus, the Lord of Bethlehem (love themes had been part of the *bhakti* tradition and were also evident in Sastri's preference for the *Song of Songs* in the Old Testament). The poem, however, also had a didactic side: Sastri used parts of it to introduce Copernican astronomy to his Tamil audiences at a time when it was still under suspicion from Hindu pundits. Sastri's hymns, set to Tamil rhythms and melodies, have retained their appeal and are performed to this day.[33]

Despite his established reputation, Sastri faced increasing difficulties in the 1820s and 1830s, difficulties that were faced by thousands of Tamil Christians in the face of increasing British penetration of the subcontinent. The waning of Danish power meant that their support of Protestant missions was gradually transferred to Anglican organizations, some of which had quite different ideas on what it meant to be a Christian. In some cases, the transition could be radical and abrupt – from Lutheran- to Calvinist-type influence. Thus, to again quote Frykenberg, "By fiat, some 20,000 mostly Pietist Tamils found themselves 'converted' overnight into Anglican Protestants–forced to read different translations, sing strange new songs, and recite from an unknown Book of Common Prayer."[34] Sastri found himself in the cross-fire – over the issue of caste. When the new Anglican missionary ordered him to end the separate seating arrangements and order of taking communion, he objected and was dismissed. Some 3,000 Vellalars were excommunicated for the same reason in 1834.[35] Sastri soon found employment as the court poet of his childhood friend Serfoji, despite the fact that the latter had never become a Christian. In fact, Sastri had already written a number of tracts protesting the new dispensation prior to his dismissal. He referred to the "four cruelties" – of which the denial of caste, which he viewed as the natural social order, was but one. The others were: (1) the new Bible translations, which he found to be too colloquial and contravened a hundred years of congregational practice; 2) the lack of joyfulness at festivals, such as prohibiting flowers at holidays, weddings, and burials; (3) the removal of Tamil music, lyrics, and instruments from worship.[36] All in all, Sastri presented a picture of an indigenous Christianity that had become firmly rooted and was now in increasing opposition to the ideas of foreign missionaries. He was able to cite Biblical passages enjoining Christians to have regard for local customs as they proselytized.

SEA-CHANGE OF THE EARLY NINETEENTH CENTURY

Sastri's changing fortunes were indicative of a seismic shift in missionary-indigenous relations which took place at the turn of the nineteenth century, from one of predominant accommodation to native norms such as caste to one of predominant condemnation of these as immoral and superstitious. This sea-change was accompanied by the gradual opening of doors to increased missionary activity in India over the next 30-odd years. The initiative for this change came from the British Protestant missionaries themselves – not, as one might expect, from the policies of the British East India Company. On the contrary, at the end of the eighteenth century, the Company's official position was one of religious neutrality, maintaining that any outside attempt to disturb or convert

Hindus from their established religious views would be most unwise and unfavorable to commerce. Thus when the self-taught Baptist minister William Carey wanted to travel to Calcutta in British Bengal in 1793, the Company vessel refused to take him; he arrived by Danish ship. He eventually set up shop in a small Danish outpost of Serampore, 16 miles to the north.

This attitude should be understood in the context of the Company's overall strategy of control at the time: it was to be economic and military, not cultural or political. Rather than overturning the local principalities, the British sought to cultivate loyalty to them by participating in their rituals and promoting understanding of their languages and cultures among the officers, while at the same time allowing the latter to skim as much wealth from the local economies as they could. The Governor-General from 1773 to 1785, Warren Hastings, went so far as to recruit English and indigenous scholars to study and translate indigenous languages (most famously Sir William Jones, who was known for tracing the common roots of Sanskrit and European languages), a policy known at the time as Orientalism, well before that term had acquired a pejorative meaning.[37] The governor-general at the turn of the century, Lord Wellesley, established Fort William College in Calcutta to train Company officials in these languages. Ironically, the only person they could find to teach Bengali was William Carey. In any event, the British purchased Serampore from the Danes in 1845. By that time, Carey's missionary enterprise had become recognized as one of the most effective in all of India.

This orientalist attitude was, however, beginning to collide with the missionaries' views at home, a product of that movement toward *concentration of spirituality* known as the Great Awakening. In addition to the intensification of religious feeling, it also meant intensified commitment to spread the word abroad. Millennialism also played a part, a feeling that the end times mandated the imminent conversion of heathens, Catholics, and Jews. One product of this general ferment was the formation of several new British missionary societies in the 1790s: the Baptist Missionary Society (1792), the London Missionary Society (1795), the Edinburgh and Glasgow Missionary Societies (1796), and the Anglican Society for Missions to Africa and the East (1799), the latter later known as the Church Missionary Society. By 1800, these attitudes were beginning to infiltrate the Company through a few officials, including one of the directors (Charles Grant) and one of the chaplains (Claudius Buchanan, also vice-provost at Fort William College), both of whom came to the view that the purpose of the Company should not be merely to promote commerce, but to "improve" the religion and morality of the Indian people – which only Christianity could bring about.[38] This shift from a positive to a negative opinion of Hinduism did not occur overnight, but gradually gained intensity as the issue became politicized: the Evangelicals' writings and pamphlets would be used in parliamentary debates on the occasions of the renewal of the charter of the Company over the question of whether missionaries should be officially allowed into India. Feelings ran high on both sides of this issue, and when in 1807 a mutiny occurred among Indian troops in Vellore, it was assumed – though never proven – that fear of being converted was a strong motive, setting the missionary cause back.[39] By the 1813 charter renewal, however, the Evangelicals had scored a limited but crucial victory, thanks in part to a flood of petitions. The argument that carried the day was that Christians had the right to be tolerated in India along with other faiths. At the next charter renewal of 1833, the access of missionaries was made still easier.[40] At the same time, the Orientalist position within the East India Company on teaching languages such as Sanskrit was being supplanted by the Anglicist position that education in English would be much more useful, embodied in Thomas B. Macauley's famous (or infamous) *Minute on Education* of 1835. As usual, much of that education was conducted by missionaries. Over the next decades, the influx of missionaries was accompanied by the huge influx of printed matter. The flow of books and pamphlets (on all subjects) from Britain to India was equal (in weight) to the exports of printed matter to the Americas.[41]

It is surely no coincidence that the first occurrences of the term "Hinduism" in the singular are found in missionaries' letters and essays beginning in the 1790s.[42] It may be, as Geoffrey Oddie has suggested, that this was in part simply a by-product of the expansion of missionary activity itself: in order to present the contrast between Christianity and a foreign religion to home audiences, one needed to frame the latter as integral whole (a similar argument could be made about "Confucianism" in China). Certainly the scholarly interest of Orientalists in South Asian culture encouraged thinking about its religion as a coherent system.[43] Yet this argument fails to capture one of the most significant aspects of these references, namely their derogatory *tone*. Singularization was accompanied by simplification and vilification, leading to the stereotypical thinking that Edward Said identified in his book *Orientalism* and which Jeffrey Cox has more recently labeled the "technique of defamatory synecdoche, namely taking one or a small number of characteristics of a foreign culture and using it as representative of the whole."[44] To give but one example, the shocking practice of *sati*, the killing of widows by burning, so that they could join their husbands in the afterlife, which occurred among some sectors of society some of the time, was taken to characterize the entire society and the character of its people. It is true that the Serampore missionaries attempted to collect data on how many occurrences of *sati* took place in Bengal, for example. But the numbers, whose accuracy was disputed, were accompanied by sweeping generalizations:

"Two Hindoo widows are roasted or buried alive every day in the Presidency of Bengal, in only one division of British India? ... Who shall count the groans and screams of all these widows in the scorching flames, and the tears of all these orphans. And this is Hindooism! And this is British India!"[45]

Or, to give another example:

Extreme ignorance, and the vices connected with idolatry render women in India very unfit to perform the duty nature intended for her—the care of children; for even if she can take proper care of their little bodies (which is doubtful) she infuses into their opening minds a degree of deception and willfulness which years may not be able to eradicate.[46]

How to account for this sea-change, which seems to have taken place in an emotional as well as intellectual register? One answer, surely, is that this language appeared in the heat of public debate over parliamentary legislation, deliberately designed to enflame public opinion over abuses and atrocities in India and to spur English men and women to petition their representatives to change them – and also to fund the missionary societies. Missionary pamphlets included engravings of human atrocities such as people being crushed to death dragging chariots bearing giant statues in a religious procession at the Jagannath temple in Puri. Yet one finds examples of the same vilifying rhetoric not only in pamphlets, but in longer works of considerable erudition, and in the essays by the students at Fort William College, published in 1802, before the public campaigns began. Buchanan's sermons were so incendiary that they had to be censored before they could be published.[47]

It seems to me that the exceptional intensity of this particular Orientalist discourse stemmed, at least at the conscious level, from the confluence of three rhetorically powerful master narratives that were current in England at the time and were mutually reinforcing. First, there was the anti-Catholic narrative which the Evangelicals universally shared and which was evident in the writings of missionaries such as Carey. The image of a privileged priestly elite, the Brahmins, foisting superstitions upon a poor and unthinking mass of believers, monopolizing access to a sacred text in a language accessible only to themselves, was clearly a projection of a European Protestant view of Roman Catholicism.[48] Second, there was the Enlightenment narrative of Western civilization being more advanced than those of the East. Missionaries in India, as elsewhere, tended to equate Christianity with civilization, by which they meant Western civilization, though they continued to disagree among themselves as to which should come first when it came to missionary work. Certainly missionaries accomplished a great deal in purveying Western education, and their willingness to combine education in English with vernacular languages reflected a pragmatism born of experience.[49] Nonetheless, there was the belief that the diffuse spirituality of the Hindus was less rational than the worship of one God and an only begotten son. Reason, in this case, served as Occam's razor, so to speak, in pruning away what seemed to be superfluous and superstitious elements of religion. This explains how, on this issue, the Evangelicals could be at one with the Utilitarians such as Jeremy Bentham and James Mill who, as representatives of Enlightenment rationalism would seem to be diametrically opposed to Evangelical values and who helped shape British policy in India during these years. This convergence, however, is significant in that it reveals an underlying affinity between Protestantism and enlightenment rationalism, namely the strategy of excision and reduction that we have identified as *concentration of spirituality*.[50] The third narrative was the humanitarian one: Hinduism was seen as responsible for human suffering, whether in the form of *sati*, the treatment of women in general, or the caste system. It is no coincidence that one of the leaders in the parliamentary struggle to allow missionaries into India was William Wilberforce, the leader of the antislavery campaign; the missionary efforts in Sierra Leone and India were seen as linked, and the British decree abolishing *sati* in Bengal came in 1829, when the abolitionist campaign was approaching its peak. A further example of how humanitarian considerations were linked to the defamation of Hinduism was the controversy over the procession at the Jagannath temple. The East India Company was seen to be complicit in this practice in that it managed the temples in the areas under its control, as the previous rulers had done – and collected revenues from a pilgrim tax as well. The missionaries mounted a successful campaign to dissociate the Company from these practices, both on the grounds that it was inhumane and that it promoted idolatry.[51] Indeed, it seems that the idea of idolatry served as the lynchpin which joined all these three narratives together, serving as a kind of powerful archetypal image.[52]

INDIGENOUS RESPONSES AND STRATEGIES

The wave of missionary initiatives triggered by Evangelical Protestantism provoked different responses in different sectors of Indian society. These can be said to fall into two general groups: first, those for whom Christianity acted as a stimulus to revitalize and reform their own religion, and second those for whom it served as an attractive force, leading to an improvement in their social status and in some cases to conversion. It should be noted that these trends are best viewed as additions to, rather than modifications of, the previous religious currents discussed above. In other words, Hindus continued to worship and make offerings to Vishnu, Shiva, Mahadevi, and their various avatars in their temples as before. Also, the earlier indigenous forms of Christianity (though no longer called Hindu Christianity) survived and grew: Catholicism recovered from a slump following the suppression of the Jesuits in 1773, beginning in the 1830s, and subject to increasing control from the Vatican, continuing to foster a sense of separateness from Protestantism.[53] Likewise the Thomas Christians, though subject to a series of internal divisions, continue to thrive to this day.[54]

Christianity as Stimulus: Hindu Resistance, Acculturation, and Reform

In general, the nineteenth-century Protestant challenge moved many Hindus toward *concentration of spirituality*, if only by themselves adopting the unifying label "Hinduism," thus reinforcing their self-awareness as belonging to a single religious entity. This awareness was of course a natural response to an adversarial foreign presence, and as such was by no means completely new, given India's precolonial history, but obviously received a decisive boost from the missionary attacks.[55] Not surprisingly, the new policies provoked increased incidents of *resistance* in the 1830s, '40s, and '50s, playing into the famous Uprising of 1857. The banning of *sati* brought a petition of some 30,000 notables in Bengal protesting the violation of religious freedom. In the Madras region in the south in the 1840s, a countermovement known as the "Sacred Ashes Society" arose and began attacking Christian villages.[56]

"Resistant Hinduism" also took place at the level of theological debate, as Richard Fox Young's monograph of the same title thoroughly portrays. [57] This involved both Christian theologians directly confronting Hinduism, and Hindu and Muslim scholars taking up the challenge, asserting the spiritual and moral superiority of their systems. This took some time to develop, as Brahmins themselves tended not to engage with these new foreign sources, but with increased translations into the vernacular and increased literacy, more individuals were willing to take on the task. It occurred in a variety of registers, from written treatises in response to Christian writings, to colorful outdoor preachers such as one who could draw crowds as large as 2,000 on a Bombay beach in the 1850s.[58] Hindus defended the notion of karma and the transmigration of souls as a more psychologically satisfying explanation for human suffering than the Christian idea of original sin, and found their scriptures to be more consonant with the findings of modern science than was the Bible.[59] At the same time, Muslim scholars were sharpening their defenses against missionary attacks, culminating in a highly public debate in Agra in 1854. Their tactics consisted of undermining basic Christian doctrines such as the divinity of Christ and the Trinity by calling the authenticity and consistency of the Bible into question. In this, they were more than a match for their missionary adversaries, even citing sources in modern European Biblical criticism which the Christians themselves were unaware of.[60]

A further source of resistance was the response of Brahmins and other high-caste men to the social implications of the missionary onslaught, which they regarded as highly subversive. Conversions of Brahmins were few, but even a single instance could have broad repercussions throughout an entire community.[61] A conversion tended to put the individual at odds with his family and peers, because it represented a radical break with Brahminical custom and practice. For example, it was essential for the eldest son to perform funeral rites for his father, in order to maintain continuity with the ancestors. If the son was unwilling or unable to do so, it meant his "civil death," i.e., the forfeiture of inheritance passed down from the ancestors and the breakup of family property. And because these were often people of means, such breaks led to disputes over property which involved court cases, litigation, and legislation. Thus when the British passed the so-called Caste Disabilities Removal Act of 1850, establishing the rights of inheritance for Christian converts, it was perceived as an attempt to subvert the entire religion.[62]

The 1850 law was one of several pieces of legislation that contributed, along with the offensive missionary rhetoric and the influx of printed matter, to the widespread feeling that Britain was preparing to foist

Christianity on her Hindu and Muslim subjects – one of the leading causes of the Uprising of 1857. Although the revolt was an expression of a multitude of grievances that had been building for some time, there is general agreement that the religious issue played a major role. Paradoxically, this resistance was directed less at the missionaries themselves than to the government, which was believed to be in collusion with them. Even Sir John William Kaye, a British historian second to none in his contempt for Hinduism, could write that "when it was seen that the functions of the English schoolmaster and of the Christian priest were united in the same person, and that high officers of the State were present at examinations conducted by chaplains and missionaries, a fear arose lest even secular education might be the mask of proselytism . . ."[63] Examples of army officers who were zealous in their desire to spread Christianity could be cited as well.[64] Manifestations of the religious dimension of the Uprising would include the introduction of the Enfield rifle, which triggered the revolt, involving the soldiers' biting of cartridges greased with animal fat, which was seen as a violation of both Hindu and Muslim religious practices of avoiding consumption of beef and pork respectively and a clear sign of British intent to overthrow these practices.[65] Also, when massacres occurred at Cawnpore and Delhi, the rebels deliberately targeted Christians, both indigenous and European.[66] Finally, it should be noted that the indigenous Christians, both north and south, overwhelmingly supported the government and helped put down the insurrection.[67]

Following the defeat of the Uprising in 1858, which also marked the formal establishment of the crown colony that replaced the domain of the East India Company, Queen Victoria issued a proclamation reaffirming British commitment to religious neutrality. For their part, missionaries gradually retreated from the aim of full conversion, rather reenvisioning their educational efforts as inculcating Christian values into Indian civilization. Missionary schools and colleges proliferated across India, and members of the upper castes availed themselves of the Western learning taught there.[68] During the same years, resistance took an increasingly political turn with the formation of the Congress Party (1886) and the movement for self-rule.[69]

Meanwhile, some members of the upper classes had long since been moving in the direction of *selective acculturation*. This was rooted in the very techniques that the East India Company had developed to control the subcontinent, relying as they did on the active cooperation of thousands of Indians, not only soldiers, but translators, scribes, merchants, and so on. As in West Africa, imperial penetration also meant opportunities for indigenes to build careers and wealth. Nowhere was this more evident than in Bengal, where Governor-General Charles Cornwallis's establishment of private property (1793) created a class of loyal elite landowners. For many, their exposure to things English developed into a curiosity and fascination for things Western, including its learning and science, which led to an intellectual renaissance in Calcutta in the early 1800s. Thus it is only a slight exaggeration to say that Macauley's 1835 call for the formation of a class of Indians who were "English in tastes, in opinions, in morals and in intellect" was only partially a vision imposed from Europe, but also the aspiration of an Indian elite.[70] This Indian attraction to the West remained selective, however, in that Bengali learning was by no means denigrated (unlike some of the missionaries' views).[71]

The most famous exemplar of this trend was undoubtedly Rammohun Roy (1772–1833), called "the father of modern India." It was he who channeled the Bengali learning into a reform of Hinduism utilizing *concentration of spirituality*, by founding a new movement that became known as Brahmo Samaj, the Society of Brahma. A Bengali Brahmin by birth and prodigiously gifted in languages, Roy formulated the idea as a young man that was to become his life's work: that all peoples shared a belief in a Supreme Being, however they might differ about its attributes. Along with this went the belief that the universe was rationally comprehensible. In order for this truth to shine forth, it was necessary to cut away all the superfluous rituals and superstitions that had intervened. This certainly contributed to the simplification and purification of "Hinduism," and Roy is said to have been possibly the first Indian writer to use the term.[72] He was convinced that monotheism was the true message of the *Vedas*, based on the part known as the *Upanishads*. He had the audacity to translate that sacred text into Bengali and English, thus violating the principle that their interpretation should be a Brahmin monopoly. He also used his knowledge of the Vedas to launch a public campaign against *sati* in 1818; he further protested against the treatment of women in general. All of this predictably aroused a storm of protest from orthodox Hindus. So it is not surprising that he was drawn to Christianity, being particularly drawn to the Sermon on the Mount and the ethical teachings found therein. By this time, he had also made contact with the Baptist missionaries at Serampore, who found in him an ally, both as a friend of Jesus and an enemy of *sati*. But this alliance was short-lived, as the missionaries soon realized that Roy's ethical Jesus had no room for the sacrifice on the cross, reducing rather "the Redeemer of the world to a level with Confucius and Mahomet."[73] For Roy's part, the doctrine of the Trinity seemed no more consistent with the monotheism that he was advocating than were the Hindu avatars he was fighting against. This anti-Trinitarian position led him to a second group of allies, the Unitarians. Roy himself was a cofounder of a Unitarian Committee in Calcutta in 1821, and his writings soon found a receptive audience among Unitarians in the West. But the Unitarians also considered themselves Christians and expected Roy to convert, which he did not. Moreover, their highly intellectual approach to concentrated spirituality failed to win a sizable following in Calcutta. The founding of the Brahmo Samaj in 1828 was Roy's response to this need. There was an element of imitation here, in that it involved a regular congregational meeting for worship, something new to Hindu practice, but with hymns and scripture drawn from Hindu tradition. Yet this was clearly a means to render Hinduism accessible to the universal monotheism that Roy had always advocated.

Shortly after the founding of the Brahmo Samaj, Roy departed for England, where he spent the last few years of his life. The society languished briefly but soon revived, undergoing for the remainder of the century a series of schisms, revivals, expansions, and contractions that seem to typify such new sects. While remaining a mouthpiece of the acculturated Bengali elite, it also went through a missionary phase in the 1860s and early 1870s, expanding mainly to eastern Bengal. In doing so, it moved to encompass certain further Hindu rites and beliefs, mainly from the Vaishnavas, leading among other things to a distinctive Brahmo hymnody. Hundreds of young men endured persecutions by their families and villagers in East Bengal as they joined the movement.[74] Meanwhile, as it reflected the cosmopolitanism of Calcutta, it also absorbed the multiple cultural and religious influences that streamed in from the West, as well as the identity conflicts within individuals that inevitably went with this. The society thus became a veritable cauldron for generating individual combinations of these heterogeneous strands. Perhaps best known was the work of the celebrated poet and novelist Rabindranath Tagore (1861–1941), grandson of one of Roy's closest associates and cofounder of the Society, Debendranath Tagore (1817–1905). The Brahmo Samaj was important less for the number of members it attracted than for the complicated relationships it spun with Western religious and secular beliefs and practices, including embracing Indian nationalism. It served as a way-station for several other reformers who went on to form movements of their own.

One of these was Dayananda Saraswati (1824–83), who founded a more widespread Hindu reform movement, the Arya Samaj, in 1875.

Saraswati was a Brahmin by birth who from childhood was profoundly dissatisfied with orthodox practices. As a wandering ascetic *(sannyasin)* in his formative years, he had investigated the multiple religious movements in his environment in an attempt to attain spiritual truth. A four-month sojourn with the Brahmo Samaj in 1872 transformed his approach from ascetic to reformer.[75] His new society resembled the Brahmos in many respects: belief in the monotheism of the Vedas, rejection of idolatry and caste, and the uplifting of women. Yet there was one crucial difference: whereas the Brahmos held that all religions strive toward the worship of the same God and thus contain basic truths, Dayananda chose to emphasize the falsehoods of religions other than Vedic Hinduism. To him the Vedas were the infallible basis of truth, and other religions must be measured against it. He believed that the God represented there was eternal and immutable, so that any religion based on contingent historical events – including Judaism, Christianity, and Islam – contained falsehoods by comparison. Dayananda's criticisms of Christianity reflected his literal reading of the Bible, making it easy to point out its contradictions and irrational assertions.[76] He sought to win people back to Hinduism through a process of re-conversion, and adopted a purification ritual *(shuddhi)*, derived from traditional Brahminic practice, in order to do so. The results were meager, but its symbolic significance was great. As a revitalization movement, the Arya Samaj had a much wider appeal than the rival Brahmos, particularly in the Punjab, where Hindus were in a minority, surrounded by Muslims, Sikhs and an ever-growing Christian population. As they took to street-preaching, imitating the missionaries, the Aryas contributed to an atmosphere of militancy, as each major religion competed with each other on the streets of cities like Lahore.[77]

Dayananda was but one of several reformers who came out of the Hindu tradition of itinerant asceticism and who used this to create a message for contemporary society, both Indian and Western. The best known of these was Swami Vivekananda (1863–1902), a disciple of the Bengali saint Ramakrishna (1836–86), who founded the Ramakrishna monastic order. Vivekananda traveled to North America and Britain to present Hinduism as an alternative to Western materialism. At his sensational address to the World Parliament of Religions in Chicago in 1893, he announced, "I am proud to belong to a religion that has taught the world both tolerance and universal acceptance. We believe not only in universal toleration, but we accept all religions as true."[78] Like Dayananda, he presented the Vedas as more compatible with modern science than were Judeo-Christian-Muslim views.[79] His attitude toward

Christianity combined a veneration of Jesus himself with an often-scathing critique of Christians for failing to live up to his ideals. He chided missionaries for failing to give aid in times of famine and noted the defamatory images of Indians in American Sunday school textbooks.[80] Responding to attacks from missionary periodicals while in the United States, he delivered a passionate rejoinder, from the perspective of an ascetic:

Now goes the missionary, a married man, who is hampered because he is married. The missionary knows nothing about the people, he cannot speak the language, so he invariably settles in the little white colony . . . Were he not married, he could go among the people and sleep on the ground if necessary.[81]

Vivekananda embraced, as did a number of other Indian intellectuals, an inverted and indigenized Orientalism, pitting Asian spirituality against Western materialism. This led him, for example, to make the following claim about Jesus:

Many times you forget . . . that the Nazarene himself was an Oriental of Orientals. With all your attempts to paint him with blue eyes and yellow hair, the Nazarene was still an Oriental . . . The voice of Asia has been the voice of religion. The voice of Europe is the voice of politics . . . No wonder, the oriental mind looks with contempt upon the things of this world . . . and, as for Prophets, you may also remember that without one exception, all the Messengers were Orientals.[82]

To be sure, the same cross-cultural fermentation that led to these Hindu reformers also produced a number of creative and insightful indigenous Christian thinkers and leaders.[83] Some of them saw Christianity as actually reinforcing Indian nationalism, strengthening the nation through its infusion of Western humanistic values.[84] But the impact of this group on Indian opinion was far outweighed by the negative association of the foreign missionaries with British domination – even as the missionaries themselves were softening their views on Hinduism and turning to the Social Gospel of alleviating poverty and disease as their main focus.[85] The negative aspect was of course magnified as the *resistance* to British domination grew in the first half of the twentieth century. Naturally, the attitudes of Mohandas Gandhi (1869–1948) toward Christianity and missionaries were crucial in this respect, and these virtually mirrored those of Vivekananda. In his autobiography, Gandhi tells of hearing missionaries denigrating Hindus on the streets of his hometown and how one prominent Christian convert promptly adopted Western dress and began to eat beef and drink liquor – in Gandhi's view, hardly marks of moral superiority.[86] Later, in England

and South Africa, Gandhi befriended Christians and worked with them, but noted their recurrent attempts to convert him. Like Vivekananda and Roy, he learned to treasure Jesus, particularly the Sermon on the Mount, but held to the view that each religion has its own equally valid way to God. For Gandhi, conversion to a foreign religion usually occurred for materialistic reasons, and led people to spurn their own nationality and heritage.[87] Although he was willing to credit missionaries as having a positive indirect effect on India – "it has forced us to put our own houses in order" – he became more critical of proselytization efforts over time, particularly beginning in the mid-1930s.[88]

Christianity as an Attractive Force: Women, Untouchables, Ethnic Minorities

As in so many parts of the world, the attraction of Christianity reached first those groups who were marginalized in their own society. In the Indian case, we can point to three such groups: (1) women, (2) untouchables, and (3) ethnic minorities, particularly in the northeast.

The project of uplifting the lot of Indian women may be counted as one of the missionaries' greatest successes. At the beginning of the nineteenth century, opposition to upper-caste women's education and literacy was widespread. Reading and writing was considered more appropriate for courtesans and temple dancers than for respectable wives and mothers. An educated girl, it was believed, would have fewer chances of finding a husband. Moreover, the custom of early marriage, beginning around age nine, militated against any extended formal schooling. In addition, missionaries' success in attracting lower-caste converts diminished the attractiveness of their schools for the upper castes.[89]

These attitudes changed gradually in the course of the century. While missionaries were not the only advocates of women's education, they were generally ahead of other groups (such as government officials) in doing so. One can point to several stages. By the 1830s, several day schools were established with attendance in the hundreds, in which missionary wives played a prominent role. Beginning in the 1850s, a more concerted effort was made to reach upper-caste women. Since many of these practiced *purdah* (seclusion in the part of the home known as *zenana*, or women's quarters), the so-called zenana missions developed, in which female missionaries, accompanied by native literate or semi-literate converts ("Bible women"), would visit these women in their homes, often for an extended period of time, and would both read Bible lessons and convey practical skills such as reading and needlework. This was fueled by the influx of women missionaries from Europe and North America in the second half of the century. Even so, the number of women reached by this very labor-intensive system was relatively small – an estimated 2,000 for India as a whole in 1873.[90] After the turn of the century, the zenana missions tended to be eclipsed by more efficient teacher training schools, though the numbers also remained small. Nevertheless, women benefitted from the spread of elite education, as a number of women's colleges were founded.[91] Thus one can point to a movement from the home to the school.

Another area of great demand that was met by Western missionary women was medicine. Again, the mores surrounding female seclusion and modesty meant that women would not allow male doctors to examine them. This in turn meant opportunities for female physicians that were often greater than in England or America. In central India in the 1890s, more than one-third of women missionaries were doctors. There followed several large women's hospitals and a women's medical college. By World War II, according to one estimate, the Christian hospitals supplied 90 percent of all trained nurses in India.[92]

If these numbers are indices of changing attitudes of Indian women, it by no means follows that they and the missionaries shared a common interpretation of what the numbers meant. Missionaries began by seeing schools and visitations and even medical consultations as means of evangelization, with women occupying a particularly strategic position in the process. To quote a zealous missionary, speaking at a conference in Calcutta in 1883: "Let us in our Master's name lay our hand on the hand that rocks the cradle, and tune the lips that sing the lullabies. Let us win the mothers of India for Christ, and the day will not long be deferred when India's sons also shall be brought to the Redeemer's feet."[93]

Yet all these efforts, insofar as they were directed at upper-caste women, usually stopped short of conversion, thanks to the *resistance* of the Indian women. If in the mission schools any one of the girls converted, the other parents withdrew their daughters and the school was often forced to close down. Although there were cases of secret conversions in which the wives did not tell their husbands, the zenana visits rather afforded an opportunity for wives to engage in secular pursuits such as learning English.[94]

More generally, the schools and visits continued to mask profound differences in views about family, marriage, and social hierarchy. There is no better illustration of this than the so-called Breast Cloth controversy of

1858 in the southern princely state of Travancore. It arose with the upwardly mobile toddy-tappers in the south, the Shanars, now rebranded as Nadars. As untouchables, they had suffered under multiple restrictions, including not being allowed to wear clothing above the waist or below the knee. Clothing was a sign of status, nakedness a sign of humility and shame. The missionaries of course urged the newly converted Nadar women to cover themselves in the name of modesty, which they were only too happy to do in the name of status elevation. But the upper castes regarded this as a sign of insolence and responded by burning down chapels and publicly stripping the women. Indignation naturally ran high in the British press, since the practice seemed to illustrate all the stereotypes of Indian barbarity. Eventually the courts and the local maharaja ruled in favor of the covering, as long as the specific fashion did not imitate that of high-caste women.[95]

The controversy illustrates an important point, namely that despite vast divergences of views on gender and society, there were specific points on which Indians and Westerners could converge, however different the meanings they attached to them. Female modesty was one of these; another was domesticity, which fit the nineteenth century Western middle-class view of women's place (insofar as the growth of factories in the West only accentuated the separation of home and workplace and hence of male and female spheres). Women's status could be changed and upgraded without altering their basic anchor in the home. Still, the effects of missionary activity were beginning to show in the early twentieth century: Christian women had higher rates of literacy than their Hindu counterparts, and fewer of them were marrying at an early age.[96] Insofar as these women were gaining a sense of their own self-worth, one can label this process one of *acculturation*, albeit a highly selective one.

One of the fruits of the Christian engagement with Indian women was the appearance of a distinguished indigenous Christian feminist who gained international fame and defied both Indian and Victorian gender expectations, Pandita Ramabai Sarasvati (1858–1922). Ramabai's family upbringing was at once a product of deep-seated Brahmin traditions and a conscious defiance of these. Her father, a learned Brahmin, believed in educating women and taught his wife and daughter to read and memorize some of the sacred writings; Ramabai could give public recitations of them by age 15. Her parents lived a life of mendicant asceticism, crossing the country on foot without possessions, reciting the sacred writings and prayers in return for offerings. Ramabai experienced great personal tragedy in her young years, losing both her parents to starvation and later her brother and husband to cholera. After exposure to the ideas of Brahmo Samaj, she became disillusioned with orthodox Hinduism and its views on women, particularly the treatment of child widows, and was attracted to Christianity, accepting baptism in 1883. English missionaries regarded this as a triumph, but she steadfastly resisted their attempts to channel her to a particular denominational rite or creed. For this she aroused opposition both from Anglicans and from Hindu nationalists (including Vivekananda). In the 1880s she traveled to England and the United States to promote women's education in India. She launched a foundation to provide funding for a boarding school for child widows, and her book, *The High Caste Hindu Woman*, became a bestseller. In her later years, she turned increasingly to studying the Bible, and translated it into her native Marathi in a style that would be simple and accessible to common people.[97]

If missionaries were the active agents in reaching out to Hindu women, just the opposite was true of the outcaste groups, variously known as untouchables, depressed classes, *Harijans* ("children of God," Gandhi's term), *Dalits* (the "broken" or "oppressed"), or, later, "scheduled tribes." Here the contacts were often initiated by the outcastes themselves.[98] Mass conversions from these groups began, as we have seen, in the south. From the 1860s and 1870s, they accelerated and spread to almost every region of India, nearly quadrupling the number of Christians in India by 1931.[99] Untouchables suffered religious as well as economic and social discrimination: according to Brahminical practice, they were not allowed to enter a Hindu temple or even hear, much less read, the Vedas – not to mention such things as exclusion from water sources used by the upper castes.[100] This, as well as their massive poverty, formed a favorable condition for such conversion. So too was the well-known opposition of most Protestant missionaries to the caste system. Beyond that, it is difficult to make generalizations about it. Certainly it was not uniformly true: there were many more outcastes who did *not* convert to Christianity (in 1992 the percentage of Indian Christians who were *Dalits* stood at 66 to 75 percent, while only 10 to 15 percent of *Dalits* were Christians).[101] Nor can one always find a neat correlation between conversions and economic crises such as famines, although these obviously played a role in some instances. The key seems to be the presence of local leadership. In some cases the initiative came from a group of elders who made a decision to convert;[102] in others from a member of a slightly higher caste who was exceptionally dedicated to those below;[103] in still others from religiously gifted illiterate members of the outcastes themselves.[104]

The initial conversions of outcastes often happened quickly and in groups, spreading via networks of extended family members. This took the missionaries themselves by surprise, especially where the latter had been focusing on developing – none too successfully – a core of converts among the upper castes. Whereas they had envisioned a top-down conversion process, just the opposite in fact occurred.[105] But if foreign missionaries did not initiate such conversions, they nevertheless found themselves thrust into playing an important role in them, as protectors and advocates for the poor. As one Lutheran missionary noted in 1897, "Any missionary who wants to work successfully among these people must be prepared to become to them not only a teacher, but also a pleader and an almoner."[106] An American missionary couple who published a memoir of their time in a northern Indian village in the 1930s wrote, "If we had supported all the litigation to which we were invited by our Christian brethren during our first six months among them, we would have been bankrupt both as to time and money."[107] They claim that, in accepting baptism, the untouchables were establishing a relationship of finding a patron, modelled on the relationship with the landowner who provided them with a pittance of food in return for work, but more advantageous. This suggests a strategy, at least initially, of *selective incorporation*, namely improvement of conditions within the caste system rather than rejecting the system itself. Yet the missionaries also chronicle a "vague reaching out for something better," exemplified in a desire for a schools and teachers, which worked as long as the boundaries dividing the untouchables from the other castes were not transgressed.[108]

As one might expect, the conversion process at first was uneven, and several studies record vacillations between Christianity and worship of Hindu or local deities. One such study of Travancore in the south in the nineteenth century tracked the relation between baptismal records and years of famine, finding that, while baptisms generally increased during famines, there was also a reverse movement of newly converted Christians back to worshipping their old gods, on the assumption that the latter were angry for not having been propitiated.[109] Over time, however, a sense of Christian identity became firmer at the expense of the local gods, who were either subordinated to God or Jesus or disappeared entirely.[110] According to another study from the 1930s, very few "idols" were to be found in the homes of *Dalit* converts.[111] This study concluded – as have most studies since – that the Christian doctrine of God's and Christ's love gave the outcastes a sense of self-worth and dignity they had previously lacked and which Hinduism had failed to provide. This in itself provided the motivation for whatever material improvement they were able to attain.

The growth of *Dalit* Christianity became highly controversial in the first half of the twentieth century, as the issue of the status of the untouchables became intertwined with the move toward independence. By this time, the *Dalits* had gained a powerful spokesman in the person of Vedanayagam Samuel Azariah (1874–1945), who became India's first native Anglican bishop. Azariah's grandfather was a Nadar of the toddy-tapper caste, but was a merchant, which set him apart from the others. He came from an area that had been exposed to missionary Christianity; Azariah's father went to a missionary school, converted, and became a village pastor. The son was able to take advantage of further educational opportunity and attend Madras Christian College. Vedanayagam resolved to be a missionary himself in his 20s and found a vehicle in the Indian YWCA, which had rapidly become an international movement with some 25 associations in India alone. He worked in that organization until 1906, when he left to become missionary to outcastes in Dornakal, an isolated impoverished area just north of Madras. He soon turned it into the fastest growing diocese in all of South Asia, continuing to work there during his bishopric, which began in 1912.[112]

Azariah's missionary activity drew criticism from Gandhi, who saw it as undermining Hinduism. Gandhi held that such conversions were insincere and matters of convenience rather than genuinely spiritual. At the same time, another powerful *Dalit* leader emerged, the economist and jurist B. R. Ambedkar (1891–1956), who criticized Christianity on opposite grounds from Gandhi, namely that Christianity had failed to agitate sufficiently for overcoming *Dalit* oppression (Ambedkar would eventually convert to Buddhism).[113] These differences became complicated by the British policy of creating limited representation for Indians in the colonial parliament, with separate seats earmarked for different social and religious groups. Thus arose the concept of the "scheduled castes." After independence, this concept was continued in the form of "compensatory discrimination," which reserved a number of places in education and government for *Dalits*. But Christian *Dalits* were explicitly excluded from these scheduled castes, on the grounds that Christianity did not recognize untouchability. Perhaps the most impressive demonstration of the spiritual integrity of the *Dalit* Christians came when these communities held together in the face of these exclusions.[114]

The people in India who proved to be by far the most receptive to Christianity were the ethnic minorities, known as *Adivasi* (aboriginals), or tribal peoples. Officially recognized as "scheduled tribes" in the Indian Constitution, they often live in remote or heavily forested areas, retain their distinct languages and cultures, and have frequently successfully resisted assimilation into broader Indian culture. According to the 2011 census, 32.8 percent of the *Adivasi* are Christians, compared to 2.3 percent of the Indian population as a whole. They are particularly concentrated in several mountainous northeastern provinces – Mizoram, Meghalaya, and Nagaland – where they represent between 70 and 90 rcent of the population.[115]

The process of Christianization in the last of these, Nagaland, which lies on the eastern border with Burma, has particularly drawn scholarly attention, in part because of the especially high rate of conversion in the face of what would seem to be a remote and isolated locale.[116] The rugged topography of the region, which consists of a series of valleys separated by steep ridges, created a dozen or so microcosmic societies, each with a language that was mutually unintelligible to the others. These were also warrior headhunter societies, in which preserving the skulls of enemies was considered essential to ensure crop fertility. Thus the worldview and religion of each of these societies was focused on its own local area and gods, viewing those of any neighboring groups with fear and mistrust. The Nagas periodically raided the agricultural societies in the plains and successfully resisted conquest until the coming of the British in the mid-nineteenth century.

The British were initially drawn to confront the Nagas in order to protect their tea plantations from raids by the mountain warriors. Attempts to conquer them militarily failed, but in the 1870s the British developed a new strategy, namely offering their services as mediators in disputes among the Naga villages. This proved to be attractive to a number of chiefs who made alliances with the outsiders, and the British gradually extended their claims as administrators to the entire region. Also in the 1860s, the first missionaries, American Baptists, appeared, having been frustrated by failure to convert the people of the plains, and also managed to establish a presence using peaceful means (one of the first, it is said, faced down a group of spear-bearing Nagas by taking out his violin and starting to play and sing).[117] The timing of the missionaries' arrival, occurring just as the Nagas were thrust into contact with the wider world by the British, explains much of their success.

As elsewhere, the main means the missionaries used to spread Christianity were literacy and education. The Baptists quickly went to work creating written vernaculars for several of the Naga languages, using Roman, rather than Sanskrit, characters. This had the effect of reducing the number of languages by elevating a few to written status, and this in turn broke down barriers of isolation. Schools offered practical training as well as religious education. One missionary wrote, "with a mission school there immediately follows a Sunday school and out of that grows a church."[118]

Richard M. Eaton views the massive conversion of the Nagas to Christianity over a hundred-year period as essentially corroborating the thesis of the Africanist Robin Horton.[119] Horton claimed, it will be recalled, that contact with the wider world shifted attention and worship from such local gods to deities whose powers extended over a wider, even universal region, even if these broader deities had had been present but inactive in the local religion all along. The Nagas were soon drawn back into war at the macrocosmic level, as some 2,000 men were drafted to serve in the trenches in World War I. In World War II their land became a theater of mechanized warfare as the Japanese attempted to invade India. Eaton attributes the dramatic increase in conversions in the 1940s and 1950s – from 17.9 percent to 52.9 percent – to this ordeal.[120] By this time the Nagas had developed a unified national consciousness which resulted in the formation of a single state within independent India.

As with the *Dalits*, the process was by no means smooth. There was backsliding and dual participation, as Naga men chafed at the missionaries' prohibitions, such as drinking rice beer. Some of the missionaries, despite their accomplishments, showed contempt for Naga ways. But Eaton maintains that, in the long run, the missionaries' cultural attitudes mattered little. Rather what was important was their ability to convey the notion of a high God in language that spoke to the evolving beliefs of each particular linguistic group – a feat, basically, of *vernacular translation*. By comparing several such groups among the Nagas, who converted at different times and at different rates, Eaton is able to suggest this as a key explanatory factor.[121] Thus the Nagas serve to illustrate a more general, if obvious, conclusion: the introduction of literacy itself via Christianity was a tremendously powerful factor in conversion; in comparison, the relative imperviousness of Hindus, Buddhists, and Muslims to the missionaries may be attributed to the fact that their spirituality had long since been anchored in the written word.[122]

INDEPENDENCE AND AFTER

An enduring problem for Indian Christians since independence in 1949 has been their association, in many people's minds, with foreign influence, whether via missionaries or funding of schools and hospitals, and thus indirectly with European colonialism. Indian Christian leaders had long been painfully aware of this stigma and had made moves for church autonomy dating back to the mid-nineteenth century. One can find examples of lay participation in Catholic worship, for example, well before it became prevalent in the West.[123] Among Protestants, a landmark was the formation of the National Missionary Society in 1905, showing a commitment both to patriotism and evangelization. By 1930, it had 116 missionaries in eight provinces.[124] For Indian Protestants, ecumenism had a strong appeal, leading to the formation of a Church of South India in 1947, which nevertheless was far from immune to denominational fragmentation. This was conceived both as a means to church autonomy and to further the work of proselytization within India.[125] Indian Christians were, however, generally careful in their embrace of nationalism, avoiding extremist or violent versions.[126]

Nationalism in India has tended to take one of two forms. The first was that of a secular state, as represented by the first prime minister, Jawaharlal Nehru, and the Congress Party and inscribed in the Indian constitution. This guaranteed freedom of religion and recognized the plurality of faiths, languages, and cultures that comprised India. The second was identification of the nation with Hinduism, known today as *Hindutva*, or "Hindu-ness." It has been characterized as aiming to create "One Nation, One State, One Culture, One Religion, and One Language" for South Asia,[127] and thus represents the antithesis of the inclusiveness that has characterized Hindu spirituality for so much of its long life – a shift in other words, from diffuse toward concentrated spirituality. It embraces a theology of "eternal order" based on the Vedas, including the hierarchical notions underlying the caste system. It views conversion with particular horror, as it supposedly subverts the cosmic order that assigns everyone his or her place. Although politically in the ascendant since the 1990s, it has its roots in the early twentieth century as part of the *resistance* to missionary Christianity. Despite the constitutional protections of freedom of religion, already in the 1950s, Christians in central India were reporting harassment, and a state-sponsored report in one province claimed that missionaries were getting outside funding to lure the lower castes with material benefits. Under such pressures the government of Prime Minister Nehru reluctantly enacted restrictions on foreign missionaries in 1954.[128] Christian successes among the ethnic minorities in border regions increased fears of separatism such as had occurred with Muslims and Sikhs.[129] The growth of the *Hindutva* movement has led to acts of violence, first against

Muslims and increasingly against Christians since the 1990s, in one case (Orissa) creating some 20,000 refugees in 2008.[130]

Pitted against this *resistance*, there is evidence that Indian Christianity continues to be a dynamic and growing movement, feeding on and sustaining the missionary impulse. Frykenberg estimates the number of missionaries in India, including Pentecostal groups, to be between 40,000 and 100,000.[131] Much of this success remains among the *Adivasi* and *Dalit* groups, the latter having mobilized massively for their rights as

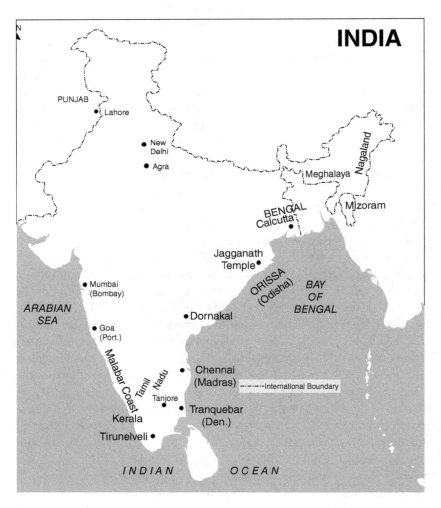

Figure 6.1 India
Source: Drawn by the author

citizens since independence. The churches have supported this movement, and it has even generated a *Dalit* theology, a branch of Liberation Theology. It claims that the essence of Christ's life and message is to uplift the oppressed, and that the Bible as a whole is a *Dalit* book.[132] It should also be mentioned that many who identify with Christianity forego baptism, in order to avoid being excluded as a scheduled caste.[133]

Christianity is still a minority religion in India, representing around 2–4 percent of its population.[134] But its influence is undeniably greater than what these numbers suggest. As we have seen, some of that influence has been paradoxical, in eliciting a movement toward *concentrated spirituality* within Hinduism itself. Yet Christianity also serves as a foil to the Hindu worldview, insofar as the latter is based on caste.

Meanwhile, the original Thomas Christians remain strong, numbering around 8.69 million, divided into eight separate churches (compared to 11.8 million Roman Catholics).[135] In parts of India where Catholicism is strong, masses of Hindus ignore the *Hindutva* strictures and continue to worship in Catholic shrines and participate in festivals honoring the Virgin Mary and the infant Jesus, along with Shiva or Vishnu, as they have done for centuries. These processions have become more popular in recent years.[136] And charismatic gurus continue to incorporate Christian figures and symbols into their practice, following the principle of one God, many paths. Thus, despite having acquired a unitary label, Hinduism remains, more than ever, a container of contradictions. The same might be said of Indian Christianity itself.

7

East Asia

China, Japan, and Korea

East Asian encounters with missionary Christianity since 1500 have encompassed a full spectrum of strategies, from passionate *acceptance and commitment* to equally impassioned and uncompromising *resistance.*[1] In order to discern a pattern in these changing relationships, one must understand something of Confucianism, a religion that, along with Buddhism and to a lesser extent Taoism, has put its stamp on the entire East Asian region. As mentioned in the previous chapter, "Confucianism" is a nineteenth-century Western term stemming from the Jesuits in the sixteenth century. It was a Latinization of the name Kong Fuzi (551–479 BCE), who represented but by no means originated a tradition known by the Chinese as the school of *Ru* (scholars). This encompassed the classic writings that preceded Kong, not to mention the neo-Confucian movements that followed him. While the label, like "Hinduism," thus included a number of heterogeneous elements and combinations, this never reached the degree of luxuriant growth that one finds in Hinduism. Rather, as befits a scholarly enterprise, there was an emphasis on order, regularity and symmetry among the parts, which found expression in numerology and correlative thought. John Henderson has identified the latter as finding "systematic correspondences among aspects of various orders of reality, or realms of the cosmos, such as the human body, the body politic, and the heavenly bodies"– elements one could find in Hinduism and other traditions as well, but worked out here to a much greater degree.[2] Still, over time, Confucianism has taken on a variety of colorations: open to influences from Buddhism and Taoism in the Song and Ming dynasties, identified with hidebound conservatism in the nineteenth century and, more recently, with high educational standards that give Asians an edge in economic development. As for the relationship between Christianity and Confucianism, it too has oscillated widely over the centuries between antagonism and conciliation, inscribing a pattern that one might perhaps describe as a slow-motion dance, with the partners alternately approaching and distancing from each other over time.[3] In describing and explaining these complex patterns, two cardinal points should be kept in mind.

First, East Asian religions predominately take the form of diffuse spirituality, in contrast to Christianity, with the by-now-familiar proviso that neither system is reducible to a simple formula. Nevertheless, the sociologist C. K. Yang, writing in 1961 on the eve of Mao Zedong's Cultural Revolution, used the term "diffused" to characterize Chinese religion in general. He states, "[T]here was not one corner in this vast land of China where one did not find temples, shrines, altars, and other places of worship."[4] His fieldwork in eight localities scattered across the country yielded 1,786 major temples, encompassing a range of functions from welfare of families (including ancestors) and kinship groups to communities, the state, agriculture, crafts, commerce, health, and the general moral order. Many if not most of these temples were autonomous, run by local lay leaders, i.e., independent of Confucianism, Buddhism, or Taoism.

For a metaphysical underpinning of this system, one may turn to Stephen F. Teiser, who, in his introduction to Chinese religion, has characterized the fundamental beliefs as follows:

The basic stuff out of which all things are made it called *qi*. Everything that ever existed, at all times, is made of qi, including inanimate matter, humans and animals, the sky, ideas and emotions, demons and ghosts, the undifferentiated state of wholeness, and the world when it is teeming with different beings ... [This] indicates that there is no unbridgeable gap separating humans from gods or, for that matter, separating spirits from demons ... Humans are born with the capacity to transform their spirit into one of the Gods of the Chinese pantheon.[5]

In Japan, diffuse spirituality is seen in the approximately 80,000 officially recognized Shinto shrines (plus many unofficial ones) that dot the countryside, memorials to the *kami*, or nature spirits – although the notion that Shinto existed as the original primordial Japanese religion has been put to rest by scholars.[6] Given this fluidity, East Asian spirituality often finds expression more in ritual than in creeds, leaving the exact nature and number of deities undefined. Thus, Confucius is notable for the relative, albeit not complete, absence of a God-term in his writings, though he makes eighteen references to an impersonal heaven in the *Analects*. His concentration on affairs of this world has led some to classify him as a secular humanist, though many have found an unmistakably transcendent dimension in his invocation of heaven.[7]

One consequence of this diffuse spirituality was an openness to foreign religious influences – most strikingly in the East Asians' assimilation of Buddhism over an extended period of time – and in efforts to find points of concordance and harmony among multiple religious traditions. Thus it is common to refer to the "three teachings" of Chinese religion: Confucianism, Taoism, and Buddhism. Japanese imperial rulers around 750 CE similarly sought to harmonize Buddhism and Shinto. Here, the notion of syncretism finds ready application, although it is no less of an umbrella-like concept here than elsewhere, covering a variety of moves.[8] Thus. the harmonization of traditions did not exclude competition and rivalry between and among them. But such competitions typically involved the engagement with the opposing doctrine through debate and dialogue, so that each party had to take account of others' views.[9] These interactions were facilitated by the existence of a common written language among the elite, in China a product of the imperial bureaucracy and the examination system, whose impact could even be felt at the village level.[10] Of course, such interactions were not all sweetness and light, as both China and Japan underwent periods of disunity, civil strife, and centralizing despotism, which could lead to persecutions such as the massive destruction of Buddhist temples in China in 845 CE. But during the Ming Dynasty (1346–1644), the conciliatory tendencies were in the ascendant, including the extension of correlative thought.[11]

Second, much of East Asian religion, particularly Confucianism, was intimately bound up with the state and its vicissitudes. This was true in a practical sense, inasmuch as the Confucian classics served as curriculum for the civil services examinations of the imperial bureaucracy. The Chinese emperor, the "Son of Heaven," occupied a key position in maintaining the human connection with the divine, and his legitimacy was determined by the "Mandate of Heaven." The rituals that he performed ensured the orderly cycles of nature and protection from natural disasters. Moreover, local religion frequently bore the imprint of a bureaucratic metaphor in the form of a hierarchical ordering of the spirits. Thus, as Teiser observes:

At the apex of the divine bureaucracy stands the Jade Emperor ... in Heaven, corresponding to the human Son of Heaven (*Tianzi*, another name for emperor) who rules over earth ... The local officials of the celestial administrations are the

Gods of Walls and Moats, and below them are the Gods of the Hearth, one per family, who generate a never-ending flow of reports on the people under their jurisdiction. They are assisted in turn by gods believed to dwell inside each person's body ... carrying with them the records of good and evil deeds committed by their charges.[12]

The Japanese imperial rulers also established a heavenly basis of legitimacy in the seventh century CE, as did the Tokugawa shoguns in the seventeenth.[13]

By the same token, when the emperor failed to execute Heaven's mandate, e.g., in times of economic hardship, natural disasters, or political instability, religion served as an outlet for popular protest and even rebellion. Religious sects, often meeting in secret, were a recurring feature of Chinese culture; in a sense they mirrored the political values of the state in that they stepped in when the state failed to live up to its mandate. These sects provided venues for *concentration of spirituality*: intensity, ascetic practices, small-group exclusivity, and, above all, millennialism – the belief that present signs indicated an imminent cataclysm followed by a new age of peace and prosperity for the surviving righteous. Such hopes were found in Buddhism in the belief in the *Maitreya Buddha* – the Buddha of the future – long before the coming of Christianity; during the Song Dynasty (960–1279 CE), some of them acquired the name *White Lotus*, which remained into the nineteenth century. Needless to say, popular Christianity could readily merge with them.[14]

Such unrest, and the threat of it, naturally provoked a repressive reaction on the part of state authorities. In this way, the state placed limits on openness to new forms of religious expression – when such forms were perceived to undermine the established order of state and society. The alternation of openness and repression forms the basic outline for the narrative of East Asian negotiation with Christianity, both missionary-inspired and local, down to the present day, with the precise rhythms and intensity determined by particular historical circumstances.

EARLY MODERN JAPAN

Nowhere were these gyrations as great, nor the consequences as cataclysmic, as in early modern Japan. Statistics give the bare outlines of the story: following the arrival of the first three Jesuit missionaries in 1549 (including Francis Xavier from India), Japan had an estimated 500 Christians by the mid-1550s. By 1571, the number had jumped to 30,000; by 1583, to 150,000; and at its height in 1614, roughly 300,000, representing about

1.5 percent of the entire population. At this time there were 143 European missionaries plus 250 native catechists (*dojuku*). The contrary tide of persecutions may be dated from 1597, when 26 Christians were publicly executed in Nagasaki. The numbers increased sharply after 1614, with 265 executions by 1620; 773 by 1630; and 912 by 1640.[15] By 1650, Christianity had been largely wiped out, except for about 30,000, meeting as secret congregations.[16]

These numbers are explained by the timing of Christianity's arrival toward the end of a period of civil war among local and regional lords (*daimyo*), from 1467 to 1567, characterized by widespread lawlessness and impoverishment, and overlapping with political reunification of Japan at the hands of three successive military leaders: Oda Nobunaga, Toyotomi Hideyoshi, and Tokugawa Ieyasu (1568–1614), the last of whom took the title of shogun (military governor) and founded a dynasty that lasted to 1868. The missionaries came on Portuguese merchant ships which carried goods from China, where the Portuguese had obtained an enclave at Macao. The impoverished *daimyo* of the southeastern island of Kyushu, closest to China, vied with each other for that trade, and under these circumstances Christianity became most attractive. The official Jesuit supervisor, called a visitor, to Japan, Alexander Valignano, had no illusions about the process. He observed in 1580:

For as the lords of [Kyushu] Japan are very poor ... and the benefits they derive when the ships come to their ports are very great, they try hard to entice them to their fiefs. And since they have convinced themselves that they will come to where there are Christians and churches ... many of them, even though they are heathen, seek to get the padres to come thither ... And since the Japanese are so much at the disposal of their lords, they readily become converted when told to do so by their lords and they think it is their wish. This is the door by which entered most of those who were baptized in the beginning ...[17]

Of course, such numbers of converts could evaporate just as quickly if and when such a lord was overthrown by a rival. Nevertheless, one of them, Omura Sumitada, was baptized as Dom Bartholomeu in 1563, burning down the local Buddhist temple in commemoration. Twelve years later, he ordered all his subjects to convert as well, netting some 60,000 souls; more temples were either destroyed or made into churches. What is more, in 1580 he donated the harbor town of Nagasaki to the Jesuits, making it the favored port of the merchant ships and providing a stable colony for Christians.[18]

It would be tempting to conclude from such incidents that the motives for Japanese conversion were purely economic or political – or the result of compulsion. But the evidence does not completely support this. One has only to point to the mass demonstrations, sometimes extending to self-flagellations, in the face of the persecutions and executions as they began to mount in the early 1600s, signs of *acceptance and commitment.*[19] Missionaries themselves noted the extraordinary devotion of many Japanese. To again quote Valignano, "But they all have this in common, that after they become Christians they pay no regard whatsoever to their idols, and in this point they far surpass those of India, who even after their conversion are greatly prone to hanker after their idols."[20] Valignano himself deserves no small credit for this result, as he instituted a policy of strict accommodation on the part of the missionaries to Japanese customs, following Xavier's example. Valignano's instructions were exceedingly specific: Jesuits should imitate the natives in dress, housing, diet, etiquette, and cleanliness. They were to avoid ostentatious display of religious artifacts, including crosses, and steer away from controversial issues. In this way, the Japanese could more easily transfer their veneration for Buddhist monks, who were also supposed to lead ascetic lives but who were widely regarded as a danger, to the new clergy from abroad – a good example of *conservation of form.* The use of beads in prayer was popular in both traditions – a *cultural hook* – and Christian converts would bring in their Buddhist beads to be burned and traded for rosary ones.[21] Indeed, it is hardly surprising that initially some Japanese thought that the missionaries represented a sub-sect of Buddhism – as some Chinese were also to do.[22]

Such accommodation stopped short, however, of any concessions to Buddhism on creedal matters. The Jesuit catechisms began with the assertion of a "personal and infinite Creator" as opposed to the falsehoods of beliefs in many gods. The missionaries claimed that the defects of Japanese religion were manifest in the prevalence of war, pestilence, and famine that the country was suffering from – an argument that undoubtedly had an appeal. So did the discipline and hierarchical structure of the Jesuit order itself, which was not unattractive to the Samurai warrior class.[23] Indeed, the first of the great unifiers, Nobunaga, himself an agnostic and no friend of Buddhism, positively encouraged the missionaries and supported the extension of the area in which they could proselytize.[24]

Part of this missionary strategy of accommodation was the decision to target the ruling class – not only the rulers themselves but the people directly under them, from whom the *dojuku* were largely recruited. Valignano went so far as to close a hospital that catered primarily to the poor on the grounds that it would give the Jesuits a bad name.[25] But while he strove to create from this upper class of converts an educated native clergy who could meet Jesuit standards of learning (including mastery of Latin), this was more than he could manage, at least before the persecutions began. This proved to be a serious weakness, because many of these *dojuku*, who had done the brunt of the work for the mission, became resentful that they could not become priests. One of them, a certain Fabian Fucan, having been a leading spokesman for the Jesuits, became a vigorous anti-Christian polemicist in 1620.[26]

Into this rather controlled mission environment, in the 1590s, came the Franciscans from the Philippines, which had recently been claimed by Spain. Their tactics were just the opposite of the Jesuits: they ministered directly to the poor and sick, and they did not hesitate to flaunt the outward signs of their faith. Thus was introduced a rivalry between missionaries that became part of a larger one between Spanish and Portuguese. To these were soon added the voices of Dutch and English merchant-adventurers, who were eager to denounce all forms of Catholicism to the Japanese. The effect was to sow seeds of suspicion among the rulers who were in the process of unifying the country. Particularly worrisome was the possibility that one of these foreign powers would give military aid to one of the southern Christian *daimyo* to overthrow the central authority.

Faced with such prospects, both Hideyoshi and later Ieyasu wavered. On the one hand, they continued to recognize the importance of the Portuguese trade and the language skills of the Jesuits in maintaining it – although this became less crucial as the years went on; on the other, a specific incident or intrigue could tip the scales in favor of suspicion and repression. Thus, Hideyoshi issued a decree banning missionaries in 1587 but did not enforce it; but when a Spanish ship ran aground off the coast of Japan, it provided the pretext for the executions of 1597. Conditions eased again under Ieyasu in the 1600s, but an accumulation of court intrigues involving Christians sorely tried his patience until he finally issued a decree completely banning Christianity from Japan in 1614, two years before his death.

The language of both Hideyoshi's and Ieyasu's decrees indicates that more than trade and national security were at stake; there was also the preservation of Japan's religious identity. They contain the refrain that "Japan is the land of the gods (*kami*)." The 1614 document goes on to maintain: "Japan is also called the country of Buddha ... *kami* and buddhas are different in name but one in their intentions ... That clique

of padres contravenes our polity, traduces Shinto, calumniates our righteous teachings, destroys our sense of justice, and corrupts our virtue ...
They are the enemy of *kami* and buddhas."[27] All Japanese were now
required to become a member of a Buddhist sect, which was empowered
to certify annually that parishoners had not fallen away. This remained in
place until 1868.

Under Ieyasu's son and especially his grandson, the persecutions escalated in scope and cruelty. Unfortunately the missionaries at first seriously
underestimated the determination of the shoguns and continued to work
underground or to penetrate Japan from abroad, disguised as merchants.
This only increased the rulers' suspicions, leading to more executions. For
their part, the Japanese underestimated the appeal of martyrdom to
Christians; underground tracts exhorted potential victims to imagine
Christ on the cross. Eventually this led to a shift in emphasis from
execution to torture in order to get the victims to commit apostasy; one
hand was left free to give the signal as their bodies were immersed in hot
sulfur springs or suspended upside down in pits of excrement. But all this,
though effective up to a point, also had the effect of spreading the faith, as
Christians fled from the areas where they had been concentrated to the
north and east where they were previously unknown. The peasants and
fishermen tended to remain steadfast more than the upper classes – to the
great annoyance of the shoguns.[28]

Annoyance turned to alarm as the Tokugawa faced an unexpected
rebellion, involving some 37,000 people, in the Shimabara Peninsula near
Nagasaki. Although triggered by economic grievances and the treatment
of peasants by the *daimyo*, it quickly adopted Christian slogans to mobilize its followers. The result was a bloodbath, as the rebels were besieged in
a castle for six months and were summarily executed, but with heavy
losses on the Tokugawa side as well. The immediate aftermath was the
complete cessation of the Portuguese trade. Moreover, as the government
realized it faced an indigenous movement, not simply promulgated by
missionaries, it added inquisitional methods, such as annual temple
inspections throughout the country to ascertain there were no secret
Christians, e.g., by forcing peasants to walk on images of the virgin and
other holy icons. Rewards were given to people who informed on
Christians.[29] Nevertheless, the "hidden Christians" (*kakure*) managed
to survive, without priests, into the nineteenth century and the fall of
the Tokugawa. Local leaders assumed the responsibility of baptism, and
nineteenth-century missionaries could still recognize some of the prayers
the *kakure* had passed on through seven generations, although they had

lost any knowledge of their meaning. At the same time, elements from Shinto, Buddhist, and popular religion were conserved and incorporated in the *kakure* rites, illustrating, as Ann Harrington writes, "what Japanese had been doing for centuries."[30]

EARLY MODERN CHINA

The Court and the Literati

One of the initial Japanese objections to Christianity was that if it were true, the Chinese would have known about it.[31] In fact, Nestorian Christians had been present in China during the Tang Dynasty (618–907 CE) and the Mongol Yuan Dynasty (1271–1368), catering primarily to foreign merchants and other ethnic groups but leaving little impact on the Han Chinese people; on the contrary, the greatness of Chinese civilization exerted a magnetic attraction for these outsiders – a process known as "Sinicisation."[32] In any case, it was not until the seventeenth century that the Chinese themselves began to interact with missionary Christianity on a significant scale.

The initiative for this process came first from the Jesuits, in what must be ranked as among the most thoroughly planned and skillfully executed missions in modern history – in the face of adverse conditions. There were approximately 60 failed attempts of missionaries to penetrate China beyond the Macau enclave between 1552 and 1583, involving some 50 missionaries.[33] Once again, Valignano provided the winning set of strategies: (1) accommodation to Chinese culture, including learning the language; (2) focusing on the elite, which consisted of the *literati* schooled in the classics required of imperial bureaucrats, and ideally the emperor himself; (3) using Western science and technology as a means to attract these; (4) being tolerant of Chinese moral values. The individual who most successfully executed these policies was Matteo Ricci, who after nineteen years of study and effort, obtained permission to reside in Beijing in 1601. Among the Western innovations he introduced were machines like the clavichord and the clock, the last of which came to be in great demand; a world map that flatteringly placed China at the center;[34] examples of realistic Western art; and most profoundly, knowledge of Western mathematics and astronomy. The latter proved to be especially valuable to the emperors, whose heavenly mandate involved bringing the human realm into harmony with the cyclical movements of the planets and stars. Moreover, Ricci immersed himself in the study of the literary language and the Chinese classics; his translations of Christian prayers remained in use into the twentieth century.

Ricci's method of harmonizing Christianity and Confucian ideas was to selectively focus on a number of references in Confucius's writings to a Sovereign-on-High (*Shangdi*), or Master of Heaven (*t'ien*), claiming these to be identical with the personal Christian creator-God. This, he argued, was Confucius's original meaning; the attributions of heaven as an impersonal organism came from later misinterpretations (the so-called Neo-Confucianism of the Song Dynasty). The Western religion filled in, so to speak, the bare outlines of Chinese picture. Ricci relied heavily on the argument from design, portraying God as the designer and first cause of the universe. If Ricci was dismissive of Neo-Confucianism, he was even harsher on Buddhism and Taoism, which, he claimed, traced the origins of the universe to a "voidness" or "nothingness." Ricci was even more deliberately selective in his presentation of Christianity, mentioning Jesus only briefly at the end of his major polemical work, *The True Meaning of the Lord of Heaven*. Thanks probably to Ricci, the Chinese name for Christianity at the time bypassed Jesus in favor of "Heavenly Studies" (*tianxue*).[35]

Ricci's arguments found a positive reception among a number of high-ranking literati, some of whom were baptized and served as patrons and propagators. This was true not only in the capital, but in several provincial cities, thanks in large part to Ricci's building a network of friends and supporters before he reached Beijing. Europeans and Chinese both wrote treatises and prefaces promoting the Christian philosophy, reinforcing the impression of commonality among literati across the continents.[36] To quote one of them:

The kingdoms of the West are scores of thousands of *li* distant from China. Since the beginning of the world, we have never communicated through interpreters. Our language and writing are different. But one fine day, these people, taking great care over what they brought with them, translated it into Chinese, and there was then, as it were, the discovery of a perfect correspondence with the idea of our Saints and Sages when they declare that one must respect and fear Heaven ... It is just as our Confucianism says: "There is nothing that is not included and covered by this marvel that is Heaven's work of creation-transformation."[37]

Especially compelling was the confluence of Christian and Confucian teachings on morality. One could point to a significant overlap between Christianity and Confucianism on ethical values, e.g., between the Fourth Commandment to honor one's parents and the Confucian doctrine of filial piety. Granted, this weave was not seamless: Christians condemned the practice of taking a concubine, which was common among the literati, and was justified in case one's spouse failed to produce a son.[38] Nonetheless, the Jesuits managed to convert 140 members of the extended imperial Ming family by 1636.[39] The fame of Ricci is shown in that one of his writings found its way into the *Imperial Encyclopedia* in the eighteenth century, and Ricci himself was deified as the patron saint of the clockmakers of Shanghai.[40]

This acclamation, however, was far from universal, and the more the literati became familiar with Christian doctrine and practices, the more voices were raised against it. Anti-Christian writings began to surface within a few years of Ricci's death in 1610. Their arguments were basically that the notion of a creator-God was at odds with that of an impersonal order of Heaven and Earth (as Fucan was also arguing in Japan). The Christian story introduced all sorts of irrationalities, for example, the sin of Adam and Eve, which showed that God's creation was flawed from the beginning. In the words of one critic, "This is like an artisan who has built an unsuited tool. We [the Confucianists] would not say that it is the fault of the instruments, but that the artisan has poor skill."[41] Moreover, the Ten Commandments contradicted the hierarchical Confucian order in a fundamental way: obedience to one's Heavenly Father took precedence over obedience to one's natural father and to the monarch. Even more disturbing, from the point of view social hierarchy, was the idea that God could be incarnate in the low-born person of Jesus and the fact that he was crucified as a common criminal. In the words of a Manchu prince:

I was enchanted by the order, clarity and weight of the arguments that proved the existence of a sovereign being, the creator of all things ... But when I reached the place where it was taught that the son of God became a man, I was astonished that people so enlightened in other respects should have mixed in with so many truths a doctrine which seemed to me so improbable and which shocked my reason.[42]

To these arguments could be added some fundamental anxieties, e.g., that Christians posed a threat to Chinese sexual mores by creating ritual situations (baptism, communion, confession) involving close physical proximity between male priests and female congregants. And even more, the suspicion of Christianity as a foreign religion, possibly part of a plot to overthrow the Chinese Empire.[43]

The increasing number of anti-Christian writings, stemming from high officials, thus gave rise to a series of imperial bans on missionaries over the next two centuries, creating a pattern not unlike Japan's, although much more protracted in time and milder in their execution.[44] The missionaries typically were exiled to Macau or Canton or went into hiding. As with Japan, this was no simple linear process, but the result of pressures working in contrary directions. The expertise of some Jesuits in astronomy proved to be the chief mitigating factor, actually drawing the missionaries closer to the emperors even as they lost the support of the literati. This enabled the missionaries to survive the transition from the Ming dynasty to the Qing dynasty in the 1630s and '40s – a transition marked by war and upheaval and, as in Japan, opportunities for missionary expansion in some areas.[45] Although the new rulers tended to be more suspicious of foreign influences, they relied on Jesuits Johann Adam Schall and Ferdinand Verbiest for advice on the calendar, resulting in their appointment as directors of the royal Bureau of Astronomy (Schall even had a chapel established within the Forbidden City).[46] Needless to say, this provoked a reaction among the literati, leading to a particularly dramatic moment when in 1664 one of them accused Schall of making a false prediction. Schall was sentenced to death, only to be saved by an earthquake which struck the imperial palace the next day; but four other Chinese converts paid with their lives.[47]

These contrary tendencies were especially evident during the long reign of the Kangxi emperor (1661–1722). At first, the trajectory was upward: the Jesuits' value was demonstrated not only in astronomy, but also in diplomacy and artistic endeavors – several Jesuit painters introduced Western techniques of perspective and portraiture. Kangxi rewarded them with an edict of toleration in 1692, not extending to proselytization, but claiming that they at least did not pose a threat to the kingdom.

This goodwill was soon undermined, however, by the famous rites controversy, a classic confrontation between expressions of diffuse and concentrated spirituality. It may be traced back to the arrival of the Franciscans and Dominicans who, as in Japan, took a more confrontational approach to native customs than the Jesuits. These friars were shocked by the Chinese custom of making offerings to wooden tablets in their homes, which embodied the spirits of their ancestors, or in larger ceremonies in ancestral halls belonging to a given lineage. The Jesuits preferred to view this as a civic rite, an expression of veneration for one's departed relatives; the friars saw it as idolatry.[48] The controversy dragged on for some 60 years, involving Chinese Christian literati as well as Westerners. In 1704 the pope ruled decisively against the Jesuits, forbidding Christians from performing these rites. The papal emissary, Charles de Tournon, who conveyed the ruling to the emperor, lacked knowledge of Chinese and behaved in a high-handed way, disillusioning the otherwise tolerant Kangxi. The emperor issued a licensing procedure in response, requiring missionaries to subscribe to the policies of Ricci. Relations continued to deteriorate until Kangxi's son, the Yongzheng emperor, declared Christianity illegal in 1724, shortly after ascending the throne. This effectively shut down Christian publications, but did not lead to massive persecutions on the scale of Japan – only intermittent bursts, depending again on circumstances. Jesuit astronomers and artists remained at court – a good example of *selective incorporation* – and Christianity remained tolerated in Beijing until 1811. The official proscription remained, however, until the 1840s, while the papal ban on ancestral rites held until 1939.[49]

Beyond the Court

Meanwhile, Christianity had learned to survive underground. Table 7.1 represents the best estimates of the (admittedly inexact) numbers of foreign missionaries, Chinese clergy, and native Christians in the early modern period. It demonstrates the overall inability of the imperial bureaucracy to enforce the ban, either in substantially reducing the number of clergy or the number of Christians in the long run. Missionaries evaded detection by moving from place to place, staying in peoples' homes. This meant that more Chinese were drawn to the clergy themselves, and also that, for most of the time, native Christians were thrown back on their own resources, which proved to be sufficient to maintain the practice of the religion. To be sure, there were apostasies, but the remarkable fact was that these Christian communities survived into the nineteenth century and beyond.[50] Moreover, these were not necessarily poor or socially marginal groups; in one study, the percentage of degree-holders who were Christians matched the percentage in the population as a whole. That said, the majority of Chinese Christians were undoubtedly poor peasants.[51]

These figures are admittedly misleading in that they remained relatively constant during a period when the population of China is said to have doubled, namely in the late eighteenth and early nineteenth centuries. They also suggest that the foundation for this survival had already been established by the turn of the eighteenth century, before the ban. The Jesuits, beginning with Ricci, drew on their European experience to create groups of laymen ("confraternities") and networks which in turn

Table 7.1 *Estimated numbers of missionaries, Chinese clergy, and Christians in China, 1590–1820*[52]

Decade	Missionaries (Chinese in parentheses)	Christians
1590s	4	100
1600s	15 (7)	2,000
1610s	18 (6)	6,000
1620s	26 (3)	13,000
1630s	44 (6)	60,000
1640s	–	70,000
1650s	36 (5)	–
1660s	38 (2)	110,000
1670s	43 (4)	–
1680s	–	100,000
1690s	97 (10)	200,000
1700s	148 (6)	196,200
1710s	89 (4)	–
1720s	90 (4)	
1730s	109 (26)	–
1740s	–	120,000
1750s	–	–
1760s	101 (44)	135,000
1770s	71 (28)	–
1790s	–	150,000
1800s	76 (50)	–
1810s	113 (78)	217,000

Nicolas Standaert, ed. *Handbook of Christianity in China*, Vol. 1: *635-1800* (Leiden: Brill, 2001), pp. 307–8, 382–83.

spawned communities; it is a misconception to think that they only catered to the elites.[53] But they succeeded because they could tap into a rich Chinese associational tradition of benevolent societies and lay religious organizations. Another strong contributing factor was the Confucian emphasis on filial piety, which established strong intergenerational bonds. Thus one common form of association was the extended family or lineage; once such a family adopted Christianity, it tended to remain so, often ignoring the Western prohibition of ancestor veneration.[54] Sometimes confraternities served as surrogates for family associations when people had to move to escape persecution.[55] Others served specific religious functions, such as praying for the souls of the departed in purgatory, thereby earning them indulgence.[56] Still others served as venues for ascetic practices, such as the Confraternity of the Passion, which imitated the sufferings of the crucified Christ.[57] One can conclude that such Christianity was *selectively incorporated* into preexisting Chinese traditions and practices.[58] Christianity came to be regarded less as a foreign religion than as an indigenous sect, the Heavenly Lord sect.[59]

At the local level, these traditions and practices sometimes overlapped with those of Buddhism and Taoism, embracing heterodox ideas that officials viewed with a combination of tolerance and suspicion. Such sects were frequently open to participation by women, which went against the traditional insistence on subordination of women to men. Chinese Christianity fit this pattern: given the taboos on the sexes congregating in churches, women began to meet in secret already in the late Ming era; in other cases, separate churches were built for them.[60] Soon women's associations and confraternities developed, enabling them to play an active role in the spread of Christianity. Wealthy widows, such as Candida Xu (1607–80), donated substantial funds for the building and decoration of churches.[61] Moreover, Christianity offered role models for women in the stories of the virgin saints such as Catherine of Siena, stories that were definitely subversive in the Confucian context. Given that women's duty was to marry and bear children, a number of Christian converts refused to do so, eventually forming celibate orders such as the *beatas* in Fujian or the Institute of Christian Virgins in Sichuan.[62] The latter eventually became a teaching order. Such women were often persecuted initially for refusing to marry, but over time the orders came to be accepted as part of the heterodox landscape.

Because Christians shared this landscape with other religious groups that were more politically subversive, and because they themselves often met in secret, they suffered a certain amount of guilt by association in the eyes of the state. This was especially true with respect to their relations with the White Lotus movement, although this was more an umbrella-like term covering a variety of sects. Some White Lotus groups did indeed seek cover for their own activities by using Christian labels such as the Lord of Heaven Teaching; a massive influx of some 5,000 newly baptized Christians in Shandong Province in 1714, totally out of proportion to normal conversion rates, has no other plausible explanation.[63] Such opportunism did not preclude, however, at times a genuine blending of Christian and non-Christian characteristics, given the fluidity and fragmentation of these sects.[64] Whatever the case, Christians faced the threat of persecution whenever a sectarian uprising occurred, as happened increasingly by the early nineteenth century. Local officials, however, often looked the other way, especially if suitably bribed. There are remarkably few accounts of popular outbursts against Christians in the seventeenth and eighteenth centuries–in marked contrast to a century later.

NINETEENTH-CENTURY CHINA

Shortly after proscribing Christianity in 1724, the Yongzheng emperor addressed a group of missionaries as follows:

> You want all the Chinese to become Christians. I know well that this is something required by your religion. But if that happens, what will we become? The subjects of your kings? Your Christians only recognize you, and in time of trouble they will listen only to your voice. I know well that there is nothing to fear now. But when more and more boats come from your countries, then there could be disorders.[65]

These words proved to be prophetic: as a result of defeat in the Opium War (1839–42) against Britain and the subsequent treaties with Britain, the United States, and France (1842–44), missionaries gained reentry into the five port cities that were now open to foreign access. In those cities, Westerners now had the right to build churches and schools and to reclaim buildings that had been Catholic before the ban. In addition, missionaries were now under foreign protection, immune from prosecution under Chinese law, by virtue of the principle of extraterritoriality. A second round of war and treaties came in 1858–60, guaranteeing missionaries freedom to proselytize throughout China.[66] Moreover, missionary attitudes toward the Chinese now tended to be the exact opposite of the sixteenth century; rather than admiring Chinese civilization, they viewed it as backward and inferior to the West.

Concentration and Conservation: The Taiping Rebellion

The interaction of missionary initiative and native agency proved explosive with the appearance of Protestant missionaries, which began in 1807. As elsewhere, the Protestants put great stock in translating the Bible into the vernacular; missionaries produced two complete translations by 1840, often with largely unacknowledged native assistance, and several more followed by the end of the century. This difference of approach from the Catholics is reflected in the fact that, to this day, the Chinese classify Catholicism and Protestantism as two separate religions rather than as one: the Lord of Heaven teaching and the Christ teaching (*Tianzhujiao* and *Jidujiao*).[67]

The Protestants were also prolific in their use of the printing press, producing thousands of copies of Christian tracts in addition to the Bible. Not waiting for permission to enter, several missionaries traveled along the coast and up inland rivers, distributing these. The reception accorded Edwin Stevens, an American Baptist, on one of these journeys, has been described by Jonathan Spence:

The books left Stevens' hands as fast as they could be unloaded and carried ashore. On some days the crowds were eager and smiling, neat and courteous, as the decorous distribution proceeded; on others, they pressed around with such uncontrollable force that Stevens clambered up on walls to escape the grasping hands ... Sometimes, as if in anticipation of baptismal rites, the Chinese waded out through the water to his boat before he could go ashore, and asked him for their copies.[68]

The flamboyant German missionary and gifted linguist Karl Gützlaff established a network of paid Chinese to distribute tracts, which, although subject to much embezzlement, had a wide reach. Gützlaff's use of the term *Shangdi* for God, the term found in the Confucian texts – as distinct from the Catholic *Tianzhu* – gave it a special effectiveness among the people.[69] Of course, both Stevens and Gützlaff realized that not all such enthusiasts were motivated by spiritual hunger; simple curiosity played a role as well. Yet by this time the missionaries had already found a single fervent and influential convert who would become a pastor, pamphleteer, and missionary himself. This was Liang Fa (or Afa) (1789–1855), whose tract, *Good Words to Admonish the Age*, consisting mostly of Bible translations, appeared in 1832. Liang's spiritual journey reminds one of Martin Luther's, combining a sense of individual sinfulness with an acute moral critique of his society and finding the available religious solutions of Confucianism, Buddhism, and Taoism to be inadequate to assuage either one. Christianity provided a simple and powerful answer: worship One God rather than images, believe in Jesus Christ and the transformative power of the Holy Spirit, and follow the Ten Commandments, and be rewarded in heaven; the alternative was eternal punishment in hell.[70] Liang developed the confrontational strategy of going to cities and towns where the civil service examinations were held, distributing his tracts to the candidates in the hope of sowing random seeds. One such candidate was a young man named Hong Huoxiu, later renamed Hong Xiuquan, who journeyed to Canton from his village to take the examinations in 1836 – the first of four tries, all failures. A foreigner – in all probability Stevens – handed him Liang's *Good Words* at that time, though at first he paid it scant attention. That single deed, however, planted the fuse, so to speak, that would later ignite the most destructive war in nineteenth-century China, the Taiping Rebellion.

To understand how this could happen, one must note the increasingly unstable domestic conditions in China in the early nineteenth century. The doubling of population was outstripping the ability of the bureaucracy to provide basic services like flood control or grain distribution. In parts of the country government had more or less completely abdicated control to bands of pirates and robbers, particularly in frontier zones. As a result, rebellions multiplied, and with them the millennial belief in end times. An extended White Lotus rebellion lasted from 1796 to 1804 and was but one of several uprisings. But none were as extensive or destructive as the Taiping Rebellion, which lasted from 1851 to 1864. At its height it occupied an area in east-central China the size of France. The death toll from the civil war that defeated it has been estimated at between 20 and 30 million, with some estimates even higher.[71] Religion was not the only factor in accounting for this intensity – ethnic tensions were also key – but it nevertheless played a central role.

The question of whether the Taiping movement was genuinely Christian has been long debated. In terms of our vocabulary, it is fair to say that it represented a hybrid of several strategies, mainly *selective incorporation* and *concentration of spirituality* – not in static combination, but in a dialectical process, which was eventually resolved through *conservation of form*. One can begin to trace this in the mind of the founder, Hong Xiuquan. In 1837, upon returning from one of his failed examinations, he experienced an extended period of hallucinations and near-death lasting some 40 days, in which he had an extended and vivid dream of being in Heaven and facing a Heavenly father who ordered him to return to Earth to slay the evil demons there. After the battle, Hong returned to Heaven to be welcomed by the father, his wife, an elder brother, and a sister-in-law. The father and elder brother ordered him, against his own inclination, to return to Earth once more to continue fighting evil and to usher in a period of great peace (*Taiping*). Most, though not all, of these dream images were quite comprehensible in terms of a larger body of Chinese writings that would have been familiar to Hong. At first, he tended to dismiss the vision and resumed his life as a schoolteacher. But in 1843, he picked up Liang Afa's tract, which, as he read it, provided a remarkable key to the vision and reinforced its authenticity: the father was Jehovah, the elder brother was Jesus, and Hong himself was God's second son. Hong was further convinced of this by a

partial coincidence of Chinese characters between the transliteration of
Je-ho-vah and Hong's own name – a mode of persuasion that has been
dubbed "glyphomancy" and has been found in other cases of Chinese
conversion as well.[72] As another local study has shown, Hong was by no
means idiosyncratic in having such visions and incorporating a few
Christian concepts within Chinese beliefs about the supernatural.[73]

At the same time, Liang's version of Christianity conveyed the exclusivity of worshiping One God that set it apart from other Chinese religions.
One of Hong's first acts upon assuming his new calling was to smash the
tablets to Confucius in the school where he had taught – a gesture to be
imitated, incidentally, 40 years later by a youthful admirer of Hong who
would go on to lead a national revolution, Sun Yat-Sen.[74] Throughout the
rebellion, Hong and his followers destroyed images and temples to local
divinities as well as Buddhist and Taoist shrines, thus setting himself in
opposition to much Chinese popular religion. Such radicalism soon drove
Hong into the remote interior of Guangxi Province, where he established
a small sect called the Society of God-Worshippers at a place called
Thistle Mountain. In 1847, he returned to Canton, however, to receive
further instruction at the hands of another missionary, and came back
with the Gūtzlaff translation of the Bible. Thus, the Protestant Christian
identity was firmly established in his mind.

In the minds of the followers at Thistle Mountain, however, the mix
was quite different. The new religion quickly merged with the visionary
and shamanistic aspects of local religion, with Jehovah competing against
other gods in ways that Hong could not control. Spirit possession was
widespread, and others came forward claiming to be the mouthpieces of
Jesus and God himself; Hong found he had to share his charismatic
authority with them.

Around 1850, a number of changes took place that Max Weber would
have called the routinization of charisma: the leaders succeed in putting
an end to the waves of popular visions and trances by concentrating spirit
possession in the hands of a few; concentration was further served as the
movement acquired a political focus in that the demons to be slain became
the Qing Dynasty, enabling the rebellion proper to be launched; and the
leaders now proclaimed a new Heavenly kingdom with Hong as king.
From this point on, the Taiping ideology combined punitive and fearsome
aspects of the Old Testament God and the Book of Revelations with strict
military discipline in a highly effective way that reminded Weber of
Cromwell's model army in the English Puritan Revolution.[75] The regime
exhibited other puritanical features, such as segregation of the sexes and

taboos on drugs.[76] The Taipings were egalitarian in their economic ideas, establishing a common treasury of pooled wealth in the capital city. This phase of the rebellion exhibits elements of *conservation of form*: having set up a Heavenly capital city in Nanjing in 1853, Hong incorporated further rituals and hierarchical structures from the imperial tradition he knew so well: a new calendar, a hierarchy of titles and regalia, palaces, silk robes, concubines, and a new set of civil service exams, though based on the Bible.[77]

Observers noted that Christianity was the most conspicuous new feature of the regime. Reading the Confucian classics was banned, on pain of death by decapitation. In their place, the Taipings unleashed a torrent of printed Christian literature, including Gützlaff's Bible, involving the labors of 600 craftsmen.[78] Sunday worship was compulsory and included prayers, hymn singing, and sermons. The ferocity of their battles against the imperial troops was based on the notion that the emperors had committed blasphemy in taking the title "Lord of Heaven" for themselves, a title reserved for God. Routine proclamations referred to Hong as king, not emperor, with Jesus consistently invoked as the "Heavenly elder brother."

The rigid and authoritarian theocracy that developed in Nanjing soon lost popular support, and the regime lost power as it failed to deliver on its utopian promises. A key factor was rivalry among the charismatic leaders themselves, which eventually led to fratricidal warfare, decisively undermining the Taipings' control of their territory after 1856. The peculiar nature of the Taipings' concentration of spirituality played a role as well. A Confucian-like ideology minus Confucius himself was unacceptable to the gentry and bureaucracy and mobilized support for the Qing that would otherwise have been lacking. The Taiping challenge in fact spurred a revitalization of Confucian doctrine and practice under the leadership of the Qings' most brilliant general, Zeng Guofang.[79] And a Christianity with more than one begotten son proved to be an equally decisive barrier to enlisting help from the European powers in the port cities – an alliance the Taiping leaders earnestly desired. The feelers between the two sides are quite revealing on this point: the theocratic language of the Taiping dispatches only convinced the British that they were dealing with a group of unstable and superstitious rebels who had no proper understanding of politics.[80]

As the power of the Heavenly Kingdom waned, Hong Xiuquan retreated increasingly into his private palace. While most scholars interpret this as a retreat into mental illness, Jonathan Spence argues that

Hong was working on a *vernacular translation* of the Bible, bringing its stories into line with his original vision and hence legitimizing his lineage and ultimately his dynasty. He came to believe he was the incarnation of King Melchizedek, mentioned fleetingly in Genesis 14 as "priest of the Most High God" at the time of Abraham.[81]

Resistance: The Boxer Uprising

In the later decades of the nineteenth century, one sees an increasing number of violent attacks on missionaries and native Christians in China, including the burning of churches and Christian homes. The Boxer Uprising of 1900 was the most famous and extensive, but local incidents numbered in the thousands.[82] This was in part a result of what Daniel Bays has called "the Taiping hangover" among the elite, namely the tendency to identify all Christians with that radical sect they had just fought.[83] But it is also clear that, in rural areas, Chinese often did not need official incitement in order take action against Christians. For example, a study of Christianity among the Hakka people in southeastern China documents that persecution of Christians increased when European missionaries arrived in 1862.[84] The Chinese were responding to the increasingly haughty behavior of the missionaries and their adversarial stance toward indigenous practices, including the Christian virgins.[85]

The Chinese also came to associate such missionary haughtiness with foreign imperialism, a link that was by no means unfounded. The French in particular, who wanted a share of the spoils that Britain had gained from the Opium War, sought to increase their influence by claiming themselves to be the protectors of Catholic interests abroad – including both missionaries and Chinese Catholics themselves. This became formalized in the treaties of 1858 and 1860: Catholic missionaries were now issued French passports, regardless of their nationality.[86] Their numbers increased greatly in the following years, from 250 to 886 between 1870 and 1900.[87] The French pursued a confrontational politics of space: by claiming property that had been in Christian hands earlier, they deliberately generated conflicts between Catholics and other Chinese, intervening with the imperial government on behalf of the Catholics, demanding indemnities for any property violations. A major source of irritation was the missionaries' claim that Christians should be exempt from contributions to local temples and religious festivals, which the Chinese saw as much a civic obligation as a religious one.[88] Church architecture was another source of conflict: the tall spires were thought to interrupt the flow of *feng shui,* the forces of nature which were supposed to determine the proper location of buildings, cemeteries, and so on. Over time, these disputes had a cascading effect, bringing the imperial government and foreign missionaries and officials to bear on local issues, thereby heightening the level of resentment. When this erupted into violence, it created the pretext for more foreign intervention, creating a vicious cycle. Moreover, as in the past, people who were in trouble with the law now saw such foreign-protected Christianity as a means of escaping prosecution and tended to convert in large numbers. This led one official to claim in 1867 that "[t]he Catholic religion ... takes in the scum and filth and perpetrates every kind of evil."[89]

In some provinces, Catholics tended to see their missions as enclaves of Christianity in an alien society and to view conversion optimally as a process of quarantining new Christians in order to protect them from the pressures and frequent hostility of their families and friends.[90] One extreme application of this was the founding of orphanages. The Catholics believed that infants who were baptized and near-death would automatically go to heaven. Those who survived could be protected from pagan influences, instructed in the true faith, and receive the sacraments. This process of sequestering only increased curiosity and spurred the imagination of the Chinese as to what went on inside, all of which helped feed a semi-pornographic literature about Christian practices. Rumors about an orphanage helped ignite one of the most violent incidents, the Tientsin Massacre of 1870, in which some 60 people were killed.[91]

The influx of Protestant missionaries was even more dramatic in the years following the treaties, from 189 in 1864 to 3,445 in 1905, coming primarily from Britain and America.[92] They tended to be more cautious about baptism, but were more likely to mix with the people—especially with Hudson Taylor's China Inland Mission after 1866 – setting up street chapels near the mission stations and offsetting the impression of secrecy of the Catholics (Taylor also insisted on his missionaries' adopting Chinese dress and customs). They had some success in gaining converts in areas affected by a terrible famine in 1876–79, where they did much relief work.[93] Nevertheless, Protestant attitudes toward indigenous religions varied little from those of the Catholics; they generally saw Christianity as identical with Western civilization and sought to remake China in that image. Both groups became targets during the Boxer Uprising at the turn of the century.

This uprising (not strictly speaking a rebellion, since its slogan was "Preserve the Qing, destroy the foreigner"), which swept the north China plain and involved the deaths of an estimated 30,000 Chinese Christians plus some 250 foreigners – mostly missionaries – resulted from a confluence of factors.[94] First, an escalation of foreign intervention in the late 1890s, following the defeat of China by Japan in the war of 1894–95. The pretext was again provided by the murder of two German missionaries in 1897, which provided the Germans the excuse they had been seeking to establish a colony, followed by a "scramble for concessions" on the part of other foreign powers. Second, a quick succession of environmental disasters: a Yellow River flood in 1898 and a drought the following year. Such disasters were still commonly attributed to the anger of the gods, and the Christian refusal to contribute to temple and festival rites became the preferred explanation for these occurrences. The following text was reported to have been posted throughout northern China:

On account of the Protestant and Catholic religions the Buddhist gods are oppressed, and our sages thrust into the background. The Law of Buddha is no longer respected, and the Five Relationships [of Confucius] are disregarded. The anger of Heaven and Earth has been aroused and timely rain has consequentially been withheld from us. But Heaven is now sending down eight millions of spiritual soldiers to extirpate these foreign religions, and when this has been done there will be timely rain.[95]

The "spiritual soldiers" were of course the boxers, who combined traditions of martial arts and spirit possession, which some believed rendered them invulnerable to bullets, into a ritual, easily learned and passed on, of working themselves into a state of frenzy.[96] By 1900, they were drifting to Beijing, at which point the Qing government sided with them and declared war on the foreigners. The boxers then laid siege to the North Church and legation quarters where Christians and foreigners were confined for six months existing on starvation rations. The siege was ended by an eight-nation Western expeditionary force, which quickly defeated the Qing forces. There followed an extended foreign occupation of northern cities, with much looting in which missionaries were also complicit.

Selective Acculturation

At the same time as resistance to Christianity was peaking, another contrary movement had been gradually brewing since mid-century, which turned to missionaries as transmitters of Western secular knowledge. As might be expected, this originated in the treaty port cities, where Westerners were present and where missionaries and their institutions were most heavily concentrated. These cities served as cultural bridge-heads, as it were, for the penetration of Western influences into the interior. In a seminal article, Paul A. Cohen has portrayed this as part of a long-term confrontation between the Chinese "littoral" and the "hinterland," where Confucian values and traditions predominated.[97] One might also legitimately see this as a case of "cultural imperialism," since the missionaries saw themselves not simply as bearers of Christ's message but also as agents of cultural transformation on Western lines. But this label makes it easy to neglect native agency and empowerment, in the attraction that Western culture held for increasing numbers of Chinese – not only in terms of ideas but also economic behavior.[98] Thus, as Cohen points out, by 1881, 17 of the 20 largest firms in Hong Kong were owned by Chinese, prompting the British to worry about a "Chinese takeover."[99]

Cohen highlights the role that Christianity played in this process by focusing on eight Chinese pioneer "reformers" who were products of missionary education or who converted. All but one of them studied or traveled abroad, either in the United States, Britain, France, or Japan. Given the anti-Christian sentiment of the time, they preferred to keep their religion secret.[100] But they began to have an impact, together with several prominent missionaries, on a few reformers such as Kang Yu-Wei in Beijing, which led to the "hundred days" of reform on the eve of the Boxer Uprising. Another individual who fit this profile was Sun Yat-Sen, who worked for the overthrow of the Qing Dynasty and became the first president of the Chinese Republic after the monarchy fell in 1912. Born in a village in the Pearl River Delta near Hong Kong, Sun's initial exposure to Christianity came in Hawaii, where he lived with his elder brother, illustrating the important role of diasporas in the acculturative process. He was baptized in 1884 in Hong Kong, and is reported to have said, "I do not belong to the Christianity of the churches, but to the Christianity of Jesus who was a revolutionary," anticipating Liberation Theology.[101]

It is of course debatable how much of these Western influences were specifically Christian, since by the late nineteenth century they were also present in the writings purely secular intellectuals. Also, the military defeat by Japan in the war of 1895 did much to convince Chinese authorities of the need to modernize. Still, the Christian role in this acculturation was undeniable, and was strengthened by a simultaneous shift in the attitudes among missionaries themselves – a pendulum swing away from emphasis on individual sin and salvation and back toward Ricci's original ideas of appealing to the literati and emphasizing Western science as a means of persuasion.[102] This coincided with a shift in Western Protestant sentiment, at least in the United States, toward improving conditions in society which found expression in the Social Gospel movement. To be sure, this shift did not occur smoothly or overnight, or evenly between Catholics and Protestants. The latter were largely in the forefront, while individual Catholic missionaries had an uphill fight against French and papal orthodoxy.[103]

All this can most vividly be seen in the area of education. Earlier in the century, missionaries established schools as places for religious instruction, perhaps the only way they could get a regular audience; Catholics were primarily concerned with holding on to their existing flock. But some of the missionaries discovered quite early that the Chinese were quite indifferent to their message unless accompanied by non-religious information. In order to recruit students at all, they had to offer instruction in the Chinese classics as well. A typical pattern was to hire a Chinese instructor in the morning, and to teach religion in the afternoon. Both relied on repetition and rote memorization, methods already familiar to the Chinese. As long as missionaries themselves were the teachers, this did not prove very effective in winning people to the new religion. In the port city of Fuzhou, for example, it took missionaries nine years before winning a single convert in 1856, after no less than 35 missionaries had come and gone.[104]

One solution to this impasse was to hire and train more native helpers to teach, which in turn required more schools to train them. It also involved girls schools, originally to provide Christian wives for these teachers.[105] A turning point came in 1877 at a conference of Protestant missionaries in Shanghai, when Presbyterian Calvin Mateer urged emphasis on more secular subjects, particularly science, as the only effective way to combat heathenism. This was still a minority view: another prominent missionary, Griffith John, spoke for the majority when he declared, "We are here, not to develop the resources of the country, not for the advancement of commerce, not for mere promotion of civilization, but to do battle with the powers of darkness, to save men from sin, and conquer China for Christ."[106] Nevertheless, a committee was established to standardize textbooks, and by the next conference in 1890, opinion had shifted markedly. It was native demand as much as changing attitudes in the West which drove the shift. A strong indicator was the Chinese desire for instruction in English, the main language of commerce. There was also a demand for science; mission presses published more books on science than on all other non-religious subjects combined.[107] A third area was medicine, where the effectiveness of Western techniques and cures overcame Chinese skepticism.[108] The number of medical missionaries went from 10 in 1874 to 300 in 1905.[109] By 1911, there were 26 medical schools offering training in Western medicine, 14 of which were run by missions.[110]

Thus was gradually built an extensive network of primary and secondary Protestant schools, numbering more than 2,500 in 1906, providing an institutional foundation which would accommodate the shift toward acculturation. Catholics reported similar numbers in 1900.[111]

As in India, women especially benefitted from these improvements.[112] The uplift of Chinese women from such backward-seeming customs as foot-binding, concubinage, and female infanticide was a staple of missionary propaganda and fundraising in Europe and America; not surprisingly, missionaries took the lead in advocating such reforms. At first, progress was slow, but accelerated in tandem with the mounting number of female missionaries, both married and single, coming to China. Missionary women turned to Chinese women as their natural audience, as they needed help with the language and with making contacts. Thus arose a formidable cohort of "Bible Women" – hundreds of thousands by one estimate – who performed a variety of tasks from medical assistants to teaching to counseling.[113] Missionary attitudes toward women changed slowly, holding to the domestic ideal of training women to be better wives and mothers – the "gospel of gentility," to quote the title of a book on the subject.[114] Yet paradoxically, they were laying the institutional foundations for a social change that would go far beyond this by establishing a network of hospitals and schools. The upward mobility that eventually resulted was certainly in no small part the product of missionary enterprise, probably to a greater degree than missionaries are given credit for. Here, too, however, the foundations are also to be found in Chinese society itself. For even as women were subordinate in the Confucian hierarchy, its emphasis on education fostered a considerable degree of social and geographical mobility.[115] Women would eventually benefit from this, as attitudes began to change in the early twentieth century: Chinese parents now found that Western education made their daughters more eligible as marriage partners.[116] In the words of Jessie G. Lutz, "more than one semiliterate grandparent could boast of his granddaughter who was a physician, a college teacher, or YWCA secretary."[117]

These trends of acculturation increased greatly during the two decades following the defeat of the Boxer Uprising. Here too a comparison with

India is apposite. India had experienced an uprising against a Western imperial power in 1857, which had also failed. But at this time, the movements of Hindu reform, embodying as they did the energizing power of concentrated spirituality, were just taking shape and growing, eventually contributing to the struggle for independence. China had had a similar surge in the Taiping Rebellion at the same time, but it was directed against the Qing Dynasty itself rather than a foreign power. Its failure left the Confucian orthodoxy still in power. But when the dynasty then backed the Boxers against the West and it too failed, Confucianism lost much of its prestige, leaving acculturation as the only viable alternative. The result was a dramatic reversal of attitudes in favor of the West.[118]

The Qing government recognized this and enacted a modernization agenda in the 1900s, including a national education program in 1904, modeled on that of Japan, and the ending of the civil service exams in 1905. This was accompanied by a campaign against "superstition" – a new term in the Chinese vocabulary – in the name of science, and the destruction of temples and images under the slogan "destroy temples to build schools."[119] This trend continued, albeit sporadically, after the fall of the monarchy during the interwar years and into the communist era.[120] In a way it represented an internalization by Chinese officials of the attitudes that the missionaries had been propagating, but also had the potential to be directed against Christianity itself, as would later be the case.

The Qing modernization initiative opened the floodgates to study abroad, with some 13,000 Chinese students in Japan in 1906, and also the United States and France.[121] Mission schools provided opportunity for those who could not afford to travel, and missionary organizations kept pace with this expanding demand. By this time China had eclipsed the Middle East as the most favored destination in the evangelical imagination, and the number of Protestant missionaries and their associates in China rose from about 3,500 in 1905 to over 8,000 in the 1920s.[122] This was a reflection of a surge of missionary enthusiasm and optimism in the West, as exemplified in the Student Volunteer Movement and its slogan the "evangelization of the world in this generation."[123]

This focus on China also generated a huge amount of foreign financial support for the missions, which funded doctors and teachers as well as proselytizers, not to mention personal contacts between congregations at home and missionaries in the field. American mission property in China in 1915 was valued at $25 million.[124] In the words of Valentin H. Rabe, "The multimillion-dollar budgets and complex interrelationships of this world-wide conglomerate were the characteristics less of a spontaneous movement than of a giant service industry."[125] One prominent product of this philanthropy was the group of 16 Chinese Christian colleges, run by foreign mission and denominational boards, which enrolled about 15 percent of the Chinese student population in the 1920s.[126] Moreover, the energetic work of Christian missions in education and philanthropy set an example for Buddhists, Taoists, and Confucians who came to imitate them.[127]

All this resulted in a substantial growth of Chinese Christians – although nothing like the utopian hopes of the young missionaries of converting all of China. Catholics rose from between 700,000 and 800,000 around 1900 to over 1.4 million in 1912. Protestants grew from about 100,000 in 1900 to 246,000 in 1912.[128] Still, the number of Chinese who participated in these institutions far exceeded the number of converts. In the words of John Fairbank, "Chinese patriots found they could make a selection of foreign ways to adopt or emulate. They discovered that no special faith was required to operate steamships."[129] Nevertheless, it seems that for the 1910s, the forces of Chinese patriotism, cosmopolitan internationalism, secular knowledge, and Christian idealism coexisted in a somewhat precarious synthesis.

LATE NINETEENTH-CENTURY JAPAN

As is well known, the Japanese government deliberately pursued a policy of *selective acculturation* in the second half of the nineteenth century, adopting the slogan "civilization and enlightenment (*bunmei kaika*)." Forced to open Japan to foreign trade in the wake of US Commodore Matthew Perry's initial demands of 1854, the authority of the Tokugawa shogunate soon disintegrated, succumbing to an oligarchy of young samurai from two southern clans, the Satsuma and Choshu, in 1868. They ruled in the name of the emperor Meiji, claiming in the Charter Oath of 1868 not only that "knowledge shall be sought throughout the world in order to strengthen the foundations of imperial rule," but also that "all classes, high and low, shall unite in vigorously carrying out the administration of the affairs of state."[130] To that end, the oligarchs abolished the privileges of their own samurai class by 1873.

Acculturation did not, however, extend to religion. The new rulers remained suspicious of Christianity and retained the Tokugawas' ban on it in the first few years. Moreover, they sought to establish a national religion of Shinto to buttress the emperor's authority, claiming him to be a living god (*kami*).[131] This involved the disestablishment and demotion of Buddhism: whereas subjects had been required to register with Buddhist temples under the shogunate, now they were required to register at Shinto shrines. Thousands of Buddhist temples were destroyed in an attempt to undermine the privileges of their priests, which had stoked much popular outrage. Soon, however, the clash between these policies and those of modernization became evident, and the government backed down by the mid-1870s in the face of Buddhist resistance and Western condemnation. As we will see, the government did not give up on the project of creating a national religion in subsequent decades, but developed a way of dealing with Buddhists and Christians through a strategy of cooption rather than repression. In terms of creating undying loyalty to the regime, this proved to be brilliantly successful, although during World War II, cooption mutated into repression.

Missionaries played an important role in the early stages of this process. Both Catholics and Protestants had eagerly awaited and prepared for the opening of Japan and took advantage of the initial treaties between Japan and the United States, Britain, and France to establish themselves. These resembled the initial Chinese port city arrangements that allowed for foreigners to practice their religion in these limited locations, while the ban remained in place for Japanese. The missionaries immediately began pushing the envelope, importing Christian literature and secretly meeting with interested Japanese prospects, who were no less eager to learn about the forbidden faith. The French provocatively erected a Church of the Twenty-Six Martyrs in Nagasaki in 1865, commemorating the persecutions under Hideyoshi. Immediately some of the thousands of *kakura* Christians began presenting themselves. The Japanese soon resumed persecutions, exiling these Christians to other parts of Japan over the vigorous protests of Western diplomats. Only in 1873 was the ban on Christianity quietly dropped and religious freedom proclaimed.[132] At the same time, the Russian Orthodox church was also gradually winning converts, more than anywhere else outside Russia, thanks largely to one Nicolai Kasatkin (1836–1912), an energetic bishop who insisted on accommodation to Japanese ways and involvement of Japanese catechists and priests. By 1912, it had gained 32,000 followers.[133]

The Protestant expansion illustrates well the attraction that the foreign religion held for a select but important group. Almost all the converts in the first decade were from the samurai class, and for the Meiji period as a whole (to 1912), they made up 30 percent.[134] Initially they came from the groups that had fought for the shoguns against the Satsuma and Choshu clans and were consequently dispossessed and alienated from the Meiji society. Christianity offered an alternate route to Western acculturation. Moreover, many of the missionaries and schoolmasters who came to Japan in the early years were from New England and retained a good bit of Puritan asceticism, high ideals, and devotion to duty, traits that resonated with samurai values. Thus a number of young samurai from all over Japan coalesced around these role models, forming several bands of converts – one in in the north (Sapporo), one in the center (Yokohama), one in the south (Kumamoto). They went on to form a generation of vigorous Christian clergy who soon became independent of foreign tutelage. The most dramatic example was Niijima Jo (1843–90), who escaped Japan in 1864 as a stowaway on an American ship, studied at Amherst College and Andover Theological Seminary in Massachusetts, became an ordained Congregationalist minister before returning to Japan in 1875 to found a Christian college in Kyoto.[135]

The lifting of the ban in 1873 ushered in a wave of foreign missionary organizations – 14 during the rest of the decade and 13 in the 1880s, as compared with 7 between 1861 and 1872.[136] Certainly the old anti-Christian attitudes did not disappear, and the ruling oligarchy itself was divided as to the value of Christianity. Westernization, it was realized, could also come in secular form, as represented, for example, by Fukuzawa Yukichi, whose attitudes toward Christianity, in the words of Charles W. Iglehart, "swung back and forth like a weather-vane."[137] Nevertheless, the 1880s witnessed the high tide of imitation of Western culture among the urban elites of Japan, and Christianity likewise gained increased acceptance. As elsewhere, missionaries brought hospitals and schools, including girls' schools, the YMCA, and initiatives for social reform.[138] Missionaries may also have been responsible for introducing Western music, as they introduced hymn singing. In seven years, church membership increased from c. 4,000 to 30,000.[139] Much of this growth had an evangelistic fervor to it, which the Japanese called *ribaibaru*, from "revival."[140] Nevertheless, there remained serious limits to Christianity's appeal, which was largely restricted to urban elites, not affecting the Buddhist and Shinto loyalties in the countryside. In addition, the Christians' insistence on conversion went against the Japanese habit of mixing different religious loyalties as suited their needs. Moreover, the missionaries brought with them a denominational focus, rather than working toward a strong united Japanese church, reminding the Japanese that Christianity was still a foreign import.[141] These factors notwithstanding, the presence of Christianity among the urbanized middle and upper classes gave it a prominence in national life that was impossible to ignore. This remains the case today.

The 1890s witnessed a certain reaction to excessive admiration of the West, and anti-Christian polemics became more prominent. Partisans of Confucianism in education had already raised their voices in the previous decade, and the government once again faced the dilemma of recognizing religious pluralism while continuing its effort to establish a religious basis for national loyalty to the regime in Shinto. They arrived at an ingenious solution: they divided Shinto into a "religion" and a "non-religion." The former consisted of the 13-odd existing Shinto sects ("sect Shinto"), and was protected under the freedom of religion in the 1889 Constitution, while the latter consisted of patriotic rituals ("state Shinto" or "shrine Shinto"), and was entirely government-run and regulated. Ironically this echoed the Jesuits' argument in the Chinese rites controversy two centuries before that some rites could be considered "civic" rather than "religious," and this time the Vatican responded by allowing Catholics to participate, demonstrating the effectiveness of the government's cooption strategy.[142]

The government further promulgated nationalism through the Imperial Rescript on Education, issued in 1890, to be displayed with the emperor's portrait and recited in every school. Much of the language was Confucian, making several references to filial piety. It enjoined the children to "respect the Constitution and observe the laws," offer themselves "courageously to the State" in an emergency, and "guard and maintain the prosperity of Our Imperial Throne coeval with heaven and earth."[143] This gave rise to an impassioned debate over whether Christianity, with its doctrine of universal love, was compatible with the patriotism of the Rescript.[144] This debate was cut short, however, when in 1895 the Sino-Japanese War broke out, giving Christian churches and missions the opportunity to demonstrate their loyalty by giving aid to the troops.[145] The same was true of the Russo-Japanese War a decade later; perhaps the most vivid example of successful cooption was the Russian Orthodox archbishop in Japan urging his followers to be loyal to Japan and pray for their soldiers.[146]

Not all Japanese Christians conformed to the imperial script, however. The most famous of those who did not was Uchimura Kanzo (1861–1930), a lonely prophet who developed a distinctive "non-church" Christianity movement (*Mukyokai*). Born a low-ranking samurai who became a Christian through the Sapporo band, he journeyed to the United States to study at Amherst and Hartford Theological Seminary. Disillusioned with American society with its un-Christian ways, he returned to Japan in 1888. He became infamous when, as a schoolteacher, he refused to bow deeply before the Imperial Rescript at a public ceremony and was discharged. His thinking evolved toward pacifism and he opposed the Russo-Japanese War. He eventually was able to support himself by publishing a monthly journal devoted to Bible study. This became famous enough to attract hundreds of followers to his lectures. By 1918 he had become convinced of Jesus' second coming and devoted a series of lectures and writings to this topic. His idea of a true Christian was one with a direct relationship to God, eschewing any institutionalized structure. Despite his dissent from Japanese nationalism, he was no less a patriot, believing Japan was uniquely positioned to reform Christianity. He once wrote, "Christianity grafted upon *bushido* [the way of the warrior] will yet save the world," and proclaimed his loyalty to two J's – Jesus and Japan.[147] His story may be seen as a variation on the theme of Japanese national religion rather than in opposition to it.

A word should be added about Christian relations with Buddhism in this period. The Meiji revolution revealed Buddhism as a religion in crisis. It had, after all, been deeply associated with the Tokugawa past, and part of that past had been anti-Christian. Thus when the ban against Christianity was lifted, Buddhists felt increasingly threatened and launched anti-Christian campaigns. As Christianity gained support in the '80s, these became more extreme, calling for "extermination of Christianity" and harassing Christians at meetings.[148] A particularly difficult issue was the treatment of the dead. Buddhist rituals were still widely practiced at the local level as a way of honoring and propitiating ancestors – not only at the time of death but in periodic times when spirits were said to return. All this was alien to missionary Christianity, where the focus on individual salvation cut the converts off from their families. Christians were often refused burial in Buddhist graveyards.[149] Gradually, however, the intense hostility declined, as Buddhist scholars traveled to the West and returned with ideas on how to preserve and reform their religion. Japanese Buddhists made an appearance at the World Parliament of Religions in 1893, which preached a message of tolerance and understanding. By 1896, Buddhists and Christians were ready to hold a joint conference.[150] In 1911, the government convened a Conference of the Three Religions to share in moral guidance of the nation – Shinto, Buddhism, and Christianity – a clear recognition that the latter had arrived. This too would be undermined in the course of the twentieth century.

In short, the overall strategy of Meiji Japan in dealing with the West has been labeled "defensive modernization," enabling her to preserve her traditions even while undergoing radical change.[151] In our terminology, one can view this as *selective acculturation* in the service of *incorporation*.

TWENTIETH-CENTURY CHINA AND JAPAN

The fall of the Chinese imperial monarchy in 1912 ushered in 60 years of upheaval, while at the same time the vaulting ambitions of its Japanese counterpart resulted in catastrophic defeat in 1945 – without, however, bringing down the monarchy itself. In China, the establishment of a republic gave way to a brief, unsuccessful attempt to reestablish a Confucian-based monarchy in 1917. This was followed by a period of rule by local warlords, until partially replaced by a coalition of Nationalists (Guomindang) and Communists – in the so-called Northern Expedition. Then the Nationalists turned against the Communists in 1927, until brought together again by the Japanese invasion in 1937, followed by a return to civil war between 1945 and 1949. In that year the Communist Peoples Republic of China was established, with the Nationalists exiled to Taiwan. The upheaval continued under the Communist rule under Mao Zedong and only stabilized after his death.

All this meant turmoil in the cultural, intellectual and spiritual realms as well, as the convergences that had seemed to be emerging in the early part of the century became unraveled. One might indeed characterize the period, at least until 1945 in China, as one of a series of religious-ideological cocktails, in which every conceivable mixture of creed and doctrine was tried at one time or another.

The rupture of good feeling between China and the West came with the Treaty of Versailles in 1919, which awarded the former German colony in Shandong to the Japanese instead of returning it to China. This unleashed the student demonstrations of May Fourth, an event that lent its name to a movement of intellectual experimentation that followed. As students became familiar with secular ideologies such as Marxism, they increasingly associated Christianity with irrationality and superstition. In addition, there was the inevitable association with foreign imperialism. These *resistances* came together in 1922, when the World Student Christian Federation held a conference in Beijing, triggering the formation of an

Anti-Christian Student Federation, which soon became broadened to the Great Federation of Anti-Religionists.[152] At the same time, a collection of essays by moderate Chinese Christian leaders entitled *China Today Through Chinese Eyes* for the benefit of the attendees, underscored many of the same points of how missionary Christianity was stifling indigenous developments.[153] A movement to "restore educational rights" soon followed, requiring schools to be registered with the government and prohibiting compulsory religious education in them. This gathered strength with the nationalist-communist collaboration, as churches and schools also came under direct attack. A tipping point came in 1927, when the Western vice president of Nanjing College was killed, leading to a massive exodus of over 2000 missionaries from China.[154]

Under these circumstances there occurred, not surprisingly, an efflorescence of independent Chinese churches, usually with Pentecostal and/or millenarian features. Some owed their origins to like-minded missionaries from abroad (who sometimes believed that the "gift of tongues" would instantly make them fluent in Chinese); some were probably crossovers from non-Christian sects; many were formed in reaction to the missionary churches – at least they could not be accused of being "running dogs of imperialism." Bays estimates that some 25 percent of Chinese Protestants belonged to these churches by 1949.[155] These can be seen as part of a broader canvass of expressions of *concentration of spirituality* in China that extended well beyond Christianity, including the so-called "redemptive societies," which were dedicated to such causes as abstinence from alcohol and opium, moral improvement, not to mention various combinations of elements from the Three Teachings of Confucianism, Buddhism, and Taoism. The adherents to these movements vastly outnumbered those of the Christians, especially in the years between 1945 and 1949, as nationalists and communists vied for control of China.[156] Nevertheless, some of the charismatic leaders from this period were able to exert their influence posthumously in the communist era post-1949.

The anti-Christian mood subsided after 1927, when the Nationalists under Chiang Kai-Shek turned against the communists. Chiang Kai-Shek himself came from a Confucian background, but was baptized in 1930, thanks to the influence of his Christian wife.[157] At the same time, the new regulations on education meant that Christian schools were becoming less distinguishable from secular ones. The Social Gospel tradition remained alive, however, as several Christian institutions sought to address China's impoverished peasantry with rural reform initiatives, though their impact was quite limited.[158] Realizing the need to inspire masses of followers to compete with communism, the Guomindang fashioned the New Life Movement, which one writer has called "a hybrid composite of Confucian, fascist, Japanese, and Christian elements, which could not but help appeal to certain sections of American Protestantism."[159] It combined military-style youth movements with appeals for orderliness and cleanliness. Its spread was cut short by the Japanese invasion of the mainland in 1937. As in Japan itself, the wartime situation gave Christians a chance to prove their patriotism. An estimated 50,000 members of denominational churches, as well as the church organizations and universities, traveled westward from the coastal provinces to escape the enemy.[160] Even the communists dropped their hostility, as part of a united front against the Japanese.[161] During the period from 1937 to 1942, when Japan was not at war with the United States, missionaries and their institutions were relatively unmolested in the occupied territories; this obviously changed after Pearl Harbor.[162] All these developments, however, had the result of making the Chinese Christians less dependent on Western benefactors and more in charge of Chinese institutions.

In Japan meanwhile the government's strategy of cooption proved successful in bringing most religious organizations (and intellectuals) to support its imperialist expansion. The process also demonstrated how easily cooption could become coercion. A "spiritual mobilization" campaign launched in 1937 brought increased government control of information, and in 1939 it issued the Religious Organization Law requiring registration and merging of Protestant denominations into a unified Church of Christ in Japan (known as the *Kyodan*), as well as a Catholic church under a Japanese bishop, subject to control by the Ministry of Education. A unified church, it should be noted, had long been the goal of many Japanese Protestants. Missionaries were allowed to remain, until after Pearl Harbor, when they were interned and then repatriated. The pressure to conform to State Shinto increased steadily throughout the war, with churches required to conduct a "people's ceremony" at the beginning of each service, bowing to the emperor and singing the national anthem. In the final years the government issued mandatory sermon topics to mobilize national sentiment, and references to God as creator and judge were excised from hymnals. The Ministry further sought to alter the Apostles' Creed to substitute "Father of Jesus Christ" for "Father Almighty, Maker of Heaven and Earth," but the *Kyodan* never acquiesced in this fundamental change.[163]

Japan in 1945 certainly experienced a severe disorientation as its semi-divine monarchy went down to defeat. Although the American occupation authorities decided to retain the exalted status of the emperor (while denying he was literally a god), State Shinto was dis-established. This did indeed open the door to a proliferation of new religions – a "rush hour of the gods," as it was called.[164] There was an increase of interest in Christianity as part of this phenomenon, but it proved to be ephemeral. Although missionaries poured in in the early 1950s – some 1,500 by one estimate – the results in terms of numbers was disappointing.[165] The *Kyodan* still existed, though some denominations left, and had to face the consequences of having supported the war effort, an issue that remained controversial. By contrast, the new religions flourished, being free from state regulation for the first time and untainted by cooperation with the wartime regime.

This is not to deny the real influence that Christianity wielded that was disproportionate to its numbers. It remained based in the urban middle classes, many of whom hold important positions in business, universities, and parliament. As of 1983, three of Japan's prime ministers were Christians.[166] As in the prewar years, Christians continued to excel in building schools, including for women, and in providing social services to the underprivileged.[167] In addition, these limitations have not prevented Japanese from appropriating certain Christian festivals and practices, including Christmas, Valentine's Day, and most notably marriage – not only the paraphernalia of wedding dresses, but also the deeper meaning of an emotional bond between two people.

To return to China, large numbers of missionaries reentered following the Japanese defeat, numbering some 4,000 by 1949.[168]At the same time, the independent churches and redemptive societies flourished. As the civil war intensified, most missionary organizations sided with the Christian Chiang Kai-Shek against the atheistic communists; for their part, however, the communists did not pursue an actively anti-Christian agenda at this time.[169] Disillusionment with Guomindang policies was widespread, however, and many hoped to achieve a modus vivendi with the communists as their victory became imminent.

The story of Chinese Christianity during Mao Zedong's reign again illustrates how quickly a strategy of cooption can become one of coercion and repression. Despite the anti-religious stance of the party, the communists began by organizing and preserving the main existing faiths as long as they did not contradict official policies. In the case of Christianity this meant "purging imperialist influences from within Christianity itself," to quote a manifesto that Christians were encouraged to sign beginning in 1950, and many Protestants did.[170] To reinforce the notion of independence, the official organization was christened the Three Self Reform Movement, drawing on an idea originating with nineteenth-century British and American idealistic missionaries to work for indigenous churches that would eventually be "self-organizing, self-financing, and self-propagating." The Catholics, on the other hand, under the Vatican's direction, maintained unbending opposition to the communists, with the result that over 1,500 Catholics in Shanghai were in prison by 1955.[171]

Whatever possibilities for a modus vivendi between missionary Christianity and communism that might have existed were squelched by the Korean War, which pitted Chinese and American soldiers against each other on the battlefield. This meant the end of missionary presence in China and also the cutting of any support for the Christian colleges, which were now absorbed by the government. Worse, it meant that the campaign against any trace of Western influence shifted into high gear, so that anyone who had studied abroad, for example, could be subject to group denunciation and humiliation.[172] In the late '50s, these were extended to the independent churches. By the 1960s, the government dropped all pretense of toleration for Christians: the Great Leap Forward of 1958 subjected the population to unremitting work to increase production, leaving no time for religion: 90 percent of the churches were closed. In the Cultural Revolution that followed, Christianity came under direct attack as part of the "Four Olds" – old ideas, old culture, old customs, old habits. The most visible signs of the religion were, in Lian Xi's words, "bonfires made of Bibles and hymnbooks, in decapitated cathedral spires, in sealed doors of church buildings ... and in parades of 'reactionary priests and ministers, wearing dunce caps, through city streets.'"[173] It seemed that Christianity in China was dying.

The decline of Mao's version of communism following his death and the drastic changes that ensued created a crisis in orientation for many Chinese, in which one hardly knew what to believe or how to act. In this situation, the vacuum was filled by a variety of religious revivals, from local temple reconstruction to Confucianism, including a spectacular growth of Protestant Christianity. The numbers are difficult to determine, but one conservative estimate is an increase from 1 million in 1949 to at least 30 million by the turn of the century and growing.[174] The observations of sociologist Fenggang Yang give a vivid picture:

During my fieldwork research since 2000, I have visited many Christian churches in coastal cities and inland provinces. In almost all of these places, I observed churches filled beyond capacity. In Beijing, each of the churches even offered multiple Sunday services to accommodate the growing number of worshippers ... Some churches had overflow rooms with closed-circuit TV sets transmitting the service from the main sanctuary ... In the southwestern mountainous city of Nanchong, Sichuan ... Many people would arrive one or two hours before the scheduled start of service in order to obtain a seat in the sanctuary ... A waiting list for baptism was common in most of the churches I visited.[175]

It should be noted that this revival was not unique to Christianity. Buddhist and Taoist temples experienced a similar increase, if not as steep. Redemptive societies proliferated as well, as can be seen in the evolution of the phenomenon known as *Qigong*, a way of channeling *qi* (mentioned at the beginning of the chapter) through a combination of exercise, meditation, and healing not unlike some New Age movements. In the 1990s, this morphed into Falun Gong, a moral critique of Chinese materialism and corruption. As such it proved threatening to the government, which turned against it, banning it in 1999, arresting and torturing adherents, claiming it to be a cult and attributing to it far more organization than it probably possessed.[176]

Paradoxically, the Cultural Revolution itself gave birth to growth of Christianity, as the intensity of persecution drove people to join house churches, and the very crushing of official church organizations left the house churches willy-nilly in charge of their own ritual and liturgy. Just as in earlier Tokugawa Japan, persecution triggered *acceptance and commitment*. In this atmosphere, the seeds planted by charismatic leaders from the 1930s and '40s such as Watchman Nee and John Sung quickly germinated, and millennialist and Pentecostal forms spread, with the help of literature coming from Taiwan. Protestantism even spread to new provinces within China, as evangelists like Li Tian'en held an underground training camp for some 4,000 leaders in 1975, who then traveled to some 30 provinces and municipal regions.[177] Meanwhile, in the late '70s, the government lifted the prohibitions on religion and re-instated the official church organizations. In 1982, it issued a directive, known as Document 19, addressing the role of religion in the Marxist-Leninist state. It acknowledged that religion would remain for a long time under socialism, but also made a distinction between "normal" and abnormal religious practices, such as the house churches, which should not be allowed, but that "this prohibition should not be too rigidly enforced."[178] Thus, the communists reinstated the division between orthodoxy and heterodoxy, as well as the ambiguous and sometimes tense relation between them, that had previously characterized imperial China for centuries.[179]

China's Catholics and Protestants experienced these changes some-what differently. Catholics had long been concentrated in rural villages where, it will be recalled, they tended to operate in the same manner as a popular sect. The Vatican's pronouncement in 1950 that Catholics should resist the communist regime gave them tremendous strength to resist when the Cultural Revolution occurred, but it also made them suspicious of the subsequent lifting of the prohibition. The numbers of Catholics did rise with the increase in population, but did not generally expand beyond their previous boundaries until very late in the twentieth century when massive urbanization occurred. Moreover, the Vatican remained steadfast in its refusal to recognize communist China, supporting rather the under-ground church.[180] The Protestant resurgence also began in the country-side but was more widely dispersed. Although many of their healing and millennialist practices also coincided with popular folk religion, their Biblical emphasis added a new dimension to such practices. More remark-ably, Protestants were able to negotiate the huge social change that was taking place in China as people moved from rural areas to the cities. As they did so, aspects of folk religion tended to recede in favor of Western models. The prestige of being associated with the modern West was now an attractive feature, in contrast to the earlier twentieth century. For example, in an article entitled "Lost in the Market, Saved at McDonald's," Fenggang Yang concludes that Christian groups chose Macdonald's restaurants for Bible study because both were associated with "modernity and cosmopolitanism." More importantly, Christianity provided a moral compass in an increasingly capitalist society where choices were multiplying and outcomes increasingly uncertain.[181] In other words, *selective acculturation* continued to be a powerful force, taking precedence over incorporation.[182] Ryan Dunch has observed that this Chinese Protestantism is less distinctively Chinese and more like Christianity in other industrializing market economies.[183]

Nevertheless, in a country as large and variegated as China, Christianity cannot be reduced to a single formula. As in India, for example, Christianity has had an appeal to many ethnolinguistic minor-ities. By the end of the nineteenth century, there were already eleven different regional translations of the Bible in addition to classical Chinese.[184] Of course, ethnic marginality by no means automatically meant conversion; studies that have compared different ethnic minorities in this respect point to two factors that favor acceptance: 91) a minority group is undergoing oppression, and 92) it has a decentralized communal structure that makes it more open to outside penetration.[185]

CASE OF KOREA

In his study of twentieth-century Christianity, Brian Stanley has noted the exceptionalism of Korea, in that Christianity, especially Protestantism, became identified with nationalism rather than being viewed primarily as a foreign or colonial import.[186] In explaining the origins of the appeal of Christianity to Koreans, other scholars frequently point to her "self-evangelization," the fact that the earliest converts took the initiative to embrace the religion in advance of being visited by foreign missionaries. This was true both of Catholicism, which arrived in 1784, and Protestantism, which came about a century later. While true, this account perhaps underestimates the degree to which Korea was part of the Chinese cultural orbit, where it was exposed to missionary Christianity that was already in play.[187] The Choson Dynasty, which had ruled since 1392, practiced a strict Confucianism, paying great attention to the proper performance of ritual. A delegation from the court of the Korean king made an annual journey to Beijing to pay tribute to the Chinese emperor, where they came in contact with Western learning, including the works of Ricci, not to mention images of Christ in art and church architecture. They regularly visited the Jesuit mission, which prepared astronomical tables for them, and brought back over 60 Catholic tracts. At first, they tended to accept Ricci's interpretation that Christianity was compatible with and complemented original Confucianism. The first Korean to be baptized accompanied his father on one such journey in 1783 and was given the charge by a French missionary to spread the faith in Korea. By this time, however, the differences with Confucianism were becoming evident, both to the converts and their opponents – including the Choson rulers. The notion of God's love being bestowed on all people regardless of station contradicted their hierarchical view of society, while it attracted women and eventually members of the lower classes.[188] A letter from the French bishop in Beijing in 1790 informing the Christian community that they could no longer perform the customary mourning ritual put them on a collision course with the monarchy, and massive persecutions began in earnest in 1801.[189] As in China, these were intermittent through the nineteenth century, but they were severe: between 1866 and 1871, for example some 8,000 Christians were executed. These persecutions seemed only to stiffen the resolve of the Christians, however, whose numbers had increased to 15,000 by 1856. By 1882, there were 12,500 believers, and by 1910, there were 73,000.[190]

In the case of late nineteenth-century Protestantism, there was already an extensive literature of Christian tracts in classical Chinese that were in circulation in Korea, which remained the predominant written language until the 1900s, although accessible only to the elite.[191] The Scotch Presbyterian John Ross, working with a group of Korean merchants in Manchuria, broke new ground by translating the New Testament into Korean in the 1880s, using a distinctive phonetic alphabet. Soon other translations of Christian literature followed, making it available to more than the upper class. The first American and European missionaries arrived in Korea in the same years. They found a country where the traditions of the Chosons were beginning to disintegrate and foreign influences were streaming in; missionaries found a ready reception for their schools and hospitals. This activity was concentrated in the north, in and around Pyongyang, adjacent to Manchuria.

The fact that missionaries arrived later in Korea than in China and Japan gave some of them a certain advantage in cultural sophistication: they were more ready to accept local customs and less likely to be condescending than their predecessors. Thus, for example, despite the importation of Western medicine, missionaries gradually learned also to value indigenous traditions of exorcism and healing, finding confirmation in Jesus's own practices.[192] One of their most ingenious innovations was to invent a new Korean name for God, *Hananim* (Great One), which was neither foreign nor indigenous, but an indigenous-sounding neologism, giving Protestants a distinctive sense of identity and differentiating them from Catholics, who used a Chinese term.[193] Another innovation was their use of the so-called Nevius Method, named for an American Presbyterian missionary in China, which stressed the threefold goals of self-government, self-financing, and self-propagation. This gave Protestants a taste for democratic habits, which proved to be crucial in the twentieth century.

Another ingredient which entered into Korean Protestantism was shamanism, an aspect of Korean folk religion that featured charismatic spiritual leaders, many of them women, who had found there a religious outlet that had been closed to them under Confucianism. As missions involved increasing numbers of women, including Korean Bible women, these practices became incorporated into an emotional, revivalistic style of worship. Millennialism was likewise a feature of Korean folk religion, which Protestants quickly picked up, linking it to prophecies of the Second Coming.[194]

As a result of all these factors, Protestant growth outstripped that of Catholicism by 1910. Nevertheless, despite increases of both faiths,

Christianity amounted to little more than a sect, comprising less than 2 percent of the population. Its later catapult to one of the largest religions in the country, roughly equivalent to Buddhism, was largely the result of a series of political turns that together continued to cast Christianity as a target of persecution and cemented its association with national feeling.

The ending of Korea's isolation exposed her geopolitical vulnerability, lodged between powerful neighbors, Russia and Japan, and unable to rely further on Chinese protection. Awareness of this position led to a nationalist movement in the 1890s in which Protestants were heavily involved (among them Syngman Rhee, later president of the Republic of South Korea). Japan's victory over Russia in 1905 awarded her Korea as a sphere of influence, leading to outright annexation in 1910. Koreans in Pyongyang responded to this humiliation with the "Great Revival" of 1907, which astonished observers by its intensity. Less a resistance movement to the Japanese, its mass confessions of sinfulness were more a self-reflection of the country's weakness.[195] Christians found a pun-based parallel between the Choson dynasty and the "chosen" people of Israel, who had also been punished for turning their back on God.[196] In any event, the Japanese quickly perceived Christianity as a threat to their colonial designs, which eventually involved the extension of state Shinto to Korea. In 1915, the Bible was excluded from private school curricula and instruction was to take place in Japanese rather than Korean. In 1919, inspired by Woodrow Wilson's program for self-determination, a number of Koreans issued a Declaration of Independence, accompanied by massive street demonstrations (the March 1 movement). Half of the signers were Protestants. More arrests followed, 41 Presbyterian leaders were shot, and a Christian village was burned to the ground.[197] Both sides proceeded more cautiously in the 1920s, but in the '30s the government began a campaign to launch state Shinto in Korea. To many Christians, this constituted idolatry, but most churches went along in response to extreme pressure and intimidation.[198] The repression continued throughout World War II, with arrests and executions, and records indicate the army was planning a massacre of Christians on August 15, 1945 – the very day the Japanese surrendered.[199]

Korea was divided politically after 1945 into a Russian and American occupation zone. The Russians immediately instituted a policy of suppressing church leaders as a means of eliminating opposition to a one-party state.[200] This was continued under the Democratic People's Republic of Korea under Kim Il Sung, and into the Korean War (1950–53). Kim's ideology of *Juché* (self-reliance) posited humans as masters of their own destiny, eliminating any dependence on God.[201] All of this prompted a massive migration of Christians from the north, heretofore the center of Korean Christianity, to the south. During the war, several hundred Protestant clergy were taken prisoner, marched north, and never heard from again.[202]

Christianity's phenomenal catapult in the south began in the 1960s and extended through the '80s. The percentage of Christians grew from 3 percent in the 1950s to 26 percent in the mid-90s, three-fourths of these being Protestants.[203] These figures can be easily correlated with South Korea's breakneck transition from a poor, agricultural, war-torn country to an urbanized industrial power. Churches provided a community in an otherwise impersonal environment. Women constituted a majority of members, and churches helped them negotiate the contradictions in role expectations between traditional and modern society. According to one study, "God / Jesus replaces the husband as the primary intimate companion and the locus of male authority in a woman's life."[204] To meet these needs, small sects proliferated; at the same time, huge megachurches arose, the largest in the world, but able to extend outreach to their congregants in small groups. The Yoido Full Gospel Church in Seoul had over 900,000 members, 700 ministers, and 50,000 neighborhood groups.[205] As might be expected, many of these churches were strongly anti-communist, but many also developed a strong ethos of social and political justice, particularly in opposition to the authoritarian regime of Park Chung-Hi in the 1970s. From these protests developed a particularly Korean theology, *Minjung* (the people), similar to Liberation Theology in Latin America. Central to it was the Exodus story, one of liberation from oppression and expressing a long-standing Korean sense of connection with the ancient Israelites as both a suffering and a chosen people.[206] Pope John Paul II underscored the point in another way when he canonized 103 Korean martyrs in 1984 – the largest number so honored at any one time.[207]

The 1990s witnessed a diminution of growth and a certain disillusionment with the churches as having grown too materialistic and corrupt. At the same time, the gospel of prosperity found its place, as in so many other parts of the world.[208] Also at the same time, the Korean missionary impulse exploded, going from just 93 missionaries abroad in 1979 to over 8,000 in 2000 and almost 15,000 in 2006, making it the second-largest missionary country behind the United States.[209] These Koreans clearly see their story as a chosen and prosperous Christian nation as applicable to much of the developing world. When they visit places like

Uganda or the Congo, they are reminded of what their life had been like in the not-too-distant past – which also means that they are no less likely to project their own experiences onto other cultures, as Western missionaries had often done.²¹⁰

CONCLUSION

In his book *Korean Spirituality*, Don Baker points to a trend that I believe can be tested with respect to much of East Asia. In 1916, a census revealed that only 3 percent of Koreans identified themselves as belonging to a particular religion. One would of course not conclude that the remaining 97 percent were irreligious, only that they interacted with multiple spirits from whatever tradition was ready at hand, as was typical of diffuse spirituality. By contrast in 2005, the number of Koreans claiming a specific religious affiliation was 53 percent, much of this change having occurred since 1960, the period of urbanization. The number of Protestant churches had gone from 6,785 in 1962 to 58,046 in 1997; the number of Buddhist temples from 2,306 to 11,561 in the same time. This, of course, did not mean that multiple religious participation had disappeared; many Koreans are still capable of making a pilgrimage to a Buddhist temple or consulting a shaman for a personal problem or to have one's fortune told – without being labeled a Buddhist or a Shamanist.²¹¹ But the shift in emphasis from diffuse to *concentrated spirituality* is unmistakable.

Baker attributes the origin of this shift to the advent of Christianity. It was the first Korean religion to define itself by a set of beliefs sincerely held rather than a set of rituals properly performed. Moreover, the inerrant source of these beliefs was found in a single collection of writings, the Bible, rather than a plurality of writings as found in most other religions. This formed the basis for exclusive, faith-based communities, bound together by belief, rather than by belonging to a family, lineage, or political unit. The effectiveness of these bonds, particularly in an urban environment, set an example for others to follow – not only Buddhism, but also a multitude of smaller New Religions defined as faith-based communities.²¹²

Turning to postwar Japan into the 1970s and '80s, one also finds signs of a trend toward concentration of spirituality, much of it connected to urbanization. In Shinto, although there were still many shrines in the countryside, the number of priests servicing them declined, leading to a shortage. On the other hand, major shrines continued to attract large numbers of pilgrims (one of them, the Yasakuni shrine for war dead, continues to be the focus of controversy over the relation of Shinto to the government, whose constitution mandates the separation of church and state).[213] Another conspicuous indication of the trend was the growth of so-called New Religions during this period (although some date back to the nineteenth century). These attracted huge numbers within a short amount of time, often with the help of mass media, so that estimates range between 10 percent and 30 percent of the population.[214] These differed from the Korean case in that many of their concerns, such as miracles and spirit possession, are closer to Japanese folk religion and illustrate the strong pull of tradition and also of multiple affiliation (some local ministers doubled as Shinto priests).[215] They provided networking, vitality, and a sense of community, especially in an urban environment, which was missing in Shinto and Buddhism.[216] Women were able to assume leadership positions, and there was an emphasis on personal counseling. Nevertheless, the tradition of multiple religious loyalties remained strong: during the 1980s, about three-fourths of households reported having a Shinto or Buddhist altar at home, or both.[217] While this may account in no small part for the lack of growth in Christianity, the *selective incorporation* of Christian marriage rites and holidays into Japanese religious practice demonstrated the ongoing vitality of its pluralistic, diffuse spirituality.

While the governments of South Korea, Japan, and also Taiwan, have broken with the historic pattern of state control of religion and adopted a laissez-faire policy, the Chinese communist government has continued that pattern, while having to live with the reality of fervent spiritual expression beyond its control. Officially China remains an atheist state, while recognizing and regulating five religions: Buddhism, Daoism, Islam, Catholicism and Protestantism. Outside of this, there has been a proliferation of both diffuse and concentrated spirituality. On the one hand, many local temples have been reconstructed, reversing the trend that had begun in the last years of the Qing Dynasty.[218] A survey from 2007 of religious practices revealed more instances of people venerating ancestral spirits at gravesites than all visitations of Christian, Buddhist, Taoist, and Confucian temples combined.[219] On the other hand, as in South Korea and Japan, urbanization has brought with it a multiplication of sites of concentrated spirituality – in Vincent Goosaert's and David Palmer's terms, "a shift in the relative importance of preexisting forms of Chinese religiosity, from the ascriptive communal cults employing religious specialists to voluntary, congregational, and body-cultivational styles."[220] They identify four major movements that exemplify this trend: body-cultivation movements such as *Qigong*, redemptive societies, Lay Buddhism, and Christianity. These can further be seen as a microcosmic case of the broader trend in modernizing societies toward the carving out of a distinctive religious sphere from the broader socio-cultural matrix, as we have seen in the emergence of "religion" itself as a distinct category. Goosaert and Palmer point to the parallel with India in this respect.[221]

In this context, the revival of Confucianism that has occurred since the repression of Falun Gong in the late 1990s is especially intriguing, as it reverses the trend of much of the previous twentieth century when Confucius had fallen into discredit.[222] This has happened at a variety of levels, from academic scholarship to the formation of private academies and study groups, to a popular TV series and bestselling book as a Confucian self-help key to success (to the disdain of scholars), to the invention of new rituals at Confucian temples in which women are also active, to state initiatives such as the formation of Confucian Institutes abroad for Chinese language study – some 353 of them in 104

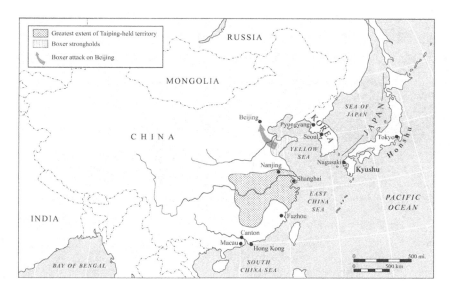

Figure 7.1 East Asia
Source: Drawn by Mary Lee Eggart

countries.[223] At the end of the second decade of the twenty-first century, there are signs that this trend is being combined with an increased repression of independent Christian churches under the name of "Sinicization" – a further instance of the long-term oscillation of relations between Christianity and the state that has gone on since the sixteenth century.

8

The Pacific

The spread of Christianity across the vast Pacific region must surely count as one of its most remarkable successes. Statistics for the year 1970, probably at the height of Christian influence, registered 93.6 percent of the people from Polynesia to the Philippines as Christians.[1] Of the 12 Pacific island states that have achieved independence, 11 invoke God in their constitutions, and, of these, 5 explicitly refer to Christian principles.[2] In attempting to account for this success, the anthropologist John Barker offers a suggestive initial clue: the missionaries arrived on the scene in advance of the colonial powers (though not usually in advance of individual merchants and sailors) and were therefore not only relatively untainted by them but also utterly dependent on the indigenes for material support – which inclined them to patience and compromise.[3] This holds true for much of Polynesia but is less so for other parts of the region. In Australia, in fact, the opposite was the case: missionaries lagged behind the initial British prisoner colony and experienced long years of failure. In Melanesia, the missionaries also arrived in advance, but did not get very far until the colonial powers came along. As late as 1910, 83 percent still adhered to their indigenous religion. And in the Philippines, religion and colonial conquest may be said to have gone hand in hand. Thus, we are faced with a variety of situations and explanations.

PHILIPPINES

The Philippines are not usually classified as part of Oceania, the customary geographical term for the Pacific islands, but the division between the latter and Asia is quite arbitrary in terms of ethnohistorical origins: the ancestors of most Filipinos, as well as Melanesians, Micronesians, and Polynesians, were from Southeast Asia.[4] In any case, Christianity clearly came to the Philippines not from Asia, but from the opposite direction.

According to the Philippine Statistical Authority in 2014, 92 percent of the country's population is Christian, with 81 percent being Roman Catholic (Muslims make up 5.6 percent, concentrated mostly in the south).[5] These figures clearly reflect the imprint of Spanish colonization, which lasted from 1564 (1521, if one counts Magellan's visit) to 1898. Many secondary sources refer to the "Hispanization" of Philippine society, although some also simultaneously invoke "Philippinization" of certain aspects, such as Catholicism.[6] Given this situation, syncretism suggests itself as a convenient expression of the combination, and one could argue that it applies more readily to the Philippine situation than to others, particularly where there is a genuine blending of elements. Yet, as elsewhere, the term masks the variety of strategies that Filipinos have actually used, not to mention the strong regional differences within the archipelago that still exist.

Consisting of some 7,100 islands, the bulk of the Philippine landmass and population is concentrated in 11 of them. These, however, have an extremely varied topography, which resulted in number of far-flung, fragmented communities with no central authority prior to the Spanish conquest. According to Benedict Anderson, their leaders were unaware of each other's existence, or if they were, regarded them as hostile.[7] The notion of Filipino – as the name, derived from the Spanish king Phillip II, indicates – had not yet been born. Yet because of its location vis-à-vis Asia, the Philippines were accessible by sea from the south, the north, and the west. The original inhabitants were related to the peoples of Malaya and Indonesia. They were literate, using the Malayan alphabet, written in a variety of dialects, although very little of it survives.[8] From the twelfth century, Chinese traders were present as well.

The fragmentation of society was reflected in religion. Although traces of Hinduism and Buddhism can be found, stemming from the influence of several Malayan empires, neither established a permanent presence, due in large part to the spread of Islam from India. Aside from expanding Islam in the south, the spirituality of the people was extremely diffuse, with a variety of benevolent and malevolent spirits inhabiting the landscape, varying from village to village, with no fixed temples, and a remote, uninvolved Supreme Being. The people were adept in the arts of music, weaving, sculpture, and dancing, which were part of festivals that marked major rites of passage. The Spanish commented on much drinking on such occasions as well, though, according to one source, not to excess.[9]

The Spanish administered the Philippine colony from Mexico, of which it was considered a province, and lessons learned in the Americas clearly contributed to the missionaries' success on the other side of the Pacific. This included the decision to train missionaries of different orders in different vernacular languages, facilitating the teaching and printing of Christian literature and thereby eventually sustaining a literate elite (one of these, Tagalog, from the ethnic group around Manila, eventually became the national language).[10] Still, the dispersed Filipino population both facilitated Spanish penetration in some respects and inhibited it in others. On the one hand, fragmentation meant that the Spanish did not need to rely as heavily on military force as in Mexico or Peru, and also that deadly disease did not spread as easily. On the other, the Spanish were spread even more thinly, forcing them to rely on agreements with local chieftains to a greater extent; only 10 percent of the population came to speak Spanish by the nineteenth century.[11] Economically, the province became a drain on Mexican finance, so that over time the main justification for remaining was religious. At first the Spanish tried the strategy of reduction, i.e., resettling the Filipinos into towns with churches, but this met with sullen *resistance*.[12] Faced with failure, the missionaries turned to a strategy of enticement, drawing people into the churches from surrounding villages with ceremony and spectacle that outshone anything that precolonial religion or Islam could offer. This developed into a cycle of feast days (*fiestas*), in which church bells, processions, music, theater, dancing, even fireworks became standard elements. This was *concentration of spirituality* at work, in the sense of creating sacred spaces and times. The events of Holy Week became especially significant, with people re-enacting the story of Christ's last days and resurrection throughout the streets. Over time, these fiestas also became linked with Spanish political celebrations such as royal weddings and coronations, and with secular activities such as markets, accompanied by popular entertainments such as cockfighting and gambling.[13]

Such exercises, while appealing to indigenous sensibilities, clearly had the effect of transforming Philippine society in the direction of Hispanization (*acculturation*) and, ultimately, by bringing people together, toward shaping a Filipino identity. If one looks for signs of Philippinization, one finds it in a *conservation of form*.[14] In other words, the interchange with spirits dwindled gradually, but the need for such interchange remained and became fastened to Christian rituals and symbols. Examples would be finding curative powers in baptism and holy water, or women dancing in front of a statue of the virgin in order to become pregnant.[15] And, as in so many other parts of the Catholic world, seeking intercession through Mary and the saints conserved a relationship of interaction that had formerly obtained in the human/spirit world.[16]

An example of genuine blending can be found in the Chinese Christian minority in Manila.[17] The growing market for Spanish-American silver in China led to a flourishing trade – and the presence of 20,000 Chinese in the capital city, compared to only 1,000 Spanish in the seventeenth century. The Chinese experienced segregation and discrimination, which erupted in several rebellions, only to be suppressed. One exit from this situation for a man was to marry a Filipino woman, a step which required conversion to Catholicism. This growing class of Chinese *mestizos* gradually became accepted as Filipinos. Both parents of José Rizal, the most renowned Filipino intellectual of the nineteenth century, traced such an ancestry.[18] This community came to venerate a particular image of St. Nicolas, who was said to have performed the miracle of rendering three Chinese invisible in one of the rebellions, saving them from being killed. A fiesta soon developed, coinciding with the Chinese mid-autumn festival in mid-September. In addition, an image of the Madonna was found in a fisherman's net in 1603 and likewise became an object of veneration. The Chinese identified her with Mazu, the goddess of fishermen. Both of these sites drew visitors from throughout the Philippines in the nineteenth century – Filipinos and Europeans, as well as the Chinese.

Such cases may be viewed as rudimentary examples of *vernacular translation*; the Filipinos were to develop more extended forms of it as they became more familiar with the Christian message. Vicente Rafael has traced this process in his book *Contracting Colonialism*, which presents the Tagalog encounters with Spanish colonialism as a series of translations, beginning with initial gropings or "fishings," as he calls them, and evolving to more sophisticated combinations of narratives and rituals, always retaining an indigenous interpretation. A key moment in this process was the publication in 1703 of an extended epic poem by a member of the literate elite, Don Gaspar Aquino de Belén, the *Sacred Passion (Pasyong Mahal)*, narrating the events of Holy Week. In 1812, a more popular version of Belén's *Pasyong* appeared, suitable for being recited and sung. It told the story of Jesus as the son of a humble carpenter, who met his death by confronting authority. It became memorized by common people and sung not only during Holy Week, but at funeral services and even in courtship.[19]

In the course of the nineteenth century, the anti-authoritarian aspect of the *Pasyong* became more pronounced and implicitly directed at the Spanish colonial authorities. The Spanish missionary clergy were prominent targets, as they had amassed a great amount of power outside the church by this time, including ownership of large landed estates, and creating a system that resembled a police state.[20] The Spanish clergy resisted the advancement of native clergy, who served only 181 of the 792 parishes in 1870. The orders reserved for themselves the larger and more prosperous ones and tended to look down on the Filipinos. According to Horacio de la Costa, SJ, "the average Filipino priest received just enough education to resent the suspicion and contempt with which he was treated, but not enough to perceive the real causes for such treatment, or how to rise above it."[21]

During the nineteenth century, the Philippines became increasingly involved in the world market, which it experienced primarily through increased demand for its agricultural products. This meant commercialization of large tracts of land, extending into the previously uncultivated interior, leveling many regional differences, decimating native communities, and creating vast disparities of wealth.[22] At the same time, the educated elite, known as the *illustrados*, became exposed to European liberal and democratic ideas, which the Spanish perceived as a threat. The *illustrados* tended to make common cause with the native clergy in *resistance*, while the missionary orders remained loyal to Spain. These tensions escalated when, in 1872, three native priests were accused of having conspired in a mutiny and were executed. Rizal met the same fate in 1896.

At the turn of the twentieth century, the Philippines were struck by the convergent upheavals of indigenous revolution and modern Western imperialism, as Filipino leaders declared independence from Spain in 1898, followed immediately by forceful and bloody annexation by the United States. These events combined to alter the religious constellation significantly. Anti-clericalism directed against the missionary orders had played a large role in the overthrow of Spain, and at one point some 400 friars were held prisoner.[23] A Philippine national church was formed, which attracted many of the poor. At the outset it attracted an estimated one-quarter of the population. The members occupied the Catholic churches, cemeteries and buildings, but the supreme court eventually ruled against them in favor of the Roman church as owners, which caused a massive exodus from the Independent Church, showing the attachment to the Catholic mass and the ritual.[24] The arrival of the Americans in

1898 brought an influx of Protestant missionaries in the ensuing years; according to one local study, they had an appeal in the rural areas that had not previously converted to Catholicism.[25] Under American pressure, the influence of the Spanish Catholic clergy was somewhat lessened and the church became more receptive to native priests, as well as from other countries.[26] The American-influenced constitution of 1935 provided for separation of church and state. The influence of the Catholic Church remained strong, however. An indication is seen in the liturgy that the national church eventually adopted in the 1950s, which adhered to the Roman rite.[27] The continuing prestige and power of the church was evident in 1986, when its radio station urged the people to peacefully demonstrate against dictator Ferdinand Marcos, which led to his ouster.

POLYNESIA

The term "Polynesia," originally coined by Europeans in the eighteenth century (from the Greek for "many islands"), was applied at first to all the Pacific Islands, but was later narrowed to the area stretching roughly from New Zealand in the southwest to Hawaii in the northeast, and eastward to Easter Island, forming a triangle with sides of a thousand miles each, distinct from Melanesia ("black islands") to the west. The vast area of Polynesia had been reached by native mariners with superb navigational skills and settled by people with similar languages, beliefs, and culture.

While the nature and degree of *acceptance and commitment* to Christianity in the early to mid-nineteenth century varied among Polynesians as anywhere else, two things are striking about it when compared to other parts of the world. First was the relative speed with which it spread. Most Polynesians became Christians within about two decades of the first missionary arrivals, beginning in 1797. Second was the large number of newly converted and literate Christians who quickly took to evangelizing other islands in the Pacific. They were usually called "teachers," but their duties were pastoral and evangelical as well as educational. While the missionaries – a term still reserved for Westerners – realized they would have to train such "teachers" in order to cover such a far-flung area, this does not explain the enthusiasm, even restlessness, with which these Polynesians (and later Melanesians) took up the task.[28] According to Hermann Hiery, "from the first third of the 19th century to the middle of the 20th century, there were far more than 1000 Christian missionaries—maybe even approaching double that number–[who were] Pacific islanders...The numerical ratio of European and indigenous Pacific missionaries lay in the range between app. 1:4 and 1: 10."[29] Hawaiians, for example, played a prominent role in evangelizing Micronesia, the island region between Hawaii and the Philippines; it is estimated that one-fourth of the ordained Hawaiian ministers served outside of Hawaii in the first 50 years.[30] In some cases, the indigenous "teachers" arrived at an island in advance of the foreign missionaries and were generally better able to understand the customs of their charges. Thus on the Melanesian island of Lifu, a part of the Loyalty Islands, the word for Protestant is "Praying Samoa," while the word for Catholic is "Praying Oui-Oui," reflecting the French colonial presence.[31]

The Polynesians' embrace of Christianity is all the more striking in view of the contrast between their mores and attitudes and those of the missionaries who initially introduced it. The latter were Calvinist and Methodist Protestants, products of the evangelical revival around the turn of the nineteenth century both in England and America, who adhered to a high standard of virtue and concentration of spiritual energies. They subscribed to the notion of inherent human sinfulness, the need for repentance and for being inwardly reborn in order to partake in the gift of salvation. Their catalog of sinful behavior was extensive and included dancing, the theater, certain kinds of music, not to mention the more obvious infractions of the Ten Commandments such as polygamy, infanticide, human sacrifice, and cannibalism, all of which they found in the South Seas. Most of the missionaries had little knowledge of or interest in the particularities of the societies they were seeking to convert.[32]

It is thus difficult to imagine a more extreme cultural clash than what occurred in the initial encounter. The experience of John Harris, one of 30 missionaries who sailed to the Pacific as part of an initial London Missionary Society expedition in 1797, sums it up. On his first night ashore, a chief, showing customary hospitality, left him his wife. Harris insisted he did not want the woman, who was mystified by this behavior and at first doubted his masculinity. Having summoned some female companions, they removed his clothing while he was asleep to satisfy their curiosity. He awoke, terrified, and fled back to the ship the next day.[33]

Polynesians generally believed in a multiplicity of spirits, both benevolent and malevolent, that governed every aspect of their daily lives. One commonly shared notion was that of *manu* (or *mana*), variously translated as efficacy, fecundity, even luck or success. It flowed from spirits to humans, and was manifest in such things as victory in battle. If *manu* represents a fluid, diffuse aspect of spirituality, then another common concept, *tapu* (*kapu* in Hawaiian; introduced as "taboo" in English in 1777 by Captain James Cook), expresses concentration and boundedness of the sacred.[34] It might refer to certain sacred or dangerous places that were reserved for priests and where most people were forbidden from visiting on pain of death. It could also be manifest, for example, in certain foods that were reserved for nobility but denied to commoners, or the practice in Hawaii of men and women eating separately. As the larger islands developed hierarchical societies, *tapu* became a means of the nobility's exerting social control over the commoners via draconian punishments. Such notions also gave ample sanction to warfare and violence, which was widespread. According to K. R. Howe, "the Hobbesian view of island life—'continuous fear and danger of violent death; and the life of men solitary, poor, nasty, brutish and short'—is closer to the mark than the romantic views of the philosophers who saw in island living echoes of arcadian golden ages."[35]

Needless to say, the Polynesians' acceptance of Christianity was not instantaneous. The immediate response ranged from incomprehension to contempt. Missionaries, who could barely understand the language, had nothing concrete to offer them. One common conclusion was that Jehovah may be the God of the white men, but was irrelevant to the islanders. As one Fijian chief put it, "if He were our God we also would have white skins."[36]

How then does one explain the change?

The first thing to note is that missionaries were not the first Westerners to have contact with the islanders. They were preceded by explorers and merchants since the middle of the eighteenth century. While the initial appearance of white men in tall ships undoubtedly created the impression that they were descended from the gods, it did not take long for this to dissipate – as shown most dramatically in Captain Cook's being feted as a god, when he entered a sacred cove in Hawaii in 1778, only to be stabbed to death and dismembered a few weeks later.[37] More enduring was the islanders' fascination with European manufactured goods: metal products such as nails, axes, fishing hooks, and of course weapons. Europeans also introduced a variety of foodstuffs, livestock, and alcoholic beverages that had not been seen before. Much of Polynesia quickly became swept up in the transpacific trading network, supplying sandalwood to China and pork to Australia, not to mention serving as stations for the New England whaling industry.

From the outset, contact was sexual as well as commercial. The willingness of women to offer themselves to the sailors at first was probably due to their belief that having a child by a more powerful god or chief would be a way of securing a higher place in society for themselves, and the number of mixed births in a place like Tahiti was undoubtedly high.[38] Close contact, sexual or otherwise, also brought multiple diseases – influenza, whooping cough, measles, mumps, smallpox, cholera, tuberculosis, and later leprosy – from which the Polynesians had no immunity, resulting in severe decline of populations.[39]

In addition, the islands attracted a certain number of "beachcombers," Westerners who preferred to stay rather than return home – including escapees from the prison colony in Australia. The indigenes often treated them with contempt, but some were valued for their artisanal skills. In any case, they served as an additional channel of cross-cultural contact.

More significant were the number of Polynesians who boarded ships and traveled with Westerners to foreign ports. By the 1840s, over 1,000 Hawaiians were so engaged annually.[40] Some of them had narrowly escaped death at home due to warfare or from having violated *kapu*. Among them a boy named Opukaha'ia, who found his way to New England at the time of the Second Great Awakening and was moved to bring Christianity back to Hawaii – a project he pursued with single-minded zeal. He persuaded four other Hawaiian refugees to join him. Thus when the first contingents of American missionaries sailed to the Sandwich Islands, as they were then called, in 1820, 1823, and 1828, they were accompanied by native Hawaiians (sadly, Opukaha'ia died of typhus shortly before the first voyage).[41]

By this time, it was clear that all the contact with Westerners in Polynesia had effectively undermined the system of *tapu* (*kapu*). The traders had trespassed on sacred spaces without suffering any retribution, and the observances had failed to protect the highborn from the diseases that struck everyone. It is significant that the queen-regent of Hawaii ordered the abolition of *kapu* in 1819, *before* the arrival of missionaries.[42] Some years later, another member of the royal family confided to a missionary wife that the old priesthood knew that *kapu* was fraudulent, but perpetuated it to keep the lower classes in tow.[43]

This "twilight of the gods" would seem to have created an obvious opening for Christianity, the religion of the Westerners whose immunity to *kapu* (and the diseases) was evidence of a more powerful God, a higher degree of *manu*. This is true, yet the story is not quite so simple: the old spirits did not immediately disappear from people's beliefs, but were rather subordinated to the higher power. The decisive factor in much of the area was religio-political: the more powerful God and the missionaries became associated with a more powerful chief who was consolidating his rule over a group of islands – as was the case in Tahiti, Hawaii, and Tonga. The exact sequence varied from one to another, but the end result was the same (one could also add Fiji, which was ethnically Melanesian but had more in common with typical Polynesian political patterns).[44]

In Tahiti, church and state grew more or less simultaneously, as the missionaries fastened on the Pomare family. They had previously cultivated ties with Europeans, who mistakenly took them for kings. Despite the fact that the Pomares showed no interest in Christianity at first and continued to practice human sacrifice to the god Oro, the missionaries stuck with them. A few remained loyal even after Pomare II was overthrown in 1808 and went into exile.[45] During that period, the chief gradually distanced himself from Oro (as many other Tahitians were doing) and declared his conversion to Christianity in 1812 – in time to wage a victorious battle over his rivals in 1815 and establish his rule in the name of the Lord. By the 1820s most Tahitians had obediently become Christian.

In Hawaii, political centralization had occurred first, in a series of bloody battles under King Kamehameha I, who died in 1819. It was his widow, Ka'ahumanu, who abolished *kapu*, partly to forestall any further strife over the succession. The first missionaries arrived from Boston the following year. The conversion process that followed was more gradual than in Tahiti: the new king, Kamehameha II, showed little interest, and the missionaries were granted only probationary permission to stay at first. Ka'ahumanu meanwhile cultivated close relationships with the missionary wives, building trust through activities such as dressmaking.[46] In 1823, the king left on a state visit to England, only to die there of measles the following year. Ka'ahumanu, faced again with the prospect of political strife, wasted little time in promulgating Christianity and accepted baptism in 1825. With the cooperation of the missionaries, she enacted laws forbidding drunkenness, gambling, violating the Sabbath – in effect a Christian *kapu*.[47]

In Tonga, one finds a third sequence: the first LMS missionaries arrived in 1797 in the midst of a civil war and soon abandoned it after several were killed. The British Wesleyans sent two further expeditions in the 1820s but met with little success; only around 1830 did they begin to attract followers. Around this time they also attracted genuine interest from several members of a leading family. One of them was an ambitious young man, Taufa'ahu, who began to seriously investigate Christianity in the late 1820s and sought missionary instruction. He was baptized in 1831 and took the title of King George. He took his religion seriously, and proceeded to burn down god-houses and destroy effigies in his unification of the islands. His political skill set Tonga on a long-term path of independence – unlike Tahiti and Hawaii which eventually succumbed to colonial annexation.[48]

One sees in these stories a certain aping of British monarchy, evidence of *selective acculturation* that is also apparent in the rulers' adoption of European dress.[49] Nevertheless, K. R. Howe points out that each of these "kings" attained their power within the structures of their indigenous political systems. This did not, however, diminish the importance of Christianity and the missionaries in legitimizing and solidifying their control once having attained it.[50] A crucial element in doing so was establishing a code of law, which again followed European models, and here the missionaries were thrust, not always willingly, into the role of political consultant, drawing up legal codes and even constitutions.[51] These were particularly important in gaining credibility and recognition for these kingdoms abroad, part of a strategy which Philip Curtin has called "defensive modernization." This is an intentional *selective acculturation* on the part of the rulers as a way of fending off a foreign threat – sometimes successful, sometimes not.[52]

A major exception to the above pattern was Samoa, which never developed a rigid class structure or central political authority, but consisted of many autonomous villages of 200–500 people. Yet its story only serves to highlight further the appeal of Christianity in the region as a whole. The Samoans had gained a reputation for ferocity among the European traders, who largely avoided it until about 1830. Yet individual Samoans traveled to other islands in the Pacific and had heard about the new religion. One named Sio Vili returned as a prophet and cult figure, announcing the coming of a new religion which would bring material abundance.[53] Another chief named Fauea traveled to Tonga and became convinced of Christian superiority, which he conveyed to his fellow Samoans in the following way:

Only look at the English people. They have noble ships while we have only canoes. They have strong, beautiful clothes of various colours while we have only *ti* leaves; they have iron axes while we use stones; they have scissors, while we use the shark's teeth; what beautiful beads they have, looking glasses, and all that is valuable. I therefore think that the god who gave them all things must be good, and that his religion must be superior to ours. If we receive this god and worship him, he will in time give us these things...[54]

While in Tonga, Fauea met the LMS missionary John Williams (dubbed the "Ulysses of Protestantism in the Pacific," because he traveled from island to island, spreading the Gospel in his self-built boat), and persuaded him to stop at Samoa. More missionaries appeared in the next decade. Despite Williams's attempt to groom a single leader, the missionaries were forced to go village by village, which made the need for native teachers all the more imperative. By 1839, there were 11 missionaries and 138 teachers, traveling to villages other than their own.[55] The teachers eventually rose up demanding a salary, and the new churches took up a separate collection for them. Samoan Christianity thus developed a grassroots character that limited the influence of the Europeans, unlike the situation in the monarchies. This enthusiasm proved a fertile breeding ground for indigenous missionaries to Melanesia, where the Samoans were perceived as arrogant and condescending.[56]

The key element that was common to the Samoan case and the others in explaining the appeal of Christianity was literacy. The word repeatedly used to describe Polynesian perception of the written word was "magic," and the desire to acquire it was frenetic and unstoppable. This was something the missionaries could deliver as could no one else, and thus the association of literacy and Christianity was firm. Aside from translating the Bible into several languages, missionaries provided educational materials in the vernacular. The arrival of a printing press in Tahiti in 1817 was greeted with a wave of popular enthusiasm. Presses turned out 8 million pages in Samoa and 20 million in Hawaii. Statistics for Tonga show 17,000 books mostly religious, within the first year of operation.[57] A European observer noted the impact in Honolulu in the 1820s: "[Every street] has more than one school house. In each of these, about a hundred scholars of both sexes are instructed by a single native teacher, who, standing on a raised platform, names aloud every letter, which is repeated in a scream by the whole assembly. No other sounds are heard in the streets..."[58]

By 1834, Hawaii had 900 schools and 50,000 pupils; in Samoa, there were 20,000 copies of the Bible sold by the end of the century.[59] Another link between education and religion was healing: many Polynesians came to appreciate the efficacy of Western medicine, which missionaries likewise dispensed.[60]

In general, the Polynesians' acceptance of Christianity consisted of a combination of *selective acculturation* and *conservation of form*. On the first count, they adopted the missionaries' styles of worship. Barker writes, "visitors to Tonga were impressed (or dismayed) by commodious village churches, by the black-frocked native pastors exhorting their congregations during the long services to honour Jehovah and give generously to his mission, and by the melodious church choirs raising their voices to heaven."[61] At the same time, they exercised selectivity in rejecting the Protestants' sexual mores and puritanical ideas, even in the face of the missionaries' most strenuous educational efforts.[62] Perhaps the most graphic example was the Hawaiian response to the leprosy epidemic. The government established a colony on a remote promontory on the island of Molokai and decreed, in accordance with the medical practices of the time, that patients should be isolated, a policy which the Congregational church endorsed. Hundreds Hawaiians regularly violated it, choosing to spend their days with family even at the risk of contracting the disease.[63] On the second count, *conservation of form*, certain Christian practices reinforced the previous Polynesian religion, most notably the strict observance of the Sabbath, which could easily be understood as a form of *tapu*. The Tonga Constitution of 1875 states, "the Sabbath Day shall be sacred in Tonga for ever and it shall not be lawful to work, or artifice, or play games, or trade on the Sabbath."[64] Another custom which transferred easily was the display of *manu* through generosity in donations to the churches.[65] Polynesians assimilated Christianity through ritual practices, but showed little interest in doctrinal issues; nor did they exhibit the deep-seated sense of sin and rebirth that the missionaries hoped for. The previous belief that the spirit world could be both benevolent and malevolent was mirrored in the Old Testament notion of a God who was both angry and loving. It would be going too far, however, to deny Christians teaching any influence on Polynesian beliefs and values. Missionaries in Hawaii did succeed in reversing the practice of infanticide. And the balance between God's anger and love could be seen as gradually tipping in favor of the latter. The statement of a young convert-missionary from Rarotonga named Ta'unga in 1833 reveals the delicate balance:

God showed great love in giving his beloved son to the world. If he had refused to give his son, men could not have lived on. . . . The shedding of his blood made God angry. . .It was the boundless anger of God and the sins of man which descended upon Jesus. The anger of God did not strike mankind because Jesus became a shield against the anger of his Father, and Jesus carried the burden and so he was overcome by death. Thus mankind was saved because he took death upon himself.[66]

   In the course of the nineteenth century, Polynesians became exposed to
a greater diversity of Christian denominations as Catholics made their
appearance, followed by Anglicans, Mormons and Seventh-Day
Adventists. In Hawaii, these alternatives were an especially welcome
alternative to the stern doctrines of the Congregationalists; by 1864,
one-third of the population had become Catholic, and this trend continued as Protestantism became associated in the minds of Hawaiians
with American annexationist pressure.[67] The Mormons meanwhile had
established a holy city on the island of Lana'i. The notion that they were a
chosen people gave consolation to many Hawaiians in the years following
the loss of their monarchy and the immigration of Asian workers to the
islands. By 1913, 22 percent of the Hawaiian ethnic population had
become Mormons.[68]

The Case of New Zealand

The story of the native New Zealanders' engagement with Christianity
strongly resembled that of their fellow Polynesians up to a point in time,
around 1840, after which it diverged in a new, creative direction. Known
as Maori, they had migrated from eastern Polynesia in the thirteenth
century CE; they had to adjust to a radically different, colder climate
and variegated topography, which perhaps contributed to a fragmented,
competitive culture where *mana* could be acquired by individual achievement, including of course victory in war.[69] These qualities would win
them the admiration of the Europeans when they appeared in the eighteenth century (later, in a bit of social-science fantasy, the claim was made
that they were actually of Aryan descent).[70] The Anglican cleric Samuel
Marsden of Sydney judged them to be ripe candidates for "civilization"
that would lead to their conversion and dispatched several missionaries to
an isolated settlement on the North Island in 1814 at the invitation of a
chief. The Maori were willing to allow missionaries to settle as long as
they would facilitate trade in Western goods. And the good they most
desired at first was muskets. The missionaries had no choice but to engage
in this morally compromising trade, because they were utterly dependent
on the Maori for survival. The Anglicans' main benefactor in the early
1820s, Hongi Heka, was also the most powerful warrior, and the muskets
he had acquired on a trip to England greatly increased the lethality of
these wars, killing an estimated 20,000.[71] Hongi himself considered
Christianity a fit religion for slaves, not warriors. The open displays of
contempt for missionary preaching were an expression Maori confidence
in the superiority of their power.[72]

The Maoris' turn to Christianity and their frenzy to acquire literacy around 1830 was as sudden and dramatic as elsewhere in Polynesia, but the pattern resembles more the grassroots movement of Samoa than the consolidated-rule phenomenon of Tahiti, Hawaii, and Tonga. Several factors were at work: (1) the missionaries were multiplying and were increasingly supplied by ships from Australia, thus becoming less dependent on their Maori hosts for survival; they were able to turn their attention to mastering the language and translating the Bible, with a New Testament appearing in 1827; (2) the musket wars wound down after 1828, partly due to the proliferation of muskets themselves, which acted as a deterrent to overly ambitious warriors; Hongi Heka himself was assassinated in 1828, triggering a massive migration of former war prisoners and slaves to their home areas. Many of these had been exposed to Christianity, and they carried it with them in advance of the missionaries themselves; (3) the competitive rivalry among chiefs now became directed toward acquiring missionary teachers, a strategy which worked hand-in-glove with the competition among Anglicans, Methodists, and Catholics, each finding different patrons outbidding each other for the new *mana*.[73]

Certainly the willingness of Polynesian peoples to cast off and bury old gods when their *mana* had declined was nothing new – multiple examples can be found.[74] What is remarkable about this case is the way Biblical stories and imagery now suffused the Maori imagination, overlaying and perhaps even eclipsing earlier beliefs about the gods – a case of *vernacular translation*. The fact that reading and writing was learned almost exclusively via the Bible was of great importance here. This was in part the missionaries' doing: they had insisting on teaching the Bible in Maori in order to shield them from secular influences that might creep in if English were taught.[75] It must be said that they were successful. Thus we find numerous religious movements in which the Maori internalized and identified with Biblical stories and characters – with the aim of creating an alternative version of Judeo-Christianity to that presented to them by the missionaries. There are written references to some 60 such new religious movements from the 1830s on, and probably many more went unrecorded.[76]

Many of these variants of the Biblical message were Old Testament prophet-centered, a fact which should not be surprising in the light of Maori belief in prophecy prior to European contact. As a corollary, it seems that the figure of Jesus had little appeal. As Bronwyn Elsmore, an expert on the prophetic movements put it, "no aspect of his related to what was desirable in the Maori tradition...A man who was not a successful warrior – and in fact not a warrior at all – and who had been killed (for the Maori found it difficult to believe in a physical resurrection) was not a figure who could command great respect on traditional grounds."[77] On the other hand, the Old Testament and the Jews were of much greater interest, not only because of the prophets, but also because Jehovah, the God of the Hebrews, who led his people to victory in war, was much more accessible. Once the Old Testament had become fully translated by 1858, the elaborate set of rules and rituals in Leviticus separating the clean and the unclean corresponded to the notions of *tapu*. The Maori identified with the Jews – to such an extent, in fact, that many of these movements viewed the Maori as actually descended from the lost tribes of Israel – a notion in fact introduced by some of the missionaries themselves.[78]

This narrative would gain appeal in the subsequent decades as the English took steps to acquire New Zealand as a colony. The Treaty of Waitangi (1840) formally subjected the Maori to the British monarch. Missionaries were involved in the process of translating the terms of the treaty to the Maori chiefs, but the different interpretations of the treaty and its language has made it a bone of contention into the present century. Gradually, increasing numbers of settlers arrived, acquiring more and more Maori land. In this context, the Old Testament presented a narrative of liberation, of an oppressed people struggling to retain hold of their land. Casting themselves as Israelites, the Maori could see themselves as God's chosen.[79]

The 1840s brought a certain disillusionment with the missionaries, as the new religion and the written word failed to deliver the well-being that Maori expected from them. In this situation, some Maori prophets managed to interweave their newfound Jewish identity with their own pre-contact traditions and customs and fashion a *resistance* to Christianity in the process. One can see this in the first large-scale prophetic movement, Papahurihia ("One who relates wonders"). Its visionary founder called himself Te Atua Wera, or "the fiery God." His strategy of rejecting the new religion can be seen as one of inversion: taking the things the missionaries regarded as bad and reevaluating them as good. Thus Te Atua claimed to be the mouthpiece of the serpent in the Garden of Eden, the agent of Satan. He used the traditional means of the Maori priests (*tohunga*) to convey this, such as holding séances and ventriloquism. His followers called themselves Jews; what was known of the Jews at that time, based on the translations of Matthew, Acts, and Corinthians, was that they had rejected Christ. Similarly, Te Atua's portrayal of heaven, in which missionaries were excluded, appears to be an act of deliberate heresy: "Everything is found in plenty, flour, sugar, guns, ships; there too murder and sensual pleasure reign."[80] Te Atua served as a *tohunga* for a chief who was involved in a revolt against the British in the late 1840s.

The 1860s were, again, a decade of warfare, though not as violent as those of the 1820s. By now the sale of land to white settlers had reached sufficient proportions that something had to be done to stop it. This gave rise to a movement to unite some of the tribes under a Maori king–again, under clear inspiration of the Old Testament, whose historical books on the Hebrew kings were just appearing in print. This, however, was a clear challenge to the imperial rule of the British, who sent in over 20,000 troops to put it down.[81] As with the Indian uprising of 1857, the Maoris were not united; many tribes fought on the British side (and some Irish fought for the Maoris). The British outnumbered the Maoris and were able to weaken the king movement but not to overrun it completely. Guerilla resistance continued until 1872.

Religious prophetic movements were part and parcel of this story. The most famous was Pai Marire ("good and peaceful"), which attracted some 10,000 followers at its height in the mid-1860s – about one-fifth of the Maori population.[82] Its founder, the prophet Te Ua Haumene, had a visitation from the Angel Gabriel in 1862. Scholars have variously labeled this movement Jewish or Christian – the evidence is ambiguous.[83] But it is clear that its founder identified New Zealand as the land of Canaan and the Maori as God's chosen people. Te Ua's intent was to forge a new unity among the Maori tribes and a sense of identity distinct from that of the whites. He taught that the Maori Israelites were descended from Noah's son Shem, while the Europeans were descended from Japheth, and this led each to develop different gods, namely Jahweh and Jesus respectively.[84] Te Ua's message was apocalyptic: Gabriel was the angel of the Book of Revelations, as was the Archangel Michael, the god of war. Although both were given Maori names, there is little or no reference to the major gods of the Maori pantheon. The central ritual, which consisted of dancing around a tall pole called a *niu*, which resembled a European flagpole. Streamers attached to the pole were channels by which angels could communicate to the celebrants. There is a connection with Maori creation mythology here, in that poles were said to have lifted up the sky as it separated from the earth, like a tent. British flagpoles were the object of Maori violence in the 1840s.[85] In any case, the dancing was supposed to endow the participants with extraordinary power, including resistance to bullets (not unlike the Boxers in China or the Ghost Dancers in the US). The chants were imitations of English prayers in a kind of pidgin. The overall effect was one of ecstatic intensity and even ferocity, leading one scholar to call it "the first expression of . . .Pentecostalism in New Zealand."[86]

The wars of the 1860s constituted the last attempt to resolve Maori-white issues by force. In the decades that followed, the two groups settled into a pattern of largely separate coexistence. The Maoris often practiced some combination of Christianity and indigenous practices. Prophetic movements for autonomy continued to sprout, but when they protested white infringements, they did so peacefully. A striking example was the religious evolution of the most famous and feared guerilla warrior of the '60s, Te Kooti, who had seen himself as Moses and Joshua combined. Having taken sanctuary in territory controlled by the King movement, Te Kooti renounced violence after 1872 and turned his attention to developing his new religion (Ringatu, or "Upraised Hand"). It consciously interwove both native and Christian traditions and drew from them in rituals, while deriving its church calendar from the Anglican Prayer Book.[87]

It should be emphasized that these movements took place against a background of increasing Maori despair. They continued to lose land to white settlers, and the population declined from an estimated 100,000–120,000 in the late 1700s to a low of 42,000 in 1896. Many whites claimed they were bound for extinction. Although the numbers increased thereafter, their proportion of the total population declined in the face of continuing white settlement – from 8.6 percent of the total population in 1880 to 4.5 percent in 1921. Although a minority of Maori became assimilated into white society, even taking seats in parliament and forming the Young Maori party, they had little influence on the rural majority, which continued to live in great poverty. This was dramatically underscored by the influenza pandemic of 1918, which affected the Maori about seven times more severely than the whites.[88]

This was the setting for the last great Maori prophet, Tahupotiki Wiremu Ratana. He came from a family of landowning chiefs who belonged to the Anglican and Methodist churches. The vision which launched his calling came to him just after the flu pandemic, which had wiped out much of his family.[89] Ratana's way out of the impasse which the Maori had reached in 1920 was to direct his charisma against many remnants of the old religion, promoting greater assimilation while maintaining an independent Maori church. His focus, however, remained clearly Christian. Photographs always show him in western dress. Ratana's ingenious solution to the Jesus question was to expand the notion of the Trinity to a "quinquinity," by elevating angels to equal status with the Father, the Son, and the Holy Spirit. These were needed, in his view, to serve as additional mediators to a people used to many gods. The fifth element was Ratana himself, who called himself the *Mangai* (mouthpiece) of God, sent specifically to the Maori people. His movement encompassed material and political concerns. Ratana's designated disciples ran for the four Maori seats in parliament and won, forming a coalition the Labour Party. This led to a number of advances in legislation during the 1930s and '40s. At its height in 1936, the Ratana church became the second-largest of the Maori churches after the Anglican, with almost 20 percent of the population.[90]

The second half of the twentieth century saw a dramatic reversal of Maori fortunes as compared to first half, a movement from relative isolation and impoverishment to greater *acculturation* and resurgence. The turning point was World War II, when the Maori War Effort Organization mobilized about 30 percent of its population for military recruitment and war-related work; the Maori battalion distinguished itself on the battlefield.[91] The postwar decades saw a steady trend toward urbanization – from 17 percent of the Maori population in 1936 to 83 percent 50 years later. In 1960, 42 percent of Maori marriages in Auckland were to *Pakeha* (whites).[92] The resurgence took several forms: (1) a fivefold population growth from 1936 to 1986, thanks largely to better health and sanitation; (2) social activism and protest; (3) a cultural renaissance, which also included a greater *Pakeha* appreciation of Maori customs. New Zealand was becoming a pluralistic society in those years in any event, as more Asians and Pacific Islanders migrated to the country.

One casualty of this massive transformation was the decline of organized religion among both Maori and *Pakeha*. New Zealand followed the pattern of Western Europe in a trend toward secularization. Christianity, which had provided such a source of strength and survival to the Maori in earlier times, no longer seemed as relevant: the Ratana church, for example, had dropped to 5.6 percent of the Maori population in 2013, and the total number of Christians stood at 46.4 percent – almost exactly equivalent to those Maori professing no religion (46.2%) and virtually equal to the whites in the same category (47%).[93] Paradoxically, however, indigenous religion appeared to be re-entering "through the backdoor," in Eric Kolig's words, in the form of Maori rites being performed on state ceremonial occasions, and Maori language creeping into legislation on land use and resource management.[94] Christianity, however, seems to have been subordinated in this process.

AUSTRALIA

The contrast between the reception of Christianity by the Polynesians and the Australian Aborigines could hardly be greater. In the early nineteenth century, when the former were already embracing Christianity in large numbers, the latter saw little or no reason to do so. The explanation is not far to seek: the Europeans regarded the native Australians as "the most degraded of the human race," in the words of Rev. Samuel Marsden, senior Anglican cleric of New South Wales.[95] In contrast to his view of the Maori, Marsden did not believe them sufficiently advanced to receive the Christian message at all. Others debated whether the Aborigines were fully human. The view that they were not found legal confirmation in Britain's declaration of Australia as *terra nullius*, i.e., uninhabited and therefore open to settlement. Unlike Native Americans, Aborigines were not considered capable of negotiating treaties.[96]

In fact the genealogical distance between the European and Australian branches of the human species was as great as any in history. DNA samples collected in 2011 point to the Aborigines' leaving Africa between 62,000 and 75,000 years ago, well before Eurasians did so.[97] Questions of how and when they migrated to Australia are still debated, but a widely accepted date is at least 40,000 years ago. Rising sea levels at the end of the last ice age gradually cut off the land bridge between New Guinea and Australia and likewise separated Tasmania from the Australian mainland beginning around 6000 BCE, leaving the inhabitants to evolve largely on their own. Over time they developed a fine-tuned understanding of the land and what it could produce, enabling a nomadic lifestyle based on gathering and hunting. That lifestyle was sufficient to impress Captain Cook, who found them to be "far happier than we Europeans...they think themselves provided with all the necessaries of life."[98] They lived in relatively small groups of tribes and sub-tribes, averaging 500 persons, which were generally divided into smaller "hordes" of 30–40.[99] As they spread across Australia's varied landscape, they developed some 250 distinct languages. Yet, contrary to the Europeans' impressions, they were neither static nor isolated. They engaged in networks of trade, ritual, and marriage that could extend over hundreds of miles. Rules governing marriage were especially elaborate, involving multiple cross-tribal considerations – so much so that Aborigines tended to look down on Europeans for their indiscriminate mating customs (an Aboriginal male once jokingly compared Europeans to dogs, because neither had any decent marriage rules).[100] Such rules did not, however, exclude the trading of women for goods as part of networks of exchange in these patriarchal societies.

Aboriginal religion was similarly complex, a fact missed for a long time by Western anthropologists, who were fascinated by the relations between humans, animals, and plants that went under the name of totemism, but thereby mistook these symbols for the narratives and meanings underlying them.[101] As with Native Americans, Aboriginal mythology tended to be intimately tied to landscape, with dramatic ruptures such as rock outcroppings, caves, and water holes often serving as sites for the emergence of ancestral spirits from underground. The myths of such emergences were collectively labeled "dreamtime" by anthropologists, though this was not universally recognized by Aborigines themselves.[102] The label expressed the belief that contact with the spirits is replenished on an ongoing basis through dreams, when the human spirit is said to wander away from the body and can journey to the ancestors – a process that is required if the continued life and health of humans, plants, and animals is to be maintained.[103] Mythical narratives are carried on by oral traditions, particularly in song, in which geographical references play a major role.[104] The willingness, even eagerness of Aborigines to share these stories beyond their local tribe is illustrated by the initial contact between the LMS missionary Lancelot Threlkeld and the Awabakal people in New South Wales in 1824, before large numbers of colonial settlers had reached their region. The Awabakals sang imitations of Christian church music, invited Threlkeld to a ritual dance, and eventually exchanged religious stories and place names through one of their number who had learned English when captured as a boy.[105]

Aboriginal religion also had its dark side, contravening Captain Cook's rosy picture. Sickness and death were also caused by spirits that could be manipulated by a person wishing to do harm, and justice demanded that such persons be sought out and punished, often by killing. Many tribes had a special ritual executioner to carry out this function (*kadaitja*). According to an Aboriginal Christian writing in 1987, "people thus lived in fear of the spirit world, in fear of people who might be manipulating the spirit world to do them harm, in fear of being wrongly implicated in someone's death and illness, and therefore in fear of the *Kadaitja* killing them in the pay back for someone's death. The missionaries came into all this, and gave the Gospel to the people. The Gospel was truly a God-send."[106]

It took over a century, however, for this message to be assimilated by large numbers of Aboriginal people. There was no complete translation of the New Testament into an Aboriginal language until 1989.[107]

In 1788, the British landed some 700 convicts and 300 jailers near present-day Sydney, the first of several penal colonies, followed in the early 1800s by free settlers, creating, in one writer's words, an "alcoholic, violent, greedy, lonely, crude and cruel world where the only feminine solace was in the bodies of Aboriginal girls and women."[108] A year after the first landing, smallpox ravaged the native population; other epidemics were to follow. If whites tended to place Aborigines beyond the pale of humanity, Aborigines quickly learned that these newcomers were outside the norms of human-spirit relationships they had been used to. Violence was the common result: native *resistance* brought white retribution seven times over, with an estimated 3,000 whites killed by Aborigines and 20,000 Aborigines killed by settlers.[109] Massacres were not uncommon, and in the case of Tasmania, attempted genocide. A white constable summed up the settlers' attitude toward native women, "Men would not remain so many years in a country like this if there were no women, and perhaps the Almighty meant them for use as he has placed them wherever the pioneers go."[110] The kidnapping and abuse of women should not blind us to the fact that Aborigines sometimes continued to treat sex as an element of exchange for goods, and that women sometimes did voluntarily enter into such relationships. Whatever the path, the outcome was frequently the scourge of venereal disease, which peaked in the middle of the century.[111] Given the cycle of disease and death, it is no wonder that the Aboriginal population declined drastically, by about one third every decade by 1843.[112]

Missionaries shared in the low estimation of Aborigines as an inferior race. But they did draw the line when it came to questioning their humanity. Although they were slow to take up the Aborigines' cause, they did speak out against the worst abuses by the 1820s and '30s, often at odds with the settlers, and established eight missions in New South Wales by mid-century. They all failed.[113]

One principal reason was the unrealistic expectation that Aborigines would "improve" by turning to settled agriculture, which the missionaries viewed as a prerequisite for genuine conversion. Aborigines saw little reason to give up their freedom of movement in exchange for the drudgery of planting and harvesting crops. Nor did they see the advantage of Western learning. They viewed missions as part of the system of exchange, i.e., they were willing to oblige the missionaries by attending church and school in return for such things as food and tobacco. But the missions were in competition with the cities for these and other goods, and Aborigines generally chose the latter. In addition, preaching about sin made little sense in the light of settler transgressions. Why were not the missionaries preaching to the whites?

The missionaries' failure to evangelize in the early nineteenth century did not necessarily mean that the Aborigines learned nothing from them. In a provocative, if speculative, study, Tony Swain has argued that the rupture of colonial settlement led the southeastern tribes to a radical revision of their cosmology. Now, in addition to the ancestral spirits from the earth, they posited a creator sky-god who was beyond the regeneration of the dream journeys and whose ways were not tied to a particular location, resulting in a duality between heaven and earth. Swain further suggests that Christian references acted as an initial stimulus, but were then *incorporated* into native mythologies rather than leading toward Christianity itself.[114]

After 1850, the situation changed somewhat. As settlers moved into the northern and western parts of the continent, the patterns of violence and degradation repeated themselves. But in the south and east, the killings subsided, and authorities began to think about reservations to protect the remaining Aborigines. Missionaries were prime movers in this process; they doubtless shared the prevailing view that Aborigines were bound for extinction, but that this should happen in a peaceful manner. Thus, a new generation of missions arose which were genuine havens from the surrounding violence, and numbers of Aborigines consciously chose to give up their freedom for the protection offered – including the care of their children. When granted sufficiently large tracts of land, these missions became successful agricultural and ranching operations which guaranteed a steady supply of rations, and the residents became part of these operations. Moreover, missionary teachers invariably found that Aboriginal children were bright and able to adapt to new ways. Although the Europeans continued to struggle with the culture they found abhorrent, they gradually learned to respect aspects of it – although there was wide variation from one mission to another.[115] These missions produced a few Aboriginal evangelists, one of whom, Moses Tjalkabota, actually directed the Hermannsburg mission among the Arrerntes in central Australia in the 1920s in the absence of a European.[116]

In the first half of the twentieth century these humanitarian impulses were swept up in the growing tide of racist thinking in which the notion of "protection" of Aborigines was stretched and twisted into something quite the opposite: it became a euphemism for constricting the Aborigines' freedom of movement in the name of keeping the races separate. Of course legitimate concerns about sexual abuse of

Aboriginal girls did not disappear and were not imaginary – although missionaries generally did not distinguish this from consensual sexual relationships.[117] But over time, "protection" was extended to include protection from one's own aboriginal family and culture. In the words of a government-run official in 1902, children in rural districts should be removed "at once to the Missions, etc., where their future welfare and happiness are assured from the day they enter till the day they die."[118] Of particular concern were the so-called half-castes, children of mixed race, whose valuable white blood was not to be degraded because of Aboriginal upbringing. Thus arose the policy of removing children from Aboriginal families and putting them in institutions. At first this was done by missionaries with parental consent; in some cases the families lived at the mission station as well and were allowed to see their children once a week. But the state took an increasingly interventionist role after 1900, and a 1905 law banned intercourse with non-Aborigines and required special permission for interracial marriage; by 1911, all state governments had "protection" legislation on their books, and in 1915 the Aborigines Protection Board received authorization to remove children from their homes without parents' consent.[119] Between 1916 and 1969, at least 5,000 Aboriginal children were removed, creating countless stories of trauma and grief. Although the state itself rather than the missionaries ran many of these institutions, missionaries played an active role in shaping the policies. This is not to say that all missionaries were uncaring, but the very scale of the operation brought out authoritarian tendencies. According to Christian historian John Harris, "I have spoken to hundreds of middle-aged and elderly Aboriginal people in widely separated parts of Australia and the memories of regimentation and oppression run as a common thread through the majority of their stories."[120] If Christianity had an impact in these years, it seemed to be primarily through the institution of monogamous marriage within the mission stations, where missionaries arranged and conducted marriages between inmates, creating islands of stable families in the midst of uprootedness. These marriages frequently violated Aboriginal taboos, however, which created conflicts and even an occasional killing.[121]

These segregation policies were undermined by World Wars I and II, which of necessity threw the races together to meet the demand for soldiers and laborers. World War II, in particular, seemed to demonstrate that Aborigines who had lived on mission stations as opposed to government-run institutions were at an advantage in having more job skills and being better able to communicate with whites.[122]

After the wars, Aborigines were less willing to accept inferior status and began organizing for equal rights. Meanwhile, the realization had dawned on whites – already in the 1920s – that Aborigines were *not* dying out, and that therefore the alternative to extinction was assimilation into white society. This became official government policy in the 1950s and '60s, even as the removal of children from their families continued, but eventually culminating in full citizenship rights in 1967.

Assimilation was itself soon undermined, however, in the 1970s by the reawakening of interest Aboriginal culture and the reassertion of its value. This transition was not always easy, particularly for the generation that had grown up in the boarding schools in ignorance of that culture. Their process of rediscovery entailed the painful realization of what had been taken away; thus arose the narrative of the "stolen generations," which gained national prominence in the 1980s and '90s.[123] Meanwhile the state had taken over many of the educational and medical facilities that had been run by the missions, significantly reducing the latter's institutional presence.

Some observers faulted the missionaries for having unwittingly contributed to secularization by so denigrating Aborigines' religion as to leave them without a spiritual foundation. Others claim that the fate of Aborigines would have been worse were it not for the missionaries.[124] In any case, the closing of missionary institutions has created room for the growth of an increasingly autonomous Aboriginal Christianity. A 2006 census revealed that 73 percent of Aborigines identified with Christianity, compared to 63.9 percent of the population as a whole. At the same time, 24 percent reported no religious affiliation as compared to 19% of the non-indigenous population.[125] As is so often the case, these numbers raise more questions than they answer as to what such identification means. According to Hans Mol, "there is ample evidence that the many Christian baptisms, confirmations, marriages, and funerals were, for the Aborigines, ways to dutifully meet Western expectations...without much effect on identity and motivation."[126] It is also clear that acceptance of Christianity does not mean total rejection of Aboriginal religion. In fact, a collection of studies published in 1988 reveals a wide spectrum of negotiations, from *resistance* to *selective incorporation* and *dual participation*.[127] One can further point to several cases of *concentration of spirituality* in the form of revival movements which have proven effective in reducing alcoholism, a widespread affliction in Aboriginal Australia.[128] There is further evidence of *vernacular translation*, as Bible stories are transposed to take place on Australian soil. Distant memories of the sea-level rise after the last ice age made stories of the flood especially appealing; Aborigines point to remnants of Noah's ark on opposite sides of the continent, one on a mountaintop in New South Wales, another at the edge of a desert in the northwest. Locals there dismiss the idea that the ark landed somewhere in Egypt (sic) as a vicious Western lie, designed to keep Aborigines in submission.[129] Such stories illustrate the fact that the speed and traumatic impact of European invasion could not wipe out thousands of years of cultural evolution. In his sweeping study of the topic, Robert N. Bellah concludes, "the world still has much to learn from the Aborigines."[130]

MELANESIA

Two things are immediately striking about Melanesia, the chain of islands of various sizes in the western Pacific extending from New Guinea in the west to Fiji in the east. One is the extreme complexity of its linguistic map: while occupying only .9 percent of the earth's landmass, it contains between one-fourth and one-third of its distinct languages.[131] The other is the relative recency of extended contact with the West in many parts, especially the highlands of New Guinea, which were not "discovered" until the age of air travel. Both of these have to do the region's extremely rugged, often corrugated terrain, which both harbors an extraordinary diversity of plant and animal species and creates isolated valleys and pockets of human habitation. This diversity makes easy generalization about cultural patterns extremely hazardous; nevertheless, many scholars feel confident about ascribing certain common patterns that hold more or less to the area as a whole.[132] In a 1965 anthology of studies of mostly New Guinean religions, the editors noted a broad similarity but with considerable regional variation between highlands and coastal areas. They also emphasized a certain this-worldliness to the religions, in that the "most important representatives – gods, ghosts, ancestors, demons, and totems – are generally said to live on the earth, often near human settlements."[133] This gave religion a pronounced pragmatic slant, in which spirits were closely associated with material benefits or lacks. Belief in *mana* was widespread, as in Polynesia.

Another common feature is the extreme fragmentation of socio-political units. Much of Melanesia (except for New Caledonia and Fiji in the south) consisted of hamlet or village communities of 70–300 inhabitants, with little in the way of social hierarchy. Authority was established by individual achievement, such as amassing wealth or victory in war; the winners in this competitive environment were the so-called big men, while the losers were thought of as little better than slaves.[134] A male-dominated warrior ethos prevailed, in which killing one's enemy was a mark of prestige. Women lived often segregated from men and were barred from major religious rituals, although they had their own rituals surrounding the menstrual cycle from which men were excluded.[135] Although this warrior ethos was compatible with extensive trade networks among the islands, outsiders were generally greeted with suspicion and hostility – a fact that led European explorers largely to bypass the area in favor of the friendlier islands further east. Retribution and revenge were prominent values, as noted not only by Europeans, but also by Polynesian missionaries like Ta'unga, who wrote, "These islands have no equal when it comes to vengeance. Their very natures are truly vindictive. That is why all forms of evil are widespread here. Vindictiveness is the real cause of them; that is what causes wars and cannibalism…" His journal contains grisly descriptions of the latter practice (although it had also been practiced in his native Raratonga).[136] Human flesh was considered a source of *mana*. Moreover, the ethos of retribution justified killing not only an individual enemy, but also a member of the group to which the enemy belonged. Add to this the fact that foreigners were frequently bearers of disease, which the Melanesians attributed to sorcery on their part.[137]

All of this put early missionaries in an especially vulnerable position. Although they did not fit either familiar category of outsider, namely warrior or trader, they were subject to guilt by association with these and to accusations of sorcery. So it is not surprising that they were killed and eaten with some regularity in the nineteenth century, beginning with the clubbing of John Williams in 1839.[138] The popular stereotype of missionaries as victims of cannibalism goes back to this incident, although it was untrue for most parts of the world. Of course, missionaries were themselves vulnerable to disease, particularly malaria, which also contributed to their deaths. In New Guinea, at least 130 out of 250 Polynesian teachers died within 26 years, not to mention their wives and children.[139] A successful Presbyterian mission on the island of Aneityum in the New Hebrides was wiped out by a measles epidemic in 1861, killing thousands.[140]

This unremittingly dark portrayal of Melanesian society deserves correction in that retribution was part of a larger value, namely reciprocity. There were positive mechanisms of compensations for loss and fair exchange. Generosity was also deeply imbued, and it was the mark of a "big man" to be conspicuously magnanimous, with gifts, presented in elaborate ceremonies, serving as visible signs of his power and prestige. The willingness to make sacrifices to both the living and the dead also served as signs of ethical character. Both the positive and negative aspects of reciprocity ultimately served a higher good, namely that of the community, defined as the familial or kinship group to which one belonged, but not further. According to Garry Trompf, "Melanesians lacked 'the concept of the person' in the broad sense, perhaps, since people outside their own families or primary and affinal groups were thought 'less-than-human' in varying degrees."[141]

Nineteenth-century missionaries generally greeted these cultural patterns with incomprehension. Their experiences in Polynesia, with its kings ruling over a wide area, had little or no counterpart here; nor did the bewildering multiplicity of languages. One individual, however, who attempted to change this situation was George A. Selwyn, the Anglican bishop of New Zealand, who inaugurated a scheme to take young Melanesian men out of their home environment, train them in a special school in New Zealand, and send them home again. One hundred seventy-five such "scholars" made the journey between 1849 and 1859. They were probably motivated more by a sense of adventure than a desire to learn about Christianity; in any case, the type of Christianity presented to them was thoroughly European, with an appeal to the intellect rather than the heart or the will. Selwyn's successor, John Patteson, made a greater effort to understand the attitudes of the Melanesians; he transferred the school from Auckland to Norfolk Island, midway between New Zealand and New Caledonia. With great effort, he managed to baptize about 300 natives on one island. But his stamina was already wearing thin when he met his death by clubbing in 1871. These converts faced difficulty in reentry into their home environments. The cultural gap remained insurmountable.[142]

An exception to the above pattern occurred in the southernmost islands in the chain: New Caledonia, the Isle of Pines, and the aptly named Loyalty Islands. This was a malaria-free zone, and the language obstacles were not as great. Above all, the political structure on these islands resembled more the Polynesian pattern, with strong rulers controlling a greater expanse of territory. The situation was complicated, or rather reinforced, by the appearance of Catholic Marist missionaries, which introduced denominational rivalry into the area. These soon reinforced existing tribal rivalries, which actually led to more islanders accepting Christianity.[143]

Despite these successes, the overall result of missionary efforts at the end of the century was paltry: only about 6 percent of the islands' inhabitants had accepted Christianity.[144] A sea change, however, was about to take place. By 1910, some 14,125 persons had converted to Anglicanism alone, compared to 8,929 in 1894. By 1942, that number had become approximately 35,000.[145]

The explanation of such figures lies in the fact that only around 1900 were massive numbers of Melanesians exposed to Western material goods, technologies, and customs – in contrast to Polynesia, where this had occurred in advance of the missionaries. Timing was everything, and the spread of Christianity in this period may be viewed as part of a three-pronged initiative by the West, the other two being plantation-type economic activity and outright colonization. These occurred simultaneously and reinforced each other – and paradoxically found widespread acceptance from the people in their initial phase of fascination.[146]

Although parts of Melanesia had seen whalers, sealers, and especially sandalwood traders in the early nineteenth century, there were still islands which had not much changed since the days of Captain Cook. An early Melanesian Christian, George Sarawaia, describes the wonder and terror he felt when first meeting a white man, Bishop Selwyn, "I looked at the feet of all the people on the ship, and thought it was really their feet, but it was only leather shoes they were wearing. I said to myself that these men were made partly of clamshell, and my bones quaked."[147]

European interest in the region began to be aroused in the 1860s and '70s. France established a penal colony in New Caledonia; the accessible parts of New Guinea attracted trading companies – including from newly unified Germany – who fantasized about untold wealth, much as in central Africa at the same time. White Australians and New Zealanders had similar ambitions and schemes and encouraged the British to enter in. As many of these schemes failed, colonial protectorates were established to prop them up – Germany established a protectorate in northeastern New Guinea in 1884 and the British promptly followed suit in the southeast. The British and the French agreed to a joint policing effort in the New Hebrides in 1906.

Melanesians first felt the impact of these changes in the form of labor recruitment. Between 1860 and 1906, owners of cotton and sugar plantations in Queensland in Australia imported over 100,000 indentured workers from the Melanesian islands (others went to Fiji). These operations had a very bad press – missionaries were outraged – accusing recruiters of kidnapping and violence, which certainly went on. But this cannot hide the fact that many of these young men went voluntarily, in search of new experiences; many signed up for repeated terms. At the end of the three-year term, they received payment from which they purchased tobacco, tools, gunpowder, mirrors, fish hooks, and other items. In 1904, Australia ended the arrangement, leading to a flood of returning Melanesians replete with goods.[148] Some also returned as Christians, thanks in part to the vigorous missionary efforts of one Florence Young, whose family ran a Queensland plantation. She had worked in Hudson Taylor's China Inland mission, and brought an intense, puritanical Christianity back with her. When the Melanesians were expelled in 1904, she went with them, setting up the South Sea Evangelical Mission on the island of Malaita.[149] These returnees became proselytizers and teachers themselves.[150]

By 1914, Melanesia's isolation was past. Steamships now plied the waters between Sydney and the islands; the larger merchant companies did business there, and plantations had reached the islands themselves. Darrell Whiteman writes, "Gone forever were the days of the lone mission vessel *Southern Cross* carrying missionaries who enticed islanders away to school with a few fish hooks."[151]

In this setting, Christianity played an important role in easing the process of *selective acculturation*. Charles Forman put it succinctly, "The old religion had not been designed to account for the great changes that were taking place with the European impact. In consequence it lost vitality and its great ceremonies decayed, while the Christian religion commended itself as a way of accounting for the new."[152] This might be seen as a continuation of the Melanesians' past materialistic values, but it also necessitated important ruptures with that past. For example, as firearms became widely circulated in the new economy, revenge warfare became even more destructive until the costs clearly outweighed the benefits. Christianity provided a clear alternative in preaching peace.[153] Missionaries, including wives and missionary women, presented a new, relatively more elevated model of women's role and status, although its success was not as clear.[154] In these respects and many others, missionaries reinforced the efforts of colonial authorities to establish order – a collusion often greeted positively by the people themselves. To have a European missionary in one's village was regarded as a status symbol.[155]

The close connection between commerce and Christianity was illustrated in another way. People interested in Christianity tended to move to the coast from the interior, establishing Christian villages as they did so. People who remained inland were more likely to adhere to traditional religion.[156] Roger M. Keesing writes of an area on Malaita where this dichotomy and tension was still in place in 1989. The women of the interior were particularly offended by the Christians' mixing of the sexes and failure to observe segregation during menses.[157]

As in so many other parts of the world, Christianity's attraction lay first and foremost as a purveyor of education and literacy. As a Solomon islander put it to a Western observer, "You white men are like us ... You have only two eyes, two hands, two feet. How are you different? Because you can read books ... If we could read your books we would have money and possessions."[158] Villages invited missionaries on the condition that they build a school. These schools were not always of good quality – in a case from Papua New Guinea, for example, they depended for teachers on Melanesians returning from Queensland who were barely literate themselves and could only teach by rote.[159] Missionaries' emphasis shifted to more centralized regional boarding schools. They were able to surmount the problem of fragmented language by first adopting Motu, a language used by native traders on the coast of New Guinea and thus comprehensible across a wider area. The debate over Motu versus English as the language of instruction continued throughout the early twentieth century, with English winning out in 1931.[160] After World War II, another lingua franca came into use: Tok Pisin (pidgin talk), which had originated among migrant workers in Samoan coconut plantations. Missionaries were averse to it at first, but eventually gave in, eventually resulting in a Bible translation.[161]

It seems that one of the major lessons taught in the schools was that of discipline. John Barker writes,

> The elder Maisin I interviewed in the 1980s remembered little of the lessons or the services they attended in the station as children. However they vividly recalled parading in formation into class, mending fences, cleaning classrooms, working in the teacher's garden or fishing for him. The described in exquisite detail the punishments they received...for tardiness, slacking on the work details and skipping classes. They did not learn much, however, they said, quite simply, that the teachers were good men and their parents wanted them to go to the school and be baptized. The work was hard, but one man told me "It was good doing these things because later when we married we knew how to do the work well. [The teacher] made us into hard-working people."[162]

One may question the depth of understanding of Christianity that was conveyed through these processes. But one may equally question whether missionaries expected much of the Melanesians in this regard.[163] This was the era, after all, of high imperialism and civilizing mission, where missionaries' regard for native cultures were generally at a low ebb, despite some outstanding exceptions. The belief that peoples like Melanesians belonged to dying races was widespread.

Beginning in the 1920s, there were signs that this Christian-colonial honeymoon was starting to wane, as inequalities between the Europeans and Melanesians persisted and grew. The German colony in New Guinea was handed over to the Australians after World War I, and the natives found them to be far more racist in their attitudes than the Germans. A violent tax revolt on Malaita in 1927 prompted a punitive British reprisal which included destruction of ancestral shrines. (Meanwhile, in Samoa, a terrible outbreak of influenza, part of the worldwide pandemic, was blamed on the New Zealand administrator's failure to quarantine a ship, and a militant nationalist uprising followed which was also directed against the London Missionary Society – although an emissary from that society succeeded in mediating an end to the uprising.[164]) In the 1930s, the Great Depression made an impact through the fall of export prices, leading to a reduction in wages. From all these indicators, it was clear that the promise of Christianity's bringing wealth to the islands was not being fulfilled – the whites were evidently withholding the true secrets of their power. This belief gave rise to *resistance* in the form of the famous cargo cults, which looked forward to the return of the ancestors which would bring the wealth but without the Westerners – the retribution motif that Trompf identified with payback.[165] There were examples of these cults already in the interwar period.[166] Christian millennialist references and images were interwoven with these movements, but by no means dominated them.[167]

With World War II, parts of Melanesia found themselves in the center of combat operations, with major battles such as Guadalcanal and with hundreds of thousands of foreign troops pouring into the area. Missionary activity ground virtually to a halt, with many interned and executed by the Japanese. Native Christians were also harshly treated, as they were suspected of collaborating with the allies. Christianity had taken sufficient root, however, for local congregations to be able to survive on their own, without clergy or buildings, instilling confidence in their ability to exist without foreign missionaries. Moreover, the war-time conditions brought different denominations together, including Catholics and Protestants, foreshadowing a later ecumenicism.[168] The encounter with American troops proved especially eye-opening, for they displayed an informality and egalitarianism, including between whites and blacks, that contrasted with the colonial overlords – not to mention the fact that it was Americans, not the British or French, who actually liberated the islands from the Japanese. And they brought tons of "cargo" – seemingly endless supplies of military equipment in the supply centers.

The war generally undermined further the Melanesians' trust and respect for the colonial powers. It also shaped the rhetoric and emphasis of the cargo movements, given the actual experience of massive amounts of material goods being bestowed and then withdrawn. The hope that the Americans would return in their airplanes tended to replace hope in return of the ancestors. Nevertheless, commentators have emphasized that these movements were deeply rooted in precontact belief and custom, which expressed a hope not merely in goods, but also in knowledge and redemption from present circumstances.[169]

Cargo cults were in fact part of a spectrum of responses to the general restlessness. These included strictly charismatic movements such as the one led by Silas Eto, a Methodist who developed trances and visions and eventually led his flock out of the church, proclaiming himself "Holy Mamma," an incarnation of the Holy Spirit.[170] Others were more secular, demanding a more equal share in colonial wealth and power, such as the "Marching Rule" in the Solomon Islands.[171] Still others were more utilitarian, seeking to emulate Western capitalist habits (*"bisnis"*).[172]

Nevertheless, the vitality of missionary-led Christianity remained strong, due in part to indigenous evangelizing movements such as the Melanesian Brotherhood, which began in the 1920s.[173] Also, the influx of foreign missionaries, mostly from the United States and Australia, increased dramatically in the postwar years. The number of missionaries in 1960 was 4,500, compared to 1,700 in 1930.[174] They tended to be less paternalistic than their forebears. Catholic missions in New Guinea became more involved in providing social services in the villages, even opening stores to facilitate economic activity.[175] While education remained a high priority, governments were gradually edging out churches as providers of education – often against the wishes of the natives themselves.[176]

Part of the explanation for this influx was the opening of the New Guinea highlands. Though isolated, these valleys were heavily populated, with tens of thousands of people living there. Missionaries were among the first to penetrate the region in the early 1920s, followed closely by mineral prospectors. The missionaries had learned from past mistakes and did not attempt to squelch native religion, except for such practices as cannibalism and warfare. Thus, the highlanders were receptive, and matters progressed until two missionaries were killed in 1934. The government banned any further missionary activity for a decade, but penetration resumed after the war and Christianity spread rapidly. The Catholics had inherited an airstrip near its main compound in the coastal area, which at its height was sending fourteen flights a day.[177]

The fast tempo of radical change in Melanesia continued into the later decades of the twentieth century, as the region became exposed to electronic communication and to global social and cultural fashions. As elsewhere in the world, the islands partook of the struggle for political independence, though this was usually not as violent as in parts of Africa, for example. And, as elsewhere, there was a countermove in the form of a reassertion of the value of native customs as expression of a national identity. Yet the quick tempo of change guaranteed that many of these customs had persisted more than originally thought, however much they may have been modified. For example, the belief in human sorcery as the cause of sickness and death was almost universally held; many people adhered to their belief in spirits.[178] At the same time, Christianity continued to grow by leaps and bounds. Much of the discussion surrounding Christianity in Melanesia in the late twentieth century focuses on this paradox.

One partial answer is that much of this growth took the form of revival movements such as Pentecostalism, amounting to a Melanesian "great awakening" in the 1970s and early '80s. The prevalence of visions, dreams, and trances provided links to native religion, even if they assumed new forms such as spirit possession. Visitation by the Holy Spirit became for many Melanesians the true core of the Christian message.[179] Many of the new evangelical missionaries, it is true, showed little tolerance for a multiplicity of spirits. But, as Trompf points out, "by turning the ancestors, minor deities, place spirits, and such like into 'Satans', moreover, as most missionaries have tended to do, they have kept them very much alive at the village level–admittedly, often as forces to be overcome by a Higher Power, but still to be feared and still to be dealt with as integral to the cosmos."[180] On the other hand, the spread of Seventh Day Adventists – some 800,000 strong in Papua New Guinea – represented extreme *concentration of spirituality*, totally rejecting indigenous traditions.[181] In one remote community in the New Guinea highlands, millennial expectations were kept on constant alert in response to daily developments in the world news.[182]

When it comes to the question of how villagers interpreted these mixed messages, the answers are probably as varied as the different villages themselves. Yet the issue of whether Christianity is sufficiently compatible with native customs as to be smoothly *incorporated* in them, or is fundamentally different so as to allow only for juxtaposition or *dual participation* has been a matter of scholarly controversy in anthropology.[183] There is strong evidence to support both claims. On the one hand, Christian voices and messages have been found to enter into dreams, a prime medium for communication with spirits among one group of highlanders.[184] Another point of contact is that of sacrifice: the taking of Holy Communion, a reenacting of Christ's sacrifice, is viewed as a way of acquiring *mana*.[185] Priests are also viewed as possessors of *mana*, exemplars of big men.[186]

On the other hand, the gap between Christian precepts and Melanesian mores, at least as presented to the Melanesians by evangelicals, could be impossibly large, not only with respect to warfare and marriage, but also especially with the whole idea of original sin. In the case of one highland village (Urapmin) studied by Joel Robbins, the inhabitants had so internalized the missionaries' preaching that they were sinners that they viewed themselves as inferior blacks to European whites.[187] Another point of incompatibility is the individualistic notion of sin and repentance in Christian theology as contrasted with a collective or relational viewpoint in Melanesia. Robbins concludes that attempts to live the completely Christian life are doomed to failure.[188] The only way for them to do so, then, is to compartmentalize, that is *dual participation*. Barker, in his study of another group, the Maisin, on the New Guinea north coast, reaches the same conclusion: dual participation is marked by a spatial divide between the village and the mission station.[189]

Compartmentalization, however, does not preclude the possibility of interaction, and it is clear that Christian doctrine has significantly modified Melanesian mores and customs. People still believe in sorcerers, but fear them much less than before. The role of missionaries in reducing violence has already been pointed out. Churches have admitted women to their schools and administration, and patterns of segregation in sleeping and eating have largely been eliminated. That said, the male orientation remains strong.[190]

In a purely quantitative sense, Christianity may be said to have succeeded in Melanesia: the percentage of Christians grew from 87.3 percent of the population in 1970 to a projected 92.1 percent in 2020.[191] More important than these figures, Christianity has undoubtedly instilled a broader notion of humanity than previously existed among

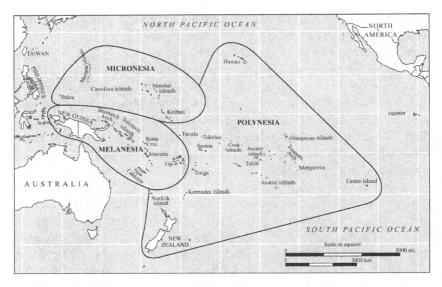

Figure 8.1 The Pacific
Source: Modified from Karuhoa, Pacific Culture Areas, Wikimedia Commons, 2015. Drawn by Mary Lee Eggart

Melanesians. The notion that outsiders are less than human has been discarded, and even the Urapmin, while they regard themselves as inferior, nevertheless take solace in being part of a worldwide community of the faithful.[192] If the heart of the Christian message is God's love for humanity, it may be said to have succeeded in Melanesia.

Conclusion: Reflections on Concentrated and Diffuse Spirituality

In this conclusion, I pose the following question: What inferences or generalizations can one draw from this traversal of cross-cultural interactions between indigenes and missionaries? In particular, what light can this study shed back on the state of religion and spirituality in the West? Given that the study of World Christianity seeks to overcome the barrier between the "West" and the "rest" by noting the reciprocal effects of one on the other in an interdependent world, this question is an important one.[1]

We can begin by noting that many, if not most, of the religious traditions with which missionary Christianity came in contact did not make the same dividing line between the sacred and profane aspects of existence as did the West, nor were the divisions that existed always as sharp. Oppositions such as spiritual/material, transcendent/immanent, and religious/secular did not find ready counterparts in Africa, Asia, or Oceania. Thus, it should not be too surprising that, as the boundaries between Western and non-Western cultures have become more permeable in recent decades, these divisions should be subject to scrutiny in the West as well.

The contrasting yet complementary concepts of *concentrated* and *diffuse spirituality*, alluded to throughout the book, provide a suitable framework for discussing these relationships. I have argued that both types of spirituality are likely to be present, in one form or another, in any given society, sometimes in complementary, sometimes in dialectical relationship. This hypothesis is intended to provoke a reexamination of unidirectional theories of religious evolution and to suggest a broader interpretation based on data from a greater variety of cultures.

This argument would appear to be a difficult one to make in the face of strong evidence to the contrary. We have noted a strong shift in favor of concentrated spirituality in places such as India and East Asia. And it is incontrovertibly true that religious diversity has declined worldwide in favor of a few world religions. To quote Alan Strathern:

A handful of religious systems now dominates our planet: Christianity, Islam, Hinduism, and Buddhism account for the vast majority of the religiously affiliated, while Judaism, Sikhism, and Jainism mop up a far smaller number. Survey takers must then find a name for the forlorn category of the residuum: adherents of 'folk religions,' which in 2015 made up only 5.7 per cent of the world's population. Thus the countless, nameless traditions of ritual performance and mythic elaboration that lay outside the world religions, and that provided the distinct habitats of meaning in which humanity lived for most of its history, have been subject to a merciless winnowing.[2]

In the West, the story of the shift toward concentration has been told via the grand narrative of modernization since c. 1500. Although it has been relatively easy for historians to puncture holes in it, both with respect to its relation to the prior Middle Ages and to later developments in the nineteenth and twentieth centuries, it is difficult to deny its core of truth .[3] The increasing human control of the natural environment through scientific and technological advances has indisputably diminished our dependence on the operations of spirits, be they natural or supernatural. The belief in spirits has by no means disappeared, but it is safe to say that it has become marginalized. This is evident from the several labels that scholars have invented to illuminate this phenomenon, beginning with Max Weber's "disenchantment."[4] "Disenchantment" can be seen as the withdrawal of spirits, and our magical interaction with them, from the everyday world. Weber used it to mean the substitution of rational calculability to replace such interventions. As noted in the chapter on India, this substitution involved the pruning and reduction of multiple aspects of human existence to a concentrated few.[5] This was not necessarily irreligious, as it could lend support to concentration of spirituality in the form of deism, i.e., the notion of a God as master designer, creating the world to run on scientific laws – as seen, for example, in William Paley's widely read *Natural Theology*.

Another version of the evolutionary narrative goes back further in time to the so-called Axial Age (beginning 800–200 BCE), first adumbrated by Karl Jaspers, when notions of "transcendence" were supposedly lifted out of their mundane context in a number of world religions. Strathern, following this version, contrasts "Transcendentalism" with

"Immanentism," a contrast that closely maps that between concentrated and diffuse spirituality. He claims, however, that Immanentism never really goes away in modern times.[6]

Finally, the narrative persists in the notion of secularization, i.e., the apparent decline of religion itself. Long thought to be more or less an inevitable concomitant of modernization, this notion lost credibility in the 1980s and 1990s with such events as the Iranian Revolution and the fall of communism. But it continues to be the focus of passionate debate, as empirical data documenting declining church attendance and affiliation with organized religious bodies continue to mount, even in a supposedly religious country such as the United States.[7] Much of this discussion is carried on by social scientists as well as scholars in religious studies, but historians are remarkably largely absent.[8] The formidable *Oxford Handbook of Secularism*, which appeared in 2017, lists not a single historian among its 53 contributors. As noted in Chapter 1, however, the whole notion of the secular originated as a Christian concept and thus bears the imprint of Christianity through *conservation of form*, preserving the sharp division between the spiritual and the temporal.

My basis for undercutting these powerful narratives is to claim that *the relationships between concentrated and diffuse spirituality may best be understood by looking at the full range of behaviors and pronouncements that go under the name of religion, not merely their belief systems.* I find that these behaviors and pronouncements can be grouped into four basic categories or dimensions, which taken together may be thought of as comprising a kind of phenomenology of the subject. I call these dimensions (1) the theoretical, (2) the practical, (3) the experiential, and (4) the political.[9] The predominance of one type of spirituality in one dimension often leads to an opposite and compensating emphasis in another. Let me briefly comment on each of them.

(1) The *theoretical*, plainly enough, are the beliefs one holds about God, gods, spirits, incarnation, the relation of the supernatural to the natural, and so on. Such beliefs may be expressed in terms of creeds and doctrines, but no less importantly through narrative myths of origin and development. Such beliefs are often taken to be the defining benchmark of religion, and this assumption continues to haunt the debate over secularization. Thus, the sociologist Steve Bruce, a leading proponent of the secularization thesis in the West, claims that "religion diminishes in social significance...*except where it finds work to do other than relating individuals to the*

supernatural" [italics in original].[10] The implication that such "other work" is somehow not "really" religious, a notion that the multidimensional view of religion can serve to correct.

(2) The *practical* refers to the actions, ritual or otherwise, that one performs in the name of religion/spirituality. One might assume that such actions follow upon beliefs, but this is not always the case. The repeated performance of ritual over time, for example, creates physical and mental habits, which may be more indicative of the living pulse of one's religion than belief itself. This can lead to some striking discrepancies – for example Sweden, often cited as a textbook case of secularism, nevertheless has very high rates of baptism, confirmation, and church weddings – pointing to the particular significance of rites of passage from one major stage of life to another.[11] More central is the power of the act of worship itself in shaping the mind. The religious scholar Joachim Wach writes, "worship is, in fact, so integral to religion that it is doubtful if the latter could continue to exist without it."[12] He decries the tendency to put intellectual formulations ahead of such practice as the defining characteristic of religion.

(3) The *experiential* refers to those psychological states that, in one way or another, touch or grasp the whole person. This has been the subject of a rich literature in the West, from Meister Eckhart to Friedrich Schleiermacher, William James, Rudolf Otto, and Carl Jung, among others. James writes, "If religion is to mean anything definite for us...[it should be an] added dimension of emotion, this enthusiastic temper of espousal."[13] To this, I would add a pinch of Emile Durkheim, namely the idea that such enthusiasm may also be experienced collectively, in public ceremonies and festivals – or megachurches.[14] Ever since James, there has been an increasing tendency to elevate the experiential aspect as the defining characteristic of religion altogether, with Otto's definition of it as the experience of the "numinous" frequently serving as the benchmark. This "numinous" emphasizes the feeling of awe in the presence of a higher power, which can also encompass its fearsome and even violent aspects, a recognition of the fact that human experience includes pain, suffering, and malevolence that no meaningful religion can afford to ignore.[15]

(4) By *political*, I do *not* mean primarily the relation between church and state, but rather the structure of religious or spiritual authority itself: who gets to pronounce on and define what religion is and on

Table 9.1 *The varieties of concentrated and diffuse spirituality*

Category	Concentrated	Diffuse
Theoretical	Monotheism	Polytheism
Practical	Ritual, yoga	Being-in-the World
Experiential	Revivals, cults, altered states of consciousness	Privatization; feeling of collective identity
Political	Specialist	Communal

what grounds. The centrality of authority in religious matters is perhaps understudied, but Clifford Geertz gives a perceptive estimation of its importance:

[Religion] is a matter of affirming, or at least recognizing, the inescapability of ignorance, pain, and injustice on the human plane while simultaneously denying that these irrationalities are characteristic of the world as a whole...[Thus] religious belief involves not a Baconian induction from everyday experience—for then we should all be agnostics—but rather a prior acceptance of authority which transforms that experience.[16]

Religious institutional structures will vary according to how this question of authority is answered. Once these structures are understood, the issue of church-state relations becomes more readily comprehensible.

How, then, do the two types of spirituality enter in to these four dimensions? This may be summarized in Table 9.1.

1. **Theoretical.** The contrast between the two types of spirituality would seem superficially to be exemplified in the contrast between monotheism and polytheism. Yet the complementarity of concentration and diffusion within each of these belief systems becomes evident on closer examination. Students of polytheistic societies acknowledge that many of them posit a supreme being, not infrequently a sky god whose power undergirds the multiple spirits on the earth. But this god is generally remote and unconcerned with the daily travails of human beings and therefore does not receive ritual invocation, except as a last resort.[17] And conversely, the monotheistic deities, while denying or excluding the powers of lesser or local gods and spirits, are seen as having a much greater or even universal reach or "scope," embracing all humanity, thus diffuse in a spatial sense.[18] Furthermore, it hardly needs mentioning that the lesser or local spirits reappear in many (though not all) versions of monotheism in the form of semidivine intercessors or miracle workers, such as the ubiquitous saints in Roman Catholicism or Sufi Islam.

2. Practical. I would define "ritual" as concentrated practical spirituality (yoga would be another example). For one thing, rituals generally involve the setting aside of a specific place and time, whether it is at the level of a worship service or a broader "cultural performance" such as fasting at Ramadan or performing a Chinese opera in honor of a temple deity. For another, rituals tend to be highly structured activities that involve a high degree of formality. Rituals typically involve repetition of vocalizations and movements at regular intervals (including singing), designed to create familiarity and reassurance among the participants. The prescribed body movements (including speech) create muscle memory that fixates contents and meaning. It is widely recognized that such repeated actions lend strength to creeds that contemplation alone cannot deliver. To again quote Geertz, "it is, primarily at least, out of the context of concrete acts of religious observance that religious conviction emerges on the human plane."[19]

Diffuse practical spirituality, on the other hand, might be called being-in-the-world, to use Martin Heidegger's phrase. It encompasses the various activities that people perform in the name of religion outside their sacred spaces and times (while admitting that these can also be purely secular, i.e., performed without invoking religion). These would include such things as (1) healing and medicine, (2) education, (3) moral and legal norms and codes, and (4) engagement in causes of social change or in politics. (Education, to which missionaries have devoted a great portion of their time, seems to me actually a hybrid of the concentrated and diffuse, in that it typically takes place in bounded spaces and involves much heavily scripted activity). Within Christianity, the "worldliness" of such activity has frequently elicited a contrary reaction in favor of concentrated spirituality, namely an emphasis on otherworldly salvation – such as the controversy between modernists and fundamentalists in the United States in the early twentieth century.[20] We have seen this controversy play out in numerous situations involving missionaries; but for indigenes coming from traditions of diffuse spirituality, there was often no contradiction between material improvement and religious efficacy. Thus, missionaries spent increasing proportions of time and money running hospitals and schools.[21]

3. Experiential. The most obvious examples of concentrated experiential spirituality are religious revivals and cults, and the altered states of consciousness that frequently accompany them (e.g., hallucinations, trances, speaking in tongues). Beyond this, mystical experiences have been described throughout history as being in the presence of a higher power.

One should also include the intense experience of beauty, i.e., the feelings of sublimity and grandeur that a spectacular sunset or mountain vista or work of art can evoke that are commonly called religious.[22] These examples also tell us that, in the experiential realm, the line between religious and nonreligious spirituality is fuzzy indeed. The same goes for the feeling of being transported that can occur at mass political rallies such as occurred at Nuremberg during the Nazi years.

The contrasting diffuse spirituality can be seen as the same kinds of experiences but spread out in space and time and consequently less intense. This can happen in one of two directions. The first is that of so-called privatization, the cultivation of religious experience by individuals apart from any institutional setting, such as in the home. In the West, for example, this became associated with femininity as the home became separated from the workplace during the Industrial Revolution.[23] The second, opposite direction is the feeling that one's religion is central to one's collective identity, hence closely associated with other markers of identity such as nation or race. Thus, it is no coincidence that, in American culture, God and country are frequently mentioned in the same breath. This need not entail such things as participation in mass parades or rallies, but can simply exist in one's imagination – what Benedict Anderson calls an imagined community.[24] Other examples of such diffuse identity feelings may be found in Israeli and Indian nationalism, where Jewish*ness*, as an ensemble of customs and habits, can be distinguished from Judaism, or Hindutva from Hinduism.[25] These examples also point to the fact that, under the right conditions, such identifications can easily intensify, to a point where diffuse experiential spirituality becomes highly emotional and thus concentrated. This is likely to occur when a society faces a crisis, in which the normal patterns of everyday life are disrupted or threatened.

4. Political. The contrast between concentrated and diffuse spiritual authority may be framed as one between specialists (experts) and non-specialists. The former gain their qualifications through extensive preparation and training, either through education, apprenticeship, or disciplines of initiation and purification. The phenomenon of the shaman, a man or woman with special access to the spirits, is found in many polytheistic religions throughout the world, illustrating the complementarity of diffusion at the theoretical level and concentration at the political. The model of the Roman Catholic hierarchy also comes to mind, as do the Yoruba diviners (*Babalawo*), who have memorized at least a thousand verses to apply their divination.[26] Such knowledge is often kept deliberately inaccessible to the laity, as also with Hindu Brahmins. In the nonspecialist case, authority rests in the congregation or community of believers – or, alternatively, with a charismatic individual who feels directly called by God to gather a community of followers around him or her. Of course, the best-known of these go on to found religions of their own – Wach calls them "'soloists' in the sublime orchestra of the communion of worship."[27] But in many other cases, the success of one charismatic figure opens the door to others who make the same claim. The result is a multiplication and diffusion of authorities and institutions, be they denominations or individual autonomous churches.[28] We have seen this in the cases of the Aladuras in West Africa and the Taipings in China; another example would be European Protestantism in the sixteenth and seventeenth centuries, where Luther's reform inspired a number of mystics who claimed individual communion with the spirit, as well as sectarian congregations such as the Anabaptists, who claimed authority to interpret the Bible on their own and to excommunicate members who did not fit in.[29] In these cases, concentration of experiential and theoretical spirituality went hand in hand with diffusion of religious authority–precisely the opposite pattern from Roman Catholicism, which retained its diffuse intercessor spirits, even as it concentrated authority in the papacy. A comparable example from Buddhism might be the contrast between the more narrowly focused Theravada path, based on monastic authority and discipline, vs. the Mahayana, which emphasizes a multitude of Buddhas and bodhisattvas as modes of access to nirvana.

These contrasting modes of authority have shaped the history of church-state relationships to a great degree. In many premodern societies, religious and political authority were one: kings sometimes functioned simultaneously as high priests (Assyria), or as divine figures in their own right (China). In the modern West, Protestantism and Catholicism went their separate ways, leading to differing relationships with the state. Put oversimply, the proliferation of Protestant churches and denominations led to quarreling, which eventually forced the state to take a neutral or separatist position (England, United States), while the monopoly that resulted from concentration of authority in Catholic countries led to a backlash in terms of a militant secularism which sought to de-throne the church, as in France, Spain, and Latin America.[30]

To what extent, then, can these hypotheses serve to qualify the modernization narrative, especially – though not exclusively – in the West?

The story of disenchantment has been modified by studies of popular culture, particularly in the nineteenth century, have pointed to widespread examples of popular piety and revival, manifest in such practices as pilgrimages to sites of miracles among Catholics. This can be seen as dialectical response to rationalistic religion and contained a strong experiential component.[31] The identification of Christianity with nationalism was also evident, particularly in times a crisis, as shown in the churches' support for World War I. According to Michael Snape writing about 1914, "it was an early and almost universal expectation among the major churches of the belligerent nations that the idealism and anxieties of war would produce an abundant harvest of souls and a powerful antidote to the secularizing tendencies of the modern age."[32]

In the realm of practical spirituality, we find much energy devoted to charitable work as part of the Protestant and Catholic revivals and later to the Social Gospel movement. The same impulse spurred the waves of missionary expansion to the non-Western world. As noted throughout the book, many missionaries set out with a mindset of concentration: simply preaching the word would convince indigenes of the truth of the Christian message. But experience on the ground soon taught them otherwise.

The decade of the 1960s is rightfully regarded as a turning point in the history of secularization and its bearing on religion.[33] The heightened level of cross-cultural interaction in the second half of the twentieth century that goes under the name of globalization was a contributing factor to the intense ferment of those years. The result was something quite extraordinary from a religious perspective: *a shift toward diffuse spirituality in all four dimensions simultaneously.* At the theoretical level, the influence of Hinduism, Buddhism, and Daoism promoted a holistic orientation, linking personal growth to a harmonious physical and metaphysical cosmos, popularly labelled "New Age." Practically, more and more clergy saw involvement in social and political causes as a major part of their mission, as seen in the civil rights movement in the United States and Liberation Theology in Latin America. Experientially and politically, the trend to privatization and diffusion was carried to new extremes, embodied in the phrase "spiritual but not religious." According to Robert Fuller, those attracted to secular spirituality, as he called it, it "consider[ed] it not just their right, but even their duty, to establish their own criteria for assessing the merits of religious beliefs or practices."[34]

Concomitantly, the established institutions of the Christian churches saw a diminution of their authority, particularly in regard to their previous teachings on marriage, divorce, abortion, homosexuality, and contraception. For many feminists, organized religion represented patriarchy. Although Roman Catholicism continued to represent concentrated spiritual authority, even this was diffused to an extent by Vatican II, with its embrace of ecumenism and vernacular language for ritual.

The result was a dramatic decline in church attendance, as well as marriages and baptisms, trends that continued in subsequent decades. In England, where approximately half the population had attended church in 1851, that number declined to 12 percent in 1979 and 6 percent in 2005.[35] In the United States, where 49 percent of the population reported attending church in 1957, the number dropped to 42 percent in 1972, and only 28 percent among young people.[36] Clearly these figures indicate a disillusionment with organized religion; whether they represent a departure from all religion is less clear. A 2012 poll in the United States showed that 64 percent of those who claimed no religious affiliation still believed in God.[37]

In any case, it was not long before a dialectical reaction set in in favor of concentration, appearing in different ways in different parts of the world. There was a resurgence of orthodoxy among US Protestants, an overt reaction to secularism, which was decried as materialistic and morally deficient.[38] The term has had similar connotations in the Middle East, where it is seen as a tool of American colonialism.[39] A similar situation obtains in India, which has a secular constitution but where the notion of a secular society has come under fire from the Hindutva movement. Among African Christians, there has been a strong reaction against liberal Western attitudes on the role of women and homosexuality – something that is likely to continue in the light of the demographic shift to the southern hemisphere.[40] In the experiential dimension, the growth of Pentecostalism at a rate four times that of the world's Christian population as a whole is a powerful indication of the ongoing attraction of concentrated spirituality.[41] In the practical dimension, on the other hand, religion retains its diffuse orientation by virtue of its active engagement in political, social, and moral issues, again largely in reaction to the secularist challenge. José Casanova has called this trend the "de-privatization" of religion.[42]

The question of the relative strength of secularization vis-à-vis that of religion worldwide tends to be answered today based on survey data on religious affiliation, including the option of "none." This approach, however, is elusive at best, given unreliable data (especially for China), as well as the different ways of asking questions from one survey to another, and consequently the discrepancies of results.[43] It seems safe to say, however, that the religiously unaffiliated population, while growing, tends to be concentrated in areas of the world with lower fertility rates, resulting in a declining share of the world's population as compared to the religiously affiliated.[44] In other words, from a global perspective, religion is growing faster than secularization. It seems further true that in the global south, where much of the population growth is occurring, pluralism is giving way to the dominance of a single religion, either Christianity or Islam, which are estimated together to encompass 56.6 percent of the world's population in 2020.[45] This represents a significant shift in the direction of concentration at the theoretical level, while still allowing for a variety of combinations of concentration and diffusion in the other dimensions.[46]

Finally, returning to the industrialized West (including by extension Australia and New Zealand), one may ask whether these countertendencies toward concentration are strong enough to compensate for those of diffusion that have continued since the 1960s. This is the question that Steve Bruce, a tireless advocate for secularization, cogently poses. Without a firm institutional basis, he argues, diffuse spirituality lacks the capacity to sustain itself from generation to generation, or to provide a sufficient basis for faith-based action and commitment. He predicts that religion in the future will resemble "the world of New Age spirituality: a world in which individuals select from a global cafeteria of ideas, rituals, and therapies that appeal to them...Precisely because they are so individualized, diffuse beliefs will have very little impact even on those who carry them, let alone on their wider societies."[47] But the luxury of such an approach, as Bruce himself admits, presupposes a sufficient level of prosperity and stability that the affluent parts of the world currently enjoy. There is, however, no guarantee that this will continue, or that the West will be immune to deep crisis, be it military, political, epidemiological or environmental. While rational approaches to such crises are urgently called for, the human need for hope will probably demand a mobilization of energies and commitments that only concentrated spirituality can provide. But unless that concentration is tempered by the affirmation of plurality that is at the heart of diffuse spirituality, reason does not stand much of a chance.

The argument for the preservation of such cultural diversity parallels, I believe, the argument for biological diversity. Both represent centuries of accumulated adaptation to their environments and thus constitute a knowledge base for a broader range of solutions to the challenges we are likely to face as a species than a few hegemonic cultures and religions can provide.

Endnotes

CHAPTER I

1 Philip Jenkins, *The Next Christendom: The Coming of Global Christianity*. 3rd ed. (Oxford: Oxford University Press, 2011), 2–3.
2 For the terminological differences between these two, see Sebastian Conrad, *What Is Global History?* (Princeton, NJ: Princeton University Press, 2016), chap. 4. The extensive overlap of these fields will be evident from a perusal of the contents of their two journals: *Journal of Global History* and *Journal of World History*.
3 David J. Bosch, *Transforming Mission: Paradigm Shifts in Theology of Mission*, Twentieth Anniversary Edition (Maryknoll, NY: Orbis Books, 2011), 233.
4 I use the term "indigenous" broadly, simply to mean the "other" who were the targets of missionaries' efforts. It is a term that appears to be relatively free of value-judgments or pejorative connotations that can attach even to terms such as "native." Nonetheless, it differs from a widely accepted meaning of the term, which refers to original inhabitants of a region – "first peoples" – and further characterizes them much as the colonial powers did–living in small scale units, tied to a specific place, conservative, preindustrial, among other things. See Ken S. Coates, *A Global History of Indigenous Peoples* (New York: Palgrave Macmillan, 2004), 13–14. Yet the Han Chinese and Japanese, for example, were original inhabitants who do not fit this depiction.
5 Norman Etherington, ed., "Introduction," in *Missions and Empire* (Oxford: Oxford University Press, 2005), 7; David Maxwell, "Historical Perspectives on Christianity Worldwide," in *Relocating World Christianity*, ed. Joel Cabrita, David Maxwell, and Emma Wild-Wood (Leiden: Brill, 2017), 54–56.
6 William H. McNeill, "The Changing Shape of World History," *History and Theory* 34, no. 2 (May, 1995): 8–26 (15, 18).

7 Patrick Manning, *Navigating World History* (New York: Palgrave Macmillan, 2003), 248. Compare, Cabrita, Maxwell, Wild-Wood, *Relocating World Christianity*, 27 ("world historians have been slow to engage with religious history").

8 C. A. Bayly has convincingly demonstrated that this gap was already evident in historians' treatment of the nineteenth century, as people responded to modernization worldwide by firming up their religious doctrines and institutional structures. He claims, "in retrospect, this process is as important as, if not more important than, the theme of the rise of nationalism or liberalism, which has so often dominated studies of this period." See his *The Birth of the Modern World 1780-1914* (Oxford: Blackwell, 2004), chap. 9, esp. 363–64.

9 Robert A. Yelle, in *The Language of Disenchantment: Protestant Literalism and Colonial Discourse in British India* (Oxford: Oxford University Press, 2013), 14, 163, characterizes disenchantment as a myth, but one that is widely accepted and hence a cultural reality. I make a similar argument with respect to secularization below, pp. 30–32 .

10 Dipesh Chakrabarty, in *Provincializing Europe: Postcolonial Thought and Historical Difference* (Princeton, NJ: Princeton University Press, 2000), 14, points out that in over one hundred cases of peasant rebellions in British India between 1783 and 1900, one side or the other evoked gods and spirits.

11 Stephen Prothero, *God Is Not One* (New York: HarperOne, 2010), 131. Prothero provocatively highlights a further variation of the secular bias. It is the wishful assumption that all religions ultimately believe in the same truth(s), and that differences among religious traditions can likewise be explained away. However desirable it may be to find commonalities in the name of religious peace, Prothero claims, such an approach is bound to backfire because it trivializes the profound differences which actually exist among these traditions. Prothero also points to the need to study religions as they impinge on each other rather than as isolated cases.

12 David Lindenfeld, "The Concept of 'World Religions' as Currently Used in Religious Studies Textbooks," *World History Bulletin*, 23, no. 1 (Spring 2007): 6–7.

13 Tomiko Masuzawa, *The Invention of World Religions, or How European Universalism Was Preserved in the Language of Pluralism* (Chicago: University of Chicago Press, 2005), 266; Rosalind Shaw, "The Invention of 'African Traditional Religion'," *Religion* 20, no. 4 (1990): 339–53 (340–42).

14 Jacob K. Olupona and Terry Rey, eds. *Òrìṣà Devotion as World Religion* (Madison: University of Wisconsin Press, 2007); Prothero, *God Is Not One*, chap. 6.

15 See "AHR Conversation: On Transnational History," *American Historical Review*, 111, no. 5 (Dec. 2006): 1441–64, for an airing of these concerns among six historians.

16 Cabrita and Maxwell, "Introduction," in *Relocating World Christianity*, 14.

17 See Andrew Porter, *Religion versus Empire? British Protestant Missionaries and Overseas Expansion, 1700-1914* (Manchester: Manchester University Press, 2004), 2–4, for those studies pertaining to British colonies.

18 E.g., Lindenfeld, "Indigenous Encounters with Christian Missionaries in China and West Africa, 1800-1920: A Comparative Study," *Journal of World History* 16, no. 3 (Sept. 2005): 327–69; Lindenfeld and Miles Richardson, eds. *Beyond Conversion & Syncretism: Indigenous Encounters with Missionary Christianity, 1800-2000* (New York: Berghahn Books, 2012).

19 For other examples, see Jenkins, *Next Christendom*, 53–55.

20 See, for example, Ryan Dunch, "Beyond Cultural Imperialism: Cultural Theory, Christian Missions, and Global Modernity," *History and Theory* 41, no. 3 (Oct. 2002): 301–25.

21 Dana L. Robert, *Christian Mission: How Christianity Became a World Religion* (Chichester, UK: Wiley-Blackwell, 2009), 81–87, 114–18, 159–71, points to several examples, including the famous David Livingstone, Annalena Tonelli, who ran a tuberculosis hospital in Somalia, and Bernard Mizeki, missionary to the Shona in Zimbabwe, whose martyrdom is now the focus of an annual pilgrimage.

22 See Porter, *Religion versus Empire?*, chap. 4, for a discussion of how these debates took shape in the early nineteenth century.

23 Etherington, "Introduction," in *Missions and Empire*, 3. Cooperation did increase, however, during the interwar period. See Kevin Ward, "Christianity, Colonialism, and Missions," in *World Christianities c. 1914-c. 2000*, ed. Hugh McLeod, Vol. 9 of *The Cambridge History of Christianity* (Cambridge: Cambridge University Press, 2006), 72.

24 Hendrik Kraemer, *World Cultures and World Religions. The Coming Dialogue* (Philadelphia: Westminster Press, 1960), 90–91; Peter van der Veer, *Imperial Encounters: Religion and Modernity in India and Britain* (Princeton, NJ: Princeton University Press, 2001), 23.

25 Jean Comaroff and John Comaroff, *Of Revelation and Revolution: Christianity, Colonialism, and Consciousness in South Africa*, 2 vols. (Chicago: University of Chicago Press, 1991, 1997), 2: 411.

26 Comaroff and Comaroff, *Of Revelation and Revolution*, 2: 22.

27 Comaroff and Comaroff, *Of Revelation and Revolution*, 1: 314; 2: 28.

28 For the first, see Elizabeth Elbourne, "Word Made Flesh: Christianity, Modernity, and Cultural Colonialism in the Work of Jean and John Comaroff," *American Historical Review* 108, no. 2 (April 2003): 435–59, which contains citations of other reviews; for the second, see Dunch, "Beyond Cultural Imperialism," 311–13. The Comaroffs respond to the critics of volume 1 in the opening chapter of volume 2.

29 Vijay Mishra and Bob Hodge, "What is Post(-)colonialism?," in *Colonial Discourse and Post-colonial Theory. A Reader*, ed. Patrick Williams and Laura Chrisman (New York: Columbia University Press, 1994), 284–86.

30 Dunch,"Beyond Cultural Imperialism," 311; Robert, *Christian Mission*, 96. For applications of postcolonial theory to missionary studies, see R. S. Sugirtharajah, *The Bible and the Third World. Precolonial, Colonial and Postcolonial Encounters* (Cambridge: Cambridge University Press, 2001), chap. 8; William B. Taylor, "Two Shrines of the Cristo Renovado: Religion and Peasant Politics in Late Colonial Mexico," *American Historical Review* 110, no. 4 (Oct. 2005): 945–74.

31 Mishra and Hodge, "Post(-)colonialism," 287.

32 Jehu J. Hanciles, "New Wine in Old Wineskins. Critical Reflections on Writing and Teaching a Global Christian History," *Missiology: An International Review* 34, no. 3 (July 2006): 361–82 (375).

33 Philip D. Curtin, *The World and the West: The European Challenge and the Overseas Response in the Age of Empire* (Cambridge: Cambridge University Press), 2000, 1.

34 According to the William H. Brinner's article on "conversion" in *The Oxford Encyclopedia of the Modern Islamic World*, ed. John L. Esposito. 4 vols. (Oxford: Oxford University Press, 1995), 1: 318, joining Islam is seen as a *return* to a natural state that had been interrupted since birth. See also Richard W. Bulliet, *Conversion to Islam in the Medieval Period* (Cambridge, MA: Harvard University Press, 1979), 33.

35 Lewis Rambo, *Understanding Religious Conversion* (New Haven, CT: Yale University Press, 1993); Robert W. Hefner, ed. *Conversion to Christianity: Historical and Anthropological Perspectives on a Great Transformation* (Berkeley: University of California Press, 1993).

36 On the former, see the essays by Saurabh Dube and C. Mathews Samson on India and Guatemala respectively in Lindenfeld and Richardson, *Beyond Conversion and Syncretism*. On the latter, see, e.g., Joel Robbins, "Anthropological Perspectives on World Christianity," in Cabrita, Maxwell, Wild-Wood, *Relocating World Christianity*, 243–46. In a seminal article, Robbins pitted this Christian emphasis on discontinuity against the prevailing assumptions of cultural anthropology, at the expense, as he admitted, of creating an ideal-typical model of how Christianity operates. See his "Continuity Thinking and the Problem of Christian Culture: Belief, Time and the Anthropology of Christianity," *Current Anthropology* 48, no. 1 (February 2007): 5–38.

37 Hefner, "Introduction: World Building and the Rationality of Conversion," in *Conversion to Christianity*, 34.

38 Hefner, *Conversion to Christianity*, 19.

39 The theme of transcendence is taken up by Alan Strathern in *Unearthly Powers: Religious and Political Change in World History* (Cambridge: Cambridge University Press, 2019), 7, 47–81. His extended comparison of Christianity and Buddhism in this respect is especially valuable. He insists, however, that "transcendent" world religions never dissociate themselves

from their conceptual opposite, namely "immanentism," a point borne out by the contributions to the Hefner volume. Cf. my contrasting concentrated and diffuse spirituality in the conclusion.

40 J. R. McNeill and William H. McNeill, *The Human Web* (New York: W. W. Norton, 2003), 322; cf. Frances Kartunnen and Alfred W. Crosby, "Language Death, Language Genesis, and World History," *Journal of World History* 6, no. 2 (Fall 1995): 157–74; John R. McNeill, *Something New under the Sun* (New York: Norton, 2000), 262–64.

41 Robin Horton, "African Conversion," *Africa* 41, no. 2 (1971): 85–108 (101–5); "The Rationality of Conversion," *Africa.*, 45, nos. 3–4 (1975), 219–35, 373–99. For critical perspectives on Horton, see Terence Ranger, "The Local and the Global in Southern African Religious History," in Hefner, *Conversion to Christianity*, 65–98; Elizabeth Isichei, *A History of Christianity in Africa* (Grand Rapids, MI: William B. Eerdmans Publishing Co., 1995), 96, 228; Birgit Meyer, *Translating the Devil: Religion and Modernity among the Ewe in Ghana* (Trenton, NJ: Africa World Press, 1999), xxiii, 109–10; Deryck Schreuder and Geoffrey Oddie, "What Is 'Conversion'? History, Christianity and Religious Change in Colonial Africa and South Asia," *The Journal of Religious History*, 13, no. 4 (Dec. 1989): 496–518 (514); Richard Fox Young, "Horton's 'Intellectualist Theory' of Conversion, Reflected on by a South Asianist," in Lindenfeld and Richardson, *Beyond Conversion*, 120.

42 *Merriam-Webster's Collegiate Dictionary*, 10th ed. (Springfield, MA: Merriam-Webster, 1999), s.v. "syncretism"; Morton Klass, "Seeking Syncretism: The Case of Sathya Sai Baba," in, *Reinventing Religions: Syncretism and Transformation in Africa and the Americas*, ed. Sidney M. Greenfield and André Droogers (Lanham, MD: Rowman & Littlefield, 2001), 212. Plutarch attributed the term to the custom of the Cretans to make up their internal differences when faced with a common external threat. For a fuller treatment of the term, see Lindenfeld, "Syncretism," in *Vocabulary for the Study of Religion*, ed. Robert A. Segal and Kocku v. Stuckrad, 3 vols. (Leiden: Brill, 2015), 3: 442–47.

43 Harold W. Turner, "New Religious Movements and Syncretism in Tribal Cultures," in *Dialogue and Syncretism: An Interdisciplinary Approach* ed. Jerald Gort et al. (Grand Rapids, MI: Eerdmans, 1989), 108; Sheila S. Walker, "Everyday and Esoteric Reality in the Afro-Brazilian Candomblé," *History of Religions*, 30, no. 2 (Nov. 1990): 103–28 (113–14); Rosalind Shaw and Charles Stewart, eds. "Introduction: Problematizing Syncretism," in *Syncretism/Anti-Syncretism. The Politics of Religious Synthesis* (London: Routledge, 1994), 7–9.

44 J. D. Y. Peel, "Syncretism and Religious Change," *Comparative Studies in Society and History*, 10, no. 2 (January 1968), 121–41.

45 Eliade, *A History of Religious Ideas*, 3 vols. (Chicago: University of Chicago Press, 1987), 2: 277.

46 Shaw and Stewart, *Syncretism/Anti-Syncretism*, 21–22.
47 E.g., James O. Gump, "A Spirit of Resistance: Sioux, Xhosa, and Maori Responses to Western Dominance, 1840-1920," *Pacific Historical Review* 66, no. 1 (Feb. 1997): 21–52 (21–23).
48 Joseph W. Esherick, *The Origins of the Boxer Uprising* (Berkeley: University of California Press 1987), 95, 136, 215, 271, 282; Paul A. Cohen, *History in Three Keys: The Boxers as Event, Experience, and Myth* (New York: Columbia Univ. Press, 1997), 86, 173; Henry Warner Bowden, *American Indians and Christian Missions: Studies in Cultural Conflict* (Chicago: University of Chicago Press, 1981), chap. 2, esp. 55.
49 Susan M. Deeds, "Indigenous Responses to Mission Settlement in Nueva Vizcaya," in *The New Latin American Mission History*, ed. Erick Langer & Robert H. Jackson (Lincoln: University of Nebraska Press, 1995), 95–6.
50 Rambo, *Understanding Religious Conversion*, 35.
51 Donald K. Pollock, "Conversion and 'Community' in Amazonia," in Hefner, *Conversion to Christianity*, 168–69; Peter Gow, "Forgetting Conversion. The Summer Institute of Linguistics Mission in the Piro Lived World," in *The Anthropology of Christianity* ed. Fenella Cannell (Durham, NC: Duke University Press, 2006), 214.
52 Gow, "Forgetting Conversion," 236–37. Cf. Pollock, "Conversion and 'Community,'" 188.
53 On Latin American Christianity, see Edward L. Cleary, "The Transformation of Latin American Christianity, c. 1950-2000," in Mcleod, *World Christianities, c. 1914-c.2000*, 366–84; Ondina E. Gonzáles & Justo L. Gonzáles, *Christianity in Latin America: A History* (Cambridge: Cambridge University Press, 2008), chap. 9.
54 For a discussion of Catholic and ecumenical interpretations of inculturation, see Peter C. Phan, *In Our Own Tongues. Perspectives from Asia on Mission and Inculturation* (Maryknoll, NY: Orbis Books, 2003), 3–10.
55 London: Routledge, 1994, 102–4.
56 James Axtell, *The Invasion Within: The Contest of Cultures in Colonial North America* (New York: Oxford University Press, 1985), 8–10; for other references to the same idea, cf. Richard Gray, *Black Christians and White Missionaries* (New Haven, CT: Yale University Press, 1990), 6 (for West Africa); Bronwyn Elsmore, *Mana from Heaven: A Century of Maori Prophets in New Zealand* (Tauranga, NZ: Moana Press, 1989), 21; Strathern, *Unearthly Powers*, 234–36.
57 Turner, "The Hidden Power of the Whites. The Secret Religion Withheld from the Primal Peoples," *Archives des sciences sociales des religions*, 46, no.1 (July–Sept. 1978), 41–55.
58 See Jenkins, *Next Christendom*, 157–59, for examples.
59 Willy de Craemer, Jan Vansina, Renée C. Fox, "Religious Movements in Central Africa: A Theoretical Study," *Comparative Studies in Society and*

History 18, no. 4 (Oct. 1976): 458–75 (466); Danilyn Rutherford, "The Bible Meets the Idol. Writing and Conversion in Biak, Irian Jaya, Indonesia," in Cannell, *Anthropology of Christianity* 250. Cf. Strathern, *Unearthly Powers*, 286.

60 Walter E. A. van Beek, ed. *The Quest for Purity* (Berlin: Mouton de Gruyter, 1988), 3.

61 Max Weber, *Economy and Society: An Outline of Interpretive Sociology*, ed. Guenther Roth and Claus Wittich, trans. Ephraim Fischoff et al., 3 vols. (New York: Bedminister Press, 1968), 2: 541.

62 Anthony F. C. Wallace, "Revitalization Movements," *American Anthropologist*, 58, no. 2 (April 1956): 264–81, esp. 270.

63 C. G. Jung, *Psychology and Religion West and East*, 2nd ed. trans. R.F.C. Hull. Vol. 11 of *The Collected Works of C.G. Jung*, ed. Sir Herbert Read et al. (Princeton, NJ: Princeton University Press, 1969), 7–9.

64 Erika Bourguignon, ed. *Religion, Altered States of Consciousness, and Social Change* (Columbus: Ohio State University Press, 1973), 9–11. Bourguignon found that the percentages varied by region, lower in the Mediterranean area, Sub-Saharan Africa, and South America (80%, 82%, and 85%, respectively), higher in East Eurasia, the Pacific islands, and North America (94%, 94%, and 97%, respectively).

65 Axtell, *Invasion Within*, 135–37.

66 Julia J. S. Sarreal, *The Guaraní and Their Missions: A Socioeconomic History* (Stanford, CA: Stanford University Press, 2014), 1, 21–22. The Guaraní missions were portrayed in the 1986 film *The Mission*.

67 Strathern, *Unearthly Powers*, 150.

68 Lian Xi, *Redeemed by Fire. The Rise of Popular Christianity in Modern China* (New Haven, CT: Yale University Press, 2010), 15–16, 72–74, 233–41.

69 E.g., Eva Keller, "Scripture Study as Normal Science. Seventh-Day Adventist Practice on the East Coast of Madagascar," in Cannell, *Anthropology of Christianity*, 272–93.

70 See, e.g., Meyer, *Translating the Devil*, 83–85.

71 Strathern, *Unearthly Powers*, 4, 7, 27–47.

72 Lorraine Aragon, *Fields of the Lord: Animism, Christian Minorities, and State Development in Indonesia* (Honolulu: University of Hawaii Press, 2000), 22, 28, 38.

73 Aragon, 203, 233–35, 322, 324.

74 See Talal Asad, *Formations of the Secular: Christianity, Islam, Modernity* (Stanford, CA: Stanford University Press, 2003).

75 See Michael D. Bailey, *Magic and Superstition in Europe: A Concise History from Antiquity to the Present* (Lanham, MD: Rowman & Littlefield, 2007). Bailey argues that the excesses of the witch trials of the early modern period led to a skepticism about witchcraft and magic in general, which helped facilitate Enlightenment rationalism.

76 Asad, *Formations of the Secular*, 25, 55. It has often been pointed out that Marxism preserves the form of the Christian millennialist narrative by positing a similar eschatology of the victory of the righteous in a climactic battle.

77 Saurabh Dube, "Conversion, Translation, and Life-History in Colonial Central India," in Lindenfeld and Richardson, *Beyond Conversion and Syncretism*, 27–49; Vicente L. Rafael, *Contracting Colonialism. Translation and Christian Conversion in Tagalog Society under Early Spanish Rule* (Ithaca, NY: Cornell University Press), 1988.

78 In Williams and Chrisman, *Colonial Discourse and Postcolonial Theory*, 104.

79 A related formulation comes from Walter D. Mignolo, who adopts the term "transculturation" from the Cuban writer Fernando Ortiz. See Mignolo & Freya Schiwy, "Beyond Dichotomies. Translation/Transculturation and the Colonial Difference," in *Beyond Dichotomies: Histories, Identities, Cultures and the Challenge of Globalization*, ed. M. Elizabeth Mudimbe-boyi (Albany: State University of New York Press, 2002), 251–52.

80 Andrew F. Walls, *The Missionary Movement in Christian History* (Maryknoll, NY: Orbis Books, 1996), 27.

81 Lamin Sanneh, *Translating the Message: The Missionary Impact on Culture* (Maryknoll, NY: Orbis Books, 1989), 31.

82 Sanneh, 245–49.

83 For an in-depth comparative study of such double translation, see Anne Keary, "Colonial Constructs and Cross-cultural Interaction: Comparing Missionary/ Indigenous Encounters in Northwestern America and Eastern Australia," in Lindenfeld and Richardson, *Beyond Conversion and Syncretism*, 243–98 .

84 See Elliott P. Skinner, "The Dialectic between Diasporas and Homelands," in *Global Dimensions of the African Diaspora*, 2nd ed., ed. Joseph. E. Harris (Washington, DC: Howard University Press, 1993), 11–13. In a classification of African religious movements from 1967, H. W. Turner specified "Hebraist" as a distinct type: "A Typology for African Religious Movements," *Journal of Religion in Africa*, 1, fasc. 1 (1967): 1–34 (8–10).

85 Bronwyn Elsmore, *Like Them That Dream: The Maori and the Old Testament* (Otumoetai, NZ: Turanga Press, 1985); Sugirtharajah, *Bible and Third World* 87–90.

86 Raynaldo Clemeña Ileto, *Pasyon and Revolution: Popular Movements in the Philippines, 1840-1910* (Quezon City: Ateneo de Manila University Press, 1979), chap. 1.

87 Walls, *Missionary Movement*, 135.Walls has also put forth an eightfold typology of responses of "primal" religions to missionary Christianity since World War II. I see his terms as partially overlapping with mine, with exceptions at either end of the spectrum. At one end, Walls does not consider resistance; at the other, he includes "appropriation," the way "primal" religions become adopted by others, as for example in the Western appreciation

---

of native religions. As stated, I do not deal with this type of interaction in the interest of economy. Walls's other terms I view as roughly synonymous with mine: "Recession" would translate into my acceptance or commitment, "absorption" into selective acculturation; "restatement" and "invention" fall under vernacular translation. "Reduction" of native forms resembles my dual religious participation. "Adjustment" I would call selective incorporation, and "revitalization" comes under concentration of spirituality. See Walls, 131–39.

88 David K. Jordan, "The Glyphomancy Factor: Observations on Chinese Conversion," in Hefner, *Conversion to Christianity*, 287–88. On the materiality of words and objects as signifiers, see Webb Keane, "Anxious Transcendence," in Cannell, *Anthropology of Christianity*, 310–13.

89 Jordan, "Glyphomancy," 287.

90 For an overview of the dialogue process, see the essays in Gort, *Dialogue and Syncretism*, particularly those of Maurice Friedman (76–84) and Dirk C. Mulder (203–11).

91 William K. Powers, *Beyond the Vision: Essays on American Indian Culture* (Norman: University of Oklahoma Press, 1987), 106.

92 Marla N. Powers, *Oglala Women: Myth, Ritual, and Reality* (Chicago: University of Chicago Press, 1986), 185–88.

93 Edward H. Spicer, "Acculturation," *International Encyclopedia of the Social Sciences*, ed. David L. Sills. 17 vols. (New York: Macmillan, 1968), 1: 21. See also Stewart, "Syncretism and its Synonyms. Reflection on Cultural Mixture," *Diacritics* 23, no. 3 (Autumn 1999): 40–62 (49–51).

94 Ashis Nandy, *The Intimate Enemy. Loss and Recovery of Self under Colonialism* (Delhi: Oxford University Press, 1983), 3.

95 Comaroff & Comaroff, *Revelation and Revolution*, vol. 2, passim. Cf. Asad, *Formations of the Secular*, 154. For another example from the Pacific Northwest, see Michael Harkin, "The House of Longing: Missionary-led Changes in Heiltsuk Domestic Forms and Structures," in *Indigenous Peoples and Religious Change*, ed. Peggy Brock (Leiden: Brill, 2005) 205–26. Harkin depicts how the communal longhouses of the Heiltsuk were viewed by missionaries as crowded and unsanitary, characteristic of savages. The missionaries built a new settlement with Victorian-style houses with big windows and fewer residents (4.3 as compared to c.30 in the longhouses). The windows also made it easier for missionaries to inspect.

96 Comaroff & Comaroff, *Revelation and Revolution*, 2: 368. On assimilation of forms see 1: 30, 213, 311.

97 Powers, *Beyond the Vision*, 113; Lindenfeld, "Indigenous Encounters," 355.

98 See Julia Hauser, "From Transformation to Negotiation: A Female Mission in a 'City of Schools'," *Journal of World History* 27, no. 3 (Sept. 2016): 473–96 (477). See also chap. 5.

99 Robbins, "Anthropological Perspectives on World Christianity," in Cabrita, Maxwell, & Wild-Wood, *Relocating World Christianity*, 247–48.

100 Claude A. Clegg III, *The Price of Liberty: African Americans and the Making of Liberia* (Chapel Hill: University of North Carolina Press, 2004), 240.
101 Clegg, 242.
102 Rambo, *Understanding Religious Conversion*, 160–62.
103 I know of one comparative study by Peggy Brock of five biographies of "new Christians" as evangelists, from southern Africa, Australia, the Pacific Islands, and the Pacific Northwest. She finds that each of them were both products of their respective societies and also critics of them from the inside, in ways that foreign missionaries would often miss. Beyond this, there is little they appear to have in common, aside from the act of evangelization itself. Peggy Brock, "New Christians as Evangelists," in Etherington, *Missions and Empire*, 132–52.
104 Jenkins, *Next Christendom*, 2–3, 108–12, 277–78 n.2. The note cautions readers against too exclusive reliance on the widely quoted *World Christian Encyclopedia*.
105 Walls, *Missionary Movement*, 132. Jenkins makes the same point, *Next Christendom*, 93–94.
106 Daniel H. Bays & James H. Grayson, "Christianity in China, Korea and Japan," in *World Christianities, c.1815–c.1914*, ed. Sheridan Gilley & Brian Stanley. Vol. 8 of *The Cambridge History of Christianity* (Cambridge: Cambridge University Press, 2006), 509.
107 Peter Cho Phan, "Christianity in Indochina," in Gilley and Stanley, 513–23.
108 Timothy S. Lee, "Beleaguered Success. Korean Evangelicalism in the Last Decade of the Twentieth Century," in *Christianity in Korea*, ed. Robert E. Buswell and Timothy S. Lee (Honolulu: University of Hawaii Press, 2006), 341.
109 John Garrett, *To Live Among the Stars: Christian Origins in Oceania* (Geneva: World Council of Churches, 1982), 159.

CHAPTER 2

1 Daniel T. Reff, *Plagues, Priests, Demons: Sacred Narratives and the Rise of Christianity in the Old World and the New* (Cambridge: Cambridge University Press, 2005), 125–27. Reff draws the parallel between the success of Christianity in the Roman world and in Mexico by pointing to the coincidence with massive epidemics in both cases. On the unprecedented nature of these plagues in the native mind, see Serge Gruzinski, *The Conquest of Mexico*, trans. Eileen Corrigan (Cambridge: Polity Press, 1993), 80–81.
2 Cf. John Leddy Phelan, *The Millennial Kingdom of the Franciscans in the New World*, 2nd ed., rev. (Berkeley: University of California Press, 1970), 24.
3 Robert Ricard, *The Spiritual Conquest of Mexico*, trans. Lesley Byrd Simpson (Berkeley: University of California Press, 1966), 47–49.
4 Frances Kartunnen, "Nahua Literacy," in *The Inca and Aztec States, 1400–1800: Anthropology and History*, ed. George A. Collier, Renato I. Rosaldo, and

John D. Wirth (New York: Academic Press, 1982), 400. Cf. Gruzinski, *Conquest*, 46–47.

5 Louise M. Burkhart, *Holy Wednesday: a Nahua Drama from Early Colonial Mexico* (Philadelphia: University of Pennsylvania Press, 1996), 55–66. The history of the College of Santa Cruz of Tlatelolco is revealing of the ambivalence of the missionary attitude and its underlying paternalism. Latin was taught, but not Spanish, lest Indians compete with Spanish settlers for positions. When it appeared that the students were forming their own interpretations of the Bible and demanding to be priests themselves, the Franciscans withdrew their support.

6 Joseph Kroger and Patrizia Granziera, *Aztec Goddesses and Christian Madonnas: Images of the Divine Feminine in Mexico* (Farnham, UK: Ashgate, 2012), 221.

7 Ricard, *Spiritual Conquest*, 186–87. For an extended treatment of these mock battles, see Max Harris, *Aztecs, Moors and Christians: Festivals of Reconquest in Mexico and Spain* (Austin: University of Texas Press, 2000). On "exuberance" and the excesses that accompanied it, seeWilliam B. Taylor, *Magistrates of the Sacred. Priests and Parishioners in Eighteenth-Century Mexico* (Stanford, CA: Stanford University Press, 1996), 60, 253.

8 Reff, *Plagues, Priests, and Demons*, 162, 177–82.

9 On a controversy over this issue, see Ricard, *Spiritual Conquest*, 91–94, and Harris, *Aztecs, Moors, and Christians*, 144–45.

10 Burkhart, *The Slippery Earth: Nahua-Christian Moral Dialogue in Sixteenth-Century Mexico* (Tucson: University of Arizona Press, 1989), 23–24.

11 Burkhart, *Slippery Earth*, 11. Cf. Charles Gibson, *The Aztecs under Spanish Rule* (Stanford, CA: Stanford University Press, 1964), 117; Reff, *Plagues, Priests, and Demons*, 165–66.

12 Camilla Townsend, "Burying the White Gods: New Perspectives on the Conquest of Mexico," *American Historical Review* 108, no. 3 (June 2003): 659–87; Susan D. Gillespie, *The Aztec Kings* (Tucson: University of Arizona Press, 1989), 200.

13 James Lockhart and Stuart B. Schwartz, *Early Latin America* (Cambridge: Cambridge University Press, 1983), 109.

14 Gibson, *Aztecs*, 282–85; Lockhart, *The Nahuas After the Conquest* (Stanford, CA: Stanford University Press, 1992), 44–46.

15 Gibson, *Aztecs*, chap. vii., 306, 403. Cf. Lockhart and Schwartz, *Early Latin America*, 113–18.

16 Gruzinski, *Conquest*, 15–18; Ricard, *Spiritual Conquest*, 268.

17 Gibson, *Aztecs*, 111.

18 Quoted in Ricard, *Spiritual Conquest*, 269.

19 Jorge Klor de Alva, in "Spiritual Conflict and Accommodation in New Spain: Toward a Typology of Aztec Responses to Christianity," in Collier, Rosaldo, Wirth, *Inca and Aztec States*, 359, 361, maintains that covert practice of indigenous religion was much greater than previously thought.

20 Fray Diego Durán, *Book of the Gods and Rites and the Ancient Calendar*, trans., ed. Fernando Horcasitas and Doris Heyden (Norman: University of Oklahoma Press, 1971), 53–54, 410–11. Based on the latter passage, De Alva ("Spiritual Conflict," 355) gives this anomic state a special name, "nepantlism," although he claims it was a temporary condition.

21 Durán, *Book of the Gods*, 150.

22 Taylor, *Magistrates of the Sacred*, 64–67.

23 Gibson, *Aztecs*, 101.

24 This is particularly graphic in the case of Durán, who, in his disillusionment, drew the conclusion that such idolatrous practices had to be eliminated root and branch. Ironically, in his will to believe the coherence of the Christian narrative as he understood it, he also came to the belief that Quetzalcoatl was actually the Apostle Thomas, who had come to Mexico to fulfill Christ's injunction to carry his message to the remote corners of the world. Durán also believed, as did many of his contemporaries, that the Indians were descended from the lost tribes of Israel. See Durán, *Book of the Gods*, 25; Carmen Bernand and Serge Gruzinski, *De L'Idolâtrie: Une Archéologie des Sciences Religieuses* (Paris: Éditions du Seuil, 1988), 112; Jacques Lafaye, *Quetzlcoatl and Guadalupe: The Formation of Mexican National Consciousness 1531-1813*, trans. Benjamin Keen (Chicago: University of Chicago Press, 1976), 158.

25 This applies to Klor De Alva's analysis as well. He defines conversion as "a radical change in values, customs, and world view" ("Spiritual Conflict," in *Inca and Aztec States*, 362). Other responses which do not meet this standard are classified as "incomplete conversion" or "overt conversion."

26 Klor de Alva, "Aztec Spirituality and Nahuatized Christianity," in *South and Meso-American Native Spirituality*, ed. Gary H. Gossen (New York: Crossroad, 1993), 182; Martin Austin Nesvig, ed., "Introduction," in *Local Religion in Colonial Mexico* (Albuquerque: University of New Mexico Press, 2006), xviii.

27 Gibson, *Aztecs*, 120–21; Lockhart, *Nahuas*, 209.

28 Lockhart, *Nahuas*, 210–12, 216–17.

29 Lockhart, *Nahuas*, 212–14; S.L. Cline, *Colonial Culhuacan, 1580-1600: A Social History of an Aztec Town* (Albuquerque: University of New Mexico Press, 1986), 26, 33, 143, 164.

30 Gibson, *Aztecs*, 127–32; Lockhart, *Nahuas*, 218–29.

31 John K. Chance, "Civil-Religious Hierarchy," in *The Oxford Encyclopedia of Mesoamerican Cultures: The Civilizations of Mexico and Central America*, ed. David Carrasco. 3 vols. (Oxford: Oxford University Press, 2001), 1: 223–25.

32 Burkhart, *Slippery Earth*, 28–34, 38–39.

33 Burkhart, *Slippery Earth*, 30–31, 142.

34 Ricard, *Spiritual Conquest*, 117–20; Burkhart, *Slippery Earth*, 141–46, 181–83.

35 Gossen, "Introduction," in *South and Meso-American Spirituality*, 19–21. Nancy M. Farriss employs it effectively in her study of the Yucatan, where conditions were different from central Mexico, in *Maya Society under Colonial Rule: The Collective Enterprise of Survival* (Princeton, NJ: Princeton University Press, 1984), 299, 312–19. The leading exponent of syncretism as applied to central Mexico is Hugo Nutini, who combines a valuable ethnographic study of the cult of the dead with a historical account, *Todos Santos in Rural Tlaxcala: A Syncretic, Expressive, and Symbolic Analysis of the Cult of the Dead* (Princeton, NJ: Princeton University Press, 1988). His use of the term, however, is very wide-ranging and introduces several sub-types. For a critique of the historical part, see Lockhart, *Nahuas*, 549–50.

36 Most vehemently, David Carrasco, who calls it a "ubiquitous and lazy category," in "Jaguar Christians in the Contact Zone. Concealed in Narratives in the Histories of Religions in the Americas," in *Beyond Primitivism: Indigenous Religious Traditions and Modernity*, ed. Jacob K. Olupona (New York: Routledge, 2004), 129. Inga Clendinnen is equally scathing, who sees in it a "mix and match model ... [which] subject[s] a lived faith to vivisection, carving it into transportable, stateable, teachable propositions: a disturbing, dispiriting, and finally effectively disabling business." See "Ways to the Sacred: Reconstructing 'Religion' in Sixteenth Century Mexico," *History and Anthropology* 5, no. 1 (1990): 105–41 (109). The most extensive and penetrating critique is in Taylor, *Magistrates of the Sacred*, 53–62. Cf. also Ricard, *Spiritual Conquest*, 276; Burkhart, *Slippery Earth*, 7; Gruzinski, *Conquest*, 226.

37 Lockhart, *Nahuas*, 235. See also Antonio Rubial García, "Icons of Devotion. The Appropriation and Use of Saints in New Spain," in Nesvig, *Local Religion*, 37–61.

38 Lockhart, *Nahuas*, 420; Burkhart, *Slippery Earth*, 20–21; John McAndrew, *The Open Air Churches of Sixteenth-Century Mexico* (Cambridge, MA: Harvard University Press, 1965).

39 Gruzinski, *Conquest*, 238.

40 Gruzinski, *Conquest*, 247.

41 Lockhart, *Nahuas*, 239; Gibson, *Aztecs*, 130; William Madsen, *The Virgin's Children: Life in an Aztec Village Today* (reprint, New York: Greenwood Press, 1969 [1960]), 102.

42 Rubial García, "Icons of Devotion," in Nesvig, *Local Religion*, 43.

43 Klor de Alva, "Spiritual Conflict," in *Inca and Aztec States*, 348.

44 Indeed, the friars were at first reluctant to put Jesus in the foreground, since they feared his blood sacrifice would only reinforce the Nahua predisposition to the same (Kroger and Granziera, *Aztec Goddesses*, 138).

45 A comparison with the veneration of saints in Spain is worth noting. According to William J. Christian, *Local Religion in Sixteenth-Century*

Spain (Princeton, NJ: Princeton University Press, 1981), 31, 96, the main form of communication with a saint in Spain was the vow. One made a promise to a saint to do a good work in return for answering one's prayers in time of crisis or disaster. This, however, did not preclude an offering as part of the agreement.

46 Stanley Brandes, "Sugar, Colonialism, and Death: on the Origins of Mexico's Day of the Dead," *Comparative Studies in Society and History* 39, no. 2 (April 1997): 270–99. Brandes makes a strong case for the Day of the Dead as primarily colonial in origin, its peculiar prominence in Mexico being traceable to the enormous suffering and loss of life that occurred there in the sixteenth century.

47 Burkhart, "The Cult of the Virgin of Guadalupe in Mexico," in Gossen, *South and Meso-American Spirituality*, 210.

48 Clendinnen, "Ways to the Sacred," 127; Burkhart, "Cult of the Virgin," 207–9. Kroger and Granziera, in *Aztec goddesses and Christian Madonnas*, make an argument for syncretism, but their visual material, which demonstrates the vast distance between the portrayal of the two, undercuts their argument.

49 Burkhart, "Cult of the Virgin," 206.

50 For example, Lockhart (*Nahuas*, chap. 7) has traced the development of the Nahuatl language in colonial times as an indicator of this process. He posits three stages: (1) from 1519 to 1540–1550, when the language remained unchanged, as the Spanish were in the process of learning it; (2) the next century, when many Spanish nouns entered the language; (3) from about 1650 to the present, when many other parts of speech entered as well and more and more natives became bilingual.

51 For an in-depth study of this phenomenon, see Yanna Yannakakis, *The Art of Being In-between: Native Intermediaries, Indian Identity, and Local Rule in Colonial Oaxaca* (Durham, NC: Duke University Press, 2008).

52 On the development of the cult in general, see Stafford Poole, *Our Lady of Guadalupe: The Origins and Sources of a Mexican National Symbol, 1531-1797.* (Tucson: University of Arizona Press, 1995); and D. A. Brading. *Mexican Phoenix: Our Lady of Guadalupe: Image and Tradition across Five Centuries* (Cambridge: Cambridge University Press, 2001).

53 James M. Taggart, *Nahuat Myth and Social Structure* (Austin: University of Texas Press, 1983), 7, 30–33, 97–99, 109, 115. Cf. Madsen, *Virgin's Children*, 125; and Alan R. Sandstrom, *Corn is Our Blood: Culture and Ethnic Identity in a Contemporary Aztec Indian Village* (Norman: University of Oklahoma Press, 1991), 242–44, for examples of incorporation.

54 Ricard, *Spiritual Conquest*, 281.

55 Maureen Ahern, "Martyrs and Idols. Performing Ritual Warfare on Early Missionary Frontiers in the Northwest," in *Religion in New Spain*, ed. Susan Schroeder and Stafford Poole (Albuquerque: University of New Mexico Press,

2007), 284. In the same volume, Kevin Terraciano and David Tavárez refer to several uprisings against the Spanish in Oaxaca. On the northwest, see also Ricard, *Spiritual Conquest*, 264; William L. Merrill, "Conversion and Colonialism in Northern Mexico: The Tarahumara Response to the Jesuit Mission Program, 1601-1767," in *Conversion to Christianity*, ed. Robert W. Hefner (Princeton, NJ: Princeton University Press, 1993), 129–64 (139–40).

56 Henry Warner Bowden, "Spanish Missions, Cultural Conflict, and the Pueblo Revolt of 1680," *Church History*, 44, no. 2 (June 1975), 217–28 (221).

57 Robert H. Jackson, "Introduction," in *The New Latin American Mission History*, ed. Erick Langer and Robert H. Jackson (Lincoln: University of Nebraska Press, 1995), viii–ix; David Sweet, "The Ibero-American Frontier Mission in Native American History," 16–24.

58 Susan M. Deeds, "Indigenous Responses to Mission Settlement in Nueva Vizcaya," in Langer and Jackson, *New Latin American History*, 78–80.

59 Reff, *Plagues, Priests and Demons*, ch. 3; Merrill, "Conversion and Colonialism," in *Conversion to Christianity*, 140–41, 147–48, 155–56. According to Merrill, members of the Tarahumara continue to identify themselves as "baptized Tarahumaras" but not as Catholics or Christians. Thomas E. Sheridan disagrees on the latter point but concurs in the basic interpretation, in *Paths of Life. American Indians of the Southwest and Northern Mexico*, ed. Sheridan and Nancy J. Parezo (Tucson: University of Arizona Press, 1996), 156.

60 Clendinnen, *Ambivalent Conquests: Maya and Spaniard in Yucatan, 1517-1570*, 2nd ed. (Cambridge: Cambridge University Press, 2003), 52, 58, 73, 90–91, 169–89. Clendinnen discusses the issue of how much these accusations were the product of the mindset of the priests and of the torture that followed.

61 Clendinnen, *Ambivalent Conquests*, 76–79.

62 Farriss, *Maya Society*, 292, 313. Farriss sees this as a syncretic merging with pre-Columbian religion.

63 Clendinnen, *Ambivalent Conquests*, 174–75; Manuel Gutiérrez Estévez, "The Christian Era of the Yucatec Maya," in Gossen, *South- and Meso-American Spirituality*, 264–71; Farriss, *Maya Society*, 315, 328–29. Farriss characterizes this as a syncretic synthesis, "a set of horizontal, mutual exchanges across comparable levels" (295).

64 Taylor, *Magistrates of the Sacred*, 56; Farriss, *Maya Society*, 107.

65 Farriss, *Maya Society*, 386.

66 Carolyn Dean, "The Renewal of Old World Images and the Creation of Colonial Peruvian Visual Culture," in *Converging Cultures: Art and Identity in Spanish America*, ed. Diana Fane (New York: Harry N. Abrams, 1996), 174–77; Sabine MacCormack, *Religion in the Andes: Vision and Imagination in Early Colonial Peru*. (Princeton, NJ: Princeton University Press, 1991), 148–49.

67 MacCormack, 335–36; Kenneth Mills, *Idolatry and Its Enemies: Colonial Andean Religion and Extirpation, 1640-1750* (Princeton, NJ: Princeton University Press, 1997), chaps. 2–3.

68 Nicholas Griffiths, *The Cross and the Serpent. Religious Repression and Resurgence in Colonial Peru* (Norman: University of Oklahoma Press, 1996), 79, 165.

69 Griffiths, *The Cross and the Serpent*, 204–5.

70 Griffiths, *The Cross and the Serpent*, 215. On present day instances, see Olivia Harris, "The Eternal Return of Conversion. Christianity as Contested Domain in Highland Bolivia," in *The Anthropology of Christianity*, ed. Fenella Cannell (Durham, NC: Duke University Press, 2006), 51–76 (61, 65).

71 On a comparison, see Alfredo López Austin, "Guidelines for the study of Mesoamerican Religious Traditions," in Olupona, *Beyond Primitivism*, 118–27.

72 See, for example, n. 45 above.

73 E.g., Christian, "Catholicisms," in Nesvig, *Local Religion*, 259–68.

74 On Mesoamerica, Merrill, "Conversion and Colonialism," in *Conversion to Christianity*, 153–54; Clendinnen, "Ways to the Sacred," 110–11. On Europe, Richard Fletcher, *The Barbarian Conversion: From Paganism to Christianity* (New York: Henry Holt, 1997), 515; James C. Russell, *The Germanization of Early Medieval Christianity* (New York: Oxford University Press, 1994), 155.

75 Fletcher, 250–53, 271; Russell, *Germanization*, 88.

76 For a summary of these developments, see Carlos M.N. Eire, "The Concept of Popular Religion," in Nesvig, *Local Religion*, 4–11.

77 Nesvig, "The 'Indian Question' and the Case of Tlatelolco," in *Local Religion*, 74–75, 79, 80–84.

78 The terms "elite" and "popular" religion – however slippery in themselves – have served as expressions of this tension over the centuries, as Carlos M. Eire has admirably summarized in "The Concept of Popular Religion," in Nesvig, *Local Religion*, 1–35.

79 Edward L. Cleary, "The Transformation of Latin American Christianity, c. 1950-2000," in *World Christianities, c. 1914-2000*, ed. Hugh McLeod, Vol. 9 of *The Cambridge History of Christianity* (Cambridge: Cambridge University Press, 2006), 372.

80 Much of this was the work of the Summer Institute of Linguistics, a mission founded by a Presbyterian minister in the 1930s. On this organization and the controversies surrounding it, see David Martin, *Tongues of Fire: The Explosion of Protestantism in Latin America* (Oxford: Blackwell, 1990), 98–101, 212–13.

81 Brian Stanley, *Christianity in the Twentieth Century: A World History* (Princeton, NJ: Princeton University Press, 2018), 309.

82 Martin, *Tongues of Fire*, 65. This, it should be noted, proved quite compatible with authoritarian leadership *within* a given church. Martin contextualizes the

Pentecostals by linking them to Methodism in belief and technique, while R. Andrew Chesnut, *Competitive Spirits: Latin America's New Religious Economy* (Oxford: Oxford University Press, 2003) persuasively views the same phenomenon in terms of free-market competition for religious consumers based on the theories of Rodney Stark. See the latter's *A Theory of Religion* (New York: Peter Lang, 1987).
83 Stanley, *Christianity in the Twentieth Century*, 304.

CHAPTER 3

1 The figures are from Henry Warner Bowden, *American Indians and Christian Missions: Studies in Cultural Conflict* (Chicago: University of Chicago Press, 1981), 22.
2 R. Murray Thomas, *Manitou and God: North-American Indian Religions and Christian Culture* (Westport, CT: Praeger, 2007), 35.
3 Michel Foucault, *Power/Knowledge*, ed. Colin Gordon (New York: Pantheon Books, 1980), esp. 96–99.
4 Thomas N. Ingersoll, *To Intermix with Our White Brothers* (Albuquerque: University of New Mexico Press, 2005), 67. For a description of an initiation ceremony of whites into Indian society, see James Axtell, *The Invasion Within. The Contest of Cultures in Colonial North America* (New York: Oxford University Press, 1985), 311–14.
5 E.g., see Daniel K. Richter, *The Ordeal of the Longhouse: The Peoples of the Iroquois League in the Era of European Colonization* (Chapel Hill: University of North Carolina Press, 1992), 32–36;
6 See chap. 1, n. 33.
7 Richard White, *The Middle Ground: Indians, Empires, and Republics in the Great Lakes Region, 1650-1815* (Cambridge: Cambridge University Press, 1991), x.
8 Richter, *Facing East from Indian Country: A Native History of Early America* (Cambridge, Mass.: Harvard University Press, 2001), 171.
9 James Belich, *Replenishing the Earth: The Settler Revolution and the Rise of the Anglo-World, 1783-1939* (Oxford: Oxford University Press, 2009), 82.
10 Belich, *Replenishing the Earth*, 182.
11 Robert F. Berkhofer, Jr., *The White Man's Indian* (New York: Knopf, 1978), 27–28.
12 Jace Weaver, "From I-Hermeneutics to We-Hermeneutics. Native Americans and the Post-Colonial," in *Native American Religious Identity: Unforgotten Gods*, ed. Jace Weaver, ed. (Maryknoll, NY: Orbis Books, 1998), 3.
13 George E. Tinker, *Missionary Conquest: The Gospel and Native American Cultural Genocide* (Minneapolis: Fortress Press, 1993).
14 Tinker, 3.

15 E.g., James Treat, ed., *Native and Christian: Indigenous Voices on Religious Identity in the United States and Canada* (New York: Routledge, 1996), 9-10; Kenneth Morrison, *The Solidarity of Kin: Ethnohistory, Religious Studies, and the Algonkian-French Religious Encounter* (Albany: State University of New York Press, 2002), 81.

16 Berkhofer, *Salvation and the Savage: An Analysis of Protestant Missions and American Indian Response, 1787-1862* (Lexington: University of Kentucky Press, 1965), 111. Cf. the controversy between Morrison, cited above, and James Axtell over whether natives were actually "converted" (Morrison, *Solidarity of Kin*, chap. 8).

17 John Webster Grant, *Moon of Wintertime: Missionaries and the Indians of Canada in Encounter since 1534* (Toronto: University of Toronto Press, 1984), 17.

18 James P. Ronda and James Axtell, *Indian Mission: A Critical Bibliography* (Bloomington: Indiana University Press 1978), 8. Cf. Richter, *Facing East*, 86 for a similar view.

19 Axtell, *Invasion Within*, 122, 276. Slightly higher proportions obtain for the Haudenosaunee: 3,000 baptisms between 1668 and 1679, 1,200 of these close to death. See Richter, *Ordeal of the Longhouse*, 116.

20 Axtell, *Invasion Within*, 24.

21 Nancy Bonvillain, *Native Nations. Cultures and Histories of Native North America* (Saddle River, NJ: Prentice Hall, 2001), 104–5.

22 Axtell, *Invasion Within*, 10, 19, 49–50.

23 Axtell., 26–28.

24 Allan Greer, "A Wandering Jesuit in Europe and America. Father Chaumonot Finds a Home," in *Empires of God: Religious Encounters in the Early Modern Atlantic*, ed. Linda Gregerson and Susan Juster (Philadelphia: University of Pennsylvania Press, 2011), 113.

25 Emma Anderson, "Blood, Fire, and 'Baptism'. Three Perspectives on the Death of Jean de Brébeuf, Seventeeth-Century Jesuit 'Martyr,'" in *Native Americans, Christianity, and the Reshaping of the American Religious Landscape*, ed. Joel W. Martin and Mark A. Nicholas (Chapel Hill: University of North Carolina Press, 2010), 144–46; Christopher Vecsey, *The Paths of Kateri's Kin* (Notre Dame, IN: University of Notre Dame Press, 1997), 59–60.

26 Urs Bitterli, *Cultures in Conflict: Encounters Between European and Non-European Cultures, 1492-1800*, trans. Ritchie Robertson (Stanford, CA: Stanford University Press, 1989), 106.

27 Axtell, *Invasion Within*, 100–106; White, *Middle Ground*, 26; Roger M. Carpenter, *The Renewed, the Destroyed, and the Remade: The Three Thought Worlds of the Iroquois and the Huron, 1609-1650* (East Lansing: Michigan State University Press, 2004), 53.

28 Axtell, *Invasion Within*, 107. Cf. Vecsey, *Paths of Kateri's Kin*, 28, who attributes the Jesuits' reputation as "rabid relativists" to Recollect propaganda.

29 Eleanor Leacock, "Montagnais Women and the Jesuit Program for Colonization," in, *Women and Colonization: Anthropological Perspectives,* ed. Mona Etienne and Eleanor Leacock (New York: Praeger, 1980), 32, 35, 37.

30 Axtell, *Invasion Within*, 58, 61; Vecsey, *Paths of Kateri's Kin*, 51–53.

31 Axtell, *Invasion Within*, 61–62, 125.

32 Anderson, "Blood, Fire," 143; Bowden, *American Indians*, 90; Grant, *Moon of Wintertime*, 40–41.

33 Carpenter, *Renewed, Destroyed, Remade*, chaps. 8–9.

34 See Carpenter chap. 9; Bowden, *American Indians*, 91–95; on the Haudenosauneee, see Richter, *Longhouse*, 58–64.

35 Anderson, "Blood, Fire," 125–58.

36 Katherine Ibbett, "Reconfiguring Martyrdom in the Colonial Context. Marie de L'Incarnation," in Gregerson and Juster, *Empires of God*, 179, 184.

37 Richter, *Longhouse*, 116–18.

38 Quoted in Bonvillain, *Native Nations*, 82.

39 On this history, see Vecsey, *Paths of Kateri's Kin*, 99–108; Allan Greer, *Mohawk Saint: Catherine Tekakwitha and the Jesuits* (New York: Oxford University Press, 2005).

40 On the following, see Grant, *Moon of Wintertime*, 58–70; Morrison, *Solidarity of Kin*, chaps. 3–4; Axtell, *Invasion Within*, 111, 277.

41 Axtell, *Invasion Within* 254.

42 Grant, *Moon of Wintertime*, 53, 68–69.

43 Berkhofer, *Salvation and the Savage*, 59.

44 Axtell, *After Columbus: Essays in the Ethnohistory of Colonial North America* (New York: Oxford University Press, 1988), 50; On New France, Edward E. Andrews, *Native Apostles. Black and Indian Missionaries in the British Atlantic World* (Cambridge, MA: Harvard University Press, 2013), 18.

45 Neal Salisbury, *Manitou and Providence: Indians, Europeans, and the Making of New England, 1500-1643* (New York: Oxford University Press, 1982), 183, 225. Contrasting interpretations of Puritan strategy in dealing with Indians may be seen by comparing Alden T. Vaughan, *New England Frontier: Puritans and Indians, 1620-1675* (Boston: Little, Brown, 1965), with Francis Jennings, *The Invasion of America: Indians, Colonialism, and the Cant of Conquest* (Chapel Hill: University of North Carolina Press, 1975).

46 Salisbury, *Manitou and Providence*, 225.

47 Meanwhile, in England the upheaval of civil war, regicide, and Puritan government under Cromwell in England raised millennialist expectations: a prophecy that Christ's second coming would occur in 1650 brought with it an urge to convert the Jews, and speculation centered on the Indians as possible descendants of the lost tribes of Israel gave missionary work an extra urgency. By 1660 donations to the Society for the Propagation of the Gospel in New England exceeded £15,900. See Gregerson, "The Commonwealth of the

Word: New England, Old England and the Praying Indians," in Gregerson and Juster, *Empires of God*, 71, 77; Kristina Bross, "From London to Nonantum. Mission Literature in the Transatlantic English World," ibid., 129.

48 Cf. Vaughan, *New England Frontier*, 238, Axtell, *Invasion Within*, 107.

49 Quoted in Richard W. Cogley, *John Eliot's Mission to the Indians before King Philip's War* (Cambridge, MA: Harvard University Press, 1999), 57.

50 Quoted in Richter, *Facing East*, 126.

51 On the estimate, see Bross, *Dry Bones and Indian Sermons: Praying Indians in Colonial America* (Ithaca: Cornell University Press, 2004), 22, 213 (n.72).

52 Ironically, Eliot's imperfect grasp of the language meant that the Bible was little read. See Bross, *Dry Bones*, 53.

53 Axtell, *Invasion Within*, 142. On the fine, see 220. Mention should also be made of Thomas Mayhew and his son, who established a mission on the island of Martha's Vineyard and won more converts than did Eliot. See Cogley, *John Eliot's Mission*, 172–81.

54 Andrews, *Native Apostles*, 28.

55 Axtell, *Invasion Within* 234–25; Cogley, *John Eliot's Mission* , 125–26; According to Bowden, "Algonkian rituals provide us with a better under-standing of their religion than their mythology does because their myths are quite diffuse and contain varying details." (*American Indians and Christian Missions*, 108). On the way Christian rituals cut across native patterns, see Harold W. van Lonkhuyzen, "A Reappraisal of the Praying Indians: Acculturation, Conversion and Identity at Natick, Massachusetts, 1646-1730," *New England Quarterly* 63, no. 3 (Sept. 1990): 396–428 (416–17).

56 Morrison, *Solidarity of Kin*, chap. 2. Morrison is here discussing Ojibwa religion, but in the context of his work on the Canadian Algonkians. See Richter, *Facing East*, 128, for a reading of the Natick confessions in the light of this interpretation.

57 Axtell, *Invasion Within*, 232–33.

58 Axtell, *Invasion Within*, 223–24.

59 Cogley, *John Eliot's Mission*, 118, 168–69.

60 Compare Axtell, *Invasion Within*, 276, 285 and Cogley, *John Eliot's Mission*, 246, who claimed that much native culture was preserved, to Bowden, *American Indians and Christian Mission*, 123, 128 and Lohnkuyzen, "Reappraisal," 411–17, who claimed that the native culture was disintegrating.

61 Axtell, *Invasion Within*, 174.

62 Richter, *Facing East*, 96–104

63 Bross, *Dry Bones*, 164.

64 Daniel R. Mandell, *Behind the Frontier: Indians in Eighteenth-Century Eastern Massachusetts* (Lincoln: University of Nebraska Press, 1996), 62; Douglas L. Winiarski, "Native American Popular Religion in New

England's Old Colony," in Martin and Nicholas, *Native Americans*, 93–124. Cf. Colin Calloway, *The American Revolution in Indian Country* (Cambridge: Cambridge University Press, 1995), 2–4, for a similar picture of Eastern Indians generally at this time.

65 Winiarski, "Popular Religion," 113.
66 See Linford D Fisher, *The Indian Great Awakening: Religion and the Shaping of Native Cultures in Early America* (Oxford: Oxford University Press, 2012).
67 Richter, *Facing East*, 181–12, 189–90; Mandell, *Behind the Frontier*, 202.
68 Calloway, *American Revolution*, 280–81.
69 On revitalization, see Chapter 1, pp. 25–26.
70 Axtell, *Invasion Within*, 188; Fisher, *Great Awakening*, passim.
71 Bernd C. Peyer, *The Tutor'd Mind: Indian Missionary Writers in Antebellum America* (Amherst, MA: University of Massachusetts Press, 1997), 67; Axtell, *Invasion Within*, 211.
72 Andrews, *Native Apostles*, 162–64.
73 Not to be confused with the Mohegans of Connecticut.
74 David J. Silverman, "To Become a Chosen People. The Missionary Work and Missionary Spirit of the Brotherton and Stockbridge Indians, 1775-1835," in Martin and Nicholas, *Native Americans*, 256.
75 Rachel Wheeler, *To Live Upon Hope: Mohicans and Missionaries in the Eighteenth-Century Northeast* (Ithaca, NY: Cornell University Press, 2008), 247.
76 Charles Hudson, *The Southeastern Indians* [Knoxville]: University of Tennessee Press, 1976, 148, 317.
77 Fred Gearing, *Priests and Warriors. Social Structures for Cherokee Politics in the 18th Century*, Memoir 93. The American Anthropological Association 64, no. 5.2 (Oct. 1962): 26–28, 31–32, 47–53.
78 Leonard Bloom, "The Acculturation of the Eastern Cherokee: Historical Aspects." *The North Carolina Historical Review* 19, no. 4 (Oct. 1942): 327–48 (343–44).
79 A notable exception was one Christian Gottlieb Priber, a German who claimed to be a Jesuit and was an agent of the French. Priber lived among the Cherokee for five years, learned their language, and sought to unify them under French auspices. He was eventually arrested by the English and died in prison. See James Adair, *The History of the American Indians* (1775) reprint, ed. Samuel Cole Williams (Johnson City, TN: Watauga Press, 1930), 252–57. According to Native historian Emmet Starr, *History of the Cherokee Indians* (Oklahoma City, The Warden Company, 1921), 23–24, the Cherokee learned Bible stories from Priber and incorporated them into their own mythology, to the surprise of missionaries who came later.
80 Raymond D. Fogelson, "Cherokee Notions of Power," in *The Anthropology of Power*, ed. Raymond D. Fogelson and Richard N. Adams (New York: Academic Press, 1977), 188.

81 Stanley W. Hoig, *The Cherokees and Their Chiefs in the Wake of Empire* (Fayetteville: University of Arkansas Press, 1998), 44–45. This is a good general history of the nation, to be preferred to Grace Steele Woodward's *The Cherokees* (Norman: University of Oklahoma Press, 1963) for the colonial period.

82 See n. 79 above; also Ulrike Kirchberger, *Konversion zur Moderne? Die britischen Indianermission in der atlantischen Welt des 18.Jahrhunderts* (Wiesbaden: Harrasowitz, 2008), 158–65.

83 Quoted in Steven J. Oatis, *A Colonial Complex: South Carolina's Frontiers in the Era of the Yamasee War, 1680-1730* (Lincoln: University of Nebraska Press, 2004), 92.

84 Woodward, *Cherokees*, 63–64.

85 Theda Perdue, "Cherokee Planters: The Development of Plantation Slavery before Removal," in *The Cherokee Indian Nation: A Troubled History*, ed. Duane H. King (Knoxville: University of Tennessee Press, 1979), 112. On intermarriage as a women's tool of diplomacy, see Cynthia Cumfer, *Separate Peoples, One Land: The Minds of Cherokees, Blacks, and Whites on the Tennessee Frontier* (Chapel Hill: University of North Carolina Press, 2007), 26–27.

86 James Mooney, *James Mooney's History, Myths, and Sacred Formulas of the Cherokees*, intro. George Ellison. Originally published 1900 by Bureau of American Ethology (Fairview, NC: Historical Images, 1992), 36.

87 Another missionary from the Society in Scotland for Propagating Christian Knowledge arrived out the outbreak of one of these wars in 1758 and gave up after three months. See Kirchberger, *Konversion*, 239.

88 Calloway, *American Revolution*, 182, 211.

89 Douglas C. Wilms, "Cherokee Land Use in Georgia before Removal," in *Cherokee Removal: Before and After*, ed. William L. Anderson (Athens: University of Georgia Press, 1991), 7.

90 William G. McLoughlin, *Cherokees and Missionaries, 1789-1839* (New Haven, CT: Yale University Press, 1984), chap. 2. The settlement lasted until 1833, and eventually 65 Indians converted.

91 McLoughlin, chap. 6; Joel W. Martin, "Crisscrossing Projects of Sovereignty and Conversion. Cherokee Christians and New England Missionaries during the 1820s," in Martin and Nicholas, *Native Americans*, 72.

92 McLoughlin, *Cherokees and Missionaries*, 187–89.

93 These differences in criteria make the statistics for conversion in this period very unreliable. In 1830, for example, the Methodists claimed 1028 converts, compared to 61 Baptists, 180 Congregationalists, and 46 Moravians. See McLoughlin, *Cherokee Renascence in the New Republic* (Princeton, NJ: Princeton University Press, 1986), 382.

94 McLoughlin, *The Cherokees and Christianity, 1794-1870*, ed. Walter H. Conser Jr. (Athens: University of Georgia Press, 1994), 120.

95 McLoughlin, *Cherokees and Missionaries*, 142.

96 Peyer, *Tutor'd Mind*, 188.

97 One of these occurred in 1811–13, as Tecumseh's influence was at its height, and was labeled by James Mooney as a Ghost Dance. Another, known as White Path's Rebellion, occurred in the 1820s, as legislation leading up to the constitution was being enacted by the mixed bloods. To traditionalists, it seemed that these laws (such as banning polygamy) were designed to turn the Cherokee nation into a Christian polity. See McLoughlin, *Cherokees and Missionaries*, chaps. 4 and 9.

98 McLoughlin, *Cherokees and Christianity*, 185.

99 McLoughlin, *Champions of the Cherokees: Evan and John B. Jones* (Princeton, NJ: Princeton University Press, 1990), 179.

100 For statistics, see Grant Foreman, *The Five Civilized Tribes* (Norman: University of Oklahoma Press, 1934), 365–66; on the temperance movement, 382–89.

101 McLoughlin, *Cherokees and Christianity*, 185, 193. On its foundation for ecumenicism within the modern Indian movement, see James Treat, *Around the Sacred Fire: Native Religious Activism in the Red Power Era* (New York: Palgrave Macmillan, 2003), 41, 57–58, which discusses the Cherokee background of Bob Thomas, a leader in that movement.

102 McLoughlin, *Cherokees and Christianity*, chap. 7 for what follows.

103 McLoughlin, *Cherokees and Missionaries*, 163. Cf. Hudson, *Southeastern Indians*, 324–25.

104 McLoughlin, *Cherokees and Christianity*, 199–200, 211.

105 McLoughlin, *Champions of the Cherokees*, 71–78.

106 McLoughlin, *Cherokees and Christianity*, 212–13.

107 McLoughlin, *Champions*, 345–46. See also *Cherokees and Christianity*, chaps. 9–10.

108 These were Lewis Downing (1867–1872), whose conciliatory approach helped heal the factional divisions from the War, and Charles Thompson (Oochelata) (1875–79), who embraced a populist platform. See the strongly Christian tone of Downing's proclamation of a day of fasting in 1870 in McLoughlin, *Cherokees and Christianity*, 306–10.

109 Albert J. Wahrhaftig and Jane Lukens-Wahrhaftig, "New Militants or Resurrected State? The Five County Northeastern Oklahoma Cherokee Organization," in King, *Cherokee Indian Nation*, 238. The authors describe a spontaneous revitalization movement of the 60s that again brought Baptists and traditionalists together. See also Treat, *Around the Sacred Fire*, 40–41.

110 Wilma Mankiller and Michael Wallis, *Mankiller: A Chief and Her People* (New York: St. Martin's Griffin, 1993), 220.

111 Quoted in McLoughlin, *Cherokees and Christianity*, 187.

112 Bowden, *American Indians and Christian Mission*, 179; Guy Gibbon, *The Sioux* (Oxford: Blackwell, 2003), 2–3; Raymond J. DeMallie and Douglas R. Parks claim, however, in their introduction to *Sioux Indian Religion:*

Tradition and Innovation (Norman: University of Oklahoma Press, 1987), 6–7, that there is no historical evidence for Nakota being a separate dialect among the Yankton/Yanktonais, but that Santee and Yankton are both Dakota.

113 William H. Wassel, "The Religion of the Sioux," quoted in Thomas E. Mails, *Fools Crow* (New York: Doubleday, 1979), 232–33. Cf. Philip J. Deloria, "Vine V. Deloria Sr.," in *The New Warriors: Native American Leaders since 1900*, ed. R. David Edmunds, ed. (Lincoln: University of Nebraska Press, 2001), 81 for a similar estimate of Episcopalians.

114 Gordon Macgregor, *Warriors without Weapons* (Chicago: University of Chicago Press, 1946), 93.

115 DeMallie and Parks, *Sioux Indian Religion*, 14.

116 Frederick E. Hoxie, "The Reservation Period, 1880-1960," in Bruce G. Trigger and William E. Washburn, *The Cambridge History of the Native Peoples of the Americas: North America*. 2 vols. (Cambridge: Cambridge University Press, 1996), 2: 227.

117 Weaver, "I-Hermeneutics," 6.

118 Gibbon, *Sioux,* 81–83, 109; Gary Clayton Anderson, *Kinsmen of Another Kind: Dakota-White Relations in the Upper Mississippi Valley 1650-1862* (Lincoln, NB: University of Nebraska Press, 1982), 203, 256.

119 Stephen R. Riggs, *Mary and I: Forty Years with the Sioux* , 1880. Reprint (Williamstown, MA: Corner House Publishers, 1971), 103. For an overview of this phase, see Berkhofer, *Salvation*, 118–19, 144–47.

120 Quoted in Beaver, *Church, State and the American Indians* (St. Louis: Concordia Publishing House, 1966), 196–97. On Williamson and Riggs, see Robert Stahl, "Carrying the Word to the Sioux: The Williamson and Riggs Families," in *South Dakota Leaders From Pierre Chouteau, Jr. to Oscar Howe*, ed. Herbert T. Hoover and Larry J. Zimmerman (Vermillion, SD: University of South Dakota Press, 1989), 65–79.

121 Robert Warrior, *The People and the Word: Reading Native Nonfiction* (Minneapolis: University of Minnesota Press, 2005), 104.

122 Margaret D. Jacobs, *White Mother to a Dark Race: Settler Colonialism, Maternalism, and the Removal of Indigenous Children in the American West and Australia, 1880-1940* (Lincoln, NB: University of Nebraska Press, 2009), 31. Jacobs emphasizes the role that white women played in breaking up Native family structures.

123 Weaver, "I-Hermeneutics," 2.

124 Roy W. Meyer, *History of the Santee Sioux* (Lincoln, NB: University of Nebraska Press, 1967), 175.

125 Vine Deloria, Jr. *Singing for a Spirit: A Portrait of the Dakota Sioux* (Santa Fe, NM: Clear Light Publishers, 2000), 41–42.

126 Herbert T. Hoover, *The Yankton Sioux* (New York: Chelsea House, 1988), 61. See also Gibbon, *Sioux,* 83–86, 108–9.

127 Richard White, "The Winning of the West: the Expansion of the Western Sioux in the Eighteenth and Nineteenth Centuries," *Journal of American History* 65, no. 2 (Sept. 1978): 319–43 (330). See also Gibbon, *Sioux*, 86–94.

128 James O. Gump, *The Dust Rose Like Smoke: The Subjugation of the Zulu and the Sioux* (Lincoln: University of Nebraska Press, 1994), 102. He adds, "but not the desire for Indian labor," thereby drawing a contrast with the Zulu case.

129 Beaver, *Church, State*, chap. 4.

130 Ross Alexander Enochs, *The Jesuit Mission to the Lakota Sioux* (Kansas City, MO: Sheed and Ward, 1996), 19.

131 On Hare and Marty, see Gerald W. Wolff, "First Protestant Episcopal Bishop of South Dakota: William Hobart Hare," in Hoover and Zimmerman, *South Dakota Leaders*, 81–105; Ann Kessler, "First Catholic Bishop of Dakota: Martin Marty, the Blackrobe Lean Chief," ibid., 107–23.

132 Leslie Spier, *The Prophet Dance of the Northwest and Its Derivatives: The Source of the Ghost Dance* (Menasha, WI: George Banta Publishing, 1935). For another instance in British Columbia, see Susan Neylan, *The Heavens are Changing: Nineteenth-Century Protestant Missions and Tsimshian Christianity* (Montreal: McGill-Queens University Press, 2003), chap. 7.

133 Rani-Henrik Andersson, *The Lakota Ghost Dance of 1890* (Lincoln, NB: University of Nebraska Press, 2008), 53–54.

134 Jeffrey Ostler, *The Plains Sioux and U.S. Colonialism from Lewis and Clark to Wounded Knee* (Cambridge: Cambridge University Press, 2004), 274; Mooney, *The Ghost-Dance Religion and the Sioux Outbreak of 1890*, abridged (Chicago: University of Chicago Press, 1965), 200.

135 Andersson, *Lakota Ghost Dance*, 171; Elaine Goodale Eastman, *Sister to the Sioux* (Lincoln: University of Nebraska Press, 1978), 140.

136 Ostler, *Plains Sioux*, 345.

137 DeMallie, "Lakota Belief and Ritual in the Nineteenth Century," in DeMallie and Parks, *Sioux Indian Religion*, 42–43. Cf. Julian Rice, *Before the Great Spirit: The Many Faces of Sioux Spirituality* (Albuquerque: University of New Mexico Press, 1998), 13.

138 Rice, 153 and chap. 10 for an overview; DeMallie, "Lakota Belief and Ritual," 29. The sixteen aspects are: A) the gods Sun, Sky, Earth and Rock; B) their associates moon, wind, the feminine, and thunder; C) their subordinates the buffalo, bear, the four winds, and the whirlwind; D) four spiritual components of the human soul: the godlike, the spirit, the ghost, and the spirit-like.

139 Quoted in Robert M. Utley, *The Last Days of the Sioux Nation* (New Haven, CT: Yale University Press, 1963), 34. Cf. Clyde Holler, *Black Elk's Religion: The Sun Dance and Lakota Catholicism* (Syracuse, NY: Syracuse University Press, 1995), 213.

140 Ostler, *Plains Sioux*, 230–31.

141 For an in-depth discussion of one reservation, see Harvey Markowitz, "Converting the Rosebud. Sicangu Lakota Catholicism in the Late Nineteenth and Early Twentieth Centuries," *Great Plains Quarterly* 32, no. 1 (Winter 2012): 3–23 (12).

142 Black Elk, *The Sacred Pipe*, ed. Joseph Epes Brown (Norman: University of Oklahoma Press, 1953), pp. 3–9, esp. n. 12. Also Paul B. Steinmetz, *Pipe, Bible, and Peyote among the Oglala Lakota*, dissertation, University of Stockholm, 1980, 52–54; Marla N. Powers, *Oglala Women* (Chicago: University of Chicago Press, 1984), 42–52.

143 Vecsey, "A Century of Lakota Sioux Catholicism at Pine Ridge," in *Religious Diversity and American Religious History: Studies in Traditions and Culture*, ed. Walter H. Conser and Sumner B. Twiss (Athens: University of Georgia Press, 1997), 266.

144 DeMallie, "Lakota Belief and Ritual," 34–42.

145 Ostler, *Plains Sioux*, 169.

146 Holler, *Black Elk's Religion*, chaps. 2–3, esp. 73, 96; William K. Powers, *Oglala Religion* (Lincoln: University of Nebraska Press, 1975), 95–100. On the sweat lodge, see Raymond A. Bucko, *The Lakota Ritual of the Sweat Lodge* (Lincoln, NB: University of Nebraska Press, 1998).

147 Ostler, *Plains Sioux*, 178; Vecsey, "Century," 273; Arthur Amiotte, "The Lakota Sun Dance," in DeMallie and Parks, *Sioux Indian Religion*, 75.

148 William K. Powers, *Beyond the Vision: Essays on American Indian Culture* (Norman: University of Oklahoma Press, 1987), 94–125.

149 Vine Deloria, Jr., *Singing for a Spirit*, 70.

150 Enochs, *Jesuit Mission*, 67.

151 Vecsey, "Century," 276–80; Enochs, *Jesuit Mission*, 125.

152 Wolff, "First Protestant Episcopal Bishop," 87; Mary E. Cochran. *Dakota Cross-Bearer: The Life and World of a Native American Bishop* (Lincoln: University of Nebraska Press, 2000), 18.

153 The missionary sources make no mention of this, however; they refer rather to German precedents. Karl Markkus Kreis, ed., *Lakotas, Black Robes and Holy Women: German Reports from the Indian Missions in South Dakota, 1886-90*, trans. Corinna Dally-Starna (Lincoln: University of Nebraska Press, 2007), 172.

154 Enochs, *Jesuit Mission*, 59; Vecsey, "Century," 274.

155 Riggs, *Tah-koo Wah-kan, or the Gospel among the Dakotas*, 1869. Reprint (New York: Arno Press, 1972), 343.

156 Stahl, "Carrying the Word," 77.

157 Todd Kerstetter, "Spin Doctors at Santee: Missionaries and the Dakota-Language Reporting of the Ghost Dance at Wounded Knee," *Western Historical Quarterly*, 28, no. 1 (Spring 1997): 45–67 (46–48). The paper split into separate English and Dakota papers, substantially different in content, in 1884.

158 On the Episcopalian paper, see Virginia Driving Hawk Sneve, *That They May Have Life: The Episcopal Church in South Dakota, 1859-1976* (New York: Seabury Press, 1977), 63. On the Catholic, see Enochs, *Jesuit Mission,* 89–90.

159 Enochs, 91–93; Vecsey, "Century," 266–27; Kreis, *Lakotas, Black Robes and Holy Women,* 64–66.

160 Horowitz, "Converting the Rosebud," 6. As in the colonial Northeast, the Sicangu Lakota had an initial fear of baptism, which they associated with death.

161 Stahl, "Carrying the Word," 75.

162 Kerstetter, "Spin Doctors," 51.

163 Enochs, *Jesuit Mission,* 22–23; William K. Powers, *Beyond the Vision,* 113–14.

164 Philip J. Deloria, *Indians in Unexpected Places* (Lawrence, KS: University Press of Kansas, 2004), 116.

165 Beatrice Medicine, *Learning to Be and Anthropologist and Remaining "Native,"* ed. with Sue-Ellen Jacobs (Urbana: University of Illinois Press, 2001), 22.

166 Macgregor, *Warriors without Weapons,* 40, 44; chaps. 12–13.

167 Ella Deloria, *Speaking of Indians,* 1944. Reprint (Lincoln: University of Nebraska Press, 1998), 112–13.

168 Markowitz, "The Catholic Mission and the Sioux. A Crisis in the Early Paradigm," in DeMallie and Parks, *Sioux Indian Religion,* 125–27; Joseph H. Cash and Herbert T. Hoover, eds., *To Be an Indian: An Oral History* (New York: Holt, Rinehart and Winston, 1971), 108–9.

169 See Holler, ed. *The Black Elk Reader* (Syracuse, NY: Syracuse University Press, 2000) for selections from these different points of view.

170 According to William K. Powers, the Lakota who remembered Black Elk did not regard him as an exceptional figure, but one of a number of Native catechists. See "When Black Elk Speaks, Everybody Listens," in *Religion in Native North America,* ed. Christopher Vecsey (Moscow: University of Idaho Press, 1990), 140–47.

171 The full transcripts were later published under the name *The Sixth Grandfather,* edited by the anthropologist Raymond J. DeMallie (Lincoln: University of Nebraska Press, 1984). De Mallie's introduction constitutes the fullest biographical source for Black Elk.

172 *Sixth Grandfather,* 294; cf. 123, 214.

173 Philip Deloria, *Indians in Unexpected Places,* 69–70.

174 Powers, "When Black Elk Speaks," 141; *Sixth Grandfather,* 14; Michael F. Steltenkamp, *Black Elk: Holy Man of the Oglala* (Norman: University of Oklahoma Press, 1993), 34.

175 *Sixth Grandfather,* 14, 135–37.

176 Steltenkamp, *Black Elk,* 62–67, 88.

177 The outside study in the 1940s led by Gordon Macgregor concluded that young people on the reservation did not look to priests or ministers for leadership or guidance. Macgregor, *Warriors without Weapons*, 201–2.

178 *Sixth Grandfather*, 60; Steltenkamp, *Black Elk*, chap. 6.

179 *Sixth Grandfather*, 64.

180 Black Elk, "Foreword," in Brown, *The Sacred Pipe*, xix–xx.

181 Black Elk had steadfastly refused to perform it for Neihardt, despite the latter's repeated requests. See *Sixth Grandfather*, 15n.

182 *Sixth Grandfather*, 91.

183 Bucko, *Lakota Ritual*, pp. 83, 171; Marla Powers, *Oglala Women*, p. 191; Waziyatawin Angela Wilson, *Remember This! Dakota Decolonization and the Eli Taylor Narratives* (Lincoln: University of Nebraska Press, 205), 117.

184 Vine Deloria, Jr., *God Is Red: A Native View of Religion*, 3rd ed. (Golden, CO: Fulcrum, 2003), 77.

185 Deloria, Jr., *God Is Red*, 304.

CHAPTER 4

1 The lower 2010 figures are from *Christianity in its Global Context, 1970-2020* (Hamilton, MA: Center for the Study of Global Christianity, Gordon Conwell Theological Seminary, 2013), https://archive.gordonconwell.edu/ock enga/research/documents/ChristianityinitsGlobalContext.pdf, 22. The 1910 figures are from Pew Research, Religion & Public Life Project, *Tolerance and Tension: Islam and Christianity in Sub-Saharan Africa*, www .pewforum.org/2010/04/15/executive-summary-islam-and-christianity-in-sub-saharan-africa/, as are the higher 2010 figures, illustrating the difficulties in arriving at exact numbers. Another Pew report issued a year later, gives the percentage of Christians in sub-Saharan Africa in 2010 as 63 percent (*Global Christianity: A Report on the Size and Distribution of the World's Christian Population*), www.pewforum.org/2011/12/19/global-christianity-exec/.

2 For example, J. D. Y. Peel, "The Christianization of African Society: Some Possible Models," in *Christianity in Independent Africa*, ed. Edward Fasholé-Luke et al. (Bloomington: Indiana University Press, 1978), 448–49; Ogbu H. Kalu, ed., "Introduction: The Shape and Flow of African Church Historiography," in *African Christianity. An African Story* (Trenton NJ: Africa World Press, 2007), 8.

3 "Appendix. Address by Professor E.A. Ayandele..." in Fasholé-Luke, *Christianity in Independent Africa*, 611–12. For other examples, see B. A. Pauw, *Christianity and Xhosa Tradition: Belief and Ritual among Xhosa-speaking Christians* (Cape Town: Oxford University Press, 1975), 56–59, 65, 224–27, 231–34; Flora Edouwaye S. Kaplan, "Understanding Sacrifice and Sanctity in Benin indigenous Religion, Nigeria," in *Beyond Primitivism:*

Indigenous Religious Traditions and Modernity, ed. Jacob K. Olupona (New York: Routledge, 2004), 196.

4 Stephen Ellis and Gerrie ter Haar, "Religion and Politics in Sub-Saharan Africa," *Journal of Modern African Studies*, 36, no. 2 (June 1998): 175–201 (177).

5 Quoted in Devaka Premawardhana, *Faith and Flux. Pentecostalism and Mobility in Rural Mozambique* (Philadelphia: University of Pennsylvania Press, 2018), 101. The man was Premawardhana's research assistant.

6 David Gordon, *Invisible Agents: Spirits in a Central African History* (Athens: Ohio University Press, 2012), Introduction.

7 Gerrie Ter Haar, ed. *Imagining Evil. Witchcraft Beliefs and Accusations in Contemporary Africa* (Trenton, NJ: Africa World Press, 2007), esp. chaps. 4, 12.

8 See, e.g., Birgit Meyer, *Translating the Devil: Religion and Modernity among the Ewe in Ghana* (Trenton, NJ: Africa World Press, 1999), 195, 204–12, 216; J. Kwabena Asamoah-Gyadu, "Witchcraft Accusations and Christianity in Africa," *International Bulletin of Missionary Research*, 39, no. 1 (Jan. 2015): 23–27.

9 Adrian Hastings, *African Catholicism* (London: SCM Press, 1989), 24.

10 Ellis and Ter Haar, "Religion and Politics," 188–89; Baffour K. Takyi, "Secular Government in Sub-Saharan Africa," in *The Oxford Handbook of Secularism*, ed. Phil Zuckerman and John R. Shook (Oxford: Oxford University Press, 2017), 201–13. Takyi concludes, "a separation of church and state exists in many parts of Africa only in the area of rhetoric" (210).

11 See Willy de Craemer, Jan Vansina, and Renée C. Fox, "Religious Movements in Central Africa: A Theoretical Study," *Comparative Studies in Society and History*, 18, no. 4 (Oct. 1976): 458–75 (460, 468–89).

12 Ann Swidler, "Where Do Axial Commitments Reside? Problems in Thinking About the African Case," in *The Axial Age and Its Consequences*, ed. Robert N. Bellah and Hans Joas (Cambridge, MA: Harvard University Press, 2012), 224–27.

13 See John L. and Jean Comaroff, *Of Revelation and Revolution: The Dialectics of Modernity on a South African Frontier*, 2 vols. (Chicago: University of Chicago Press, 1991, 1997), 2: 27.

14 David Maxwell, "Christianity without Frontiers: Shona Missionaries and Transnational Pentecostalism in Africa," in *Christianity and the African Imagination: Essays in Honour of Adrian Hastings*, ed. David Maxwell and Ingrid Lawrie (Leiden: Brill, 2002), 295. Two studies of Christianity in East Africa both emphasize the connection between conversion and movement from place to place. See also Premawardhana, *Faith and Flux* and Derek Peterson, *Ethnic Patriotism and the East African Revival: A History of Dissent, c. 1935-1972* (Cambridge: Cambridge University Press, 2012).

15 This interpretation differs in emphasis from that of Lamin Sanneh, who stresses the contrast between Christianity's promotion of vernacular languages and Islam's insistence on the nontranslatability of the Quran. See his "Translatability in Islam & in Christianity in Africa: A Thematic Approach," in *Religion in Africa: Experience & Expression*, ed. Thomas D. Blakely, Walter E. A. van Beek, and Dennis L. Thompson (London: James Curry, 1994), 23–45.

16 To the best of my knowledge there is very little comparative scholarship on the two, except for Noel Q. King's brief but insightful narrative, *Christian and Muslim in Africa* (New York: Harper & Row, 1971), and Simon Ottenberg's local study of the Bafodea chiefdom in northern Sierra Leone, "Two New Religions, One Analytic Frame," in *Igbo Religion, Social Life and Other Essays by Simon Ottenberg*, ed. Toyin Falola (Trenton, NJ: Africa World Press, 2006), 519–38. Ottenberg finds the same religious pluralism there as mentioned above. For an account of Muslim penetration, see Nehemia Levtzion & Randall L. Pouwels, eds. *The History of Islam in Africa*. (Athens, OH: Ohio University Press, 2000), chap. 3.

17 Hastings, *The Church in Africa, 1450-1950* (Oxford: Clarendon Press, 1994), 332–34.

18 For a penetrating critique of these tendencies, see Okot p'Bitek, *African Religions in Western Scholarship* (Kampala: East African Literature Bureau, [1971]); also Robin Horton, *Patterns of Thought in Africa and the West. Essays on Magic, Religion and Science* (Cambridge: Cambridge University Press, 1993), chap. 6; James H. Sweet, *Recreating Africa: Culture, Kinship and Religion in the African-Portuguese World, 1441-1770* (Chapel Hill: University of North Carolina Press, 2003), 106–8,

19 Humphrey Fisher, "Conversion Reconsidered: Some Historical Aspects of Religious Conversion in Black Africa," *Africa* 43, no. 1 (Jan. 1973): 27–40. Fisher was responding to Robin Horton's theory of African conversion (see above, pp. 15–16). For an in-depth application of Fisher's model to a single case, see Patrick J. Ryan, S. J., *Imale. Yoruba Participation in the Muslim Tradition: A Study of Clerical Piety* (Missoula, MT: Scholars Press, 1978).

20 See below, p. 49.

21 Craemer, Vansina, and Fox, "Religious Movements in Central Africa," 458–75, esp. 466.

22 See, e.g., Hastings, *Church in Africa*, 336–37, for an elaborate description of such a moment from the Ivory Coast.

23 Levtzion, "Patterns of Islamization in west Africa," in *Conversion to Islam*, ed. Nehemia Levtzion (New York: Holmes and Meier, 1979), 208; Mervyn Hiskett, *The Development of Islam in West Africa* (London: Longman, 1984), 56–57.

24 Cf. Noel King's remark in *Christian and Muslim in Africa*, 68: "'Swahili' Islam has been likened to rain from the Indian Ocean: it comes gently but persistently, and in the end goes deep."

25 Quoted in Hastings, *Church in Africa*, 278.

26 Sanneh, *West African Christianity: The Religious Impact* (Maryknoll, NY: Orbis Books, 1983), 20. For other summaries of the period, see Elizabeth Isichei, *A History of Christianity in Africa* (Grand Rapids, MI: Eerdmans, 1995), chap. 2; Kalu, ed., *African Christianity*, chaps. 6–7.

27 Symptomatic of the quarantine stage was the life of Philip Quaque (1741? – 1816), an African-born missionary from the Gold Coast, educated in London, who returned to the Gold Coast to serve both as chaplain to the British slave-traders there and as missionary to the surrounding population. He failed in the latter capacity, having lost the ability to speak his native language and looking down on African religion as primitive. Like the Muslim merchants who were involved in a trans-Saharan network, Quaque was involved in a trans-Atlantic one, corresponding with those who wanted to send American slaves to Africa. See Edward E. Andrews, *Native Apostles: Black and Indian Missionaries in the British Atlantic World* (Cambridge, MA: Harvard University Press, 2013), 125–49, 199–204.

28 Sanneh, *West African Christianity*, 37–39; Hastings, *Church in Africa*, 77–78.

29 Sanneh, *West African Christianity*, 48–49. See also Isichei, *History of Christianity*, 61–62.

30 Wyatt MacGaffey, *Religion and Society in Central Africa: The BaKongo of Lower Zaire* (Chicago: University of Chicago Press, 1986), 198–99.

31 Hastings, *Church in Africa* , 79–80.

32 John Thornton, *Africa and Africans in the Making of the Atlantic World, 1400-1800*, 2nd ed. (Cambridge: Cambridge University Press 1998), 257.

33 Thornton, *The Kongolese Saint Anthony: Dona Beatriz Kimpa Vita and the Antonian Movement, 1684-1706* (Cambridge: Cambridge University Press, 1998), 29; Hastings, *Church in Africa*, 92.

34 Thornton, "The Development of an African Catholic Church in the Kingdom of the Kongo, 1491-1750," *Journal of African History* 25, no. 2(1984): 147–67 (159).

35 Isichei, *History of Christianity*, 65. Afonso petitioned that clergy should be allowed to marry on the grounds that the tropical climate made celibacy impossible. See also Thornton, "African Catholic Church," 158.

36 Linda Heywood and John Thornton, *Central Africans, Atlantic Creoles, and the Foundation of the Americas, 1585-1660* (Cambridge: Cambridge University Press, 2007), 62–63, 100–101.

37 Cf. MacGaffey, *Religion and Society*, 205–7. By the eighteenth century, however, the accent appeared to be shifting toward *selective acculturation*, as the urban elite and eventually the common people adopted European names, dress, food and drink, music, etc. (Heywood and Thornton, *Central Africans*, 185, 208–21). There is no evidence, however, that this was accompanied by a shift in religious observance.

38 One should also mention Queen Njinga in Angola, the kingdom immediately to the south, whose conversion to Catholicism in 1656 was partly a way of making peace with the Portuguese. See Heywood and Thornton, *Central Africans*, 125–27.

39 Thornton, *Kongolese Saint Anthony,* 216. Cf. MacGaffey, *Religion and Society*, 208–12, who emphasizes the continuities with pre-Christian religion.

40 Jason R. Young, *Rituals of Resistance: African Atlantic Religion in Kongo and the Lowcountry South in the Era of Slavery* (Baton Rouge, LA: Louisiana State University Press, 2007), 68–70.

41 Hastings, *Church in Africa,* 385–88.

42 Heywood and Thornton, *Central Africans,* 159–68, 222.

43 Heywood and Thornton, *Central Africans* , 225. In the Kongo, baptism was incorporated into indigenous belief in the following way: salt was viewed as preventing evil, and the priests began administering salt as part of the ritual. This led to a great demand for baptism, which was interpreted as a remedy for evil rather than a washing away of sins. See Sweet, *Recreating Africa*, 94–97.

44 Laënnec Hurbon, "The Church and Afro-American Slavery," trans. John Cumming, in *The Church in Latin America 1492-1992*, ed. Enrique Dussel (Maryknoll, NY: Orbis Books, 1992), 364; Heywood and Thornton, *Central Africans,* 186.

45 Richard Gray, *Black Christians and White Missionaries* (New Haven, CT: Yale University Press, 1990), chaps. 1–2; Isichei, *History of Christianity,* 71.

46 See, for example, Leslie G. Desmangles, *The Faces of the Gods: Vodou and Roman Catholicism in Haiti* (Chapel Hill: University of North Carolina Press, 1992), 26–28; Joseph M. Murphy, *Santería: An African Religion in America* (Boston: Beacon Press, 1988), 120–24; Roger Bastide, *The African Religions of Brazil,* trans. Helen Sebba (Baltimore: Johns Hopkins University Press, 1978), 21; chap. 12.

47 Joseph M. Murphy, "Santa Barbara Africana: Beyond Syncretism in Cuba," in *Beyond Conversion and Syncretism*, ed. David Lindenfeld and Miles Richardson (New York: Berghahn Books, 2011), 138–39; Paul Christopher Johnson, *Secrets, Gossip, and Gods. The Transformation of Brazilian Candomblé* (Oxford: Oxford University Press, 2002), 71–72; Luis Nicolau Parés, "The 'Nagoization' Process in Bahian Candomblé," in *The Yoruba Diaspora in the Atlantic World*, ed. Toyin Falola and Matt D. Childs (Bloomington: Indiana University Press, 2004), 194, 196–98; Christine Ayorinde, "Santería in Cuba: Tradition and Transformation," ibid., 224.

48 Olabiyi Babalola Yai, "Yoruba Religion and Globalization. Some Reflections," in *Òrìṣà Devotion as World Religion. The Globalization of Yoruba Religious Culture*, ed. Jacob K. Olupona and Terry Rey (Madison: University of Wisconsin Press, 2008), 237.

49 Sweet, *Recreating Africa*, passim.

50 Bastide, *African Religions,* 155.

51 Murphy, *Santeria*, 26. On the different work environments in Brazil, see Bastide, *African Religions*, 48–52.
52 Stephen Prothero, *God Is Not One* (New York: Harper One, 2010), 210–11. The counting of *orishas* varies widely. One text, according to Prothero, refers to 3200. Joseph Murphy gives the figure of 1700 (*Santería*, 12).
53 Bastide, *African Religions*, 53–54, 120; Thornton, *Africa and Africans*, 203–04.
54 Johnson, *Secrets, Gossip, and Gods*, 75.
55 Murphy, *Santería*, 28–30.
56 Desmangles, *Faces of the Gods*, chap. 2.
57 Bastide, *African Religions*, 83–90; Thornton, *Africa and Africans*, 269.
58 Jean-Baptiste Labat, quoted in Desmangles, *Faces of the Gods*, 27.
59 Bastide, *African Religions*, 272.
60 Murphy, *Santería*, 40.
61 Johnson, *Secrets, Gossip, and Gods*, 38.
62 See Murphy, "Santa Barbara Africana," in Lindenfeld and Richardson, *Beyond Conversion and Syncretism*, 144.
63 Bastide, *African Religions*, 262–67.
64 Bastide, *African Religions*, 14, esp. 322–24; see also Margarite Fernandez Olmos and Lisbeth Paravisini-Gebert, *Creole Religions of the Caribbean* (New York: New York University Press, 2003), chap. 7.
65 On Candomblé, Johnson, *Secrets, Gossip, and Gods*, 122–23; on Vodou, Desmangles, *Faces of the Gods*, 9, 75–76, 87–88.
66 Albert J. Raboteau, "African Religions in America: Theoretical Perspectives," in *Global Dimensions of the African Diaspora*, ed. Joseph E. Harris, 2nd ed. (Washington, DC: Howard University Press, 1993), 72–73.
67 Murphy, *Santería*, 137; Prothero, *God Is Not One*, 238.
68 The *ifa* divination involves a specialist (*babalawo*) shuffling sixteen palm nuts 256 times to arrive at a distinct combination, which is a key to a poem or poems that the *babalawo* has memorized. It has been compared to the *I Ching* in China.
69 Mechal Sobel, *Trabelin' On: The Slave Journey to an Afro-Baptist Faith* (Westport, CT: Greenwood Press, 1979), xxii.
70 Raboteau, *Slave Religion: The "Invisible Institution" in the Antebellum South* (New York: Oxford University Press, 1978), 64. Raboteau also discusses Catholicism among blacks, but this tended to be limited to Maryland and Louisiana. Although orders of black nuns arose in both places, there was little opportunity to incorporate dance and song into Catholic ritual, nor for African Americans to enter the priesthood (271–75).
71 Michael A. Gomez, *Exchanging Our Country Marks: The Transformation of African Identities in the Colonial and Antebellum South* (Chapel Hill: University of North Carolina Press, 1998), 267.
72 Gomez, 275–88. See also Jermaine O. Archer, "Bitter Herbs and a Lock of Hair: Recollections of Africa in Slave Narratives of the Garrisonian Era," in

Diasporic Africa. A Reader, ed. Michael A. Gomez (New York: New York University Press, 2006), 84–104.

73 Young, *Rituals of Resistance,* 125.

74 Sobel, *Trabelin' On,* xxi–xxii.

75 Gomez, *Exchanging Our Country Marks,* 260–61.

76 Sylvia R. Frey and Betty Wood, *Come Shouting to Zion: African American Protestantism in the American South and British Caribbean to 1830* (Chapel Hill: University of North Carolina Press, 1998), chap. 3, esp. 76–77.

77 Sobel, *Trabelin' On,* 98.

78 Raboteau, *Slave Religion,* 133.

79 Frey and Wood, *Come Shouting to Zion,* 106–10.

80 *Journal of John Wesley,* quoted in Frey and Wood, 90.

81 Sobel, *Trabelin' On,* 133–35; Raboteau, *Slave Religion,* 231–39.

82 Frey and Wood, *Come Shouting to Zion,* 176.

83 Gomez, *Exchanging Our Country Marks,* 272–74.

84 Sobel, *Trabelin' On,* 128–29; Raboteau, *Slave Religion,* 196; Frey and Wood, 190, 201.

85 Sobel, *Trabelin' On,* 101; Raboteau, *Slave Religion,* 251, 311, 318.

86 Raboteau, *Slave Religion,* 295–96. On the white counteroffensive, see chap. 4.

87 For a full discussion of these events and trends, see Daniel C. Littlefield, "Revolutionary Citizens: 1776-1804," in *To Make Our World Anew. A History of African Americans,* ed. Robin D.G. Kelley and Earl Lewis (Oxford: Oxford University Press, 2000), 108–40.

88 Gomez, *Exchanging Our Country Marks,* 255.

89 Roswith Gerloff, "The African Diaspora in the Caribbean and Europe from pre-emancipation to the present day," in *World Christianities c. 1914-2000,* ed. Hugh Mcleod. Vol. 9 of *The Cambridge History of Christianity* (Cambridge: Cambridge University Press, 2006), 224. This article provides an excellent overview of African Christianity in Jamaica.

90 Mary Turner, *Slaves and Missionaries: The Disintegration of Jamaican Slave Society, 1787-1834* (Urbana, IL: University of Illinois Press, 1982), 201–2.

91 Gerloff, "African Diaspora," in McLeod, *World Christianities,* 227–29.

92 Sanneh, *Abolitionists Abroad. American Blacks and the Making of Modern West Africa* (Cambridge, MA: Harvard University Press, 1999), 50–52.

93 John Peterson, *Province of Freedom: A History of Sierra Leone, 1787-1970* (Evanston, IL: Northwestern University Press, 1969), 32–37.

94 Filomina Chioma Steady, "The Role of Women in the Churches in Freetown, Sierra Leone," in Fasholé-Luke, *Christianity in Independent Africa,* 151–63; Sanneh, *West African Christianity,* 69.

95 Sanneh, *Abolitionists Abroad,* 99.

96 Claude A. Clegg III, *The Price of Liberty: African Americans and the Making of Liberia* (Chapel Hill: University of North Carolina Press, 2004), 6, 35, 70.

97 Alexander Crummell, *The Future of Africa*. Reprint (New York: Negro Universities Press, 1969 (1862)), 9, 19.

98 Clegg, *Price of Liberty*, 88, 111.

99 Clegg, *Price of Liberty*, 217, 239, 242.

100 Yekutiel Gershoni, *Black Colonialism: The Americo-Liberian Scramble for the Hinterland* (Boulder, CO: Westview Press, 1985), 24; J. Gus Liebenow, *Liberia The Quest for Democracy* (Bloomington: Indiana University Press, 1987), 53–54.

101 Liebenow, *Liberia*, 81–2. It should hardly be surprising that an American anthropologist, doing fieldwork in the interior of Liberia, found that people viewed Christianity cynically, "as something to be used for one's advantage, and nothing more." Se Benjamin G. Dennis, *The Gbandes: A People of the Liberian Hinterland* (Chicago: Nelson-Hall, 1972), 180.

102 Barbara E. Harrell-Bond, Allen M. Howard, David E. Skinner, *Community Leadership and the Transformation of Freetown (1801-1976)* (The Hague: Mouton, 1978), 3, 20–27.

103 John Peterson, *Province*, 239–40; Harrell-Bond, *Community Leadership*, 122, 135. See also Gibril Cole, *The Krio of West Africa: Islam, Culture, Creolization and Colonialism in the Nineteenth Century* (Athens: Ohio University Press, 2013), chap. 2.

104 Despite the apparent resemblance to "creole," the term has an entirely different origin, from the Yoruba term "to trade." See Cole, *Krio*, chap. 1.

105 Akintola J. G. Wyse, "The Sierra Leone Krios: A Reappraisal from the Perspective of the African Diaspora," in Harris, *Global Dimensions*, 355–58.

106 Harris, *Global Dimensions*, 346; Sanneh, *Abolitionists*, 214.

107 John Peterson, *Province*, 46, 78–79.

108 For differing interpretations of MacCarthy's governorship, see Peterson, *Province*, chap. 3 and Cole, *Krio*, chap. 2.

109 John Peterson, *Province*, 63.

110 Hastings, *Church in Africa*, 339.

111 Quoted in Frieder Ludwig, *Kirche im kolonialen Kontext: Anglikanische Missionare und afrikanische Propheten im südöstlichen Nigeria, 1879-1918.* (Frankfurt/M: Peter Lang, 1992), 133.

112 Cole, *Krio*, chap. 2; Andrew F. Walls, "Africa as the Theatre of Christian Engagement with Islam in the Nineteenth Century," in Maxwell and Lawrie, *Christianity and the African Imagination*, 49 –54.

113 J. A. Ade Ajayi, *Christian Missions in Nigeria 1841-1891: The Making of a New Elite* (Evanston, IL: Northwestern University Press, 1965), 73.

114 Ajayi, 27–28.

115 See E. A. Ayandele, *The Missionary Impact on Modern Nigeria 1842-1914* (New York: Humanities Press, 1967), chaps. 1–3.

116 On Abeokuta, see J. D. Y Peel, *Religious Encounter and the Making of the Yoruba* (Bloomington: Indiana University Press, 2000), 135–36; on Lagos,

Michael A. C. Echeruo, *Victorian Lagos: Aspects of Nineteenth Century Lagos Life* (London: Macmillan, 1977); on the Ijebu, Ayandele, *Missionary Impact*, 68.

117 On this group, see Robin Law, "Yoruba Liberated Slaves Who Returned to West Africa," in Falola and Childs, *Yoruba Diaspora*, 349–65; S. Y. Boadi-Siaw, "Brazilian Returnees of West Africa," in Harris, *Global Dimensions*, 421–39; Isichei, "An Obscure Man: Pa Antonio in Lagos (c. 1800[–]1880)," in Isichei, ed. *Varieties of Christian Experience in Nigeria* (London: Macmillan, 1982), 28–33.

118 T. G. O. Gbadamosi, *The Growth of Islam among the Yoruba, 1841-1898* (Atlantic Highlands, NJ: Humanities Press, 1978), 26–28, 51–52, 70; Peel, *Religious Encounter*, 140–50.

119 Peel, *Religious Encounter*, 242.

120 Peel, *Religious Encounter*, 186; Gbadamosi, *Growth of Islam*, 146.

121 Peel, *Religious Encounter*, 195.

122 Peel, *Religious Encounter*, 250–55. A thorough study of this mindset is Birgit Meyer's work of the Ewe in present-day Ghana, who were evangelized by the North German Missionary Society: *Translating the Devil*, 98.

123 Hastings, *Church in Africa*, 209–15; on Yoruba, see Ajayi, *Christian Missions*, 108–24; chap. 5. on the Ewe, see Meyer, *Translating the Devil*, 8, 20.

124 Chinua Achebe, *Things Fall Apart* (New York: Random House, 1994), 152. Achebe is the son of a Christian catechist.

125 Peel, *Religious Encounter*, 265–77; Ayandele, *Missionary Impact*, 15.

126 Peel, *Religious Encounter*, 217–18; Hastings, *Church in Africa*, 274–78, 313–17.

127 Peel, *Religious Encounter*, 223.

128 Hastings, *Church in Africa*, 403.

129 Kenneth Scott Latourette, *A History of the Expansion of Christianity*, 7 vols. (New York: Harper, 1937–45), 5: 438.

130 Latourette., 5: 450–51. See also James Bertin Webster, *The African Churches Among the Yoruba, 1888-1922* (Oxford: Clarendon Press, 1964), 97–101.

131 Hastings, *Church in Africa*, 457, 540–45.

132 P. B. Clarke, "The Methods and Ideology of the Holy Ghost Fathers in Eastern Nigeria, 1885-1905," in *The History of Christianity in West Africa*, ed. Ogbu Kalu (London: Longman, 1980), 51–53. See also Ayandele, *Missionary Impact*, chap. 5.

133 Quoted in Hastings, *Church in Africa*, 480. See Ayandele's excellent biography, *Holy Johnson: Pioneer of African Nationalism, 1836-1917* (London: Frank Cass, 1970). Also Peel, *Religious Encounter*, 279–83.

134 For a survey of the African interpretations, see Kalu, "Ethiopianism in African Christianity," in Kalu, *African Christianity*, chap. 10.

135 Quoted in Ayandele, *Missionary Impact*, 215.

136 See the table in Webster, *African Churches*, 91.

137 Peel, *Religious Encounter*, 294–95; Ayandele, *Missionary Impact*, 256.

138 See Hollis R. Lynch, *Edward Wilmot Blyden: Pan-Negro Patriot 1832-1912* (Ibadan, Nigeria: Oxford University Press, 1967), 180–82, 196, 199.

139 Teshale Tibebu, *Edward Wilmot Blyden and the Racial Nationalist Imagination* (Rochester: University of Rochester Press, 2012), 17, 76–77, 93, 108–12.

140 Allan H. Anderson, *African Reformation: African Initiated Christianity in the 20th Century* (Trenton, NJ: Africa World Press, 2001), 12, 14. This helpful survey proceeds by region. Classificatory attempts include H. W. Turner, "A Typology for African Religious Movements," *Journal of Religion in Africa*, 1 (1967): 1–34. For a discussion of the merits of typologies in general, see Stephanie R. Douglas, "Bringing Order to Chaos: The Role of Typologies in the Study of African Christian Movements," *Mission* 5, no. 2 (1998): 257–73. For an alternative classification from a Christian perspective, see Kalu, *African Pentecostalism. An Introduction* (Oxford: Oxford University Press, 2008), chap. 4.

141 On Harris, see Gordon Mackay Haliburton, *The Prophet Harris* (London: Longman, 1971); Sheila S. Walker, *The Religious Revolution in the Ivory Coast: The Prophet Harris and the Harrist Church* (Chapel Hill: University of North Carolina Press, 1983). On Braide, see G. O. M. Tasie, *Christian Missionary Enterprise in the Niger Delta 1864-1918* (Leiden: E. J. Brill, 1978), chap. v.

142 See Marie-Louise Martin, *Kimbangu: An African Prophet and His Church*. Trans. D. M. Moore (Oxford: Basil Blackwell, 1975 [1971]); on its size, see Anderson, *African Reformation*, 125.

143 The discussion of the Aladuras is drawn primarily from Peel, *Aladura: A Religious Movement among the Yoruba* (London: Oxford University Press, 1968); Turner, *The History of an African Independent Church*, 2 vols. (Oxford: Clarendon Press, 1967); Akinyele Omoyajowo, *Cherubim and Seraphim. The History of an African Independent Church* (New York: NOK Publishers, 1982); Afeosemimi U. Adogame, *Celestial Church of Christ: The Politics of Cultural Identity in a West African Prophetic-Charismatic Movement* (Frankfurt am Main: Peter Lang, 1999).

144 Quoted in Turner, *Independent Church*, 1: 12.

145 Peel, *Aladura*, 164, 169–70, 174. Cf. Adogame, *Celestial Church*, 162; Turner, *Independent Church*, 2: 122–40.

146 Turner, *Independent Church*, 2: 122. Cf. Peel, *Aladura*, 72–73; Adogame, *Celestial Church*, 186–91. On the centrality of the Bible, see Hastings, *Church in Africa*, 527–28, 533.

147 Turner, *African Independent Church*, 1: chap. 5; Kalu, *African Pentecostalism*, 76–77. See also Omoyajowo, *Cherubim*, chap. 4, esp. 82; Peel, *Aladura*, 269–76.

148 Hastings, *Church in Africa*, 516. See also Tasie, *Christian Missionary Enterprise*, 176 on Braide, and Walker, *Religious Revolution*, 37, 40, on Harris.

149 Omoyajowo, *Cherubim*, 16.

150 Omoyjowo, 157; Turner, *African Independent Church*, 2: 79–82.

151 David D. Laitin, *Hegemony and Culture: Politics and Religious Change among the Yoruba* (Chicago: University of Chicago Press, 1986), 87. Adogame, *Celestial Church*, 131.

152 MacGaffey, "Kimbanguism & the Question of Syncretism in Zaïre," in Blakely, van Beek, and Thompson, *Religion in Africa*, 247, offers an interpretation of Kimbanguism's rules from both a native and European perspective.

153 Peel, *Aladura*, 86–88, 216, 228, 293. Cf. Walker, *Religious Revolution* on Harris, 166.

154 Laitin, *Hegemony*, 72. See Deidre Helen Crumbley, "Impurity and Power: Women in Aladura Churches," *Africa*, 62, no. 4 (1992): 505–22.

155 Omoyajowo, *Cherubim*, 154–55.

156 Turner, *African Independent Church*, 2: 70.

157 Peel, *Aladura*, 119–20.

158 Peel, *Aladura*, 96–97; Omoyajowo, *Cherubim*, 60. Cf. Turner, *African Independent Church*, 2: 361–63.

159 Adogame, *Celestial Church*, 146–47.

160 Gray, *Black Christians*, chap. 5; Meyer, *Translating the Devil*, 211–16.

161 Adogame, "Clearing New Paths into an Old Forest: Aladura Christianity in Europe," in Olupona and Rey, *Òrìṣà Devotion*, 256–57.

162 Gabriel I. S. Amadi, "Continuities and Adaptations in the Aladura Movement: the Example of Prophet Wobo and his Clientele in South-Eastern Nigeria," in *New Religious Movements in Nigeria*, ed. Rosalind I. J. Hackett (Lewiston, NY: E. Mellen Press, 1987), 75–91. Cf. Meyer, *Translating the Devil*, 175, for Ghana.

163 Gordon Conwell Seminary, *Christianity in Its Gobal Context*, 24.

164 Issichei, *History of Christianity*, 230.

165 Gordon Conwell Seminary, *Christianity in Its Global Context*, 26.

166 Hastings, *The Church in Africa*, 581. On the White Fathers, 254–55, 564–67.

167 To cite a few examples referenced elsewhere in this chapter: Devaka Premawardhana on Mozambique (n. 5); Derek Peterson on Kenya (n. 14); David Maxwell on Zimbabwe (n. 224).

168 Philip Jenkins, *The Next Christendom*, 3rd ed. (Oxford: Oxford University Press, 2011), 114, lists Protestants as 41 percent, Catholics 42 percent.

169 D. A. Low, *Religion and Society in Buganda, 1875-1900* (Kampala: East African Institute of Social Research [n.d.]), 3; M. S. M Semakukla Kiwanuka, *A History of Buganda from the Foundation of the Kingdom to 1900* (New York: Africana Publishing Corp., 1972), 106–10; Michael Wright, *Buganda in the Heroic Age* (Nairobi: Oxford University Press, 1971), passim.

170 Low, *Religion and Society*, 5. There is some evidence of Mutesa's sincere interest in Christianity, but in the end it was determined by pragmatic considerations (Kiwanuka, *History*, 174–79, 182).

171 Hastings, *Church in Africa*, 375–76.

172 The reference to slavery comes from Aylward Shorter, *Cross & Flag in Africa: The "White Fathers" during the Colonial Scramble (1892-1914)* (Maryknoll, NY: Orbis Books, 2006), 10.

173 Roland Oliver, *The Missionary Factor in East Africa*, 2nd ed. (London: Longmans, 1965), 186. Cf. Shorter, *Cross & Flag*, 142, on the logistics of catechist training.

174 Shorter, *Cross & Flag in Africa*, 185.

175 For a personal recollection of life at Masaka in the 1950s, see Hastings, *African Catholicism*, 69–81.

176 M. Louise Pirouet, *Black Evangelists: The Spread of Christianity in Uganda 1891-1914* (London: Rex Collings, 1978), 36. The book is an account of this process. See also Hastings, *Church in Africa*, 468–75.

177 Hastings, *Church in Africa*, 597; see also Graham Duncan & Ogbu U. Kalu, "*Bakuzufu*: Revival Movements and Indigenous Appropriation in African Christianity," in Kalu, *African Christianity*, 254–57.

178 Derek Peterson, *Ethnic Patriotism*, 38–40, 62, 65.

179 Jenkins, *Next Christendom*, 182.

180 Stanley, *Christianity in the Twentieth Century*, 163–69.

181 Isichei, *History of Christianity*, 103–4. For a perceptive comparative study of Khoi-settler relations with those of the Haudenosaunee of North America, see Elizabeth Elbourne, "Christian Soldiers, Christian Allies: Coercion and Conversion in Southern Africa and Northeastern America at the Turn of the Nineteenth Century," in Lindenfeld and Richardson, *Beyond Conversion*, 79–114.

182 King, *Christian and Muslim*, 154; Isichei, *History of Christianity*, 100.

183 Hastings, *Church in Africa*, 424–27. In Kenya, missions controlled over 90,000 acres in 1910; in Rhodesia over 400,000 in the 1920s.

184 On this and the following, see Richard Elphick, *The Equality of Believers. Protestant Missionaries and Racial Politics of South Africa* (Charlottesville: University of Virginia Press, 2012).

185 Isichei, *History of Christianity*, 100.

186 William H. Worger, "Parsing God: Conversations about the Meaning of Words and Metaphors in Nineteenth-Century Southern Africa," *Journal of African History*, 42, no. 3 (2001): 413–47 (424–28); Norman Etherington, *Preachers Peasants and Politics in Southeast Africa, 1835-1880* (London: Royal Historical Society, 1978), 55–58.

187 Elphick, *Equality*, 37.

188 See Elbourne, *Blood Ground: Colonialism, Missions, and the Contest for Christianity in the Cape Colony and Britain, 1799-1853* (Montreal: McGill-Queen's University Press, 2002).

189 J. B. Peires, "Nxele, Ntsikana and the Origins of the Xhosa Religious Reaction," *Journal of African History*, 20, no. 1 (1979): 51–61.

190 Peires, "The Central Beliefs of the Xhosa Cattle-Killing," *Journal of African History*, 28, no. 1 (1987): 43–63.

191 Quoted in Worger, "Parsing God," 427–28.

192 Hastings, *Church in Africa*, 366. For a picture of Christianity under Khama, see Paul Stuart Landau, *The Realm of the Word: Language, Gender, and Christianity in a Southern African Kingdom* (Portsmouth, NH: Heinemann, 1995).

193 Isichei, *History of Christianity*, 118.

194 Isichei, 114; Comaroff and Comaroff, *Revelation*, 1: 245.

195 Elbourne, *Blood Ground*, 162–64; Etherington, *Preachers*, 92–93.

196 Etherington, *Preachers*, 116–17, 124–26.

197 Elphick, *Equality*, 109, 188.

198 Quoted in Elphick, *Equality*, 279.

199 Etherington, *Preachers*, 67–69, 178–79; Hastings, *Church in Africa*, 364–65; Isichei, *History of Christianity*, 301–2.

200 Elphick, *Equality*, 377, n.37. The figures broke down as follows: 191, 952. Catholics, 135,022 Methodists, 93,207 Anglicans, and 43,578 Dutch Reformed.

201 Bengt G. M. Sundkler, *Bantu Prophets in South Africa*, 2nd ed. (London: Oxford University Press, 1961), 41.

202 J. Mutero Chirenje, *Ethiopianism and Afro-Americans in Southern Africa, 1883-1916* (Baton Rouge, LA: Louisiana State University Press, 1987), 111; chap. 5.

203 Steve De Gruchy, "Religion and Racism: Struggles around Segregation, 'Jim Crow' and Apartheid," in McLeod, *World Christianities*, 394.

204 Anderson, *African Reformation*, 96–97, 100.

205 Joel E. Tishken, *Isaiah Shembe's Prophetic Uhlanga: The Worldview of the Nazareth Baptist Church in Colonial South Africa* (New York: Peter Lang, 2013), 15, 94–95, 119. Shembe's prophetic vision consisted of a direct experience of God, who announced His covenant with "my Brown people" and instructed Shembe to preach to "all nations under the sun" (120). Sundkler, in his pioneering study, claims that Shembe saw himself as an incarnation of Jesus, but Tishken questions this based on evidence. See also Anderson, *African Reformation*, 107–8. Sundkler's perspective was that of a missionary and his statements need to be read with caution.

206 Anderson, *African Reformation*, 103–6; Sundkler, *Bantu Prophets*, 304, 307. On the role of women, see Sundkler, 139–44 and also Landau, *Realm of the Word*, 91–101.

207 Eugene M. Klaaren, "Creation and Apartheid: South African Theology since 1948," in *Christianity in South Africa. A Political, Social, and Cultural History*, ed. Richard Elphick and Rodney Davenport (Berkeley, CA: University of California Press, 1997), 371–72, 377–79.

208 For a summary, see De Gruchy, "Religion and Racism" in McLeod, *World Christianities*, 392–400; Peter Walshe, "Christianity and the Anti-Apartheid Struggle: The Prophetic Voice within Divided Churches," in Elphick and Davenport, *Christianity in South Africa*, 383–99.

209 Anderson, *African Reformation*, 93.

210 Paul Gifford, *Ghana's New Christianity: Pentecostalism in a Globalizing African Economy* (Bloomington: Indiana University Press, 2004), 7, 13; Basil Davidson, *The Black Man's Burden: Africa and the Curse of the Nation-State* (New York: Times Books, 1992), 206; chap. 8. Davidson offers insightful comparisons with Eastern Europe.

211 Maxwell, "Post-Colonial Christianity in Africa," in McLeod, *World Christianities*, 401.

212 Maxwell, "Post-Colonial Christianity," in McLeod, *World Christianities*, 409–10.

213 Meyer, "Christianity in Africa: From African Independent to Pentecostal-Charismatic Churches," *Annual Review of Anthropology* 33 (2004): 447–74 (448).

214 Matthews A. Ojo, "Transnational Religious Networks and Indigenous Pentecostal Missionary Enterprises in the West African Coastal Region," in *Christianity in Africa and the African Diaspora: The Appropriation of a Scattered Heritage*, ed. Afe Adogame, Roswith Gerloff, and Klaus Hock (London Continuum, 2008), 168. The figure refers to Africa as a whole. Cf. Matthew Engelke, "Past Pentecostalism: Notes on Rupture, Realignment, and Everyday Life in Pentecostal and Africa Independent Churches," *Africa* 80, no. 2 (2010): 177–99, who also takes exception to Meyer's characterization, finding similar traits in the Africa Independent Churches.

215 Matthew Schoffeleers, "Pentecostalism and Neo-Traditionalism: The Religious Polarization of a Rural District in Southern Malawi," in Maxwell and Lawrie, *Christianity and the African Imagination*, 263. On the role of women in general, see Kalu, *African Pentecostalism*, chap. 8. For a more skeptical view of the liberating tendencies in these churches, see Philomena N. Mwaura and Damaris S. Parsitau, "Perception of Women's Health and Rights in Christian New Religious Movements in Kenya," in *African Traditions and the Study of Religion in Africa*, ed. Afe Adogame, Ezra Chitando, and Bolaji Bateye (Farnam, UK: Ashgate, 2012), 175–85.

216 J. Kwabena Asamoah-Gyadu, "'I Will Put My Breath in You, and You Will Come to Life': Charismatic Renewal in Ghanaian Mainline Churches and Its Implications for African 'Diasporean' Christianity," in Adogame, Gerloff, and Hock, *Christianity in Africa*, 193–207.

217 See p. 7 above.
218 Ruth Marshall, *Political Spiritualities. The Pentecostal Revolution in Nigeria* (Chicago: University of Chicago Press, 2009), 69–70.
219 Kalu, *African Pentecostalism*, 76–79.
220 Anderson, *African Reformation*, 224–25. Premawardhana, *Faith and Flux*, 65–66.
221 Asamoah-Gyadu, "'Born of Water and the Spirit': Pentecostal/Charismatic Christianity in Africa," in Kalu, *African Christianity*, 350.
222 Marshall, *Political Spiritualities*, 71, 112.
223 Marshall, 85.
224 Martin Meredith, *The Fate of Africa* (New York: Public Affairs, 2005), 580. For another study that emphasizes this point, see Maxwell, *African Gifts of the Spirit: Pentecostalism & the Rise of a Zimbabwean Transnational Religious Movement* (Oxford: James Currey, 2006).
225 Marshall, *Political Spiritualities*, 172.
226 David Martin, "The Relevance of the European Model of Secularization in Latin America and Africa," in *Secularization and the World Religions*, ed. Hans Joas and Klaus Wiegandt, trans. Alex Skinner (Liverpool: Liverpool University Press, 2009), 294.
227 Premawardhana, *Faith and Flux*, 13, 17, 100, 150, 160–61.
228 Meyer, *Translating the Devil*, 211–12, 214–15. Cf. Premawardhana, *Faith and Flux,* chap. 6.
229 Asoamah-Gyadu, "Symbolising Charismatic Influence: Contemporary African Pentecostalism and Its Global Aspirations," in Cabrita, Maxwell, and Wild-Wood, *Relocating World Christianity*, 303.
230 Adogame, "African Christian Communities in Diaspora," in Kalu, *African Christianity*, 437–39.

CHAPTER 5

1 *Christianity in Its Global Context, 1970-2020* (Hamilton, MA: Center for the Study of Global Christianity, Gordon Conwell Theological Seminary, 2013), archive.gordonconwell.edu/ockenga/research/documents/ChristianityinitsGlobalContext.pdf , 42–43.
    Iran is not included. The 2050 projections are from Pew Reseach Center, *The Future of World Religions. Population Growth and Predictions, 2010-2050*, www.pewforum.org/2015/04/02/middle-east-north-africa/, April 2, 2015, [p. 16]. The Pew study, which groups the Middle East together with North Africa but omits Turkey and Iran, lists the following percentages for 2010: 93 percent Muslims, 3.7 percent Christians, and 1.6 percent Jews.
2 Samuel P. Huntington, *The Clash of Civilizations and the Remaking of World Order* (New York: Simon and Schuster, 1996), esp. 209–18; for a rebuttal,

Richard W. Bulliet, *The Case for Islamo-Christian Civilization* (New York: Columbia University Press, 2004). It should be noted that the term *jihad* (struggle), as used in the Qu'ran, is much more variegated in meaning, including inner psychological struggles, than the term "crusade."

3 For example, Bernard Heyberger, *Les Chrétiens du Proche-Orient au Temps de la Réforme Catholique* (Rome: École française de Rome, Palais Farnèse, 1994), 54 (residential proximity in Aleppo); Amnon Cohen, "On the Realities of the *Millet* System: Jerusalem in the Sixteenth Century," in *Christians and Jews in the Ottoman Empire. The Functioning of a Plural Society*, ed. Benjamin Braude and Bernard Lewis. 2 vols. (New York: Holmes and Meier, 1982), 2: 11, 15 (economic ties); Bruce Masters, *Christians and Jews in the Ottoman Arab World: The Roots of Sectarianism* (Cambridge: Cambridge University Press, 2001), 25 (sharing of rituals and saints); Karen Barkey, *Empire of Difference: The Ottomans in Comparative Perspective* (Cambridge: Cambridge University Press, 2008), 41–42 (military collaboration); Chad F. Emmett, *Beyond the Basilica: Christians and Muslims in Nazareth* (Chicago: University of Chicago Press, 1995). Both Masters and Barkey use the term "syncretism."

4 James W. Laine, *Meta-Religion: Religion and Power in World History* (Berkeley: University of California Press, 2014), chaps. 4–5, esp. 81, 103.

5 Quoted in Richard M. Eaton, *Islamic History as Global History* (Washington, DC: American Historical Association, 1990), 22.

6 See Françoise Micheau, "Eastern Christianities (eleventh to fourteenth century): Copts, Melkites, Nestorians and Jacobites," in *Eastern Christianity*, ed. Michael Angold. Vol. 5 of *The Cambridge History of Christianity* (Cambridge: Cambridge University Press, 2006), 375–78; Heyberger, *Les Chrétiens*, 14–17; Sidney H. Griffith, *The Church in the Shadow of the Mosque: Christians and Muslims in the World of Islam* (Princeton, NJ: Princeton University Press, 2008), 131–40.

7 John Tolan, Gilles Veinstein, and Henry Laurens, *Europe and the Islamic World*, trans. Jane Marie Todd (Princeton, NJ: Princeton University Press, 2013), 93.

8 Marshall G.S. Hodgson, *The Venture of Islam: Conscience and History in a World Civilization*. 3 vols. (Chicago: University of Chicago Press, 1974), 1: 226, 252.

9 Griffith, *Church in the Shadow of the Mosque,* 11.

10 Griffith, *Church in the Shadow of the Mosque,* chaps. 4–5.

11 Tarif Khalidi, *The Muslim Jesus: Sayings and Stories in Islamic Literature* (Cambridge, MA: Harvard University Press, 2001), 9–16, 25–26.

12 Albert Hourani, *History of the Arab Peoples* (Cambridge, MA: Harvard University Press, 1991), 187–88. Hodgson, *Venture of Islam*, 1: 447–48; According to Hodgson, reading the Bible was actually forbidden in certain literary circles in the ninth century. For an early Shi'ite text on Jesus, see

Mahmoud Ayoub, *A Muslim View of Christianity*, ed. Irfan A. Omar (Maryknoll, NY: Orbis Books, 2007), chap. 12.

13 Emmett, *Beyond the Basilica*, 21.

14 For the following, see C. E. Bosworth, "The Concept of *Dhimma* in Early Islam," in Braude and Lewis, *Christians and Jews*, 1: 37–51.

15 Masters, *Christians and Jews*, 21–23. It was variously attributed to the second caliph, Umar ibn al-Khattab (634–44) and to the later Umayyad caliph Umar II (717–20).

16 Hodgson *Venture of Islam*, 1: 308; Micheau, "Eastern Christianities," in Angold, *Eastern Christianity*, 401–2.

17 Micheau, "Eastern Christianities," 388; Kenneth Cragg, *The Arab Christian: A History in the Middle East* (London: Mowbray, 1991), 98–105. For a cautionary review of this book, see Griffith, "Kenneth Cragg on Christians and the Call to Islam, *Religious Studies Review* 20, no. 1 (Jan. 1994): 29–35.

18 Robert M. Haddad, *Syrian Christians in Muslim Society: An Interpretation* (Princeton, NJ: Princeton University Press, 1970), 8.

19 Tolan, Veinstein and Laurens, *Europe and the Islamic World*, 102–3. According to Tolan in *Saint Francis and the Sultan. The Curious History of a Christian-Muslim Encounter* (Oxford: Oxford University Press, 2009), 305, "Francis was never a preacher of crusading as Bernard of Clairvaux, for example, had been or as were numerous later Franciscans. But nor does anything indicate any particular hostility toward crusading: in his writings, it is money and women who inspire disgust in him, far more than war."

20 Giuseppe Buffon, "Les Franciscains en Terre Sainte: de l'espace au territoire, entre opposition et adaptation," in *New Faith in Ancient Lands. Western Missions in the Middle East in the Nineteenth and Early Twentieth Centuries*, ed. Heleen Murre-van den Berg (Leiden: Brill, 2006), 75.

21 On the Armenians, see S. Peter Cowe, "The Armenians in the Era of the Crusades 1050-1350," in Angold, *Eastern Christianity*, 424–27.

22 Barkey, *Empire of Difference*, 123–5. Barkey also mentions other cases of forced conversions, 125–28.

23 The origin of the *millet* system is the subject of controversy, centering on whether the early formation of such recognized communities was an *ad hoc* arrangement or the execution of a consistent policy. See Benjamin Braude, "Foundation Myths of the *Millet* System," in Braude and Lewis, *Christians and Jews,* 1: 69–88, who argues for the former, and Barkey, *Empire of Difference*, 115–16, for the latter view.

24 On the contentiousness of the eighteenth century, see Masters, *Christians and Jews*, chap. 4. On the nineteenth century, see the several articles in Braude and Lewis, *Christians and Jews*, 1: parts III and IV.

25 Kemal H. Karpat, "*Millets* and Nationality: the Roots of the Incongruity of Nation and State in the Post-Ottoman Era," in Braude and Lewis, *Christians*

and Jews, 1: 146; Cragg, *The Arab Christian*, 117–18; Febe Armanios, *Coptic Christianity in Ottoman Egypt* (Oxford: Oxford University Press, 2011), 23. According to Armanios, relations between Armenians and Copts in Cairo were friendly as they viewed themselves as "fellow anti-Chalcednonians" (20).

26 Tijana Krstić, *Contested Conversions to Islam: Narratives of Religious Change in the Early Modern Ottoman Empire* (Stanford, CA: Stanford University Press, 2011), 13–14.

27 Krstić, *Contested Conversions to Islam*, 14, 168–72; Barkey, *Empire of Difference*, 70–72.

28 Heyberger, *Les Chrétiens*, chap. 6; Tolan, Veinstein and Laurens, *Europe and the Islamic World*, chap. 8; Charles A. Frazee, *Catholics and Sultans: The Church and the Ottoman Empire 1453-1923* (Cambridge: Cambridge University Press, 1983), chap. 1. According to Heyberger, the number of printed books in French devoted to the Turks between 1480 and 1609 were twice as many as devoted to the Americas (193).

29 Tolan, Veinstein and Laurens, *Europe and the Islamic World*, 178–81. The Ottomans also used the term *gazā*, referring to more limited campaigns, but with the same end in view, namely extending the reach of Islam at the expense of the infidel.

30 Krstić, *Contested Conversions to Islam*, chap. 5.

31 Krstić, *Contested Conversions to Islam*, chap. 3.

32 Paschalis M. Kitromilides, "Orthodoxy and the west: Reformation to Enlightenment," in Angold, *Eastern Christianity*, 188–201.

33 Frazee, *Catholics and Sultans*, 139.

34 Tolan, Veinstein and Laurens, *Europe and the Islamic World*, 211–13.

35 Haddad, *Syrian Christians*, 31–32.

36 Tolan, Veinstein, and Laurens, *Europe and the Islamic World*, 216–18, 233.

37 Frazee, *Catholics and Sultans*, 26–28, 67–68; Tolan, Veinstein, and Laurens, *Europe and the Islamic World*, 231.

38 Masters, *Christians and Jews*, 87.

39 Masters, *Christians and Jews*, 82.

40 Heyberger, *Les Chrétiens*, 459

41 Heyberger, *Les Chrétiens*, 366.

42 Heyberger, *Les Chrétiens*, 434, 479–80.

43 Masters, *Christians and Jews*, 96.

44 Ussama Makdisi, *Artillery of Heaven: American Missionaries and the Failed Conversion of the Middle East* (Ithaca, NY: Cornell University Press, 2008), chap. 2; Heyberger, *Les Chrétiens*, 130–32.

45 Frazee, *Catholics and Sultans*, 140–41; Heyberger, *Les Chrétiens*, 189.

46 Heyberger, *Les Chrétiens*, 408–9. The numbers fluctuated between 9 and 24 in the early years, peaking between 1690 and 1730.

47 Heyberger, *Les Chrétiens*, 409, my translation. A list of written materials sent from Rome to the Maronite patriarch includes, in addition to New Testaments

and breviaries, an Arabic translation of *Imitatio Christi* by Thomas A Kempis. (406–7).

48 Already in the fifteenth century, the Maronites had 110 copyists (Heyberger, *Les Chrétiens*, 146).

49 Heyberger, *Les Chrétiens*, 209.

50 Frazee, *Catholics and Sultans*, 148.

51 Frazee, *Catholics and Sultans*, 60–63, 145–48; Heyberger, *Les Chrétiens*, 216.

52 Heyberger, 173–75. For a modern account of the different interpretations of pilgrimage, see Glenn Bowman, "Contemporary Christian Pilgrimage to the Holy Land," in *Palestinian Christians: Religion, Politics, and Society in the Holy Land*, ed. Anthony O'Mahony (London: Melisende, 1999), 141–65.

53 O'Mahony, "Coptic Christianity in Modern Egypt," in Angold, *Eastern Christianity*, 5: 488–92; Doris Behrens-Abouseif, "The Political Situation of the Copts, 1798-1823," in Braude and Lewis, *Christians and Jews*, 2: 186–87; Thomas Philipp, "Image and Self-Image of the Syrians in Egypt: From the Early Eighteenth Century to the Reign of Muhammad Ali," in Braude and Lewis, 2: 167–84; Frazee, *Catholics and Sultans*, 63–64, 148–50, 216–19.

54 Armanios, *Coptic Christianity*, chap. 5.

55 Armanios, *Coptic Christianity*, 99–103.

56 Haddad, *Syrian Christians*, 50.

57 Masters, *Christians and Jews*, 113–15; Heyberger, *Les Chrétiens*, 516–22; Makdisi, *Artillery of Heaven*, 77–78. Masters suggests that her mystical beliefs may have had Sufi roots; he views the movement as an example of popular syncretism.

58 This is the conclusion both of Masters, *Christians and Jews*, 97, 112, and Heyberger, *Les Chrétiens*, 155–60, 557–58.

59 Edward W. Said, *Orientalism* (New York: Random House, 1979), 70.

60 See for example , Makdisi, "Reclaiming the Land of the Bible: Missionaries, Secularism, and Evangelical Modernity," *American Historical Review* 102, no. 3 (June 1997): 680–713.

61 Heather J. Sharkey, *A History of Muslims, Christians, and Jews in the Middle East* (Cambridge: Cambridge University Press, 2017), 164–65.

62 This survey makes no claims to completeness. Important cases such as northern Africa and western Anatolia are left out.

63 Samil Khalaf, "Communal Conflict in Nineteenth-Century Lebanon," in Braude and Lewis, *Christians and Jews*, 2: 129; Masters, *Christians and Jews*, 130.

64 Thomas Philipp, "Image and Self-Image," in Braude and Lewis, *Christians and Jews*, 2: 175, 177; Masters, *Christians and Jews*, 157.

65 Khalaf, "Communal Conflict," in Braude and Lewis, *Christians and Jews*, 2: 109–10.

66 Imperial rescript, 1856, in *The Human Record: Sources of Global History*, ed. Alfred J. Andrea and James H. Overfield, 3rd ed. (Boston, MA: Houghton

Mifflin, 1998), 311. For an analysis of these reforms, see Carter Vaughn Findley, *Turkey, Islam, Nationalism, and Modernity* (New Haven, CT: Yale University Press, 2010), 44–45, 91–93 . For changing Ottoman attitudes toward the West in the early nineteenth century, see Cemil Aydin, *The Politics of Anti-Westernism in Asia: Vision of World Order in Pan-Islamic and Pan-Asian Thought* (New York: Columbia University Press, 2007), 16–24.

67 Master, *Christians and Jews*, 158–61. Cf. 162 on a similar incident in Nablus, a Palestinian market town.

68 On the following, see Makdisi, *The Culture of Sectarianism: Community, History and Violence in Nineteenth-Century Ottoman Lebanon* (Berkeley: University of California Press, 2000), chaps. 5–6.

69 Sharkey, *History*, notes that only Christians in poorer neighborhoods were spared, underlining the economic factor (165).

70 Heleen Murre-van den Berg, "The Middle East: western missions and the Eastern churches, Islam and Judaism," in *World Christianities, c. 1815-1914*, ed. Sheridan Gilley and Brian Stanley. Vol. 8 of *The Cambridge History of Christianity* (Cambridge: Cambridge University Press, 2006), 466. She mentions Turkey and Iran as the recipients, so that Syria may well have represented an additional amount.

71 See Makdisi, *Culture of Sectarianism*, 22–23, 88–94; A. L. Tibawi, *American Interests in Syria, 1800-1901* (Oxford: Clarendon Press, 1966), 92–95.

72 Makdisi, "Reclaiming the Land of the Bible," 700–703 .

73 So concludes Murre-van den Berg in her introduction to *New Faith in Ancient Lands*, 16.

74 There is some dispute over how important this goal was to American missionaries, although their initial aim was to establish a mission in Jerusalem. See Christine Lindner, "The Flexibility of Home. Exploring the Spaces and Definitions of the Home and Family Employed by the ABCFM Missionaries in Ottoman Syria from 1823 to 1860," in *American Missionaries and the Middle East: Foundational Encounters*, ed. Mehmet Ali Dogan and Heather J. Sharkey (Salt Lake City: University of Utah Press, 2011), 36. Most accounts, however, include conversion of the Jews as an initial goal.

75 Tibawi, *British Interests in Palestine, 1800-1901* (Oxford: Oxford University Press, 1961), 64. Cf. a similar anathema in Baghdad, home of a sizeable and wealthy Jewish community: Reeva Spector Simon, "The Case of the Curse: The London Society for Promoting Christianity amongst the Jews, and the Jews of Baghdad," in *Altruism and Imperialism: Western Cultural and Religious Missions in the Middle East*, ed. Eleanor H. Tejirian and Reeva Spector Simon (New York: Middle East Institute, Columbia University, 2002), 53.

76 For example, the Sarah Society, founded in 1854 in Jerusalem by three English women, one of whom was murdered in 1858 under mysterious circumstances.

See Nancy L. Stockdale, "Danger and the Missionary Enterprise: The Murder of Miss Matilda Creasy," in Murre-van den Berg, *New Faith in Ancient Lands*, 113–32.

77 Emmett, *Beyond the Basilica*, 25.

78 Makdisi, *Artillery of Heaven*, 102.

79 Makdisi, *Artillery of Heaven*, 2–3.

80 Tibawi, *American Interests*, 42, 65; Khalaf, "On Doing Much with Little Noise: Early Encounters Of Protestant Missionaries in Lebanon," in Tejirian and Simon, *Altruism and Imperialism*, 18–19.

81 Khalaf, "On Doing Much," 26.

82 Tibawi, *American Interests*, 143.

83 Ellen Fleischmann, "Evangelization or Education: American Protestant Missionaries, the American Board, and the Girls and Women of Syria (1830-1910)," in Murre-van den Berg, *New Faith in Ancient Lands*, 265–69.

84 Khalaf, "On Doing Much," in Tejirian and Simon, *Altruism and Imperialism*, 21; and Lindner, "Flexibility of Home," in Dogan and Sharkey, *American Missionaries*, 48–51.

85 Tibawi, *American Interests*, 121; Habib Badr, "American Protestant Missionary Beginnings in Beirut and Istanbul: Policy, Politics, Practice, and Response," in Murre-van den Berg, *New Faith in Ancient Lands*, 234–25.

86 Tibawi, *American Interests*, 54–57, 69–70, 147–49.

87 Makdisi, *Culture of Sectarianism*, 89–94.

88 Marwa Elshakry, "The Gospel of Science and American Evangelism in Late Ottoman Beirut," in Dogan and Sharkey, *American Missionaries*, 176.

89 Quoted in Tibawi, *American Interests*, 134.

90 Deanna F. Womack, "Conversion, Controversy and Cultural Production. Syrian Protestants, American Missionaries, and the Arabic Press, ca. 1870-1915." (PhD. diss., Princeton Theological Seminary, 2015), 155.

91 Makdisi, *Artillery of Heaven*, 193, 196–99, 206–8; Jens Hanssen, *Fin de Siècle Beirut: The Making of an Ottoman Provincial Capital* (Oxford: Clarendon Press, 2005), 164–68.

92 Tibawi, *American Interests*, 183. On a general assessment of Abdulhamid's rule, see Findley, *Turkey, Islam, Nationalism*, chap. 3; Sharkey, *History*, chap. 5.

93 The main proponent of the missionary role was George Antonius in *The Arab Awakening: The Story of the Arab National Movement* (New York: G.P. Putnam's Sons, 1946); Tibawi has taken pains to refute this, showing that the missionary press did *not* publish works of Arab literature (*American Interests*, 252–53). See also Masters, *Christians and Jews*, 173–74.

94 See Hourani, *Arabic Thought in the Liberal Age 1798-1939* (London: Oxford University Press, 1962), 114; Carolyn McCue Goffman, "Masking the Mission: Cultural Conversion at the American College for Girls," in Tejirian and Simon, *Altruism and Imperialism*, 93, 119.

95 On fiction, see Elizabeth M. Holt, "Narrative and the Reading Public in 1870s Beirut," *Journal of Arabic Literature* 40, no. 1 (2009): 37–70 (66); on emigration, Akram Fouad Khater, *Inventing Home: Emigration, Gender, and the Middle Class in Lebanon, 1870-1920* (Berkeley: University of California Press, 2001), 1, 8. Among the emigrants was the Maronite poet Kahlil Gibran.

96 Khater, 137–38.

97 Quoted in Fleischmann, "Evangelization," in Murre-van den Berg, *New Faith in Ancient Lands*, 280.

98 Letter of Henry Jessup, 6 January 1863, quoted in Tibawi, *American Interests*, 168; subcommittee report, 23 January 1862, ibid., 161. Protestants had previously established Robert College in Istanbul in 1863.

99 Womack, *Protestants, Gender and the Arab Renaissance in Late Ottoman Syria* (Edinburgh: Edinburgh University Press, 2019), chap. 3; Womack and Lindner, "'Pick Up the Pearls of Knowledge and Adorn Ourselves with the Jewelry of Literature': An Analysis of Three Arab Woman Writers in *Al Nashra al-Usbu'iya*," *Living Stones [of the Holy Land Trust] Yearbook*, 2014, 148–49. The articles were entitled "Diligence and Perseverance," "Caution and Attentiveness," and "The Necessity of Libraries." See also Elshakry, "Gospel of Science," in Dogan and Sharkey, *American Missionaries*, 183–90.

100 Womack, *Protestants*, 109–11.

101 On these attempts, see Sharkey, *History*, 222–26.

102 The quote is from the pamphlet *Bulgarian Horrors and the Question of the East* (1876), quoted in Jeremy Salt, *Imperialism, Evangelism and the Ottoman Armenians, 1878-1896* (London: Frank Cass, 1993), 45; the cartoon is reproduced on p. 126. On missionary attitudes toward Islam, see Andrew Porter, *Religion versus Empire? British Protestant Missionaries and Overseas Expansion, 1700-1914* (Manchester: Manchester University Press, 2004), 292–99.

103 Tibawi, *American Interests*, 171–76, 254–70.

104 E.g., also among Syrian Protestants. See Womack, *Protestants*, chap. 4.

105 Elie Kedourie, "The American University of Beirut," in *Arabic Political Memoirs and Other Studies* (London: Frank Cass, 1974), 67; Philippe Bourmaud, "Public Space and Private Spheres: the Foundation of St Luke's Hospital of Nablus by the CMS (1891–1901), in Murre-van den Berg, *New Faith in Ancient Lands*, 132–50.

106 Elshakry, "Gospel of Science," in Dogan and Sharkey, *American Missionaries*, 190–96.

107 Aydin, *Politics of Anti-Westernism*, 82–89.

108 Aydin, 64–68.

109 Aydin, 62–63; Findley, *Turkey, Islam, Nationalism*, 148–50; Salt, *Imperialism*, 147.

110 Sharkey, *History*, 208, 238–42.
111 There were estimated 5,000–6,000 Catholic Copts in 1980 and 5355 Evangelicals (Presbyterians) in 1897. See Frazee, *Catholics and Sultans*, 310; Sharkey, *American Evangelicals in Egypt: Missionary Encounters in an Age of Empire* (Princeton, NJ: Princeton University Press, 2008), 18, 71–83.
112 Sharkey, "American Missionaries, the Arabic Bible, and Coptic Reform in Late Nineteenth-Century Egypt," in Dogan and Sharkey, *American Missionaries*, 243. Sharkey has also studied the distribution of Bibles throughout North Africa in a multitude of vernacular dialects that could appeal to the rural poor and especially women. See her "The Gospel in Arabic Tongues. British Bible Distribution, Evangelical mission, and Language Politics in North Africa," in *Cultural Conversions*, ed. Sharkey (Syracuse, NY: Syracuse University Press, 2013), 203–21. On the British missionary effort, see Paul D. Sedra, "Modernity's Mission. Evangelical Efforts to Discipline the Nineteenth-Century Coptic Community," in Tejirian and Simon, *Altruism and Imperialism*, 208–35. On the influx of Catholics, Frazee, *Catholics and Sultans*, 308–11.
113 Sharkey, "American Missionaries," in Dogan and Sharkey, *American Missionaries*, 245.
114 Sedra, "Modernity's Mission," in Tejirian and Simon, *Altruism and Imperiaism*, 230.
115 Behrens-Abouseif, "Political Situation of the Copts," in Braude and Lewis, *Christians and Jews*, 2: 194–99.
116 On the terminological complexity, see John Joseph, *The Modern Assyrians of the Middle East: Encounters with Western Christian Missions, Archaeologists, and Colonial Powers* (Leiden: Brill, 2000), 1–20; Adam Becker, *Revival and Awakening: American Evangelical Missionaries in Iran and the Origins of Assyrian Nationalism* (Chicago: University of Chicago Press, 2015), 48–50.
117 Joseph, *Modern Assyrians*, chap. 3.
118 Tejirian and Simon, *Conflict, Conquest, and Conversion: Two Thousand Years of Christian Missions in the Middle East* (New York: Columbia University Press, 2012), 134.
119 Joseph, *Modern Assyrians*, 138; Becker, *Renewal and Awakening*, passim.
120 Becker, chap. 8; Joseph, *Modern Assyrians*, 15–26.
121 Becker, *Renewal and Awakening*, 1–4, 286–95.
122 E.g., Kenneth Scott Latourette, *A History of the Expansion of Christianity*, 7 vols. (New York: Harper & Brothers, 1937–45) 6: 62–63; Murre-van den Berg, "The Middle East," in Sheridan and Gilley, *World Christianities, c. 1815-1914*, 470.
123 Cowe, "Church and Diaspora: the Case of the Armenians," in Angold, *Eastern Christianity*, 439; Tejirian and Simon, *Conflict*, 64; Frazee, *Catholics and Sultans*, 223.

124 Hagop Barsoumian, "The Dual Role of the Armenian *Amira* Class within the Ottoman Government and the Armenian *Millet* (1750–1850), in Braude and Lewis, *Christians and Jews*, 1: 179; Cemal Yetkiner, "At the Center of the Debate. Bebek Seminary and the Educational Policy of the American Board of Commissioners for Foreign Missions (1840-1860)," in Dogan and Sharkey, *American Missionaries*, 74; Habib Badr, "American Protestant Missionary Beginnings," in Murre-van den Berg, *New Faith in Ancient Lands*, 221.

125 Giragos H. Chopourian, *The Armenian Evangelical Reformation: Causes and Effects* (New York: Armenian Missionary Association of America, 1972), 92–94. Communicant members increased from 140 in 1846 to 13,891 in 1914.

126 Findley, "The Acid Test of Ottomanism: The Acceptance of Non-Muslims in the Late Ottoman Bureaucracy," in Braude and Lewis, *Christians and Jews*, 1: 343, 347.

127 See Avedis K. Sanjian, *The Armenian Communities in Syria under Ottoman Dominion* (Cambridge, MA: Harvard University Press, 1965), 37–45.

128 Barbara J. Merguerian, "'Missions in Eden': Shaping the Educational and Social Program for the Armenians in Eastern Turkey (1855-1895)," in Murre-van den Berg, ed., *New Faith in Ancient Lands*, 241–61.

129 Tejirian and Simon, *Conflict*, 153.

130 Ronald Grigor Suny, *"They Can Live in the Desert but Nowhere Else": A History of the Armenian Genocide* (Princeton, NJ: Princeton University Press, 2015), 131. Suny believes that the massacres of 1895–96 were done largely by government troops. Heather Sharkey, on the other hand, doubts that the sultan personally ordered the killings, though he did nothing to stop them (*History*, 267–70).

131 David Gaunt, Naures Atto, and Soner O. Barthoma, eds., "Introduction," in *Let Them Not Return: Sayfo—The Genocide against the Assyrian, Syriac and Chaldean Christians in the Ottoman Empire* (New York: Berghahn, 2017), 19–20. According to these authors, "Genocide in the Ottoman Empire was not accomplished in the set-up of a modern bureaucratic system as was the Jewish Holocaust, but depended instead mainly in the enthusiasm of brutal local leaders who could build up an *ad hoc* organization of volunteer death squads, reinforced in places by pardoned criminals" (13–14).

132 Salt, *Imperialism*, 117, 133.

133 Michael B. Oren, *Power, Faith, and Fantasy: America and the Middle East, 1776 to the Present* (New York: Norton, 2007), 285; Tejirian and Simon, *Conflict*, 138. As might be expected the massacres prompted a massive outpouring of sympathy, outrage, and aid from the United States.

134 Suny, *"They Can Live in the Desert,"* 172.

135 Latourette, *History*, 7: 272.

136 Findley, *Turkey, Islam, Nationalism*, 202.
137 Aydin, *Politics of Anti-Westernism*, 92–97; Tolan, Veinstein, and Laurens, *Europe and the Islamic World*, 345–48; 356–59. One might also mention the Austrian annexation of Bosnia and the French penetration of Morocco.
138 Tejirian and Simon, *Conflict*, 170–72.
139 Michael Zirinsky, "Onward Christian Soldiers: Presbyterian Missionaries and the Ambiguous Origins of American Relations with Iran," in Tejirian and Simon, *Altruism and Imperialism*, 242–43.
140 The literature on the Armenian genocide is abundant; the Syrian Orthodox story is much less well known, but a number of documentary sources that appeared in the 1980s and 1990s have provided a clear picture. As with the Armenians, these massacres were also foreshadowed by earlier ones in 1895. Part of the confusion stems from the fact that Syrian Orthodox were found throughout the Middle East, not exclusively or even primarily in Syria, and are sometimes lumped together with Assyrians. See Sebastian Brock, "The Syrian Orthodox Church in Modern History," in *Christianity in the Middle East: Studies in Modern History, Theology, and Politics,* ed. Anthony O'Mahony (London: Melisende, 2008), 17–38.
    On the Lebanese Christians, O'Mahony writes in "Syriac Christianity in the Modern Middle East," in Angold, *Eastern Christianity*, 522, "To the estimated 100,000 murdered between 1900 and 1914 must be added the countless victims of the atrocities committed under the aegis of the Young Turks, which only came to an end with the arrival in September 1918 of General Allenby and the forces under his command. To this must be added the victims of famine and disease which affected Christian and Muslim alike."
141 Oren, *Power, Faith, and Fantasy*, 330. For similar statements made to the American ambassador, see Suny, *"They Can Live in the Desert ... ,"* 268–70.
142 Brock, "Syrian Orthodox Church," in O'Mahony, *Christianity in the Middle East,* 25.
143 Joseph, *Modern Assyrians*, 139–50.
144 Gaunt, Atto, and Barthoma, "Introduction," in *Let Them Not Return*, 1. These authors classify the Syrian Orthodox as Assyrians as well.
145 Tejirian and Simon, *Conflict*, 180; Keith David Watenpaugh, *Bread from Stones: The Middle East and the Making of Modern Humanitarianism* (Berkeley: University of California Press, 2015), 50–51.
146 Quoted in Tolan, Veinstein, and Laurens, *Europe and the Islamic World*, 366.
147 On the fate of the Armenians in this period, see Watenpaugh, *Bread from Stones*, chaps. 4–6.
148 Latourette, *History*, 7: 263.
149 Joseph, *Modern Assyrians*, chaps. 7–10.

150 Latourette, *History*, 7: 267–69.

151 Joseph, *Modern Assyrians*, 207–10.

152 Elizabeth Thompson, "Neither Conspiracy nor Hypocrisy. The Jesuits and the French Mandate in Syria and Lebanon," in Tejirian and Simon, *Altruism and Imperialism*, 66–67.

153 Tejirian and Simon, *Altruism and Imperialism*, 84. On literacy rates, see William Harris, *Lebanon: A History, 600-2011* (Oxford: Oxford University Press, 2012), 238.

154 Tejirian and Simon, *Conflict*, 193.

155 Edward W. Said, *Out of Place: A Memoir* (New York: Alfred A. Knopf, 1999), 3. See also Laura Robson, "Church versus Country. Palestinian Arab Episcopalians, Nationalism, and Revolt, 1936-39," in Sharkey, *Cultural Conversions*, 49-66.

156 O'Mahony, "Palestinian Christians: Religion, Politics, Nationalism and Islam," in *Palestinian Christians*, 46–47.

157 Robson, "Church versus Country," in Sharkey, ed., *Cultural Conversions*, 65.

158 See Michael Dumper, "Faith and Statecraft: Church-State Relations in Jerusalem after 1948," in O'Mahony, *Palestinian Christians*, 56–81; Michael Prior, CM, "'You Will Be My Witnesses in Jerusalem, in all Judea and Samaria, and to the Ends of the Earth.' A Christian Perspective on Jerusalem," ibid., 118.

159 Tejirian and Simon, *Conflict*, 196.

160 Umar Ryad, "Muslim Response to Missionary Activities in Egypt: with a Special Reference to the Al-Azhar High Corps of 'Ulama (1925-1935)," in Murre-van den Berg, *New Faith in Ancient Lands*, 286–87, 292–97.

161 Sharkey, *American Evangelicals*, 129; see also Beth Baron, "The Port Said Orphan Scandal of 1933. Colonialism, Islamism, and the Egyptian Welfare State," in Sharkey, *Cultural Conversions*, 121–38. Baron points out that Hasan had contact with a member of the Brotherhood before the actual caning occurred.

162 Sharkey, *American Evangelicals*, 131–33, 183–85, 206.

163 Sharkey, *American Evangelicals*, 197.

164 Sharkey, "Gospel in Arabic Tongues," in *Cultural Conversions*, 218–21.

165 Sharkey, *American Evangelicals*, 211.

166 Karl Pinggéra, "Koptisches Christentum im subsaharischen Afrika," in *Polycentric Structures in the History of World Christianity*, ed. Klaus Koschorke and Adrian Hermann (Wiesbaden: Harrassowitz, 2014), 347–57.

167 Yaakov Ariel, *An Unusual Relationship. Evangelical Christians and Jews* (New York: New York University Press, 2013), chap. 12; "Messianic Judaism," Wikipedia, en.wikipedia.org/wiki/Messianic_Judaism.

168 David Thomas, "Relations between Christians and Muslims," in *World Christianities, c. 1914-c.2000*, ed. Hugh McLeod. Vol. 9 of *The*

Cambridge History of Christianity (Cambridge: Cambridge University Press, 2006), 494.

169 Thomas, 500–501.

170 Ayoub, *A Muslim View of Christianity*, 69; see chap. 16 for his discussion of Pope John Paul II on Islam.

171 Tejirian and Simon, *Conflict*, 207, although this trend is currently offset by the influx of migrant workers from Asia to the region, who often happen to be Christian (thus the percentage of Christians in Saudi Arabia has increased from .3 percent in 1970 to a projected 4.6 percent in 2020 (*Christianity in Its Global Context*, 42.) Lebanon might be seen as an exception, with Christians comprising 33.5% of its population (2020 projected), but down from 62.3 percent in 1970 (ibid.). On the Assyrian Christians, see Naures Atto, "The Death Throes of Indigenous Christians in the Middle East: Assyrians Living under the Islamic State," in Joel Cabrita, David Maxwell, and Emma Wild-Wood, eds., *Relocating World Christianity* (Leiden: Brill, 2017), 281–301.

172 Atto, 293–98.

173 Heyberger, "Eastern Christians, Islam, and the West: A Connected History," *International Journal of Middle East Studies* 42, no. 3 (2010), 475–78 (478).

CHAPTER 6

1 Heinrich von Stietencron, "Hinduism: On the Proper Use of a Deceptive Term," in *Hinduism Reconsidered*, ed. G. Sontheimer and H. Kulke (Delhi: Manohar, 1997), 11–12. Richard M. Eaton, in his edited volume, *India's Islamic Traditions, 711-1750* (New Delhi: Oxford University Press, 2003), 18, has effectively criticized the notion that Islam spread primarily by military conquest, or that anything resembling conversion in the Christian sense occurred. Rather he portrays it as a "slow, almost glacial process or religious evolution" which took place primarily among frontier peoples. The use of the term by non-Muslims occurred equally gradually, the first written instance occurring in 1352. See Cynthia Talbot, "Inscribing the Other, Inscribing the Self: Hindu-Muslim Identities in Pre-Colonial India," ibid., 90.

2 Stietencron, "Hinduism," 12–13.

3 Geoffrey A. Oddie, "Constructing 'Hinduism': The Impact of the Protestant Missionary Movement on Hindu self-Understanding," in *Christians and Missionaries in India: Cross Cultural Communication Since 1500*, ed. Robert Eric Frykenberg (Grand Rapids, MI: Eerdmans, 2003), 155–82. For initial use of the term, see Steven Prothero, *God Is Not One* (New York: HarperCollins, 2010), 354.

4 See Stietencron, "Hinduism," 16, 20. Stietencron insisted that Hinduism should continue to refer to a group of religions, not just one. Some years later, however, he modified this position, pointing to several common features: a belief in hierarchy, rebirth, and individual responsibility for maintaining order

in the world. See his "Hinduism," in *Secularization and the World Religions*, ed. Hans Joas and Klaus Wiegandt (Liverpool: Liverpool University Press, 2009), 134.

5 The antecedents of *bhakti* go back much earlier to the *Bhagavad Gita* (c. 200 BCE).

6 See Günther-Dietz Sontheimer, "Hinduism: The Five Components and Their Interaction," in Sontheimer and Kulke, *Hinduism Reconsidered*, 304–23. Sontheimer's five components are: (1) Brahmins and their teaching, (2) asceticism and renunciation, (3) tribal religion, (4) folk religion, (5) *bhakti*.

7 Oddie, "Constructing 'Hinduism,'" 156.

8 Frykenberg, *Christianity in India from Beginnings to the Present* (Oxford: Oxford University Press, 2008), 112.

9 Susan Bayly, *Saints, Goddesses and Kings: Muslims and Christians in South Indian Society 1700-1900* (Cambridge: Cambridge University Press, 1989), 249–52, 265, 277. Marshall Hodgson, in his magisterial study of Islam, found the same general relationship to hold between Muslims and Hindus. See his *The Venture of Islam. Conscience and History in a World Civilization*, 3 vols. (Chicago: University of Chicago Press, 1974), 3: 59–60.

10 Corinne G. Dempsey, "Lessons in Miracles from Kerala, South India: Stories of Three "Christian" Saints," in *Popular Christianity in India: Riting [sic] between the Lines*, ed. Selva J. Raj and Corinne G. Dempsey, eds. (Albany: State University of New York Press, 2002), 11; Frykenberg, *Christianity in India*, 103.

11 Stephen Neill, *A History of Christianity in India: The Beginnings to AD 1707* (Cambridge: Cambridge University Press, 1984), 226, 230.

12 Neill, 239–40; Frykenberg, *Christianity in India*, 135.

13 See Duncan B. Forrester, *Caste and Christianity: Attitudes and Policies on Caste of Anglo-Saxon Protestant Missionaries in India* (London: Curzon Press, 1980), esp. chap. 1.

14 Frykenberg, *Christianity in India*, 113.

15 Wendy Doniger, "Foreword," in Raj and Dempsey, *Popular Christianity*, xvi-xvii; Raj, "The Ganges, The Jordan, and the Mountain: The Three Strands of Santal Popular Catholicism," ibid., 47–50. Raj discerns three distinct strategies in his case study: (1) inclusion, or incorporation of Catholic elements into tribal practices or vice versa; (2) parallelism, the simultaneous coexistence of two practices; (3) traditionalization, the adoption of foreign practices after their meaning has been transformed. Raj favors the label of syncretism to cover these three, while Doniger does not.

16 Frykenberg, *Christianity in India*, 138.

17 Margaret Meibohm, "Past Selves and Present Others: The Ritual Construction of Identity at a Catholic Festival in India," in Raj and Dempsey, *Popular Christianity*, 62–63. See also Joanne Punzo Waghorne, "Chariots of the God/s: Riding the Line between Hindu and Christian," ibid., 11–37. An extensive

treatment of the Paravas is found in Bayly, *Saints, Goddesses and Kings*, chap. 9. Also valuable is David Mosse, "The Politics of Religious Synthesis. Roman Catholicism and Hindu Village Society in Tamil Nadu, India," in *Syncretism/Anti-Syncretism*, ed. Charles Stewart and Rosalind Shaw (London: Routledge, 1994), 85–107; Mosse, "Possession and Confession. Affliction and Sacred Power in Colonial and Contemporary Catholic South India," in *The Anthropology of Christianity*, ed. Fenella Cannell (Durham, NC: Duke University Press, 2006), 99–133, and Cecilia Busby, "Renewable Icons: Concepts of Religious Power in a Fishing Village in South India," ibid., 77–98.

18 Although the massive Velankanni festival is open to all castes, each local village group has a traditional ritual role to play on separate days; as the festival has grown, new layers of organization have been added to this (Meibohm, "Past Selves," 70–76). Cf. Raj's treatment of another pilgrimage at the shrine of a Jesuit martyr, St. John de Britto, "Transgressing Boundaries, Transcending Turner: The Pilgrimage Tradition at the Shrine of St. John de Britto," in Raj and Dempsey, *Popular Christianity*, 85–111. Raj argues that Victor Turner's notion of communitas at such festivals is qualified by the maintenance of caste distinctions.

19 Bayly, *Saints, Goddesses and Kings*, 360, 370. Cf. Mosse, "Politics of Religious Synthesis," in *Syncretism/Anti-Syncretism*, 93–96, for another example.

20 Bayly, *Saints, Goddesses and Kings*, 438; Louis Dumont, *Homo Hierarchicus: The Caste System and Its Implications*, rev. ed., transl. Mark Sainsbury, Louis Dumont, and Basia Gulati (Chicago: University of Chicago Press, 1980), 204, 408.

21 Frykenberg, *Christianity in India*, 167.

22 Heike Liebau, "Country Priests, Catechists and Schoolmasters as Cultural, Religious, and Social Middlemen in the Context of the Tranquebar Mission," in Frykenberg, *Christians and Missionaries in India*, 70; Frykenberg, *Christianity in India*, 167.

23 Neill, *A History of Christianity in India, 1707-1858* (Cambridge: Cambridge University Press, 1985), 335.

24 Hephzibah Israel, *Religious Transactions in Colonial South India: Language, Translation, and the Making of Protestant Identity* (New York: Palgrave Macmillan, 2011), 111.

25 Dennis Hudson, *Protestant Origins in India: Tamil Evangelical Christians, 1706-1835* (Grand Rapids MI: Eerdmans, 2000), 47, 90–91, 108–9.

26 Dumont, *Homo Hierarchicus*, 24–25; on the other examples, see chaps. 2, p. 74 and 7 below, p. 221. [AU: Incomplete reference.]

27 Oddie, *Hindu and Christian in South-East India* (London: Curzon Press, 1991), 171–72; Bayly, *Saints, Goddesses and Kings*, 410–12. The Vellalars were technically classified as Sudras, the lowliest of the four Vedic caste groupings,

but this belies their actual status. According to Bayly, the title "Vellalar" was often conferred by the Jesuits themselves as a means of recruitment.

28 See Rupa Viswanath, *The Pariah Problem: Caste, Religion and the Social in Modern India* (New York: Columbia University Press, 2014), who develops this theme for the late nineteenth and early twentieth centuries.

29 Hudson, *Protestant Origins*, 21, 38, 90, 92–94.

30 Frykenberg, *Christianity in India* 209–12, 220–21. Cf. Oddie, *Hindu and Christian*, chap. 8, esp. 153, which traces the continued growth of Christians in Tamil country to 1900.

31 See Eliza F. Kent, *Converting Women: Gender and Protestant Christianities in Colonial South India* (Oxford: Oxford University Press, 2004), 18–22.

32 Israel, *Religious Transactions*, 20, 198.

33 See Indira Viswanathan Peterson, "*Bethlehem Kuravanci* of Vedanayaka Sastri of Tanjore: The Cultural Discourses of an Early-Nineteenth-Century Tamil Christian Poem," in *Christians, Cultural Interactions, and India's Religious Traditions*, ed. Judith M. Brown and Robert Eric Frykenberg (Grand Rapids, MI: Eerdmans, 2002), 9–36; also Israel, *Religious Transactions*, 190–210; Hudson, *Protestant Origins*, chaps. 8–9.

34 Frykenberg, *Christianity in India*, 260. Neill, in *History of Christianity in India 1707-1858*, 215, paints a gentler picture.

35 Frykenberg, *Christianity in India*, 258.

36 See Hudson, *Protestant Origins*, 141–72; Frykenberg, *Christianity in India*, 260–61; Israel, *Religious Transactions*, 128–46, who attributes Sastri's favoring of literary over colloquial Tamil to his own caste heritage.

37 Edward Said, *Orientalism* (New York: Vintage Books, 1978), 78–79; cf. Frykenberg, *Christianity in India*, 302–4.

38 Andrew Porter, *Religion versus Empire? British Protestant Missionaries and Overseas Expansion, 1700-1914* (Manchester: Manchester University Press, 2004), 40, 58–75, 100–103.

39 Porter, 69; Neill, *History of Christianity in India 1707-1858*, 149–51.

40 Neill, *History of Christianity in India 1707-1858*, 173–77.

41 C. A. Bayly, *Empire and Information: Intelligence Gathering and Social Communication in India, 1780-1870* (Cambridge: Cambridge University Press, 1996), 216.

42 See n. 1 above.

43 Oddie, "Constructing 'Hinduism,'" 156–58.

44 Jeffrey Cox, *The British Missionary Enterprise since 1700* (New York: Routledge, 2008), 118.

45 W. (William) Ward [a colleague of Carey], *A View of the History, Literature and Religion of the Hindoos* (1822) quoted in Cox, *British Missionary Enterprise*, 131. On the debate surrounding *sati*, see Kenneth Ingham, *Reformers in India 1793-1833* (Cambridge: Cambridge University Press, 1956), 44–54.

46 Mary Carpenter, *Six Months in India* (London: Longman's, Green, 1868), 2: 80, quoted in Kent, *Converting Women*, 89.

47 Richard Fox Young, "Empire and Misinformation: Christianity and Colonial Knowledge from a South Indian Hindu Perspective (ca. 1804)," in *India and the Indianness of Christianity: Essays in Honor of Robert Eric Frykenberg*, ed. Richard Fox Young (Grand Rapids, MI: Eerdmans, 2009), 63–66.

48 Cox, *British Missionary Enterprise*, 81; Susan Bayly, "Race in Britain and India," in *Nation and Religion: Perspectives on Europe and Asia*, ed. Peter van der Veer and Hartmut Lehmann (Princeton, NJ: Princeton University Press, 1999), 72–73.

49 Ingham, *Reformers in India*, chap. iv, esp. 72–74.

50 Richard A. Yelle has traced in detail this affinity between Protestant iconoclasm and enlightenment rationalism in *The Language of Disenchantment: Protestant Literalism and Colonial Discourse in British India* (Oxford: Oxford University Press, 2013), chap. 2. He further explores the seventeenth-century rationalist project of a univocal language, free of ambiguity or hyperbole, and writes, "such a language would provide an antidote for the errors of language that promoted idolatry, and by ending the diversity of languages, would end as well the diversity of religions" (p. 87).

51 Ingham, *Reformers*, 39–43; Oddie, *Hindu and Christian in South-East India*, 46–56.

52 On the uses of archetypes in history, see David Lindenfeld, "Jungian Archetypes and the Discourse of History," *Rethinking History* 13, no 2 (June 2009): 217–34, esp. 223–24, 227–28. One is reminded of Jung's comment, "Our fearsome gods have only changed their names. They now rhyme with –ism."

53 Frykenberg, *Christianity in India*, chap. 12; Neill, *Christianity in India, 1707-1858*, 294; Chandra Mallampalli, "South Asia, 1911-2003," in *World Christianities, c. 1914-c. 2000* ed. Hugh McLeod. Vol. 9 of *The Cambridge History of Christianity* (Cambridge: Cambridge University Press, 2006), 423–24, 428–30.

54 See below, p. 209. Frykenberg, *Christianity in India*, 358–75; Neill, *Christianity in India, 1707-1858*, chap. 11.

55 Oddie, "Constructing 'Hinduism,'" 159–61.

56 Frykenberg, *Christianity in India*, 270, 277–80.

57 Fox Young, *Resistant Hinduism: Sanskrit Sources on Anti-Christian Apologetics in Early Nineteenth-Century India* (Vienna: Institut für Indologie der Universität Wien, 1981).

58 On the latter, Frank F. Conlon, "The Polemic Process in Nineteenth-Century Maharashtra: Vishnubawa Brahmachari and Hindu Revival," in *Religious Controversy in British India: Dialogues in South Asian Languages*, ed. Kenneth W. Jones (Albany: State University of New York Press, 1992), 18.

59 Young, *Resistant Hinduism*, 139.

60 Avril A. Powell, *Muslims and Missionaries in Pre-Mutiny India* (Richmond, UK: Curzon Press, 1993), esp. chap. 8; see also Rafiuddin Ahmen, "Muslim-Christian Polemics and Religious Reform in Nineteenth-century Bengal: Munshi Meheru'lla of Jessore," in Jones, *Religious Controversy*, 102–3.

61 These were more likely to approximate the missionaries' concept of a conversion, namely an intense interior experience of an individual. See the discussion in Saurabh Dube, "Conversion, Translation, and Life-History in Colonial Central India," in David Lindenfeld and Miles Richardson, eds., *Beyond Conversion and Syncretism* (New York: Berghahn, 2011), 29–37.

62 Oddie, "Constructing 'Hinduism,'" 171–3. On other cases and controversies regarding the legal implications of conversion, see Gauri Viswanathan, *Outside the Fold: Conversion, Modernity, and Belief* (Princeton, NJ: Princeton University Press, 1998), chap. 3; Kent, *Converting Women*, 170–80; Mallampalli, "Missionaries and Ethnography in the Service of Litigation," in *Cultural Conversions*, ed. Heather J. Sharkey (Syracuse, NY: Syracuse University Press, 2013), 67–96. On subsequent developments, see Mallampalli, *Christians and Public Life in Colonial South India, 1863-1937: Contending with marginality* (London: Routledge Curzon, 2004).

63 Sir John Kaye, *A History of the Sepoy War in India 1857-58* (London: W.H. Allen, 1864), quoted in *India in 1857. The Revolt against Foreign Rule*, ed. Ainslee T. Embree (1963; repr. Delhi: Chanakya Publications, 1987), 60–61. Other writers included in this anthology who concurred were Sir Syed Ahmad Khan (50–51), P. C. Joshi (120–21), S. B. Chaudhuri (128–29), and S. N. Sen (161).

64 According to Bruce Watson, *The Great Indian Mutiny: Colin Campbell and the Campaign at Lucknow* (New York: Praeger, 1991), 24, 15.7 percent of officers in the Bengal Army were sons of clerics. See also Christopher Hibbert, *The Great Mutiny: India 1857* (New York: Viking Press, 1978), 199 (Brig. General Henry Havelock); Stephen Neill, *History of Christianity in India, 1707-1858*, 417–18 (Lt.-Col. S. G. Wheler).

65 The missionary historian Stephen Neill points out that this suspicion occurred only in those Sepoy units which contained no Christians (Bengal), whereas those in which Christians were present showed no such hostility (Bombay, Madras), *Christianity in India, 1707-1858*, 422.

66 Andrew Ward, *Our Bodies Are Scattered. The Cawnpore Massacres and the Indian Mutiny of 1857* (New York: Henry Holt, 1996), 172–73; John C. B. Webster, "Missionary Strategy and the Development of the Christian Community: Delhi 1859-1884," in Raj and Dempsey, *Popular Christianity*, 212–13.

67 Neill, *Christianity in India, 1707-1858*, 423–26.

68 Frykenberg, *Christianity in India*, 336–43.

69 Resistance to missionaries was also reinforced by the arrival from the West of the Theosophical Society, an anti-Christian movement which became actively

364 Notes to pages 195–198

pro-Hindu under the leadership of Annie Besant, an English woman who migrated to India and became president of the Indian Congress Party. See Viswanathan, *Outside the Fold*, chap. 6, esp. 182–83, 206.

70 Thomas Babington Macaulay, *Speeches of Lord Macaulay with his Minute on Indian Education*, ed. G. M. Young (London: Oxford University Press, 1952), 359.

71 David Kopf, *British Orientalism and the Bengal Renaissance* (Berkeley: University of California Press, 1969), chap. 8.

72 Oddie, "Constructing 'Hinduism,'" 162. See also Partha Mitter, "Rammohun Roy and the New Language of Monotheism," *History and Anthropology*, 3 (1987): 177–208.

73 Iqbal Singh, *Rammohun Roy: A Biographical Inquiry into the Making of Modern India*, 2 vols. (Bombay: Asia Publishing House, 1983, 1987), 1: 225.

74 Kopf, *The Brahmo Samaj and the Shaping of the Modern Indian Mind* (Princeton, NJ: Princeton University Press, 1979), 97–100, 238 (on the hymns). The book gives a history of the multiple schisms and combinations generated by the movement.

75 Jones, *Arya Dharm. Hindu Consciousness in 19th-Century Punjab* (Berkeley: University of California Press, 1976), 34. For an overview of Arya Samaj, see Peter Van der Veer, *Imperial Encounters: Religion and Modernity in India and Britain* (Princeton, NJ: Princeton University Press, 2001), 49–52.

76 Jones, "Swami Dayananda Sarawasati's Critique of Christianity," in Jones, *Religious Controversy*, 52–74.

77 Jones, *Arya Dharm*, 47; Barbara Daly Metcalf, *Islamic Revival in British India: Deoband, 1860-1900* (Princeton. NJ: Princeton University Press, 1982), 221–34, describes how religious debates were designed not to change anyone's views, but to reinforce the beliefs of each party in their own superiority. Another group in Punjab that sought to define itself as autonomous were the Sikhs. See Tony Ballantyne, "The Persistence of the Gods. Religion in the Modern World," in *World Histories from Below: Disruption and Dissent, 1750 to the Present* , ed. Antoinette Burton and Tony Ballantyne (London: Bloomsbury, 2016), 150–51.

78 Swami Vivekananda, "Addresses at the Parliament of Religions," in *The Complete Works of Swami Vivekananda*, 8 vols., 17th ed. (Calcutta: Advaita Ashrama, 1986), 1: 3.

79 David Miller, "Modernity in Hindu Monasticism: Swami Vivekananda and the Ramakrishna Movement," *Journal of Asian and African Studies*, 34, no. 1 (Jan. 1999): 111–26 (116–19).

80 Vivekananda, "Addresses," *Complete Works*, 1: 20; "Reply to the Madras Address," 4: 344–45.

81 "Christianity in India," *Complete Works*, 8: 216.

82 "Christ, the Messenger," *Complete Works*, 4: 142–44. See also Van der Veer, *Imperial Encounters*, 47–48, 72–77, where he draws the parallels with European theosophy, which gained an enthusiastic following in India.

83 See Frykenberg, *Christianity in India*, 410–18; R. H. S. Boyd, *India and the Latin Captivity of the Church* (Cambridge: Cambridge University Press, 1974), chaps. 2, 8.

84 George Thomas, *Christian Indians and Indian Nationalism, 1885-1950* (Frankfurt/M: Peter Lang, 1979), 61–62.

85 Sushil Madhava Pathak, *American Missionaries and Hinduism* (Delhi: Munshiram Manoharlal, 1967), chap. ix. Pathak attributes this change in no small measure to Vivekananda's impact. He writes, "for nearly a decade there were few pulpits in the United States whose preachers had not something to say either for or against the teachings of Swami Vivekananda" (225).

86 Mohandas K. Gandhi, *An Autobiography. The Story of My Experiments with Truth*, trans. Mahadev Desai Reprint (*Boston: Beacon Press, 1993*), 33–34.

87 Robert Ellsberg, ed. *Gandhi on Christianity* (Maryknoll, NY: Orbis Books, 1991), chap. 3.

88 *Gandhi on Christianity*, 40; Susan Billington Harper, *In the Shadow of the Mahatma: Bishop V.S. Azariah and the Travails of Christianity in British India* (Grand Rapids, MI: Eerdmans, 2000), 315–16; Mallampalli, *Christians and Public Life*, 160–63.

89 Kent, *Converting Women*, 140–41; Aparna Basu, "Mary Ann Cooke to Mother Teresa: Christian Missionary Women and the Indian Response," in *Women and Missions: Past and Present: Anthropological ad Historical Perceptions*, ed. Fiona Bowie, Deborah Kirkwood, and Shirley Ardener (Providence, RI: Berg Publishers, 1993), 189–91.

90 Cox, *Imperial Fault Lines. Christianity and Colonial Power in India, 1818-1940* (Stanford, CA: Stanford University Press, 2002), 162, 105–8. Also Kent, *Converting Women*, 140–56; Basu, "Mary Ann Cooke," in *Women and Missions*, 199–201; Ruth Compton Brouwer, *New Women for God: Canadian Presbyterian Women and India Missions, 1876-1914* (Toronto: University of Toronto Press, 1990), 98.

91 Frykenberg, *Christianity in India*, 337.

92 Cox, *Imperial Fault Lines*, 185; Basu, "Mary Ann Cooke," in *Women and Missions*, 202–3; Brouwer, *New Women for God*, 112–19.

93 Miss Greenfield, quoted in Kent, *Converting Women*, 132.

94 Basu, "Mary Ann Cooke," in *Women and Missions*, 195; Brouwer, *New Women for God*, 99, 108; Kent, *Converting Women*, 157.

95 Kent, *Converting Women*, 204–21. Kent also argues that there was a sexual dimension to the controversy, in that low-caste women were considered objects of sexual exploitation by the upper castes – despite pollution taboos.

96 Oddie, *Hindu and Christian*, chap. 9; 226.

97 See Frykenberg, *Christianity in India*, 382–410; Viswanathan, *Outside the Fold*, 118–52; R. S. Sugirtharajah, *The Bible and the Third World* (Cambridge: Cambridge University Press, 2001), 97–105.

98 Viswanath, *The Pariah Problem*, 74.

99 Webster, *A History of the Dalit Christians in India* (San Francisco: Mellen Research University Press, 1992), 56.

100 David Mosse, *The Saint and the Banyan Tree: Christianity and Caste Society in India* (Berkeley: University of California Press, 2012), 113–15.

101 Webster, *Dalit Christians*, i.

102 E.g., the Mazhabi Sikhs in North India. See J. Waskom Pickett, *Christian Mass Movements in India* (New York: Abingdon Press, 1933), 23.

103 E.g. the "Protestant saint" Vadamanickam in southern India in the early nineteenth century. See Dick Kooiman, *Conversion and Social Equality in India: The London Missionary Society in South Travancore in the 19th Century* (Amsterdam: Free University Press, 1989), 52–53.

104 E.g., Yerraguntla Periah, from the Tellugu in East India, a leather worker who had previously been exposed to Yoga; or a lame small businessman named Ditt, also illiterate, who began a mass conversion movement among his outcaste members, the Chuhras (sweepers) in Punjab in the northwest. See Pickett, *Christian Mass Movements*, 47–49; Webster, *Dalit Christians*, 40–41, 44–45.

105 Cox, *Imperial Fault Lines*, 116.

106 Rev. J. Kabis, quoted in Oddie, *Hindu and Christian*, 138. Cf. Webster, *Dalit Christians*, 58.

107 William H. Wiser and Charlotte Viall Wiser, *Behind Mud Walls 1930-1960* (Berkeley: University of California Press, 1971) 49–50.

108 Ibid., 50–58. Cf. Viswanath, *The Pariah Problem*, 74–75.

109 Kooiman, *Conversion and Social Equality*, 80–82. Cf. Oddie, *Hindu and Christian*, 162–66.

110 Jose Kalapura, "Margins of Faith: Dalits and Tribal Christians in Eastern India," in *Margins of Faith: Dalit and Tribal Christianity in India*, ed. Rowena Robinson and Joseph Marianus Kajur (New Delhi: Sage Publications, 2010), 83–84.

111 Pickett, *Christian Mass Movements*, 168, 181–82.

112 Harper, *In the Shadow of the Mahatma*; "The Dornakal Church on the Cultural Frontier," in Brown and Frykenberg, *Christians, Cultural Interactions, and India's Religious Traditions*, 185.

113 On both of these, Webster, *Dalit Christians*, 106–10.

114 Webster, *Dalit Christians*, 155.

115 "Christianity in India. State Populations," en.wikipedia.org/wiki/Christianity in India#State_populations, as per 2011 census. By contrast, the Santals, the largest of the scheduled tribes numerically, inhabit the more accessible regions southwest of Bengal, and have developed a combination of tribal, Hindu, and

Christian practices to which the term "syncretism" may fruitfully be applied. See Raj, "The Ganges, the Jordan, and the Mountain," in Raj and Dempsey *Popular Christianity*, 39–60, esp. 57; Peter B. Andersen, "Revival, Syncretism, and the Anticolonial Discourse of the Kherwar Movement, 1871-1910," in Fox Young, *India and the Indianness of Christianity*, 127–43.

116 Frykenberg, *Christianity in India*, 422–45; Richard M. Eaton, "Conversion to Christianity among the Nagas, 1871-1971," *The Indian Economic and Social History Review* 21, no. 1 (March 1984): 1–44. A more recent but more condensed version appeared in *The Journal of World History* 8, no. 2 (fall 1997): 243–71 ("Comparative History as World History; Religious Conversion in Modern India") and was reprinted in his *Essays on Islam and Indian History* (New Delhi: Oxford University Press, 2001).

117 Eaton, "Conversion to Christianity," 7.

118 Quoted in Eaton, "Conversion," 12.

119 See above, chapter 1, pp. 15–16. For a discussion of how Horton's theories have been applied to South Asia, see Young, "Horton's 'Intellectualist Theory' of Conversion, Reflected on by a South Asianist," in Lindenfeld and Richardson, *Beyond Conversion*, 115–34. Young finds Eaton's version to be rather too mechanistic (123).

120 Eaton, "Conversion," 17, 42–43.

121 For example (Eaton, "Conversion," 23–42), in one language (Ao), rather than taking the word for "supreme being" that had previously existed, the missionaries took the more generic term for "spirit" to introduce a broader idea of God. By contrast, another group (the Sema) had already developed a serviceable term for an omnipresent deity, related to the fact that they migrated more than other Naga groups. In a third case (the Angami), the missionaries vacillated between a foreign term (Ihova) and that of a native female deity, neither of which resonated; the rate of conversion among the Angami was significantly less, despite the other indicators of their integration into the wider world. Still, according to the 1971 census, 40 percent of the Angami identified themselves as Christian.

122 Eaton, "Conversion," 32–33; Frykenberg, *Christianity in India*, 434.

123 Kenneth Ballhatchet, *Caste, Class and Catholicism in India 1789-1914* (Richmond, UK: Curzon, 1998), 68, 76.

124 Thomas, *Christian Indians and Indian Nationalism*, 151.

125 Harper, *Shadow of the Mahatma*, 240. For an overview, see Mallampalli, "South Asia, 1911-2003," in McLeod, *World Christianities c.1914-c.2000*, 422–35. Mallampalli also chronicles the Catholic reaction to these developments, both here and in *Christians and Public Life*. On the fragmentary tendencies, see Brian Stanley, *Christianity in the Twentieth Century. A World History* (Princeton, NJ: Princeton University Press, 2018), 133–40.

126 Thomas, *Christian Indians*, 152; Harper, *Shadow of the Mahatma*, 80–90. An indication of this caution was their decision to reject claiming separate

electorates for themselves as a religious minority, which the British had offered in the interwar period.

127 Frykenberg, *Christianity in India*, 473.

128 Judith M. Brown, "Indian Christians and Nehru's Nation-State," in Fox Young, *India and the Indianness of Christianity*, 232.

129 Bengt G. Karlsson, "Entering into the Christian Dharma: Contemporary 'Tribal' Conversions in India," in Brown and Frykenberg, *Christians, Cultural Interactions, and India's Religious Traditions*, 143.

130 Chad M. Bauman, "Identity, Conversion and Violence: Dalits, Adivasis and the 2007-2008 Riots in Orissa," in Robinson and Kujur, *Margins of Faith*, 265–70.

131 Frykenberg, *Christianity in India*, 464.

132 Mosse, *Saint and the Banyan Tree*, 220.

133 Jeremy Weber, "Outpacing Persecution," *Christianity Today*, 60, no. 9 (Nov. 2016), 46.

134 The official census of 2011 lists Christians as 2.3 percent of the population, 27.8 million. The Pew Research Center tabulates 31,850,000 (2010), while the Gordon Conwell Center for the Study of Global Christianity projects 67,356,000 for the year 2020 (4.9%). See "Census of India. Religion," http://censusindia.gov.in/Census_And_You/religion.aspx; Pew Research Center, "Global Christianity. A Report on the Size and Distribution of the World's Christian Population, December 19, 2011," www.pewforum.org/2011/12/19/table-christian-population-in-numbers-by-country/; Gordon-Conwell Center for Study of Global Christianity, www.gordonconwell.edu/ockenga/research/documents/ChristianityinitsGlobalContext.pdf, 38.

135 "Christianity in India. Denominations," en.wikipedia.org/wiki/Christianity_in_India; "St. Thomas Christians," en.wikipedia.org/wiki/Saint_Thomas_Christians.

136 Joanne Punzo Waghorne, "Chariots of the God/s," in Raj and Dempsey, *Popular Christianity*, 31, 34; Vasudha Narayanan, "Afterword," ibid., 260.

CHAPTER 7

1 This chapter does not attempt to cover the entire region, leaving out places like Taiwan, Vietnam, Indonesia.

2 John B. Henderson, *The Development and Decline of Chinese Cosmology* (New York: Columbia University Press, 1984), 2.

3 Recent scholarship has tended to undermine the view that the Confucian and Christian worldviews are fundamentally incompatible. E.g., D. E. Mungello, *The Great Encounter of China and the West, 1500-1800*, 4th ed. (Lanham, MD: Rowman & Littlefield, 2013), 64; Daniel H. Bays, *A New History of Christianity in China* (Chichester, UK: Wiley-Blackwell, 2012), 25. The main

target of these criticisms has been Jacques Gernet, *China and the Christian Impact: A Conflict of Cultures*, trans. Janet Lloyd (Cambridge: Cambridge University Press, 1985).

4 C. K. Yang, *Religion in Chinese Society* (Berkeley: University of California Press, 1961), 6; chap. xii.

5 Stephen F. Teiser, "Introduction. The Spirits of Chinese Religion," in *The Religions of Asia in Practice*, ed. Donald S. Lopez, Jr. (Princeton: Princeton University Press, 2002), 324, 327. For a similar take on Japanese religion, see Jacques H. Kamstra, "The Religion of Japan: Syncretism or Religious Phenomenalism?," in *Dialogue and Syncretism: An Interdisciplinary Approach*, ed. Jerald Gort et al. (Grand Rapids, MI: Eerdmans, 1989), 138.

6 John Breen and Mark Teeuwen, *A New History of Shinto* (Malden, MA: Wiley Blackwell, 2010), 219.

7 E.g., Robert N. Bellah, *Religion in Human Evolution: From the Paleolithic to the Axial Age* (Cambridge, MA: Harvard University Press, 2011), chap. 8. For a discussion of the uncertainties surrounding Confucianism as a religion, see Anna Sun, *Confucianism as a World Religion: Contested Histories and Contemporary Realities* (Princeton, NJ: Princeton University Press, 2013); also Yang, *Religion in Chinese Society*, chap. x.

8 Thus Judith A. Berling, in *The Syncretic Religion of Lin Chao-en* (New York: Columbia University Press, 1980), argues for the appropriateness of the term to underscore the importance of borrowing as more than a merely random or eclectic combination of elements. Yet she also enumerates a multiplicity of strategies that fall under the label, such as "acculturative," "adversary," and "defensive" syncretism (24–28). Cf. Conrad Totman, *A History of Japan* (Malden, MA: Blackwell, 2000), who finds a dialectical relationship between syncretic and sectarian tendencies in classical and medieval Japanese religion (128–29, 187–92).

9 Berling, *Syncretic Religion*, 17–19, 55.

10 See James Hayes, "Specialists and Written Materials in the Village World," in *Popular Culture in Late Imperial China*, ed. David Johnson, Andrew J. Nathan and Evelyn S. Rawski (Berkeley: University of California Press, 1985), 75–111.

11 Henderson, *Development and Decline*, 132–33.

12 Teiser, "Spirits of Chinese Religion," 322. Cf. Evelyn S. Rawski, "Problems and Prospects," in Johnson, Nathan, and Rawski, *Popular Culture*, 409; Henderson, *Development and Decline*, 5–6.

13 On the latter, see Herman Ooms, *Tokugawa Ideology. Early Constructs, 1570-1680* (Princeton, NJ: Princeton University Press, 1985), 65–67.

14 For a survey, see Scott Lowe, "Chinese Millennial Movements," in *The Oxford Handbook of Millennialism*, ed. Catherine Wessinger (Oxford: Oxford University Press, 2011), 307–25; Susan Naquin, "The Transmission

of White Lotus Sectarianism in Late Imperial China," in Johnson, Nathan, and Rawski, *Popular Culture,* 255–91.

15 C. R. Boxer, *The Christian Century in Japan, 1549-1650* (Berkeley: University of California Press, 1951), 78, 114, 321, 448. Edwin O. Reischauer puts the percentage of Christians even higher, between 2 percent and 3 percent in his introduction to Stuart D. B. Picken, *Christianity and Japan* (Tokyo: Kodansha International, 1983), 6.

16 Ann M. Harrington, *Japan's Hidden Christians* (Chicago: Loyola University Press, 1993), xiii.

17 Quoted in Boxer, *Christian Century,* 93.

18 George Elison, *Deus Destroyed. The Image of Christianity in Early Modern Japan* (Cambridge, MA: Harvard University Press, 1973), 88–106; Boxer, *Christian Century,* 100–103.

19 Boxer, *Christian Century,* 315, 323–24, 330, 342.

20 Quoted in Boxer, *Christian Century,* 94.

21 Harrington, *Japan's Hidden Christians,* 21.

22 Elison, *Deus Destroyed,* 33. As late as 1639, a popular anti-Christian chapbook refers to *Deus,* the God of the *Kirishitans,* as a Buddha (339).

23 Elison, *Deus Destroyed,* 41–46 on these points.

24 Boxer, *Christian Century,* 60–64.

25 Boxer, *Christian Century,* 203–4.

26 Elison, *Deus Destroyed,* chap. 6.

27 Quoted in Nam-lin Hur, *Death and Social Order in Tokugawa Japan: Buddhism, Anti-Christianity, and the Danka System* (Cambridge, MA: Harvard University Asia Center, 2007), 43–44.

28 Boxer, *Christian Century,* 334–44; 351–61.

29 Barbara Ambros, "Religion in Early Modern Japan," in *Japan Emerging: Prehistory to 1850,* ed. Karl F. Friday (Boulder, CO: Westview Press, 2012), 379; Hur, *Death and Social Order,* 14–15, 66–68, 79–86.

30 Harrington, *Japan's Hidden Christians,* 135. She gives an extended example of a *kakure* text, *Tenchi hajimari no koto* (The Beginnings of Heaven and Earth), a beautiful example of vernacular translation (77–95).

31 John D. Young, *Confucianism and Christianity: The First Encounter* (Hong Kong: Hong Kong University Press, 1983), 20.

32 Nicolas Standaert, ed. *Handbook of Christianity in China,* Vol. 1: 635–1800 (Leiden: Brill, 2001), 94; Bays, *New History,* 14. The discovery in the 1630s of a stele near Xi'an, the Tang capital, documenting the Nestorians in China helped to convince skeptics that Christianity was not merely a new-fangled Western import (ibid., 7).

33 Bays, *New History,* 21.

34 Standaert, *Handbook,* 754.

35 Gernet, *China and the Christian Impact,* 195. For a fuller discussion of Ricci's theology, see Young, *Confucianism and Christianity,* chap. 2.

36 Standaert, *Handbook*, 474–80, 604–6. On some of the initial converts, see Mungello, *Great Encounter*, 19–23; Young, *Confucianism and Christianity*, chap. 3.

37 Quoted in Gernet, *China and the Christian Impact*, 35–36.

38 Standaert, *Handbook*, 659–60.

39 Standaert, *Handbook*, 438.

40 Mungello, *Great Encounter*, 19; Gernet, *China and the Christian Impact*, 83.

41 Quoted in Young, *Confucianism and Christianity*, 67.

42 Quoted in Gernet, *China and the Christian Impact*, 224.

43 On the basis of anti-Christian feeling, see Mungello, *Great Encounter*, 53–61; Gernet, *China and the Christian Impact*, 43–47; Young, *Confucianism and Christianity*, 74–76.

44 See Standaert, *Handbook*, 506–26, for a survey.

45 Liam Matthew Brockey, *Journey to the East: The Jesuit Mission to China, 1579-1724* (Cambridge, MA: Harvard University Press, 2007), 92–93; Eugenio Menegon, *Ancestors, Virgins, and Friars: Christianity as Local Religion in Late Imperial China* (Cambridge, MA: Harvard University Press, 2009), 92, 193, 204.

46 Standaert, *Handbook*, 494. See also Mungello, *Great Encounter*, 31–35.

47 Standaert, *Handbook*, 513–15.

48 See Menegon, *Ancestors, Virgins, and Friars*, chap. 7 for a thorough discussion of the issues.

49 Standaert, *Handbook*, 317; Bays, *New History*, 28, 30.

50 This survival was regional, not uniform across all of China. The lower Yangzi region (Jiangnan province) contained 65 percent of Chinese Christians in 1700. Other centers were in the Shandong, Zhili, and Fujian provinces. Further inland, Sichuan, a frontier region with much in-migration, became a flourishing center. See Bays, *New History*, 26–27, for a brief summary; Standaert, *Handbook*, 534–72, for a more extensive treatment, including a series of excellent maps. On Sichuan, see Robert E. Entenmann, "Catholics and Society in Eighteenth-Century Sichuan," in *Christianity in China: From the Eighteenth Century to the Present*, ed. Daniel Bays (Stanford, CA: Stanford University Press, 1996), 8–23.

51 Standaert, *Handbook*, 387–91; Entenmann, "Catholics and Society," in Bays, *Christianity in China*, 22.

52 Standaert, *Handbook*, 307–8, 382–83.

53 Standaert, *Handbook*, 456; Brockey, *Journey to the East*, 47–48.

54 See Menegon, *Ancestors, Virgins, and Friars*, 177–201, for a local study from Fujian Province.

55 Lars Laamann, *Christian Heretics in Late Imperial China: Christian Inculturation and State Control, 1720-1850* (London: Routledge, 2006), 19.

56 Menegon, *Ancestors, Virgins, and Friars*, 257–58, 296. Menegon points out (299) that the rationale for such prayers was not the same as for traditional

ancestral rites. The purpose of the latter was to benefit the living and to lift the threat of ancestral punishment, whereas the former was to benefit the ancestors themselves in the afterlife.

57 Mungello, *The Spirit and the Flesh in Shandong, 1650-1785* (Lanham, MD: Rowman & Littlefield, 2001), 80. See Brockey, *Journey to the East*, chap. 10, for a treatment of the various types of confraternities.

58 Laamann extensively documents this period. His term for the overall pattern is "inculturation." It should be noted that the ensemble of religious practices that were so incorporated were little different from those of rural Europe: focusing on images and devotional objects such as crucifixes and rosaries, and looking to priests for acts of healing and exorcism.

59 Thomas H. Reilly, *The Taiping Heavenly Kingdom* (Seattle: University of Washington Press, 2004), 20–21, 42.

60 Menegon, *Ancestors, Virgins, and Friars*, 307; Standaert, *Handbook*, 395–96.

61 Standaert, *Handbook*, 394.

62 Menegon, *Ancestors, Virgins, and Friars*, ch. 8; Entenmann, "Christian Virgins in Eighteenth-Century Sichuan," in Bays, *Christianity in China,* 180–93.

63 Laamann, *Christian Heretics,* 46; Mungello, *Shandong*, 113; R. G. Tiedemann, "Christianity and Chinese 'Heterodox Sects'. Mass Conversion and Syncretism in Shandong Province in the Early Eighteenth Century," *Monumenta Serica* 44 (1996): 339–82.

64 Tiedemann, 368; Laamann, *Christian Heretics,* 83–84. Yet it does not appear that millennialism was one of the traits that was blended. Although very strong in the White Lotus movements, it was not prominent in Chinese Christianity at the time. The topic is notably absent in Standaert's otherwise encyclopedic treatment.

65 Quoted in Menegon, *Ancestors, Virgins, and Friars*, 119–20.

66 Bays, *New History*, 47–48, 56–57.

67 Bays, *New History*, 13.

68 Jonathan Spence, *God's Chinese Son: The Heavenly Kingdom of Hong Xiuquan* (New York: W. W. Norton, 1996), 19–20. On Gützlaff, see Jessie Gregory Lutz, *Opening China: Karl F.A. Gützlaff and Sino-Western Relations, 1827-1852* (Grand Rapids, MI: Eerdmans, 2008).

69 Reilly, *Taiping Heavenly Kingdom*, 80. *Shangdi* became the accepted translation in subsequent Protestant Bible translations, though not without debate. See Lutz, *Opening China*, 162–65.

70 P. Richard Bohr, "Liang Fa's Quest for Moral Power," in *Christianity in China: Early Protestant Missionary Writings*, ed. Suzanne Wilson Barnett and John King Fairbank (Cambridge, MA: Harvard University Press, 1985), 35–46.

71 Stephen R. Platt, *Autumn in the Heavenly Kingdom: China, the West, and the Epic Story of the Taiping Civil War* (New York: Knopf, 2012), 358. Much of the death stemmed from famine and disease, as both sides pursued

scorched-earth tactics destroying the other's agricultural lands. The following account of the Taiping Rebellion is also drawn from Spence, *God's Chinese Son*; Rudolf G. Wagner, *Reenacting the Heavenly Vision: The Role of Religion in the Taiping Rebellion* (Berkeley: Institute of East Asian Studies, University of California, 1982); as well as Jen Yu-Wen, *The Taiping Revolutionary Movement* (New Haven, CT: Yale University Press, 1973).

72 See chap. 1 above, p. 24.

73 Ryan Dunch, *Fuzhou Protestants and the Making of a Modern China* (New Haven, CT: Yale University Press, 2001), 7–15. Cf. Vincent Shih, *The Taiping Ideology* (Seattle: University of Washington Press, 1967). Shih's detailed discussion of the sources of Taiping ideology devotes 17 pages to Christianity and 107 pages to the Chinese classics!

74 Harold Z. Schiffrin, *Sun Yat-sen and the Origins of the Chinese Revolution* (Berkeley: University of California Press, 1968), 15; Jen Yu-Wen, *Taiping Revolutionary Movement*, 9, 544–45.

75 Max Weber, *Gesammelte Aufsätze zur Religionssoziologie*, 3 vols. (Tübingen: J. C .B. Mohr (Paul Siebeck), 1920), 1: 508.

76 Erik Zürcher, "Purity in the Taiping Rebellion," in *The Quest for Purity: Dynamics of Puritan Movements*, ed. Walter E. A. van Beek (Berlin: Mouton de Gruyter, 1988), 212.

77 Platt, *Autumn*, 54, 158.

78 Spence, *God's Chinese Son*, 179.

79 Spence, *God's Chinese Son*, 227–28; Jen Yu-Wen, *Taiping Revolutionary Movement*, 217–27; Platt, *Autumn*, chap. 6.

80 Spence, *God's Chinese Son*, chaps. 14, 18. Platt, *Autumn*, however, presents a detailed account of these negotiations, showing that Western opposition was not a foregone conclusion; prior to 1862, neutrality seemed to be an option conducive to British trade, and missionaries hoped to arrive at an understanding with the Taipings via the mediation of Hong's cousin Hong Rengan, who had been exposed to Christianity Hong Kong.

81 Spence, 254–61, 291–97.

82 Paul A. Cohen, "Christian Missions and their Impact to 1900," in *The Cambridge History of China: Late Ch'ing 1800-1911*, ed. John K. Fairbank (Cambridge: Cambridge University Press, 1978), 569.

83 Bays, *New History*, 74.

84 Lutz, *Hakka Chinese Confront Protestant Christianity, 1850-1900: With the autobiographies of eight Hakka Christians, and commentary* (Armonk, NY: M.E. Sharpe, 1998) 216–19. Cf. Lawrence D. Kessler, *The Jiangyin Mission Station* (Chapel Hill: University of North Carolina Press, 1996), chap. 2, for another example of an initial hostile reception.

85 Mungello, *The Catholic Invasion of China: Remaking Chinese Christianity* (Lanham, MD: Rowman & Littlefield, 2015), 30–37.

86 Ernest P. Young, *Ecclesiastical Colony: China's Catholic Church and the French Religious Protectorate* (Oxford: Oxford University Press, 2013), 29.
87 Cohen, "Christian Missions," in Fairbank, *Cambridge History*, 554.
88 For examples, see Charles A. Litzinger, "Rural Religion and Village Organization in North China: The Catholic Challenge in the Late Nineteenth Century," in Bays, *Christianity in China*, 41–52; Roger R. Thompson, "Twilight of the Gods in the Chinese Countryside: Christians, Confucians, and the Modernizing State, 1861-1911," ibid., 53–72.
89 Quoted in Cohen, *China and Christianity: The Missionary Movement and the Growth of Chinese Antiforeignism, 1860-1870* (Cambridge, MA: Harvard University Press, 1963), 200. See Joseph W. Esherick, *The Origins of the Boxer Uprising* (Berkeley: University of California Press, 1987), 116–24, for a detailed example of such a "conversion."
90 See, however, Richard Alan Sweeten, "Catholic Converts in Jiangxi Province: Conflict and Accommodation, 1860-1900," in Bays, *Christianity in China*, 39, who points to a rural region where Catholics mixed in with the rest of the population.
91 Cohen, *China and Christianity*, 91–92, 229–31. See also Mungello, *Catholic Invasion*, chap. 4.
92 Cohen, "Christian Missions," in Fairbank, *Cambridge History*, 555.
93 R. G. Tiedemann, "Indigenous Agency, Religious Protectorates, and Chinese Interests: The Expansion of Christianity in Nineteenth-Century China," in *Converting Colonialism: Visions and Realities in Mission History, 1706-1914*, ed. Dana Robert (Grand Rapids, MI: Eerdmans, 2008), 233–34.
94 On the Boxer Uprising, see Esherick, *Origins*, also Cohen, *History in Three Keys. The Boxers as Event, Experience, and Myth* (New York: Columbia University Press, 1997).
95 Quoted in Cohen, *History in Three Keys*, 84.
96 For a description, see Esherick, *Origins*, 293.
97 Cohen, "Littoral and Hinterland in Nineteenth Century China: The 'Christian' Reformers," in *The Missionary Enterprise in China and America*, ed. John Fairbank (Cambridge, MA: Harvard University Press, 1974), 197–225.
98 For a critique of the notion of "cultural imperialism," see Dunch, "Beyond Cultural Imperialism: Cultural Theory, Christian Missions, and Global Modernity," *History and Theory* 41, no. 3 (Oct. 2002): 301–25.
99 Cohen, "Littoral and Hinterland," in Fairbank, *Missionary Enterprise*, 214.
100 Cohen, "Littoral and Hinterland," 222. They were: Yung Wing (1828–1912), Ho Kai (1859–1914), Wang T'ao (1828–1897), Ma Chien-chung (1844–1900), Ma Liang (1840–1939), Tong King-sing (1832–1892), Cheng Kuan-ying (1842–1923), and Wu T'ing-fang (1842–1922).
101 Schiffrin, *Sun Yat-sen*, 91n.

102 Bays, *New History*, 82–84; Tsou Mingteh, "Christian Missionary as Confucian Intellectual: Gilbert Reid (1857–1927) and the Reform Movement in the Late Qing," in Bays, *Christianity in China*, 73–90.

103 See Mungello, *Catholic Invasion*, chap. 3 and his discussion of Vincent Lebbe (1877–1940), Ma Xiangbo (1840–1939), and Antoine Cotta (1852–1957). It was not until 1919 that the pope authorized the founding of a Catholic university in China. See also Young, *Ecclesiastical Colony*.

104 Ellsworth C. Carlson, *The Foochow Missionaries, 1847-1880* (Cambridge, MA: Harvard University Press, 1974), 64; for a description of teaching methods, see 50–52. See also Jessie Lutz, *China and the Christian Colleges, 1850-1950* (Ithaca, NY: Cornell University Press, 1971), 15; Dunch, "Science, Religion, and the Classics in Christian Higher Education to 1920," in *China's Christian Colleges: Cross-Cultural Connections, 1900-1950*, ed. Daniel H. Bays and Ellen Widmer (Stanford, CA: Stanford University Press, 2009), 60, 64.

105 Carlson, *Foochow Missionaries*, 86.

106 Quoted in Lutz, *China and the Christian Colleges*, 11.

107 Cohen, "Christian Missions," in Fairbank, *Cambridge History*, 578; Adrian A. Bennett and Kwang-Ching Liu, "Christianity in the Chinese Idiom: Young J. Allen and the Early *Chiao-hui hsin-pao*, 1868-1870," in Fairbank, *Missionary Enterprise*, 164–65.

108 See Spence, *The Search for Modern China* (New York: W. W. Norton, 1990), 208.

109 Cohen, "Christian Missions," in Fairbank, *Cambridge History*, 574–75; Lutz, *China and the Christian Colleges*, 138–46; Kessler, *Jiangyin Mission Station*, 31–36, 55.

110 John R. Stanley, "Establishing a Female Medical Elite: The Early History of the Nursing Profession in China," in Jessie G. Lutz, ed. *Pioneer Chinese Christian Women: Gender, Christianity, and Social Mobility* (Bethlehem, PA: Lehigh University Press, 2010), 277, 288 (n.14).

111 Bays, *New History,* 69 for Protestants; Jean-Paul Wiest, "From Past Contributions to Present Opportunities: The Catholic Church and Education in Chinese Mainland during the Last 150 Years," in *China and Christianity. Burdened Past, Hopeful Future*, ed. Stephen Uhalley Jr. and Xiaoxin Wu (Armonk NY: M.E. Sharpe, 2001), 253.

112 For an overview from an indigenous perspective, see Kwok Pui-Lan, "Chinese Women and Protestant Christianity at the Turn of the Twentieth Century," in Bays. *Christianity in China*, 194–208.

113 Ryan Dunch, "'Mothers to Our Country'; Conversion, Education, and Ideology among Chinese Protestant Women, 1870-1930," in Lutz, *Pioneer Chinese Christian Women*, 327; Ling Oi Ki, "Bible Women," ibid., 246–64.

114 Jane Hunter, *The Gospel of Gentility: American Women Missionaries in Turn-of-the-Century China* (New Haven, CT: Yale University Press, 1984).

115 Evelyn S. Rawski, "Problems and Prospects," in Johnson, Nathan, and Rawski, *Popular Culture*, 404. This is reinforced by a reading of the *Biographical Dictionary of Republican China*, ed. Howard Boorman, 4 vols. (New York: Columbia University Press, 1966–72). Although a product of American interests and the Cold War – Boorman was an ex-military officer and State Department official – its 592 biographies are a rich source of information – about the last decades of the Qing period as well as the Republic itself. Fully 82% of the subjects were born before 1900, making it likely they were educated before 1920. At least 8% of the biographical subjects came from families described as "poor." See David Lindenfeld, "China's 'Prominent Christians', a Prosopographical Analysis of the *Biographical Dictionary of Republican China*," *World History Connected*, vol. 10, no. 1 (2013), n.p. http://worldhistoryconnected.press.illinois.edu/10.1/lindenfeld.html.

116 Dunch, "Mothers," in Lutz, *Pioneer Chinese Christian Women*, 336.

117 Lutz, "Educating Women. Introduction," in *Pioneer Chinese Christian Women*, 320.

118 For a comparative study of India and China in the modern period, see Peter Van der Veer, *The Modern Spirit of Asia: The Spiritual and the Secular in China and India* (Princeton, NJ: Princeton University Press, 2014).

119 Vincent Goosaert and David A. Palmer, *The Religious Question in Modern China* (Chicago: University of Chicago Press, 2011), 47–55.

120 Goosaert and Palmer, 127–32.

121 Shirley S. Garrett, *Social Reformers in Urban China: the Chinese YMCA, 1895-1926* (Cambridge, MA: Harvard University Press, 1970), 103. The *Biographical Dictionary of Republican China* again offers an illuminating source for this trend. About 10 percent of the 592 entries were Chinese Christians, and of these 60 percent had studied in the United States; 9.2 percent studied in Japan, and 14 percent in Europe. See n. 115 above.

122 Bays, *New History*, 72, 94. See also James A. Field, Jr., "Near East Notes and Far East Queries," in Fairbank, *Missionary Enterprise*, 32, 34.

123 Andrew Porter, *Religion versus Empire? British Protestant Missionaries and Overseas Expansion, 1700-1914* (Manchester: Manchester University Press, 2004), 304.

124 Kessler, *Jiangyin Mission*, 43.

125 Valentin H. Rabe, "Evangelical Logistics: Mission Support and Resources to 1920," in Fairbank, *Missionary Enterprise*, 61.

126 For a brief summary plus a review of recent Chinese historiography on the subject, see Feiya Tao, "Christian Colleges in China: New Relations and New Perspectives since the 1980s," in *Christian Mission and Education in Modern China, Japan, and Korea*, ed. Jan A.B. Jongneel et al (Frankfurt am Main: Peter Lang, 2009), 81–87.

127 Goosaert and Palmer, *Religious Question*, 77–79.

128 Bays, *New History*, 77; Kenneth Scott Latourette, *History of The Expansion of Christianity*, 7 vols. (New York: Harper, 1937-45), 6: 293, 338.

129 Fairbank, "Introduction: The Many Faces of Protestant Missions in China and the United States," in Fairbank, *Missionary Enterprise*, 13.

130 Quoted in Joseph M. Kitagawa, *Religion in Japanese History* (New York: Columbia University Press, 1966), 184.

131 Kitigawa, *Religion in Japanese History* , 203.

132 Kitigawa, *Religion in Japanese History* , 238–39; Notto R. Thelle, *Buddhism and Christianity in Japan: From Conflict to Dialogue, 1854-1899* (Honolulu: University of Hawaii Press, 1987), 14–16.

133 Latourette, History, 6: 379–81; Andreas Müller, "Die russisch-orthodoxe Mission in Japan," in *Polycentric Structures in the History of World Christianity*, ed. Klaus Koschorke and Adrian Hermann (Wiesbaden: Harrassowitz, 2014), 335–46.

134 Irwin Scheiner, *Christian Converts and Social Protest in Meiji Japan* (Berkeley: University of California Press, 1970), 8.

135 Scheiner, chaps. 6–7.

136 Mark Mullins, *Christianity Made in Japan: A Study of Indigenous Movements* (Honolulu: University of Hawaii Press, 1998), 14.

137 Charles W. Iglehart, *A Century of Protestant Christianity in Japan* (Rutland, VT: Charles E. Tuttle Co., 1959), 61. Cf. Thelle, *Buddhism and Christianity*, 48–49.

138 On girls' schools, see Rui Kohiyama, "Women's Education at Mission Schools and the Emergence of the Modern Family in Meiji Japan," in Jongneel et al., *Christian Mission and Education*, 99–114. For a roughly parallel story to that of Niijima Jo, see Yuko Takahashi, "A Japanese American Enterprise: Umeko Tsuda's Bryn Mawr Network and the Founding of Tsuda College," in Bays and Widmer, *China's Christian Colleges*, 271–86. Tsuda was brought to the United States as part of a government program to study the West in 1871. She was six years old at the time!

139 Iglehart, *Century of Protestant Christianity*, 76.

140 Thelle, *Buddhism and Christianity*, 55. Cf. Iglehart, *Century of Protestant Christianity*, 72–74.

141 H. Byron Earhart, *Religion in Japan: Unity and Diversity*, 5th ed. (Boston: Wadsworth Cengage Learning, 2014), 223; Carlo Caldarola, *Christianity: the Japanese Way* (Leiden: Brill, 1979), 33–35.

142 Latourette, *History*, 6: 378. On the division, see Earhart, *Religion in Japan*, 202; Kitagawa, *Religion in Japanese History*, 213–14.

143 Quoted in Totman, *History of Japan*, 297.

144 Kitagawa, *Religion in Japanese History*, 243; Scheiner, *Christian Converts*, 36–37; Thelle, *Buddhism and Christianity*, 126–29.

145 Thelle, 169–72.

146 Latourette, *History*, 6: 380.
147 On Uchimura, see John F. Howes, "Japanese Christianity and the State: From Jesuit Confrontation/Competition to Uchimura's Noninstitutional Movement/Protestantism," in *Indigenous Responses to Western Christianity*, ed. Steven Kaplan (New York: New York University Press, 1995), 75–94; Caldarola, *Christianity: the Japanese Way*, 40–47; Mullins, *Christianity Made in Japan*, chap. 4.
148 Thelle, *Buddhism and Christianity*, 91, 139.
149 Thelle, *Buddhism and Christianity*, 146. On Protestant antipathy towards Japanese practices, see Mullins, *Christianity Made in Japan*, 8, 135–38.
150 Thelle, *Buddhism and Christianity*, chaps. 12–14.
151 Philip D. Curtin, *The World and the West: The European Challenge and the Overseas Response in the Age of Empire* (Cambridge: Cambridge University Press, 2000), 156–72.
152 See Bays, *New History*, 109–10; Lutz, *China and the Christian Colleges*, 215–32.
153 New York: George H. Doran Co., 1922, esp. 103–20.
154 Bays, *New History*, 112; cf. Garrett, "Why They Stayed: American Church Politics and Chinese Nationalism in the Twenties," in Fairbank, *Missionary Enterprise*, 283–310, which explains why many returned. In response to the threat of communism, some missionaries sought an alliance with Confucianism in the interwar period. See Albert Monshan Wu, *From Christ to Confucius: German Missionaries, Chinese Christians, and the Globalization of Christianity, 1860-1950* (New Haven, CT: Yale University Press, 2016), chap. 6.
155 Bays, *New History*, 105, 115, 12–40; Lian Xi, *Redeemed by Fire. The Rise of Popular Christianity in Modern China* (New Haven, CT: Yale University Press, 2010).
156 Goosaert and Palmer, *Religious Question*, 93–108, esp. 107.
157 Jay Taylor, *The Generalissimo: Chiang Kai-shek and the Struggle for Modern China* (Cambridge, MA: Harvard University Press, 2009), 12–15, 74, 91.
158 Bays, *New History*, 125–26; Lutz, *China and the Christian Colleges*, 283–99.
159 James C. Thomson, Jr., *While China Faced West. American Reformers in Nationalist China, 1928-1937* (Cambridge, MA: Harvard University Press, 1969), 152. An American missionary, George Shepherd, was put in charge of it (chap. 8).
160 Xi, *Redeemed by Fire*, 179; Lutz, *China and the Christian Colleges*, chap. X.
161 Alan Hunter and Kim-Kwong Chan, *Protestantism in Contemporary China* (Cambridge: Cambridge University Press, 1993), 111–13.
162 Timothy Brook, "Toward Independence: Christianity in China under the Japanese Occupation, 1937-1945," in Bays, *Christianity in China*, 317–37.

163 Iglehart, *Century of Protestant Christianity*, 213–58; Kitagawa, *Religion in Japanese History*, 246–48; Caldarola, *Christianity: the Japanese Way*, 164–69.

164 John W. Dower, *Embracing Defeat: Japan in the Wake of World War II* (New York: Norton, 1999), 307.

165 Iglehart, *Century of Protestant Christianity*, 341–44; Mullins, "Christianity Transplanted: Toward a Sociology of Success and Failure," in *Perspectives on Christianity in Korea and Japan. The Gospel and Culture in East Asia*, ed. Mark R. Mullins and Richard Fox Young (Lewiston, NY: Edwin Mellen Press, 1995), 63. Mullins notes an increased number of baptisms during these years, but that many left the church soon after.

166 Edwin O. Reischauer, "Introduction," in Picken, *Christianity in Japan*, 6.

167 James M. Phillips, *From the Rising of the Sun: Christians and Society in Contemporary Japan* (Maryknoll, NY: Orbis Books, 1981), chaps. 2–4. On ongoing problems in maintaining the universities, see Harry Burton-Lewis, "Christian Mission and Higher Education in Japan," in Mullins and Fox Young, *Perspectives on Christianity*, 175–89.

168 Xi, *Redeemed by Fire*, 180.

169 Hunter and Chan, *Protestantism in Contemporary China*, 112.

170 On Wu and the manifesto, see Gao Wangzhi, "Y.T. Wu: A Christian Leader under Communism," in Bays, *Christianity in China*, 338–52, esp. 344.

171 Bays, *New History*, 173.

172 Lutz, *China and the Christian Colleges*, 468–73.

173 Xi, *Redeemed by Fire*, 205.

174 On the multitude of religious revivals, see Goossaert and Palmer, *Religious Question*, 387, chaps. 10 and 11. On the pitfalls of numbers and polls, see Ian Johnson, *The Souls of China: The Return of Religion after Mao* (New York: Pantheon Books, 2017), 28–29.

175 Fenggang Yang, *Religion in China: Survival and Revival under Communist Rule* (Oxford: Oxford University Press, 2012), 144–45, 148.

176 Yang., 112–18; Goosaert and Palmer, *Religious Question*, 120–21, 286–92, 336–42.

177 Goosaert and Palmer, *Religious Question*, 381, 383.

178 Quoted in Goosaert and Palmer, *Religious Question*, 383. See also Bays, *New History*, 190–91.

179 Yang, *Religion in China*, chap. 5, has characterized this as a "gray market" for religion, in contrast to the "red market" of officially regulated churches and the "black market" of proscribed and persecuted ones.

180 Richard Madsen, *China's Catholics: Tragedy and Hope in an Emerging Civil Society* (Berkeley: University of California Press, 1998), 39–44. Also his "Beyond Orthodoxy: Catholicism as Chinese Folk Religion," in Uhalley and Wu, *China and Christianity*, 233–49. A historic 2018 agreement between the Vatican and the government stopped short of full recognition.

181 Yang, "Lost in the Market, Saved at MacDonald's. Conversion to Christianity in Urban China," *Journal for the Scientific Study of Religion*, 44, no. 4 (Dec. 2005): 423–41.

182 Hunter and Chan, *Protestantism in Contemporary China*, 171; Goosaert and Palmer, *Religious Question*, 301–2; Bays, *New History*, 199–202; Johnson, *Souls of China*, 294, 364. Indeed, the term "cultural Christian" came into fashion in the 1990s on the part of some Chinese students of Christianity to express an appreciation of the contribution of Christian faith and morality to the stability of modern Chinese society – without professing to be Christians themselves. See Zhuo Xinping, "Discussion on 'Cultural Christians' in China," in Uhalley and Wu, *China and Christianity*, 283–300.

183 Dunch, "Protestant Christianity in China Today," in Uhalley and Wu, *China and Christianity*, 215.

184 Latourette, *History*, 7: 430. One of the most successful mission stations in China at the turn of the century was the Stone Gateway school complex in Yunnan province. It was the center for creating and spreading a written language for one such group, the Hua Miao, whose language was one of the many that were not officially recognized. Soon the Hua Miao were providing active teachers and evangelists themselves. See Norma Diamond, "Christianity and the Hua Miao: Writing and Power," in Bays, *Christianity in China*, 146–47.

185 Ralph R. Covell, "Christianity and China's Minority Nationalities—Faith and Unbelief," in Uhalley and Wu, *China and Christianity*, 278–80.

186 Brian Stanley, *Christianity in the Twentieth Century: A World History* (Princeton, NJ: Princeton University Press, 2018), 40.

187 The first actual contact with Christians came during Hideyoshi's invasion of Korea in 1594, which included Japanese Christians and several Jesuits. Some Korean prisoners were taken as slaves to Nagasaki, where they formed a Christian community. They had no influence, however, on any spread of Christianity in Korea itself. See James Huntley Grayson, "A Quarter-Millennium of Christianity in Korea," in *Christianity in Korea*, ed. Robert E. Buswell Jr. and Timothy S. Lee (Honolulu: University of Hawaii Press, 2006), 8–9.

188 For divergent interpretations of the Chinese-Korean encounter, see Sebastian Kim, "'Non-Missionary Beginnings' of Korean Catholic Christianity in the Late Eighteenth Century," in Koschorcke & Hermann, *Polycentric Structures*, 73–97, which stresses continuities with Confucianism, and Cho Kwang, "Human Relations as Expressed in Vernacular Catholic Writings of the Late Choson Dynasty," in Buswell and Lee, *Christianity in Korea*, 29–37.

189 Daniel J. Adams, "Ancestors, Folk Religion, and Korean Christianity," in Mullins and Fox Young, *Perspectives on Christianity*, 97.

190 Grayson, "Quarter-Millennium," in Buswell and Lee, *Christianity in Korea*, 11–12.

191 Sung-Deuk Oak, *The Making of Korean Christianity* (Waco, TX: Baylor University Press, 2013), 223; "Chinese Protestant Literature and Early Korean Protestantism," in Buswell and Lee, *Christianity in Korea*, 72–91.

192 Oak, *Making of Korean Christianity*, 172–87.

193 Oak, *Making of Korean Christianity*, chap. 1; Donald Baker, "Sibling Rivalry in Twentieth-Century Korea," in Buswell and Lee, *Christianity in Korea*, 289–90.

194 Don Baker, *Korean Spirituality* (Honolulu: University of Hawaii Press, 2008), chap. 2; Adams, "Ancestors, Folk Religion, and Korean Christianity," in Mullins and Fox Young, *Perspectives on Christianity*, 106; Donald N. Clark, "Mothers, Daughters, Biblewomen, and Sisters: An Account of 'Women's Work' in the Korea Mission Field," in Buswell and Lee, *Christianity in Korea*, 167–89; Chong Bum Kim, "Preaching the Apocalypse in Colonial Korea. The Protestant Millennialism of Kil Son-ju," ibid., 149–66.

195 Kenneth M. Wells, *New God, New Nation: Protestants and Self-Reconstruction Nationalism in Korea, 1896-1937* (Honolulu: University of Hawaii Press, 1990), 34–35.

196 Stanley, *Christianity in the Twentieth Century*, 43.

197 Wi Jo Kang, "Church and State Relations in the Japanese Colonial Period," in Buswell and Lee, *Christianity in Korea*, 101–3.

198 Kang, "Church and State Relations in the Japanese Colonial Period," 107–10.

199 Kang, "Church and State Relations in the Japanese Colonial Period," 113.

200 Grayson, *Korea. A Religious History* (Oxford: Clarendon Press, 1989), 210–11.

201 Baker, *Korean Spirituality*, 145–51.

202 Kirsteen Kim, "South Korea as a Missionary Centre of World Christianity: Developments in Korean Protestantism After the Liberation (1945)," in Koschorcke and Hermann, *Polycentric Structures*, 116.

203 Grayson, "Quarter-Millennium," in Buswell and Lee, *Christianity in Korea*, 20; Timothy S. Lee, "Beleaguered Success. Korean Evangelicalism in the Last Decade of the Twentieth Century," ibid., 330.

204 Kelly H. Chong, "In Search of Healing. Evangelical Conversion of Women in Contemporary South Korea," in Buswell and Lee, *Christianity in Korea*, 359.

205 Richard Fox Young, "East Asia," in *World Christianities, c. 1914-c.2000*, ed. Hugh McLeod. Vol. 9 of *The Cambridge History of Christianity* (Cambridge: Cambridge University Press, 2006), 465.

206 Paul Yunsik Chang, "Carrying the Torch in the Darkest Hours. The Sociopolitical Origins of Minjung Protestant Movements," in Buswell and Lee, *Christianity in Korea*, 205, 207. For an analysis of the centrality of suffering in both individual and collective Korean religious consciousness, see Jin-Heon Jung, "Some Tears of Religious Aspiration: Dynamics of

Korean Suffering in Post-war Seoul, South Korea," *World History Connected* 12, no. 2 (June 2015), http://worldhistoryconnected.press .illinois.edu/12.2/index.html.

207 Grayson, "Quarter-Millennium," in Buswell and Lee, *Christianity in Korea*, 18.
208 Eun Young Lee Easley, "Taking Jesus Public. The Neoliberal Transformation of Korean Megachurches," in *Encountering Modernity*, ed. A.L. Park and David K. Yoo (Honolulu: University of Hawaii Press, 2014), 47–59.
209 Kim, "South Korea as a Missionary Centre," in Koschorcke and Hermann, *Polycentric Structures*, 121; Hui Judy Han, "'If You Don't Work, You Don't Eat'. Evangelizing Development in Africa," in *Millenium South Korea. Neoliberal Capital and Transnational Movements*, ed. Jesook Song (London: Routledge, 2010), 142–58.
210 Han, "If You Don't Work," 147, 153.
211 Baker, *Korean Spirituality*, 3–6. Baker adopts the terminological distinction of "religious" as meaning "belonging to an organized spiritual institution" vs. "spiritual" as more broadly meaning "interacting with invisible forces" in whatever fashion.
212 Baker, *Korean Spirituality*, 59–62, 77.
213 Breen and Teeuwen, *New History of Shinto*, 213, 219.
214 Ian Reader, *Religion in Contemporary Japan* (Honolulu: University of Hawaii Press, 1991), 195–96; Helen Hardacre, *Kurozumikyo and the New Religions of Japan* (Princeton, NJ: Princeton University Press, 1986), 3.
215 Hardacre, *Kurozumikyo and the New Religions of Japan*, 108.
216 Reader, *Religion in Contemporary Japan*, 198.
217 Totman, *History of Japan*, 493.
218 Goosaert and Palmer, *Religious Question*, chap. 10.
219 Sun, *Confucianism as a World Religion*, 149–50 (see n. 7 above)
220 Goosaert and Palmer, *Religious Question*, 304.
221 Goosaert and Palmer, *Religious Question*, 395.
222 Goosaert and Palmer, *Religious Question*, 295; Johnson, *Souls of China*, 100–101; Sun, *Confucianism as World Religion*, chaps. 7–9.
223 Sun, *Confucianism as World Religion*, 210.

CHAPTER 8

1 *Christianity in its Global Context, 1970-2020* (Hamilton, MA: Center for the Study of Global Christianity, Gordon Conwell Theological Seminary, 2013), https://archive.gordonconwell.edu/ockenga/research/documents/ ChristianityinitsGlobalContext.pdf, 40, 64. The Pew study, *The Future of World Religions*, www.pewforum.org/2015/04/02/religious-projections-2010-2050/, 143–47, treats Asia and the Pacific as a single region. It should

be noted that since the 1970s these numbers have dropped dramatically in Australia and New Zealand, to a projected figure of 65.6 percent in 2020.

2 Hermann Hiery, "Inselmissionare. Die Verbreitung des Christentums in und aus der pazifischen Inselwelt," in *Polycentric Structures in the History of World Christianity*, ed. Klaus Koschorke and Adrian Hermann (Wiesbaden: Harrasowitz Verlag, 2014), 211–12.

3 John Barker, "Where the Missionary Frontier Ran Ahead of Empire," in *Missions and Empire*, ed. Norman Etherington (Oxford: Oxford University Press, 2005), 86.

4 Keith Lightfoot, *The Philippines* (New York: Praeger, 1973), 40–41; K. R. Howe, *Where the Waves Fall: A New South Seas Islands History from the First Settlement to Colonial Rule* (Honolulu: University of Hawaii Press, 1984), 14.

5 Philippine Statistical Authority, 2014, cited in "Religion in the Philippines," *Wikipedia*, en.wikipedia.org/wiki/Religion_in_the_Philippines.

6 E.g., John Liddy Phelan, *The Hispanization of the Philippines. Spanish Aims and Filipino Responses, 1565-1700* (Madison: University of Wisconsin Press, 1959); more recently, Rainer Buschmann, Edward R. Stark, James B. Tueller, *Navigating the Spanish Lake. The Pacific in the Iberian World, 1521-1898* (Honolulu: University of Hawaii Press, 2014), 10–12, 128–30. On Philippinization, see Phelan, 72–93; John A. Larkin, "Philippine History Reconsidered: A Socioeconomic Perspective," *American Historical Review* 87, no. 3 (June 1982): 595–620 (604). Vicente Rafael argues strongly for indigenous agency without using the term specifically, preferring rather "localization," in *Contracting Colonialism. Translation and Christian Conversion in Tagalog Society under Early Spanish Rule* (Ithaca, NY: Cornell University Press, 1988), 15–16.

7 Benedict Anderson, *Imagined Communities. Reflections on the Origin and Spread of Nationalism*, rev. ed. (London: Verso, 1991), 167.

8 Lightfoot, *Philippines*, 48–49.

9 H. de la Costa, S.J. [ed.], *Readings in Philippine History* (Manila: Bookmark, 1965), 7–8.

10 Phelan, *Hispanization*, 50–51.

11 Phelan, *Hispanization*, 131.

12 Phelan, "Prebaptismal Instruction and the Administration of Baptism in the Philippines during the Sixteenth Century," in *Studies in Philippine Church History*, ed. Gerald H. Anderson (Ithaca, NY: Cornell University Press, 1969), 35–37.

13 The outstanding study of this phenomenon is Reinhard Wendt, *Fiesta Filipina. Koloniale Kultur zwischen Imperialismus und neuer Identität* (Freiburg im Breisgau: Rombach Verlag, 1997).

14 Wendt, *Fiesta Filipina*, 340; Phelan, *Hispanization*, 80.

15 On the latter, see Wendt, *Fiesta Filipina*, 341.

16 See Raul Pertierra, *Religion, Politics, and Rationality in a Philippine Community* (Honolulu: University of Hawaii Press, 1988) for a case study of how such relations persist in a rural area. There was, however, no single cult of the Virgin comparable to Guadalupe in Mexico.

17 On the following, see Wendt, *Fiesta Filipina*, 83–91.

18 Austin Coates, *Rizal. Philippine Nationalist and Martyr* (Hong Kong: Oxford University Press, 1968), 7. On the growing numbers and influence of the Chinese *Mestizos*, see Buschmann, Stark, and Tueller, *Spanish Lake*, 63–67.

19 Raynaldo Clemaña Ileto, *Pasyon and Revolution. Popular Movements in the Philippines 1840-1910* (Quezon City: Ateneo de Manila University Press, 1979), 25.

20 Coates, *Rizal*, 20–21.

21 "The Development of the Native Clergy in the Philippines," in Anderson, *Studies in Philippine Church History*, 101.

22 Larkin, "Philippine History Reconsidered," 612–19.

23 Cesar Adib Majul, "Anticlericalism during the Reform Movement and the Philippine Revolution," in Anderson, *Studies in Philippine Church History*, 166.

24 Richard L. Deats, *Nationalism and Christianity in the Philippines* (Dallas: Southern Methodist University Press, 1967), 72, 79–80.

25 Pertierra, *Religion, Politics, and Rationality*, 21–22.

26 Kenneth Scott Latourette, *A History of the Expansion of Christianity*, 7 vols. (New York: Harper 1937–43) 5: 272–74.

27 H. Ellsworth Chandlee, "The Liturgy of the Philippine Independent Church," in Anderson, *Studies in Philippine Church History*, 267.

28 For example, Maretu, a native of Raratonga in the Cook Islands, was an assistant to LMS missionary Charles Pitman, who prevented him from leaving to go proselytize, despite his wish to do so. See Peggy Brock, "Setting the Record Straight: New Christians and Mission Christianity," in Brock, ed. *Indigenous Peoples and Religious Change* (Leiden: Brill, 2005), 111.

29 Hiery, "Inselmissionare," in Koschorcke and Hermann, *Polycentric Structures*, 207–8. My translation. For a comprehensive account, see Raeburn Lange, *Island Ministers. Indigenous Leadership in Nineteenth Century Pacific Islands Christianity* (Christchurch: Macmillan Brown Centre for Pacific Studies, University of Canterbury, New Zealand, 2005).

30 Lange, 184.

31 Anna Paini, "'Praying Samoa and Praying Oui-Oui': Making Christianity Local on Lifu (Loyalty Islands), in *Common Worlds and Single Lives: Constituting Knowledge in Pacific Societies*, ed. Verena Keck (Oxford: Berg, 1998), 171–206.

32 Niel Gunson, *Messengers of Grace. Evangelical Missionaries in the South Seas, 1797-1860* (Melbourne: Oxford University Press, 1978), 47–50, 101, 181–94; Charles W. Forman, *The Island Churches of the South Pacific* (Maryknoll, NY: Orbis Books, 1982), 3.

33 Howe, *Where the Waves Fall*, 117–18.

34 Bradd Shore, "*Mana* and *Tapu*," in *Developments in Polynesian Ethnology*, ed. Alan Howard and Robert Borofsky (Honolulu: University of Hawaii Press, 1989), 137–73. The notion that *tapu* is associated with a gender division, i.e., with feminine impurity due to the menstrual cycle, is shown to be oversimplified.

35 Howe, *Where the Waves Fall*, 64–65.

36 Gunson, *Messengers of Grace*, 218. See also Howe, *Where the Waves Fall*, 134–36 for the response of the Tahitians.

37 Marshall Sahlins, *How "Natives" Think about Captain Cook, For Example* (Chicago: University of Chicago Press, 1995), ch. 1. Sahlins was responding to a critique by Gananath Obeyesekere, who claimed that the Hawaiians had never literally taken Cook to be the god Lono (*The Apotheosis of Captain Cook. European Mythmaking in the Pacific* (Princeton, NJ: Princeton University Press, 1992); most scholars since have agreed with Sahlins. For a parallel transformation of first impressions in Tahiti, see Howe, *Where the Waves Fall*, 83–88.

38 Caroline Ralston, "Changes in the Lives of Ordinary Women in Post-Contact Hawaii," in *Family and Gender in the Pacific. Domestic Contradictions and the Colonial Impact*, ed. Margaret Jolly and Marth Macintyre (Cambridge: Cambridge University Press, 1989), 55–57; Howe, *Where the Waves Fall*, 89–90.

39 James L. Haley, *Captive Paradise. A History of Hawaii* (New York: St. Martin's Press, 2014), 94, who posits a reduction by more than half by the mid-nineteenth century to about 150,000.

40 Howe, *Where the Waves Fall*, 100-1; on beachcombers, ibid., 102–8; Gunson, *Messengers of Grace*, 167–69.

41 Haley, *Captive Paradise*, xxi–xxii, 35–42.

42 Haley, *Captive Paradise*, 44–45; Howe, *Where the Waves Fall*, 163–67; Jennifer Thigpen, *Island Queens and Mission Wives. How Gender and Empire Remade Hawaii's Pacific World* (Chapel Hill: University of North Carolina Press, 2014), 87.

43 Haley, *Captive Paradise*, 64. For a similar development in Tahiti, see G. S. Parsonson, "The Literate Revolution in Polynesia," *Journal of Pacific History*, 2 (1967): 39–57 (43).

44 On Fiji, see Howe, *Where the Waves Fall*, chap. 12; Forman, 4, 29–35. Fijians had a fearsome reputation in the early nineteenth century: see Jane Samson, "Ethnology and Theology: Nineteenth-Century Mission Dilemmas in the South Pacific," in *Christian Missions and the Enlightenment*, ed. Brian Stanley (Grand Rapids, MI: Eerdmans, 2001), 107.

45 Most missionaries, it is true, fled to Sydney at this time, but one, Henry Nott, remained loyal throughout, even as Pomare's fortunes plummeted (Howe, *Where the Waves Fall*, 139).

46 Thigpen, *Island Queens*, chap. 4.

47 Howe, *Where the Waves Fall*, 169–75.

48 Howe, *Where the Waves Fall*, 186–90; Sione Latukefu, *Church and State in Tonga. The Wesleyan Methodist Missionaries and Political Development, 1822-1875* (Honolulu: University Press of Hawaii, 1974), chap. 3.

49 Dress codes, however, were subject to interpretation, with missionaries and natives having distinct notions of what to wear and when. See Patricia Grimshaw, "New England Missionary Wives, Hawaiian Woman and 'the Cult of True Womanhood,'" in Jolly and Macintyre, *Family and Gender in the Pacific*, 30–31.

50 Howe, *Where the Waves Fall*, 195–97.

51 Howe, 141–42, 173–74, 190–95; Haley, *Captive Paradise*, 140–41; Latukefu, *Church and State*, chaps. 7, 9, 11, appendices. The Tongan code of 1850 outlawed dancing and "all Heathen Customs," on pain of one month's labor for first offence, two months for subsequent ones (231).

52 Philip D. Curtin, *The World & The West. The European Challenge and the Overseas Response in the Age of Empire* (Cambridge: Cambridge University Press, 2000), 144–48. Successful examples would include Peter the Great's Russia, Buganda (see chap. 4 above), Japan, Turkey, Siam.

53 R. P. Gilson, *Samoa 1830 to 1900. The Politics of a Multi-Cultural Community* (Melbourne: Oxford University Press, 1970), 72.

54 Quoted in Gilson, *Samoa 1830 to 1900*, 72–73.

55 Howe, *Where the Waves Fall*, 241.

56 Hiery, "Inselmissionare," in Koschorke and Hermann, *Polycentric Structures*, 209–10.

57 Parsonson, "Literate Revolution," 48; Howe, *Where the Waves Fall*, 143, 188; Haley, *Captive Paradise*, 87; Barker, "Missionary Frontier," 97.

58 Quoted in Parsonson, "Literate Revolution," 53.

59 Parsonson, 54; Ian Breward, *A History of the Churches in Australasia* (Oxford: Oxford University Press, 2001), 203.

60 Gunson, *Messengers of Grace*, 254, Latukefu, *Church and State*, 73.

61 Barker, "Missionary Frontier," in Etherington, *Missions and Empire*, 99.

62 Haley, *Captive Paradise*, 106–7; Grimshaw, "Missionary Wives," 42; Ralston, "Ordinary Women," 61; Hiery, "Inselmissionare,"in Koschorke and Hermann, *Polycentric Structures*, 206; John Garrett, *To Live Among the Stars: Christian Origins in Oceania* (Geneva: World Council of Churches, 1982), 47.

63 Gavan Daws, *Holy Man: Father Damien of Molokai* (Honolulu: University of Hawaii Press, 1973), 64, 75–77, 235. The subject of the book is the Belgian Catholic priest who lived in the colony and eventually died of the disease.

64 Latekufu, *Church and State*, 253. The author writes of a childhood memory in which a neighbor would put an open Bible outside her door when her husband was away to ward off evil spirits (82).

65 Barker, "Missionary Frontier," in Etherington, *Missions and Empire*, 103; Hiery, "Inselmissionare," in Koschorke and Hermann, *Polycentric Structures*, 207.

66 R. G. and Marjorie Crocombe, eds., *The Works of Ta'unga. Records of a Polynesian Traveler in the South Seas, 1833-1896* (Canberra: Australian National University Press, 1968), 6. Cf. a recent study of schoolchildren ages seven to thriteen, in Fiji on their religious beliefs, in which 69% of girls and 64% of boys assented that God loves us. Christina Toren, "The Effectiveness of Ritual," in *The Anthropology of Christianity*. ed. Fenella Cannell (Durham, NC: Duke University Press, 2006), 189.

67 Daws, *Holy Man*, 34; Daws, *Shoal of Time. A History of the Hawaiian Islands* (New York: Macmillan, 1968), 291–92.

68 Garrett, *Footsteps in the Sea: Christianity in Oceania to World War II* (Suva, Fiji: Institute of Pacific Studies, 1992), 240–41.

69 Howe, *Where the Waves Fall*, 205.

70 James Belich, *Paradise Reforged. A History of the New Zealanders from the 1880s to the Year 2000* (Honolulu: University of Hawaii Press, 2001), 207–15.

71 Belich, *Making Peoples. A History of the New Zealanders. From Polynesian Settlement to the End of the Nineteenth Century* (Honolulu: University of Hawaii Press, 1996), 157. Belich estimates the pre-contact population of New Zealand in 1769 to be 86,000 (178).

72 Belich, *Making Peoples*, 156–57; Judith Binney, *A Legacy of Guilt. A Life of Thomas Kendall* (Auckland: Oxford University Press, 1968), 76.

73 Belich, *Making Peoples*, 64–69.

74 Te Rangi Hiroa (Sir Peter Buck), *The Coming of the Maori* (Wellington: Maori Purposes Fund Board, 1950), 519–21.

75 Bronwyn Elsmore, *Like Them That Dream: The Maori and the Old Testament* (Otumoetai, NZ: Turanga Press, 1985), 25.

76 Elsmore, *Like Them That Dream*, 94.

77 Elsmore, *Like Them That Dream*, 72.

78 Elsmore, *Like Them That Dream*, 63, 70.

79 Elsmore, *Like Them That Dream*, 73–76; Elsmore, *Mana from Heaven. A Century of Maori Prophets in New Zealand* (Tauranga, NZ: Moana Press, 1989), 166–67.

80 Quoted in Binney, "Papahurihia: Some Thoughts on Interpretation," *Journal of the Polynesian Society* 75, no. 3 (Sept. 1966): 321–31 (323). On translations of the Bible in the 1830s, see Elsmore, *Like Them That Dream*, 66.

81 Belich, *Making Peoples*, 234.

82 Paul Clark. *"Hauhau": The Pai Marire Search for Maori Identity* (Auckland: Auckland University Press, 1975), 5.

83 Cf. Elsmore, *Like Them That Dream*, 198; Lyndsay Head, "The Gospel of Te Ua Haumene," *Journal of the Polynesian Society* 101, no. 1 (March, 1992): 7–44 (12–13).

84 Elsmore, *Like Them That Dream,* 198.

85 Marshall Sahlins, *Islands of History* (Chicago: University of Chicago Press), 59–65.

86 Head, "Te Ua Haumene,"in *The Dictionary of New Zealand Biography,* ed. W. H. Oliver. 5 vols. (Wellington: Bridget Williams Books, Department of Internal Affairs, 1998–2000), 1: 513.

87 Binney, *Redemption Songs. A Life of the Nineteenth-Century Maori Leader Te Kooti Arikirangi Te Turuki* (Honolulu: University of Hawaii Press, 1997), 429–30.

88 Geoffrey Rice, *Black November. The 1918 Influenza Epidemic in New Zealand* (Wellington: Allen & Unwin, 1988), 1, 107.

89 J. McLeod Henderson, *Ratana. The Origins and Story of the Movement* (Wellington: The Polynesian Society, 1963), chap. 3. The vision, of a cloud arising from the sea, resembles that of the prophet Elijah, who was also an ardent advocate of idol-smashing (1 Kings: 18).

90 Henderson, chaps. 4–8. On church statistics over a longer period, see Hans Mol, *The Fixed and the Fickle. Religion and Identity in New Zealand* (Waterloo, Ont.: Wilfrid Laurier University Press, 1982), 42. By 1951, the Ratana had slipped to third place, behind Roman Catholicism. These figures remind us that, all throughout the waxing and waning of the prophetic movements, many Maori adhered to the European churches to which they had originally converted.

91 Belich, *Paradise Reforged,* 278–79, 475–76.

92 Belich, *Paradise Reforged,* 471, 487.

93 Te Puni Kokiri, New Zealand Religion, https://tpk.idnz.co.nz/tpk/religion; Carl Walrond, "Atheism and Secularism," revised April 20, 2018, *Te Ara. Encyclopedia of New Zealand.* https://teara.govt.nz/en/atheism-and-secularism.

94 Eric Kolig, "Coming through the Backdoor? Secularisation in New Zealand and Maori Religiosity," in *The Future of Christianity. Historical, Sociological, Political and Theological Perspectives from New Zealand,* ed. John Stenhouse and Brett Knowles (Adelaide, Australia: ATF Press, 2004), 192, 199–201.

95 John Harris, *One Blood. 200 Years of Aboriginal Encounter with Christianity: A Story of Hope* (Sutherland, *Australia: Albatross Books,* 1990), 22

96 For an insightful comparison of the two cases, see Anne Keary, "Colonial Constructs and Cross-Cultural Interaction: Comparing Missionary/ Indigenous Encounters in Northwestern America and Eastern Australia," in *Beyond Conversion and Syncretism. Indigenous Encounters with Missionary Christianity, 1800–2000,* ed. David Lindenfeld and Miles Richardson (New York: Berghahn Books, 2011), 243–98.

97 Morten Rasmussen et al., "An Aboriginal Australian Genome Reveals Separate Human Dispersals into Asia," *Science,* 334, no. 6052 (Oct. 7, 2011), 94–97.

98 Quoted in Harris, *One Blood,* 23.
99 Kenelm Burridge, *Encountering Aborigines. A Case study: Anthropology and the Australian Aboriginal* (New York: Pergamon Press, 1973), 66.
100 Aram A. Yengoyan, "Religion, Morality, and Prophetic Traditions: Conversion among the Pitjantjatjara of Central Australia," in *Conversion to Christianity,* ed. Robert W. Hefner (Berkeley: University of California Press, 1993), 238. For a summary of marriage rules, see Burridge, *Encountering Aborigines,* 70–72. The importance of intertribal relations is emphasized in W. E. H. Stanner, *On Aboriginal Religion* (Sydney: University of Sydney, 1989), esp. 109.
101 Stanner, *On Aboriginal Religion,* 154, who analyzes several Aboriginal myths in depth. Burridge, *Encountering Aborigines,* 176–84.
102 Robert Bos, "The Dreaming and Social Change in Arnhem Land," in *Aboriginal Australians and Christian Missions. Ethnographic and Historical Studies,* ed. Tony Swain and Deborah Bird Rose (Bedford Park: Australian Association for the Study of Religions, 1988), 422.
103 See the articles by Robert Tonkinson, Sylvie Poirier, and Ian Keen in *Dream Travelers. Sleep Experiences and Culture in the Western Pacific,* ed. Roger Ivar Lohmann (New York: Palgrave Macmillan, 2003). See also the discussion in Robert N. Bellah, *Religion in Human Evolution. From the Paleolithic to the Axial Age* (Cambridge, MA: Harvard University Press, 2011), 147–59.
104 Fiona Magowan, "Crying to remember: reproducing personhood and community," in *Telling Stories. Indigenous history and memory in Australia and New Zealand,* ed. Bain Attwood and Fiona Magowan (Crows Nest, NSW: Allen & Unwin, 2001), 43–47.
105 Keary, "Colonial Constructs," in Lindenfeld and Richardson, *Beyond Conversion,* 244, 259–63, 275–80.
106 Rose Kunoth-Monks, "Church and Culture: An Aboriginal Perspective," in *The Gospel Is Not Western. Black Theologies from the Southwest Pacific,* ed. G.W. Trompf (Maryknoll, NY: Orbis Books, 1987), 39.
107 Harris, *One Blood,* 845.
108 Annette Hamilton, "Bond-Slaves of Satan: Aboriginal Women and the Missionary Dilemma," in *Family and Gender in the Pacific,* ed. Margaret Jolly and Martha Macintyre (Cambridge: Cambridge University Press, 1989), 258.
109 Margaret D. Jacobs, *White Mother to a Dark Race. Settler Colonialism, Maternalism, and the Removal of Indigenous Children in the American West and Australia, 1880-1940* (Lincoln: University of Nebraska Press, 2009), 19.
110 W. H. Willshire, quoted in Harris, *One Blood,* 396–97.
111 Harris, *One Blood,* 243.
112 Harris, *One Blood,* 149.

113 Harris, *One Blood*, 126–27; Jean Woolmington, "'Writing on the Sand'. The First Missions to Aborigines in Eastern Australia," in Swain and Rose, *Aboriginal Australians*, 88–99.

114 Tony Swain, *A Place for Strangers. Towards a History of Australian Aboriginal Being* (Cambridge: Cambridge University Press, 1993), chap. 3, esp. 125–33. Swain's account nicely illustrates Robin Horton's theory of religious change (see chap. 1 above). Others have challenged his bold generalizations, e.g., Jeremy Beckett in *Social Analysis.*, 40 (Sept. 1996): 11–19.

115 Compare, for example, two case studies, both from central Australia, in the collection *Indigenous Peoples and Religious Change*, ed. Peggy Brock (Leiden: Brill, 2005). Jacqueline Van Gent's study of the Lutheran Hermannsburg mission depicts widespread corporal punishment and requiring the residents to choose between traditional practices and Christianity (229–30, 238–39), contrasting with Bill Edwards's article on the Presbyterian mission at Ernabella, where decisions on what elements of the old religion to retain or give up was left up to the Aboriginal Christians themselves (139–40). See also the articles in Swain and Rose, eds. *Aboriginal Australians*, Part III.

116 Brock, "Setting the Record Straight," in Brock, *Indigenous Peoples,* 117–25.

117 Christine Choo, *Mission Girls. Aboriginal Women on Catholic Missions in the Kimberley, Western Australia, 1900-1950* (Crawley: University of Western Australia Press, 2001), 108–9.

118 Quoted in Joanna Cruickshank and Patricia Grimshaw, "'A Matter of No Small Importance to the Colony'. Moravian Missionaries on Cape York Peninsula, Queensland, 1891-1919," in *Missionaries, Indigenous Peoples and Cultural Exchange*, ed. Patricia Grimshaw and Andrew May (Brighton: Sussex Academic Press, 2010), 158.

119 Choo, *Mission Girls*, 111–16; Harris, *One Blood,* 552, 582; Jacobs, *White Mother,* 32–8.

120 Harris, *One Blood*, 591. On the missionaries' role, see Choo, *Mission Girls,* 144.

121 Jacobs, *White Mother,* 314; Cruickshank and Grimshaw, "Matter of No Small Importance," 159; Choo, *Mission Girls,* 198–99.

122 Choo, *Mission Girls,* 264. Harris, *One Blood,* 778

123 See Anna Haebich, "The battlefields of Aboriginal history," in *Australia's History. Themes and Debates*, ed. Martyn Lyons and Penny Russell (Sydney: University of New South Wales Press, 2005), 1–21; Bain Attwood, "'Learning about the Truth'. The Stolen Generations Narrative," in Attwood and Magowan, *Telling Stories,* 183–212.

124 Ronald M. Berndt, Catherine H. Berndt, "Body and Soul. More than an Episode," in Swain and Rose, *Aboriginal Australians*, 58; Harris, *One Blood,* 754.

125 "Indigenous Australians," Wikipedia, en.wikipedia.org/wiki/Indigenous_ Australians, under "Belief Systems: Recent census figures; "Christianity in Australia," Wikipedia, en.wikipedia.org/wiki/Christianity_in_Australia, under "Percentage of population since 1901"; David Hilliard, "Australia: Towards Secularisation and One Step Back," in *Secularisation in the Christian World*, ed. Callum G. Brown and Michael Snape (Farnham, UK: Ashgate 2010), 87.

126 Mol, *The Form and the Formless. Religion and Identity in Aboriginal Australia* (Waterloo, Ont.: Wilfrid Laurier University Press, 1982), 75.

127 E.g., Erich Kolig, "Mission not Accomplished. Christianity in the Kimberleys," in Swain and Rose, *Aboriginal Australians*, 376–90 (resistance); Michael Alroe, "The Pygmalion Complex among Missionaries. The Catholic Case in the Kimberley," ibid., 30–44; Peter Willis, "Riders in the Chariot. Aboriginal Conversion to Christianity at Kununurra," ibid., 308–20 (incorporation); David Thompson, "Bora, Church and Modernization at Lockhart River, Queensland," ibid., 263–76 (dual participation).

128 Maggie Brady and Kingsley Palmer, "Dependency and Assertiveness. Three Waves of Christianity Among Pitjantjatjara People at Ooldea and Yalata," in Swain and Rose, 245–47; Lynne Hume, "Christianity Full Circle. Aboriginal Christianity on Yarrabah Reserve," ibid., 255–57.

129 Guboo Ted Thomas, "The Land Is Sacred: Renewing the Dreaming in Modern Australia," in Trompf, *Gospel Is Not Western*, 91; Kolig, "Noah's Ark Revisited: On the myth-land Connection in Traditional Aboriginal Thought," *Oceania* 51, no. 2 (Dec. 1980): 118–32.

130 Bellah, *Religion in Human Evolution*, 156. See also David H. Turner, "Australian Aboriginal Religion as 'World Religion'," *Studies in Religion* 20, no. 2 (June 1991): 165–80.

131 Trompf, "Pacific Millennial Movements," in *The Oxford Handbook of Millennialism*, ed. Catherine Wessinger (Oxford: Oxford University Press, 2011), 435.

132 Mary N. MacDonald, "Thinking and teaching with the indigenous traditions of Melanesia," in *Beyond Primitivism. Indigenous Religious Traditions and Modernity*, ed. Jacob Olupona (New York: Routledge, 2004), 315–16; Trompf, *Payback. The Logic of Retribution in Melanesian Religions* (Cambridge: Cambridge University Press, 1994), xv. But see Howe, *Where the Waves Fall*, 60, who objects to characterizing these as exclusively "Melanesian" as contrasted with a "Polynesian" type: there is too much variation both within and across these regions for this to make sense.

133 P. Lawrence and M. J. Meggitt, eds., "Introduction," in *Gods Ghosts and Men in Melanesia* (Melbourne: Oxford University Press, 1965), 9.

134 Howe, *Where the Waves Fall*, 61; Trompf, *Payback*, 113.

135 Rose Kara Ninkama, "A Plea for Female Ministries in Melanesia," in Trompf, *Gospel Is Not Western*, 137–38; Brigit Obrist van Eeuwijk, "Intrusions into the Female Realm: the Medicalization of Human Procreation among the Kwanga in Papua New Guinea," in Keck, ed., *Common Worlds*, 254–59.

136 *Works of Ta'unga*, 108; ch. 10. For a comparative perspective, see Brock, Etherington, Griffiths, Van Ghent, *Indigenous Evangelists and Questions of Authority in the British Empire 1750-1940* (Leiden: Brill, 2015), 165–69. Ta'unga's writings are compared with those of another missionary from Raratonga, Maretu, who treats cannibalism more dispassionately. For a contemporary view of the culture of suspicion, see Willington Jojoga Opeba, "Melanesian Cult Movements as Traditional Religious and Ritual Responses to Change," in Trompf, *Gospel Is Not Western*, 64–65.

137 Ta'unga recorded in his journal that European traders actually sought to portray Jehovah as God of the Samoans only (not Europeans), and was responsible for the disease and destruction on the Isle of Pines (*Works*, 63).

138 Garrett, *To Live Among the Stars*, 161–67, 176, 180–81, 191, 218, 224–25. Darrell L.Whiteman, *Melanesians and Missionaries* (Pasadena, CA: William Carey Library, 1983), 1–2, 112.

139 Barker, "Missionary Frontier," in Etherington, *Missions and Empire*, 94.

140 Howe, *Where the Waves Fall*, 299–301.

141 Trompf, *Payback*, 126. Chapter 2 is devoted to reciprocity. Cf. Ennio Mantovani SVD, *The Dema and the Christ. My Engagement and Inner Dialogue with the Cultures and Religions of Melanesia.* (Siegeburg: Verlag Franz Schmitt, 2014), 29–37.

142 Howe, *Where the Waves Fall*, 303–6; Whiteman, *Melanesians and Missionaries*, chap. 3.

143 Howe, *Where the Waves Fall*, 308, 313; Garrett, *To Live Among the Stars*, 189–205; Forman, *Island Churches*, 5–7.

144 Whiteman, *Melanesians and Missionaries*, 144–45.

145 Whiteman, *Melanesians and Missionaries*, 184–85.

146 Whiteman, *Melanesians and Missionaries*, 192–93; Barker, "'We are Ekelesia': Conversion in Uiaku, Papua New Guinea," in Hefner, *Conversion to Christianity*, 203.

147 Quoted in Whiteman, *Melanesians and Missionaries*, 107–8. Howe describes in detail the impact of commerce at this time, and concludes that it was real but localized (*Where the Waves Fall*, 326). Trompf discusses the factor of wonder and awe in "On wondering about wonder. Melanesians and the cargo," in Olupona, *Beyond Primitivism*, 297–313.

148 Howe, *Where the Waves Fall*, 329–42.

149 Garrett, *To Live Among the Stars*, 299; Forman, *Island Churches*, 52.

150 For a case study, see M. R. Allen, "The Establishment of Christianity and Cash-Cropping in a New Hebridean Community," *Journal of Pacific History*

3 (1968): 25–46. This article admirably portrays the interactions between returning laborers, missionaries, and new economic patterns.

151 Whiteman, *Melanesians and Missionaries*, 176.

152 Forman, *Island Churches*, 90.

153 Whiteman, *Melanesians and Missionaries*, 191–92.

154 Whiteman, *Melanesians and Missionaries*, 177–79, 224–25.

155 Forman, *Island Churches*, 54–55; Diane Langmore, *Missionary Lives. Papua, 1874-1914* (Honolulu: University of Hawaii Press, 1989), 136; Whiteman, *Melanesians and Missionaries*, 190.

156 Whiteman, *Melanesians and Missionaries*, 186–88.

157 "Sins of a Mission: Christian Life as Kwaio Traditionalist Ideology," in Jolly and MacIntyre, *Family and Gender*, 193–212.

158 Quoted in Whiteman, *Melanesians and Missionaries*, 189.

159 Barker, "An Outpost in Papua: Anglican Missionaries and Melanesian Teachers among the Maisin, 1902-1934," in Brock, *Indigenous People and Religious Change*, 91.

160 Whiteman, *Melanesians and Missionaries*, 180–81.

161 Paul Landau, "Language," in Etherington, *Missions and Empire*, 200; Garrett, *Where Nets Were Cast. Christianity in Oceania Since World War II* (Suva: Institute of Pacific Studies, 1997), 318–20.

162 Barker, "Outpost in Papua," 103.

163 E.g., Hilliard, *God's Gentlemen. A History of the Melanesian Mission, 1849-1942* (St. Lucia: University of Queensland Press, 1978), 221–23.

164 Garrett, *Footsteps*, 399–405.

165 Trompf, *Payback*, 169–207.

166 Jean Guiart, "The Millenarian Aspect of Conversion to Christianity in the South Pacific," in *Millennial Dreams in Action. Essays in Comparative Study*, ed. Sylvia L. Thrupp (The Hague: Mouton, 1962), 123–24; Mary Taylor Huber, *The Bishops' Progress. A Historical Ethnography of Catholic Missionary Experience on the Sepik Frontier* (Washington: Smithsonian Institution Press, 1988), 118–30.

167 Trompf, "Pacific Millennial Movements," in Wessinger, *Oxford Handbook of Millennialism*, 440–43; Patrick Gesch, "The Cultivation of Surprise and Excess. The Encounter of Cultures in the Sepik of Papua New Guinea," in Trompf, ed., *Cargo Cults and Millenarian Movements. Transoceanic Comparisons of New Religious Movements* (Berlin: De Gruyter, 1990), 218–19, 231–33.

168 Breward, *History of the Churches in Australasia*, 296-97; Garrett, *Where Nets Were Cast*, 28, 44.

169 On earlier antecedents in Melanesian society, see Roderic Lacey, "Journeys of Transformation: the Discovery and Disclosure of Cosmic Secrets in Melanesia," in Trompf, *Cargo Cults*, 181–211; Opeba, "Melanesian Cult Movements," in Trompf, *Gospel Is Not Western*, 49–61.

170 Garrett, *Where Nets Were Cast*, 192–95; Esau Tuza, "The Demolition of Church Buildings by the Ancestors," in Trompf, *Gospel Is Not Western*, 67–86.
171 Whiteman, *Melanesians and Missionaries*, 250–73.
172 Huber, *Bishop's Progress*, 150–52; Barker, "'We are *Ekelesia*'," in Hefner, *Conversion to Christianity*, 220.
173 Stanley, *Christianity in the Twentieth Century. A World History* (Princeton, NJ: Princeton University Press, 2018) 74–75.
174 Katharine Massam, "Christian Churches in Australia, New Zealand and the Pacific, 1914-1970," in *World Christianities c. 1914-2000*, ed. Hugh McLeod. Vol. 9 of *The Cambridge History of Christianity* (Cambridge: Cambridge University Press, 2006), 254. Cf. Forman, *Island Churches*, 144–45. In the Anglican mission, however, the ratio of European missionaries to Melanesian workers was 1 to 29 (Whiteman, *Melanesians and Missionaries*, 295–96).
175 Huber, *Bishop's Progress*, 162.
176 Forman, *Island Churches*, 184.
177 Huber, *Bishop's Progress*, 140.
178 Trompf, *Payback*, 437–38; Whiteman, *Melanesians and Missionaries*, 351.
179 Joel Robbins, *Becoming Sinners. Christianity and Moral Torment in a Papua New Guinea Society* (Berkeley: University of California Press, 2004), chap. 3, esp. 122, 124; Breward, *History of Churches in Australasia*, 348.
180 Trompf, *Payback*, 421; Robbins, *Becoming Sinners*, 148. Cf. a similar phenomenon in Africa, see chap. 4 above, p. 139.
181 Trompf, *Payback*, 299–300; Breward, *History of Churches in Australasia*, 411–14; Monique Jeudy-Ballini, "Appropriating the Other: A Case Study from New Britain," in Keck, *Common Worlds*, 207–27. The Adventists regarded Catholics as no better than pagans.
182 Robbins, *Becoming Sinners*, 160, 168.
183 The latter position is that of Harvey Whitehouse, who claims that Christianity is based on concepts and arguments, in contrast to "iconic" or "episodic" modes of communication in Melanesian religion which are conveyed by vivid images, e.g., of rites and festivals. These two types, according to Whitehouse, can interact but not mesh. The former position is that of John Barker, who claims that such meshing can and does take place. See Whitehouse, *Arguments and Icons. Divergent Modes of Religiosity* (Oxford: Oxford University Press, 2000), and "Appropriated and Monolithic Christianity in Melanesia," in Cannell, *Anthropology of Christianity*, 295–307; Barker, "Comment," *Journal of the Royal Anthropological Institute* 5, no. 1 (March 1999): 97–100.
184 Lohmann, "Supernatural Encounters of the Asabano in Two Traditions and Three States of Consciousness," in Lohmann, *Dream Travelers*, 195–97.

185 Whiteman, Melanesians and *Missionaries*, 345–47. Ennio Mantovani, a Catholic missionary, in *The Dema and the Christ*, chap. 8, 182–83, draws the analogy between Christ's sacrifice and that of the Dema, a category of spirits. The sacrifice of the Dema is necessary in order to guarantee that life and fertility will continue, and is reenacted by an elaborate festival centered on the sacrificial slaughter of pigs.

186 Whiteman, *Melanesians and Missionaries*, 338–40, 342.

187 Robbins, *Becoming Sinners*, 171, chap. 6, esp. 215.

188 Robbins, 247–48. In a more recent article, however, Robbins emphasizes the growth among the Urapmin of "Christian individualism," in the sense that each person must interpret the Christian message for themselves. Robbins, "Anthropological Perspectives on World Christianity," in Joel Cabrita, David Maxwell, and Emma Wild-Wood, eds., *Relocating World Christianity* (Leiden: Brill, 2017), 250–51.

189 Barker, "We are *Ekelesia*," in Hefner, *Conversion to Christianity*, 204–6. Cf. Robbins, *Becoming Sinners*, 216; Whiteman, *Melanesians and Missionaries*, 345 ("split-level Christianity").

190 Margaret Jolly, "Sacred Spaces: Churches, Men's Houses and Households in South Pentecost, Vanuatu," in Jolly and Macintyre, *Family and Gender*, 213–35; Breward, *History of Churches in Australasia*, 353; Whiteman, *Melanesians and Missionaries*, 382; van Eeuwijk, "Intrusions into the Female Realm," in Keck, *Common Worlds*, 267.

191 *Christianity in Its Global Context*, 68.

192 Robbins, *Becoming Sinners*, 173, 175.

CONCLUSION

1 Joel Cabrita and David Maxwell, "Introduction. Relocating World Christianity," in *Relocating World Christianity*, ed. Cabrita, Maxwell and Emma Wild-Wood (Leiden: Brill, 2017), 37.

2 Alan Strathern, *Unearthly Powers. Religious and Political Change in World History* (Cambridge: Cambridge University Press, 2019), 1.

3 See J. C. D. Clark, "Secularization and Modernization. The Failure of a 'Grand Narrative'," *The Historical Journal* 55, no. 1 (March 2012), 161–94.

4 See Weber, "Science as a Vocation," in *From Max Weber. Essays in Sociology*, ed., trans. H. Gerth and C. Wright Mills (New York: Oxford University Press, 1946), 139.

5 See p. 191 above.

6 Strathern, *Unearthly Powers*, chap. 1. Also David Lindenfeld, "The Axial Age, Axiality and the Missionary Enterprise," *International Bulletin of Mission Research*, 41, no. 1 (Jan. 2017), 63–72; Robert N. Bellah and Hans Joas,

eds., *The Axial Age and Its Consequences* (Cambridge, MA: Belknap Press of Harvard University Press, 2012).

7 On the shift, compare the earlier work of sociologist Peter Berger: *The Sacred Canopy* (Garden City, NY: Doubleday, 1967) with his subsequent *The Desecularization of the World* (Washington, DC: Ethics and Public Policy Center, 1999). On the 1980s as the pivotal decade, see José Casanova, *Public Religions in the Modern World* (Chicago: University of Chicago Press, 1994, 3-6. On recent debates, *The Oxford Handbook of Secularism*, ed. Phil Zuckerman and John R. Shook (New York: Oxford University Press, 2017), 7–8; Steve Bruce, *God Is Dead. Secularization in the West* (Malden, MA: Blackwell, 2002), 63–69 (on Great Britain). And not only in the West: compare Ian Reader's conclusion in his study *Religion in Contemporary Japan* (Honolulu: University of Hawaii Press, 1991), that "religious matters, and religiosity, are very much part of Japanese life" (243) with the same author's 2012 article, "Secularisation R.I.P.? Nonsense! The 'Rush Hour Away from the Gods' and the Decline of Religion in Contemporary Japan," *Journal of Religion in Japan* 1 (2012), 7–36.

8 An exception is David A. Hollinger, "Christianity and Its American Fate: Where History Interrogates Secularization Theory," in *The Worlds of American Intellectual History*, ed. Joel Issac et al. (New York: Oxford University Press, 2016), 280–303.

9 This classification is close to that of Bruce Lincoln, *Holy Terrors: Thinking about Religion after September 11*, 2nd ed. (Chicago: University of Chicago Press, 2006), 5–7.

10 Bruce, *God Is Dead*, 30.

11 Erik Sidenvall, "A Classic Case of De-Christianisation? Religious Change in Scandinavia, c.1750-2000," in *Secularisation in the Christian World. Essays in Honour of Hugh McLeod* ed. Callum G. Brown and Michael Snape (Farnham, UK: Ashgate, 2010), 119–33.

12 Joachim Wach, *Sociology of Religion* (Chicago: University of Chicago Press, 1944), 26.

13 William James, *The Varieties of Religious Experience*. Reprint (New York: The Modern Library, 1994), 55.

14 Emile Durkheim, *The Elementary Forms of the Religious Life*, trans. Joseph Ward Swain. Reprint (New York: Free Press, 1965 (1915), 475.

15 Rudolf Otto, *The Idea of the Holy*, 2nd ed., trans. John W. Harvey (London: Oxford University Press, 1950), chaps. ii–iv.

16 Clifford Geertz, *The Interpretation of Cultures* (New York: Basic Books, 1973), 108–9. This emphasis on authority and the political might serve as an alternative formulation to the more commonly accepted emphasis on association and the sociological, as elaborated in Wach's treatise. The contrast between church and sect, as formulated by Ernst Troeltsch – the one reaching out to the masses, the other delimited as an intense set of believers – can also

serve to illustrate the difference between diffuse and concentrated spirituality. See his *The Social Teaching of the Christian Churches*, trans. Olive Wyon, 2 vols. (London: Allen & Unwin: 1931), 2: 993.

17 G. Van der Leeuw, *Religion in Essence and Manifestation*, trans. J. E. Turner (Princeton, NJ: Princeton University Press, 1986), 159–68; Mircea Eliade, *The Sacred and the Profane. The Nature of Religion* (San Diego: Harcourt, 1959), 121–25.

18 Rodney Stark and William Sims Bainbridge, *A Theory of Religion* (New York: Peter Lang, 1987), 85–6.

19 Geertz, *Interpretation of Cultures*, 112–13. For a comprehensive survey of rituals, see Catherine Bell, *Ritual: Perspectives and Dimensions* (New York: Oxford University Press, 1997).

20 Brian Stanley, *Christianity in the Twentieth Century* (Princeton, NJ: Princeton University Press, 2018), 28–33; this had repercussions abroad where missionaries were heavily involved, such as in China. See Daniel Bays, *New History of Christianity in China* (Malden, MA: Wiley-Blackwell, 2012), 104–6.

21 According to Kenneth Scott Latourette, by the 1930s about half the personnel and money provided by Western churches to missionaries went to education. See his *A History of the Expansion of Christianity*, 7 vols. (New York: Harper & Brothers, 1937–45), 7: 54

22 Otto, *Idea of the Holy*, 65–71.

23 Casanova, *Public Religions*, 64. See also Colleen McDannell, *Material Christianity. Religion and Popular Culture in America* (New Haven, CT: Yale University Press, 1995).

24 Benedict Anderson, *Imagined Communities. Reflections on the Origin and Spread of Nationalism*, rev. ed. (London: Verso, 1991), 5, 35–36.

25 See Guy Ben-Porat, "Secularization in Israel," in Zuckerman and Shook, *Oxford Handbook*, 173; Vidhu Verma, "Secularism in India," ibid., 225.

26 Stephen Prothero, *God Is not One: The Eight Rival Religions That Run the World—and Why Their Differences Matter* (New York: Harper One, 2010), 204–5. Wach, *Sociology*, 385–88, provides a survey of religious hierarchies worldwide.

27 Wach, 333.

28 I must confess that I owe this idea to having spent most of my adult life in the American south, where the landscape is dotted with myriads of small independent Baptist churches every few miles.

29 Ernst Troeltsch provides an extensive roster of these mystics and sectarians in *Social Teaching of the Christian Churches*, 2: 691–799.

30 For a more variegated and nuanced version, see David Martin, *A General Theory of Secularization* (New York: Harper Colophon, 1978), esp. 18–21.

31 On religious revivals and popular culture, see the articles by Mary Heimann and David M. Thompson in *World Christianities, c. 1815-1914*, ed. Sheridan

Gilley and Brian Stanley. Vol. 8 of *The Cambridge History of Christianity* (Cambridge: Cambridge University Press, 2006), 70–84, 197–214.

32 Michael Snape, "The Great War," in *World Christianities, c. 1914-c.2000*, ed. Hugh McLeod. Vol. 9 of *The Cambridge History of Christianity* (Cambridge: Cambridge University Press, 2006), 132.

33 On the following, see Mcleod, "The Crisis of Christianity in the West: Entering a Post-Christian Era?" in Macleod, *World Christianities c. 1914-c.2000*, 323–47; and Brown and Snape, *Secularisation in the Christian World*.

34 Robert Fuller, "Secular Spirituality," in Zuckerman and Shook, *Oxford Handbook*, 578; *Spiritual But Not Religious* (New York: Oxford University Press, 2001).

35 Bruce, *Secular Beats Spiritual* (Oxford: Oxford University Press, 2017), 3. On baptisms, Macleod, "Crisis," 324.

36 Macleod, "Crisis," 331.

37 Fuller, "Secular Spirituality," in Zuckerman and Shook, *Oxford Handbook*, 572. This should not be interpreted as saying that people who declare themselves to be secular are "really" religious, any more than claiming that liberal Protestants, for example, are "really" secular. One should take people at their word.

38 R. Scott Appleby, "Rethinking Fundamentalism in a Secular Age," in *Rethinking Secularism*, ed. Craig Calhoun, Mark Jurgensmeyer, and Jonathan VanAntwerpen eds. (Oxford: Oxford University Press, 2011), 325–50.

39 Juergensmeyer, "The Imagined War between Secularism and Religion," in Zuckerman and Shook, *Oxford Handbook*, 80–81.

40 Philip Jenkins, *The Next Christendom. The Coming of Global Christianity*, 3rd ed. (Oxford: Oxford University Press, 2011), chap. 9.

41 *Christianity in Its Global Context, 1970-2020* (Hamilton, MA: Center for the Study of Global Christianity, Gordon Conwell Theological Seminary, 2013), https://archive.gordonconwell.edu/ockenga/research/docu ments/ChristianityinitsGlobalContext.pdf, 19.

42 Casanova, *Public Religions*, chap. 8.

43 Casanova, *Public Religions*, 242, n.44. A comparison of the World Values Survey data for 2010 with the Pew Research Center's findings show the following disparities in percentages of people for whom religion is unimportant (WVS) or who are unaffiliated (Pew): Japan: 34.3% (WVS), 57% (Pew); South Korea, 18.5% (WVS), 46.4% (Pew); Russia, 22.4% (WVS), 16.2% (Pew). Inglehart, R., C. Haerpfer, A. Moreno, C. Welzel, K. Kizilova, J. Diez-Medrano, M. Lagos, P. Norris, E. Ponarin, B. Puranen et al. (eds.). 2014. World Values Survey: Round Six – Country-Pooled Datafile Version: www .worldvaluessurvey.org/WVSDocumentationWV6.jsp. Madrid: JD Systems Institute; Pew Research Center, April 2, 2015, The Future of World

Religions: Population Growth Projections, 2010–2050, http://www.pewforum.org/2015/04/02/religious-projections-2010-2050/, 81.

44 Pew Research Center, Future of World Religions, full report, 9; Gordon-Conwell Theological Seminary, *Christianity in its Global Context*, 12.

45 Todd M. Johnson and Gina A. Zurlo, *World Christian Encyclopedia*, 3rd edition (Edinburgh: Edinburgh University Press, 2019), 6.

46 The case for the latter is made by Eller, "Varieties of Secular Experience," in Zuckerman and Shook, *Oxford Handbook*, 499–514. Nevertheless, according to Philip Jenkins, *Next Christendom*, 135, the spreading Christian churches in the global south have remained recognizably Christian.

47 Bruce, *God Is Dead*, 240.

General Bibliography

Works listed here are relevant to more than one world-region. Works specific to such regions may be found in the notes to the individual chapters.

Anderson, Benedict. *Imagined Communities. Reflections on the Origin and Spread of Nationalism*. Rev. ed. London: Verso, 1991.

Andrews, Edward E. *Native Apostles. Black and Indian Missionaries to the British and Atlantic World*. Cambridge, MA: Harvard University Press, 2013.

Angold, Michael, ed. *Eastern Christianity. The Cambridge History of Christianity, vol. 5*. Cambridge: Cambridge University Press, 2006.

Asad, Talal. *Formations of the Secular. Christianity, Islam, Modernity*. Stanford, CA: Stanford University Press, 2003.

Aydin, Cemil. *The Politics of Anti-Westernism in Asia. Vision of World Order in Pan-Islamic and Pan-Asian Thought*. New York: Columbia University Press, 2007.

Ballantyne, Tony. "The Persistence of the Gods: Religion in the Modern World." In *World Histories from Below. Disruption and Dissent, 1750 to the Present*, edited by Antoinette Burton and Tony Ballantyne: 137–67. London: Bloomsbury, 2016.

Bayly, C. A. *The Birth of the Modern World 1780–1914*. Oxford: Blackwell, 2004.

Belich, James. *Replenishing the Earth. The Settler Revolution and the Rise of the Anglo-World, 1783–1939*. Oxford: Oxford University Press, 2009.

Bellah, Robert N. *Religion in Human Evolution. From the Paleolithic to the Axial Age*. Cambridge, MA: Harvard University Press, 2011.

Bellah, Robert N. and Hans Joas, eds. *The Axial Age and Its Consequences*. Cambridge, MA: Harvard University Press, 2012.

Berger, Peter. *The Sacred Canopy*. Garden City, NY: Doubleday, 1967.

— *The Desecularization of the World*. Washington: Ethics and Public Policy Center, 1999.

Bitterli, Urs. *Cultures in Conflict. Encounters between European and Non-European Cultures, 1492–1800*. Translated by Ritchie Robinson. Stanford, CA: Stanford University Press, 1989.

Bonnell, Victoria E., and Lynn Hunt, eds. *Beyond the Cultural Turn.* Berkeley: University of California Press, 1999.

Bosch, David J., *Transforming Mission: Paradigm Shifts in Theology of Mission, Twentieth Anniversary Edition.* Maryknoll, NY: Orbis Books, 2011.

Bossy, John. *Christianity in the West, 1400–1700.* Oxford: Oxford University Press, 1985.

Bourguignon, Erika, ed. *Religion, Altered States of Consciousness, and Social Change.* Columbus: Ohio State University Press, 1973.

Bowie, Fiona, Deborah Kirkwood, and Shirley Ardener, eds. *Women and Missions: Past and Present. Anthropological and Historical Perspectives.* Providence, RI: Berg, 1993.

Brock, Peggy, ed. *Indigenous Peoples and Religious Change.* Leiden: Brill, 2005.

Brock, Peggy, Norman Etherington, Gareth Griffiths, and Jacqueline Van Gent. *Indigenous Evangelists and Questions of Authority in the British Empire 1750–1940.* Leiden: Brill, 2015.

Brown, Callum G. and Michael Snape, eds. *Secularisation in the Christian World: Essays in Honour of Hugh McLeod.* Farnham, UK: Ashgate, 2010.

Bruce, Steve. *God Is Dead: Secularization in the West.* Malden, MA: Blackwell, 2002.

— *Secular Beats Spiritual.* Oxford: Oxford University Press, 2017.

Cabrita, Joel, David Maxwell, Emma Wild-Wood, eds. *Relocating World Christianity. Interdisciplinary Studies in Universal and Local Expressions of the Christian Faith.* Leiden: Brill, 2017.

Calhoun, Craig, Mark Jurgensmeyer, Jonathan VanAntwerpen, eds. *Rethinking Secularism.* New York: Oxford University Press, 2011.

Cannell, Fenella, ed. *The Anthropology of Christianity.* Durham, NC: Duke University Press, 2006.

Casanova, José. *Public Religions in the Modern World.* Chicago: University of Chicago Press, 1994.

Chakrabarty, Dipesh. *Provincializing Europe. Postcolonial Thought and Historical Difference.* Princeton, NJ: Princeton University Press, 2000.

Christian, William A. *Local Religion in Sixteenth-Century Spain.* Princeton, NJ: Princeton University Press, 1989.

Coates, Ken S. *A Global History of Indigenous Peoples: Struggle and Survival.* New York: Palgrave Macmillan, 2004.

Colpe, Carsten. "Syncretism," in *Encyclopedia of Religion.* Edited by Mircea Eliade, 16 vols., 14: 218–27. New York: Macmillan, 1987.

Comaroff, Jean, and John Comaroff. *Of Revelation and Revolution. Christianity, Colonialism, and Consciousness in South Africa.* 2 vols. Chicago: University of Chicago Press, 1991, 1997.

Conrad, Sebastian. *What Is Global History?* Princeton, NJ: Princeton University Press, 2016.

Cox, Harvey. *The Secular City: Secularization and Urbanization in Theological Perspective,* rev. ed. New York: Macmillan 1966.

Cox, Jeffrey. *The British Missionary Enterprise since 1700.* New York: Routledge, 2008.

Curtin, Philip D. *The World and the West. The European Challenge and the Overseas Response in the Age of Empire*. Cambridge: Cambridge University Press, 2000.

Dunch, Ryan. "Beyond Cultural Imperialism: Cultural Theory, Christian Missions, and Global Modernity." *History and Theory* 41 (2002): 301–25.

Durkheim, Emile. *The Elementary Forms of the Religious Life*. Translated by Joseph Ward Swain. New York: Free Press, 1965. First published 1915 by George Allen & Unwin.

Eisenstadt, Shmuel M. "The Axial Age: The Emergence of Transcendental Visions and the Rise of Clerics." *Archives européenes de Sociologie* 23 (1982): 294–314.

Eliade, Mircea. *A History of Religious Ideas*. 3 vols. Chicago, IL: University of Chicago Press, 1987.

— *The Sacred and the Profane. The Nature of Religion*. San Diego, CA: Harcourt, 1959.

Etherington, Norman, ed. *Missions and Empire*. Oxford: Oxford University Press, 2005.

Etienne, Mona, and Eleanor Leacock, eds. *Women and Colonization. Anthropological Perspectives*. New York: Praeger, 1980.

Firth, Raymond. *Religion: A Humanist Interpretation*. London: Routledge, 1996.

Fletcher, Richard. *The Barbarian Conversion. From Paganism to Christianity*. New York: Henry Holt, 1997.

Foucault, Michel. *Religion and Culture. Selected and edited by Jeremy R. Carrette*. New York: Routledge, 1999.

Fuller, Robert. *Spiritual, But Not Religious*. New York: Oxford University Press, 2001.

Geertz, Clifford. *The Interpretation of Cultures*. New York: Basic Books, 1973.

Gilley, Sheridan, and Brian Stanley, eds. *World Christianities, c. 1815–1914*. Vol. 8 of *The Cambridge History of Christianity*. Cambridge: Cambridge University Press, 2006.

Gordon Conwell Theological Seminary. *Christianity in Its Global Context. Society, Religion, and Mission*. Hamilton, MA: Center for the Study of Global Christianity, 2013. www.gordonconwell.edu/ockenga/research/docu ments/ChristianityinitsGlobalContext.pdf.

Gort, Jerald D., Hendrik Vroom, *et al.*, eds. *Dialogue and Syncretism. An Interdisciplinary Approach*. Grand Rapids, MI: Eerdmans, 1989.

Gregerson, Linda, and Susan Juster, eds. *Empires of God: Religious Encounters in the Early Modern Atlantic*. Philadelphia: University of Pennsylvania Press, 2011.

Greenfield, Sydney M., and André Droogers, eds., *Reinventing Religions: Syncretism and Transformation in Africa and the Americas* Lanham, MD: Rowman & Littlefield, 2001.

Grimshaw, Patricia, and Andrew May, eds. *Missionaries, Indigenous Peoples and Cultural Exchange*: Brighton, UK: Sussex Academic Press, 2010.

Gump, James O. "A Spirit of Resistance: Sioux, Xhosa, and Maori Responses to Western Dominance, 1840–1920." *Pacific Historical Review* 66 (1997): 21–52.

Hanciles, Jehu J. "New Wine in Old Wineskins. Critical Reflections on Writing and Teaching a Global Christian History." *Missiology: An International Review* 34 (2006): 361–82.

Harkin, Michael E., ed. *Reassessing Revitalization Movements. Perspectives from North America and the Pacific Islands.* Lincoln: University of Nebraska Press, 2004.

Hefner, Robert A., ed. *Conversion to Christianity. Historical and Anthropological Perspectives on a Great Transformation.* Berkeley: University of California Press, 1993.

Horton, Robin. "African Conversion." *Africa* 41 (1971): 85–108.

— *Patterns of Thought in Africa and the West. Essays on Magic, Religion and Science.* Cambridge: Cambridge University Press, 1993.

— "The Rationality of Conversion." *Africa* 45 (1975): 219–35; 373–99.

Hodgson, Marshall G. S. *The Venture of Islam. Conscience and History in a World Civilization.* 3 vols. Chicago: University of Chicago Press, 1974.

Jacobs, Margaret D. *White Mother to a Dark Race: Settler Colonialism, Maternalism, and the Removal of Indigenous Children in the American West and Australia, 1880–1940.* Lincoln: University of Nebraska Press, 2009.

James, William. *The Varieties of Religious Experience.* New York: The Modern Library, 1999. First published 1902 by Longmans, Green.

Jenkins, Philip. *The Next Christendom: The Coming of Global Christianity.* 3rd ed. Oxford: Oxford University Press, 2011.

Joas, Hans, and Klaus Wiegandt, eds. *Secularization and the World Religions.* Translated by Alex Skinner Liverpool: Liverpool University Press, 2009.

Jung, C. G. *Psychology and Religion: West and East.* 2nd ed. Translated by R. F. C. Hull. Vol. 11 of The Collected Works of C. G. Jung. Princeton, NJ: Princeton University Press, 1969.

Kaplan, Steven, ed. *Indigenous Responses to Western Christianity.* New York: New York University Press, 1995.

Koschorke, Klaus, and Adrian Hermann, eds. *Polycentric Structures in the History of World Christianity/Polyzentrische Strukturen in der Geschichte des Weltchristentums.* Wiesbaden: Harrasowitz Verlag, 2014.

Kraemer, Hendrik. *World Cultures and World Religions: The Coming Dialogue.* Philadelphia: Westminster Press, 1960.

Laine, James W. *Meta-Religion. Religion and Power in World History.* Berkeley: University of California Press, 2014.

Latourette, Kenneth Scott. *A History of the Expansion of Christianity.* 7 vols. New York: Harper, 1937–45.

Lincoln, Bruce. *Holy Terrors: Thinking about Religion after September 11.* 2nd ed. Chicago: University of Chicago Press, 2006.

Lindenfeld, David. "The Concept of 'World Religions' as Currently Used in Religious Studies Textbooks." *World History Bulletin* 22, no. 1 (2007): 6–7.

— "Indigenous Encounters with Christian Missionaries in China and West Africa, 1800–1920: A Comparative Study." *Journal of World History*, 16 (2005): 327–69.

— "Jungian Archetypes and the Discourse of History." *Rethinking History*, 13, no. 2 (2009): 217–34.

— "Syncretism." In *Vocabulary for the Study of Religion*. Edited by Kocku von Stuckrad and Robert Segal. 3 vols. 3: 242–47. Leiden: Brill, 2015.

— "The Axial Age, Axiality, and the Missionary Enterprise." *International Bulletin of Mission Research* 41 (2017): 63–72.

Lindenfeld, David and Miles Richardson, eds. *Beyond Conversion & Syncretism: Indigenous Encounters with Missionary Christianity, 1800–2000.* New York: Berghahn, 2011.

Manning, Patrick. *Navigating World History.* New York: Palgrave Macmillan, 2003.

Martin, David. *A General Theory of Secularization.* New York: Harper & Row, 1978.

Masuzawa, Tomiko. *The Invention of World Religions, or How European Universalism Was Preserved in the Language of Pluralism.* Chicago: University of Chicago Press, 2005.

McLeod, Hugh, ed. *World Christianities c. 1914–2000.* Vol. 9 of *The Cambridge History of Christianity.* Cambridge: Cambridge University Press, 2006.

McNeill, J. R., and William H. McNeill. *The Human Web: A Bird's Eye View of World History.* New York: W. W. Norton, 2003.

McNeill, William H. "The Changing Shape of World History." *History and Theory* 34, no. 2 (May, 1995): 8–26.

Mudimbe-boyi, M. Elizabeth, ed. *Beyond Dichotomies: Histories, Identities, Cultures and the Challenge of Globalization.* Albany: State University of New York Press, 2002.

Nandy, Ashis. *The Intimate Enemy. Loss and Recovery of Self under Colonialism.* Delhi: Oxford University Press, 1983.

Neill, Stephen. *A History of Christian Missions.* 2nd ed. Revised by Owen Chadwick. London: Penguin Books, 1990. First published 1986 by Pelican Books.

Nongbri, Brent. *Before Religion. History of a Modern Concept.* New Haven, CT: Yale University Press, 2013.

Olupona, Jacob K., ed. *Beyond Primitivism: Indigenous Religious Traditions and Modernity.* New York: Routledge, 2004.

Otto, Rudolf. *The Idea of the Holy.* 2nd ed. Translated by John W. Harvey. London: Oxford University Press, 1950. First published in 1923.

Pew Research Center. *The Future of World Religions: Population Growth Projections, 2010–2050.* www.pewforum.org/2015/04/02/religious-projec tions-2010-2050/.

Phan, Peter C. *In Our Own Tongues: Perspectives from Asia on Mission and Inculturation.* Maryknoll, NY: Orbis Books, 2003.

Porter, Andrew. *Religion Versus Empire? British Protestant Missionaries and Overseas Expansion, 1700–1914.* Manchester: Manchester University Press, 2004.

Prothero, Stephen. *God Is Not One: The Eight Rival Religions That Run the World – and Why Their Differences Matter.* New York: HarperCollins, 2010.

Rambo, Lewis. *Understanding Religious Conversion.* New Haven, CT: Yale University Press, 1993.

Reff, Daniel T. *Plagues, Priests, and Demons: Sacred Narratives and the Rise of Christianity in the Old World and the New.* Cambridge: Cambridge University Press, 2005.

Robert, Dana L. *Christian Mission: How Christianity Became a World Religion.* Malden: Wiley-Blackwell, 2009.

Robert, Dana L., ed. *Converting Colonialism: Visions and Realities in Mission History, 1706–1914.* Grand Rapids, MI: Eerdmans, 2008.

Robbins, Joel. "Continuity Thinking and the Problem of Christian Culture: Belief, Time and the Anthropology of Christianity," *Current Anthropology* 48, no. 1 (February 2007): 5–38.

Russell, James C., *The Germanization of Early Medieval Christianity.* New York: Oxford University Press, 1994.

Said, Edward W. *Orientalism.* New York: Vintage Books, 1978.

Sanneh, Lamin. *Translating the Message. The Missionary Impact on Culture.* Maryknoll, NY: Orbis Books, 1989.

Schreuder, Deryck, and Geoffrey Oddie. "What Is 'Conversion'? History, Christianity and Religious Change in Colonial Africa and South Asia." *The Journal of Religious History*, 13 (1989): 496–518.

Sharkey, Heather J., ed. *Cultural Conversions. Unexpected Consequences of Christian Missionary Encounters in the Middle East, Africa, and South Asia.* Syracuse, NY: Syracuse University Press, 2013.

Shaw, Rosalind. "The Invention of 'African Traditional Religion.'" *Religion*, 20 (1990): 339–53.

Smart, Ninian. *The Phenomenon of Religion.* London: Macmillan, 1973.

Smith, Wilfred Cantwell. *The Meaning and End of Religion.* Minneapolis: Fortress Press, 1991.

Spicer, Edward H. "Acculturation." In *International Encyclopedia of the Social Sciences*, edited by David L. Sills, 17 vols. New York: Macmillan, 1968. 1: 21–27.

Stanley, Brian. *Christianity in the Twentieth Century: A World History.* Princeton, NJ: Princeton University Press, 2018.

Stanley, Brian, ed. *Christian Missions and the Enlightenment.* Grand Rapids, MI: Eerdmans, 2001.

Stark, Rodney, and William Sims Bainbridge. *A Theory of Religion.* New York: Peter Lang, 1987.

Steinmetz, George. *The Devil's Handwriting: Precoloniality and the German Colonial State in Qingdao, Samoa, and Southwest Africa.* Chicago: University of Chicago Press, 2007.

Stewart, Charles and Rosalind Shaw, eds. *Syncretism/Anti-Syncretism: The Politics of Religious Synthesis.* London: Routledge, 1994.

Strathern, Alan. *Unearthly Powers: Religious and Political Change in World History.* Cambridge: Cambridge University Press, 2019.

Sugirtharajah, R. S. *The Bible and the Third World. Precolonial, Colonial and Postcolonial Encounters.* Cambridge: Cambridge University Press, 2001.

Taylor, Charles. *A Secular Age*. Cambridge, MA: Harvard University Press, 2007.

Thrupp, Sylvia J., ed., *Millennial Dreams in Action. Essays in Comparative Study*. The Hague: Mouton, 1962.

Trompf, Garry, ed., *Cargo Cults and Millenarian Movements: Transoceanic Comparisons of New Religious Movements*. Berlin: De Gruyter, 1990.

van Beek, Walter E. A., ed. *The Quest for Purity: The Dynamics of Puritan Movements*. Berlin: Mouton de Gruyter, 1988.

Van der Leeuw, G. *Religion in Essence and Manifestation*. Translated by J. E. Turner. Princeton, NJ: Princeton University Press, 1986. Originally published 1933 as *Phänomenologie der Religion*.

Van der Veer, Peter. *Imperial Encounters. Religion and Modernity in India and Britain*. Princeton, NJ: Princeton University Press, 2001.

— *The Modern Spirit of Asia: The Spiritual and the Secular in China and India*. Princeton, NJ: Princeton University Press, 2014.

Van der Veer, Peter, ed. *Conversion to Modernities: The Globalization of Christianity*. New York: Routledge, 1996.

Van der Veer, Peter, and Hartmut Lehmann, eds. *Nation and Religion: Perspectives on Europe and Asia*. Princeton, NJ: Princeton University Press, 1999.

Wach, Joachim. *Sociology of Religion*. Chicago: University of Chicago Press, 1944.

Wallace, Anthony F. C. "Revitalization Movements." *American Anthropologist*, 58 (1956): 264–81.

Walls, Andrew F. *The Missionary Movement in Christian History: Studies in the Transmission of Faith*. Maryknoll, NY: Orbis Books. 1996.

Weber, Max. *From Max Weber: Essays in Sociology*. Translated and edited by H. H. Gerth and C. Wright Mills. New York: Oxford University Press, 1946.

— *Gesammelte Aufsätze zur Religionssoziologie*. 3 vols. Tübingen: J. C. B. Mohr, 1920–21.

Wessinger, Catherine, ed. *The Oxford Handbook of Millennialism*. Oxford: Oxford University Press, 2011.

Williams, Patrick, and Laura Chrisman, eds. *Colonial Discourse and Post-colonial Theory: A Reader*. New York: Columbia University Press, 1994.

World Values Survey. Wave 6 (2010–2014). www.worldvaluessurvey.org/WVSDocumentationWV6.jsp.

Yelle, Robert A. *The Language of Disenchantment: Protestant Literalism and Colonial Discourse in British India*. Oxford: Oxford University Press, 2013.

Zuckerman, Phil, and John R. Shook, eds. *The Oxford Handbook of Secularism*. Oxford: Oxford University Press, 2017.

Index

CPSIA information can be obtained
at www.ICGtesting.com
Printed in the USA
LVHW022018240521
688348LV00015B/726

9 781108 926874